A dynamic interpersonal relationships program from Goodheart-Willcox

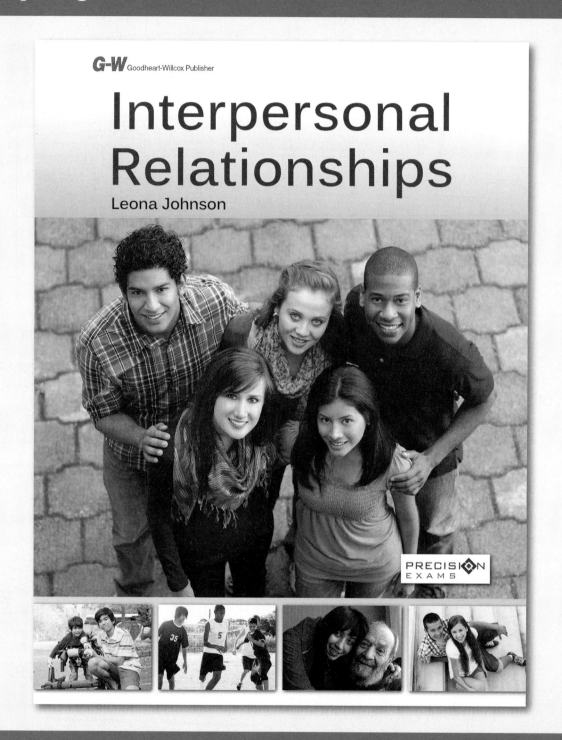

G-W Goodheart-Willcox Publisher

Interpersonal Relationships

Leona Johnson

PRECISION EXAMS

rich with opportunities for discussion and application

Captivates interest with real-world applications

Case Studies introduce unit topics with realistic stories about peer, family, work, and multicultural relationships from around the world.

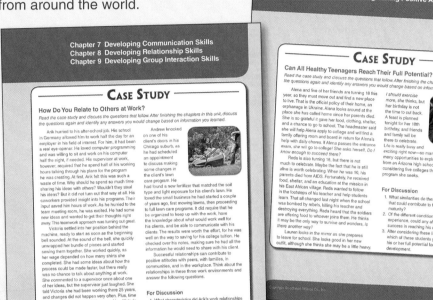

Chapter 1 A Close-Up View of You
Chapter 2 Your Growth and Development
Chapter 3 Strengthening Positive Attitudes

Case Study

Can All Healthy Teenagers Reach Their Full Potential?

Read the case study and discuss the questions that follow. After finishing the chapters in this unit, discuss the questions again and identify any answers you would change based on information you learned.

Alena and five of her friends are turning 18 this year, so they must move out and find a new place to live. That is the official policy of their home, an orphanage in Ukraine. Alena looks around at the place she has called home since her parents died. She is so grateful it gave her food, clothing, shelter, and a chance to go to school. The headmaster said she will help Alena apply to college and will find a family offering room and board in return for Alena's help with daily chores. If Alena passes the entrance exam, she will go to college! She asks herself, *Do I know enough to succeed there?*

Reda is also turning 18, but there is not much to celebrate. Maybe the fact that he is still alive is worth celebrating. When he was 10, his parents died from AIDS. Fortunately, he received food, shelter, and an education at the mission in his East African village. Reda wanted to follow in the footsteps of his teacher and help students learn. That all changed last night when the school was bombed by rebels, killing his teacher and destroying everything. Reda heard that the soldiers are offering food to whoever joins them. He thinks it may be the only way to survive and wonders, *Is there another way?*

Lauren looks in the mirror as she prepares to leave for school. She looks good in her new outfit, although she thinks she may be a little heavy. *I should exercise more*, she thinks, but her birthday is not the time to cut back. A feast is planned tonight for her 18th birthday, and friends and family will be there to celebrate. Life is really busy and exciting right now—so many choices to make, so many opportunities to explore. She will graduate from an Arizona high school this year and is considering five colleges that offer the specialized program she seeks.

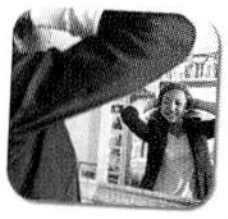

For Discussion

1. What similarities do these students share that could contribute to their growth toward maturity?
2. Of the different conditions these students experience, could any affect an individual's success in reaching his or her full potential?
3. After considering these life stories, explain which of these students you believe will reach his or her full potential for personal growth and development.

MJTH/Shutterstock.com

Chapter 7 Developing Communication Skills
Chapter 8 Developing Relationship Skills
Chapter 9 Developing Group Interaction Skills

Case Study

How Do You Relate to Others at Work?

Read the case study and discuss the questions that follow. After finishing the chapters in this unit, discuss the questions again and identify any answers you would change based on information you learned.

Arik hurried to his after-school job. His school in Germany allowed him to work half the day for an employer in his field of interest. For him, it had been a real eye-opener. He loved computer programming and was willing to sit and work on his computer half the night, if needed. His supervisor at work, however, required that he spend half of his working hours talking through his plans for the program he was creating. At first, Arik felt this was such a waste of time. Why should he spend so much time sharing his ideas with others? Wouldn't they steal his ideas? But it did not turn out that way at all. His coworkers provided insight into his programs. Their input saved him hours of work. As he hurried to the team meeting room, he was excited. He had some new ideas and wanted to get their thoughts right away. This teamwork approach was turning out great.

Victoria settled into her position behind the machine, ready to start as soon as the beginning bell sounded. At the sound of the bell, she quickly unwrapped her bundle of pieces and started sewing them together. She worked quickly, as her wage depended on how many shirts she completed. She had some ideas about how the process could be made faster, but there really was no chance to talk about anything at work. She commented to a supervisor once about one of her ideas, but the supervisor just laughed. She told Victoria she had been working there 25 years, and changes did not happen very often. Plus, time was money, and she should keep working. Victoria wondered if all the factories in her city in Belize operated the same way. She had heard from one of her classmates that some of the factories were starting work teams, where groups worked together on projects. She liked the idea of being able to offer improvements and make things better.

Andrew knocked on one of his client's doors in his Chicago suburb, as he had scheduled an appointment to discuss making some changes in the client's lawn care program. He had found a new fertilizer that matched the soil type and light exposure for his client's lawn. He loved the small business he had started a couple of years ago, first mowing lawns, then proceeding to full lawn care programs. It did require that he be organized to keep up with the work, have the knowledge about what would work well for his clients, and be able to communicate with his clients. The results were worth the effort, for he was well on the way to saving for his college tuition. He checked over his notes, making sure he had all the information he would need to share with his client.

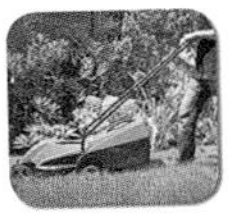

Successful relationships can contribute to positive attitudes with peers, with families, in communities, and in the workplace. Think about the relationships in these three work environments and answer the following questions.

For Discussion

1. What characteristics did Arik's work relationships have that contributed to his success?
2. How did the relationships in Victoria's work environment limit her ability to grow as a person or reach personal goals?
3. How did Andrew use relationship skills to build his own business?

Dejpixel/Shutterstock.com

Getting Started introductions bring students into the minds of people who are experiencing the events and emotions discussed in each chapter.

Getting Started

"Do you know what happened with Sam today?" Ariana asked her friend Emma. "He was upset because I said that I didn't want to go see the new superhero movie with him. I mean, I don't—I'm really tired of all those guys making poses and acting tough and all the buildings blowing up. But that's all I meant. He thought I didn't want to go out with him anymore. Can you imagine that? Now he's really hurt, and I don't know what to do. How can I fix this?"

People communicate all the time, but communicating clearly is not always easy. It is important to be clear. Poor communication can cause serious misunderstandings. Somehow, the message that is sent can differ from the message that is received. A poorly presented message conveys the wrong information or gives the wrong impression. It can hurt someone's feelings or harm relationships

Learning to communicate well is an important interpersonal skill. Effective communication is vital for developing rewarding relationships with family, friends, coworkers, and other people. Besides helping you get along with others, good communication skills can help you express yourself. Stating your thoughts and ideas clearly will help others understand you. These skills can also help you work through problems and resolve differences with other people. The end result will be improved relationships with others.

You communicate with others every day. Speaking, listening, reading, and writing are all forms of communication. Understanding the communication process will help you improve your skills in all thes

Getting Started

Joseph looked at his older brother. His brother was already 28 years old and was still living at home. He never seemed to have any money. He worked hard at his job, but still could not seem to make enough to find his own place.

"What happened?" Joseph asked his brother. "Why don't you have your own apartment?"

"I don't know," Joseph's brother replied. "Guess I'm just stupid."

Joseph knew that was not true. His brother was very gifted at fixing things. He fixed appliances in the house and kept the family car running. He was really good at working with his hands. He just could not seem to find a good-paying job.

"Why don't you go to school to become a mechanic?" Joseph asked his brother. "You could still work at nights and go to school in the daytime."

"It all takes money," his brother replied, "and I don't have any. And it just never has worked out. I'll make do."

Career success is more likely to happen with planning. Without planning, you probably will not reach your career goals. With planning and with carefully managing your time, you stand a good chance. In fact, the earlier you start with your career plan, the sooner in life you will reach career goals. But circumstances—yours and trends in society—change over time, so you also need to review and reexamine your career plan from time to time. A career plan can be started, changed, or adjusted at any time.

In this chapter, you will learn more about pursuing your career, carrying out your career plan, and finding success in the world of work. Even as you follow your career plan, you will make adjustments, set new goals, gain new experiences, and pursue more education if needed to meet your goals.

Real-Life Scenario

Facing Unemployment

Carlos's family knew that the construction season was almost over. Soon, Carlos's dad would be out of work. Thinking about another long winter with no income was causing everyone in the Sandoz family to be edgy. One Saturday evening, Carlos asked for a family meeting.

"Isn't there something we can do to help Dad keep his job?" Carlos asked.

His dad shook his head. "I don't think so, son. I'm a road builder, and not too many roads are built in the winter."

"But you have so many other skills, Dad," Carlos said. "You know how to drive those big road-building machines. Couldn't you drive trucks

Mr. Sandoz was beginning to catch Carlos's excitement. "Yes, I'd be willing to look into it," he said.

For Discussion

1. Explain how the upcoming layoff could be a potential crisis-producing event for the Sandoz family.
2. Was the source of stress for the Sandoz family external or internal?
3. What factors made it seem difficult for the Sandoz family to handle the stress and prevent the potential crisis?
4. What family resources did the Sandoz family use … hem prevent a crisis?
… actions Carlos took to cope with the … crisis.
… d Carlos have done if his father … less willing to adjust and consider … new? What other alternatives could … considered to avoid a crisis?

Real-Life Scenario

Krista's Career Choice

Krista hurried down to the high school guidance office. She had an appointment with a career specialist from the U.S. Army who was visiting the school. She was anxious to discuss careers in her area of interest.

Krista had always been interested in what she called "crawly critters." As a child, she loved to catch caterpillars and put them in a jar. She would watch them eat up the leaves in the jar and eventually spin a cocoon. Her terrarium was home for salamanders, frogs, and toads whenever she could catch them. She was always careful to treat them gently, for she had great respect for all living things.

Her biology class had confirmed her interest in living creatures. She did well in that class, finding it easy to memorize all the many facts and principles. She had also learned some techniques for studying and classifying her collection of insects.

Her biology teacher had asked her to serve as a guide for elementary school field trips in the environmental park. She enjoyed sharing her interest in living things with the children. She would guide the children through the park, pointing out the different species of insects and animals. Then she always ended the tour with a display of her bug collection.

For Discussion

1. From this description, what can you tell about Krista's personality? Include her patterns for responding to the environment intellectually, socially, emotionally, and physically.
2. What aptitudes and skills can you identify for Krista?
3. Identify as many career opportunities as you can that would match Krista's interests, personality, aptitudes, and skills. How many of these could she pursue in the U.S. Army?
4. Choose one career that you think Krista would like the most. Describe what work she would do. Explain the training or education she would need. Identify five different potential employers (agencies, companies, or institutions) that employ persons in that occupation.

Real-Life Scenarios apply chapter material to everyday situations and invite students to evaluate appropriate responses.

Illustrates concepts with a contemporary organization and look

Individual lessons present and assess information in manageable chunks.

LESSON 3.1
DEVELOPING ATTITUDES THAT LEAD TO MENTAL HEALTH

Content Terms

attitude
self-perpetuating cycle
mental health
defense mechanisms
denial
acting out
projection
rationalization
displacement
conversion
regression
idealization
conceited
fantasy
direct attack
compensation
self-talk

Academic Terms

consequence
interpret

Objectives

After studying this lesson, you will be able to

- explain how positive and negative attitudes influence behavior and contribute to mental health.
- describe defense mechanisms that people sometimes use to deal with problems.
- evaluate how defense mechanisms hinder growth.
- identify techniques used for building positive attitudes.

Focus Your Reading

1. Review the headings in this lesson. Write some questions that you think will be answered when you read each section of the lesson. As you read each part, write the answers to your questions. If you have some questions that are not answered, share them with a partner to see if he or she found the answers.
2. For each defense mechanism, identify the feelings, thoughts, and actions involved.

The study of how feelings, thoughts, and actions work together can help you understand your attitudes. **Attitudes** are patterns of thinking, feeling, and responding that people develop as they interact with their environment. Since attitudes affect behavior, your attitudes will affect your relationships in every area of life.

Positive and Negative Attitudes

Your life experiences and the way you interpret them influence your overall mental attitude (Figure 3.1). If you have positive thoughts and feelings about your experiences, your attitude will be positive. If you have negative thoughts and feelings about your experiences, your attitude will be negative. Your mental attitude will be influenced by your thoughts and feelings about life, yourself, and your worth to others.

58

Copyright Goodheart-Willcox Co., Inc.

LESSON 7.1
THE COMMUNICATION PROCESS

Content Terms

communication
sender
encoding
channel
receiver
decoding
nonverbal communication
verbal communication
body language
context
direct eye contact
communication style
I-statement
you-statement
active listening
clarifying
paraphrasing
reflecting
passive listening

Academic Terms

feedback
monitor
personal space
assertive
point of view
aggressive

Objectives

After studying this lesson, you will be able to

- describe the communication process.
- identify different forms of nonverbal and verbal communication.
- demonstrate effective speaking and listening skills.

Focus Your Reading

1. As you read, develop a profile of a good communicator. Create a graphic organizer with the heading *A Good Communicator* and two columns underneath. As you read, write qualities of a good communicator in the first column. In the second column, write what skills a good communicator uses.
2. Share an example with a partner (through words or actions) of how each content term can promote good communication.

Although it may seem simple, communication is a complex process. **Communication** is an exchange of information among two or more people. It is a two-way process that involves encoding, sending, receiving, and decoding messages (Figure 7.1).

The **sender** is the person who is the source of the message. **Encoding** a message is the process of thinking about what you want to say and how to say it and then transmitting or sending it through a **channel**. The channel may be the air, if the message is sent in person, or some form of technology or print, if the message is spoken on a phone or written on a digital device or piece of paper. The **receiver** is the person who hears or reads the message and interprets its meaning, a process known as **decoding**. **Feedback** is a signal the receiver gives back to the sender to indicate how the message was understood. Each part of the communication process is needed to make sure that good, clear communication takes place.

Both sender and receiver need to use certain skills to communicate effectively. The sender needs *encoding skills*—skills in sending clear and accurate messages. The receiver needs *decoding skills*—skills in listening to the message and interpreting it correctly. The receiver also needs to provide feedback that allows the sender to know that the message was understood.

154

Copyright Goodheart-Willcox Co., Inc.

Colorful photos and illustrations capture attention and help students visualize lesson concepts.

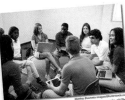

to older adults (for example, helping with lawn care or grocery shopping).

The skills gained through volunteer activities can be part of a short-term goal as you build your career plan. Volunteering can also make you more attractive to potential employers by showing that you put the time and effort into a responsible activity. Some schools offer an endorsement on a student's high school diploma for participating in a set number of volunteer hours in the school or community.

Figure 5.15 Mentor training can help you gain skills for working with people. What opportunities are there to be a mentor in your school or community?

Think About Your Reading
How could cocurricular activities that you enjoy contribute to your short-term and long-term goals for career planning?

school. Other programs offer mentoring by juniors and seniors to students in their first year of high school. Serving in various mentoring programs gives these students a chance to learn how to work with different age groups. They also learn how to act as a role model for others.

Volunteering

Every community has many opportunities for students to do volunteer work. Boy's and girl's clubs provide one-to-one mentoring with young children. Some after-school clubs give students the chance to assist younger students with homework. Peer tutoring in your high school could give you experience working with other teens.

There are also opportunities in most communities to volunteer services to the elderly. There may be a center on aging or a senior citizens center where you could volunteer to assist with activities for the elderly. Such experiences would help you gain skills working with the older population and, to some extent, working in the health care industry.

Other volunteer opportunities may be found through religious organizations in your community. These may relate to providing services for all age groups: helping with child care, teaching young children, providing recreational activities for school-age students, or offering physical services

Gain Work Experience

Part-time jobs can also help you reach some short-term career goals (Figure 5.16). They can become part of your career ladder if you can find

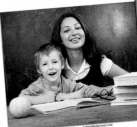

Figure 5.16 Volunteering or working part time in an after-school program can help you gain experience working with young children and families. What transferable skills could you gain from such an experience?

128   Unit 2   Setting and Reaching Life Goals

Copyright Goodheart-Willcox Co., Inc.

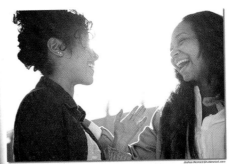

Figure 4.7 The people in your life are valuable human resources who can help you reach your goals.

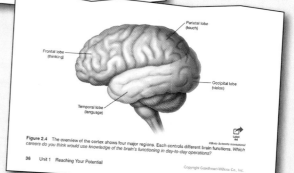

Figure 2.4 The overview of the cortex shows four major regions. Each controls different brain functions. Which careers do you think would use knowledge of the brain's functioning in day-to-day operations?

- Parietal lobe (touch)
- Frontal lobe (thinking)
- Occipital lobe (vision)
- Temporal lobe (language)

36   Unit 1   Reaching Your Potential

Copyright Goodheart-Willcox Co., Inc.

Copyright Goodheart-Willcox Co., Inc.

Reinforces learning with frequent assessment and rich activities

Comprehension Checks assess the material learned in each lesson.

LESSON 1.3
COMPREHENSION CHECK

1. Describe three characteristics of a family environment that could impact the growth of self-esteem during the early years.
2. Give two examples of how a family's cultural heritage influences a person's identity and family relationships.
3. How could sibling position in a family affect the relationships a child has with family members?
4. How can teen peers help one another mature?
5. How can the community impact a person's personal identity?
6. Explain the biological effect of a stressful environment on development.
7. What are three aspects of the environment that may become part of an adult's identity?
8. Explain what it means to respond to your hereditary and environmental background with resilience.

LESSON 5.2
COMPREHENSION CHECK

1. List six personal factors that could influence your career choice.
2. Why is it necessary to prioritize your values when thinking about a career?
3. What is an example of how interests, abilities, and personal priorities affect career choice?
4. What kind of careers might be appropriate for someone with a strong aptitude for helping other people?
5. Describe how transferable skills could benefit you in making a career choice. Give three examples.

LESSON 13.3
COMPREHENSION CHECK

1. Identify two benefits of living in a nuclear family.
2. List five ways a single-parent family may be formed.
3. Describe some challenges that single parents may have meeting the needs of their family members.
4. Explain the difference between an extended family and a modified-extended family.
5. Describe one benefit and one challenge unique to an extended family.
6. Identify two challenges faced by adoptive families.
7. Summarize how public policies and laws that impact family life could affect the family's ability to carry out its functions.

CORE SKILLS
16. **Research.** Interview an employer and ask about his or her idea of an ideal employee. In a paragraph, summarize how the employer's list is similar to or different from the list of the qualities of an effective employee listed in the text. *Group option*: Work as a team, using teamwork skills, with each member interviewing a different employer. Compare each person's findings and develop a joint list of an ideal employee from this group of employers.
17. **Research.** Create a spreadsheet listing the clubs in your school. For each club, identify its purpose, goals, and organizational structure. Include a summary of the activities of the group and identify the needs it meets in group members' lives. (Do not include the school's athletic teams.) Publish your findings on the school website where extracurricular or student activities are listed.
18. **Writing.** Create an agenda for a class meeting in which you will be leading the group in identifying problems and desired changes in the hot lunch menu. Identify what items you need on the agenda, what sources of information you will need, and what types of discussion you will use to further your agenda. Put your agenda into an electronic slide format to use in leading the class. As a class, use teamwork skills to solve the problems.

CRITICAL THINKING
11. **Make Inferences.** Create a chart or table listing the five categories of activities. For each category, list some goals that are common to teens and young adults. In a paragraph, explain how time management could help achieve each goal. *Choice*: Draw pictures that represent each category. *Group option*: Create the list with a partner.
12. **Develop a Hypothesis.** Analyze two time management tools for their value in helping you manage your time. Gather information on their cost, ease of use, and features that could help manage time. Weigh these features and make a judgment about whether they would be good tools for your personal time management needs. Write a paragraph summarizing your findings. Also analyze whether your chosen time management tools would be good for your workplace time management needs. Compare the effectiveness of the time management tools in personal and in workplace applications. *Choice*: Present your information to the class in an oral presentation.

CAREER READINESS
23. **Communicating Information.** Choose an on-the-job situation in which communication barriers result in problems between employees or between an employee and a customer. Write a short scene to illustrate the problem, ways to overcome such barriers, and strategies for improving communication on the job. *Choice*: Work with one or more partners and role-play the problem and solution for your class.

CAREER READINESS
23. **Creating a Portfolio.** Assess your interests, aptitudes, and abilities. Gather information related to past and current coursework, cocurricular activities, and work and volunteer experiences. Put together a portfolio illustrating your skills, knowledge, personal qualities, and experiences that would attract an employer's attention. Scan your artifacts, creating an electronic portfolio. *Choice*: Prepare an electronic résumé that could be e-mailed to prospective employers. Use the Internet to find guidelines to follow when creating an electronic résumé. *Group option*: Share your portfolio with a classmate and have him or her evaluate the artifacts you have contributed.

Critical Thinking and Core Skills activities invite students to engage with and dig deeper into the information taught in each chapter.

Career Readiness activities prompt students to apply their interpersonal skills to the workplace.

Engages students with critical thinking and career features

Think About Your Reading features offer frequent opportunities for discussion and critical thinking.

> **Think About Your Reading**
> When people are talking on the phone or communicating online, how could the absence of nonverbal communication affect their understanding of the message?

> **Think About Your Reading**
> How is your lifestyle affected by the work your family does?

> **Think About Your Reading**
> Think of situations in which others give you advice using a you-statement. Is there an I-statement that could give the same advice without risk of offending the listener?

> **Think About Your Reading**
> Give some examples of behaviors you would expect to see in a family that provides consistent care for a child. How might a child's growth and development be affected by care that was not consistent?

Connecting with Career Clusters features introduce students to occupations within related career clusters.

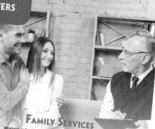

A complete program for students and teachers

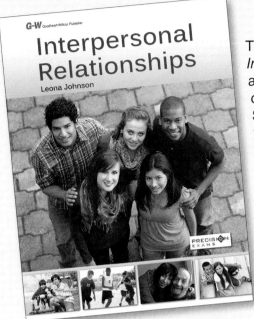

Student Textbook— Print or Online
The student edition of *Interpersonal Relationships* is available as a printed textbook or as an interactive online text. Simply choose the format that works best for your students.
www.g-wonlinetextbooks.com

Student Workbook— Print or Online
Workbook activities reinforce material presented in the textbook, offering students an application-based learning experience.

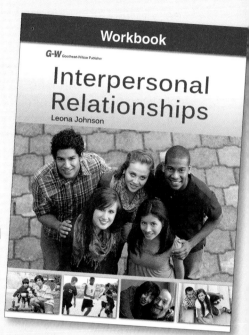

ExamView® Assessment Suite
Quickly and easily prepare and print tests with the ExamView® Assessment Suite. You can choose which questions to include in each test, create multiple versions of a single test, and automatically generate answer keys.

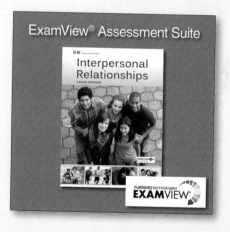

Instructor's Presentations for PowerPoint®
Visually reinforce key concepts with prepared lectures. Integrated discussion and review questions make the presentations interactive.

Instructor's Resource CD
Includes daily lesson plans, answer keys, and grading rubrics.

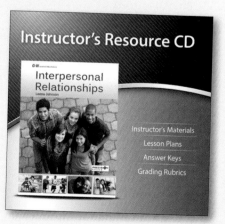

G-W integrated learning solution

The **G-W Integrated Learning Solution** offers easy-to-use resources for both instructors and students. Both digital and blended (print + digital) teaching and learning content can be accessed through any Internet-enabled device, such as a computer, smartphone, or tablet. From the following options, choose the ones that work best for you and your students.

The **G-W Learning Companion Website** for *Interpersonal Relationships* accompanies the **Student Textbook** and provides content to help students build skills and knowledge, extend textbook content, and reinforce learning. The website complements textbook chapters and is available to students at no charge.

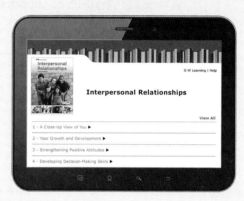

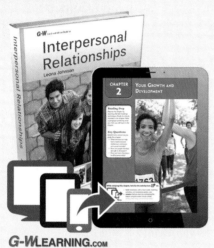

The **Online Instructor Resources** provide extensive support for instructors. Included in the online resources are Answer Keys, Lesson Plans, Instructor's Presentations for PowerPoint®, ExamView® Assessment Suite, and much more. These resources are available as a subscription and can be accessed at school or at home. They are also available on CDs.

The **Online Learning Suite** for *Interpersonal Relationships* is available as a classroom subscription. It includes the online student text, the companion website content, and the digital workbook.

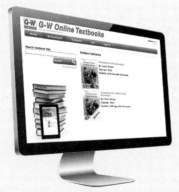

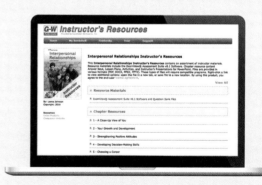

Looking for a **Blended Solution**? G-W offers the Online Learning Suite bundled with the printed textbook in one easy-to-access package for school districts and instructors seeking a combination of print and digital tools. With this option, individual students and instructors have the flexibility of using solely print, solely digital, or a combination of print and digital versions of the *Interpersonal Relationships* educational materials to best meet their particular learning and teaching styles.

Goodheart-Willcox Publisher Welcomes Your Comments

A leader in educational publishing since 1921, Goodheart-Willcox Publisher is continuously developing print and digital products for Family and Consumer Sciences courses. This new *Interpersonal Relationships* textbook program is one of the first of its kind.

If you teach a family and consumer sciences class, and you have been unable to find a suitable text for your students, please let us know. We are eager to develop high-quality, innovative products that fill the unmet needs of family and consumer sciences educators. Your suggestions may lead to the development of digital or print materials that benefit teachers and students across the country.

With each new product, our goal at Goodheart-Willcox Publisher is to deliver superior educational materials that effectively meet the ever-changing, increasingly diverse needs of students and teachers. To that end, we welcome your comments and suggestions regarding *Interpersonal Relationships* and its supplemental components.

Please send any comments and suggestions to the managing editor of our Family and Consumer Sciences Editorial Department. You can send an e-mail to editorial@g-w.com, or write to:

Managing Editor—FCS
Goodheart-Willcox Publisher
18604 West Creek Drive
Tinley Park, IL 60477-6243

Interpersonal Relationships

by

Leona Johnson, EdS
Esko, Minnesota

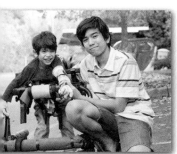
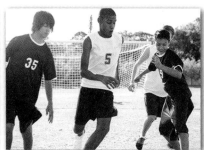
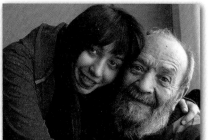
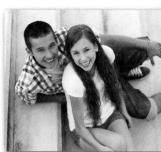

Publisher
The Goodheart-Willcox Company, Inc.
Tinley Park, IL
www.g-w.com

ABOUT THE AUTHOR

Leona Johnson, EdS, currently resides in Northeastern Minnesota, where she pursues and maintains healthy interpersonal relationships with friends and family in her community. Her career includes being the PK-12 Director of Curriculum and Instruction and elementary principal in her former district, and she continues to provide input into local educational initiatives, as well as into community endeavors. Johnson has implemented many varied initiatives in K-12 curriculums, and she has practiced firsthand her knowledge and skills in using the best teaching and learning practices in multiple subject areas, leading collaborative work groups, facilitating consensus building in group decision making, and participating in group goal setting with both staff and community members. As a teacher, principal, parent, and grandparent, she has experienced the challenges and joys of guiding youth toward reaching their potential. As a friend and lifelong spouse, she continues to contribute much to the lives of those around her.

A participating member of several professional and community organizations, Johnson has received recognition for her various academic and professional endeavors, including a Kohl Fellow Scholarship and Award of Excellence for her contributions to teaching secondary family and consumer sciences. In her years serving the educational community, she brought in several million dollars in grant monies for various educational programs and initiatives. A native of Canada, Johnson previously taught individual and family relations at the University of Wisconsin-Stout, where she also served as a research specialist.

REVIEWERS

Goodheart-Willcox Publisher would like to thank the following instructors who reviewed selected manuscript chapters and provided valuable input into the development of this textbook program.

Ann Bottoms
Family and Consumer Sciences Instructor
Trigg County High School
Cadiz, Kentucky

Samantha Cosper
Family and Consumer Sciences Instructor
Cassville High School
Cassville, Missouri

Tish Dimick
Family and Consumer Sciences Instructor
Goddard High School
Goddard, Kansas

Amelia Dorsey
Family and Consumer Sciences Instructor
Texas High School
Texarkana, Texas

Angelia Ford
Family and Consumer Sciences Instructor
Bearden High School
Knoxville, Tennessee

Mary Funk
Family and Consumer Sciences Instructor
Newman Smith High School
Carrollton, Texas

Linda Halsell
Family and Consumer Sciences Instructor
Livingston Academy
Livingston, Tennessee

Wendee Kilgore
Family and Consumer Sciences Instructor
Grundy County High School
Coalmont, Tennessee

Sharon Mang
Family and Consumer Sciences Instructor
Greensburg Community High School
Greensburg, Indiana

Elisa McIntire
Family and Consumer Sciences Instructor
Elkins High School
Missouri City, Texas

Marcy Minnick
Family and Consumer Sciences Instructor
Palmyra High School
Palmyra, Missouri

Krystal Sallee
Family and Consumer Sciences Instructor
Macon County High School
Lafayette, Tennessee

Bonnie Thomson
Family and Consumer Sciences Instructor
Skyline High School
Dallas, Texas

Erika Vargas
Family and Consumer Sciences Instructor
Garland High School
Garland, Texas

CONTENTS IN BRIEF

CONTENTS

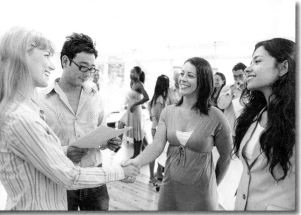

stockphoto mania/Shutterstock.com

Rawpixel.com/Shutterstock.com

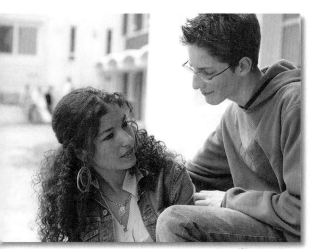
Monkey Business Images/Shutterstock.com

auremar/Shutterstock.com

Unit 5　Family Relationships

©iStock.com/DragonImages

Unit 6　Family Relationships Over Time

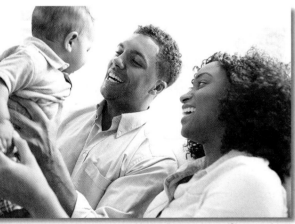

Monkey Business Images/Shutterstock.com

Unit 7 Fulfilling Family, Career, and Community Roles ... 500

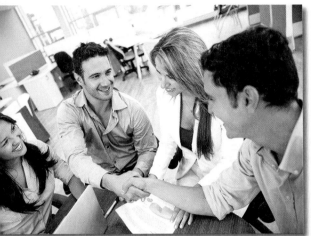

Andresr/Shutterstock.com

Precision Exams Certification

Goodheart-Willcox Publisher is pleased to partner with Precision Exams by correlating **Interpersonal Relationships** to the Standards, Objectives, and Indicators for Precision Exams' *Interpersonal Relationships* exam. Precision Exams were created in concert with industry and subject matter experts to match real-world job skills and marketplace demands. Students who pass the exam and performance portion of the exam can earn a Career Skills Certification™. To see how **Interpersonal Relationships** correlates to the Precision Exam Standards, please visit www.g-w.com/interpersonal-relationships-2018 and click on the Correlations tab. For more information on Precision Exams, please visit www.precisionexams.com.

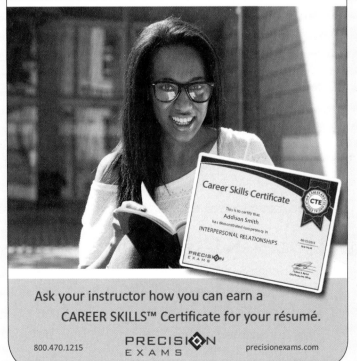

I earned a CAREER SKILLS™ Certificate in INTERPERSONAL RELATIONSHIPS. You can earn one, too!

Career Skills Certificate

This is to certify that
Addison Smith
has demonstrated competency in
INTERPERSONAL RELATIONSHIPS

PRECISION
EXAMS

Ask your instructor how you can earn a CAREER SKILLS™ Certificate for your résumé.

PRECISION EXAMS

800.470.1215   precisionexams.com

BONNINSTUDIO/Shutterstock.com

SPECIAL FEATURES

INTRODUCTION

Interpersonal Relationships is designed to help you grow and develop, strengthening both knowledge and skills so that you can build and maintain strong and healthy relationships with multiple groups of people throughout your life. Healthy relationships with others will help you experience a quality of life that contributes to your well-being. This is true whether those personal relationships are with members in the immediate family, other relatives, friends, or others in the community. Relationship skills also can impact success in the workplace, as you relate to coworkers and colleagues, bosses and supervisors, customers and clients, or employees. Thus, the benefits of studying *Interpersonal Relationships* include understanding and skills that can be applied throughout your life.

Personal growth to maturity establishes a strong foundation for healthy interpersonal relationships. This foundation includes understanding and accepting who you are; taking steps to mature and reach your potential; learning to set goals and make good decisions, whether alone or in a group; communicating clearly and effectively in various settings; and developing skills for solving problems and resolving conflicts. Skills for developing healthy relationships apply to friendships with peers, romantic relationships, spousal relationships, parent-child relationships, and relationships with others in your community. These skills also can impact success as you participate in the workforce, both as a team member and as a team leader. *Interpersonal Relationships* can also help you develop lifelong skills for managing areas of your life. With help from this text, you can acquire the skills needed for adjusting to change, choosing and building a successful career, managing stress, responding to crises, meeting the relational and financial challenges of daily living, and balancing the demands of various family and career roles. All of these skills will help you build, maintain, and manage the diverse relationships and experiences you will encounter.

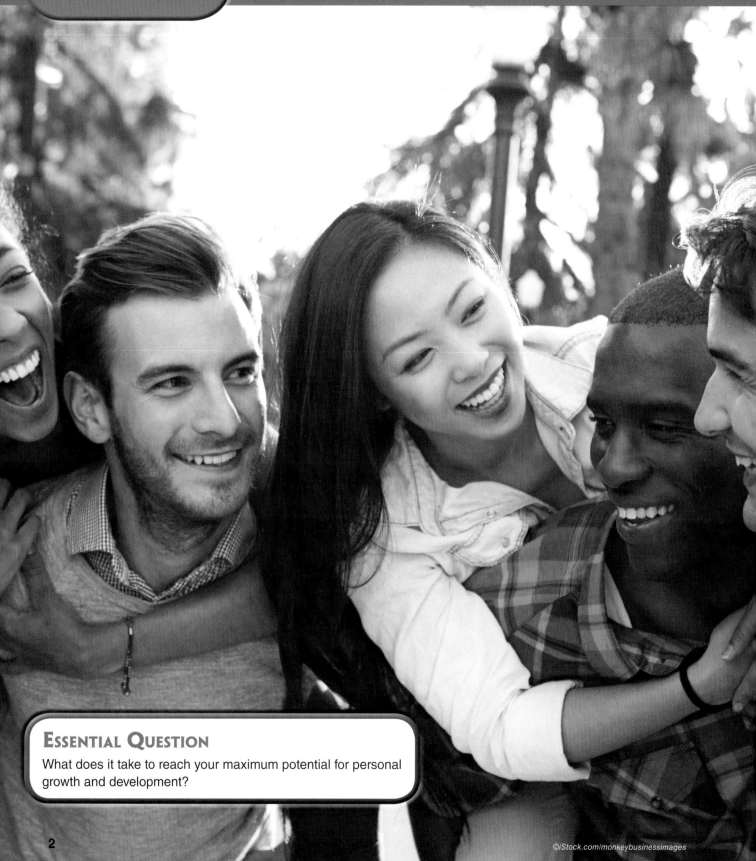

UNIT 1

REACHING YOUR POTENTIAL

ESSENTIAL QUESTION

What does it take to reach your maximum potential for personal growth and development?

CASE STUDY

Can All Healthy Teenagers Reach Their Full Potential?

Read the case study and discuss the questions that follow. After finishing the chapters in this unit, discuss the questions again and identify any answers you would change based on information you learned.

Alena and five of her friends are turning 18 this year, so they must move out and find a new place to live. That is the official policy of their home, an orphanage in Ukraine. Alena looks around at the place she has called home since her parents died. She is so grateful it gave her food, clothing, shelter, and a chance to go to school. The headmaster said she will help Alena apply to college and will find a family offering room and board in return for Alena's help with daily chores. If Alena passes the entrance exam, she will go to college! She asks herself, *Do I know enough to succeed there?*

Reda is also turning 18, but there is not much to celebrate. Maybe the fact that he is still alive is worth celebrating. When he was 10, his parents died from AIDS. Fortunately, he received food, shelter, and an education at the mission in his East African village. Reda wanted to follow in the footsteps of his teacher and help students learn. That all changed last night when the school was bombed by rebels, killing his teacher and destroying everything. Reda heard that the soldiers are offering food to whoever joins them. He thinks it may be the only way to survive and wonders, *Is there another way?*

Lauren looks in the mirror as she prepares to leave for school. She looks good in her new outfit, although she thinks she may be a little heavy.

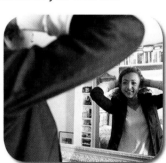

I should exercise more, she thinks, but her birthday is not the time to cut back. A feast is planned tonight for her 18th birthday, and friends and family will be there to celebrate. Life is really busy and exciting right now—so many choices to make, so many opportunities to explore. She will graduate from an Arizona high school this year and is considering five colleges that offer the specialized program she seeks.

For Discussion

1. What similarities do these students share that could contribute to their growth toward maturity?
2. Of the different conditions these students experience, could any affect an individual's success in reaching his or her full potential?
3. After considering these life stories, explain which of these students you believe will reach his or her full potential for personal growth and development.

MJTH/Shutterstock.com

A CLOSE-UP VIEW OF YOU

Reading Prep

Arrange a study session to read the chapter aloud with a classmate. At the end of each lesson, discuss any words you do not know. Take notes of words you would like to discuss in class.

Key Questions

Questions to answer as you study this chapter:

- What is *personal identity*?
- Why is it important to know who I am?
- How did I get to be the way I am?

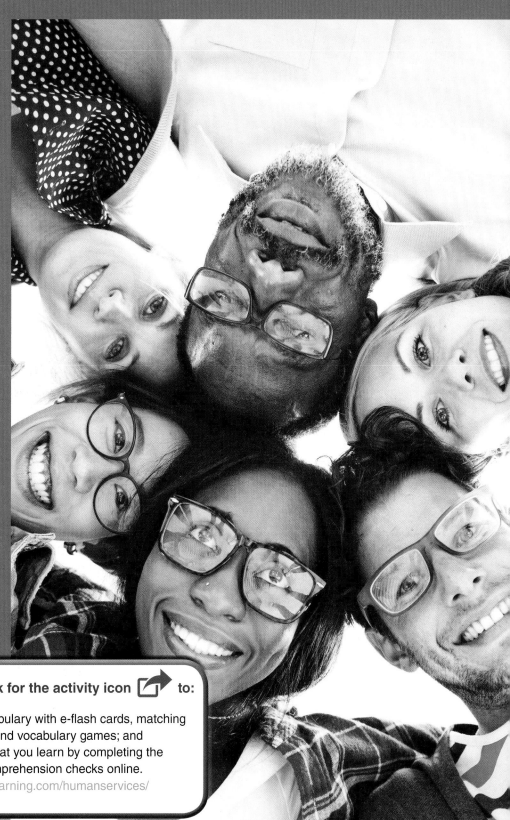

While studying this chapter, look for the activity icon 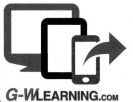 **to:**

- **build** vocabulary with e-flash cards, matching activities, and vocabulary games; and
- **assess** what you learn by completing the lesson comprehension checks online.

G-WLEARNING.com

www.g-wlearning.com/humanservices/

Rawpixel/Shutterstock.com

AFTER STUDYING THIS CHAPTER, YOU WILL

KNOW:

- Key terms related to *personal identity*, *heredity*, and *environment*.
- The major developmental tasks of the teen years.
- Hereditary and environmental factors impacting development and personal identity.

UNDERSTAND:

- How studying this text can help prepare you for life changes.
- How life paths are unique and interdependent with others.
- How the major developmental tasks of the teen years relate to future changes over the course of life.
- How heredity and environment influence growth and development.

BE ABLE TO DO:

- Evaluate the influence of heredity on personal characteristics.
- Analyze global environmental influences for their impact on growth and development.
- Project ways to respond to hereditary and environmental factors with resilience.
- Demonstrate skills for preparing for change.

GETTING STARTED

"What are you going to do after graduation?" Ava asked her friend Molly.

Molly's response was eager and excited. "I plan to go to the state university next fall and get a degree in teaching. I've been working in an after-school child care center and love to work with kids. I think I can keep working there part-time while I go to college. I'm sure the experience will help me get a teaching job when I graduate. Then, I'd really like to stay in the Miami area when I begin my career," Molly said.

Molly sure has her life together, *Ava thought as she listened to all of Molly's plans. Molly was known for setting goals and accomplishing them. Ava had no doubt she would achieve her dreams for the future.*

"I'm still trying to figure out who I am," Ava said to herself. "Where am I going? Will I be a success at what I do someday?"

Have you ever questioned yourself about your future? Almost all young people ask questions like the ones Ava asked as they try to learn more about themselves. They want to know how they will fit into the world beyond school. They want to plan for the future and set directions for their lives.

Planning for the future requires gaining the knowledge and skills related to human growth and development for reaching your maximum potential. As you grow to maturity, this knowledge and these skills can help you make choices that enable you to reach your goals in life. Other knowledge and skills can help you relate more confidently to people. By knowing how to develop positive relationships, you can have success in family and community life and in school and career interactions. Good relationship skills will benefit all areas of your life.

The future may seem frightening because it is unknown. For example, will you know when you are really in love? Will you have a happy family life? Will you find a job you like, and will you succeed at it? Unfortunately, life does not come with a set of answers or directions, but this book provides information that can help you as you make decisions in the future related to these important life events.

People who succeed in life know how to find the information they need and use it wisely. They develop certain skills that help them in their personal relationships. This book uses their experiences to identify the knowledge and skills that will be useful to you.

YOUR LIFE PATH

Content Terms

Build Vocab

gene
DNA
adolescence
developmental task
personal identity
self-esteem

Academic Terms

life span
unique
interdependent

Objectives

After studying this lesson, you will be able to

- **identify** how your life path is unique.
- **relate** major developmental tasks of the teen years to future changes.
- **describe** the steps in preparing for change.

Focus Your Reading

1. As you read, list key points under the following headings: *Qualities of Your Life Path*, *Changes in the Teen Years*, and *Preparing for Change*.
2. Pick an object that you think describes you and explain how it relates to your identity. Include your strengths as well as areas you need to improve.

Life can be thought of as a path. Your birth marks the beginning of your path in this world. Death marks the end of this path. The time between these endpoints is called your *life span*.

No one knows just how long his or her life span will be. The average life span today for men is 76 years; for women, it is 81 years. These are the averages expected for people who are teens today.

You will have many life experiences similar to others along your life path. You will pass through similar stages as you grow from being a baby through childhood to becoming a teen and then move into adulthood (**Figure 1.1**). In these stages, you will experience many life events similar to those that others do. Your life path is also *unique*, unlike that of any other person. You started your life path with your own set of genes, received from your parents. A **gene** is the basic unit of heredity, which you will learn more about in the next lesson. Your unique pattern of genes is known as your **DNA**. It is so distinctive that it can be used as a method of identification.

Your life experiences can be unique to you as you have different opportunities and make personal choices. For example, how you apply yourself to your schoolwork affects how you move from

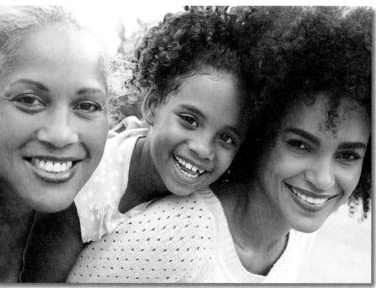
Figure 1.1 The grandmother, mother, and daughter in this image represent the older adult, adult, and elementary years of the life span.

©iStock.com/Cathy Yeulet

grade to grade. What you learn will also have an effect on your future career options.

The relationships you have along your life path will also result in a unique "you." No one has the exact same interactions in their relationships as you, for you are a unique individual in your family and among your circle of friends. Your life path crosses the life paths of other people every day. You are affected by others in your life and you also have an impact on them. In this way, you are *interdependent* with people around you.

Some people have a direct influence on your life path. They may give you food, clothes, and shelter so you feel warm and secure. They may give you a hug or praise so you feel loved. Such actions and words affect you in a direct way and shape how you feel about yourself as well as how you interact with others. People's actions can also affect you indirectly. For example, have you ever known someone who was hurt by not being invited to a classmate's party? This is an example of an indirect effect.

Your words and actions can also directly or indirectly impact others. How you interact with others affects your relationships and how others see you. Who you are, what you say, and what you do or do not do are all important. Your interactions with others help to create a unique "you."

Think About Your Reading
Think of the last item you purchased. Who was directly affected by your purchase? Who was indirectly affected by it?

Developmental Tasks of Adolescence

Adolescence refers to the teen years. As a teen, you have major developmental tasks to achieve. A **developmental task** is a skill that society expects of individuals at various stages of life. Six tasks are the focus of the teen years (**Figure 1.2**). Accomplishing these tasks successfully helps you become an adult.

Understanding and Accepting Yourself

One developmental task of the teen years is to figure out who you are. Asking the question "Who am I?" helps you clarify your **personal identity**. This is a sense of your individuality and your personality—what makes you, you. Exploring the answers to this question will help you feel that you have worth and value. Your feelings of value and importance are your **self-esteem**.

Identifying who you are is the first step toward accepting yourself. When you accept yourself, it is easier to believe that others will accept you as you are. There is no need to pretend—you can let others know the real you. Accepting yourself can help you feel more confident when relating to others.

Developmental Tasks of Adolescence

- Understand and accept who you are.
- Make healthful choices that help you grow to maturity.
- Develop mature relationships.
- Prepare for a career.
- Prepare for independence.
- Prepare for marriage and family living.

Figure 1.2 There are six tasks that society expects teens to accomplish during adolescence. *What information could help in mastering these tasks?*

Growing to Maturity

Knowing your personal identity also allows you to make choices that will help you grow to maturity. When you know and accept yourself as you are, you recognize your good and bad points. You can use your strengths to make choices that help you reach personal goals. You can also make choices to improve the areas in which you are weak.

It is important to grow to maturity in all areas: physical, intellectual, social, and emotional. Maturity in these areas will help you adjust to life changes, develop positive relationships, and increase your quality of life.

Developing Mature Relationships

During the teen years, your position in the family changes. Your relationship with your parents becomes one of decreasing dependence and increasing independence. You gain a new respect for your parents as you mature. They develop more trust and confidence in your judgment as you show you can act responsibly.

Friendships also change and mature. True friendships, which involve care and concern for a friend's well-being, become important.

In addition, many teens develop relationships with people at work. As you get your first job and gain work experience, you learn to become a contributing member of a work team. You may also learn skills for communicating well with customers. Learning to work well with everyone you meet at work makes you a valuable employee and will help you enjoy success in your future work life.

Preparing for a Career

Adolescence is a time to prepare for the future and look ahead to living on your own. Of course, living independently requires having a job that provides a good income. Many people want more than just an income—they want a career that provides enjoyment, interesting tasks, meaningful work, and advancement opportunities. A very important task of the teen years, therefore, is to prepare for a career that will use your strengths and interests while meeting your personal and financial goals.

Preparing for Independence

Many responsibilities and adjustments are associated with living as an independent adult. Living on your own requires planning and preparation. Paying for rent, heat and electricity, water, phone and Internet access, clothing, food, and transportation requires more than having enough income. You also need to gain the skills for managing that income. You may have a part-time job that provides some income now. As you learn to manage your money now, you are increasing your skills for successfully living on your own. Also, learning to care for your own food, clothing, and transportation needs will help you prepare for living independently.

Preparing for Marriage and Family Living

Adolescence is also a time to develop skills that help you get along with others. When you work on group projects or solve problems with a partner, you learn to share ideas, listen to each other, consider another person's point of view, and collaborate. These are skills that can help you develop long-lasting relationships.

During the teen years, you can also learn how to help others grow and develop. What is needed to help someone grow to maturity? How can you help others reach their potential? Developing these skills will help you prepare for marriage and family living.

Think About Your Reading

How could having a job help you achieve developmental tasks of the teen years? How could being in a school sport or club help you with these tasks?

Preparing for Change

Change is a normal part of life. Many people fear change, though, because it brings unknowns. People prefer individuals and experiences they know because they feel more comfortable. When change comes, it brings new experiences that can make a person feel uncomfortable or afraid. You

can avoid these feelings by learning about change and using the right skills to manage it (**Figure 1.3**).

Gathering Information

Learning as much as possible about upcoming changes can help you prepare for them. For instance, it is helpful to know what changes to expect as your body grows and develops during adolescence. When these changes occur, you will not be upset by them because you know they are normal.

When you get your first job or apartment, you can expect many changes. Couples experience change when they start going out, get engaged, or get married. Still more changes occur when people become parents.

What information will help you adjust to life's changes? What can be expected? What have others felt as they went through these changes? Knowing what to expect is the first step in preparing for change.

Developing Skills to Adjust to the Change

As you gather information about a change, you will identify skills needed to be successful in the new situation. Developing these skills is the second step in preparing for change. For example, a new job may require skills for managing time or relating to customers. As you prepare for a change in a relationship, you may need to develop skills for sharing your inner feelings or better listening skills. With patience and practice, new skills can be developed.

Managing the Change

The third step in preparing for change is to develop a plan to manage it. This step can help make the experience a positive one. For example, what changes might occur when you get your first full-time job? Will your family expect you to buy

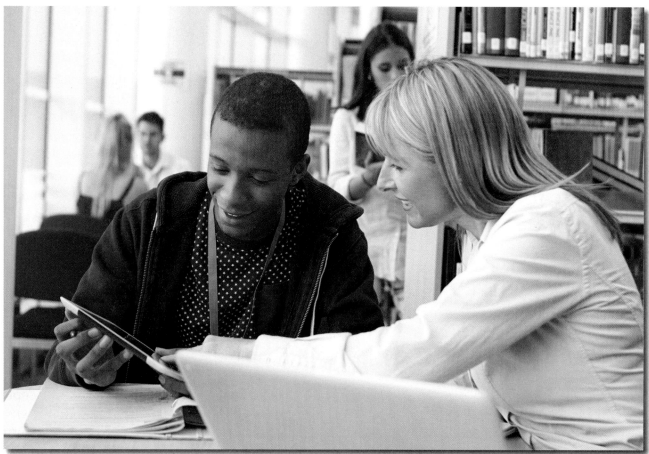

Monkey Business Images/Shutterstock.com

Figure 1.3 Preparing for change as you mature to adulthood can help you feel confident. *What steps do you think teens should take to get prepared?*

all your own clothes? If so, you will need to budget so you have money to purchase them. How would your personal schedule change? You may need to plan a schedule that includes time to work, relax, see friends, and enjoy your family. Planning can help you manage the increased demands on your time (**Figure 1.4**).

Completing high school will begin a time of many changes for you. How will you prepare for them? What information will you gather in advance to help you grow in a positive way? Will it be information related to getting more education, finding a job, or living on your own? What skills will you need to successfully achieve your goals? What plan will you develop for managing all these choices?

The more you know about the coming changes, the more confident you will be to face them. Planning for change will make you less likely to fear it.

Think About Your Reading

Identify a change you will be facing in the near future. What questions would you like answered before this change takes place?

LESSON 1.1

Assess

COMPREHENSION CHECK

1. Explain how your life path is similar to the paths of others and how it is unique.
2. List three benefits of knowing your identity.
3. Describe six developmental tasks of the teen years.
4. What adjustments and responsibilities are associated with independent living?
5. Identify three steps a person can take to prepare for and manage an expected change.

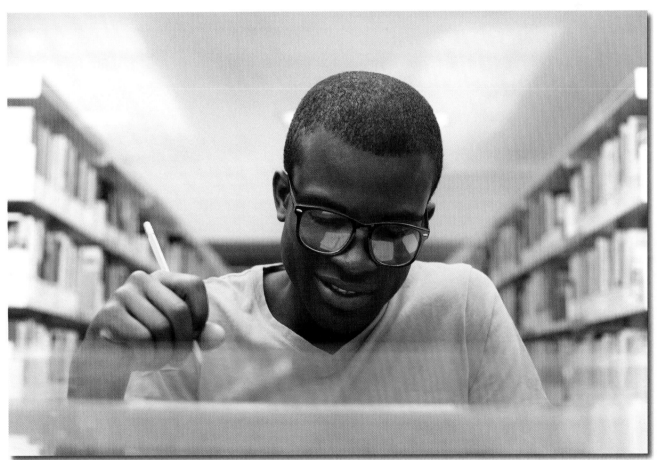

Diego Cervo/Shutterstock.com

Figure 1.4 Developing a plan can help you manage new changes.

Objectives

After studying this lesson, you will be able to

- **identify** hereditary traits that could impact personal identity.
- **explain** what promotes brain development.
- **identify** issues related to hereditary diseases.

Focus Your Reading

1. Create a chart with two columns. In the first column, identify all the traits you have that you think you inherited from your parents. As you read this lesson, record in the second column specific information about genetics that supports (or refutes) your list of inherited traits.

2. Prepare a drawing that shows how information flows in the brain from one nerve cell to another.

When planning for the future, it can help to look at the influences that shape your life. One main factor that affects personal development is **heredity**. Your heredity is the sum of the characteristics that were passed from your ancestors through your parents to you (**Figure 1.5**). The characteristics you inherit make you a unique human being.

Heredity and Personal Identity

Some obvious characteristics that are inherited are physical and seen in your appearance. Your hair color, facial features, and height are examples. These contribute to the way you see yourself and become part of your personal identity.

Other inherited physical traits that may be less obvious can impact your health and your ability to fight diseases. Some impact your ability to develop certain skills and your capacity for intelligence. These traits that impact what you can do will also influence your personal identity.

Content Terms

Build Vocab

heredity
genetics
chromosome
genotype
Punnett square
intelligence
neuron
dendrite
axon
synapse
neurotransmitter
carrier
family tree

Academic Terms

trait
dominant gene
recessive gene
window of opportunity

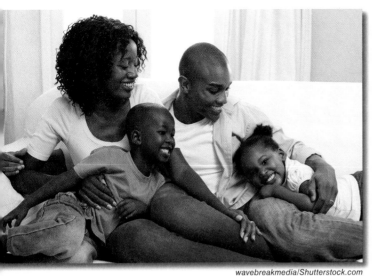

Figure 1.5 What physical characteristics do these family members have in common? *For each shared trait, identify if it is dominant or recessive.*

Heredity is a major factor in your personal growth and development. Your heredity influences your rate of development and the patterns in which you grow and develop. Some of these patterns influence the way you feel, think, and behave and become part of your personal identity. (This topic is covered in-depth in Chapter 2.) Knowing about the characteristics you inherit will give you some insight to your own potential development. You will also pass on to your children part of what you inherit from your parents.

Genes

The science that studies heredity is called **genetics**. Each human being begins life with his or her own set of genetic material. A person normally inherits 23 rod-shaped structures called **chromosomes** from each biological parent.

Chromosomes carry hereditary information from each parent. The father and mother each contribute 23 chromosomes, so the child inherits a total of 46 chromosomes. Each chromosome contains many genes, which determine all inherited characteristics, or *traits*. This genetic "blueprint" exists in the nucleus of every cell in the body.

Because of inherited genes, your personal traits may be similar to a brother, sister, or another family member. The genes that come from both parents combine in different patterns in their children. As a result, brothers and sisters have different traits.

Dominant and Recessive Genes

Genes are classified as either dominant or recessive. *Dominant genes*, when present, determine how a certain trait is expressed in a person. A dominant gene always overrules a recessive gene. *Recessive genes* determine the nature of a trait only when two of them are present. The child must receive one recessive gene from each parent for the recessive characteristic to be expressed. **Figure 1.6** lists some examples of physical traits that are dominant and recessive.

Scientists use letter combinations such as *DD* or *dd* to identify a person's genotype for various traits. A **genotype** is the genetic makeup of an individual or group. A capital letter signifies a dominant trait, such as dimples in one's cheeks. A lowercase letter signifies a recessive trait, such as no dimples on the cheeks. A person with two dominant genes, genotype *DD*, will have dimples. A person with one dominant and one recessive gene, genotype *Dd*, will also have dimples because the dominant *D* gene will be expressed. Only a person with two recessive genes, genotype *dd*, will have no dimples.

Examples of Dominant and Recessive Traits			
Dominant Traits		**Recessive Traits**	
Dimples in cheeks	Freckles	No dimples in cheeks	Lack of freckles
Free earlobes	Widow's peak hairline	Attached earlobes	Straight hairline
Cleft chin	Hitchhiker's thumb	Chin with no cleft	Straight thumb
Blood types A and B		Blood type O	Cystic fibrosis

Figure 1.6 This chart shows some of the inherited traits that are dominant or recessive. *Can you recognize any of your personal traits as dominant or recessive?*

Scientists use a graphic called a **Punnett square**, invented by R.C. Punnett, to determine what possible gene pairs may result from combining two genes (**Figure 1.7**). The genes of the parents are identified along two adjacent sides of the square—one parent per side. Each possible combination is recorded in a box inside the square. A total of four combinations are possible. Consequently, each offspring has a 25 percent chance of having the genotype indicated in each box.

Many traits are influenced by more than one pair of genes. For example, height seems to be determined by at least four pairs of genes. When several genes influence a trait, children of the same parents may show several variations.

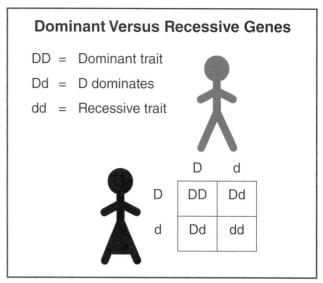

Dominant Versus Recessive Genes

DD = Dominant trait
Dd = D dominates
dd = Recessive trait

	D	d
D	DD	Dd
d	Dd	dd

Figure 1.7 A Punnett square illustrates the possible combinations of a pair of inherited genes. The parents in this example each have one dominant and one recessive gene.

Think About Your Reading

What are some ways you think genetic research might help humankind in the future? What are some possible negative effects of this kind of research?

Brain Development and Intelligence

The way your brain grows, develops, and functions is affected not only by your genes, but also by factors in your environment. Your brain development, in turn, affects your intelligence. **Intelligence** is your capacity for mental activity. It affects your ability to learn, understand, reason, and think. Knowing some key principles about how your brain works can help you make decisions that lead to maximum growth and development.

How Your Brain Functions

Each person is born with over 100 billion nerve cells called **neurons** in his or her brain (**Figure 1.8**). A neuron has four parts: a cell body, dendrites, an axon, and a myelin sheath. The cell body has all the person's genes plus genetic information the neuron needs to carry out the cell's functions. From the cell body, the **dendrites** branch out in

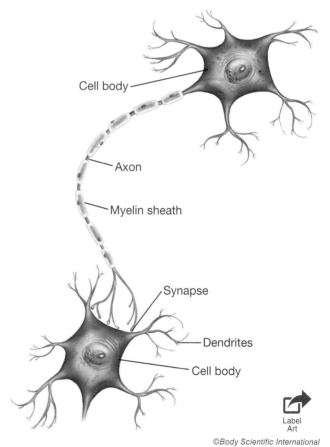

Cell body
Axon
Myelin sheath
Synapse
Dendrites
Cell body

Label Art

©*Body Scientific International*

Figure 1.8 Each brain cell or neuron connects to thousands of other brain cells and can send 250 to 2,500 nerve impulses each second.

extensions that look like fingers or tentacles. Their job is to receive information from other cells. The **axon** is a long fiber that carries information away from the cell body to the dendrites of other nerve cells or to other cells in the body. The myelin sheath is a coating along the axon that helps transmit information along the neuron.

Each neuron connects with thousands of other neurons in the brain. Each new experience you have results in new connections made between neurons. As more signals are sent and received between neurons, these connections grow stronger. The result is that information can be transmitted between neurons faster. This speeds thinking and reaction time.

The space between the axon of a sending neuron and the dendrite of a receiving neuron is called a **synapse**. The body makes chemicals in the synapses that allow messages to be carried from one neuron to another. These chemicals are called **neurotransmitters**.

Different neurotransmitters result in different types of messages. For example, some messages speed up a body response; others slow it down. Some chemicals produce a positive feeling, while others help information flow to different parts of the brain. The way your body responds is controlled by the neurotransmitters.

The chemicals that are produced in your synapses can be affected by both your heredity and your environment. For example, your body produces certain chemicals when you sleep and others when you are awake. Other chemicals are produced when you are in danger or in a stressful situation. These responses are genetic. Environmental factors—like the food you eat and how physically active you are—can also affect which chemicals are produced in the synapses.

How Your Brain Grows and Develops

As you grow and develop, your brain continues to strengthen the pathways that are used. The more you use a pathway, the quicker and stronger the neural connections become. You can see these results when, for example, your performance steadily improves by practicing a skill over and over (**Figure 1.9**). Parts of the brain that are not used

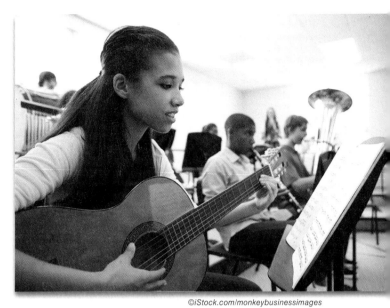

©iStock.com/monkeybusinessimages

Figure 1.9 With practice, your neural connections for a task become stronger, improving your performance. *In what areas have you improved your performance through practice?*

decline as nerve cells die off. This healthy removal of unused cells allows the often-used brain connections to strengthen, which speeds their signals. Thus, your choices can make a physical difference in the structure of your brain.

The most efficient time for learning to take place is called a *window of opportunity*. If the window is missed, nerve cells often die off and the related development may take longer or not take place at all. For example, you are born with the capacity to learn any language. The brain connections that are used to learn the language you speak continue to develop, but the parts you could use to learn other languages die off because of nonuse. After age 10, you are still able to learn another language, but it may take you more time or effort to master that new language than if you had learned it earlier.

Although your heredity determines the number of brain cells you start with, your environment affects the number of connections made among them. Good nutrition and plenty of rest are important for brain development. As you will see in the next lesson, a stimulating environment is just as important. To reach your full intellectual potential, both hereditary and environmental factors need to come together.

Hereditary Health Conditions

Certain diseases and disorders are genetic, meaning they are inherited. With advances in medicine, scientists can study a person's genetic makeup to identify the presence of these genes. Scientists can take a sample of someone's DNA and compare it to DNA from people with various diseases. For instance, scientists know that some conditions result from a change in the sequence of genes on a chromosome.

Some people are **carriers** of a disease or disorder. This means they can pass the condition to their children, but never have it themselves. This situation occurs because they have one recessive gene carrying the condition and a dominant gene carrying a healthy trait. When both parents are carriers, their children have one chance in four of inheriting that disorder.

Each person is likely to carry some defective genes, but no problems result in most cases because the dominant genes are healthy. The defective genes affect a person only when they are combined with defective genes from both parents. This is why marriage between blood relatives is discouraged. Children of these marriages have a higher chance of inheriting pairs of defective genes that may result in disabilities at birth or even in death.

Genes are also a major factor in some intellectual disabilities in children (**Figure 1.10**). Down syndrome is a chromosome disorder that occurs mostly in children born to women over 40 years old. As women age, their DNA molecules may be altered in some way. Altered DNA passed on to a child may result in the disorder occurring in that child.

Real-Life Scenario

A Hereditary Disease

Linda is a sophomore in high school and has already lived longer than most people with her condition. She has cystic fibrosis. Her parents do not have the disease, nor do her brother or sister, however, the disease is hereditary.

Linda appears healthy to those who meet her, but she does not have much longer to live. Every day she undergoes therapy to thin the mucus that affects her breathing and digestion.

Her family members help her with the daily treatments. They have grown very close to one another, realizing that Linda's life will be short. They have also tried to help her live a normal life. She does very well in school and has won honors for her achievements.

The constant stress caused by Linda's condition affects her family. Frequent visits to the hospital strain family finances. The daily therapy routines take time and energy. Family members also feel the emotional strain of not knowing how long Linda will live.

For Discussion

1. Who in Linda's family are carriers of cystic fibrosis? Using *D* for a dominant healthy gene and *d* for a gene for cystic fibrosis, identify a genotype for both her mother and her father.
2. What are the chances that each child in this family would have cystic fibrosis? What are the chances that Linda's brother and sister are carriers of cystic fibrosis? (Use a Punnett square to diagram the answer.)
3. Why might Linda's siblings seek genetic counseling before getting married and starting their own families?
4. Linda's family environment has been affected by her disease. Because of Linda's disease, in what areas might the growth of other family members be slowed? In what areas might their personal growth be enhanced?
5. Citing evidence from the text, explain how Linda's disease could impact her success in completing the developmental tasks of adolescence.

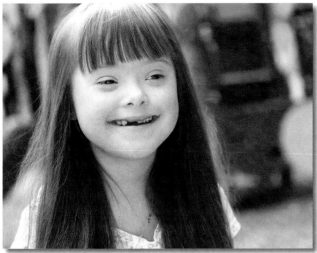
©iStock.com/DenKuvaiev

Figure 1.10 Down syndrome results when a child inherits an extra chromosome. One of the effects of this condition is an intellectual disability.

Think About Your Reading

How might researchers and doctors use DNA information to help identify causes of and cures for hereditary diseases?

Genetic Counseling

Genetic counselors help people understand how hereditary diseases and conditions are passed on and their risk of transmitting one of these conditions to their children. Some people may know that a hereditary condition exists in their family. They may seek out a genetic counselor to see how likely they are to have a child with that condition. Couples who have a child with an inherited disease or disorder may want to seek genetic counseling before having more children. Also, couples related by blood may want to seek genetic counseling before having a family.

Your **family tree** is a list of your blood relatives for several generations. By tracing your family tree, you can identify conditions that could be hereditary in your family. You can also trace other dominant or recessive traits that are passed from one generation to the next.

Medical Research Versus the Right to Privacy

New technologies make it possible to gather information about people's genetic makeup. These technologies can help health care workers identify genetic conditions before they develop. With that information, they can begin treating the condition in some cases. Even if treatment is not possible, individuals and families can prepare themselves for adapting to the condition. Meanwhile, researchers are working to understand these conditions. This research holds the promise of trying to find a way to minimize the impact on people's lives.

At the same time, these advances raise some concerns about the well-being of private citizens. The ability to use a technology to gather such information must be weighed against a person's right to keep the information private and confidential. For instance, if you have a genotype similar to that of a person with a life-threatening disease, would you want to know this? Would you want your health insurance company, your employer, or others to know? Could such information lead to discrimination against you? Concerns for the personal well-being and rights of individuals must be considered. Such issues will continue to be raised as genetic-related technology becomes more advanced.

LESSON 1.2

Assess

COMPREHENSION CHECK

1. Name five characteristics that a person inherits and explain how they could affect personal identity.
2. Explain the difference in the effects of a dominant gene and a recessive gene on the way a trait is expressed.
3. Describe how a pathway in the brain can be made stronger and faster.
4. Explain why a marriage between close relatives is a health risk.
5. Under what circumstances might a couple seek genetic counseling?

Objectives

After studying this lesson, you will be able to

- **identify** the environmental factors that impact personal identity.
- **explain** how factors in the environment can influence growth and development.
- **describe** ways to respond to heredity and environment with resilience.

Focus Your Reading

1. Create a graphic organizer with the lesson headings listed on the left side. As you read, summarize how each environmental factor could affect personal identity.

2. Create a concept web showing how each term relates to growth and development. Include a brief definition or example of each term where it appears in the web.

Content Terms

Build Vocab

environment
prenatal
cultural heritage
peer
resilience
brain plasticity

Academic Terms

sibling
technology
media

Your **environment** includes everything in your surroundings (**Figure 1.11**). Family, friends, home, school, and community are part of your environment. All these factors influence your experiences. As a result, they affect who you are and how you grow and develop. They join with heredity to help shape your personal identity. You inherit certain traits that influence how you look and behave, but then your environment takes over. Your heredity determines your potential for development, but your environment determines if or how that potential is reached.

The Influence of the Family Environment

The family is usually the major human influence in a person's life. This is especially true during the preschool years, when children spend most of their time with parents and other family members. Thus, healthy relationships within the family are important for maximum growth and development as well as for healthy personal identity and self-esteem.

Environmental Factors Affecting Growth and Development
• Family
• Cultural heritage and society
• School
• Peers
• Community
• Religion
• Technology
• Media and electronic entertainment
• Stress and violence

Figure 1.11 Many factors in the environment influence growth and development. *Which of these factors influence you more than the others?*

The Prenatal Environment

Prenatal refers to the months before birth. How well a woman cares for herself during pregnancy affects her baby's prenatal environment. Eating and resting properly and avoiding harmful drugs and medications increase a woman's chance of having a healthy baby.

Poor health practices, on the other hand, can have a negative, long-term impact on the child. Substance abuse by a pregnant woman, poor nutrition, alcohol use, or exposure to harmful radiation can permanently affect a baby's health and brain development.

The Family and the Early Childhood Years

Relationships within the family need to be strong enough that the family can meet children's needs. Families need to create a safe environment for a baby to grow, learn, explore, create, and develop. They need to take care of the baby, keep the baby warm and fed, and protect him or her from harm. This care needs to be provided consistently, 24 hours a day.

Babies need more from their environment than just physical care, however. They also need an environment that makes them feel secure and loved. This helps them grow emotionally and socially. Families need to hold, cuddle, talk to, and play with the baby, and respond to the baby's cries. When children receive warm, loving, and consistent care, they tend to feel safe and secure (**Figure 1.12**).

Children also need a stimulating environment to reach their growth potential. Having a variety of sights, sounds, smells, and textures to explore promotes intellectual development. Parents can contribute to children's intellectual growth in other ways, too. For instance, studies show that parents who read aloud to infants help their children develop language skills. A parent who encourages a child to practice athletic, artistic, or other skills helps that child develop those skills.

A child's environment should promote the growth of independence. As children explore, they discover they can do things on their own. Families can provide tasks for children to do by themselves, such as picking up toys or getting dressed. When children are not allowed to try some tasks on their own, they may doubt their abilities. They may feel ashamed of their lack of skills. Instead of growing toward independence, they become more dependent on others.

Families can also help children learn how to fit into their surroundings. An environment with well-defined limits helps young children learn to control their behavior. For instance, they discover that when they kick something, it moves. With guidance from parents, they can learn that it is okay to kick balls, but not to kick brothers and sisters. In this way, they learn that some activities are safe and acceptable while others are not.

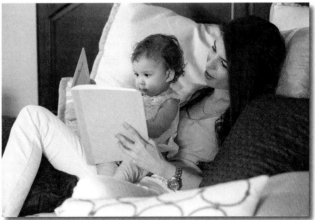
antoniodiaz/Shutterstock.com

Figure 1.12 Children enjoy having stories read to them. *Why do you think being read to makes children feel secure and loved?*

The Family and the Teen Years

The family can help teens through the changes of adolescence by providing a loving and caring environment that encourages growth. Such an environment will help both you and your family cope with changes as you become more independent. A caring environment will also help you accept your identity and develop positive relationships with others.

One way a family can encourage a teen's growth is to allow the teen more opportunities to make personal decisions. Suppose, for instance, a teen wants to go on a school-sponsored trip. After discussing it with his parents, he could take the responsibility for making the needed arrangements. Earning the money for the trip could be his responsibility, too. Taking more responsibility helps the teen develop his own capabilities for decision making (**Figure 1.13**).

Parents also need time to adjust as teens develop and mature. Adolescents may be changing faster than their parents can keep up with. Teens

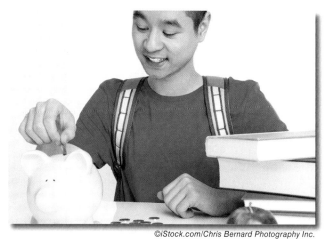

©iStock.com/Chris Bernard Photography Inc.

Figure 1.13 Assuming more responsibility, such as the responsibility for paying for a trip, can help teens develop decision-making skills.

can help their families maintain a loving family environment by showing respect for the ideas, requests, and feelings of their parents. This will help them listen and show respect for the teens' thoughts and feelings. Honest, open communication between teens and parents can help prevent problems from arising.

Family Structure

The structure of a family can influence many areas of a child's life. A family may include any combination of father, mother, children, grandparents, or other relatives. Many families include stepparents and stepchildren as well. Changes in family structure often affect the family's ability to provide a stimulating environment. For instance, after a divorce, there may not be enough money for all the children's needs. The addition of a newborn is likely to reduce the amount of time parents have to listen, share, encourage, and guide other children. Changes in family structure can also introduce new relationships, as when single parents marry and a stepparent enters the family.

Whatever the family structure may be, it is important that the family fulfills its functions and meets the needs of each family member. Sometimes others, such as grandparents, older siblings, or stepparents, help make this happen. Sometimes families turn to resources outside the family, such as child care centers, babysitters, or community youth leaders.

The Influence of Siblings

A *sibling* is a brother or sister. Siblings can be a source of fun and understanding, but they can also be a source of conflict and competition.

A family environment that includes siblings can be beneficial because siblings can learn much from each other. An older sibling can teach a younger sibling certain skills. Siblings often become good

companions who play together and learn to share as they play. They can learn to work together to do a task. These experiences can help children learn to get along with others. Of course, siblings can sometimes be rivals for parents' attention or for family resources.

Sibling Position

Being the first, the last, or a middle child in the family can make a difference in a child's development. Being an only child may also affect development.

Parents are usually idealistic with their first child. They have high expectations for him or her. Older siblings may be given more responsibility in the family. They may be expected to do things for themselves. They may be required to set an example and care for younger siblings. As a result, oldest children often get practice using skills for making decisions, organizing tasks, and supervising others (**Figure 1.14**).

The youngest child often receives a lot of attention. Older siblings may do tasks that the youngest child could and should learn to do alone. As a result, younger children may be slow to develop self-help skills such as dressing themselves. Sometimes younger children may struggle to get a chance to express themselves. When they

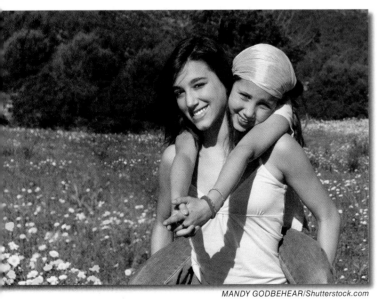

MANDY GODBEHEAR/Shutterstock.com

Figure 1.14 Often older siblings help care for younger children in the family. *How could these relationships benefit both siblings?*

do get a chance to talk, others may not take them seriously. In some families, the expectations for the youngest child are lower than for the oldest child. If families provide fewer limits and responsibilities to a youngest child, that child may appear lazy or undisciplined. In other families, the youngest child develops skills rapidly to keep up with older siblings.

The middle child is not always given the same responsibility as the oldest child or the same attention as the youngest child. Children respond to this middle position in different ways. Some middle children become peacemakers who try to settle differences between other brothers and sisters. Some put extra effort into their work, trying to outdo an older sibling. Some respond by choosing unacceptable activities that will get attention, even if it is negative attention.

> ## Think About Your Reading
> In what ways have you seen that siblings treat each other differently based on their birth position?

The Only Child

An only child does not experience the daily give-and-take of sibling relationships. He or she also does not experience the conflicts that siblings often have. As a result, this child may take longer to learn to resolve conflicts with playmates. Most families with an only child try to provide opportunities for interaction with other children so these skills are learned. These opportunities also give an only child a chance to learn how to share with others, another skill that children with siblings learn.

An only child generally spends more time with adults in one-on-one situations than does a child with siblings. This can stimulate the only child to learn adult behavior at an earlier age. At the same time, an only child may be the center of attention in those situations. When the attention stops, the adultlike behavior may be replaced with immature actions and attitudes. Providing opportunities to interact with other children of the same age can encourage the child to behave more maturely.

Twins and Other Multiple Siblings

Twins—two children born at the same time—often share more than a birthday. These siblings often have very special bonds with one another. Some twins are identical, meaning they share the exact same genetic makeup. They can still develop different personalities and personal identities, however. Some twins are no more alike than any other pair of siblings. These fraternal twins can even be of both genders. They were simply born at the same time. Whether identical or fraternal, twins often feel particularly close to each other. Some even have a sense of what the other is thinking and feeling, without words being spoken.

In other sets of multiple siblings, the children may not have that same closeness to all members of the set. Children who are part of a set of multiple siblings often begin to learn very early to share with one another.

The relationships you have within your family have a major impact on the development of your personal identity and self-esteem. The interactions between family members affect the way you grow and develop, the way you see and view yourself, and your feelings of worth and value.

The Influence of Cultural Heritage and Society

Each family environment is strongly influenced by its **cultural heritage (Figure 1.15)**. Every culture in the world has its unique way of life. The families within these cultures pass on their customs and traditions to their children. Your cultural heritage is learned behavior that is passed from generation to generation. Your family's beliefs, values, relationship patterns, and guidelines for living, based in part on that cultural heritage, shape your own. The holidays you celebrate, the foods you eat, and the traditions or ceremonies you observe are part of your culture.

In a large society like the United States, children are exposed to many different cultures. That is especially true for children who grow up in a large city. It can also be true of children in smaller towns that have a mix of cultures. A diverse community can enrich the lives of all. Sharing values

and traditions can help residents better understand one another. This can foster mutual respect for diverse opinions and lifestyles.

The values of the United States are also part of your environment. Founding documents like the Declaration of Independence and the U.S. Constitution establish that all Americans have equal rights. They also emphasize the importance of freedom in promoting happiness. American values also include the importance of respect for others' rights and tolerance and acceptance of differences.

> ## Think About Your Reading
> What multicultural influences can you identify around you? In what ways have these influences affected you personally?

The Influence of the School Environment

School-age children are busy experiencing new situations and becoming more self-reliant. They learn new skills, make new friends, and join group activities. Their activities and interests outside the family increase.

Families can help children adjust to this new environment by providing encouragement, love, and acceptance. They can help children practice skills learned at school. They can attend school events and show an interest in their children's schoolwork and classmates. This can help children develop a positive attitude about school and their learning.

A quality school environment provides a setting that encourages students to learn and grow. School facilities and after-school activities can inspire students to interact with schoolmates in clubs or sports. The curriculum should offer a wide range of courses that stimulate students' intellectual growth and prepare them for career opportunities and active citizenship.

Teachers in a quality school environment encourage students by helping them find areas in which they can succeed. Some students need a chance to learn at a slower pace. Others need

The Continuum of Cultural Views of Families	
Group Focus	**Individual Focus**
Extended family households include other relatives—such as grandparents, aunts, and uncles— who live in the same household and assist with raising children, providing income, and sharing the work of the family.	Families live independently with varying degrees of support from relatives. Some families have little or no support, while others may receive some assistance with childrearing.
Multiple generations live, play, and work together.	Young adults are expected to leave home and become independent. Self-sufficiency is valued.
Maintaining family relationships is more important than work, occupation, or income.	A high value is placed on education, hard work, and career success.
Identity, self-respect, and confidence are closely tied to one's family members or relatives.	Identity in adulthood is tied closely to one's occupation, work organization, formal education, and income.
Emphasis is on working together.	Emphasis is on competition between individuals.
Good manners, common courtesy, and sensitivity to others are highly valued.	Assertiveness, directness, and confidence are valued.
Traditions and ceremonies are honored.	Immediate needs take precedence over traditions.
Needs of the family take priority over needs of the individual.	Individuals do not feel obligated to follow the wishes of relatives.
Family values are strong and are reinforced from one generation to the next.	Family values vary by generation.
Family religious beliefs strongly impact the values and behaviors of family members.	Religious beliefs vary and are up to the individual.
Roles and responsibilities for men and women are defined with specific expectations.	Roles and responsibilities for men and women vary depending on needs, resources, and individual desires.
Parenting methods are strict as children are expected to obey.	Parenting methods are persuasive as children are urged to consider matters from the parent's point of view.

Figure 1.15 Each cultural group views the relationship of family as a group and individual members in its own way, placing it somewhere along this continuum. *Where would you place your family?*

more challenging work. All students need praise and encouragement for their achievements.

The school years are a time to stimulate brain development by exploring many different experiences and repeating them. By repeating skills, brain connections for these skills become stronger, thus promoting successful learning.

Think About Your Reading

What subjects do you find most interesting in school? What subjects do you think most stimulate your brain development?

The Influence of Peers

Peers are the people who are your age. The influence of your peers is greatest during the teen years, and your experiences with them will influence the way you see yourself. From interacting with your peers, you make judgments about how you look, how important you are, and how successful you are. Your peers can make you feel like you fit in and belong. At other times, they can make you feel left out.

Teens can offer understanding to one another as they face similar situations. They can share common experiences and feelings. Peer relationships help you learn what qualities you like or dislike in a friend. You also learn to identify such qualities within yourself. These interactions can help you understand your own identity.

Your peers can also influence the plans you make for your future. You may make decisions about your education based on your peers' choices. You might seek your best friend's opinion of your ideal career or marriage partner. Peers also influence many of your immediate actions since you often face the same decisions that affect them.

As teens spend time with their friends, they learn to develop close relationships (**Figure 1.16**). Close friends feel accepted for who they are. They are able to share and communicate deep inner feelings without fear of being embarrassed or laughed at. When young adults have trouble developing such relationships, they feel alone and isolated. Close peer relationships are important because they help prepare the young adult for marriage.

Sometimes peers may make choices that a teen feels is not right for him or her. When this happens, that teen needs to make a personal choice rather than following the group. Negative choices regarding sex, alcohol, drugs, and tobacco can affect a young person for the rest of his or her life. Skills for handling peer pressure are important for teens to develop so they can confidently make decisions that support their own goals.

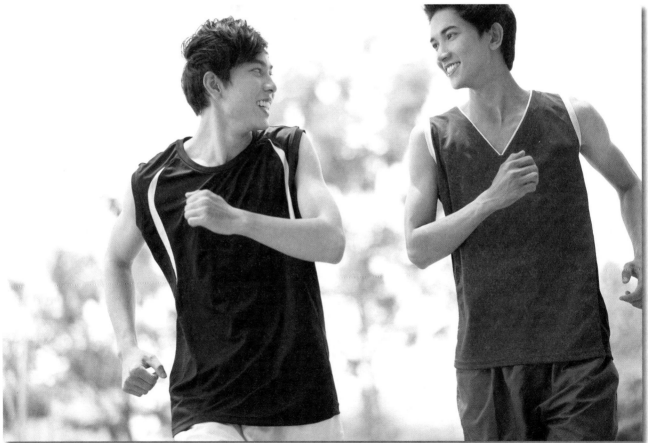

Dragon Images/Shutterstock.com

Figure 1.16 Spending time together on common interests can help develop close friendships.

Chapter 1   A Close-Up View of You   **23**

The Influence of Religious Beliefs

Your family's religious beliefs influence your outlook on life and your guidelines for living. These beliefs address important life-and-death questions, such as: What is the purpose of life? What should you try to accomplish in life? How should you live your life? What happens when you die?

Associating with others with the same religious beliefs and being an active member of a religious community are often an important part of a person's environment (**Figure 1.17**). Religious beliefs can provide meaning and direction to a person's life. The fact that many people hold different beliefs makes it important to be respectful of such differences in the larger society.

The Influence of the Community

The community in which you live is part of your environment. Many different types of communities exist, ranging from small towns to big cities. Each community has a particular influence on its residents. A community may influence the jobs people hold, the friends they make, and the activities they join.

The community environment is influenced by the resources available, such as affordable housing choices and the various industries or businesses that provide job opportunities. Schools with good teaching staffs, facilities, and programs offer quality education. Parks and recreation programs attract families with children.

Other community resources also influence the lives of residents. Clean air, water, and streets provide a healthful environment. A low crime rate makes residents feel more secure and protected. A variety of shopping facilities offer convenience and choices for obtaining needed goods and services. Opportunities to increase knowledge are provided by libraries as well as by technical colleges and universities. Various religious institutions serve people of different beliefs. A resource-rich community inspires young people to stay and build a life for themselves and their families.

> ## Think About Your Reading
> What are the benefits of staying in your home community after completing your education? Are there any drawbacks?

The Influence of Technology

Technology is a powerful element in today's environment. It influences every aspect of life. *Technology*, the practical application of knowledge, usually involves the development or use of special tools or processes to solve problems.

Look around you—technology is part of your everyday world. New technologies influence the food you eat, the clothes you wear, the car you drive, and the work you do. Communication technologies can affect your personal growth and relationships.

Today's technology allows workers, students, and family members to manage day-to-day tasks more conveniently. It provides various learning and entertainment options and instant communication with others. Because of technology, fewer people work at labor-intense jobs, and more are living longer. These effects are generally considered very positive.

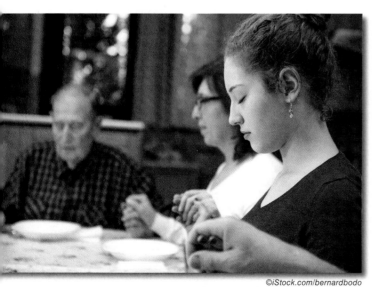

©iStock.com/bernardbodo

Figure 1.17 Religious beliefs can impact a family's values.

On the negative side, an overuse of technology may cause people to neglect personal growth and relationships. In today's fast-paced, high-tech world, people must take care not to allow technology to replace in-person contact. Also, people need to use communication technology carefully to avoid the release of private information or contact with inappropriate material or people. Parents need to monitor closely how their children use communication technology. An understanding of both positive and negative impacts can help people make choices that will lead to personal growth.

The Influence of Media

Technology has increased the types of media and entertainment sources available. *Media* include communication methods like television, magazines, and websites. These media are used to communicate with, and often entertain, large numbers of people. As people have more technology in their homes, the creators of media and entertainment can influence the public—sometimes without people realizing they are being influenced.

For many individuals, the celebrities seen daily on television become models to imitate—for making friends, developing relationships, and achieving romantic success. Think about the models you see on TV. Are they realistic? Do you agree with the values they represent? If not, you may wish to choose others to be the models for your behavior.

Some research shows a link between violent, aggressive behavior and watching violent movies or television shows or playing violent video games. When selecting entertainment options, people need to choose carefully. The choices they make may affect how well people control their emotions and actions.

Think About Your Reading

How do you feel after searching websites or playing video games for several hours? What steps can you take to be sure your entertainment media has a positive impact on your life?

Advertising is a prominent feature of most entertainment media. In fact, the dollars you spend on advertised goods help finance these media outlets. Advertising can inform you about new or improved products in the market. It can also lead people to buy goods they cannot really afford because they are trying to be seen as attractive or intelligent. Being aware of how ads try to influence you can help you make wiser choices.

Advertisers conduct research to learn why people prefer certain items over others. That information helps them develop ads that display their products in appealing ways to persuade consumers to choose their products over others (**Figure 1.18**). You might want to periodically consider how media influences your daily life. What advertising information can be useful to you in your personal growth? What messages in advertising get in the way of your growth and development?

Stress, Violence, and the Global Environment

Today's fast-paced society pressures people to succeed at school, work, and home. News stories or web messages about terrorism, war, and violence in communities can also cause stress. Some stress is positive because it prompts a person to act.

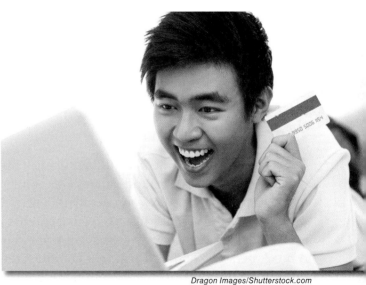

Dragon Images/Shutterstock.com

Figure 1.18 Advertising affects buying decisions, often unconsciously. *Which recent ad most impressed you?*

For example, feeling stress over a future test will probably cause you to study hard for it.

Extreme or long-term stress can have a negative effect on your growth, however. Exposure to stress and violence can trigger the *fight-or-flight response*, which is the instinctive reaction of the body to protect itself from harm by preparing to fight or fleeing to safety. This response includes a rapid heart rate and faster breathing. Even after the person is safe, these responses may persist for a while. The impact of living in this state during development is negative. A child exposed to too much negative stress may become impulsive, aggressive, and hyperactive. His or her ability to think logically and develop language skills may also decrease.

A child who grows up in a stressful environment may develop special learning needs as well. This is not necessarily the fault of anyone in particular—least of all the child. Sometimes unknown factors affect the brain's development. It is important that parents, teachers, and others who work with these children understand their special needs and the best ways to help them learn. This help is necessary for the child to reach his or her maximum potential for growth and development.

Think About Your Reading

What are some ways that violence in your environment could affect growth and development? What types of teen activities or experiences could possibly stimulate a fight-or-flight response?

The Environment in the Adult Years

An adult's environment continues to affect his or her identity, attitudes, and actions. An adult's job is a very important environmental influence on an adult's life and identity. Just like young children, adults identify themselves by what they are able to do. A person's job has a title that identifies the worker. If a person works at something that he or she feels is important and worthwhile, it increases that person's feelings of worth. Doing a job well gives workers a sense of satisfaction. The same is true about what a person does in his or her community, especially if it is extensive or extends across many years.

Many adults take a spouse and follow the path of parenting, passing on their *heritage*—their family beliefs and traditions—to their children. Children become a new influence in the adult's environment. The identity of the adult is often influenced by his or her parenting experiences and later by experiences in grandparenting. All these experiences can lead to a full and satisfying life (**Figure 1.19**).

Responding with Resilience

Many factors impact how you developed into who you are today. As you study the effects of heredity and environment on your personal identity, you may feel that there are limits to your freedom to act and choose. It is true that your genetic makeup is fixed and your environment may not be how you would like it to be. You still have great control over your life and your identity, however.

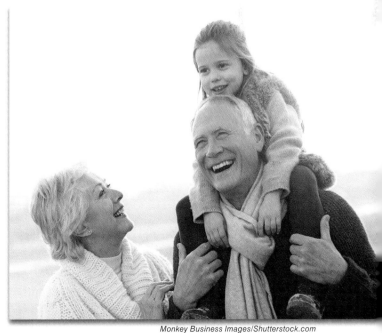

Monkey Business Images/Shutterstock.com

Figure 1.19 Sharing activities with their grandchild gives these grandparents a feeling of fulfillment.

Scientists continually make new discoveries about the brain and the human body's amazing **resilience**. This is the body's ability to adjust to misfortune or serious changes and thrive. For instance, individuals who suffer an injury to a part of the brain respond by using other parts of the brain not specialized for that role. The brain compensates for its loss as much as possible.

This ability of the brain to respond to changes is known as **brain plasticity**. This means the brain does not stay the same, but constantly changes throughout life. As people of any age learn new information, develop new skills, and interact with others in different experiences, the brain grows neurons, wires new connections, and eliminates unused connections. The brain's ability to change helps people be resilient.

Your heredity or environment may have hindered certain aspects of development. The key question is this: In what ways can you respond with resilience? What can you do to stimulate your own growth to maximum development?

The brain has potential to keep developing as it gets used. You can learn a new skill, read more, or develop new interests. As you learn something new and expand your interests, your brain develops new connections (**Figure 1.20**). Make the most of the brain power you have—and by using your brain, you will gain more.

You can make the most of your situation in other ways too. Seek positive experiences that develop your identity and enhance your personal growth and development. These experiences will help you act independently, tackle challenges successfully, and progress to maturity.

Individuals may have special needs resulting from hereditary or environmental factors. As they grow and develop their personal identity and self-esteem, they need encouragement to reach their maximum potential as well as resources that help them experience success. The family that responds with resilience will seek effective ways to help their child reach full potential. Health care professionals, teachers, community members—all can assist the family in meeting such challenges.

COMPREHENSION CHECK

1. Describe three characteristics of a family environment that could impact the growth of self-esteem during the early years.
2. Give two examples of how a family's cultural heritage influences a person's identity and family relationships.
3. How could sibling position in a family affect the relationships a child has with family members?
4. How can teen peers help one another mature?
5. How can the community impact a person's personal identity?
6. Explain the biological effect of a stressful environment on development.
7. What are three aspects of the environment that may become part of an adult's identity?
8. Explain what it means to respond to your hereditary and environmental background with resilience.

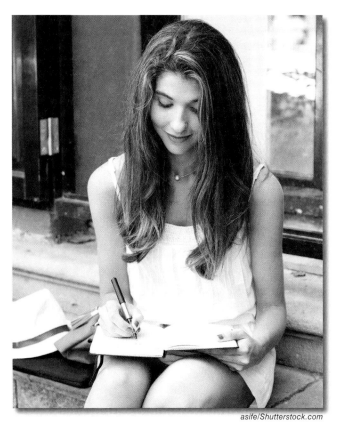

asife/Shutterstock.com

Figure 1.20 By learning and by practicing your skills, you can help your brain develop new connections. This helps you reach your full potential.

CHAPTER 1 REVIEW AND ASSESSMENT

CHAPTER SUMMARY

As a teen, several major changes in your life await you. These include developing mature relationships, having a career, living on your own, and perhaps choosing a marriage partner and raising a family. An important step in preparing for these changes is knowing and accepting your personal identity.

You inherited unique characteristics from your biological parents that influence every aspect about you. Your inherited traits can also be passed on to future generations.

The development of your inherited characteristics is influenced by your environment. Everything and everybody in your environment affect your growth and development. Your heredity and environment work together to make you a unique person. Understanding how these factors impact you can help you make wise choices that lead to developing your full potential.

VOCABULARY ACTIVITIES

1. In teams, create categories for the following terms and classify as many of the terms as possible. Share your ideas with the class.

Content Terms

adolescence (1.1)
axon (1.2)
brain plasticity (1.3)
carrier (1.2)
chromosome (1.2)
cultural heritage (1.3)
dendrite (1.2)
developmental task (1.1)
DNA (1.1)
environment (1.3)
family tree (1.2)
gene (1.1)
genetics (1.2)
genotype (1.2)
heredity (1.2)
intelligence (1.2)
neuron (1.2)
neurotransmitter (1.2)
peer (1.3)
personal identity (1.1)
prenatal (1.3)
Punnett square (1.2)
resilience (1.3)
self-esteem (1.1)
synapse (1.2)

2. Write each of the following terms on a sheet of paper. For each term, quickly write a word you think relates to the term. In small groups, exchange papers. Take turns having each person explain a term on the list until all terms have been explained. If team members disagree with any explanation, refer to a current dictionary.

Academic Terms

dominant gene (1.2)
interdependent (1.1)
life span (1.1)
media (1.3)
recessive gene (1.2)
sibling (1.3)
technology (1.3)
trait (1.2)
unique (1.1)
window of opportunity (1.2)

ASSESS

Your Knowledge

3. Define *personal identity*, *heredity*, and *environment*.
4. List the major developmental tasks of the teen years.
5. Identify the hereditary factors that affect development.
6. Identify the environmental factors that impact development.

Your Understanding

7. What can you do to prepare for future life changes?
8. How is your life path unique? How is your life interdependent with others?
9. How does each developmental task of the teen years relate to future changes in life?
10. How does heredity affect the way a person grows and develops?
11. How does a person's environment affect his or her growth and development?

Your Skills

12. Identify your personal characteristics and which are influenced by your heredity.
13. Analyze how the global environment has affected you personally and explain ways that it has affected your growth and development.
14. Predict ways you could respond with resilience to various factors in your life to stimulate your own growth to maturity.
15. Identify a change that you will face when you graduate from high school. Describe the steps you can take to prepare for and manage that change.

CRITICAL THINKING

16. **Predict Outcomes.** Choose one of the following activities and write a paragraph predicting the consequences of the activity on your environment. Explain how the action could affect other people, such as family members, friends, classmates, or teachers. Include both direct and indirect effects of the action. Cite evidence from the text to support your predictions.
    - Going camping with friends for the weekend
    - Participating in a school sport
    - Working at a part-time job after school

17. **Draw Conclusions.** Develop a collage of pictures illustrating the factors that make your life path unique. Include both hereditary and environmental factors. Cite evidence from the text to support your choice of pictures.

18. **Make Inferences.** Imagine your future and diagram on a time line what you hope will occur. Include the major events and relationships you want in your life. Cite evidence from the text that indicates how two of these events relate to developmental tasks of the teen years. Describe two major decisions you must make to achieve your time-line goals.

19. **Classify Findings.** Evaluate your present environment for factors that stimulate or hinder your personal identity, self-esteem, and ability to develop healthy relationships. Consider all areas of your environment, including family influences. Organize your findings in a graph or chart, separating the factors into positive, negative, or neutral influences on your development. Cite evidence from the text to support your evaluations. *Choice*: Analyze how the family influences all family members, including those with special needs.

CORE SKILLS

20. **Speaking, Listening, Writing.** Interview someone who has experienced a hereditary disease. Include questions related to attitudes about the disease, how the disease affects other family members, and fears about the disease affecting future generations. Consider how the disease impacts a person's ability to live alone or hold a job. Write a paper describing the impacts of the disease on the individual and his or her family. *Choice*: Identify community resources available to help people with hereditary diseases. *Group option*: Work with a partner.

21. **Reading, Writing.** Read two news articles from your local newspaper and identify how that information affects you directly or indirectly. Write a paragraph explaining your findings. Reference the source of your news article. Then respond to one article by writing a "Letter to the Editor," expressing your views on that topic. *Choice*: Share with the class how your views could impact others in the community.

22. **Writing.** Write an essay, poem, or song describing the life of a typical young person growing up in your community. Include a description of environmental factors that will influence the person's growth and development. Analyze and explore the adjustments and responsibilities they will face as independent adults. Cite and reference evidence from the text to support your description.

23. **Research, Writing.** Draw a family tree that includes you, your parents, grandparents, and great-grandparents. Identify the physical traits you possess that can be traced to members included in your family tree. Determine the average life span in your family. In a paragraph, explain how you determined the number.

24. **Research, Writing.** Identify a change that a typical teen might expect to experience in the next year and investigate what he or she would need to know about this change. Identify two or more sources of this information, including at least one Internet site. Gather information and identify what skills could help a teen adjust to this change. Use the information to prepare a multimedia presentation and present your findings to the class. Reference your sources of information in your presentation.

25. **Research, Writing.** Search the Internet to explore how technology has expanded the research on human genes and disease traits. Possible search terms include *human genome*, *genetic disorder*, and *biotechnology research*. Prepare a one-page report on one aspect of such technology, citing evidence from at least two sources.

26. **Writing, Speaking.** Develop a questionnaire you can use to survey others' feelings related to future life changes. Survey three classmates, three adults your parents' age, and three retired adults. Categorize their responses into changes that are feared and changes that are anticipated. Using a digital device, develop a chart or graph showing each age group and the number of changes feared or anticipated.

CAREER READINESS

27. **Investigating Career Requirements.** Investigate a career related to genetic counseling as well as two other counseling fields, such as school counseling and career counseling. Compare and contrast the information you find by answering these questions: What is different about the job responsibilities and required expertise? How much time, effort, and experience does it take to become proficient? What personal traits are ideal? Find information on counseling careers by searching the websites of the National Society of Genetic Counselors and the American Counseling Association. Which career area best fits with your career goals? Summarize your findings in a two-page report.

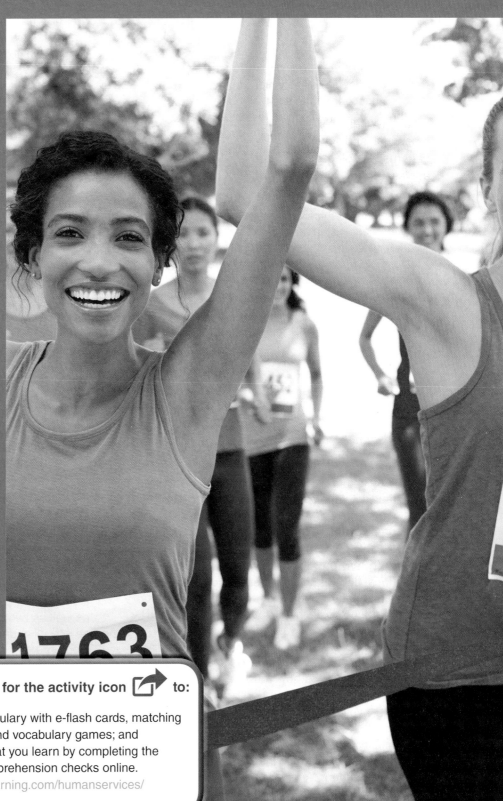

Reading Prep

Preview the chapter by scanning the text headings and images. Study the charts included in the chapter. Write a paragraph predicting what you think you will learn in the chapter.

Key Questions

Questions to answer as you study this chapter:

- What choices can help teens reach physical, intellectual, emotional, and social maturity?
- How can people develop strength in character?
- How can teens develop a healthy personality?

While studying this chapter, look for the activity icon 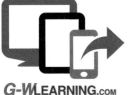 to:

- **build** vocabulary with e-flash cards, matching activities, and vocabulary games; and
- **assess** what you learn by completing the lesson comprehension checks online.
  www.g-wlearning.com/humanservices/

G-WLEARNING.COM

wavebreakmedia/Shutterstock.com

AFTER STUDYING THIS CHAPTER, YOU WILL

KNOW:

- What physical, intellectual, emotional, and social growth patterns take place in adolescence.
- Characteristics of maturity in all areas of development.
- Factors affecting the development of personality.

UNDERSTAND:

- How various factors contribute to development so a person can reach his or her growth potential in all areas.
- How self-concept and self-esteem contribute to a healthy personality.

BE ABLE TO DO:

- Project the impact of personal maturity on relationships.
- Analyze the effect personal maturity could have on job performance.
- Assess personal temperament and response patterns.

GETTING STARTED

Janine stares into space, wishing she could skip gym class. Today the class will be swimming, and she cannot bear the thought of wearing a swimsuit in front of her classmates. "They'll see how awful I look and laugh at me!" she says to herself.

She notices Rhonda is already in her swimsuit. Kim, also in her swimsuit, catches up with Rhonda. "Wow, they both look great," Janine says.

After the other girls file out of the locker room, Janine slowly changes into her swimsuit. A feeling of discomfort grips her as the bell rings. She takes one last look at herself in the mirror and realizes it is time to face her peers.

Most young people have fears from time to time about being different from others. They are afraid they will be rejected or laughed at by classmates. Teens tend to rate themselves by what they see in others their age. Compared to others, they may think, "I'm too fat (or thin)," "I'm too tall (or short)," or "Parts of me are too big (or too small)."

These differences in development may concern you and make the process of growing seem complex and difficult. In fact, all persons follow certain patterns of development—though teens follow these patterns at different rates. Learning more about these growth and development patterns can help you understand and accept your unique pattern. Growth patterns in four areas of development influence who you are and who you are becoming. Thus, they affect your personal identity.

GROWTH PATTERNS TO ADULTHOOD

Content Terms

Build Vocab

physical development
rate of development
adolescent growth spurt
puberty
intellectual development
brainstem
cerebellum
limbic system
cortex
corpus callosum
concrete thinking
abstract thinking
critical thinking
emotional development
social development
diversity
socialization
moral development
role
character
ethics
self-discipline
integrity

Academic Terms

sequence
logic
visualizing
assumption

Objectives

After studying this lesson, you will be able to

- **describe** physical, intellectual, emotional, and social growth patterns to maturity.
- **determine** factors that influence character development.
- **understand** how character is connected to ethics.
- **analyze** the potential effect of personal maturity on relationships and job performance.

Focus Your Reading

1. Organize your notes with a graphic organizer. Create a chart with these column headings: *Growth Pattern, Characteristics During Teen Years,* and *Actions to Promote Maturity.* Include these row headings: *Physical, Intellectual, Social,* and *Emotional.* As you read, fill in details along each row and under each column heading.
2. For each term related to brain structure, draw a picture, diagram, or symbol of the type of brain activity each area controls.

Human growth patterns occur in four areas:

- physical
- intellectual
- emotional
- social

Adolescence is a time when individuals see tremendous changes. The major adolescent growth patterns in each of these areas are listed in **Figure 2.1**.

Growth patterns follow an orderly *sequence*; that is, the steps occur in a specific order. For instance, babies move their arms and legs randomly at first. As their muscles develop, they learn to use their arms and legs to pull themselves around along the floor. Next, they learn to crawl on hands and knees. Finally, the toddler reaches the stage of walking. This is an example of a physical growth pattern, but patterns occur in all areas of development.

Adolescent Growth Patterns

Physical	• Hormone production increases: estrogen in females and testosterone in males.
	• Growth spurt resulting in increased height and weight.
	• Primary sex characteristics develop: reproductive organs mature.
	• Secondary sex characteristics develop.
	    Hair grows under the arms and in the pubic area.
	    Male voice lowers in pitch.
	    Males develop facial hair and hair on chest.
	    Breast formation increases in females.
	    Females experience widening of hips.
	• Body makeup changes due to distribution of fat and muscle.
	• Strength and ability to exercise increase due to changes in circulatory and respiratory systems.

Intellectual	• Sudden growth spurt occurs in brain cells. • Formal thinking skills increase. • Abstract ideas are used. • Logical reasoning improves. • Ability to visualize the future increases.
Emotional	• Intense emotions are felt and expressed. • Emotions fluctuate. • Ability to verbally identify emotions increases. • Ability to control emotional behavior increases. • Realistic sense of self-identity forms.
Social	• Social skills improve. • More ideas are shared. • Others' viewpoints are considered. • Ability to cooperate to complete tasks increases. • Close relationships with peers develop. • Personal identity is formed. • Personal standards develop.

Figure 2.1 Growth patterns explain the unique way teens grow. *How could differences in rate of development affect personal identity as a person goes through these growth patterns?*

Although normal growth follows a pattern, each person proceeds through the stages of the growth sequence at his or her own pace. This pace is that person's **rate of development**. For instance, some teens develop physically at an earlier age than others. Some grow taller or more muscular before others. Some are well developed before others barely begin to develop.

Your rate of development does not affect the limits of your overall development. Someone who develops early will not necessarily grow taller or bigger or be more intelligent than classmates. For instance, in eighth grade, one boy may be 6 feet tall while another is closer to 5 feet tall, but several years later, when both finish growing, they may be the same height.

Reaching your full growth potential, or the greatest growth possible, depends on several factors. Heredity and environment both influence your overall growth and development. For instance, a teen with relatively short parents is not likely to grow to be very tall. How that teen takes care of

herself determines how she meets her growth potential, though. Environmental influences like having a nutritious diet and good health care will help her grow to her full potential height.

Think About Your Reading

How do you think different growth rates affect the feelings that young teens have about themselves?

Physical Development

Physical growth patterns are the easiest to observe during the teen years. **Physical development** refers to the growth of and changes to your body. These changes affect your internal body systems as well as your height and weight and other external characteristics. Physical development continues from birth to adulthood, but the changes that take place in adolescence are dramatic.

Adolescent Growth Spurt

One change that takes place during the teen years is a period of sudden growth called the **adolescent growth spurt**. Noticeable body changes occur during this growth period. Adolescent girls usually start their growth spurt before adolescent boys. They grow rapidly in height and weight. The average age for girls to reach adult height is 17. Boys become stronger as their muscles develop rapidly, their shoulders widen, and their waists narrow. They generally reach adult height at about age 21.

The adolescent growth spurt occurs at puberty. **Puberty**, when reproductive organs mature, takes place between 9 and 16 years of age for most persons. Hormones bring about sexual maturity and other physical changes within the body. Figure 2.1 lists these changes, called *primary and secondary sex characteristics.*

Reaching Physical Maturity

Factors such as accidents, disease, and illness can prevent complete physical growth and development from occurring. To avoid health risks, take good care of yourself and get periodic physical checkups. Get the rest you need, and get regular physical activity. Eat nutritious meals. Avoid harmful substances and activities, and take safety precautions. Make wise decisions about what you do and where you go. By taking these steps, you should be able to reach physical maturity and live a long, healthy life (**Figure 2.2**).

Think About Your Reading

How could your daily choices affect your ability to reach physical maturity?

Intellectual Development

A second area of growth is intellectual development. **Intellectual development** refers to the growth of the brain and mental skills. These skills include your ability to use words, numbers, and ideas. You take information into your brain through your five senses—what you see, hear, taste, touch, and smell. You then use this information to reason, solve problems, make decisions, and think creatively and to respond to your experiences.

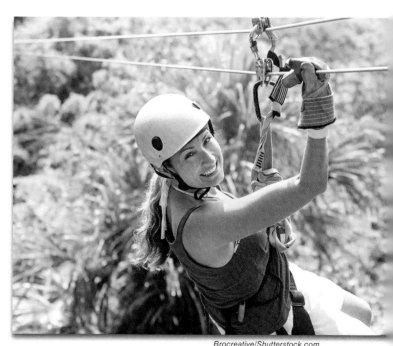

Brocreative/Shutterstock.com

Figure 2.2 Being active and adventurous is natural during the teen years. *How could following safety precautions help you reach your physical potential?*

Parts of the Brain and Their Functions

The diagram in **Figure 2.3** shows some parts of the brain. The brainstem, midbrain, and cerebellum control actions. The limbic system controls emotion-related responses. The cortex and cerebellum carry out thinking and movement. As you mature, you develop the thinking part of your brain so it controls your responses to your environment.

- The **brainstem** controls life functions such as the beating of the heart and breathing. The brainstem is involved in getting information out to different body parts and producing a physical response. When there is a threat to the body, the brainstem controls the body's responses and ensures survival.

- The **cerebellum** controls automatic movements. For instance, once you learn to ride a bike, you do it automatically. You have stored this information in the cerebellum and draw on it without consciously thinking about it. The cerebellum also appears to be involved in coordinating complex thinking processes—ones used in mature intellectual activities. This part of the brain appears to continue developing well into a person's early twenties.

- The *midbrain*, located at the upper end of the brainstem, controls some reflex actions and is involved in some voluntary movements.

- The **limbic system** consists of four main structures in the brain that control emotions and hormone production as well as eating, drinking, and sleeping. This system is also involved in long-term memory storage.

- The **cortex**, also known as the *cerebrum*, is the part of the brain that controls thinking, decision making, and judgment. This is the part of the brain people usually refer to when they talk about intellectual development. It is divided into different regions, some of which are connected to processing information from

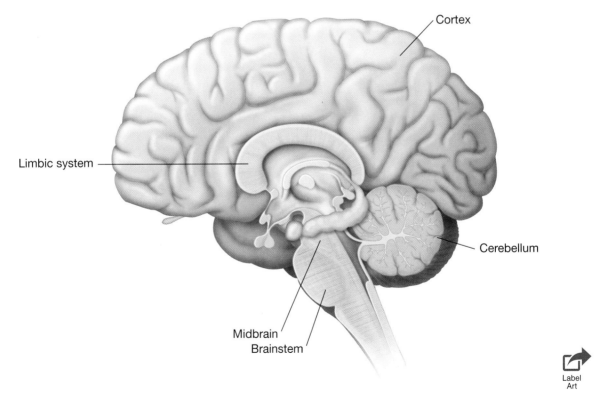

Label Art

©*Body Scientific International*

Figure 2.3   The side view of the brain shows the three major areas: the brainstem and cerebellum, which control movement and motor responses; the limbic system, which controls emotions and their interactions with other parts of the brain; and the cortex, which controls thinking, decision making, and judgment. *How could understanding how your brain works help you increase your performance?*

the senses. See the diagram of the cortex in **Figure 2.4** to learn what brain functions each region controls.

The cortex is divided in half vertically, so each region has a left brain half and a right brain half. Each half processes information from a different perspective. The two halves of the cortex communicate continuously as you take in information and process it. Together, the two halves help you get a clear picture of the stimuli you are receiving. The **corpus callosum** is the cable of neurons that connects the two halves of the brain. This area appears to change and grow during the teen years.

The Development of the Adolescent Brain

The parietal lobe (touch), occipital lobe (vision), and temporal lobe (language) are quite developed by the teen years. Your abilities to sense and process touch, vision, and language stimuli are mature. Just as important physical changes take place in the body, though, some areas of the brain undergo major changes in adolescence. A major growth spurt takes place in the frontal lobes of the cortex around age 11 for girls and 12 for boys. These areas are the part of the brain responsible for thinking, problem solving, planning, and making judgments. The frontal lobes do not fully mature until young adulthood. Therefore, the teen years are important in developing this part of the brain. After a growth spurt, your brain again starts to prune the neural connections that have not been put in use. The pathways you use create more connections with other parts of your brain. The pathways you do not use get pruned, and the connections die off.

The physical growth of brain cells and the connections between them is directly related to mature intellectual skills. When people develop intellectually, they can think in abstract ways. They can use logic and judgment and are able to visualize the future.

> **Think About Your Reading**
> What opportunities during the teen years are critical for intellectual growth to maturity?

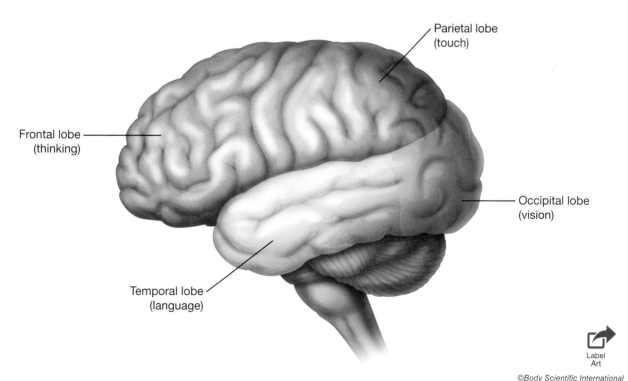

Label Art

©*Body Scientific International*

Figure 2.4 The overview of the cortex shows four major regions. Each controls different brain functions. *Which careers do you think would use knowledge of the brain's functioning in day-to-day operations?*

Thinking Abstractly

The development of thinking skills proceeds through stages, beginning with **concrete thinking**. This type of thinking is related to specific objects that can be seen or touched. Suppose a school-age child sees water in a pan heated and steam rising from it. The child can then recognize that water, when heated, turns into steam.

During adolescence, teens develop the ability to think about more abstract ideas. **Abstract thinking** refers to thoughts about something you cannot see, touch, taste, smell, or hear. Love is an example of an abstract idea. You cannot touch or examine it, but you can think about it and experience it. Concepts such as love, happiness, friendship, loyalty, and bravery are all abstract ideas.

Developing Logic

As young people mature, they begin to use abstract ideas in a logical manner. This process of using *logic* involves connecting several abstract ideas to support a decision or build a viewpoint. For instance, Doug wonders if he is in love. He likes Erika and enjoys talking to her. He thinks she is friendly and cute. He feels happy when she is around and likes being with her. He concludes that these feelings could be the beginning signs of love. Doug has connected several thoughts about his relationship with Erika and about love into a logical conclusion.

Developing Judgment

Maturity also brings an increase in a young person's ability to judge if a viewpoint is strong or weak. New information may cause them to change their position on a question or issue. For instance, Doug gains some new information about himself when Melissa stops by his locker to talk. He learns that he likes talking with her, too. She is friendly and interesting, like Erika. After talking to Melissa, he begins to question his first conclusion about his feelings for Erika.

Visualizing the Future

Thinking about the future and your place in it is also part of mature thinking. *Visualizing* the future is a process in which you try to picture in your mind how things might be. Doug can think about his future relationship with Erika. He can consider his feelings for her now and how these feelings may change over time. He can visualize himself in college and think about how a relationship with Erika might affect that. Visualizing can help you identify possible consequences of a decision (**Figure 2.5**).

Think About Your Reading

What factors in your environment could make it hard to use mature thinking skills? What are some activities you could do to increase your use of mature intellectual skills?

Reaching Intellectual Maturity

Learning and developing new skills uses your intelligence and helps you develop intellectual maturity. There are eight different types of intelligences (**Figure 2.6**). Most people possess all eight in varying degrees but perform better in certain areas than others. For instance, people with more musical intelligence may excel in playing instruments or writing music. Those with more interpersonal intelligence may interact extremely well

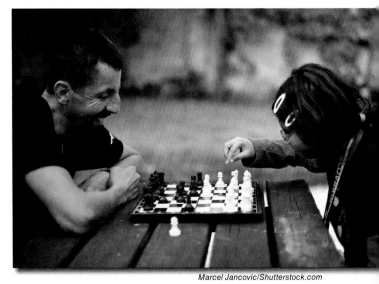

Marcel Jancovic/Shutterstock.com

Figure 2.5 Learning to play challenging games can help develop skills for thinking with logic, making good judgment calls, and visualizing what will happen if you make certain choices. *What games do you enjoy that use mature thinking skills?*

The Eight Human Intelligences		
Type of Intelligence	Description	Examples
Linguistic (verbal)	Using words; communicating through language	Edit, interpret, speak, read
Logical (mathematical)	Using math concepts, logic skills, or abstract reasoning	Analyze, calculate, propose theories
Musical	Using sounds to create meanings; hearing patterns in sounds	Compose, harmonize, sing, play an instrument
Spatial (visual)	Perceiving images and transforming them; recreating images from memory	Draw, design, map, sketch, sculpt, create fine art
Kinesthetic (bodily)	Moving the body in highly skilled ways	Dance, mime, use complex tools skillfully, show athletic talent
Intrapersonal	Understanding oneself	Reflect, set goals, improve behavior
Interpersonal	Relating to other people	Persuade, motivate, teach, inspire
Naturalist	Classifying and using features of the environment	Observe, discover, cultivate, harvest, hunt

Dr. Howard Gardner, Harvard University

Figure 2.6 To reach intellectual maturity, seek ways to use all eight of your intelligences. *What activities could you do to develop your brain in each area of intelligence?*

with all types of people. By seeking ways to use all eight intelligences, you can reach your intellectual potential in multiple areas.

Learning to think critically will help you develop intellectual maturity. **Critical thinking** is the active process of improving your own thinking. It includes analyzing your own ideas and comparing them with others', assessing the accuracy of your logic, judging the likelihood of your projections being true, and then restructuring your own thoughts based on your reasoning and reflection.

The teen years are the time to grow intellectually. Expand your knowledge base by reading more, talking with friends about different ideas, talking with people who think differently than you, and exploring the pros and cons of different viewpoints. Think about new ideas and connect them to what you have already learned. Evaluate your *assumptions*, the ideas you take for granted. Evaluate your successes in predicting the consequences of various options. This process will

help you improve your own thinking and move toward intellectual maturity.

Think About Your Reading

Examine the eight multiple intelligences and analyze your own preferences for learning. What type of intelligence do you think you prefer using?

Emotional Development

Emotional development refers to the ability to experience and express emotions. It also involves the ability to control emotional behaviors. During the teen years, your emotions are continually changing. Sometimes you feel loved and accepted. You may feel happy and excited when others give you positive comments and encouragement. Then there are times when you feel insecure, left out, and alone. You may think no one really cares about

you. At times like these, you may feel discouraged and unhappy.

Emotions usually arise from your interactions with others. Understanding how your brain responds to emotional stimuli in your environment can help you understand your own emotions and how to control them. Maturing emotionally will help you develop healthy relationships.

Your Brain and Your Emotional Responses

When you see an event, you process your emotional reaction to it through the limbic system. The connections between the limbic system and your actions or responses are fast. This system is designed to provide protection to your body. In times when you are not in danger, you still may react before your brain has had time to think about the benefits and drawbacks of different responses. Some people call this quick automatic response the "low road." Learning to control your emotions and the responses that go with them takes practice. This means getting the "high road" to function. The *high road* is the term some people use to refer to the connections between the limbic system and the thinking cortex. Using the high road takes a little more time because you think instead of acting immediately. As you learn to think about what you are feeling before you respond, you will have a more controlled reaction.

Identifying Your Emotions

Emotional responses become more controlled as the thinking part of your brain takes over. A first step is to recognize your emotions. Practice sharing your emotions when you are not upset. Say "I am happy today" or "I'm so glad to see you" when you feel those positive emotions (**Figure 2.7**). If you become accustomed to expressing emotions in this way, it will be easier to say "I feel angry" or "I feel upset" when you are under stress. Sometimes others can help you recognize your emotions by identifying them for you.

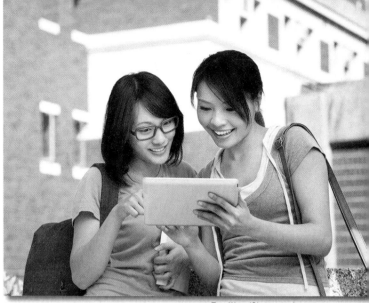

Tom Wang/Shutterstock.com

Figure 2.7 If you practice sharing your emotions when you are not upset, it will be easier to share emotions while under stress.

Controlling Your Emotional Responses

Controlling emotional behavior means communicating your feelings in acceptable ways. For instance, if you are angry because someone used your phone without your permission, you can say "I am really angry because you used my phone without asking if it's okay." This is an acceptable, healthy response—a high-road response. Uncontrolled responses—low-road responses—include yelling or taking something that belongs to the other person to get even.

Another controlled response is to remove yourself from the situation. You may decide to take a walk or go to your room, giving yourself time to cool down and think through your feelings. Consider what you are feeling and why you are feeling that emotion. In this way, you can think about your response and the effects it will have on others before deciding on a particular course of action.

Think About Your Reading

Think of an example when you responded quickly with an emotional response. What could you have done to slow down that response?

Reaching Emotional Maturity

Emotionally mature persons experience mature emotions such as love, self-esteem, concern, and empathy. They are able to activate their thinking brain enough to control their emotional responses. What factors help a person grow to emotional maturity?

A strong supportive family network is important in the development of mature emotions (**Figure 2.8**). Being in such an environment helps a person develop positive emotions, such as feelings of being loved and considered valuable to others. Positive feedback and warm, affirming touches from others actually affect the chemicals produced in the brain. Growing up in such an environment helps a person develop mature emotions.

Some people do not share the experience of a nurturing home like this. They can still be helped to develop emotional maturity, though. Having a close relationship with at least one significant adult has been found to stimulate the development of mature emotions. Is there at least one adult with whom a teen can develop a warm and caring relationship—someone who cares about her, talks with and listens to her, and encourages her to grow to be the best she can be? This person might be a parent, grandparent, youth leader, religious leader, or teacher. It takes only one close relationship to stimulate the growth of mature, positive emotions.

Another strategy for promoting emotional maturity is to reduce stress in your life. Work at eliminating whatever stress you can, perhaps with music, video games, movies, and time with friends.

You can also promote emotional maturity by avoiding the use of alcohol or other controlled substances. Such substances slow down and dull the functioning of the thinking parts of your brain. People whose thinking processes are slowed or

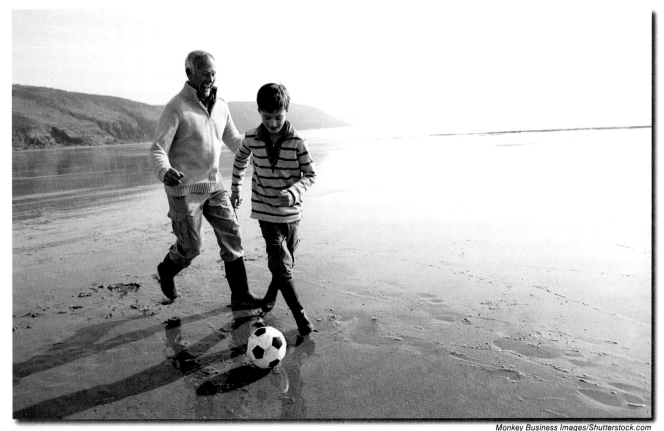

Figure 2.8 Sharing activities in a warm, loving, and caring relationship promotes the development of the emotional center of the brain.

dulled by these substances may express themselves in ways they do not like or want.

Focus on learning new facts and skills that make you feel more positive about yourself and find areas in which you can succeed. As you succeed, these positive emotions will be stored in your long-term memory along with the new skills learned. This focus on growth will help you develop more mature emotions and sharpen your ability to control your responses.

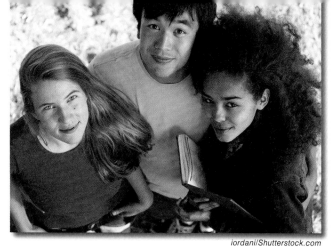
iordani/Shutterstock.com

Figure 2.9 Friendships can help you develop skills for building close relationships.

Think About Your Reading
What factors in your environment could hinder growth to emotional maturity? What steps could you take to reduce their impact?

Think About Your Reading
Which of the skills involved with social development use the thinking part of the brain? Which social skills involve the maturation of the limbic system?

Social Development

Social development involves relating to others with greater ease and understanding. When you were very young, you related to others from your own point of view. Your ideas centered on yourself and concerned your possessions or your parents. When you began to play with other children, you had to consider them and their feelings. You had to share the ball during recess or take turns jumping rope. By considering the feelings of others, you were beginning to develop social skills. As you grew and developed, you learned how to consider the thoughts and ideas of others as well.

During the teen years, you continue to mature socially. You learn give-and-take as you consider others' viewpoints. You use social skills as you try to understand and accept others even though they do not share your views. You develop an appreciation for **diversity**, or for the unique qualities of people from different backgrounds. This helps you foster friendships with people outside your social circle (**Figure 2.9**).

Social development continues throughout your lifetime as you meet new people and face new personalities. You will have to work at understanding people and helping them understand you as well.

Socialization and Roles

Socialization is the way you learn the behavior that society accepts. Learning the shared beliefs and standards of society begins with your family. In your family, you learn what will be expected of you in the many roles you will have in life. You will also learn how to distinguish between good and bad, or acceptable and unacceptable, behaviors. This aspect of socialization is sometimes called **moral development** and includes the development of a person's character and ethics.

A **role** is a way of acting to fulfill certain responsibilities. One role you have now is that of son or daughter. In this role, you may be expected to talk to your parents, show them love and respect, and help do household tasks. At school, your role of student means you are expected to participate in class, read assignments, write papers, and take exams. Your future roles might include husband or wife, parent, employee or employer, and community leader. Each of these roles will have certain responsibilities.

By observing family members and interacting with them, you learn how to respond to various

life situations. You learn what is important, what guidelines to use, and what actions are acceptable.

Young people develop socially as they adopt the family's beliefs and standards as their own. Part of this process includes thinking about and questioning parents' standards. By providing answers and reasons for their standards and beliefs, parents can help children understand their future roles.

Character and Ethics

Character is the set of principles and beliefs that shape one's conduct. It develops as part of socialization. Desirable character traits that contribute to social maturity help people make choices that not only benefit themselves, but also others around them and society as a whole.

Ethics are the moral principles or standards used to judge what is right and wrong. Society sets some of these standards in the form of laws to protect the public welfare. Parents and family members teach some of these moral principles to help children learn acceptable behavior. Often these standards are based on the family's traditions and religious beliefs. These standards serve to guide and protect you, your family, and others.

When people make choices and decisions that benefit only themselves, usually someone ends up being hurt. It may even be the person making the choice. For example, if someone takes money belonging to another, they hurt the owner, but they will themselves be punished by the law. Ethical behavior, on the other hand, protects everyone's welfare.

Character Traits

Some inner traits and moral qualities define a person's character and contribute to ethical behavior.

- **Self-discipline** is the ability to control your behavior. For instance, can you control your desire to watch television until your homework is done? This takes self-discipline, which is also called *self-control.*
- *Dependability* means that you are reliable and true to your word. When you do what you promise and handle your responsibilities without reminders, you are dependable.

- *Responsibility* means answering for your behavior and obligations. For instance, do you do your part of a group assignment well and deliver it on time? This shows you are responsible (**Figure 2.10**). More importantly, do you uphold the laws of society and respect the rights of others? This shows that you treat your civic duties responsibly.
- **Integrity** is the quality of being completely honest, doing the right thing in a reliable way. People with integrity can be trusted because they handle matters truthfully and do not favor some people over others.
- *Initiative* moves a person to do what needs to be done without reminders. Addy shows initiative when she spends her spare time playing the piano to prepare for a music competition. Sometimes initiative causes a person to go beyond what is expected. For instance, Manuel offers to carry Lori's books because he wants to meet her and maybe date her.
- *Fairness* moves a person to show regard for the rights of others. Often fairness is displayed with compassion. A sense of compassion is reflected in treating others in a caring way, showing respect for their views and opinions.

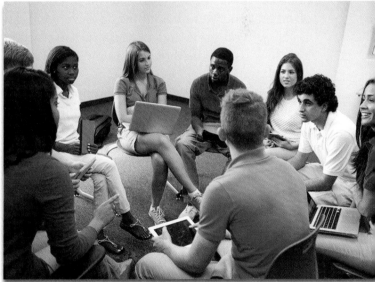

Monkey Business Images/Shutterstock.com

Figure 2.10 Doing your part in team class projects shows you are able to be responsible. *How could the character trait of initiative help you be more responsible?*

People who often show these desirable traits are considered strong in character. They respond with social maturity and ethical behavior. A person who rarely shows these traits is considered weak in character.

Think About Your Reading

How could immature character development affect society as a whole?

The Development of Character

Character development starts when a child is young and continues throughout life. The teaching, training, and examples provided by families are the first influences on a child's character development. Many character traits, such as being kind to others or telling the truth, are learned through direct teaching by parents (**Figure 2.11**). The family also teaches character by setting behavior guidelines.

For instance, a teen might be expected to finish homework before being allowed to go out with friends. When parents require that children follow behavior guidelines, they are helping the child learn responsibility.

Families reinforce their teaching through training. This is a second way that families teach character. Children are provided opportunities to practice how to act responsibly. They may be given responsibilities around the house, such as helping with household chores or caring for siblings. Caring for a family pet can teach children to carry out daily responsibilities as well. All these experiences help children develop strength in character.

Families also teach their children by example. Certain adult character traits may be modeled, or copied, by young family members. For instance, a sense of fairness can be taught by example. When children are treated fairly, they usually learn to treat others the same way. When children see adults act with integrity, they tend likewise to be honest.

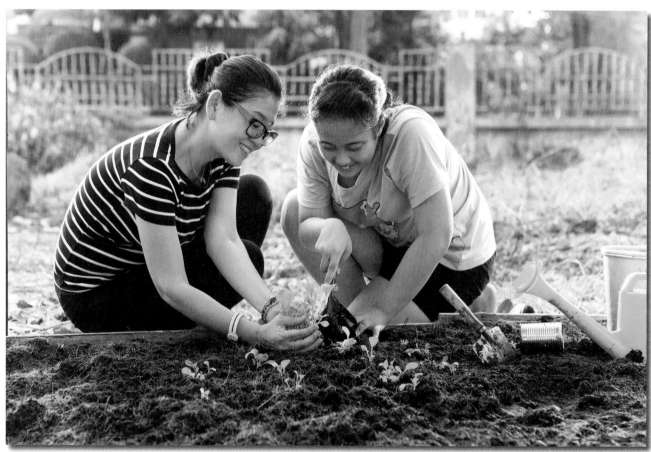

stockphoto mania/Shutterstock.com

Figure 2.11   Many people learn character traits from their parents through direct teaching.

Religious beliefs can be a strong influence in character development. Various religious faiths teach standards of right and wrong. Many people feel these standards give meaning and direction to their lives and serve as a foundation for their character formation.

Schools also influence character development. Students learn dependability and responsibility

Examining Character Traits	
Trait	**Questions**
Self-discipline	Do I accomplish what I plan to do? Can I say no to myself? Do I keep myself neat, clean, and appropriately dressed?
Dependability	Do I arrive on time for a date or appointment? Can I be counted on to get a job done?
Responsibility	Do I do my share of the work when assigned to a group project? Do I feel that I have a part in helping others grow to their potential? Do I carry out my jobs without being reminded?
Integrity	Do I try to be honest? Do I present a truthful picture?
Initiative	Do I believe that hard work is useful and worthwhile? Am I enthusiastic about my work? Do I find satisfaction in a job well done?
Sense of fairness	Do I feel compassion when others are ill-treated? Do I help others when I see others in need? Am I able to look beyond my own desires to consider the welfare of others?

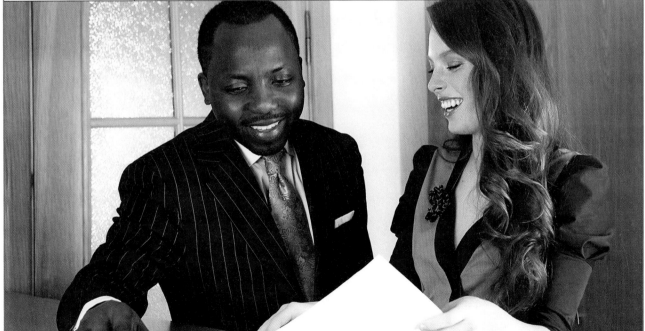

Gromovataya/Shutterstock.com

Figure 2.12 These questions help you examine your character traits. Your answers can identify areas that you may want to develop.

through homework assignments and group projects. Schools set standards for acceptable behavior, too. Such standards encourage integrity and self-discipline by requiring students to do their own work. Standards of responsibility and initiative help students learn to do a job well. Standards for treating other students with caring and respect teach a sense of fairness and compassion. Teachers influence character development by modeling strong character traits that support these standards.

Think About Your Reading

What other sources of training, modeling, and examples might affect the growth of children's character?

Developing Strength in Character

A person's character is not shaped in a day, a week, or even a year. You may have certain traits that you want to change. Developing new character traits takes effort and time, but it can be done.

1. The first step in improving your character is to identify the trait you want to change or develop. Questions similar to those listed in **Figure 2.12** can help you identify such a trait. Any question to which you answer "mostly never" may pinpoint an area needing improvement.

2. After you identify a weak area, focus on specifics about it. For instance, if dependability is sometimes a problem, identify the circumstances when you are not dependable. Is it when doing homework? Is it when doing a household task? Is it when trying to be on time for appointments?

3. Next, develop a plan that addresses the trait. List some specific actions to take to improve the trait, focusing on only one trait at a time.

4. As part of your plan, choose someone to make regular checkups. A person who is close to you could check your progress without offending you. Regular checkups by a friend will help you implement your plan.

Think About Your Reading

How do you think being involved in a community service project could help you develop your character and grow in social maturity?

Reaching Social Maturity

Developing a strong character helps you achieve social maturity. A socially mature person can relate to many different people, listen to and accept differences in others, share and cooperate with others, and relate to others ethically. This set of qualities will make you an enjoyable companion and help you develop strong relationships. When you have social maturity, the important people in your life will be able to count on you, depend on you, and trust you. They know you will also consider their well-being when making decisions. They know you will respond with ethical behavior.

Being involved in community service projects can help you grow socially. Such projects are usually group efforts that focus on helping others and satisfying some of their needs. Community service projects can help you see situations from other points of view. In what group projects have you participated? Is there some type of need in a person's life that you could help fill? Perhaps you could be the one to step in and make a difference. As you help others, you grow socially and become more mature.

LESSON 2.1

Assess

COMPREHENSION CHECK

1. Name the four typical growth patterns and summarize the characteristics of each.
2. When are differences in growth rates most obvious?
3. List three steps that an adolescent can take to promote physical growth to maturity.
4. List three characteristics of intellectual development.
5. List three strategies that could help a person reach intellectual maturity.
6. Describe an emotionally mature person.
7. Describe three characteristics of a socially mature person.

Content Terms

Build Vocab

personality
self-concept
temperament
extrovert
introvert

Academic Terms

continuum
motivation

Objectives

After studying this lesson, you will be able to

- **identify** factors that influence personality formation.
- **explain** how personality is related to self-concept, self-esteem, temperament, and human needs.
- **analyze** personal temperament and response patterns.

Focus Your Reading

1. Use the equation "All you are + All you do = Personality." Under each part of the equation, summarize the key points from the text that illustrate each of the two parts of personality.
2. For each content term, write some words that people use to describe that trait or concept in a person.

If your best friend were asked to describe you, what would your friend say? "He's a lot of fun, rather quiet, but a true friend." "She is tall, very outgoing, and a starter on the basketball team."

When your friend describes you, he or she is listing different parts of your personality. Your **personality** is the sum of all your personal and behavioral traits. These traits combine to make you a unique person with your own personality.

Many researchers have studied the factors that affect personality. Some look at how a person's view of "self" affects behavior. Others study the patterns that people naturally use to express themselves. Still others study personality by looking at how people respond to their human needs. Your personality will be influenced in some way by each of these factors.

The Influence of Self-Concept

Your **self-concept** is the mental picture you have of yourself (**Figure 2.13**) and is also sometimes called *self-image*. If you like the way you see yourself, you will have a positive self-concept. If you do not like what you see, you will have a negative self-concept.

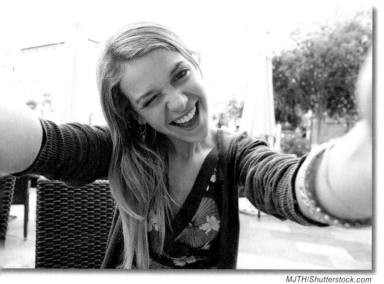
MJTH/Shutterstock.com

Figure 2.13 Your personality is influenced by how you see yourself and feel about that mental image.

Your self-concept affects your *self-esteem*, your feelings of your own worth and value. A positive self-concept indicates high self-esteem. A negative self-concept shows low self-esteem. High self-esteem means you respect yourself, have self-confidence, and feel secure in your world. You value yourself as a person.

If you have a positive self-concept, you will find it easier to accept yourself as you really are—a worthwhile person (**Figure 2.14**). When you know and accept yourself, you can be realistic about judging your personal traits. You know your good points and feel positive about them. You also know that you have areas to improve. You feel good about who you are, even though you know you have room to grow.

With a negative self-concept or self-image, you do not feel good about yourself. This may cause you to feel insecure or less important as a person. A lack of confidence makes it hard to try to improve. You may not want to try new experiences because you fear failure.

Three factors influence the development of your self-concept or self-image: (1) how you see your physical traits or appearance, (2) how you see what abilities you have, and (3) how people respond to you. Knowing how these factors influence your self-concept and self-esteem will help you understand how your personality is formed.

Physical Traits

Your height, weight, appearance, and sexuality are traits that influence your self-concept. How do you see yourself? Are you tall, short, or average? Are you thin, heavy, or in between? Are you cute or plain? Your responses to these questions form a part of your self-concept. If you feel good about your appearance, you are more likely to have a positive self-concept.

Skills and Talents

What you are able to do is also a part of your self-concept. Can you play football, tennis, soccer, baseball, or basketball? Can you draw, sing, write, or play the piano? Are you good at math, computer programming, or woodworking? You might include your abilities when you describe yourself. These various skills and talents form a part of your self-concept and, in turn, your personality (**Figure 2.15**).

A Positive Self-Concept or Self-Image	
I enjoy getting up in the morning.	I look at the positive side of things.
I am usually in a good mood.	I enjoy what I do.
I like the way I look.	My life is interesting.
Most people like me.	I plan to do something important in life.
Others think I am attractive.	Others like to have me with them.
I am happy with my friends.	Others care about my opinions.
I can laugh at my mistakes.	I can tell others how I feel.
I am continuing to grow and change.	I can talk to others with ease.

Figure 2.14 This list describes some of the thoughts and feelings expressed by a person with a positive self-concept.

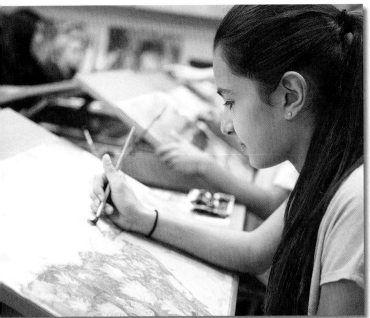

Monkey Business Images/Shutterstock.com

Figure 2.15 Your skills and talents form a part of your self-concept. *What skills and talents influence your self-concept?*

How do you feel about your skills? Whatever they are, these feelings affect your self-esteem. If you feel capable of doing a good job in some area, your feelings of worth increase. Your confidence in your ability to succeed grows. This expression of confidence is part of your personality and affects the plans you make for yourself.

Responses from Others

Your overall view of yourself is also affected by the way others respond to you. Are they friendly to you? Do they compliment you? Do they show you respect? Do they recognize your achievements? Their responses or feedback help you form your self-concept. If the feedback you get from others is positive, you likely see yourself as worthwhile. That view adds to your positive self-concept and increases your self-esteem. If the responses of others toward you are negative, you may judge yourself in a negative way. For instance, your height may be average according to your doctor's chart. If a peer calls you short, though, you may think of yourself as too short.

You can see how your self-concept forms part of your personality. It affects the way you feel about

yourself and the way you express your thoughts and feelings to others. When you relate to others positively, with praise or compliments, you build their self-esteem and promote their positive self-concept. Often they will return positive feedback to you, building your positive self-concept. Thus, your self-concept can affect your ability to develop positive relationships with others.

Your Temperament's Influence

Individuals tend to relate to others in a consistent manner. In other words, their individual behavior is predictable. Your family and friends generally know how you will respond in given situations. This consistency of behavior is based on your **temperament**, which is an inborn pattern of responses.

Although you inherit your temperament, the environment has a strong effect on how your behavior patterns develop. For instance, behavior patterns that are encouraged and accepted by parents, siblings, or peers are likely to become stronger. Patterns that are ignored or not accepted by others tend to become weaker. Your environment shapes the way these behavior patterns develop during your life.

The Four Areas of Temperament

Temperament patterns are related to basic behavior in the following four areas:

- how you express yourself intellectually
- how physically active you are
- how you feel and express your emotions
- how sociable you are

Your intellectual behavior pattern relates to how you use words, numbers, and images and how you plan and organize your ideas. For instance, you may be able to describe and explain your ideas very clearly when speaking. Another person may be better at organizing thoughts on paper. Yet another person may have difficulty with words and ideas, but feel at ease with math concepts. These differences reflect individual patterns of intellectual expression (**Figure 2.16**).

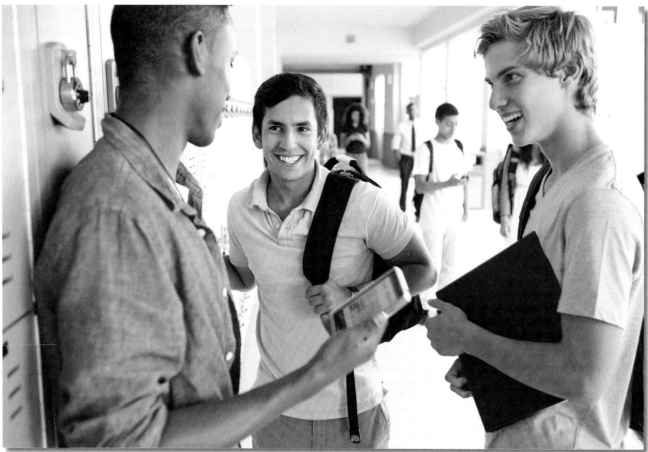
Monkey Business Images/Shutterstock.com

Figure 2.16 People have different ways of communicating intellectually.

Think About Your Reading

What is your strongest response pattern for expressing yourself intellectually? Is it similar to one of the multiple intelligences?

Physical behavior patterns range from being very active to very inactive. You may be a person who is always moving, working on one task or another. You may enjoy active sports such as running, basketball, or tennis. On the other hand, you may be a person who prefers quieter activities such as reading, playing the piano, or building models. Working on projects that require great thought and precision might appeal to you.

Emotional behavior patterns vary widely. Some people are more sensitive to their emotional feelings. They may also be more aware of the feelings of others. On the other hand, some people are considered insensitive. They seem less aware of their own emotions or the feelings of others. Without realizing it, they may hurt other people's feelings or offend them. Emotional behavior patterns also include how people show their emotions. Strong emotional feelings can cause some people to express anger quickly or lose control and cry. Others tend to hide their emotions, keeping everything inside and presenting a calm face regardless of the situation.

Think About Your Reading

How could a person's emotional behavior patterns affect his or her social relationships?

Social patterns relate to how outgoing a person is. An **extrovert** is a person who is very outgoing and enjoys being with people (**Figure 2.17**). Such a person is usually friendly and seems to have a lot of friends. An **introvert** is a person who is more

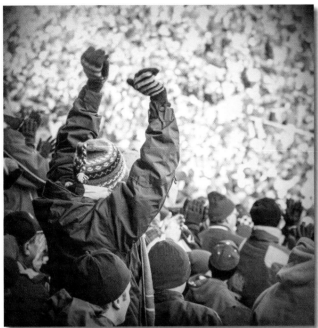
Suzanne Tucker/Shutterstock.com

Figure 2.17 An extrovert is socially outgoing. This trait can be a strength when trying to get to know someone. *In what settings could being an extrovert be a weakness?*

withdrawn. This person may be shy and anxious about meeting new people. An introvert usually likes to be alone or with a very small group of familiar people. Introverts may have fewer friends than extroverts, but they can still have very strong friendships.

All areas of your temperament—intellectual, physical, emotional, and social—affect your personality. Your intellectual and physical patterns affect the way you approach a task and complete your work. Your emotional patterns affect the way you feel about others' responses to you and about the situations you face. Your emotional and social patterns both affect the way you relate to others.

Understanding Your Response Patterns

Have you been able to see yourself in any of these temperament patterns? The list in **Figure 2.18** identifies some characteristics of two types of common temperament patterns. The first pattern describes an aggressive, hardworking, impatient,

Real-Life Scenario

Response Patterns

Gwen was neat and well organized. She was an excellent student at school, particularly in math. At home, her room was the neatest place in the house. She loved to organize items. She had files for all her favorite cards, pictures, and music.

Although they shared some interests, Dana was different from Gwen. Dana enjoyed school, but had trouble with math. Her favorite subject was history. She especially liked talking about current affairs. At home, Dana had items all over her room. Her clothes were in one pile. Her homework and favorite magazines were in another.

Gwen and Dana had other friends, but spent most of their time together. Neither had much interest in activities that involved exercise, so they both were a bit overweight. They often went to movies and concerts together and discussed books they had read. Sometimes they would invite another girl, Roxanne, to join them. Roxanne spent much of her time alone, so they hoped their invitation would help her feel happier.

For Discussion

1. What natural patterns of physical activity can you identify in Gwen and in Dana? How were their physical patterns evident in the activities they enjoyed?
2. What intellectual patterns can you identify? How did their intellectual patterns affect their favorite subjects in school and the way they organized their rooms?
3. What social patterns can you identify in Gwen and Dana? What emotional patterns can you identify? How did these patterns affect their choice of friends?
4. How might Gwen's and Dana's behavior patterns have been affected by their parents? What behaviors do you think their parents may have encouraged?

and competitive person. The second describes a person who tends to respond in a calmer, quieter, and more relaxed manner. Most people fit somewhere between these two patterns, on a *continuum* between the two extremes.

One type of temperament is not better or more desirable than the other. Each pattern of responding has both strengths and weaknesses. For instance, a person who is talkative and enthusiastic may be seen as lively and energetic in some situations and loud and obnoxious in others. A sensitive person may sometimes be considered touchy, but at other times may be seen as very considerate to others. The situation may determine whether the quality is a strength or a weakness.

Knowing your typical response patterns can be helpful. You can make choices that will focus on your strengths. This will help you experience success. For instance, you may be required to be a leader in class. If you are a quiet and reserved person, volunteer to lead a small group rather than the whole class. Having success in that situation will also give you more confidence the next time you have to be a leader. When you know your natural response patterns, you can also make choices that will help you present yourself in a positive way to others.

Think About Your Reading

How could you use your knowledge of your temperament to help you choose a project you could complete successfully?

Behavior Patterns
Type 1: Aggressive, hardworking, impatient, and competitive
I often do several things at the same time.
I ordinarily work quickly and energetically.
I persist at working on a problem even though it seems overwhelming.
I often hurry.
I become impatient when someone slows me down.
In conversation, I often gesture with my hands.
I really like challenges.
I walk quickly.
Sometimes I speak too quickly and put words in another person's mouth.
I often try to persuade others to my point of view.
Type 2: Calm, quiet, relaxed, and easygoing
In comparison to others, I am fairly easygoing.
I usually do not plan more work than I can finish.
I am a good listener and hear people well.
I am relaxed when I work.
I am bothered when people rush me.
Most people consider me quiet.
I like to eat slowly and enjoy my meals.
I can usually wait patiently.
I usually speak more softly than most people.
I rarely worry about being late.

Figure 2.18 The natural way people respond to their environment is influenced by their temperament. Some common behavior patterns are described here.

The Influence of Human Needs

How you respond to your environment is shaped by human needs. All people have certain needs that they strive to fulfill. The manner in which human needs are met influences your personality as well as your physical, intellectual, social, and emotional development. Each person attempts to meet the following needs in different ways:

- *The need for food, clothing, and shelter surpass all other needs.* Life's basic physical needs provide strong *motivation* (drive) for action. When people are starving, their only thought is finding food. When they are freezing, they search for warmth and protection. These physical needs must be met before other needs are even recognized.

- *The need to feel safe and secure causes people to act in certain ways.* For instance, if a tornado is near, people seek immediate shelter and stay there until danger has passed. People need to feel secure in their relationships, too. A warm family environment satisfies this need. Feelings of security develop as you learn you can trust others to care for you and guard your well-being. As you mature, feeling secure helps you reach out to others by showing care and concern for them.

- *The need to be loved and accepted by others is a powerful motivator.* Some teens will join a school club because of their desire to belong to a particular group. The need to feel loved and accepted by family and friends is very important. These feelings help you accept yourself, and in turn, love and accept others (**Figure 2.19**).

- *The need for recognition and respect also influences personality.* Why does a person try so hard to be the winner of a game or have the best costume at a party? This inner drive may be a need for personal achievement or recognition. Meeting this need can bring satisfaction and a feeling of success. These feelings of success increase as your skills increase. When you and others recognize your skills and success, you see yourself as a capable and worthwhile person.

When people meet all or most of their needs, they continue to strive to reach their full potential. They try to be the best they can be. They work hard at their jobs. They continue to perfect their talents and skills. They become more concerned for others. Although their personalities are well developed, they continue to learn and grow from their experiences.

Think About Your Reading

How could a person's needs change over time and, therefore, change the way his or her personality appears to others?

A Healthy Personality

Many factors contribute to a healthy personality. A positive self-concept and a sense of worth

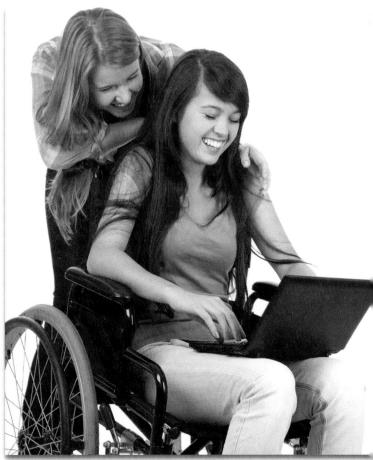

photomatik/Shutterstock.com

Figure 2.19 Sharing experiences with friends satisfies the need to be accepted.

and value are important. Accepting yourself, with all your strengths and weaknesses, is also part of a healthy personality. These lead to feelings of "I am lovable" and "I am capable."

A healthy personality means you have a realistic personal identity. You know who you are and where you hope to go in the future. You know you are not perfect, but you keep trying to improve. You are aware that learning and growing from your experiences can help you become a better person (**Figure 2.20**).

Some people put too much emphasis on a single aspect of their personality. They may be overly concerned about how they look. They may have feelings of importance based on just one area of their lives. Maybe they are too concerned about what others say and do. By focusing on just one part of their personality, they miss the chance to

see other areas where they have strengths or that could benefit from change.

How can you develop or change parts of your personality? You can start by looking at yourself. Are there things you can change about the way you look or act? Are there skills that you would like to develop? Would these changes help you think more of yourself? Would they increase your self-concept and self-esteem?

Think about your temperament—how you express your personality to other people. Would you prefer not to be shy in a group of your peers? Does feeling angry when you are criticized by someone bother you? Would you like to be a better listener? If you answer yes, you are ready to begin the change. Make a plan for improving that behavior and find a supportive family member or friend to check your progress.

Personality development continues throughout your life. Your self-concept, patterns of interacting, responses to your needs—all these can change. Knowing how personality is formed and how to change it will help you develop a healthier personality.

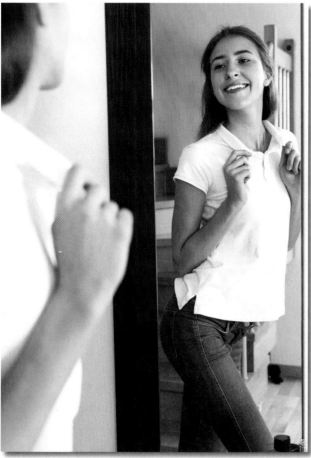
Iakov Filimonov/Shutterstock.com

Figure 2.20 A healthy personality is characterized by realistic self-assessment and an understanding of yourself—that is, a realistic personal identity.

LESSON 2.2
Assess

COMPREHENSION CHECK

1. How can personality be defined?
2. Explain how self-concept, or self-image, and self-esteem are affected by physical traits, personal skills, and the responses of other people.
3. How do responses from others, including responses from community, workplace, and family members, influence self-esteem and personality?
4. Give an example of a trait in each of the four areas of temperament: physical, intellectual, social, and emotional.
5. List four human needs that could make a difference in the way a person responds to the environment.
6. Summarize the factors that influence personal identity, self-esteem, and personality.

CHAPTER SUMMARY

The growth of the human body follows certain patterns, but each person develops at his or her own rate. Rapid physical growth and development of primary and secondary sex characteristics mark the teen years. Taking care of your health can help you reach physical maturity and your full growth potential.

A teen's intellectual growth is related to brain development and greater ability to grasp abstract ideas and use logical reasoning. These formal thinking skills enable you to make more accurate judgments and predict the future consequences of a decision. Try to learn something new every day to help yourself reach your intellectual potential.

Emotional development in the teen years is characterized by an increased ability to identify feelings and control the responses that go with them. Emotional maturity will help you establish close, long-lasting relationships.

Social development is seen as teens learn give-and-take in relationships and develop close friendships with their peers. They also learn to fulfill the expectations that go with various roles in the society.

As teens grow in all these areas, they develop unique personalities. Your personality is strongly influenced by your view of yourself and by your temperament. How you respond to meeting human needs also affects personality. As you learn and grow from your experiences, you may realize a need to change poor behaviors. Feeling good about yourself and continually trying to improve are signs of a healthy personality.

VOCABULARY ACTIVITIES

1. With two classmates, divide the terms into groups of three. Study your terms so you are thoroughly familiar with the meaning of each one and can use them to discuss human development or personality. Take turns teaching your terms to your two partners to make sure all three of you understand all the terms.

Content Terms

abstract thinking (2.1)	cortex (2.1)
adolescent growth spurt (2.1)	critical thinking (2.1)
brainstem (2.1)	diversity (2.1)
cerebellum (2.1)	emotional development (2.1)
character (2.1)	ethics (2.1)
concrete thinking (2.1)	extrovert (2.2)
corpus callosum (2.1)	integrity (2.1)

intellectual development (2.1)	rate of development (2.1)
introvert (2.2)	role (2.1)
limbic system (2.1)	self-concept (2.2)
moral development (2.1)	self-discipline (2.1)
personality (2.2)	social development (2.1)
physical development (2.1)	socialization (2.1)
puberty (2.1)	temperament (2.2)

2. Write a sentence in which you use each of the following terms, but leave the term out of the sentence. List the terms at the top of the paper. Exchange your sentences with a partner and fill in each of the missing words. Discuss any disagreements over the meaning of the terms, consulting a dictionary.

Academic Terms

assumption (2.1)	motivation (2.2)
continuum (2.2)	sequence (2.1)
logic (2.1)	visualizing (2.1)

ASSESS

Your Knowledge

3. What major physical changes take place during the teen years?
4. What is the difference between a person who is emotionally immature and one who is emotionally mature?
5. What can a teen do to help his or her brain reach its full intellectual potential?
6. What three factors affect a person's self-concept and self-esteem?
7. What is temperament? How does temperament affect a person's behavior?

Your Understanding

8. How is the development of character stimulated?
9. How does the maturing brain help the development of emotional maturity?
10. How does the development of character traits contribute to long-term relationships?
11. How does a society promote ethical behavior?
12. How does a person's self-concept affect his or her personality?

Your Skills

13. Analyze how a marriage relationship would be affected if both partners were intellectually immature.
14. Evaluate how emotional immaturity could affect a friendship.

15. Describe a socially immature person and analyze how those characteristics could impact the person's performance on a job.

16. Analyze your own personal response patterns in the four areas—physical, intellectual, emotional, and social. Explain how your temperament influences your personality.

CRITICAL THINKING

17. **Create a Solution.** Choose an aspect of physical, intellectual, social, or emotional development that you would like to improve. Using critical thinking skills, develop a strategy that you think would strengthen this area. Identify a person who could check your progress. Write a paragraph describing your plan of action. *Choice:* Share your plan of action with a partner and discuss possible obstacles.

18. **Draw Conclusions.** Write a paper analyzing your personal response patterns in the four areas of temperament. Include how active you are physically, how you express yourself intellectually, how you express your emotions, and how you relate socially. Cite evidence from the text to support your analysis. *Choice:* Present your information in a format other than a paper, like a song, a rap, an artistic drawing, or a multimedia display.

19. **Predict Outcomes.** Write a paper on how personal maturity contributes to success in relationships at home and work. Explain how personal maturity in social, emotional, and intellectual areas can help you succeed in family relationships at home. Also explain how maturity in these areas could benefit your professional relationships on the job. Cite evidence from the text to support your statements. *Group option:* Complete this paper with two partners, with each of you focusing on one area of development.

CORE SKILLS

20. **Research, Writing.** Read several newspaper articles involving human behavior aimed at meeting one of the following needs: basic needs (food, clothing, and shelter), safety, or security. For each story, write an explanation how the person's behavior helped him or her meet that need. *Choice:* Find articles describing behaviors that responded to the need for love and acceptance and the need for respect and recognition.

21. **Research.** Interview a community leader on the topic of how to build a strong character. Summarize the interview in a report. Include in your report a list of resources and opportunities in your community for building character.

22. **Writing.** Choose a community service project and volunteer at least three hours. Describe the project in a one-page report. Include a description of your feelings before, during, and after the project. Also explain how participating in such a project can help a person mature. Cite evidence from the text to support your explanation.

23. **Research.** Search the Internet for a personality inventory. Take the personality test and print the results. Then, summarize your thoughts about the inventory in a paragraph. Was it thorough enough? Did it provide an accurate picture of your personality? Explain why you agree or disagree with the inventory results.

24. **Research, Writing.** Survey the senior high school class for height and weight data. Collect current data from every student as well as eighth-grade data. Use numbers rather than names for each survey so data is confidential. Enter the data in a computer to create a line graph for average heights and weights in grades eight and twelve. Prepare averages for the whole class as well as separate averages for males and females. Were males or females taller or heavier in eighth grade? in twelfth grade? Write a paragraph drawing some conclusions about rate of development and overall growth. *Group option:* Complete the activity as a class project, with each group member interviewing only some of the students.

25. **Technology.** Design a digital flyer to advertise yourself to a future employer. Include your strengths, abilities, skills, interests, and any other information you think would help you get a job. Use a format with at least two folds in your flyer. *Choice:* Insert digital pictures in your flyer.

CAREER READINESS

26. **Investigating Career Requirements.** Search for information about a psychology career, such as school psychologist, clinical psychologist, social worker, or a career that focuses on developing young adults. Identify the type of work done, the personal qualities and educational requirements needed for job success, and the job outlook for the career. Prepare a report with this career information. *Choice:* Post your report on the guidance website in your school.

CHAPTER 3

STRENGTHENING POSITIVE ATTITUDES

Reading Prep

Divide the chapter among yourself and two partners. Each of you should take responsibility for preparing a study guide for one lesson and distribute that guide to your partners.

Key Questions

Questions to answer as you study this chapter:

- How can a person develop attitudes that lead to mental health?
- How can difficult events and emotions be handled in a healthful way?
- How does stress impact individuals and relationships?

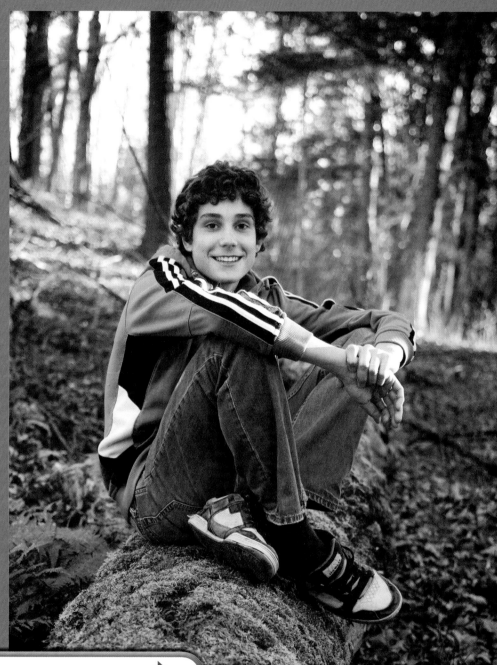

While studying this chapter, look for the activity icon to:

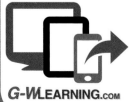

- **build** vocabulary with e-flash cards, matching activities, and vocabulary games; and
- **assess** what you learn by completing the lesson comprehension checks online.

www.g-wlearning.com/humanservices/

G-WLEARNING.com

Lesson 3.1 Developing Attitudes That Lead to
Mental Health
Lesson 3.2 Managing Stress
Lesson 3.3 Handling Difficult Events and Emotions

57

AFTER STUDYING THIS CHAPTER, YOU WILL

KNOW:

- The attitudes that lead to mental health.
- The defense mechanisms that people sometimes use to deal with problems.
- The causes of stress.
- The signs of major depression.

UNDERSTAND:

- How attitudes develop.
- Ways stress can be handled to reduce its effects on the body.
- How to build positive attitudes.
- How stereotypes lead to negative attitudes and poor mental health.

BE ABLE TO DO:

- Evaluate how defense mechanisms hinder growth.
- Apply techniques for building positive attitudes.
- Apply techniques for handling negative feelings or events.

GETTING STARTED

The bell rang and the class ended. "You will have an exam tomorrow," the teacher announced.

"Not another test," several students moaned.

"I give up," Lindsay said. "The last one nearly killed me. It better not include the hard stuff we covered this week."

"Are you kidding? The last test was a snap," Craig replied. Nan and Vicky nodded their heads in agreement.

"I wonder what the test will be like this time," Ryan said. "Will there be a lot of short questions or a few really hard ones? I hope I get a good grade."

"The tests in this class are not all that hard," Kevin replied. "All you have to do is just keep up with your homework."

How many different attitudes would there be in your classroom if an exam were announced for the next day? Would some students be worried, depressed, or afraid of the results? Would some be confident they would do well? What would be your attitude?

LESSON 3.1

DEVELOPING ATTITUDES THAT LEAD TO MENTAL HEALTH

Content Terms

Build Vocab

attitude
self-perpetuating cycle
mental health
defense mechanisms
denial
acting out
projection
rationalization
displacement
conversion
regression
idealization
conceited
fantasy
direct attack
compensation
self-talk

Academic Terms

consequence
interpret

Objectives

After studying this lesson, you will be able to

- **explain** how positive and negative attitudes influence behavior and contribute to mental health.
- **describe** defense mechanisms that people sometimes use to deal with problems.
- **evaluate** how defense mechanisms hinder growth.
- **identify** techniques used for building positive attitudes.

Focus Your Reading

1. Review the headings in this lesson. Write some questions that you think will be answered when you read each section of the lesson. As you read each part, write the answers to your questions. If you have some questions that are not answered, share them with a partner to see if he or she found the answers.

2. For each defense mechanism, identify the feelings, thoughts, and actions involved.

The study of how feelings, thoughts, and actions work together can help you understand your attitudes. **Attitudes** are patterns of thinking, feeling, and responding that people develop as they interact with their environment. Since attitudes affect behavior, your attitudes will affect your relationships in every area of life.

Positive and Negative Attitudes

Your life experiences and the way you interpret them influence your overall mental attitude (**Figure 3.1**). If you have positive thoughts and feelings about your experiences, your attitude will be positive. If you have negative thoughts and feelings about your experiences, your attitude will be negative. Your mental attitude will be influenced by your thoughts and feelings about life, yourself, and your worth to others.

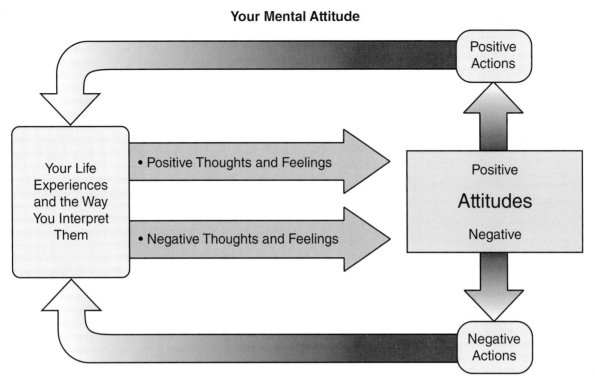

Your Mental Attitude

Figure 3.1 Your attitudes are influenced by what you think about your life experiences.

People with positive attitudes think about themselves and their lives in favorable ways. They feel their actions are important. They believe they can have a positive influence on other people or their community, even if it is minor.

Some people have a negative mental attitude. People like this usually have a low opinion of themselves. They believe that it really does not matter what they do or think. They feel they have no control over the events in their lives. They have no sense of direction and feel powerless. These feelings and thoughts produce a negative attitude.

You may feel positive about some parts of yourself and negative about others. For instance, you may feel confident about your ability to get good grades. However, you may have a negative attitude about your appearance. As you will see, keeping your positive attitude—and developing one in areas where you do not have it—can strongly influence how you act.

Think About Your Reading

What examples can you identify where your feelings about an event gave you a bad attitude?

Attitudes Affect Behavior

As the diagram in Figure 3.1 shows, your attitudes affect how you behave. How you take care of yourself, relate to others, or do your work are all influenced by your attitudes.

Behaviors have *consequences*. For example, if a student does not study a school subject, she may fail an exam in that subject as a consequence. If a teen eats a lot of unhealthy food, he may feel sick as a consequence. Understanding how your attitudes affect what you do can help you take steps to control your behaviors and their resulting consequences.

For instance, someone feeling down and depressed may have negative attitudes. A person with a negative attitude about his ability to make friends may not expect anyone to act in a friendly way toward him. When a group invites him to sit with them at lunch, he may feel suspicious. He may think they just want to make fun of him. With that worry, he is likely to turn them down—and miss an opportunity to connect with people. Negative attitudes tend to have a negative effect on people's actions.

Attitudes can produce actions that may cause those same attitudes to increase. This is called a

self-perpetuating cycle. For example, positive attitudes can influence your actions in a positive way. When you feel good about yourself, you may take time to look your best (**Figure 3.2**). You greet your friends with confidence. You tackle your work with energy. Your positive attitudes will likely help you experience success in your day. If you think you can succeed, you will likely put more effort into your work. Greater effort usually brings more success. In this way, positive attitudes influence you to act in ways that increase your positive feelings. In contrast, someone who starts her day with a negative attitude may feel bad and dress the way she feels. When she looks in the mirror, her feelings are confirmed. Not only does she feel bad, but what she sees confirms that. At school, that girl may grumble and complain to friends. They decide to avoid her because of her bad attitude. In turn, their behavior causes her to feel worse about herself. The self-perpetuating cycle continues, but this time in a negative way.

Think About Your Reading

Draw a diagram of a self-perpetuating cycle of positive attitudes and actions. Then draw a diagram of a similar cycle using negative attitudes and actions.

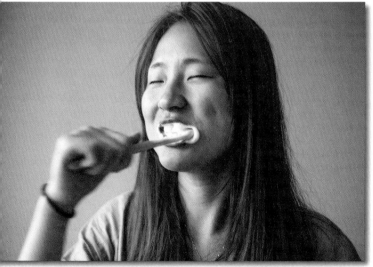

LIUSHENGFILM/Shutterstock.com

Figure 3.2 Taking time to groom yourself in the morning demonstrates a positive attitude.

How Mental Attitudes Develop

Past experiences affect the development of your mental attitudes. Parents influence their children in many ways. As family members spend time together, they share their thoughts, beliefs, and desires. They also model a *mental attitude*, or a way of thinking and responding to life situations. Children pick up that attitude and adopt it as their own. If parents act in a way that suggests that problems can be solved and challenges met, their children will absorb those attitudes.

Other people can also influence the development of your mental attitude. Can you think of a person who has made a big impact on your life? A teacher, club leader, religious leader, author, or entertainer might have affected you. What particular advice or attitudes did these people express that influenced you?

Your friends also can have an impact on your attitudes. Do your friends help you think positively about life experiences? Do they encourage you to take positive actions? Spending time with others who are kind, encouraging, supportive, and understanding can help you develop a positive attitude.

How would you identify your mental attitude? Do you see yourself in control of your life path, or do you feel powerless and swept along by events outside your control? Teens who adopt a positive mental attitude view themselves as valuable people, able to make a difference and able to make choices that help them reach their goals in life. They have a purpose and direction for living.

Mental Health

Your self-concept, self-esteem, and overall attitudes contribute to mental health. **Mental health** describes the overall condition of your social and emotional well-being. The state of your mental health depends on how well you deal with feelings about yourself, others, and the world around you (**Figure 3.3**).

Characteristics of Mental Health

Mentally healthy people have a positive mental state. They possess certain qualities that help them

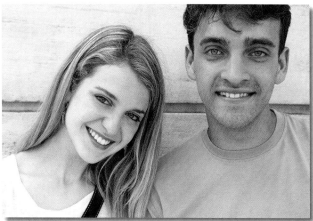

Figure 3.3 Mentally healthy people accept themselves as they are, with both strengths and weaknesses. *What influences in the environment might make it difficult to accept personal weaknesses?*

deal with life. They can accept themselves as they are, with both strengths and weaknesses. They feel equal to and liked by others. They believe they can handle most situations.

Being mentally healthy does not mean always being happy. Mentally healthy people can experience hard times that cause negative feelings, too. At times they feel sadness, hurt, or disappointment. The key is how they handle these feelings. Building positive attitudes as you cope with life's experiences is a sign of a healthy mental state.

Think About Your Reading

Think of people who have had a major influence on your life. What kind of attitudes do they portray? How do their attitudes affect their actions?

The Use of Defense Mechanisms

A positive mental attitude can help people deal with most problems in a positive way. However, dealing with daily problems and situations can be difficult at times, even for someone with a positive attitude. When people have problems they cannot solve, they may react by using defense mechanisms to protect themselves.

Defense mechanisms are methods people unconsciously use to deal with life situations. Sometimes they use these defenses to hide from

problems, to protect their self-esteem, or to reduce tension (**Figure 3.4**). Nine defense mechanisms are commonly used. These include denial, acting out, projection, rationalization, displacement, conversion, regression, idealization, and fantasy.

Denial

People use **denial** when they refuse to accept the reality of something that has happened. They do not admit that the situation ever occurred or deny that they have feelings or thoughts about the event. For example, a student who fails a test may say, "I did not fail that test. That's impossible. I knew all the answers." Responding to a loss with denial is a common initial reaction. If people get stuck in denial, however, problems will arise. The student who does not accept the reality of a failed test and study more for the next one will continue to fail. Denial keeps people from solving their problems.

Acting Out

When people are not able to express their feelings or thoughts in words and express themselves with an extreme behavior instead, they are **acting out**. For example, instead of saying, "I am

---

Defense Mechanisms

- **Denial**—refusing to accept reality
- **Acting out**—using an extreme behavior to express thoughts or feelings
- **Projection**—placing blame on others
- **Rationalization**—giving excuses to defend a behavior
- **Displacement**—taking out one's feelings on someone else
- **Conversion**—transferring an emotion into a physical symptom
- **Regression**—returning to immature behavior
- **Idealization**—assigning excess value to someone or something
- **Fantasy**—meeting needs through the imagination

Figure 3.4 Sometimes people use defense mechanisms as a way to escape the pain of a negative situation. *How could using defense mechanisms limit personal growth?*

angry," a child gets mad and throws a book across the room. The act of physically acting out releases inner pressure the child feels, but it does not solve the problem or help that child to grow. Remember that growing to emotional maturity includes being able to identify and express emotions and control the behavior that goes with them. People may on occasion act out as they are learning to identify and manage their emotions, but using acting out as a frequent means to solve problems will not lead to growth (**Figure 3.5**).

Sometimes people act out when the emotions they are experiencing are so painful, they cannot express them. Self-injury behaviors are an example. People who hurt themselves inflict physical pain to dominate and help cover the deep emotional pain they feel. If you know people who hurt themselves, seek out a counselor on their behalf. Your school counselor can intervene and help the person take steps to resolve their problems and grow in healthy ways.

Projection

Sometimes people place the blame for their failures on others. This is called **projection**. People may project the blame for their problems or shortcomings to someone or something else to avoid admitting their faults. For example, Steve blamed his coach after he lost an important track event. The real problem, though, was Steve had not practiced enough before the event. By blaming his coach, Steve is avoiding the real problem—his own lack of discipline and effort.

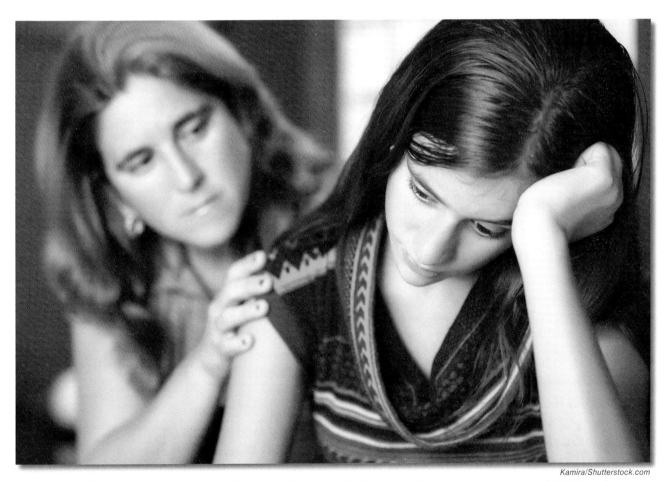

Figure 3.5 Some extreme behaviors that people use for defense mechanisms appear very childish and immature; other behaviors may be harmful to oneself or to others. *How could acting out as a way to solve problems affect relationships?*

Rationalization

Explaining weaknesses or failures by giving socially acceptable excuses is called **rationalization**. People who use excuses to defend their behavior are not being honest with themselves. For instance, Jenny tried out for a singing part in the school play and was not accepted. She responded by saying, "If they had picked a different song for me to sing, I would have gotten the part." She is using rationalization to cover her disappointment.

Displacement

When people take out their feelings on someone or something else rather than face the real problem, they are using **displacement**. For instance, Rodney's parents asked how much gas was left in the family car after he used it to get to and from his job. He may respond, "You're always checking up on me." The real problem may be that Rodney does not know and does not want to bother checking. He may actually be upset about something else that took place during his school or workday. By taking out his frustrations on his parents, he is not addressing his real problem. In fact, he may be creating more negative feelings.

Conversion

Transferring an emotion into a physical symptom is called **conversion**. If Irina feels anxious about her first day at a new job, she might develop a headache. It is a real physical symptom caused by being anxious (**Figure 3.6**).

Regression

Returning to childish or immature behavior when difficulties or frustrations occur is known as **regression**. Cindy wants to meet her friends at the basketball game. Her parents want her to stay home to babysit her younger sister. She reacts by crying and calling her sister names. This kind of behavior can create more problems for Cindy. She may lose the respect of others as well as her own self-respect.

Idealization

Valuing someone or something far more than it is worth is called **idealization**. If people idealize

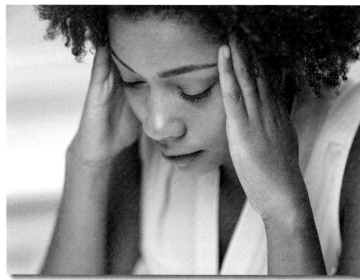

Syda Productions/Shutterstock.com

Figure 3.6 Feeling sick just before exam time often results when a student is not prepared. This is a common example of conversion.

themselves, they may act **conceited**, or think they are better than others. In other cases, they might idealize another person or group. They see the person or group as having more positive qualities than really exist. Material things, such as expensive cars, are sometimes idealized. Spending too much time idealizing someone or something can limit personal growth.

Fantasy

Fantasy becomes a defense mechanism when people use their imaginary thoughts as an escape to fill their personal needs. For instance, a young girl who is unhappy with her social life may spend too much time watching TV shows or movies to fulfill her need for love. In her mind, she may pretend she is living a romantic life. Sometimes people use this defense mechanism so often they begin to believe their fantasies. These people may need help in identifying the real needs they are trying to cover up and work on meeting them.

> ## Think About Your Reading
> What are some examples of times when you have used defense mechanisms? Did using the defense mechanism make you feel better? Did it help you solve a problem?

Building a Positive Attitude

Defense mechanisms can help people feel better about a situation but only for a short time. Negative feelings are temporarily covered up, avoided, or acted out. The problem that caused the person to adopt that defense mechanism remains, however. Using defense mechanisms too often can become a habit that slows personal growth because it does not result in a person learning to solve problems in a mature way. A more positive approach is to recognize and solve the problems that cause negative feelings. This can help in building a positive attitude.

You can use several techniques to help build positive feelings or attitudes. These techniques involve thinking about yourself, observing what you do, when you do it, and why you do it, and then taking action to help yourself grow (**Figure 3.7**).

Directly Attacking an Issue

Direct attack is a method used to face a problem, recognize it, and try to solve it. For instance, Bailey tries out for first chair in the trumpet section of the band but does not earn the place. She feels bad but believes that she can improve and adds 15 minutes to her daily practice. Bailey has used

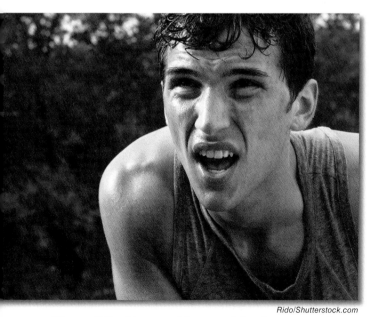

Rido/Shutterstock.com

Figure 3.7 *How could strength in character traits help a person keep a positive attitude and attack a problem?*

direct attack to address her problem. Her actions give her a chance to reach her goal in a positive way.

Compensating

What is another way you can handle a negative view of yourself? **Compensation** is a technique in which you focus on a strength in one area to make up for a weakness in another area.

For instance, Rico is on the high school football team. He has a small build and is not very muscular. As a result, he feels inferior when he compares himself to other team members. Rico could build his self-esteem by trying another sport for which he is better suited, such as tennis or swimming. He could also develop his skills in some other areas outside athletics that he enjoys.

Sometimes negative feelings are related to personal qualities that you cannot change. These are times to compensate and focus on strengths and abilities you do have.

Setting Reasonable Expectations

When people expect too much from themselves or others, their expectations may be difficult to reach. Their chances for experiencing success will decrease. For instance, some students may expect to get an A in every subject. If they cannot meet that expectation, they may become discouraged. On the other hand, some people limit their goals, choosing experiences in which they are certain to succeed. They do not want to take chances but want guaranteed success. By limiting their opportunities, they may limit their personal growth.

A little challenge is helpful for building self-esteem. When you try something new and do a good job, your confidence grows. You believe that you will probably do well the next time you try something new. Reasonable expectations can help you build positive attitudes. If Rico changes his focus from football to tennis, where he has a chance to succeed, he is setting reasonable expectations for himself.

Using Positive Self-Talk

The little messages that you send to yourself are called **self-talk**. These messages usually are not

spoken aloud. When you say to yourself, "Good job!" you are sending yourself positive messages. As a result, you will feel more positive about yourself. In the same way, negative messages such as "How stupid!" will increase your negative feelings about yourself. Use positive self-talk whenever you can.

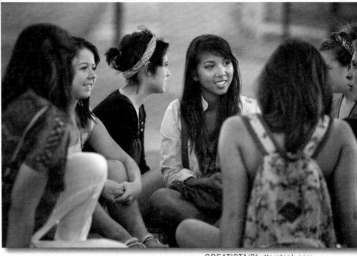
CREATISTA/Shutterstock.com
Figure 3.8 Choosing friends who share your interests can help you develop positive attitudes.

Think About Your Reading

What are some of the most common messages that you send yourself? What impact do those messages have on your attitudes?

Interpreting Information

The way you *interpret* information can affect your self-esteem and your attitudes. When you try to interpret facts in a positive way, your self-esteem can increase. For instance, a friend may say, "You should have worn a different shirt today." You could interpret that negatively and think, *She doesn't like my shirt*. You could also interpret that statement positively: *She thinks I should save this shirt for special occasions*. Of course, this approach is only useful if you have a solid reason for the positive interpretation.

Another way to think positively is to use positive sounding terms that have the same meaning. For instance, saying you are being determined sends a more positive message than calling yourself stubborn. Focusing on positive thoughts or speech can increase your positive attitudes.

Selecting Your Friends

You can stimulate your own personal growth and enhance your self-esteem by your choice of friends (**Figure 3.8**). Your friends share many feelings, experiences, and interests with you. Friends who accept you help you accept yourself. Their positive attitudes can encourage you to feel positive about yourself. By listening and sharing their thoughts with you, they can make you feel important. Friends can encourage you to reach your potential. Friends who consistently act in this way

are your true friends. They are the friends you should spend the most time with.

Friends can also affect your attitudes in a negative way. Their actions can sometimes create bad feelings. In some situations, you may feel left out or inferior to them. Learning to handle your negative feelings in a positive way can help you cope when these situations occur. People who often make you feel this way are probably not suitable to be your close friends.

Assess

LESSON 3.1

COMPREHENSION CHECK

1. List two characteristics of people with positive attitudes.
2. Using an example, explain how positive attitudes can produce a self-perpetuating cycle of positive actions.
3. Describe the reaction of mentally healthy people to life events that cause sadness, hurt, or disappointment.
4. Name and describe five types of defense mechanisms.
5. Explain why the continued use of defense mechanisms may slow a person's personal growth.
6. List and describe five techniques for building positive attitudes.

MANAGING STRESS

Content Terms

Build
Vocab

stress
routine stress
transitional stress
fight-or-flight response
stress hormones
chronic stress

Academic Terms

potential
traumatic

Objectives

After studying this lesson, you will be able to

- **identify** types of stress.
- **describe** the impact of stress on individuals and relationships.
- **practice** techniques for managing stress.

Focus Your Reading

1. Create a list of the things that cause you stress in your life. As you read, compare your list to the causes and effects of different types of stress.
2. Match each item on your list of things that cause you stress with a content term that identifies the type of stress.

The events of daily living can cause stress in your life. **Stress** is your body's response to demanding life events that cause physical, mental, or emotional tension. Simple everyday events such as oversleeping can be stressful. Major events such as a divorce, death of a family member, or serious illness definitely cause stress. You can feel stress in both good and bad situations. Even happy events like a graduation or wedding can be stressful.

Stress has the *potential* to impact you physically and mentally, and thereby can affect your relationships throughout life. The effects of stress will depend on the source of the stress as well as your responses to it. The amount of stress an event causes can be affected by your attitude as well. The way you think about the event, feel about the event, and respond to the event affects how stressful the event is to you.

Types of Stress

Everyday events that demand a change in response from you can cause **routine stress**. An upcoming test, large amount of homework, or deadline for a project are examples of events that cause routine stress. Routine stress usually decreases once the event is over: The test is turned in, homework is done, or the project is

completed. Such normal stress can come from positive as well as negative events. The excitement of winning a race is a positive event, but missing a bus can be a negative event. The chart in **Figure 3.9** lists some examples of routine changes in life that could be stressful.

Some of life's changes result from the normal process of growing and developing. The stress resulting from the demands placed on a person by these changes is called **transitional stress**. For example, the changes that adolescents go through as they become adults can cause transitional stress. Changes that couples go through in the early years of marriage cause this kind of stress also. The effects of transitional stress can be drawn out, extending over a period of time. Preparing for change (as discussed in Chapter 1) can help reduce some of the stress experienced during expected transitions.

Traumatic events are usually negative events that cause emotional upset and represent major changes in life. Some common traumatic events that cause stress are listed in the chart in **Figure 3.10**. The effects of traumatic stress can be deep and long-lasting.

The more sources of stress you experience at one time, the greater is their combined effect. When Paul's family moved to a new neighborhood, he faced a stressful change. Going to a new school

Traumatic Events
• Death in the family
• Divorce
• Marital separation
• Jail term
• Unemployment
• Fired from job
• Loss of home
• Major injury or illness
• Major surgery

Figure 3.10 Stressful events that could lead to crises are often caused by major changes in a person's environment. *What are some examples of strong emotions that a person might feel when experiencing some of these traumatic events?*

after the move caused yet more stress. If his parents then decided to divorce, his stress level would increase further.

Stress is a normal part of life, but too much stress can be unhealthy. Developing skills for handling stress can help you manage and maintain your health and well-being.

Think About Your Reading

What are some events in your life that are causing you transitional stress?

Sources of Routine Stress
• Change in health of family member
• Change in finances
• Change in friendships
• Change in daily schedule
• Starting school
• Ending school
• Change in social activities
• Personal illness
• Change in eating habits
• Change in work hours
• Change in responsibilities at home
• Change in living conditions

Figure 3.9 *What common changes do you find most stressful? How could preparing for life changes help reduce stress in life?*

Effects of Stress

The body's natural response to stress—the **fight-or-flight response**—can be lifesaving. In this response, the body reacts to a perceived danger by sending out stress hormones to give the body increased strength and speed. **Stress hormones** are chemicals that cause the heart to beat harder and faster, open wide the airways to the lungs, increase metabolism, increase the flow of blood to large muscles, and suppress the immune system. After the perception of danger goes away, the body returns to its normal state.

Everyday events that cause routine stress may result in some of these physical changes. Your heart rate may speed up and your blood pressure

may rise if you are anxious about delivering an oral presentation. Your palms may get cold and clammy. Your stomach may ache or feel upset. When the presentation is over, these symptoms go away.

Chronic stress is ongoing stress that continues over time. It may result if the small changes of everyday events are not managed, the ongoing changes of transitional stress are not handled, or the results from traumatic events are lasting. If stress builds up and continues over time, your body continues to produce the stress hormones. This can have harmful effects on your health. High blood pressure, heart attacks, and stomach ulcers are often traced to chronic stress. Some people respond to chronic stress by abusing drugs or alcohol, creating additional health problems.

In addition to the physical effects, stress can cause a variety of emotional responses such as tension, anxiety, anger, and frustration. These negative emotions can impact your intellectual functions like the ability to remember information, think logically, see another's point of view, and make good judgments. For example, taking a final exam may cause you to feel tense or frustrated. You may have a hard time even remembering simple facts for a test, even though you know the information well.

Your ability to handle stress and its effects will affect your relationships throughout life. Feeling tension, anger, and frustration can block people's ability to develop close and long-lasting friendships. These negative emotions sometimes result in people taking physical actions that hurt or abuse others. They can hinder a person's ability to think clearly and solve problems. Thus, developing skills for managing stress will help you mature emotionally and intellectually and develop and maintain healthy relationships (**Figure 3.11**).

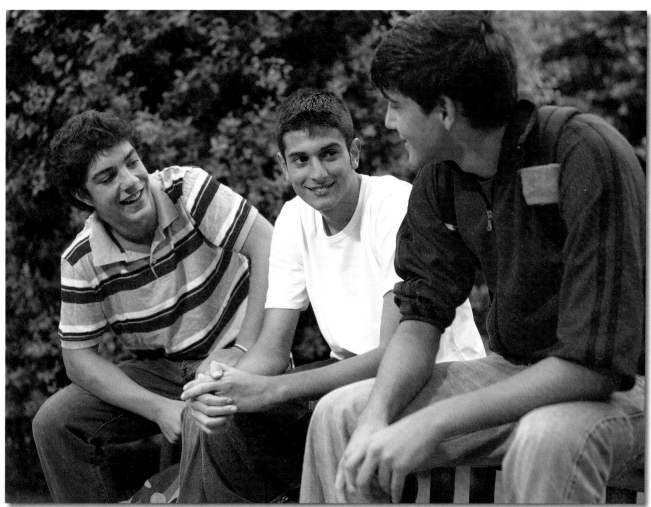

Michael Blann/Photodisc/Thinkstock

Figure 3.11 Learning to manage stress well can help you develop and maintain positive relationships.

Think About Your Reading

What physical effects have you experienced in a stressful situation? How have your emotional responses under stress affected your friendships?

Handling Stress and Problems

Your ability to handle stress and other problems is affected by your attitudes toward yourself and others. A positive mental attitude will help you handle stress in a healthful way. You will more likely learn from the experience. If you accept yourself, you will not be as threatened by these events. You will feel confident that you can work through them.

People with negative attitudes will find it more difficult to handle stress in a healthful way. They may already feel helpless, unaccepted, and worthless. In times of stress, their negative attitudes may lead to increased anger and anxiety. These attitudes may lead to more serious mental illnesses such as depression or thoughts of suicide.

Learning how to manage stress is a skill that can help you throughout life. Developing this skill takes time and effort. The keys to this skill are learning how to recognize that stress exists and then taking steps to manage it:

1. *Learn to recognize your body's signs of stress.* These may vary and could include continually lacking energy; having difficulty sleeping; or feeling depressed, tense, or easily angered. Admit any feelings that you have, even if they are negative. Acknowledging your feelings will help you accept them and prepare for the next step.

2. *Try to identify the changes or events that are the source of your stressful feelings.* When you can identify the source of your stress, you begin to feel more in control of the situation.

3. *Identify what you can do to manage the stressful situation by considering the following options:*
   - *Remove the source of the stress.* For instance, if you often find you cannot complete your

Real-Life Scenario

Managing Stress

"Would you please go and pick up some milk at the store?" Jon's mother called as he walked in the house.

"Not now!" Jon exclaimed. He threw his keys on the table. "You go get it."

Jon was tired. His feet hurt from standing and unpacking boxes at the store. He had a lot of homework and studying to do as it was near the end of the semester.

Jon's mother looked up, surprised. She did not expect such an angry reply. She knew Jon was under stress. They all were.

Jon's father was in the hospital for surgery. He would not be able to work at his construction job for a few weeks. The family finances were strained, and everyone was edgy.

Jon knew he had hurt his mother as soon as the words were out of his mouth. She was under pressure, too. "I'm sorry," he said. "I was thinking about a final paper that's due tomorrow. I'll pick up the milk before I start on it."

"Maybe I can help by typing it for you," his mother replied. "I know you've been under a lot of pressure lately."

For Discussion

1. What were some routine stressors that Jon was experiencing?
2. What was the traumatic event in Jon's family?
3. How did the stress in Jon's life affect his mental attitude and behavior?
4. How did Jon's mother handle his anger and negative attitude?
5. How could Jon's family manage the stress they were experiencing?
6. What events in your life cause you stress? How do you respond to the stress you experience? What techniques could you use to manage stress?

homework, you might cut back on your hours at your job.

- *Remove yourself from the stressful situation.* For example, if your friends decide to stay late at a party, you could leave the party on time.
- *Change your response to the stress.* Use relaxation or other creative techniques to help change a tense response to a more relaxed response.
- *Manage the stress by focusing on a part at a time* (**Figure 3.12**). Developing a plan of action to handle the stressful situation can help build positive feelings.
- *Seek help from professionals if you are feeling overwhelmed or unable to cope.* They can provide counsel or suggest ways to help you manage the stress you are experiencing.

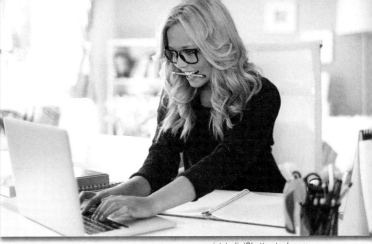
gpointstudio/Shutterstock.com

Figure 3.12 Completing a large project can be stressful. *Are there ways to break a large project into smaller ones? Managing stress by completing small steps can increase positive feelings and reduce the overall effects of the stress.*

Think About Your Reading

In what situation could you manage stress by removing yourself from a stressful event? When could you manage a stressful event by focusing on one part at a time?

- *Keep a schedule that includes physical activity.* Exercise can help you release the tension that builds up from stress.
- *Eat nutritious foods.* Stressful situations sometimes affect the way you eat. A healthful diet can improve your ability to cope with stress.
- *Get plenty of rest.* Along with exercise and a good diet, you need rest to help you feel your best during times of stress. When you are tired, you may have more negative feelings than when you are rested.
- *Spend time with people who encourage you and give you emotional support.* They can help you keep a positive attitude, interpret events in a positive way, and strengthen your feelings of being loved and cared for.

Reducing the Negative Effects of Stress

No matter what you do to try to reduce the amount of stress in your life, it will still occur. To reduce some of the negative effects of stress, use the following guidelines:

- *Practice creative techniques.* Breathing exercises and muscle relaxation can reduce the tension in your body. Take a deep breath and then slowly let it out. Tighten and then relax various muscles in your body whenever you feel tense. Think about a peaceful scene to relax your mind. These methods slow your heart rate and breathing.
- *Do something you enjoy.* Finding an activity that is enjoyable may help reduce your tension.

LESSON 3.2 Assess

COMPREHENSION CHECK

1. List three types of stressful events and give an example of each.
2. Identify physical, emotional, and relational effects that can result from stress.
3. Describe how stress could impact growth toward emotional maturity.
4. Describe five choices available for managing stress. Include some creative techniques.
5. List six strategies for reducing the negative effects of stress.

Objectives

After studying this lesson, you will be able to

- **identify** signs of major depression.
- **develop** skills for handling anger and anxiety.
- **explain** how stereotypes lead to negative attitudes and poor mental health.

Focus Your Reading

1. Create a chart with three columns labeled *Thoughts*, *Feelings*, and *Behaviors*. As you read about each difficult event, record key points about the event, feelings that are commonly felt by someone handling a difficult event, and the actions you could take to help keep a positive attitude in a similar situation.

2. Define each content term and give an example of someone a person could turn to for help if he or she had an issue related to that term.

Content Terms

anxiety

depression

self-pity

suicide

sex role

sex stereotype

Academic Terms

dwell

stereotype

M any people find that keeping a positive attitude is easy when things are going well. The challenge is keeping that attitude during difficult times. When individuals are criticized, made fun of, or yelled at in front of others, how do they handle their feelings? When they think they cannot succeed, how do they keep a positive attitude?

Many situations can make a person feel hurt, angry, worried, or depressed. It is important to be able to identify these emotions and know how to deal with them.

Anger

Anger is an emotion that occurs when people feel wronged or attacked in some way. People of all ages feel anger. A little child may become angry when the tower the child is building falls over. A teen may become angry when parents restrict driving privileges because of high insurance rates. An adult may become angry when his or her car stalls on the highway.

Think About Your Reading

Think of a time when you became angry. Identify what made you angry.

Anger is not always a negative emotion. Some people face situations that are unfair, dangerous, painful, or threatening. When a person's situation needs to be changed, anger can motivate him or her to work on the change. Handling anger in a useful way can bring positive results. For instance, people who are angry about the effects of pollution may decide to join environmental groups to work against pollution.

Problems Caused by Anger

Sometimes, however, anger is expressed in a way that is harmful to the person showing the anger or to others. Anger can destroy relationships, tear down self-esteem, or even cause physical harm. Some people blame others for their problems and try to get even. They may try to increase their own self-esteem by verbally attacking others.

Keeping anger inside can have a negative effect, too. Some people try to hide their anger by avoiding the problem causing it. Their bodies may react to the stress they feel by becoming physically ill because their anger was not resolved. Headaches, ulcers, high blood pressure, or even heart attacks can occur. Their mental health can be affected, too. Anxiety, fear, and depression may increase under the influence of stress due to hidden anger. Unresolved anger can also lead to violence if it builds up too long and a person lashes out at others.

Handling Anger

You can respond to anger in a way that builds positive attitudes. The chart in **Figure 3.13** lists steps for handling anger in a positive way.

Admitting you are angry is an important first step. You cannot get rid of anger if you try to avoid it. If you feel your emotions escalating out of control, take a time-out, remove yourself from the situation, and take time to cool down.

As you think about the situation, try to identify what exactly is making you angry. Determine what you could do to manage the situation. What action could be taken to reduce your anger? Could you look at the circumstances in a different way? Refer again to Figure 3.1. If you can think about a negative experience in a positive way, you can build positive attitudes. You might ask, "How can I learn from this? How can I grow?" Changing the way you think about the experience can impact your feelings, your overall attitude, and ultimately your behavior. Thinking clearly can be difficult when you are angry. Discussing the problem with an experienced adult or a friend can be a helpful step. He or she can help you think through your problem with logic and reason.

Even after taking these steps, you may still feel some anger. *Dwelling* (focusing your attention) on the problem will only increase your negative attitudes. If another person caused your anger, your willingness to forgive can help you get on with your life. Discussing the situation with the other person can be helpful too, as long as you both keep control of your emotions (**Figure 3.14**). If you think that might be difficult, it can be useful to have another person present to oversee the conversation and keep things calm.

Anxiety

Worries, concerns, or fears of failure produce an attitude of anxiety. **Anxiety** is the uneasy

---

Steps for Handling Anger

1. Admit your anger. Take a time-out if needed or go for a walk and cool down.
2. Identify the source of your anger.
3. Identify your choices for managing the situation.
4. Discuss the situation with a trusted adult close friend.
5. Focus on the positive; use humor to relieve tension. Practice relaxation techniques.
6. Forgive and go on.

Figure 3.13 *How could skills for handling anger help people in their relationships?*

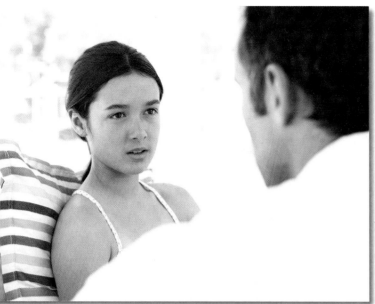
Potstock/Shutterstock.com

Figure 3.14 Talking calmly through the problem is a healthy way to handle anger.

feeling people experience when they believe something terrible will happen. Sometimes the cause of anxiety is real; sometimes it is imagined.

Mild and Major Anxiety

Normal anxiety occurs when you recognize a threat and do something about it. You respond to the threat by either removing it or moving yourself to a safer position. Such anxiety is helpful when it gets people to respond to a real concern.

On the other hand, high anxiety causes problems because it prevents people from acting in a way that corrects the problem. Freezing with fear is an example. High anxiety affects the body physically. It can result in ulcers, headaches, skin rashes, and other problems. Some people feel short of breath or cannot sleep. Some feel constantly tired and lose their appetite. Like continuous stress, ongoing cases of high anxiety can cause physical illness.

High anxiety can also influence people in other ways. It can prevent them from getting things done. It may interfere with their ability to think or hinder their ability to share thoughts or feelings with others. Anxious people also use defense mechanisms more often, which means they are not effectively addressing their problems.

Think About Your Reading

In what ways do stress and anxiety have similar effects on the body?

Handling Anxiety

The key to handling anxiety is to reduce it so you can respond to the problem underlying it. First, you need to recognize and accept your feelings. Next, you have to look at the cause of your anxiety. Sometimes, it is hard to know just what is making you feel anxious. Some of the most common sources of anxiety are listed in **Figure 3.15**.

Stressful events that cause anxiety often produce anger as well. People may become angry at the person or event that brought the stress. As they identify causes of anxiety, they may also discover sources of anger in their lives.

How can you reduce anxiety once the cause has been identified? Sometimes you cannot remove the cause. However, you can work to control the level of your anxiety in several ways.

- *Build your self-esteem.* Think about the successes you have had. Doing so will give you confidence in your ability to handle problems.
- *Use strategies for building positive attitudes.* Use those attitudes to lead you to positive actions.
- *Increase your communication skills.* Use those skills to talk about your feelings and the problem causing them.
- *Build relationships with people who support and encourage you.* Call on them when you need that support.

Causes of Anxiety
• A threat to your well-being
• Fear of failure
• Conflicts
• Fear of the unknown
• Unsatisfied needs

SpeedKingz/Shutterstock.com

Figure 3.15 *What steps in preparing for change could reduce some of these causes of anxiety?*

- *Learn techniques for relaxation.* These techniques can help you stay calm and prevent your emotions from taking over.
- *Prepare for expected changes.* Learn more about the situation that you are worried about. If you know what to expect, you might be less anxious about it. You can also learn ways to handle the challenges you will be facing.

Think About Your Reading

What are some actions you could take to build your self-esteem and reduce future cases of anxiety?

Depression

Did you ever have a day when you could not get excited about anything? You just felt down but did not know why. Having occasional negative feelings is normal. Everyone feels this way once in a while. However, if you find yourself feeling this way most of the time, you may be experiencing depression. **Depression** is an overwhelming attitude of sadness, discouragement, and hopelessness. It can cause a person to have difficulty in making decisions and in leading a normal life.

Causes of Depression

Some cases of depression are mild. The situations described earlier may lead to mild feelings of depression. More severe cases of depression may occur when a person suffers a major loss. This loss may be due to the breakup of a relationship, death, or divorce. Other causes of serious depression may relate to money problems or very low self-esteem.

Sometimes depression has a physical cause, such as a chemical imbalance, lack of sleep, or poor diet. Low blood sugar or certain drugs can also bring on depression.

Another cause of depression is a pattern of negative thinking. This may lead to feelings of anger and **self-pity**, or feeling sorry for yourself. Self-pity does not lead to positive action. Instead, it leads to more negative thoughts and often no action. This leads to a deeper state of depression.

Often there is more than one cause for a person's depression. Several factors may combine to bring on the depression. Past negative experiences can build on each other, leading to a feeling of hopelessness. It may seem impossible to change a situation for the better.

Coping with Depression

With mild cases of depression, family and friends may encourage the person to relax, get some sleep, or take a break from the daily routine. With such support, the depressed person may be able to return to normal.

When you or someone you know has several of the symptoms listed in **Figure 3.16**, and these symptoms last for more than a few weeks, that person needs professional help. Talking with a professional counselor can also help a depressed person identify the source of his or her negative feelings. He or she can then take steps to overcome those feelings, strengthen self-acceptance, and build self-esteem. If the cause of the depression is physical, a psychiatrist or medical doctor can prescribe medications to balance the chemicals in the body. Whatever the treatment, someone who is experiencing severe depression needs the help of people trained in mental health.

Suicide

A person suffering from severe depression may consider **suicide**, or taking one's own life. A person who is considering suicide as an escape often talks about it ahead of time. This can be his or her way of asking for help. If you hear someone talking about "ending it all" or "giving up," seek help for that person immediately. Your school counselor or religious leader can help. Calling a suicide hotline can also help you reach a counselor for such emergencies.

Talking about the problem can help the person think about the finality of such a choice. The goal is to cause the person to stop and think. What other choices are there? What kind of help is available for the real problem the person faces? Treatment for the depression or anxiety that often leads to suicidal thoughts is needed for a person to regain mental health.

Warning Signs of Depression

- You feel sad or cry a lot, and these feelings do not go away.
- You feel guilty for no reason or have lost your confidence.
- Life seems meaningless, like nothing good is ever going to happen again.
- You have a negative attitude most of the time, or it seems like you have no feelings.
- You do not feel like doing many things you used to enjoy, and you want to be left alone most of the time.
- You have difficulty making up your mind. You forget things and find it hard to concentrate.
- You get irritated often and overreact.
- Your sleep pattern changes; you may have trouble sleeping or want to sleep all the time.
- Your eating pattern changes; you've lost your appetite or you eat a lot more.
- You feel restless and tired most of the time.
- You think about death or have thoughts about committing suicide.

National Institute of Mental Health

Figure 3.16 Professional evaluation and help is needed for major depression.

Think About Your Reading

Why might people fail to seek help when they hear a friend make comments related to suicide?

Sex Roles and Stereotypes

As children grow up, they learn there are two sex roles in our culture: masculine and feminine. **Sex roles** are a culture's definition of how males and females should behave. The behaviors linked to each sex are learned. You watch your family, other adults, and your peers and learn from them how to carry out your sex role.

When society has rigid expectations about how males and females should act, stereotypes form. A *stereotype* is an oversimplified opinion or prejudiced attitude used to interpret a life experience or event. For example, a really short haircut may be identified as a man's haircut, or long hair may be identified as a female haircut. These are examples of stereotypes.

Sex stereotypes are oversimplified opinions or beliefs about the characteristics shared by all members of one sex. The chart in **Figure 3.17** lists some common male and female sex stereotypes.

When society expects people to show stereotyped behavior, they are not accepting people as unique persons with their own personal qualities. Harmful behaviors result when people reject one another. If someone is being forced to match a stereotype, that person is not being allowed to grow as an individual person.

LESSON 3.3

Assess

COMPREHENSION CHECK

1. List five steps for handling anger in a positive way.
2. Explain the difference between normal anxiety and high anxiety.
3. List four ways to reduce anxiety.
4. Identify three possible causes of depression.
5. Describe three feelings or attitudes that are warning signs of depression.
6. What are stereotypes and how can they affect self-concept and self-esteem?

| Sex Stereotype Characteristics ||
Men	Women
Unemotional	Emotional
Decisive	Indecisive
Strong	Weak
Independent	Dependent
Brave	Meek
Handsome	Beautiful
Muscular	Slender

Figure 3.17 Stereotype patterns for men and women often include these characteristics.

CHAPTER SUMMARY

Attitudes are learned responses that cause people to choose one behavior over another. Positive or negative attitudes can produce actions that cause those same attitudes to increase. Your self-concept, self-esteem, and overall attitudes contribute to mental health. Mental health describes the overall condition of your social and emotional well-being. Mentally healthy people who can deal with most life situations show a positive mental state.

Mental attitudes are influenced by people's thoughts about life, themselves, and their worth to others. Learning to build positive attitudes will result in actions that cause positive attitudes to increase.

Keeping positive mental attitudes when you encounter stress may be difficult. Recognizing your feelings and identifying their real cause is important. Managing the stressful situation is the next step. As you reduce the effects of stress, positive feelings will replace the negative ones and lead to positive behaviors.

All people feel anger, anxiety, and depression from time to time. Taking steps to replace negative feelings with positive attitudes can help people address the problem. If the problems causing these feelings are not addressed and the feelings build up, they may lead to serious mental illness. People in these situations need to seek professional help.

Stereotyped attitudes toward sex roles can influence your expectations for yourself and others. Overcoming these stereotypes can help you accept yourself and others as unique individuals.

VOCABULARY ACTIVITIES

1. Divide the terms evenly with a partner. Make a crossword puzzle with your set of terms. Then exchange puzzles with your partner and solve the puzzles. Discuss any questions you each have about the definitions.

Content Terms

acting out (3.1)	direct attack (3.1)
anxiety (3.3)	displacement (3.1)
attitude (3.1)	fantasy (3.1)
chronic stress (3.2)	fight-or-flight
compensation (3.1)	response (3.2)
conceited (3.1)	idealization (3.1)
conversion (3.1)	mental health (3.1)
defense	projection (3.1)
mechanisms (3.1)	rationalization (3.1)
denial (3.1)	regression (3.1)
depression (3.3)	routine stress (3.2)

self-perpetuating	sex stereotype (3.3)
cycle (3.1)	stress (3.2)
self-pity (3.3)	stress hormones (3.2)
self-talk (3.1)	suicide (3.3)
sex role (3.3)	transitional stress (3.2)

2. Create a concept web for each of the following terms. In your web, connect each term to at least three of the content terms.

Academic Terms

consequence (3.1)	potential (3.2)
dwell (3.3)	stereotype (3.3)
interpret (3.1)	traumatic (3.2)

ASSESS

Your Knowledge

3. What attitudes lead to mental health?
4. What are nine different defense mechanisms that people sometimes use to deal with problems?
5. List three factors contributing to stress in people's lives.
6. List three signs of major depression.

Your Understanding

7. How do feelings, thoughts, and actions work together to portray an attitude?
8. How can stress be handled to reduce its effects on the body?
9. Describe five examples of how you could build positive attitudes in your life.
10. How can stereotypes lead to negative attitudes and poor mental health?

Your Skills

11. Analyze two defense mechanisms and explain how they could hinder growth.
12. Write yourself a positive self-talk message that would increase your feelings of self-esteem after you took a test.
13. Write a scenario in which you think through ways to help a friend who shows signs of unresolved anger, high anxiety, or major depression.

CRITICAL THINKING

14. **Analyze and Summarize Findings.** Make a list of events that make you feel positive and identify their common qualities. Do the same for events that make you feel negative. Write a summary of the common qualities in events that make you feel positive. *Choice*: Write a paper contrasting events

that make you feel positive versus events that make you feel negative and describe steps you can take to handle the negative feelings resulting from such events.

15. **Compare Differences and Similarities.** Make a short list of your own expectations for your life. Then interview two family members and two peers about their expectations for your life. Write a paper comparing various expectations for your life. Include your own expectations, your family's expectations, and your peers' expectations. Identify the main differences and describe the feelings these differences bring about.

16. **Draw Conclusions.** Interview a person who has overcome negative life experiences to achieve success in his or her career. Write a report describing the techniques this person used to adjust to and cope with negative experiences. Compare this person's success with strategies provided in the text, citing evidence to support your comparison. *Choice*: Present your information in an oral report.

17. **Make Inferences.** Identify three to five characters, including both males and females, from popular movies or TV shows. Write a paper in which you describe the characters, and analyze what sex roles or sex stereotypes the characters represent. Conclude your paper with an analysis of whether these characters could serve as appropriate role models for teens. *Choice*: Choose three to five celebrities or entertainers for the project.

CORE SKILLS

18. **Research.** Research resources available in your community for people struggling with suicidal thoughts. List these resources and identify careers that use these resources in their professional services. *Choice*: Review a suicide hotline's website and describe the kinds of resources they have.

19. **Writing.** Write a "Dear Abby" letter seeking advice for a situation involving anger, anxiety, depression, or defense mechanisms. You can write about a real-life situation or an imaginary one. Choose a partner and exchange letters, writing a response to your partner's letter. *Group option*: Work in a small group of four and analyze the advice for techniques that build positive life attitudes, citing evidence from the text to support your analysis.

20. **Social Studies, Writing.** Interview four adults, including both men and women. Ask questions about how they interpret their roles as males or females in their home, at work, and in their community. Questions could include their thoughts on appropriate behaviors, clothing, childrearing responsibilities, work-related responsibilities, and housekeeping responsibilities. Write a paragraph summarizing your thoughts on male and female roles in your community. Do the interviewees' roles have anything in common with male and female stereotypes? Cite evidence from the text to support your opinion.

21. **Writing.** Prepare a print flyer or a multimedia presentation advertising a technique for reducing stress. Use a publishing program in a bifold or trifold format to create the flyer. Present the positive impacts of the stress reduction technique to the reader. *Choice*: Post your flyer on your class's web page or network. *Group option*: Evaluate flyers developed by classmates for their potential success in reducing stress.

22. **Research, Writing.** Search the Internet to learn about the physical effects of anger and anxiety and possible resources for dealing with these effects. Prepare a report of your findings. Describe the relationship of the physical effects of anger and anxiety to overall health and well-being. Cite references used.

23. **Social Studies, Writing.** Design and print a poster aimed at combating sex stereotyping in your school. Add digital images to help emphasize your message. *Choice*: Instead of a poster, write and produce a public service announcement on the same subject. *Choice*: Get permission to post your poster on your school's website.

CAREER READINESS

24. **Taking Initiative.** Imagine it is five years in the future and you are starting your first full-time job. Your new employer is a hospital and you know the work is fast-paced and demanding. You have watched some family members and friends suffer the effects of workplace stress on their health and wellness over the years. Your goal is to maintain health and wellness by developing a plan for handling workplace stress. Investigate and evaluate the resources on the *National Institute for Occupational Safety and Health* link on the Centers for Disease Control (CDC) website. Then write your plan for preventing job stress.

CONNECTING WITH CAREER CLUSTERS

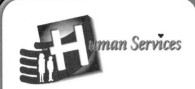

PATHWAYS

Early Childhood Development & Services

Counseling and Mental Health Services

Family and Community Services

Personal Care Services

Consumer Services

MENTAL HEALTH SERVICES

Professionals in mental health services help individuals grow to reach optimum mental health so they can achieve their potential and fully participate as productive members of society. Mental health services include a wide range of supports for persons who struggle with such issues as addictions and substance abuse; family, parenting, and marital problems; low self-esteem and thoughts of suicide; stress management; and problems associated with mental illness. Some services focus on prevention—helping persons learn skills to adjust and adapt to stresses and changes; other services focus on intervention and restoration into society.

Persons needing mental health services sometimes do not recognize their own problems. They may be referred through correctional institutions, court systems, medical providers, social services, or concerned family members. Thus, mental health services professionals need to be socially perceptive. That is, they are aware of how persons with mental health issues react, and understand why they react as they do. Negotiation skills, skills for instructing, and management skills are needed in mental health service careers.

To develop these skills, most persons working in mental health services need a college degree and may need graduate coursework, depending on the position they seek. Counseling, social work, psychology, therapy, and counseling—all are areas through which mental health services may be provided.

CAREER OUTLOOK

Persons working is this field need to enjoy actively looking for ways to help other people. These professionals need to have good communication skills, both speaking and listening. They need to use active listening to understand the issues of their clients and be able to convey information effectively as solutions are identified and implemented. Critical thinking skills, such as logic and reasoning, are needed to identify strengths and weaknesses of alternative solutions or approaches for varying needs of clients.

Employment for persons wanting to work in mental health services offers a bright job outlook, in areas that emphasize prevention as well as intervention. In 2014, the average salary for professional mental health services workers was $40,900, with salaries ranging from $26,000 to $66,900. Salaries vary depending on the training and experience required to provide specific mental health services.

EXPLORE

Internet Research

Research the mental health services available in your community to persons struggling with various emotional and mental health issues. Identify which services have a prevention focus and which services target individuals with mental health-related problems. Research the salaries earned by individuals offering different services. Prepare a summary of these services and then identify which areas of mental health you feel are not adequately met in your community.

Job Shadowing

Contact one of the mental health service providers in your community to set up a time to sit in on a group meeting as AA (Alcoholics Anonymous), Grief Share, or a similar group. Ask an adult to join you when you visit this meeting. Identify the techniques used by the group leader as he or she leads the group session. Summarize the experience by writing in a journal.

Community Service/Volunteer

See your guidance counselor about becoming involved in peer counseling. Take peer conflict-resolution training and join a peer conflict-resolution team. Help resolve peer conflicts, keeping a journal of your experiences and techniques.

Project

Create a series of posters that could be used to teach skills for coping with difficult events and emotions. See Chapter 3 for ideas to use for these posters. Posters could teach skills such as handling stress, handling anger, handling anxiety, or handling depression. Ask your guidance counselor for permission to hang these posters in the guidance office as a teaching tool to assist in preventing mental health issues.

Interview

Interview a mental health services provider for advice on entering the mental health career field. Ask questions about the types of mental health services that are provided in your community, and areas in which there is potential for job growth. Find out the provider's recommendations for good schools to attend, valuable internship opportunities, and the jobs offering the most prospects for someone eager to work hard and get ahead. Summarize your interview in a report.

Part-Time Job

Seek a part-time job in a youth summer camp or recreation program where services are provided to underprivileged children. Identify the types of activities provided in the programming. Identify responsibilities of the camp counselors and program providers. Write a report describing your experiences. Summarize how youth involvement in such programs could be beneficial for mental health and wellness.

UNIT 2

SETTING AND REACHING LIFE GOALS

ESSENTIAL QUESTION

How can day-to-day decision-making skills impact success in reaching life goals and thereby impact quality of life?

CASE STUDY

How Are Goals Influencing These Teens?

Read the case study and discuss the questions that follow. After finishing the chapters in this unit, discuss the questions again and identify any answers you would change based on information you learned.

Isa knew that a lot depended on him as he got ready to take the Chinese national placement exam. He had been studying and practicing test questions for months. It would not be long before he would need to provide for the family as his parents aged. They counted on him getting a good job so he could continue to meet the needs of the extended family. Right now, his goal was to get accepted into the University of Singapore so he could study to be a communications engineer. His dad had provided well for the family. Soon it would be his turn. Would he get accepted? Had he studied enough to get a high score on the exams?

The deadline was fast approaching for Andrea to complete her assignments. She was graduating from her high school in Alberta, Canada, with a certificate that gave her credit for completing a term of study at a technical institute in Calgary, the major city nearby. She had worked toward this program all four years of high school, taking courses that aligned with the technical institute's requirements. She had worked at an after-school job as part of her high school program and saved some money. She was excited to move on to the next phase— moving to Calgary and finishing her degree. She would be on her own soon.

Tanya looked at her younger siblings and gave them a sharp reminder to get their homework done. She knew she was needed around home for a couple more years and was glad that it worked out for her to attend the Lake Superior College after graduating from high school. She had taken training during her senior year to work in the local nursing home. She felt fortunate to have a job already and planned to keep working there while she attended

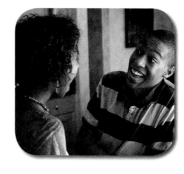

the community college. Sometimes she did feel left out while her friends talked of going away to college next year. But staying at home while she worked toward a degree seemed like the best choice for her and her family right now.

William was excited as he eagerly opened the mail. His hands shook as he unfolded the letter and read it aloud. "I've been accepted with a full scholarship," he yelled loudly as he ran into the house. He literally jumped up and down as he spoke the words. His mom wrapped her arms around him and jumped along with him, while his younger brother Jackson cheered on as well. His hard work studying in school and practicing basketball day in and day out had paid off. As the cheering quieted down, William noticed his brother Jackson was sitting quietly by the table. "We will miss you, man," Jackson told his brother. He knew William would be going to school five hours away, and he would not see his brother very often.

For Discussion

1. How are Isa's, Andrea's, Tanya's, and William's values and goals for the future similar?
2. How are their goals different?
3. In what ways did the small choices they made every day impact their potential for reaching their life goals?

Reading Prep

Before reading the chapter, copy the headings and subheadings onto a piece of paper, leaving space below each one. As you read, write the main idea of each section under the appropriate heading or subheading.

Key Questions

Questions to answer as you study this chapter:

- What can help a person make good decisions?
- What are the steps in making a good decision?
- How do decisions affect an individual's and a family's quality of life?

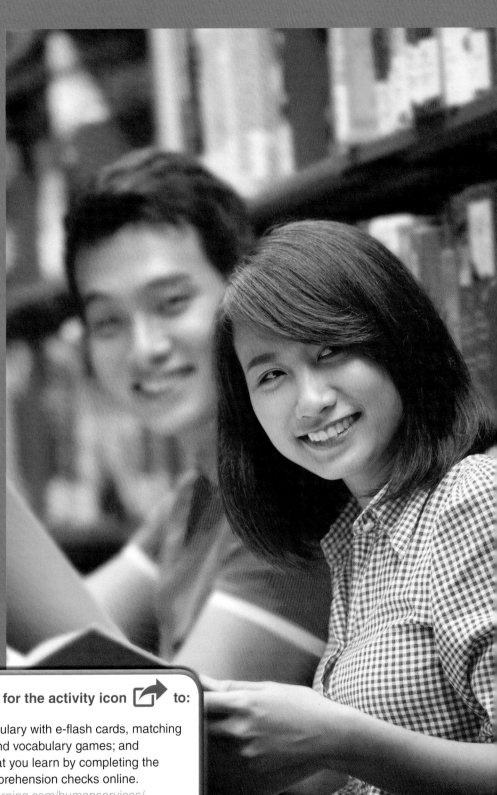

Dragon Images/Shutterstock.com

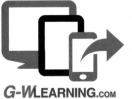

While studying this chapter, look for the activity icon to:

- **build** vocabulary with e-flash cards, matching activities, and vocabulary games; and
- **assess** what you learn by completing the lesson comprehension checks online.

www.g-wlearning.com/humanservices/

G-WLEARNING.com

Lesson 4.1 Factors Affecting Decision Making
Lesson 4.2 The Decision-Making Process

AFTER STUDYING THIS CHAPTER, YOU WILL

KNOW:

- What factors affect a person's success in making decisions.
- The steps for setting and reaching goals.
- The steps in the decision-making process.

UNDERSTAND:

- How a person's intellectual, social, and emotional maturity; values; goals; personal standards; and resources affect the ability to make good decisions.
- How decisions affect health, well-being, family, interpersonal relationships, employment, and society as a whole.

BE ABLE TO DO:

- Analyze personal, relationship, and work values.
- Use values to set personal goals.
- Apply the steps in the decision-making process.

GETTING STARTED

Hector lay on the couch, staring at the wall. His eyes were fixed on a picture, but he was not really looking at it. He was thinking about the comment Anna made to him at school that day. "Should be a great game tonight!" she said and smiled. He wondered why she said that to him. Did she like him? Did she want to go to the game with him?

Hector's thoughts were quickly interrupted. "What are you doing, Hector?" his mother called.

"Just thinking," he replied. His thoughts drifted back to Anna.

"Thinking about what?" his mother asked.

"Oh, nothing." Hector grumbled, wondering if his thoughts were important.

All your thoughts are important. When you think about a certain subject, you put together all the information you have about it. You think about the information in different ways. This helps you analyze situations, form opinions, and identify your feelings. You review your choices and the possible outcomes of each one. Whenever you make a decision, you use this process.

Your decisions affect your behaviors, what you choose to do or not to do, and as a result, have an impact on your life. Your decisions will also affect your relationships with others—and their lives. For these reasons, it is important to learn how to make good decisions. Good decisions will help you carry out responsible behaviors that help you reach your life goals. They will also help you build strong relationships. Building decision-making skills is a good way to make good decisions.

FACTORS AFFECTING DECISION MAKING

Content Terms

Build Vocab

routine decision
planned decision
values
group values
goal
short-term goal
long-term goal
subgoal
standards
human resource
nonhuman resource

Academic Terms

project
obstacle
resource

Objectives

After studying this lesson, you will be able to

- **list** factors that influence decision making.
- **explain** how values develop and influence opinions.
- **distinguish** between short-term and long-term goals.
- **develop** plans for reaching your goals.
- **explain** the relationship between standards and goals.
- **identify** human and nonhuman resources.
- **describe** skills for managing your resources.

Focus Your Reading

1. Create two columns in your notebook. As you read, list each factor affecting decision making in the first column. In the second column, summarize how that factor affects decision making.
2. For each term, identify and describe an example from your own life.

You will make many decisions throughout your life. Some will be **routine decisions**, the choices that are made every day without much thought. For instance, every morning you make a decision to get up. Most of the time you will not think about this decision for too long or you will be late for school. If you feel sick or have a headache, you may think longer about how this decision may affect you.

For a **planned decision**, you use more time and energy to make the best choice. Deciding on a career or making an expensive purchase are examples of planned decisions. These decisions are likely to have long-term effects, which is why making good planned decisions is so important.

What can help you make good decisions, ones that are responsible and lead to the end results that you want? The decisions an individual makes are influenced by the following factors:

- intellectual maturity
- social and emotional maturity
- values
- goals
- standards
- resources

Your Intellectual Maturity

In order to make good decisions, you need to be able to recognize what the effects of a decision might be. Mature thinking skills will help you do that (**Figure 4.1**).

As you grow and mature, thinking skills become more advanced. You can think about abstract ideas as well as concrete objects. You can reason about ideas and issues and draw conclusions. You can *project* thoughts about your life, or think ahead and plan ideas for the future.

Growing and maturing also bring new and different experiences. You can use information from past experiences to think through current decisions. You can identify options, figure out the likely outcomes of each, and compare the options. With experience, your ability to think of different options and to predict the future will be better. Gaining mature thinking skills leads to more satisfying decisions.

Evidence of Mature Thinking Skills

- Thinks about abstract ideas.
- Uses logical reasoning to draw conclusions.
- Projects thoughts about the future.
- Predicts possible outcomes.
- Compares ideas and thinks about which outcome might be best.

Figure 4.1 Your ability to make decisions improves as you develop these intellectual skills. *What are some situations where you practice these skills?*

Your Social and Emotional Maturity

Good decisions show evidence of mature social and emotional responses. As you mature socially, you make choices that benefit not only you, but others around you. When you consider possible options, you recognize that others in your life will be affected by your decisions. Responsible decisions consider the needs of others as well as your needs.

As you mature, you are able to recognize and control your emotional responses to a situation. This gives you time to think through a decision and make better choices. Emotional maturity will help you make responsible decisions.

Your Values

Your **values** include all the ideals and beliefs that are important to you. The values you consider important will influence the decisions you make and the actions you take. Responsible decision making requires that you consider values that are important to yourself, your family, and others in your community when making and carrying out a decision.

How Values Develop

Your values are influenced largely by those around you. The society you live in, the culture around you, the individuals and groups around you, and your family all impact your values. So does your personality.

The society in which you live shapes your values. Democracy, freedom of religion, freedom of speech, and freedom from fear and want are examples of societal values taught in the United States.

Various cultures within a society may hold additional values. For example, some cultures place a strong emphasis on intergenerational ties (**Figure 4.2**). When people of several cultures live in a society, the values of one culture may influence the members of other cultures.

Both formal and informal social groups have **group values** that are shared by everyone in the

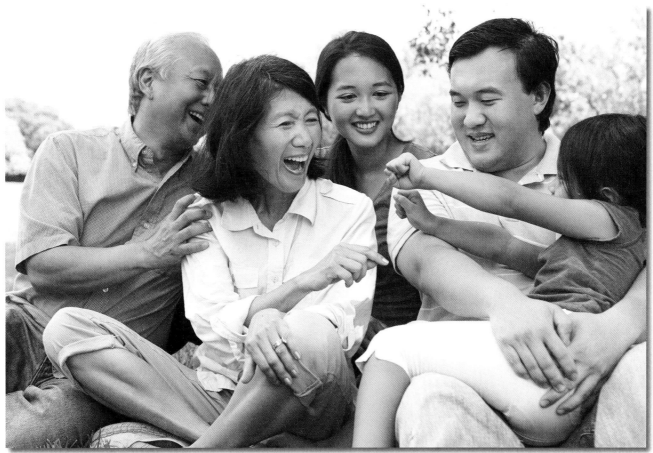

Monkey Business Images/Shutterstock.com

Figure 4.2 Some cultures place a strong emphasis on intergenerational relationships.

group. Each group that influences you may have different expectations for you. For example, your teachers may want you to spend time studying and doing your best in school while your coaches want you to practice. Your peer group holds certain values as well. They may encourage you to be more independent or to go to social activities.

The ideals or beliefs that your family emphasizes are your family's values. These will form the base from which you develop your own values. Many of your values will be similar to your family's values, though some may differ.

Your personality can influence what is important to you. For instance, if you have an outgoing temperament, being with other people might be important to you. This value leads you to spend more time with your friends. Another family member may value quiet time for thinking and reading and spend more time alone. Such differences reflect each person's unique personality.

Think About Your Reading

Identify some societal, cultural, and family values that are evident in your school.

Identifying Your Values

If you were to list your values, they would fall into different categories. You might list good health as one value. Having close friends and a good job may be others. Your values can be divided into three categories—personal, relationship, and work values. Identifying your values in each area is helpful for decision making.

Personal Values and Your Decisions

Your personal values will be seen in the decisions you make related to personal areas. What is highly important to you as an individual? a positive attitude? religious beliefs? physical attractiveness?

personal interests and hobbies? fitness? leisure? health and well-being? personal growth? Your list may include all these values and more.

Though many people cite these values, they may interpret them differently. For instance, your idea of physical attractiveness is unlikely to be the same as a friend's idea. Your idea of personal growth may be different from another's.

Relationship Values and Your Decisions

Your decisions will be impacted by the values you have regarding relationships. What values are important to you in your relationships? You might value respect, acceptance, and kindness in all your relationships. In your family relationships, you may have expectations for closeness. In those relationships, then, you might value giving and receiving love; showing warmth, caring, and trust; and sharing experiences and feelings. In friendships, you may value honesty and openness. You may also want friends to accept you for who you are (**Figure 4.3**).

Work Values and Your Decisions

The things that are important to you as you carry out your daily tasks will affect the decisions you make. As a teen, your main work tasks may be related to school, although you may have several

responsibilities related to working at home and helping out the family. Some teens may hold part-time jobs as well.

The values you hold related to your work will affect how successful you are in carrying out your work tasks. If you value the task as important, you will take the time to do a good job and complete it on time. If you enjoy doing a task, it is likely you will value it more highly.

Think About Your Reading
What values might be important for success on the job?

Values Influence Decisions

Knowing your values can help you make decisions. You will feel more confident and comfortable with your decisions if you make choices that agree with your most important values.

Values differ in their level of importance to you. Ranking your values can help you make decisions. List the most important value first. Put the least important value last on the list. Then arrange the others in between. Equally important values could be listed side-by-side. When you are faced with a decision, use this list to help you identify your most important values involved in that decision.

Some decisions are difficult to make because you experience a conflict in values. This can create stress in your life. Ranking your values can help you resolve these conflicts. As you will see, using a decision-making process can help with these difficult decisions as well.

Your Goals

Your values can help you set goals. A **goal** is something you want to do, have, or achieve. If you want to achieve the goal in the near future, it is a **short-term goal**. For instance, Adrianne wants to finish her term paper this week. If the goal will take longer to reach, it is a **long-term goal**. For instance, one long-term goal is to finish high school. Another may be to finish college or earn a promotion at work within the next year.

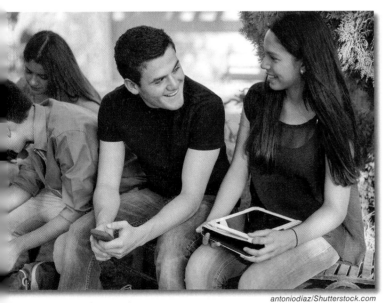

antoniodiaz/Shutterstock.com

Figure 4.3 *How would the values you have for a dating relationship be different from the things that are important in other relationships?*

A long-term goal may be broken down into several smaller subgoals (**Figure 4.4**). Each **subgoal** is a step leading toward the long-term goal. Libby has a long-term goal to save $1,000 for a down payment on a car. She has smaller short-term goals of saving $100 each month. Her monthly goals are subgoals that will help her reach her long-term goal.

Subgoals can help you keep a positive attitude as you work toward a long-term goal. As you reach each one, you will feel more confident about your ability to reach your long-term goal. As a result, your success rate for accomplishing your goals will increase.

Developing a Plan to Reach Your Goal

Use your values to set your goals. This will help you make plans that are important to you in each area of your life. Your most important values can help you identify the goals that you should work on first. Working on all your goals at one time is difficult. It is easier to choose two or three very important goals. Then take steps to reach them. As you progress toward these goals, you can add others.

See step 1 of **Figure 4.5** to see how Sean set a goal to be physically fit. This is an important value

for him. He set subgoals and then broke those down into short-term goals.

Sean then developed a plan of action (step 2 of Figure 4.5). His plan of action includes the steps he will take to reach his goal and a time frame for each step. Steps in a plan of action need to be realistic. They need to be something you are willing and able to do.

Handling Obstacles

Even if you have a plan of action, obstacles may arise to interfere. An *obstacle* is something that stands in the way as you try to reach a goal. Watching too much television could be an obstacle if your goal is to improve your grades. One way to deal with obstacles is identify them as you make your plan of action. Step 3 of Figure 4.5 shows how Sean identified some possible obstacles to his plan of action and listed actions he can take to avoid those obstacles.

Think About Your Reading

Why are subgoals and short-term goals an important part of a plan to reach a goal?

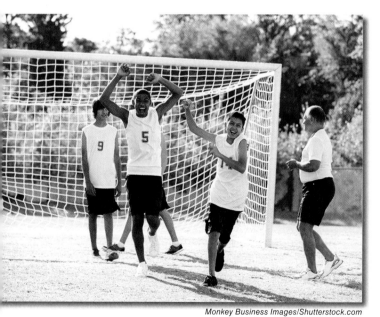

Monkey Business Images/Shutterstock.com

Figure 4.4 Breaking down a long-term goal into smaller subgoals makes it possible to see progress toward completing the long-term goal. *What could be some subgoals for a long-term goal of winning a state championship?*

Your Standards

Standards are guidelines that indicate a level of quality in a product or task. Your standards help you identify what level of quality is or is not acceptable to you. Standards can help measure your progress toward your goals. If you value getting good grades, you may set a goal to make the honor roll this semester. To help you reach that goal, you could set certain standards for yourself. These may include getting an A on most of your assignments. Meeting these standards should help you reach your goal.

Some standards are easily measured, while others are based on personal experiences. In school, you are usually required to follow the standards set for all students. For instance, you must earn credits for graduation. To do so, you need to do well on tests. These school standards are measurable.

Steps in Goal Setting	
Step 1 Identify a value and use it to set a goal.	

Value: Physical fitness
Long-term goal: To be physically fit

Subgoals	Short-Term Goals
• Lose 10 pounds. • Develop good muscle tone. • Strengthen heart.	• Lose 1 pound per week for 10 weeks. • Work out three times per week. • Run three times per week.

Step 2 Develop a plan of action to carry out goal.

Plan of Action

Goal	Steps	Time
To lose 10 pounds	1. Start watching calorie intake. 2. Identify types and quantity of foods for each meal. 3. Identify low-calorie snacks. 4. Purchase low-calorie foods.	Monday morning Monday evening Monday evening Tuesday
To work out three times a week	1. Get workout video. 2. Put time to work out on daily schedule.	Tuesday M-W-F at 7:00 a.m.
To run three times a week	1. Purchase running shoes. 2. Put time to run on agenda.	Tuesday T-Th-Sat. at 7:00 a.m.

Step 3 Identify possible obstacles. List steps to avoid obstacles.

Possible Obstacles	Steps to Avoid Obstacles
• Eating out • Getting too hungry • Sleeping late in the morning • Not enough money for all purchases	1. Choose low-calorie foods at restaurants. 2. Keep low-calorie snacks available. 3. Have someone check up on me at 6:55 a.m. 4. Borrow a friend's workout video and use my old shoes to start the program. Make purchases one at a time.

Figure 4.5 Sean's personal values can help him set and carry out his goals.

The standards you develop from your personal experiences are not so easily measured. Your standards are unique to you and may be different from the standards of others. For instance, your standard for a good movie will be different from a friend's standards.

Sometimes differences in personal standards cause conflict. Your mother's standard for a clean room may differ from yours. When setting a goal, it helps to know what the standard will be for measuring success. Then you can include steps in your plan of action to meet the standard and reach your goal.

Ethical standards are measures of proper conduct for individuals and members in society. Do your personal standards measure up to ethical standards? Will your standards help you become more trustworthy, honest, caring, and considerate of others? Such standards will help you mature socially and emotionally and make decisions that will support strong relationships.

Your Resources

A *resource* is anything available to help you carry out your decisions. When people are aware of all their resources, they are better able to make good decisions and reach their goals.

What do you have available to help you carry out your decisions? time? energy? money? a can-do attitude? special skills? There are two kinds of resources: human and nonhuman. A **human resource** comes from within a person. This includes your personal qualities and characteristics as well as the support you receive from others. A **nonhuman resource** is any item you have available to help you, such as money, a car, tools, time, and information. Some decisions may require several resources.

Human Resources

What personal qualities and characteristics help you carry out your decisions? You may have certain physical resources, such as good health, strength, and energy. Knowledge, talents, and skills are also human resources (**Figure 4.6**). Your personality and character traits are other examples. These personal traits become resources for making decisions and carrying out a task.

Your character qualities can also be considered resources. Strength in character means that you have personal qualities that will help you carry out your decisions. For instance, if you are disciplined, you will be more likely to carry out your decisions.

What skills have you developed? Skills for reading, writing, and math are resources you can acquire in school. You can also develop skills for communicating with others, solving problems, and making decisions. In addition, you probably have developed other special skills, such as preparing food or caring for children. Knowing how to maintain your car, program a computer, or play an instrument are other examples. Each personal skill can be a resource for you in some situation.

Besides your skills and abilities, you may need to use the second category of human resources—other people in your life. Family members or a friend, teacher, or religious leader can help or support you as you work toward some goals. For instance, suppose you need help to complete your homework. Would you contact a teacher? Would you ask a classmate to help you? The exact kind of support others can provide depends on the resources they have. They may offer support by helping you, encouraging you, or giving you other resources. They can combine their resources with yours to help you carry out your goals (**Figure 4.7**).

Think About Your Reading

What human resources could help a person reach a goal of physical fitness? of having good friendships? of personal maturity?

Nonhuman Resources

Money, possessions, the community, and information are examples of nonhuman resources. Every person has these resources in different amounts.

The one exception is time, the nonhuman resource everyone has on an equal basis—24 hours per day. How do you use your time? Do you use it to accomplish your goals or do you waste it? Do

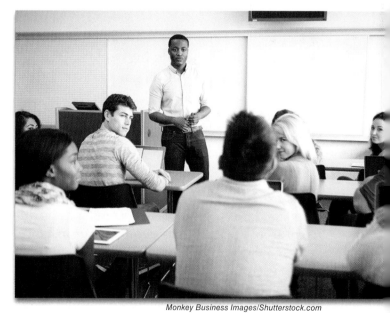

Monkey Business Images/Shutterstock.com

Figure 4.6 The knowledge gained through education is a human resource. *What knowledge have you gained recently that could help you make a decision?*

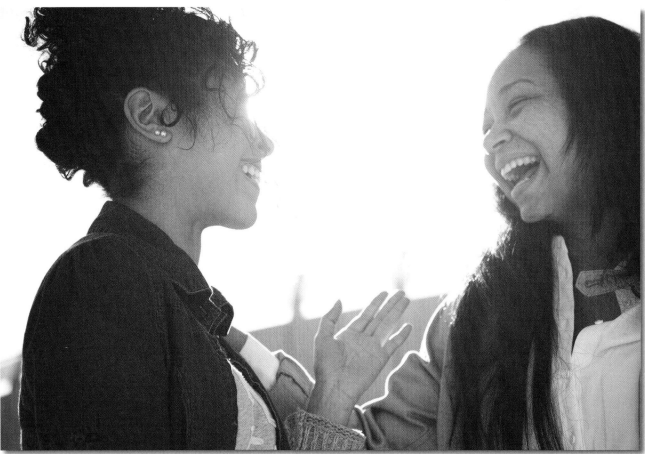
Joshua Resnick/Shutterstock.com

Figure 4.7 The people in your life are valuable human resources who can help you reach your goals.

you try to use time productively? Your time is a nonhuman resource that you can learn to manage.

Money can be used to buy goods and services. The presence or lack of money will affect the decisions you can make by shaping the options that are doable. For instance, if one option costs more money than you have, you know your decision must match what you can afford.

Personal possessions can be resources for you in some situations. A personal computer can be a resource if you want to write and edit a paper. The family car can be a resource to travel to and from a job.

Community resources, including parks, zoos, schools, museums, and stores, are shared with others. A park provides recreational services. Your school is a resource for education. Some people use public transportation to get to work instead of driving themselves.

Information is another important resource. Your ability to carry out a decision may depend on

information from a reliable source, such as a book, magazine, newspaper, or database. The Internet provides large amounts of information, but it is not always reliable. It is important to check the credibility of your sources before accepting the information in them as facts.

Think About Your Reading

What nonhuman resources in a community can help people reach personal goals of maturity?

Managing Resources

Managing your resources means using them wisely. This is a skill that can be learned. First, you must identify the resources you have and know how they might be developed. Think about your human qualities as resources. Good health, a positive attitude, and your talents are examples

of resources that are helpful. Your possessions are easier resources to identify (**Figure 4.8**). Another skill in managing your resources involves planning. Since many resources such as energy and money are limited, this is an important skill. Planning will help you use each resource in a way that will benefit you. When you do not have the skill to do what you want to do, you may need to substitute another human or nonhuman resource. You can also use time, skills, and knowledge to substitute for money in some cases. Someone who knows how to sew clothing may not need to buy a new outfit.

Think About Your Reading

What are some examples of using a human resource to reach a goal when a nonhuman resource such as money is in short supply?

Assess

LESSON 4.1

COMPREHENSION CHECK

1. Identify six factors that can influence decisions.
2. Describe five factors that influence a person's values.
3. Identify three categories of values and give an example of each.
4. Explain the difference between a short-term and a long-term goal. Give an example of each.
5. What role do standards play in setting goals? Give an example of a standard related to a goal for losing weight.
6. List three examples of nonhuman resources.
7. Identify two skills for managing resources wisely.

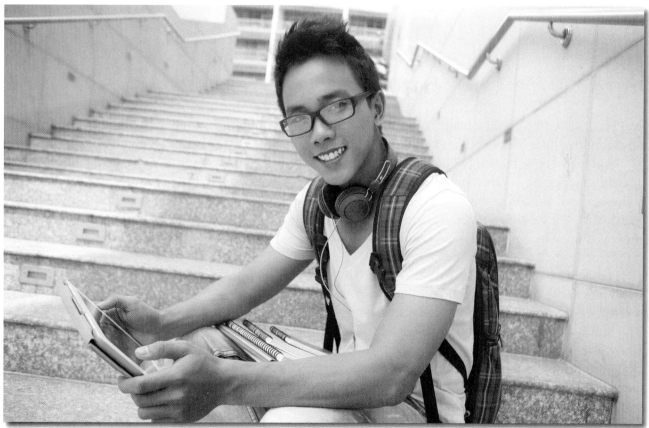

Dragon Images/Shutterstock.com

Figure 4.8 Nonhuman resources like money or a computer can help you reach your goals. *Why is management of resources needed to be successful?*

THE DECISION-MAKING PROCESS

Objectives

After studying this lesson, you will be able to

- **identify** steps in the decision-making process.
- **use** the decision-making process to make and evaluate decisions.
- **explain** the impact of decisions on health, well-being, family and interpersonal relationships, and career.
- **describe** ways individuals' decisions affect society.

Focus Your Reading

1. As you read the text, refer to the chart that shows each step in the decision-making process.

2. Choose a simple decision and brainstorm all possible alternatives and all possible consequences for that decision. List your ideas under the headings *alternative* or *consequence*.

Content Terms

Build Vocab

decision-making process
alternative
depressant
alcoholic
drug
drug abuse
addiction
withdrawal
ethical decision making

Academic Terms

available
reliable
participate

Why is it important to develop your decision-making skills? All decisions have some sort of impact on your life and lead your life path in some direction. Every choice has some type of consequence, or end result. The results of your decisions should reflect your values as you are likely to be happier with your decisions if they are consistent with your personal beliefs. Your decisions should also help you reach your goals. You will feel better about yourself if you can succeed in carrying out your plans. Thus, your decision-making skills will impact your self-concept, your self-esteem, and your quality of life.

Steps in the Decision-Making Process

The **decision-making process** is a step-by-step method to guide your thinking when you need to make a planned decision. The six steps of this process are outlined with an example in **Figure 4.9**. Using this process can help you make decisions and solve problems. Each step can help you organize your thoughts so you can make a choice or pick the best solution.

Identify the Issue

The decision-making process begins with the individual understanding the situation he or she faces. What is it about a situation that requires a decision to be made? Many situations are quite complicated and include several issues. The first step is to clarify what the issue is, as Chandra did. See step 1 of Figure 4.9.

Chandra's mother worked full-time and made enough money to meet the family's basic living expenses. Chandra, however, wanted to have some extra spending money. For her, the issue was to find a way to earn some money of her own.

Using the Decision-Making Process

Step 1   Identify the decision to be made.
Chandra wants more spending money. She sets a goal to find a job.

Step 2   Identify all possible alternatives.
Chandra knows that finding a job will be a major task. She has no previous work experience and must work limited hours. She lists four possible job alternatives. 1. Work part-time after school. 2. Work weekends only. 3. Apply for a work-study job at school. 4. Join a vocational co-op program at the high school.

Step 3   Consider each alternative.
1. Work part-time after school.

Pros	Cons
• This option offers a steady work schedule and provides the most work hours. • These jobs are more available.	• Chandra would not be able to take part in volleyball, softball, and flag squad—all of which she enjoys. • Students with after-school jobs are often scheduled to work weekends as well. This would not leave much time for studying. Chandra knew studying was important to her to reach her long-term goal of going to college.

2. Work weekends only.	

Pros	Cons
• Work would not interfere with Chandra's school schedule during the week. • She would be able to take part in more after-school activities.	• Weekend jobs are harder to find. • A weekend job would take time away from family activities.

3. Apply for a work-study job at school.	

Pros	Cons
• The work location is convenient. • She could continue with her after-school activities.	• A limited number of jobs are available. Only a few students with an interest in office occupations are chosen.

(Continued)

Figure 4.9 Developing your skill in using this process can help you make decisions or solve problems in your daily living. *What big decision will you be making in the near future?*

Using the Decision-Making Process

Step 3 Consider each alternative. *(Continued)*

4. Join a vocational co-op program at the high school.

Pros	Cons
• One of the several co-op programs offered at school is in the health field, Chandra's career interest. The teacher would help her find a job related to her career goal. • She could work an average of 15 hours per week. She would be excused from school early to go to work. She would earn credit for the work experience as well as a wage. • Job-related classroom instruction would be provided.	• Participating in the program would mean fewer chances to take elective courses during the school year. • Her work schedule would determine whether she could participate in any after-school activities.

Step 4 Make the decision.

- Chandra decided to enroll in an FCCLA co-op class. She will receive job-related classroom instruction and on-the-job training in the health services field.
- She will be working 15 hours per week.
- She will be able to participate in flag squad after school two days a week for the first quarter.

Step 5 Carry out the decision.

Chandra identified the following four steps to carry out her decision:
1. Sign up for the FCCLA class.
2. Take the job-related classroom instruction.
3. Work with the teacher-coordinator in finding a job.
4. Work with the coordinator and employer to identify goals for her work experience.

Step 6 Evaluate the decision.

- With assistance from the teacher-coordinator and the employer, she will evaluate her work experience.
- She will determine her success in reaching her job-related goals.
- She will determine her success in earning more spending money.
- Overall, she will think about how well she used the decision-making process in making her choice.

Figure 4.9 Continued.

Identify the Alternatives

The next step is to identify what choices you have in addressing the issue. A choice is called an **alternative**. At least two choices must exist before a person is faced with making a decision. At this step, you need to identify as many alternatives as you can.

Thinking about all the resources that are *available*, or possible for you to use, can help you identify alternatives. Sometimes people facing a decision need to gather more information to learn about possible alternatives. At other times, they can draw on their experience or information they have learned and remembered. For instance, Chandra remembered that staff from the co-op program had spoken to all the students in her school at the beginning of the year about what they do and what kinds of jobs they have. That helped her identify one alternative.

Chandra thought about her alternatives for earning money. She identified four possible job options. See step 2 of Figure 4.9.

Consider Each Alternative

The next step in the decision-making process is to carefully think through each alternative. You have to consider all the factors related to each choice. How does each alternative fit your values, goals, standards, and resources?

To answer these questions, gather information from reliable sources (**Figure 4.10**). In addition, you could seek out facts and opinions from others who faced a similar decision in the past, such as a family member, counselor, teacher, or friend. Your own past experiences can also provide information. *Reliable* information, information you can count on to be accurate, will help you predict the results of your decision with greater success.

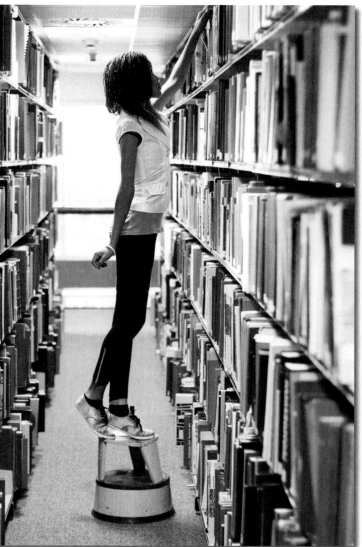

maxik/Shutterstock.com

Figure 4.10 Learning to use reliable resources can help you think through each alternative.

How will this choice affect you and others, both now and in the future? This question can help you think about the consequences of each choice. A consequence is the end result of a choice. As you think about possible outcomes, you can consider how well each choice would help you reach your goals.

You also need to think about the responsibilities that come with each alternative. How will each option affect other people? If Chandra was responsible for caring for a younger sibling after school, her options would be different. If the family had no alternative, she might have to give preference to a weekend job rather than an after-school job. In addition, each consequence creates new responsibilities. Whatever job Chandra chooses, she is making a commitment to her new employer. She is taking on the responsibility of showing up at work on time and doing her job properly while she is there.

Finally, think about what resources are needed to carry out each alternative. If you have access to the resources you need, you will have greater success at carrying out your decisions. Remember that you do not have to possess the resources yourself if you can obtain them from someone else. However, you need to be sure that those others will be willing and able to supply the resources before you can definitely count on them. If you do not have the needed resources, or access to them through others, you need to figure out a way to get them.

Chandra decided to ask some other students at school about their part-time jobs. She felt this added information would help her make a better decision. See step 3 of Figure 4.9.

Think About Your Reading
How could a person's maturity affect his or her success in considering alternatives?

Choose the Best Alternative

Making a decision takes time as you reflect on each alternative. You may find there is no perfect solution in your choices. One choice may meet

your values and help you reach your goals, but you may lack the resources you need to carry it out. Another choice may involve resources you have, but it does not completely meet your goals. You can weigh all the facts, past experiences, and valued opinions of others. Then you will be able to make the best choice (**Figure 4.11**).

Chandra weighed her four alternatives. Her after-school activities were important to her, but she realized she might not be able to *participate*, or take part, in all of them. She also wanted to be sure that her choice would not result in her neglecting her studies. She thought that 15 hours of work per week would provide the spending money she wanted. Her schedule would be tight, but she could enroll in a school-related work program in place of taking other elective classes. She especially liked the idea of gaining work experience

that would relate to her career interest. Chandra decided the best alternative would be to enroll in an FCCLA school-to-work program. This would enable her to work part-time in a health services occupation. See step 4 of Figure 4.9.

Carry Out the Decision

The next stage of the decision-making process requires developing a plan of action. In doing so, it is important to identify some of the obstacles you may meet and then think about ways to overcome them. In addition, this step includes assigning a time to carry out each part of the plan. The more specific your plan of action is, the easier it will be for you to carry out that plan.

Chandra's plan for carrying out her decision began with contacting the teacher of the FCCLA class. See step 5 of Figure 4.9. Then she had to work with the guidance counselor to set up her classes so she could carry out her plan. Because of their positions and knowledge, these human resources had to be involved in helping Chandra carry out her decision. Other plans can be put in action without needing to rely on others, of course.

Evaluate the Decision

Judging how well each decision went is a habit everyone should develop. Taking this step helps ensure that you will improve your decision-making skills over time. You can look back to see if your decision solved the problem. In step 6 of Figure 4.9, Chandra would evaluate her decision and judge how well it met her goal of earning money.

To evaluate a decision, consider these questions. Did you think of every possible alternative? Did you have enough information about each alternative? Was the information accurate? Did you recognize other alternatives after you started your plan? Could you have identified them earlier if you had approached the decision differently? Did anything unexpected happen? Were you able to follow your plan of action, or did your plan need some changes? How well did you predict the outcome of your choice? Were there some obstacles for which you did not plan or prepare?

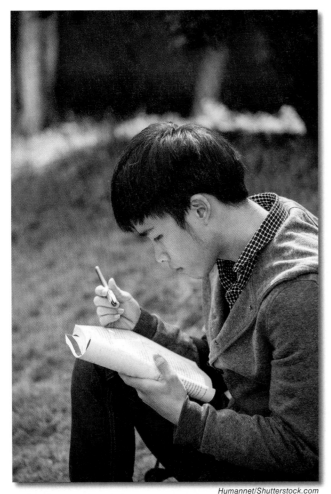

Humannet/Shutterstock.com

Figure 4.11 Journaling can be a good way to evaluate your choices when making a decision.

> ## Think About Your Reading
>
> How could evaluating a decision help you grow toward intellectual maturity?

Evaluating your decisions can help you grow. You can learn from each experience and perhaps prevent future mistakes. Your skills for using each step in the process will increase with practice.

In addition to evaluating your decision-making process, you need to evaluate the consequences of your decision as well (**Figure 4.12**). Sometimes a decision has far-reaching effects when you consider all the people affected by it. A mature, responsible decision will benefit you as well as those around you.

Throughout your life, you will encounter many choices. The decisions you make should help you reach your life goals. Some decisions may not turn out as well as others. Just remember that decision making is part of the growth process. As you mature, your skills for making effective decisions should improve.

Decision Making and Your Life Path

The consequences of your decisions will affect many areas of your life, including your health and well-being, your family and interpersonal relationships, and your future employment. For example, your decisions about what you eat and how often you exercise will affect your health and well-being. Your decisions about how you spend your time will impact your friendships and your family life. How you use your time will also have a great impact on your success at school and your future employment. Your decisions also have an

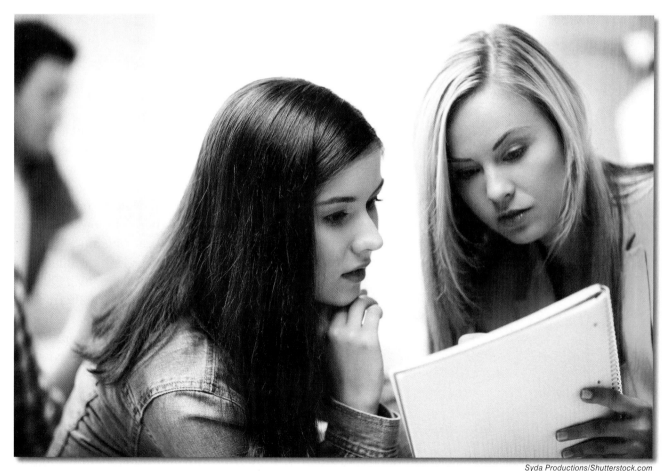

Syda Productions/Shutterstock.com

Figure 4.12 A careful evaluation of your past decisions helps you make better decisions in the future. *What could be the benefit of using a human resource to help with this evaluation?*

effect on society as a whole. Good decision making and planning is needed so that your choices take your life path in the direction you desire.

Effects of Decisions on Health and Well-Being

One of the developmental tasks of the teen years is to make healthful choices that help you grow to maturity. You need to continue to make healthful choices throughout your adult life. Maintaining your health and well-being will impact how you feel and the energy you have. Good health affects your performance at work as well as in your family and friend relationships. Thus, it is important to make good decisions related to your physical and mental health.

You can build good health by making informed decisions about what you eat, considering the nutrition your body needs, and using the resources you have to purchase and prepare food (**Figure 4.13**). Making decisions to include regular exercise in your daily routine, get enough sleep every night, manage stress, and act in a safe way will also help you promote health and well-being.

Avoiding unhealthful behaviors is also important. Your decisions related to substances like tobacco, alcohol, and other drugs need to be informed decisions based on facts. Personal opinions, gut-level feelings, or a friend's opinions are not enough. Your decisions about tobacco, alcohol, and other drugs can affect you for the rest of your life. Thinking through the consequences of using harmful substances can help you make decisions to avoid their use.

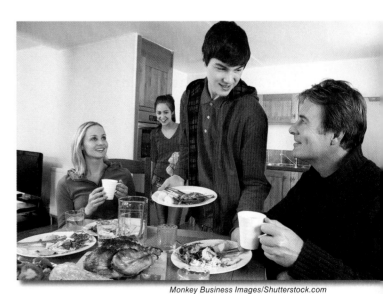

Monkey Business Images/Shutterstock.com

Figure 4.13 Making healthful food choices will help you feel better. *What obstacles could keep you from making good decisions about the food you eat?*

Decisions About Tobacco

Choosing not to use tobacco, for instance, can help you avoid the consequences of stress on the heart and increased risk of cancer. The health-related consequences of smoking led the U.S. surgeon general to require tobacco products be labeled with health warnings. To protect those who want to breathe clean air, many laws prohibit smoking in public areas. Young people under the age of 18 cannot purchase cigarettes. This is a federal law.

By choosing not to use tobacco, you are choosing the right to healthy lungs and clean air. But the benefits of not using tobacco go beyond the risk of ill health. If you do not use tobacco, your clothes will not smell, and your teeth will not yellow. In addition, you will save a lot of money compared to a person who uses tobacco.

Decisions About Alcohol

Choosing to avoid alcohol can help you avoid the consequences that alcohol has on the body (**Figure 4.14**). Alcohol is a powerful depressant. A **depressant** is a substance that slows the activity of a person's brain by knocking out control centers. Someone who drinks alcohol has slower reflexes and reduced coordination. He or she will not be

Consequences of Alcohol Use
Alcohol can
• impair thinking and reasoning
• affect coordination
• be addicting
• stifle emotional growth
• hurt relationships
• cause embarrassment
• harm reputation
• produce hangovers
• cause absenteeism from school and work
• result in arrest
• cause health problems, including birth defects, cancer, brain damage, mental disorders, loss of sexual function, liver damage, and death

Figure 4.14 Before taking an alcoholic drink, consider the consequences. Drinking alcohol can cause many types of physical and mental health problems.

as capable of interpreting messages. Since his or her judgment will be poorer, using alcohol makes it more difficult to make good decisions.

Use of alcohol affects a person's social and emotional responses as well. Brain cells control these responses. Brain cells dulled by alcohol result in fewer inhibitions. That means a person has a harder time saying "no" to impulses. For example, a person may feel happy and relaxed but also more jealous, quickly angered, and aggressive. Actions under the use of alcohol may hurt relationships, bring embarrassment, and even result in arrest.

A person's desires to reach goals may be dulled by alcohol. That may lead to skipping school or ignoring homework. Overall social and emotional growth will be stifled if alcohol is used to escape problems rather than solve them. People can become dependent on alcohol. About one out of every 10 drinkers is at risk of becoming an **alcoholic**, meaning they are addicted to alcohol and cannot control their use of it.

Decisions About Using Drugs

If you look in your medicine cabinet at home, you may find a variety of drugs used for various purposes. A **drug** is any substance that chemically changes structures or functions in a living organism. *Over-the-counter drugs* are those you can buy without a doctor's prescription. *Prescription drugs* are those prescribed by a medical doctor and purchased at a pharmacy. Both of these kinds of drugs can be used to cure or control a medical problem. They are used to improve physical or mental health.

When drugs are used in ways for which they were not intended, this is **drug abuse**. For instance, if a person uses a cold medicine to get to sleep, that drug is being abused. If a person uses a tranquilizer to avoid facing problems, it is drug abuse. The drug is being used for a purpose other than its intended use.

Think About Your Reading

What are some drugs that are commonly used for medicinal purposes in the home? Could any of these be abused?

Misusing and abusing drugs has become a crisis in the United States. The reasons that some teens use drugs are much like the reasons given for alcohol abuse. It is a way to "tune out" problems and "tune in" feelings of excitement. Drugs, however, do not solve problems; they only add to them. Thinking through the consequences of drug misuse and abuse is important to avoid making decisions that could harm your body.

Choices to misuse and abuse drugs have major consequences on health and well-being. Some consequences are physical and can end in death. Impaired judgment, destroyed brain cells, lapses in memory, slower reflexes, and the destruction of major organs are some examples (**Figure 4.15**).

Using drugs can lead to physical dependence on them. This is called **addiction**. The body physically has a need for the drug. If this need is not met, the body goes through **withdrawal**. Discomfort, nausea, pain, and convulsions may accompany the withdrawal, sometimes resulting in death.

Some drugs create a psychological dependence. The person desires the feelings that the drug gives and requires the drug to feel good. In addition to physical and psychological dependence, the drug abuser builds a tolerance to many drugs. Higher doses are needed to get the same effects. The abuser becomes more dependent, and the need for drugs becomes greater.

Another consequence of misusing and abusing drugs is their impact on a person's ability to think, make decisions, and reach goals. Because of the physical addiction or psychological dependence, individuals who abuse drugs do not think logically, do not make good decisions, and do not take care of their personal responsibilities. They may end up in trouble with the law, and as a result, their quality of life is very poor.

It is helpful to think through possible unhealthful choices, consider the consequences that such behaviors could have on your life path, and make an informed decision to avoid these. High

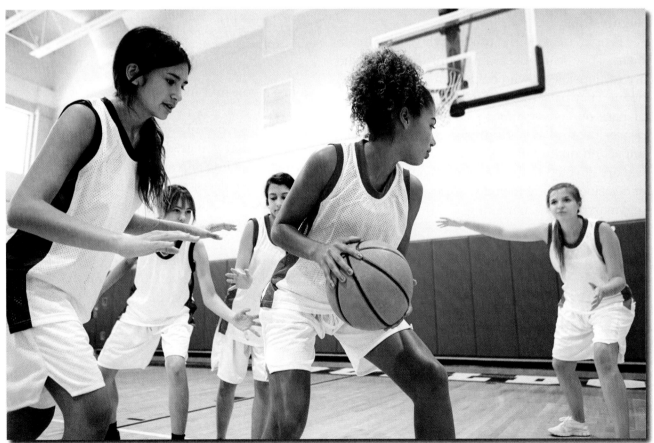

Monkey Business Images/Shutterstock.com

Figure 4.15 Misusing and abusing drugs can have negative effects on a person's physical health, including physical activities and fitness.

self-esteem, ethical personal standards, and knowing your values and goals can help you stick with this decision and make personal choices that promote health and wellness in your life.

Think About Your Reading

How could learning about food and nutrition, exercise, and the effects of tobacco, alcohol, and other drugs help people make good decisions?

Effects of Decisions on Family and Interpersonal Relationships

Making good decisions in relationships is a skill that will be used throughout your life. As a teen, you make decisions every day that affect your relationships with friends, family, teachers, classmates, and perhaps a boss and coworkers on a job. These decisions may have immediate consequences as well as long-term consequences (**Figure 4.16**).

People treat fairly others who are fair to them. They learn they can count on those who are responsible or who help them when they feel down. They trust those who do not spread rumors or pass on conversations said to them in confidence. Because relationships have such a huge impact on quality of life, several chapters in this text are devoted to these topics. Some of the areas of decision making include choices related to dating, marriage, and parenting.

Effects of Decisions on Future Employment

A major developmental task of the adolescent years is to begin preparing for a career. It may be difficult to see the connection between school today and an unknown working life in the future, but that connection is real. The schoolwork you do now affects the career options you might have.

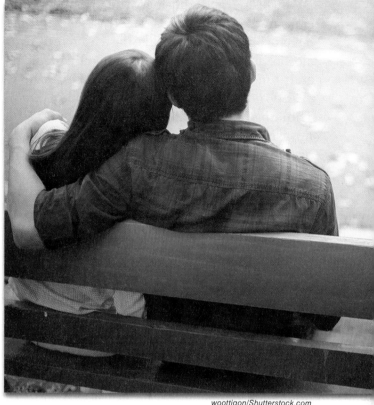

woottigon/Shutterstock.com

Figure 4.16 *Why is it important to apply decision-making skills to choices in your relationships? What impact could these decisions have on your success in reaching your life goals?*

Courses you find interesting now may lead you to consider careers in a related field. The schoolwork that you do will affect the opportunities that you have after you graduate from high school for further schooling or work training. Chapter 5 will explore these decisions in depth.

In addition, the work habits that you develop now can carry over into your work life. If you learn now to manage your time effectively, you will be able to apply that skill on the job. If you learn now to discipline yourself to focus on your schoolwork, you will have that discipline when you have a job.

Effects of Decisions on Society

The decisions that you make affect society as a whole. Drivers who obey traffic laws help keep

the streets safe for everyone to travel. The decision to help others in some way can help build a better community. For instance, teens who volunteer to tutor younger children help them learn and grow. They will be better students and better citizens. They also will have positive role models to look up to.

Your personal ethics will impact the choices you make and the steps you take to reach them. **Ethical decision making** means making personal decisions that are guided by ethical standards which help to develop communities and a society where mutual respect, honesty, caring, justice, and fairness benefit all who live there (**Figure 4.17**). Skills for making ethical decisions and applying them to all areas of life will improve your quality of life as well as the lives of those around you.

LESSON 4.2

COMPREHENSION CHECK

1. List the steps of the decision-making process. In your own words, describe each step.
2. Explain why learning to follow the decision-making process is an important skill.
3. What are three decisions a person can make to promote health and well-being?
4. Describe some consequences of using tobacco and alcohol and explain how this knowledge could help teens avoid these unhealthful behaviors.
5. Give an example of how one teen's decision affects the society in which he or she lives.

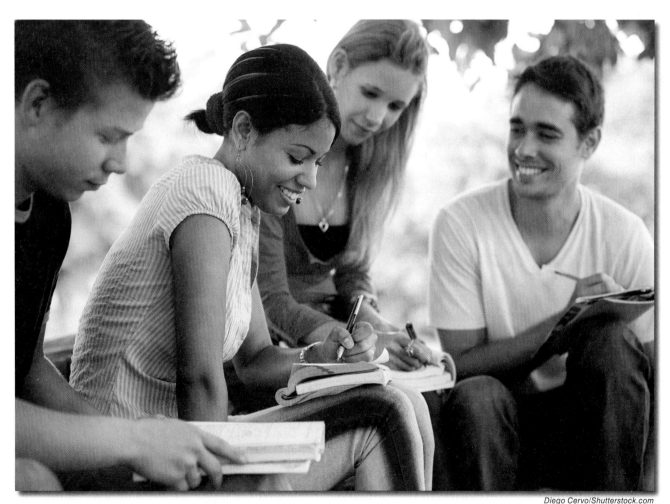

Diego Cervo/Shutterstock.com

Figure 4.17 When you make ethical decisions, you will consider the impact of your choices on others as well as yourself. *How could discussing alternatives with others help you make ethical decisions?*

CHAPTER SUMMARY

You will make many decisions throughout your life. Some will be routine; others will be planned decisions that will have long-term effects on your life. Your thinking skills, values, goals, standards, and resources will all influence the decisions you make.

Your decisions should incorporate your values as you try to reach your goals. Some of your values will help you set and carry out goals in your personal life. Other values will relate to your relationships with others or to your work. Your values are important in determining which choices to select from the many alternatives possible.

As you work toward your goals, you use your standards as a measure of your progress. Resources, both human and nonhuman, help you carry out your decisions. Knowing your resources and using them wisely can help you overcome obstacles you may face in the decision-making process.

Making decisions skillfully involves a six-step method. This process helps you to carefully analyze an issue, identify possible alternatives, choose the best one, and develop a plan to put it into action. The process also helps you judge the success of your decisions so you develop skill in making them.

Successful decision making helps you achieve your life goals. Learning to make good decisions will impact your health and well-being, your relationships, your success in your career, and the society you live in. Your decision-making skills will impact your quality of life.

VOCABULARY ACTIVITIES

1. Work with a partner to write sentences that use each of the following terms correctly.

Content Terms

addiction (4.2)
alcoholic (4.2)
alternative (4.2)
decision-making
 process (4.2)
depressant (4.2)
drug (4.2)
drug abuse (4.2)
ethical decision
 making (4.2)
goal (4.1)
group values (4.1)

human resource (4.1)
long-term goal (4.1)
nonhuman resource
 (4.1)
planned decision (4.1)
routine decision (4.1)
short-term goal (4.1)
standards (4.1)
subgoal (4.1)
values (4.1)
withdrawal (4.2)

2. Write a brief paragraph that explains how each of these terms relates to decisions.

Academic Terms

available (4.2)
obstacle (4.1)
participate (4.2)

project (4.1)
reliable (4.2)
resource (4.1)

ASSESS

Your Knowledge

3. List five factors that could affect a person's success in making decisions.

4. List and explain the steps that could be used to set and accomplish goals.

5. Summarize the six steps in the decision-making process.

Your Understanding

6. How is intellectual maturity related to a person's ability to make good decisions?

7. Why should values be part of setting goals?

8. How can standards help a person know if a goal has been met?

9. How do human resources affect the decision-making process?

10. What are the consequences and responsibilities involved in a decision to try out for a school sports team?

11. Explain how a teen's day-to-day decisions could affect his or her health and well-being over time.

Your Skills

12. List and analyze your personal values. How do they relate to your priorities in your schoolwork? How do they relate to your friendships?

13. Identify three goals that you could set that would be consistent with some of your high-priority values.

14. Choose a possible decision that you might make. Work through the decision using the decision-making process, giving examples for each step. Create a diagram to illustrate the steps taken to reach this decision.

CRITICAL THINKING

15. **Draw Conclusions.** Write a paragraph describing a situation in which you overcame an obstacle to reach a goal. Evaluate your action for its effectiveness in helping you reach your goal. In your evaluation, reference the steps in the text for evaluating a decision. *Choice*: Create a visual presentation or a rap that expresses the ideas in your paragraph.

16. **Classify and Compare Findings.** List at least three groups to which you belong. Identify each group's values and expectations for its members. Categorize your lists under personal, relationship, and work values. Then make a list of your own priorities and expectations for your life. Write a paper in which you compare the lists. Cite references from the text which support your analysis.

17. **Create an Application.** Create three separate lists of your values in the following areas: personal life, relationships, and school. Identify the most important value and a long-term goal related to it from each list. Divide the long-term goals into subgoals. Identify a plan of action that will help you reach your long-term goals. *Choice*: For each long-term goal, identify one possible obstacle and alternatives for how you could overcome it.

18. **Identify Alternatives.** Working with a partner, identify a decision that needs to be made, such as whether or not to sign up for an after-school activity, such as a sport or club, or whether or not to volunteer at a local senior center or similar location. Identify the alternatives and the advantages and disadvantages of each. Identify the values that would be likely to be important in this decision. Also identify how the decision will affect your family and interpersonal relationships.

19. **Solving Problems.** With your partner, identify a choice and a plan of action for the decision situation in the previous question. Then write down possible obstacles to that plan. Exchange your information with that of another pair. Look at the obstacles that they identified for their plan and come up with ways to address them.

20. **Make Inferences.** Identify a decision you made regarding a personal, relationship, or work-related issue. List the steps you used to make the decision. Compare your steps to those in the decision-making process. If you had followed the decision-making process, would you have made a better or more informed decision? How did your decision affect your future employment? Explain your answer.

CORE SKILLS

21. **Social Studies, Writing.** Create a list of human and nonhuman resources in your community that you could use to help you reach a goal of graduating from high school. Write a paragraph explaining how these resources will help you reach your goal. *Choice*: Create a collage of pictures or drawings to present your list.

22. **Writing.** Write a one-page paper comparing your personal values with your cultural values. Identify at least three cultural values.

23. **Reading, Writing.** Evaluate a magazine or newspaper article for different values that motivate people to act. Look for examples of societal, group, and personal values. Write a paragraph summarizing these values and their impact on the person's actions.

24. **Expressing Ideas Visually.** Choose an area in which you will be making a major decision. Research the decision using the steps for decision making. Then use a drawing program to illustrate the steps in the decision-making process in a flowchart format.

25. **Financial Literacy, Speaking.** Interview a cell-phone representative and identify the different factors to consider when making a decision to buy a cell phone. In an oral presentation, make a recommendation for purchasing a cell phone based on your analysis of the options.

26. **Writing.** Write a one-page paper explaining how nonhuman technological resources, such as cell phones, laptops, and the Internet, can increase a person's ability to access human resources.

27. **Research, Science, Speaking.** Search the Internet for information on one form of substance abuse and prepare a report on the harmful effects of that substance. Identify community resources available to help a person overcome the consequences related to the use of that drug. Present the findings of your research to the class in a two-minute summary.

CAREER READINESS

28. **Researching and Reporting on Work Values.** Visit the websites of three companies and go to the careers or employment section. Read what the companies say about what they are looking for in employees. Based on what you read, draw up a list of at least a half-dozen work values that employers expect to see in their employees. Write and deliver a brief presentation in which you identify these work values and explain why companies consider them important. *Group option*: Prepare the presentation as an expert panel discussion. *Group option*: Prepare the presentation as a job interview, with one student taking the role of an interviewer and the other taking the role of a job candidate.

CHAPTER 5

CHOOSING A CAREER

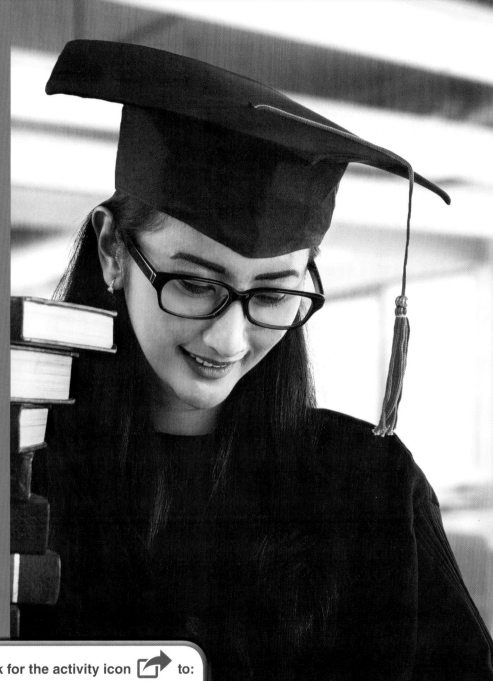

Reading Prep

Before reading the chapter, look at the three sets of objectives (what you will know, understand, and be able to do) on the next page. Write down a question you have about each objective. As you read, look for answers to the questions and record your answers on the same paper.

Key Questions

Questions to answer as you study this chapter:

* How does work help people meet life goals?
* What factors should be considered when choosing a career?
* What are the steps in developing a career plan?

While studying this chapter, look for the activity icon **to:**

* **build** vocabulary with e-flash cards, matching activities, and vocabulary games; and
* **assess** what you learn by completing the lesson comprehension checks online.
  www.g-wlearning.com/humanservices/

G-WLEARNING.com

AFTER STUDYING THIS CHAPTER, YOU WILL

KNOW:

- The reasons people work.
- Factors a person should consider when choosing a career.
- Sources of information for career planning.

UNDERSTAND:

- How career choices affect future opportunities and lifestyle.
- How the career clusters can help a person learn about careers.
- How short-term career goals can be met in high school.

BE ABLE TO DO:

- Identify employment and entrepreneurial possibilities in a chosen career field.
- Identify a career that matches personal characteristics.
- Develop a career plan that includes short- and long-term career goals.
- Develop a relevant portfolio for a chosen career.

GETTING STARTED

Ilsa hurried as she got ready to go to work. She put on her red T-shirt, part of her work uniform. Didn't have to think too long about what to wear, *she thought, smiling as she headed out the door. She was grateful for this summer job, because it was letting her save money for college. She knew that she did not want to work at this store the rest of her life, but she enjoyed helping customers find clothes that suited their tastes and their budgets. She knew that the experience she gained now could help her in the future. She worked from 3:00 in the afternoon until the store closed, usually around 10:00 at night. In the summer, that was the best time for hitting the beach! She also had to work every other weekend, missing out on some fun family activities.* At least I have a job, *she thought,* and I do like the people I work with. *Plus, the boss said she could use some extra help during the school year, too.*

Ilsa was excited that the opportunities could expand for her with this company. She had started out stocking shelves; now she was waiting on customers and running the cash register. She enjoyed listening to her boss talk about traveling to New York to purchase merchandise for the store. She could see herself doing that in the future. That did sound exciting.

Like Ilsa, you might have an idea of what you want to do in the future, and you might have a job that will help you build toward that future. On the other hand, you might be confused about what you want to do. You may ask yourself, "What type of work do I really want?" In this chapter, you will learn more about the working world and the personal factors that affect career choices. You will learn about the resources available for exploring careers. All this information will help you use the decision-making process to choose a career that is right for you.

LESSON 5.1

LEARNING ABOUT THE WORLD OF WORK

Objectives

After studying this lesson, you will be able to

- **describe** the connection between jobs and a career.
- **list** reasons people give for working.
- **explain** how career choices affect future opportunities and lifestyle.

Focus Your Reading

1. Create a graphic organizer with the heading *Why People Work*. Make branches for each heading in this lesson. As you read, write key points under the appropriate branches.

2. Create a chart with each content term listed on the left. In the first column, write your own definition for each term. Then ask a parent, grandparent, or other adult how they would define the term and write the response in the second column. As you read, write the text definition in the third column.

You will probably spend most of your adult life working. You will need to make choices about where and how you will fit into the workplace. Those choices will have a profound impact on other areas of your life. You probably already know that your job will affect your level of income and thus the way you live. The work you do also has an impact on your relationships and on how you see yourself.

What Is Work?

Work can be defined as any mental or physical activity that produces or accomplishes something. Sometimes people do work for personal reasons rather than to earn money (**Figure 5.1**). There are many different types of work. You may have a part-time job now. You may be given chores to do at home to help your family meet the needs of all its members. You may do volunteer work in your community. By considering as many different types of work as possible, you will recognize several jobs that interest you. This chapter focuses on work that is part of a job.

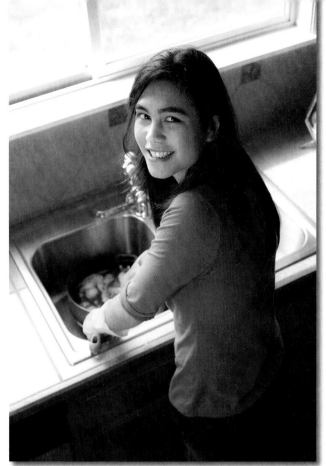
Jaren Jai Wicklund/Shutterstock.com

Figure 5.1 Much of the work that people do is for personal and family needs, satisfaction, or comfort. *How does the work of caring for the family compare to other kinds of work?*

A **job** is a position held by a person working to earn a living. You will probably have several jobs over your lifetime. For instance, you may start working as a child care provider, work as a nursing assistant while you go to college, begin your post-college work life as an addiction counselor, become a social worker, and then end your career as supervisor of case management. Each of these jobs is a particular position that has a title and clearly defined responsibilities.

A **career** refers to the work done over several years while holding different jobs within a particular field or area. A career requires careful thought and planning. Usually, each new job builds on the experiences and skills of a previous job. In this way, a person moves up a **career ladder**. Each step on the career ladder builds on the experiences of the previous step. In order to reach the higher steps on a career ladder, you need to identify the lower steps that will take you there. This is where having a career plan becomes helpful.

Why Do People Work?

People work for many different reasons. One reason is to earn an income. Most people need an income to pay for food, clothing, and shelter—all the necessities of life. Having an income enables a person to live independently. Another reason that people work is to support their *lifestyle*. This is the way a person chooses to live. People also work to satisfy personal needs such as satisfaction and recognition.

Earning Income

A person's job determines his or her income. Many of your lifestyle choices—clothing, housing, transportation, food, and leisure activities—will be influenced by your income. The following factors affect how much a job pays:

- *Education and training.* Usually, work that provides higher pay requires greater training or education (**Figure 5.2**).
- *Experience.* People with more experience generally have more skills. For their advanced skills and knowledge, they usually receive higher pay.
- *Demand and supply.* Often, advances in technology create new jobs faster than workers can be trained to handle them. Until enough workers fill all available jobs, those who are qualified are eagerly sought and well paid. Jobs that are in low demand or for which there is a large supply of available workers, on the other hand, tend to pay less.
- *Level of risk.* High-risk jobs that involve danger often command higher pay than jobs involving little danger.

> ### Think About Your Reading
> Identify and describe some high-paying jobs in your community.

Lifestyle Choices

Lifestyle is affected by a person's work. Lifestyle includes the following aspects:

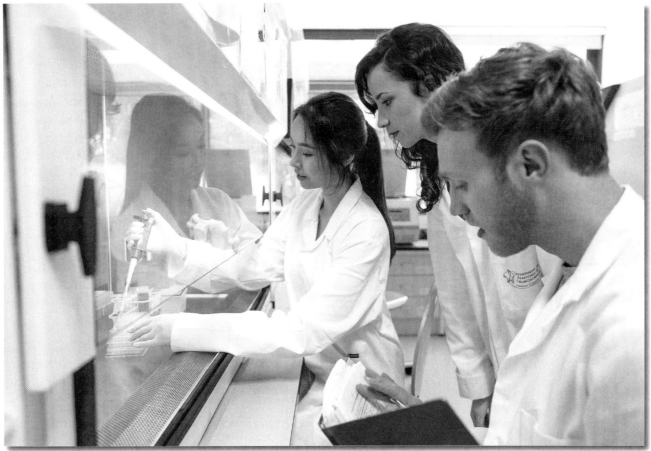

wavebreakmedia/Shutterstock.com

Figure 5.2 Some careers require six or more years of education. Usually these careers provide a higher income. *Why might a person pursue a career that requires more education, even though the pay may not be higher?*

- family relationships
- friendships and social contacts
- the area and neighborhood where a person lives
- the type and size of housing and furnishings a person has
- schools available to children
- leisure time available and activities enjoyed
- the type of food eaten
- the type of transportation a person uses

A job affects a person's status in the community and, as a result, the friends and social life one has. Work also affects family life. Some jobs require working in the evening or at night. Some require weekend work. Some require frequent travel away from home. People who work at night or on weekends or who are often away from home have less time to spend with family members.

Lifestyle choices are often affected by the amount of money you have to spend. In most cases, the more money you have, the more options you have for lifestyle choices. Thus, developing a career plan now can help you reach goals you may have for your personal lifestyle.

> ## Think About Your Reading
> How is your lifestyle affected by the work your family does?

Personal Reasons

If you asked several people why they work, you would likely hear different responses. Besides earning an income, they would probably mention

some personal reasons for enjoying their work. The following reasons are the most common:

- *Work provides personal satisfaction.* Many workers feel a sense of pride when they achieve goals at work. Workers who really enjoy their jobs feel great satisfaction in doing them well (**Figure 5.3**).

- *Work brings recognition.* Other people notice good work and *praise* (express appreciation for) workers for their accomplishments. Their respect for those workers and what they can do increases. Recognition can also lead to rewards like salary increases or promotions.

- *Work increases feelings of worth.* By working on something they believe is worthwhile, many people feel important. Their self-esteem benefits from the feeling that they are contributing to society and their community or are helping others.

- *Work provides opportunities for personal growth.* Some people are creative in their work. Many workers sharpen their abilities and learn new skills over time on a job. Work helps them express themselves and become more capable people.

- *Work provides social contacts.* Work often brings people into contact with others who have similar interests. This is why close friendships often develop on the job.

It is not likely that every job you have will fulfill all these reasons for working. As you make career choices, you will need to decide which of these factors are most important to you.

LESSON 5.1

Assess

COMPREHENSION CHECK

1. Explain what is meant by the term *work*.
2. Explain the relationship between jobs and a career.
3. Explain how a career affects the lifestyle options open to a person, including family life.
4. List three personal reasons people give for working.

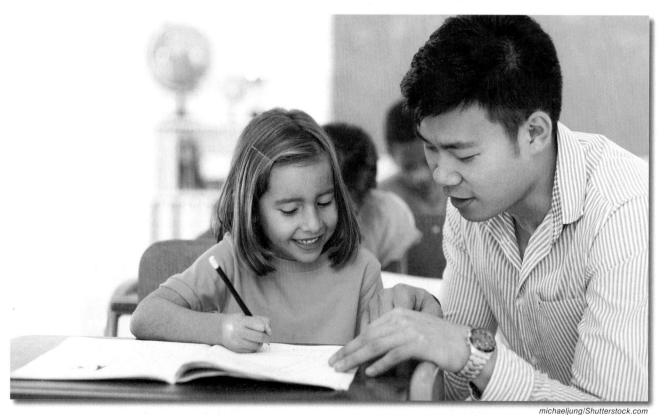

michaeljung/Shutterstock.com

Figure 5.3 Many people work for their own personal satisfaction and fulfillment. These people usually enjoy the work they do.

Content Terms

Build Vocab

interests
activities preference inventory
aptitudes
abilities
transferable skills

Academic Terms

prioritize
spatial

Objectives

After studying this lesson, you will be able to

- **recognize** personal factors that may influence your career choice.
- **identify** transferable skills.

Focus Your Reading

1. Outline this lesson using the headings as a guide. As you read the lesson, write an example of how each topic relates to your life.
2. Write sentences explaining each of the terms in your own words.

How can you know what type of career to choose? This is an important question, as there are so many choices available—and you will spend much of your life working. Choosing a career requires personal evaluation to see what type of work best suits you. Once you know what type of work you prefer, you can begin gathering information about different possible careers. When you choose one, you can develop a plan for working toward that career.

How well do you know yourself? Recognizing your unique talents and traits, examining your likes and dislikes, and deciding what you want to achieve can help you find the right career. You should consider the following personal factors when choosing a career:

- personality traits
- values
- goals
- interests
- aptitudes
- abilities

Taking time to assess yourself in each of these areas will help you achieve satisfaction and success in a career.

Personality

If the nature of your work matches your personality, you will find it easier to succeed (**Figure 5.4**). You will also find the work more satisfying. Try to identify your personality traits and choose an occupation that suits them.

Your personality is influenced by several factors, one of which is your temperament. As you learned in Chapter 2, your *temperament* is your basic patterns for interacting with your environment. A career that matches your intellectual, physical, emotional, and social temperament patterns will be a successful choice.

Tests are available to help you identify careers that could match your personality traits. The questions used in these tests are mostly designed to gather information about the various aspects of your temperament. These tests group your responses to their questions to match different personality types. Some tests use as few as 4 different personality types; some identify up to 16 types. Most types describe some combination of the ways people respond to the world intellectually, physically, socially, and emotionally.

Each person's personality has both strengths and weaknesses. To experience success, try to match your strong qualities with the demands of your work. For example, an extroverted person can be a successful salesperson. A person who cares deeply about children would be well suited to working with children's health care or in a school. You will also experience success if you choose work that is not demanding in your weaker areas.

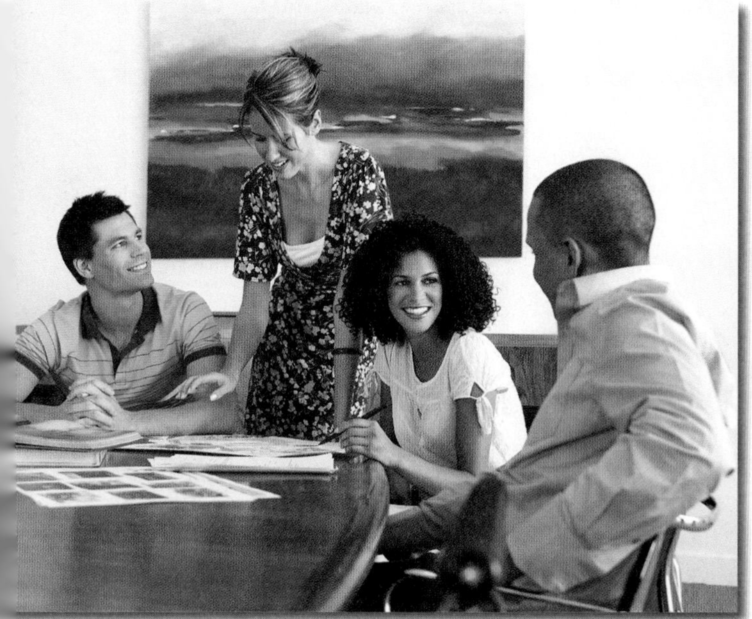

Values

As you read in an earlier chapter, the beliefs or ideals that you feel are important are your *personal values* or *personal priorities*. You may believe it is important to have a job helping others. You may also believe that it is important to work at a job that is challenging or fulfilling. These values affect your choice of a career.

How do you determine which work-related values are most important to you? You can try *prioritizing* them, or listing them in order of importance. To prioritize your values, list all your values related to work. Then compare one value to another and think about which matters most to you. Once you have decided, compare the next value on your list to both of them. Does it rank higher than both, lower than both, or in between? Continue until you have gotten through your whole list, with each value in its own position.

Ordering your work values can help you identify jobs that will match the values most meaningful to you. When the work you do matches your values, you will feel greater satisfaction. Your feelings of worth will increase when you feel that the work you do is important and meaningful.

bikeriderlondon/Shutterstock.com

Figure 5.4 *What personality traits would benefit a person working on a mental health services team?*

Think About Your Reading

What personal values will affect your career choices?

Goals

Your career choice should help you reach important life goals. *Goals* are what you want to accomplish in life and are often based on your values. Remember that the job you do affects your family

and other relationships and your lifestyle. That is why it is important to first identify what you really want to do in life. Then you can evaluate a career choice to see if it will help you attain those goals. For instance, someone whose goal is to have a high income should probably pursue a career in business. A person who wants to serve the community might consider a career in government or working for a nonprofit organization.

Interests

You will likely enjoy work more if you find it interesting (**Figure 5.5**). Therefore, identifying your interests can help you choose a career that fits them. **Interests** are the subjects, activities, or events that a person enjoys. Do you have a favorite class or subject? What hobbies or activities do you enjoy? How do you like to spend your free time? Your answers can help you identify the areas in which your interests lie and the skills you enjoy using most.

In all occupations, a worker is involved to some degree with people, ideas (data and information), and objects. For instance, a builder uses a blueprint that provides information about how the house will be built. He or she also works with people in getting all the materials and constructing the house. Then the builder works with materials and tools to carry out the plan. Making sure the customer is satisfied also requires communicating with people.

Although many jobs involve all three areas, they usually emphasize one more than the others. An accountant uses a computer and interacts with people, but most of his or her work is with data. A dietitian must know about nutrients and food preparation and uses materials to explain ideas to clients, but a major focus of his or her work is people. To find an enjoyable career, you will need to know which area interests you most. It is also helpful to know which area you like least.

Interests are learned. They also change as you grow and mature. You will not know if you have an interest in something unless you are exposed to

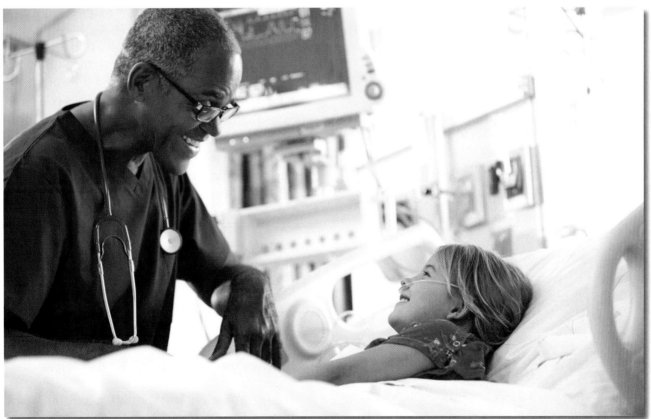

Monkey Business Images/Shutterstock.com

Figure 5.5 When work relates to your interests, you enjoy it more. *What interests would a person need to be successful at working with children?*

it. That is why it is helpful to meet new people and try new activities to see what your interests really are. Try talking to people about why they chose their careers or what they like about their work.

Another way to explore your interests is to take an **activities preference inventory**. A preference inventory is designed to help you learn whether your interests are centered on people, ideas, or objects. Your high school guidance and counseling department will likely have such a test available.

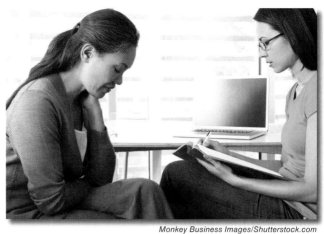
Monkey Business Images/Shutterstock.com

Figure 5.6 *What aptitudes would help a person be successful at working with people?*

Think About Your Reading

What are some jobs in your community that deal mainly with people? with ideas? with objects?

Aptitudes

Another factor affecting career choice is your aptitudes. **Aptitudes** are your natural talents. You learn certain skills quickly and easily because you have an aptitude for them (**Figure 5.6**). In other areas, it may be more difficult for you to learn. Aptitudes are similar to the eight human intelligences discussed in Chapter 2. For instance, you may have an aptitude for music, or musical intelligence, and find it easy to learn to play musical instruments. You may have an aptitude in the area of *spatial* (space-related) intelligence and find it easy to arrange shapes in a space like a graphic artist or a designer.

Consider your aptitudes when looking at careers. Your guidance counselor can help you measure your aptitudes so you can recognize which careers could be a good match.

Abilities

The final personal factor affecting career choice is abilities. Your **abilities** are skills that you learn and develop. Different jobs require different sets of skills. Through training and practice, you can increase your skills and expand your ability to get a job in a specific career. For instance, you can take a course in child care and develop skills for working with young children.

Transferable skills are basic job skills that can be applied in various work situations. Critical thinking, communicating, problem solving, negotiating, working well with people, and leading are some examples. Many computer skills are also transferable. The more transferable skills you have, the greater are the number of work opportunities that will be open to you.

Think About Your Reading

To identify your abilities, list some of your greatest accomplishments. Then think about what skills you used to achieve those accomplishments. Are any of your skills transferable?

LESSON 5.2

Assess

COMPREHENSION CHECK

1. List six personal factors that could influence your career choice.
2. Why is it necessary to prioritize your values when thinking about a career?
3. What is an example of how interests, abilities, and personal priorities affect career choice?
4. What kind of careers might be appropriate for someone with a strong aptitude for helping other people?
5. Describe how transferable skills could benefit you in making a career choice. Give three examples.

LESSON 5.3

LEARNING ABOUT CAREERS

Content Terms

Build Vocab

career cluster
career pathway
career fair
job shadow
job outlook
apprenticeship
certification
license
student and professional
    organizations

Academic Terms

high-growth industry
reap
entrepreneur

Objectives

After studying this lesson, you will be able to
- **identify** sources of career information.
- **identify** factors that affect job outlook.
- **explain** how careers have different requirements for training and education.
- **determine** opportunities for entrepreneurship in a chosen career field.

Focus Your Reading

1. Create two columns. Before reading, list everything you might want to know about a career in the first column. Then as you read, identify in the second column where you might find this information.
2. Explain the difference between a *career cluster* and a *career pathway*.

Identifying your personality, values, goals, interests, aptitudes, and abilities are important steps in career planning. They reveal your strengths and priorities so you can determine the type of work that would best match them. The next step in planning a career is to gather information about careers. Someone investigating different career choices should think about the following factors:

- *Job responsibilities.* These are the actual tasks done by people with the job.
- *Working conditions.* These refer to the environment in which the work is carried out, such as in an office or factory, or indoors or outdoors.
- *Personality traits appropriate for the job.* This factor involves the type of attitudes, behaviors, and character someone should have to do the job successfully.
- *Skills, training, and education required.* This factor refers to the type and length of school and skill-based training the career demands.

- *Places where employment can be obtained.* This factor can involve both the region of the country and the organizations that employ people with the career.

- *Employment outlook for the career.* This factor concerns the expected future demand for workers in a career.

- *Earnings potential.* This factor refers to the income associated with the career.

- *Potential for advancement.* This factor takes into account whether the career can lead to other positions that may offer higher pay and more responsibility.

Evaluating these factors can help you choose a career that will match your personality and skills and provide opportunities for reaching your goals.

Researching Careers

There are several ways you can learn about careers. The more information you gather about various careers, the more informed your decision making will be. Talking to your school guidance counselor, visiting a career fair or conference, gathering information through the Internet, and talking with and observing people who work in careers that interest you all can help you make informed decisions about your career.

Using the career clusters can help you learn about different careers. **Career clusters** are 16 broad groupings of occupational and career specialties (**Figure 5.7**). Each cluster includes several career directions, called **career pathways**. All the career choices within a pathway require a set of common knowledge and skills and should build upon each other to advance over time to higher levels of achievement in a given career. You can evaluate these career clusters for a match with your personal lists of interests, aptitudes, and abilities.

Think About Your Reading
What career cluster matches your values, goals, interests, aptitudes, and abilities?

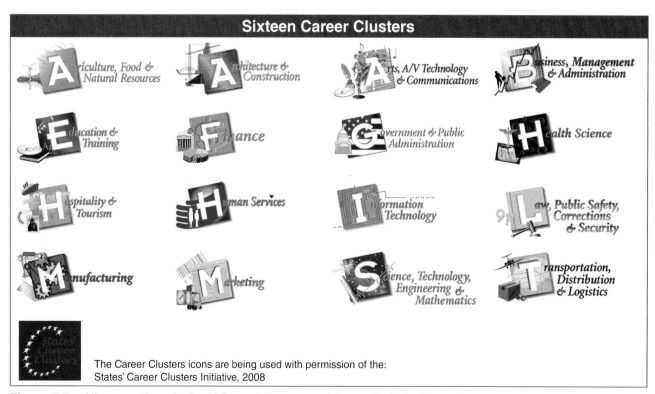

Sixteen Career Clusters

Agriculture, Food & Natural Resources

Architecture & Construction

Arts, A/V Technology & Communications

Business, Management & Administration

Education & Training

Finance

Government & Public Administration

Health Science

Hospitality & Tourism

Human Services

Information Technology

Law, Public Safety, Corrections & Security

Manufacturing

Marketing

Science, Technology, Engineering & Mathematics

Transportation, Distribution & Logistics

The Career Clusters icons are being used with permission of the: States' Career Clusters Initiative, 2008

Figure 5.7 All occupations in the U.S. workforce are addressed within these 16 career clusters.

The School Guidance and Counseling Office

School counselors can help you research careers of interest. They can help you identify career pathways that align with your personal values, goals, interests, aptitudes, and abilities. Counselors can also provide data on job descriptions, education and training requirements, and average salaries. They will have information on schools in your area that provide the education and training needed for careers that interest you. Counselors also can provide information on local apprenticeships that might be available for some careers. You can also learn more about careers that are available through the military by contacting your school counselor. Sometimes military recruiters come to the school to help students learn about military career options.

Career Fairs and Conferences

Schools sometimes provide access for students to career fairs, either by hosting the fair or sending students to one held somewhere else. A **career fair** is an event in which employers or professional organizations provide career-related information (**Figure 5.8**). There are usually many booths that attendees can visit to gather information about the careers being represented at that booth. Representatives from several industries and businesses provide information to students about the types of jobs available in their company. You can ask them any questions you might have about careers with their company. A high school career fair usually has several booths with representatives from local colleges as well. At these booths, you can gather information about possible programs of study for reaching a career goal. Military recruiters also may set up a booth at a career fair to share information about military-related careers.

Colleges sometimes offer a career conference in which specific information is provided about careers related to the majors offered at that college. These are often open for high school students to attend as well as college students. Sessions are usually offered throughout the day, and students can sign up to attend sessions of interest to them.

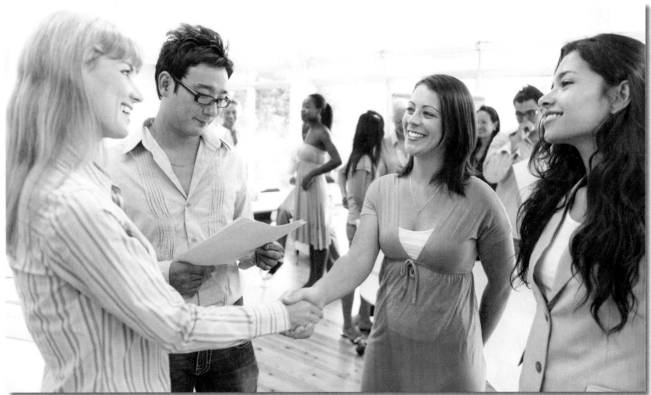

Rawpixel.com/Shutterstock.com

Figure 5.8 A career fair can provide opportunities to speak with individuals employed in many different careers. *What questions could you ask a person employed in a career area that interests you?*

The Internet

The Internet has a host of very reliable information about careers. Career information guides are available online as well as at many locations, including libraries and government offices. Three important sources of information are the Occupational Information Network, Career OneStop, and the Occupational Outlook Handbook.

- *Occupational Information Network.* The *Occupational Information Network*, also known as *O*NET*, serves as the United States' primary source of occupational information. The O*NET website is sponsored by the U.S. Department of Labor. This site provides resources for students, counselors, human resource personnel, job seekers, and other government agencies working with workforce development. Some of these resources include a variety of search options that people can use to look for an occupation that matches their skills, interests, abilities, work values, work styles, work contexts, and work activities. People can also search by career clusters, by high-growth industries, and by descriptors such as *tools and technology.* O*NET tools, such as the *My Next Move* website, contain easy-to-use search tools, career overviews, and online interest profiles.

- *CareerOneStop.* The *CareerOneStop* website is also sponsored by the U.S. Department of Labor. It features information on job trends, employment outlooks, salary ranges, and education and training requirements.

- *Occupational Outlook Handbook.* Finally, the *Occupational Outlook Handbook*, sponsored by the U.S. Bureau of Labor Statistics, describes various occupations, including the education and training needed. It also lists potential pay scales, working conditions, and future prospects for jobs.

Many professional associations and trade groups also provide reliable online information about careers in their field. For instance, the American Mental Health Counselors Association has information about jobs providing clinical mental health services, such as alcoholism and substance abuse counselors, psychotherapists, psychologists, and social workers. The National Organization for Human Services provides information about professional and paraprofessional jobs in such diverse settings as group homes and halfway houses; correctional, intellectual disability, and community mental health centers; family, child, and youth service agencies; and programs concerned with alcoholism, drug abuse, family violence, and aging. Individual companies or organizations can also provide information about their careers.

Contact with Someone in the Career

If there is a career that looks interesting to you, you can explore the career further by talking with or observing someone who has that career. It may take a call to the company to set up a meeting time, or if possible, a time to job shadow someone in the company. A **job shadow** involves following a person in a particular career for a day, listening in and observing what he or she does in the course of the job. This kind of experience exposes you to the real nature of the job responsibilities and the tasks entailed in a career. Of course, you may not see the full range of tasks or activities a worker has in a single day. Still, job shadowing can be a valuable experience. In some confidential situations, your ability to listen in and observe may be limited. In many cases, companies will arrange for a student to learn about the careers offered in their company, either through an individual discussion or a job-shadowing event.

A personal connection in the community could also help you learn about part-time jobs related to a career that interests you. Even volunteer opportunities in a related field can help you discover what it is like to work in that career (**Figure 5.9**). Such personal contact can help you gather accurate information about what it is like to work in that career area.

Think About Your Reading

What sources of information about careers are the best resources for you?

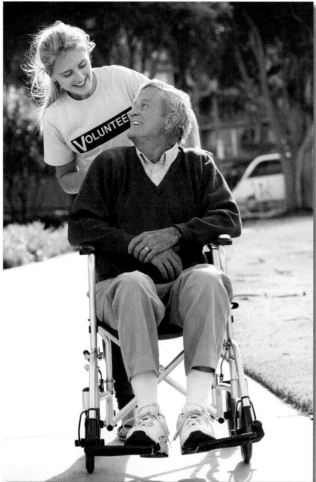

Monkey Business Images/Shutterstock.com

Figure 5.9 Volunteering in an area related to your prospective career field can help you learn about typical job responsibilities and career tasks.

Factors Affecting Job Outlook

Job outlook is an important factor in choosing a career and refers to the potential for finding a job in an area and in the future. You may not be able to find a job if you plan a career in a field with few jobs and many workers. In addition, some industries or careers are more concentrated in some parts of the country than others. Anyone interested in those industries or careers is more likely to find a job if he or she is living in those areas.

The Occupational Outlook Handbook, O*NET, and CareerOneStop provide information about industries that are growing. You can also learn what skills and knowledge are required for these jobs.

High-growth industries are those expected to provide many new job openings in the future. Most of these incorporate new technologies and

innovative ideas. As a technology spreads to various industries, new jobs are continually created. That usually means jobs using the old technology disappear.

Career opportunities are also affected by changes in society and the world. For instance, as the number of older people in the population increases, more social and health services are needed (**Figure 5.10**). Choosing a career in an expanding field will increase the likelihood of finding a job when you have finished your training.

> ## Think About Your Reading
> What is the projected outlook for jobs in the careers that interest you? Are there any high-growth industries that interest you?

Education and Training Needed

Career pathways often include several jobs that require different amounts of training. Some may be *entry-level jobs*, in which a worker receives on-the-job training after being hired. Most jobs, though, will require some specialized training. Depending on the job, you can get the needed training in different ways: through your high school coursework; through an **apprenticeship**

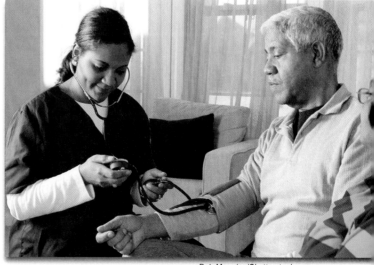

Rob Marmion/Shutterstock.com

Figure 5.10 An aging population increases the demand for workers in the health care field. *What other changes in society could impact job outlook?*

program in which you learn the skills of a trade under the supervision of a master in that field; through a one- or two-year associate's degree program at a community college or technical college; through a four-year college degree; or through military training. Some careers also require advanced degrees.

Some careers require jobholders to meet certain requirements, proving that they have the required knowledge and skills to do the job. These requirements can be either certification or licensing. **Certification** is usually granted after a person has completed a formal course of study or passed an examination. For instance, someone interested in early childhood education may need to be certified as a child care professional. Some careers require certification of all jobholders. In others, employers give preference to those who are certified. **Licenses** are issued by state governments and are required of all people pursuing the licensed career in the state. Public school teachers typically must have licenses.

Think About Your Reading
What training or education is needed for the careers that interest you?

As you research different careers, learn what additional training and education each career requires. You will also need to consider the cost and length of time for that training and education. Finally, you will need to think about the impact on future earnings.

Considering Entrepreneurship

Have you ever thought of owning your own business? Perhaps you like the idea of being your own boss and setting your own hours. The harder you work, the more you might earn. The opportunity to make all the decisions, make a long-term

REAL-LIFE SCENARIO

Krista's Career Choice

Krista hurried down to the high school guidance office. She had an appointment with a career specialist from the U.S. Army who was visiting the school. She was anxious to discuss careers in her area of interest.

Krista had always been interested in what she called "crawly critters." As a child, she loved to catch caterpillars and put them in a jar. She would watch them eat up the leaves in the jar and eventually spin a cocoon. Her terrarium was home for salamanders, frogs, and toads whenever she could catch them. She was always careful to treat them gently, for she had great respect for all living things.

Her biology class had confirmed her interest in living creatures. She did well in that class, finding it easy to memorize all the many facts and principles. She had also learned some techniques for studying and classifying her collection of insects.

Her biology teacher had asked her to serve as a guide for elementary school field trips in the environmental park. She enjoyed sharing her interest in living things with the children. She would guide the

children through the park, pointing out the different species of insects and animals. Then she always ended the tour with a display of her bug collection.

For Discussion
1. From this description, what can you tell about Krista's personality? Include her patterns for responding to the environment intellectually, socially, emotionally, and physically.
2. What aptitudes and skills can you identify for Krista?
3. Identify as many career opportunities as you can that would match Krista's interests, personality, aptitudes, and skills. How many of these could she pursue in the U.S. Army?
4. Choose one career that you think Krista would like the most. Describe what work she would do. Explain the training or education she would need. Identify five different potential employers (agencies, companies, or institutions) that employ persons in that occupation.

investment, and *reap* (gain) high rewards is available to entrepreneurs. *Entrepreneurs* are people who are self-employed and earn incomes through their own businesses.

Entrepreneurship involves starting and running your own business. To succeed, entrepreneurs need money plus a wide range of skills. Some skills are specific to the type of business. Other skills, such as good recordkeeping and management skills, are general to the overall job of operating a business. The one quality that all entrepreneurs must have is *energy* (**Figure 5.11**). Entrepreneurs work many hours for many months—often through evenings and weekends—to get a business established. Many continue to work long hours to keep the business going.

Entrepreneurs can open a wide range of businesses, from specialty stores to companies developing apps for smartphones. Many entrepreneurship opportunities exist in the field of human services. Some professionals provide family counseling services to help people in troubled families resolve their issues. Some people launch businesses providing child care or elder care services. Others open stores with educational toys for children or clothing for pregnant women. All an entrepreneur needs to do is think about what people need to build healthy families and relationships and find a way to meet that need.

Student and Professional Organizations

Student and professional organizations offer the opportunity to develop skills while learning about future careers. Participation in such organizations builds transferable skills, including leadership, communication, and problem solving. Student organizations may focus on a certain career area, such as human services, health, business, marketing, or trade occupations.

Family, Career, and Community Leaders of America, Inc. (*FCCLA*) is a student organization that prepares students to be leaders in their families, careers, and communities. Through involvement in FCCLA, you can learn about careers in the human services career cluster. These careers are in

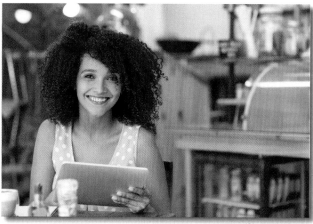
mavo/Shutterstock.com

Figure 5.11 Being an entrepreneur requires a great deal of motivation and energy.

career pathways that relate to families and human needs. You also can develop leadership skills in many different areas related to your interests by joining FCCLA.

Some professional organizations offer memberships at the student level. The American Hotel and Lodging Association is an example. Being active in a professional organization can help you stay informed about job trends and advancements in your career field. In addition, you will be able to meet professionals in your field who can offer guidance about your career plan.

> ## Think About Your Reading
> What student or professional organizations exist in career areas that interest you?

LESSON 5.3 Assess

COMPREHENSION CHECK

1. Identify four different ways to gather information about careers.
2. Identify two factors impacting job outlook for careers.
3. What do entrepreneurs need to establish a business and contribute to its success?
4. List four possible paths of education and training following high school.

MAKING A CAREER CHOICE

Objectives

After studying this lesson, you will be able to

- **apply** the decision-making steps to choosing a career.
- **identify** the components of a career plan.
- **relate** a program of study to short- and long-term career goals.
- **identify** relevant artifacts for a portfolio.

Focus Your Reading

1. List the headings of this lesson on the left side of a page. Beside each heading, identify information that you could put into your career plan.

2. Identify programs available to you in your high school that provide endorsements, certificates of completion, or advanced standing at a postsecondary college.

O nce you know about the careers you may desire, you can begin to use the decision-making process to choose a career. Developing a career plan can help you pursue whatever career you choose. Even in high school, there are steps you can take to prepare yourself for a future career.

Using the Decision-Making Process to Choose a Career

You can use the decision-making process, which you learned about in Chapter 4, to make a good decision about your career choice. To have a successful career that matches you, helps you reach your goals, and provides opportunities for you to carry out meaningful work, you need to approach choosing a career as a major life decision. The example in **Figure 5.12** illustrates how one high school student, Blair, thought through his career choice.

Blair began by assessing his own personality, values, goals, interests, aptitudes, and abilities. Then, he identified careers that

Content Terms

Build Vocab

career plan
program of study
certificate of completion
endorsement
advanced placement
internship
portfolio
letter of recommendation

Academic Terms

postsecondary
transcript
cocurricular
courteous
artifact

Using the Decision-Making Process to Choose a Career
Step 1   Identify the decision to be made.

Choose a career that matches my personal qualities.

Personal Qualities:

- *Personality*—calm under pressure; organized and detailed; enjoy working with small groups of people; sensitive to others; good verbal skills; project oriented
- *Values*—want to work with people; want to make a difference in the lives of others; want a career that is family friendly
- *Goals*—want to make a good salary; want to own a home; want to work daytime hours; want to have weekends free; want to complete a college degree
- *Interests*—reading; creating crafts; playing guitar; playing strategy games; working with children
- *Aptitudes*—verbal; musical; interpersonal
- *Abilities*—reading skills; organizational skills; musical skills; leadership skills; good communicator

Step 2   Identify all possible alternatives.

Child, Family, and School Social Worker

Substance Abuse Counselor

Marriage and Family Therapist

Step 3   Consider each alternative.

1. *Child, Family, and School Social Worker*
   - Job outlook—bright; growth projected to be much faster than average
   - Offers work with individuals and families
   - Income—median $42,120; high $72,400
   - Some freedom in scheduling
   - Most jobs require four-year degree
   - Some entry-level jobs may be available with less than a four-year degree
2. *Substance Abuse Counselor*
   - Job outlook—bright; growth projected to be much faster than average
   - Offers work with individuals and families
   - Income—median $38,620; high $64,000
   - Four-year degree required; most jobs require a master's degree
   - May be some freedom in scheduling; may also require some evening and weekend work, depending on need
3. *Marriage and Family Therapist*
   - Job outlook—bright; growth projected to be much faster than average
   - Offers work with individuals and families
   - Income—median $43,000; high $78,000
   - Four-year degree required; master's degree likely required
   - Hours can be scheduled to fit personal and family needs

(Continued)

Figure 5.12 Blair used the steps in the decision-making process to think through his choice of a career. *What other factors could have been considered when identifying alternatives?*

Using the Decision-Making Process to Choose a Career
Step 4   Make the decision.
Child, Family, and School Social Worker—potential for similar salary level without having to get a master's degree. Potential for more jobs in local area near family. Potential for related work in the field as I work toward a four-year degree.
Step 5   Carry out the decision.
• Check out schools where I can get the degree. • Meet with guidance counselor to get help with financial aid. • Get help from guidance counselor with applications for schools. • Apply and get accepted in a program for child, family, and school social work.
Step 6   Evaluate the decision.
• Did I consider all alternatives that would meet my personal qualities? • Are there any other factors I should consider? • Who hires child, family, and school social workers near where my family lives?

Figure 5.12 Continued.

matched his traits. These steps brought him to the completion of step 2 in the decision-making process with three alternatives.

> ## Think About Your Reading
> What careers can you identify as alternatives for your life? After using the decision-making steps, what career would be your first choice?

His next step was to consider factors related to each alternative. He considered the potential job outlook, how much income each career could provide along with potential for moving up a career ladder, how closely the job requirements matched him, lifestyle options each career could provide, and the education needed to follow each career path. He chose a career that he believed would best help him reach his goals. His next step is to develop a career plan to carry out his decision.

Developing a Career Plan

A **career plan** is a list of steps to take to reach a career goal. A career plan includes short-term and long-term goals for high school courses, cocurricular activities, work experience, and continued education and training (**Figure 5.13**).

Decide a Program of Study

Planning the sequence of courses for your high school career is the beginning of your career plan. This is considered a short-term career goal because it will be completed in a relatively short period of time. The sequence of courses you take in high school aligned with the courses you will take at a *postsecondary* (after high school) institution are called a **program of study**. Your school counselor can assist you in identifying the courses you should take in high school to pursue a career in a certain pathway. The courses you take can build the skills you will need for career success.

Career and technical education (CTE) teachers can also provide information about courses, including specialized courses, that relate to your planned career pathway. These courses should be included in your program of study. Several specialized courses may be available to you at your school:

- *Courses with certificates of completion.* Some courses offer **certificates of completion**, which verify that you have learned a set of specific skills. These are common in career and technical areas.
- *Courses with endorsements.* Some courses offered at the high school level result in an endorsement to indicate completion. An **endorsement** is a statement or symbol indicating mastery or completion of a specific

Career Plan for a Mental Health Counselor	
Short-Term Goals	
Education and training	• Take courses in science, math, English, psychology, sociology, interpersonal relationships, family relationships, and human growth and development.
Cocurricular activities	• Participate in student organizations that promote healthful behaviors. • Participate in student organizations that teach peers or younger students skills for preventing addiction and substance abuse. • Participate in mentor training and peer mentoring in school. • Participate in student organizations that conduct research-based activities.
Work and volunteer experiences	• Job shadow with a school counselor. • Volunteer to participate in a Juvenile Justice program. • Volunteer as a tutor for special education students. • Volunteer in a community after-school program. • Volunteer or work at a day care center, hospital, mental health clinic, or shelter.
Long-Term Goals	
Education and training	• Earn an associate's degree in substance abuse and addiction counseling. • Earn a bachelor's degree in mental health counseling. • Earn a master's degree in mental health counseling. • Complete state certification or licensing requirements.
Cocurricular activities	• Join a student association related to the field of counseling. • Obtain student membership in a professional association for mental health counselors.
Work and volunteer experiences	• Become a volunteer research assistant in the psychology or counseling department. • Obtain an internship in the mental health field. • Volunteer or work at a hospital, mental health clinic, community residential treatment center, or shelter.

Figure 5.13 A career plan can help you stay focused on the steps toward your career goals.

program. There may be endorsements available for some of the career and technical courses you take in high school.

• *Courses for college credit.* Some high school courses can be used to earn credit at a college. The college uses the student's *transcript*, or educational record, to verify that he or she took the course and received the grade required. The college then informs the student of the number of credits he or she earned.

• *Advanced placement courses.* Some colleges allow students to skip entry-level courses based on completion of certain high school courses with a specific level of success. These

are often called **advanced placement** courses. To receive the college credit, students need to pass an examination given by a national organization after completion of the course. If you know what college you plan to attend after high school, check to see what high school courses they will accept that will advance you along your career path.

> **Think About Your Reading**
> What opportunities are available in your school for earning special endorsements, certificates, or advanced standing in your area of career interest?

Align Your Program of Study with Postsecondary Options

Your guidance counselor can help you align your program of study with the postsecondary options appropriate for your career plan. Postsecondary options are opportunities available to you once you complete high school (**Figure 5.14**). These are *long-term goals* in your career plan. There are several postsecondary options available, depending on the career you choose:

- *An apprenticeship program.* As you have read, in an *apprenticeship*, the worker learns skills and gains experience while under the supervision of a master in the trade. An apprenticeship usually lasts for a set period of time to develop the skills needed to carry out the trade independently. Some classroom learning may also be required.

- *The military.* The military provides training that can be used in both military and civilian careers. Someone enlisting in the military must stay in military service for the number of years required by the terms of his or her contract.

- *A technical college.* One or two years at a technical college can provide the training needed for many jobs.

- *A two-year college program.* Two-year colleges, often called *community colleges*, offer many career-related programs of study and associate's degrees.

- *A four-year degree program.* To be a professional in many occupational fields, students must earn a degree from a four-year college or university.

Entry requirements for postsecondary options may vary depending on the option you choose. For example, a technical college will likely have different entrance requirements than a four-year college. Your guidance counselor can help you make sure you take the courses required for entrance into the postsecondary program needed to fulfill your career goals.

Participate in Cocurricular Activities

You may not think of your cocurricular activities as being part of your career plan, but they can play a significant role in helping you reach your career goals. *Cocurricular* activities include learning opportunities outside of the classroom, such as clubs, sports, leadership activities, and volunteer activities.

Clubs and Sports

Many students think of sports and recreational programs as being their main cocurricular activities. These programs provide opportunities to learn important transferable skills. For example, through group activities, students learn to work with others to set common goals and collaborate to reach those goals. In addition, sports build skills by repetition through practice. This approach develops good habits, since many job skills are developed and sharpened through practice. Clubs and sports also teach the important transferable skills of discipline and responsibility.

Leadership and Mentoring Activities

Some high schools offer leadership and mentor training to students who apply and qualify for a mentoring program (**Figure 5.15**). This training helps students develop skills useful in human services careers. These students sometimes mentor younger students in elementary or middle

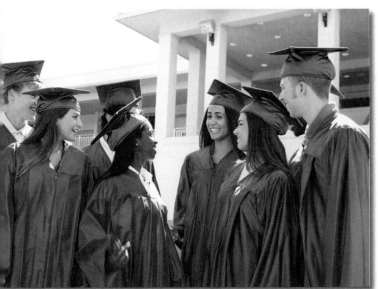

Monkey Business Images/Shutterstock.com

Figure 5.14 After you graduate high school, a number of postsecondary options may be open to you.

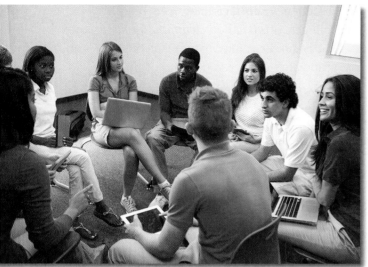

Monkey Business Images/Shutterstock.com

Figure 5.15 Mentor training can help you gain skills for working with people. *What opportunities are there to be a mentor in your school or community?*

to older adults (for example, helping with lawn care or grocery shopping).

The skills gained through volunteer activities can be part of a short-term goal as you build your career plan. Volunteering can also make you more attractive to potential employers by showing that you put the time and effort into a responsible activity. Some schools offer an endorsement on a student's high school diploma for participating in a set number of volunteer hours in the school or community.

Think About Your Reading

How could cocurricular activities that you enjoy contribute to your short-term and long-term goals for career planning?

---

school. Other programs offer mentoring by juniors and seniors to students in their first year of high school. Serving in various mentoring programs gives these students a chance to learn how to work with different age groups. They also learn how to act as a role model for others.

Volunteering

Every community has many opportunities for students to do volunteer work. Boy's and girl's clubs provide one-to-one mentoring with young children. Some after-school clubs give students the chance to assist younger students with homework. Peer tutoring in your high school could give you experience working with other teens.

There are also opportunities in most communities to volunteer services to the elderly. There may be a center on aging or a senior citizens center where you could volunteer to assist with activities for the elderly. Such experiences would help you gain skills working with the older population and, to some extent, working in the health care industry.

Other volunteer opportunities may be found through religious organizations in your community. These may relate to providing services for all age groups: helping with child care, teaching young children, providing recreational activities for school-age students, or offering physical services

Gain Work Experience

Part-time jobs can also help you reach some short-term career goals (**Figure 5.16**). They can become part of your career ladder if you can find

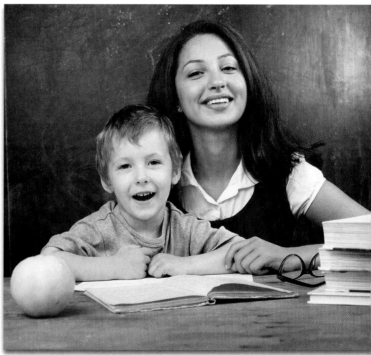

iordani/Shutterstock.com

Figure 5.16 Volunteering or working part time in an after-school program can help you gain experience working with young children and families. *What transferable skills could you gain from such an experience?*

a job related in some way to your career interest. For example, you can learn data entry skills in an office job, food preparation skills in a food service job, and child care skills in a babysitting or day care center job. Choosing a part-time job that uses skills related to your career goal can help you make progress on your career plan.

Work experience also helps you develop your set of transferable workplace skills. Skills learned on the job may relate to working with people in a *courteous* (polite) manner, handling problem situations with customers, and collaborating as a team member to reach company goals.

Another way of gaining experience is through an internship. An **internship** is on-the-job training where you learn to put to practice the skills and knowledge gained in your educational program. Internships may be paid or unpaid. It is more common to find a suitable internship after you have had some training in the field.

Building a Portfolio

As you put your career plan into action, it is important to keep a record of your activities, education, and training. A **portfolio** is a collection of materials that document your achievements over time. In a portfolio, these materials are called *artifacts*. When preparing a portfolio, include artifacts that demonstrate your academic and career skills (**Figure 5.17**). Examples are any certificates of completion, endorsements, or credits that you have earned. If you completed a notable piece of work on a job, you might include evidence of that, such as a photograph that shows the finished product. You should ask permission from your employer before including this evidence, however.

Also, include **letters of recommendation** from employers. Letters of recommendation are letters addressed to potential future employers that explain the skills and behaviors that a person showed on a job. It is a good idea to request a recommendation from any supervisor whom you think approves of the work that you did. Be sure to ask for a

---

Items to Include in a Portfolio

- career summary and goals
- list of references
- letters of recommendation that document career-related skills
- certificates of completion
- work samples that show mastery of important skills
- writing samples that demonstrate communication skills
- list of awards and special honors
- descriptions of volunteer work
- list of memberships in student organizations and related activities
- transcripts, licenses, certifications, and endorsements

Figure 5.17 Your portfolio should demonstrate your career skills to potential employers.

recommendation only when you are certain to receive a positive one.

Think About Your Reading

What items could you put into your portfolio now as you develop your career plan?

LESSON 5.4

Assess

COMPREHENSION CHECK

1. What short-term career goals can be developed while still in high school?
2. Explain how a program of study can help a person reach short- and long-term career goals.
3. Propose some short-term career goals for your field of interest.
4. Propose some long-term career goals for your field of interest.
5. List the components of a career plan.
6. What items should be collected in a portfolio?

CHAPTER 5 REVIEW AND ASSESSMENT

CHAPTER SUMMARY

People work for different reasons, including obtaining income, achieving a desired lifestyle, and gaining personal satisfaction. Work can present opportunities for growth, bring recognition, and increase feelings of self-esteem. The work that you do in your future occupation can help you meet these goals if it is interesting, worthwhile, and a good match with your personality, aptitudes, and abilities.

The career clusters are helpful in identifying broad areas of interest and outlining the knowledge and skills you will need for jobs within a cluster. Career information can be found on the Internet and through your school counseling office. When researching careers, several factors should be considered, including job responsibilities, pay, job outlook, educational requirements, and entrepreneurship opportunities.

The decision-making steps can help persons make informed career decisions that will help them reach life goals. Developing a career plan will help you reach short- and long-term career goals as you put your research into action, develop a program of study, participate in related activities, and record your progress in a portfolio.

VOCABULARY ACTIVITIES

1. Work with a partner to create a career glossary that includes definitions and examples of each of the following terms.

Content Terms

abilities (5.2)
activities preference inventory (5.2)
advanced placement (5.4)
apprenticeship (5.3)
aptitudes (5.2)
career (5.1)
career cluster (5.3)
career fair (5.3)
career ladder (5.1)
career pathway (5.3)
career plan (5.4)
certificate of completion (5.4)
certification (5.3)
endorsement (5.4)
interests (5.2)
internship (5.4)
job (5.1)
job outlook (5.3)
job shadow (5.3)
letter of recommendation (5.4)
license (5.3)
portfolio (5.4)
program of study (5.4)
student and professional organizations (5.3)
transferable skills (5.2)
work (5.1)

2. For each of the following terms, write a sentence that uses the term in the context of careers and a second sentence that uses the term in another academic field.

Academic Terms

artifact (5.4)
cocurricular (5.4)
courteous (5.4)
entrepreneur (5.3)
high-growth industry (5.3)
lifestyle (5.1)
postsecondary (5.4)
praise (5.1)
prioritize (5.2)
reap (5.3)
spatial (5.2)
transcript (5.4)

ASSESS

Your Knowledge

3. What are the reasons that people work?
4. What factors should a person consider when choosing a career?
5. What resources can be used to learn about careers?

Your Understanding

6. How can career choices affect the ability to reach life goals?
7. How can the career clusters help you choose a career?
8. Explain how choices during the high school years can contribute to your career plan.

Your Skills

9. Analyze your personal characteristics—personality; values; goals; interests; preferences for people, ideas, or objects; aptitudes; and abilities—and identify one or more careers that match your strengths.
10. Develop some short-term goals for the high school years that could contribute to a career plan in a career of your choice.
11. Develop a list of artifacts that could represent your progress toward some long-term goals in a career of your choice.

CRITICAL THINKING

12. **Make Inferences.** Interview three peers and ask them to identify four goals that a young adult in your community may have for his or her career. Ask them to identify four possible obstacles to reaching these goals. Write a paper describing these goals and obstacles, including your own ideas as well as those of your peers. Then determine four resources that could help each individual reach his or her goals.

13. **Defend Conclusions.** Assess your own personality traits, values, goals, interests, aptitudes, and abilities, and match them to at least three different jobs. In a paper, summarize your conclusions and

explain how the characteristics of each job seem suitable for you. Cite the references you used in researching these jobs. Identify the career clusters that relate to the jobs that interest you.

14. **Summarize Findings.** Analyze three career areas related to working with individuals and families and identify personality (or temperament) traits that would benefit workers in these careers. Write a paragraph summarizing your research. Cite the sources you used. *Group option*: Work in a small group and present a skit that demonstrates how certain personality traits would be useful when working with individuals and families.

15. **Develop Hypotheses.** Analyze your lifestyle expectations. Identify a house you would like to own, a car you would like to drive, vacations you would like to take, the number of children you would like to raise, and other aspects of your desired lifestyle. Estimate the average salary needed today to live that lifestyle, and identify five careers that provide it. Write a paper relating your lifestyle expectations to the job you plan to have.

CORE SKILLS

16. **Research.** Visit a guidance counselor at your school to learn the procedures that can be used to help students identify areas of work that match individual interests, personality, and aptitudes. Identify three postsecondary institutions that provide training in a career area that interests you. Summarize your research in a paper.

17. **Writing.** Research jobs in a field that interests you. Choose one job that looks interesting to you. Identify the responsibilities of the job, the earnings potential of the job, the working conditions, and the potential for advancement. Also identify the skills, training, or education required to apply for this job. Write a summary of your research about this job. *Choice*: Describe how this job does or does not match what you desire in an occupation.

18. **Social Studies, Writing.** Think about whether you are most interested in learning about jobs that involve working with people, objects, or ideas. Interview a worker who has a job with your chosen area of focus. In a report, summarize the work performed by the person and the challenges he or she faces. Then explain which of the reasons for working are met in the person's work. Cite evidence from the text to support your analysis and explanation.

19. **Writing.** On the Internet, locate a career assessment survey. Take the survey to identify careers that match your interests, abilities, and personality. Print out a copy of the results of the survey. Reflect on the results of the survey in a paragraph, summarizing which of your personal strengths matches one of the careers.

20. **Research.** Using the Internet, research a career cluster that interests you. Identify five possible occupations or entrepreneurial opportunities within the field, and describe the type of work done in each. List the aptitudes, abilities, and training or education required for each. Also, identify the personality traits needed in each. Present the information in a chart in a table format.

21. **Financial Literacy, Social Studies.** Use online resources to explore and compare potential jobs throughout the United States. Select five similar jobs available in different parts of the country, and compare salary ranges for these jobs. Prepare a chart illustrating the comparisons. Then search online to compare the cost of living in these different parts of the country. Summarize the results of your research.

22. **Math.** Find two or three careers along a career pathway that interests you. Do research to find out the average salaries and the education and training requirements for each of those jobs. Then investigate the average cost in your region of obtaining the needed education and any official certifications or other credentials needed for each career. Write a report that compares the preparation cost to the income obtained from each career. Assume that a person is in the career for at least five years. Reach a conclusion about which career you think has the best return on the investment in education. Include charts or graphs in your report.

CAREER READINESS

23. **Creating a Portfolio.** Assess your interests, aptitudes, and abilities. Gather information related to past and current coursework, cocurricular activities, and work and volunteer experiences. Put together a portfolio illustrating your skills, knowledge, personal qualities, and experiences that would attract an employer's attention. Scan your artifacts, creating an electronic portfolio. *Choice*: Prepare an electronic résumé that could be e-mailed to prospective employers. Use the Internet to find guidelines to follow when creating an electronic résumé. *Group option*: Share your portfolio with a classmate and have him or her evaluate the artifacts you have contributed.

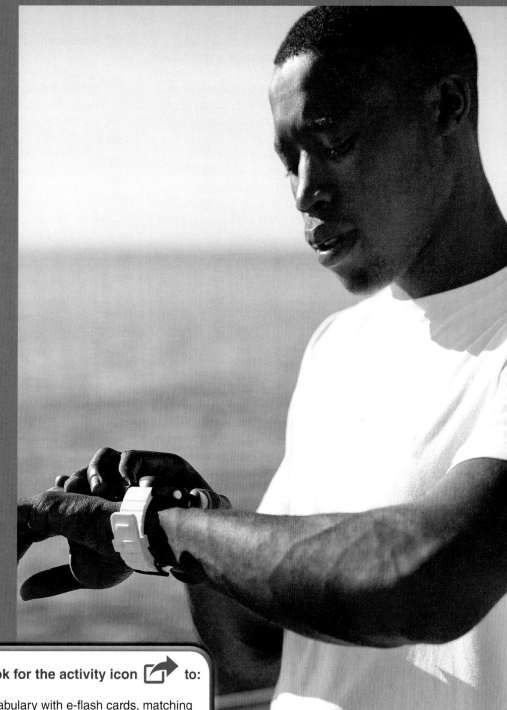

Reading Prep

Before reading the chapter, skim the headings and subheadings in each lesson. Write a sentence explaining what you think each section will be about. As you read, revise your sentences if necessary.

Key Questions

Questions to answer as you study this chapter:
- How can time management help a person achieve goals?
- What tools and skills can help a person with time management?

While studying this chapter, look for the activity icon 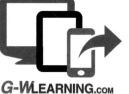 to:

- **build** vocabulary with e-flash cards, matching activities, and vocabulary games; and
- **assess** what you learn by completing the lesson comprehension checks online.

G-WLEARNING.com   www.g-wlearning.com/humanservices/

After studying this chapter, you will

Know:

- The benefits of managing time.
- The steps in developing a time management plan.

Understand:

- How a person's use of time reflects his or her values.
- How a person's use of time impacts his or her ability to reach goals.

Be Able to Do:

- Develop a time management plan.
- Analyze time management tools for their effectiveness in helping you reach goals.

Getting Started

Lea flopped across her bed, exhausted. The basketball game after school had run overtime. After the game, she and Terry had stopped to eat something. It was 8:00 p.m. already, and she still had a lot to do. She really needed to study for tomorrow's science test. Then she had some math homework. That would not take too long, but she had a history report that was due tomorrow, too.

"Why didn't I start sooner?" she mumbled to herself. She thought of the assignment that Mr. Havaro had given two weeks ago. Staring at the ceiling, Lea complained, "I always seem to leave these things to the last minute. I just wish I had more time!"

Lea's wish for more time may sound familiar to you. Why is time so valuable? Why does it make a difference how a person uses time? Here are two important reasons why time management is important:

- *Time is a limited resource.* The amount of time that each person has is limited. Every person has only 24 hours each day—and some of that has to be spent sleeping. Whatever you do in life, you have to complete it within the time you have.

- *Time is a scarce resource.* Often, there seems to be too little time to do what you want to do. The fact is, not enough time exists to do everything.

Learning to manage your time wisely is a useful skill. Time management can help you do the most important things you need and want to do. It can help you avoid wasting the scarce, limited resource that is time. Time management is a skill you can use throughout your life to help you reach your goals.

WHY MANAGE TIME?

Objectives

After studying this lesson, you will be able to

- **identify** the benefits of managing time.
- **explain** the benefits of managing time in the workplace.
- **identify** skills for managing time in the workplace.

Focus Your Reading

1. As you read, list reasons why you should manage time and then create a diagram or picture that illustrates each reason.
2. Before you read, list all the words that come to mind when you think about time management. After reading, create another list of terms that you relate to time management.

Because time is limited and the possible uses of time are many, time needs to be managed. **Time management** means controlling the way time is used. This includes planning how you will use your time and then carrying out your plan. Learning to use this skill can help you in many ways (**Figure 6.1**).

The Benefits of Time Management

Managing your time can help you do the following:

- *Ensure you accomplish important activities.* Managing your time can help you make choices so you complete important activities first. Some people make the mistake of doing easy tasks first and then find themselves without enough time to do activities that matter more to them.
- *Make it easier to reach your goals.* Managing your time can help you choose activities that move you along the path toward reaching your goals.
- *Balance your activities.* A balance of activities is important for good overall health and development. While you need to use time to meet responsibilities, you also need time for *leisure* activities, which involve enjoyment and relaxation. If

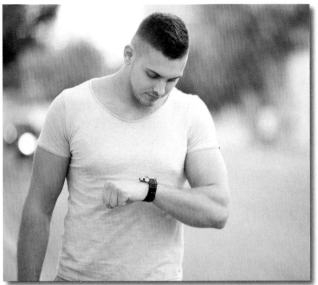

Figure 6.1 U.S. society highly values time. Everyone is expected to put time to good use. *How are others affected when you do not use your time wisely?*

fizkes/Shutterstock.com

you spend too little time in leisure activities, you will feel stressed. If you spend too much time in fun activities, you will not get enough done in other areas. Time management can help you recognize your priorities and spend time on the important areas of your life while still making sure that you enjoy a variety of different activities.

- *Avoid wasting time.* By planning and controlling the use of your time, you can avoid time wasters. Managing your time can help you spend as much time as possible doing meaningful activities.

Think About Your Reading

Think of one person you know who tries to do too many activities. How might this habit get in the way of managing time effectively?

Benefits of Managing Your Time at Work

Managing your time on a personal level helps you reach your own goals. Your use of time at the workplace is even more important because you are being paid for your time. Your use of time impacts your employer, your supervisor, your coworkers, and your reputation.

In the workplace, your employer is paying you, usually by the hour, to complete a job. The more effectively you use your time to do your job, the more valuable you are as an employee. How you manage time affects the entire workplace in the following ways:

- Your employer will benefit when you put in a full hour of work for an hour of pay. To do so, manage your personal needs so you can take care of them before or after work or during official break time. If you need to make a personal call or go to the bathroom, use your break time. Putting in your time properly also means arriving to work on time and not leaving early (**Figure 6.2**). When your employer benefits, you will benefit. Your job will be more secure. The company or business will be stronger, with more resources to provide continued work, employee benefits, and good working conditions.

- When you use your time effectively in the workplace, you will not waste your time or your supervisor's time. You listen carefully for instructions and carry them out. You do

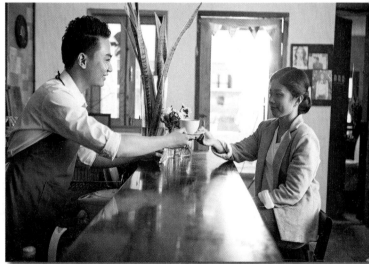

Dragon Images/Shutterstock.com

Figure 6.2 Managing your activities so you get to work on time benefits you, your employer, and your coworkers. *What might be some benefits of arriving early to work?*

not need someone to remind you to get your work done, but you take responsibility for your assigned work. Remember that your supervisor has his or her own concerns and tasks to do. Knowing that you can be counted on to do your job allows your supervisor to focus on his or her job.

- Your coworkers will also benefit when you manage your time in the workplace. Many times, you will have to work as a team member. If you do not complete your work, then others cannot complete theirs. In some cases, a team is paid for the work it completes together. Thus, your time management skills could impact the money made by others on your team as well as yourself.

- Your *reputation* is made up of the beliefs or opinions that others have of you. If you use your time effectively in the workplace, you will develop a reputation as a dependable, responsible worker. Managing your time well will help you earn the respect of others. They will see you as having a strong work ethic and being reliable. These are all qualities that make a good employee (**Figure 6.3**).

Think About Your Reading

How do you feel when a fellow student working on a project with you does not complete his or her assignments on time?

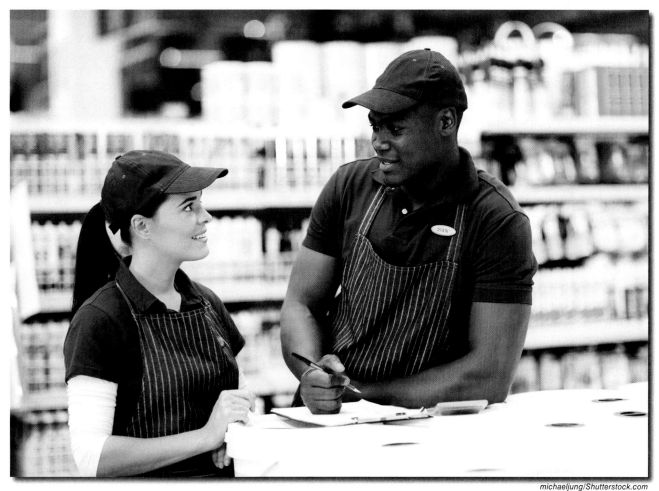

michaeljung/Shutterstock.com

Figure 6.3 High personal standards related to work can result in a good reputation on the job, with others believing in your ability to perform a job well. *What are some personal standards that could lead to a good reputation at work?*

Workplace Time Management Skills

Specific time management skills will help you balance the demands of the job with the time you have available. How to develop these specific skills is the focus of the next lesson.

Creating weekly and daily plans can help you on the job as well as in your personal life. Break large projects into smaller steps. Make sure that you reach certain points in the project in order to complete the project by the **deadline**, or the date when it must be completed. Prioritize your work. On a daily basis, identify high-priority items and put them on your activities list to do first. In some cases, your employer or supervisor will identify what they want you to complete first.

Be flexible. Even if you have goals to complete a project, your supervisor may have other work that becomes top priority. Be aware of company priorities (**Figure 6.4**). For example, your employer may have a policy that customers always come first. Even if you have a goal that you are working to complete, like stocking shelves with new products, if a customer asks you for help, you need to stop and take care of that customer's needs.

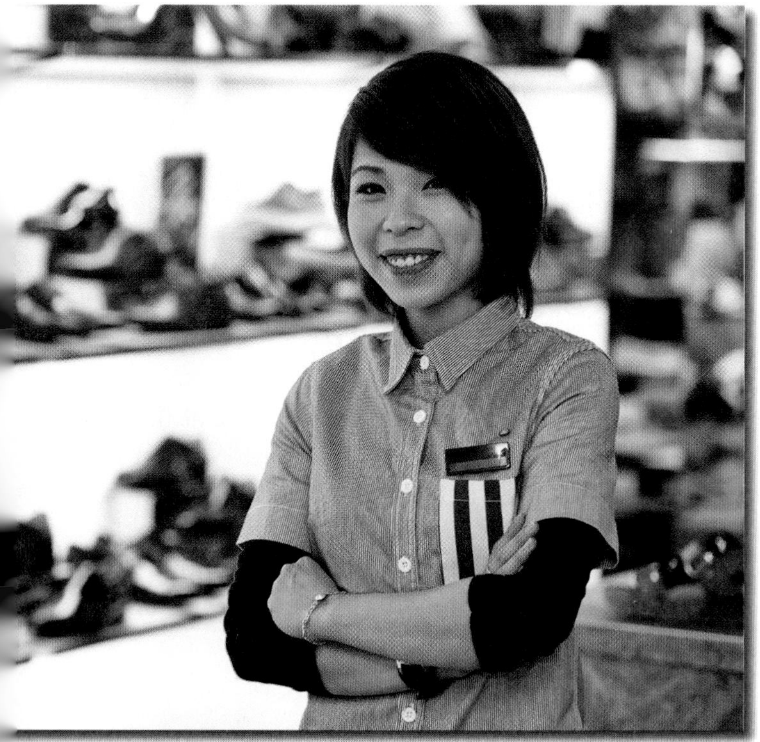

Ask questions. Clarifying issues that are uncertain can help you use your time correctly. If you are not sure when a task needs to be completed, ask your supervisor. If you are unfamiliar with the task you are being given, you might ask the person assigning it approximately how long it should take. You may also need to ask for help if more than one person gives you an assignment within the same time frame. Explain to both that you have conflicting demands and need to know which task should be done first. They may have to discuss the matter between them.

Avoid time wasters. Time needs to be used wisely on the job. If your supervisor asks you to do something, get right to it. Avoid interruptions as much as possible, stay organized, and keep your work area clean and safe. Work carefully to perform a task correctly. Having to redo work because it was done improperly or incompletely is a major time waster—and one that does not make employers happy.

Use time management tools to help you in the workplace. You can choose from calendars, to-do lists, or written instructions. You can use paper, a mobile device, a computer, or a tablet. Make sure that your employer approves whatever tools you use. Some employers may feel that the tools themselves become time wasters and may make them off limits in the workplace.

Dmitry Kalinovsky/Shutterstock.com

Figure 6.4 Following a company's policies and priorities is important when planning your use of time at work. *What are some policies an employer might have that would affect your activities at work?*

Lesson 6.1

Comprehension Check

1. Explain what is meant by the following statement: "Time is a limited resource."
2. List the four benefits of managing time.
3. What are four benefits of managing your time effectively at the workplace?
4. List three strategies that workers can use to meet goals and deadlines in the workplace.
5. What are four time wasters that need to be controlled in the workplace?

HOW TO MANAGE YOUR TIME

Content Terms

Build Vocab

inventory
service activity
procrastinate

Academic Terms

estimate
organization
commitment

Objectives

After studying this lesson, you will be able to
- **relate** the use of time to values and goals.
- **develop** a weekly and daily plan for managing time.
- **identify** ways to manage time wasters.
- **analyze** time management tools for their effectiveness in helping you manage time.

Focus Your Reading

1. Preview this section and list the three main strategies for managing time.
2. Write an explanation of how each term relates to time management.

Time is used minute by minute. Planning for every minute of every day is difficult, if not impossible. Planning the use of your time on a weekly and daily basis is much more manageable. It is one way to make the most of your time.

Making a Time Management Plan

When planning your time, you should start by looking at the overall picture of your life path and ask these questions: What in your life is important to you? What activities do you want to spend as much of your time as possible doing? What responsibilities or obligations do you have, and how much time do they require? Your answers will help you identify your priorities for the use of your time.

Make an Inventory of Your Time Use

To begin making your time management plan, you need to think about how you spend your time now. Make an **inventory**, or list, of all the activities you do in a day. You can analyze your

activities more readily by grouping them into one of the following categories:

- *Personal activities.* These include eating, sleeping, bathing, and dressing. Time spent for personal growth, such as reading, practicing an instrument or playing a sport, or for learning a new skill also belongs in this group.

- *Work activities.* These include time spent doing productive work. Being a good student by participating in classes and studying is work (**Figure 6.5**). You may also perform work at a job or by doing assigned tasks at home.

- *Relationship activities.* Anything you do to develop your relationships with parents, siblings, peers, and others is in this group.

- *Service activities.* **Service activities** include those things people do that help and benefit others, such as helping your siblings learn to read or volunteering in your community. Service activities also reflect your relationship values.

- *Leisure activities.* Examples include playing a sport, reading, or doing anything that interests you. The leisure activities you choose will reflect your values and your tastes.

Think About Your Reading

Where do you spend most of your time? Are these activities most important to you? Is your use of time balanced among the five categories of activities?

After listing each activity in the correct category, write down how much time you spend on it, on average. List the time in terms of numbers of hours per day or per week, depending on what makes sense for a given activity. You might want to note with some activities that they occur on specific days. For instance, Tonya would list the specific days she works at her after-school job and the number of hours for each of those days.

Once you have your list, ask yourself this question: Am I really spending time on things that are important to me, things I value? To help make this happen, think about your goals.

Identify Your Goals

Much of your time may be spent doing activities that you must do. You may not feel that you are getting close to reaching your goals. Looking at the big picture with your long-term goals in mind can be helpful. Think about your goals in terms of the types of activities you listed earlier—what are the goals you have in each area?

- *Personal goals.* What goals do you have for yourself? Are they good health? learning how to drive? Are you spending time in activities that support these goals?

- *Work goals.* What goals do you have for the work you do or want to do? Right now you may feel that getting through school is a big enough goal. How you spend your time now will likely affect your future choices about work. Spending time studying for good grades and taking certain courses will help prepare you for advanced education or training.

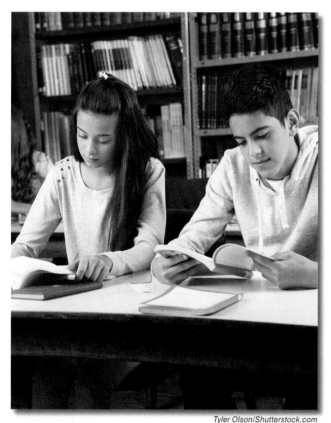

Tyler Olson/Shutterstock.com

Figure 6.5 As a student, studying is part of your work activities.

- *Relationship goals.* What activities do you do that support your relationship goals? Do you want to spend more time with grandparents or siblings? Do you want to take part in an after-school group? You need to be sure to include these activities in your time management plan also.
- *Service goals.* Do you find yourself involved in helping others, volunteering in your school or community? Is this an area you need to expand in your life? Then you may need to include that service goal in your time management plan.
- *Leisure goals.* Remember to leave some time for leisure goals. Time to relax and enjoy yourself is important for handling the effects of stress in your life.

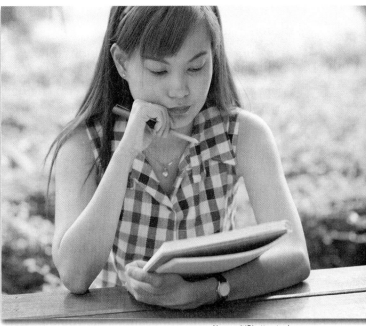

Nonwarit/Shutterstock.com

Figure 6.6 Determining and setting priorities is an important part of time management.

Think About Your Reading

Why do you think leisure and service goals are separate categories in a time management plan?

Set Priorities

Now that you have listed your current activities and looked at your goals, you are ready to make your time management plan. Begin by using your values to prioritize your goals. You want to make sure that you have time for the activities that matter to you most. Sometimes you will need to say no to activities that are worthwhile but not very important to you. This becomes necessary when you try to manage time according to priorities (**Figure 6.6**). By spending time in important activities, you will be happier with what you do. Taking this approach will also help you avoid wasting time on unimportant activities.

Working on too many goals at once can be discouraging. Identify no more than three goals to work on at one time. Choose an area where you need to see change. As you make progress in these areas, you can then add a new goal.

Finalize Your Plan

If you base your time management plan on your goals, your activities will be more meaningful to

you. Use the following steps to help you organize and finalize your time management plan:

- *Set a deadline to meet each goal.* Record the deadlines on a calendar, showing weekly, monthly, and yearly goals.
- *Break down each major goal into smaller subgoals.* What are the steps that will lead you to reaching each long-term goal? These smaller steps become monthly, weekly, or daily goals. A deadline for each step can help you complete your time management plan and progress toward your goals.
- *Be realistic about how much time each task will take.* You can draw on past experience or ask the advice of others to predict how much time some tasks will take. You will have to make an *estimate*, or guess, on tasks that you are not familiar with. If you guess too little or too much time, you can always revise your time management plan later.

Think About Your Reading

Why are deadlines important to consider when creating a time management plan?

Your Weekly Plan

To create a weekly plan, begin by listing your deadlines for the year and the monthly deadlines for your subgoals. Then, at the beginning of each month, you should draw up plans for each week that will help you build toward meeting those monthly deadlines. Each weekly plan should include a list of activities you want or need to do that week (**Figure 6.7**). It should also include a deadline for the completion of those activities.

List the activities in order of importance. Activities that must be done this week become top priority. Those that should be done, but are not as pressing, become medium priority. Those that you want to get done eventually become low priority.

Your Daily Plan

To create a daily plan, divide your weekly goals into smaller steps that can be accomplished each day (**Figure 6.8**). Number and list these items, putting the most important first. For each day,

write down one or two goals that you would like to reach.

Large projects might take several days of work before they are completed. Set aside some time in a daily plan to work on part of a big project. Schedule enough time to work on an activity to make sure it is completed by the deadline.

As you make your daily plan, block out periods of time that are the same every day. These include grooming, eating, and sleeping periods. Then add your top-priority items first and medium-priority items next. If any time is left, add your low-priority items.

Adjusting Your Plan

Before beginning each week, you will need to review the plan you made at the beginning of the month for that week. You may need to adjust it if something unexpected happens and you could not complete a task the week before. You will also need to adjust your plan if you completed a task

Weekly Time Management Plan		
Weekly Goal: Complete social studies report.		
Must Do *High Priority* • Homework • Work on social studies report • Study for math test	**Should Do** *Medium Priority* • Clean room • Help Dad mow lawn • Talk to counselor about school-to-work options	**Would Like to Do** *Low Priority* • Call friends for Friday night • Buy pizza and chips • Go shopping

Things To Do	Deadline	
Science; read pages 50–62	Sunday	
Social studies report	Monday	
Clean room	Tuesday	
Study for math test	Tuesday night	
Buy pizza and chips	Friday night	
Make appointment with guidance counselor	Thursday	
Call friends for Friday night	Thursday night	
Help Dad mow lawn	Saturday afternoon	
Go bowling	Saturday night	

Figure 6.7 A weekly plan should include the activities you want to get done and a deadline for each. *How might a person's success in reaching goals be affected if low-priority items are completed first?*

Managing Time

Chor felt overwhelmed as she stared at the tall stack of textbooks on her desk. She had brought home every book from school for the weekend. She wondered how she was going to get all her work done! She had 28 problems to do for math due Monday. She had to read a chapter of her science book by Tuesday and prepare for a quiz on the chapter on Wednesday. She had to give an oral report to her health class on Friday, which had to include library research.

She also had a piano lesson scheduled on Monday after school. She had to practice one-half hour daily for that. Her family expected her to help with household tasks for one-half hour each day as well.

Chor's friends invited her to go bowling Saturday afternoon and to a movie afterward. On Sunday, her family spent several hours at church. In the afternoon, they planned to visit her cousin, as they were all eager to see the cousin's new baby for the first time.

Chor decided she had to get organized. She had to have a plan. How else could she manage to get all those things done on time?

For Discussion

1. Identify Chor's weekly goals. Put them in a list and number them in order of importance. What must be done first?
2. Help Chor plan the use of her time in the next seven days (Saturday to Friday) by developing a weekly time schedule. Identify at least one goal for each day. Set aside time for studying and music practice on a regular basis. Include specific times to work on each major project. Include time for the following activities: building relationships, developing hobbies, and helping others.
3. How could the use of technology save time for Chor in the next week?

ahead of time. When you reach the next month, you should review your original monthly plan and revise it as needed.

Think About Your Reading

How could a weekly plan help a person use time wisely on a day-to-day basis?

Avoiding Time Wasters

A well-organized plan is beneficial only when you are able to carry it out. That means sticking to the plan. It also means avoiding obstacles that prevent you from following your schedule. Some of the major obstacles are time wasters, such as procrastination, interruptions, lack of organization, and unexpected events. You can take steps to prevent each of these obstacles from wasting your time.

Avoid Procrastinating

Sometimes people waste time because they **procrastinate**. They put off doing a task, particularly one that requires a lot of work or many steps. Instead of working on the task, they do less important activities. Then, at the last minute, they have to hurry to get the project done. Procrastination often leads to mistakes, incomplete projects, and poor quality work. It also causes stress and anxiety both while the task is being put off and when the person finally has to work in a hurry. Avoid procrastinating by dividing bigger projects into smaller tasks that you complete each day. This makes the work more manageable. You will also feel better about yourself and your ability to get things done as you complete each step.

Avoid Interruptions

When you plan work time, plan to carry it out in a quiet place away from interruptions. If you have voice mail on your phone, let your friends

Daily Time Management Plan			

Monday, February 8
Daily Goal: Read one resource for social studies project.

Time Schedule		Priorities	Things to Do Today
6:15	Shower and dress	5	Call Kallie about Friday party
7:15	Breakfast	3	Practice for band
7:30	Leave for school	1	Regular homework
8:00	School	2	Review for math test
3:30	Track practice	4	Start on social studies report
4:30	Get home	6	Pick up clutter in my room
5:00	Help prepare dinner		
5:30	Eat dinner		
6:00	Help clean up kitchen		
6:30	Relax		
	Watch TV		
7:00	Do regular homework		
7:30	Review math		
8:00	Read one resource for social studies		
8:30	Practice trumpet		
9:00	Call Kallie		
	Relax and get ready for bed		

Figure 6.8 A few minutes spent planning a day can help you reach your daily goals. *What activities in this daily time management plan could be eliminated if high-priority items are not completed?*

leave messages and return the calls after you finish studying. If you are working on a digital device, close your e-mail and sign out of instant messaging services and social networking sites while you work. If you allow yourself to concentrate on the work, you can work more efficiently and effectively.

Think About Your Reading

What are some interruptions that you experience when you are trying to work? How could you reduce those interruptions?

Stay Organized

Organization refers to arranging things in a systematic way so you can deal with them efficiently. Storing items in a specific place and

returning them after each use is a good way to stay organized. Having objects close by that you need to use on a project is another example of good organization. If you are organized, you will spend less time searching for items and will have more time to work on reaching your goals.

Be Prepared for Unplanned Events

Unplanned events often become time wasters. An accident may keep you sitting in traffic an extra hour. You may have to wait in the doctor's office while an emergency patient is treated. You can make use of these unexpected periods by always carrying some useful activity with you. It may be a book you want to read or a craft or hobby you like to do. Even if you forget one of these projects, you can use your spare time to think about your overall management plan. What

progress have you made toward your goals? What improvements would you like to make? Whether you think through or actually carry out an activity, you are using time beneficially, not wasting it.

Think About Your Reading

What could you do to wisely use your time if you were stuck in traffic?

Using Time Management Tools

Time management tools can help you organize and save time. They help you get more done with the time you have. You will be able to reach more of your goals as well as carry out tasks that are important to you. This can help you feel successful and enjoy what you do each day.

Create a Personal Calendar

A personal calendar can help you meet deadlines on time. It can also help you remember your appointments and *commitments*, or activities you have agreed to do. With a personal calendar, you can plan your priority activities so you progress toward your goals.

Your calendar can be paper or digital (**Figure 6.9**). It should include yearly, monthly, weekly, and daily goals. It should also include appointments and deadlines.

Use Technology

As technology advances, more and more tools become available to help you save time. Personal computers, tablets, and mobile devices offer possibilities to help you save time on many tasks. Technology can help you in the following ways:

- *Information gathering.* Using the Internet, you can instantly access information about any topic. Just make sure that the information you find is reliable.

- *Learning new skills.* Online classes or distance learning courses eliminate travel time to a classroom and provide the opportunity

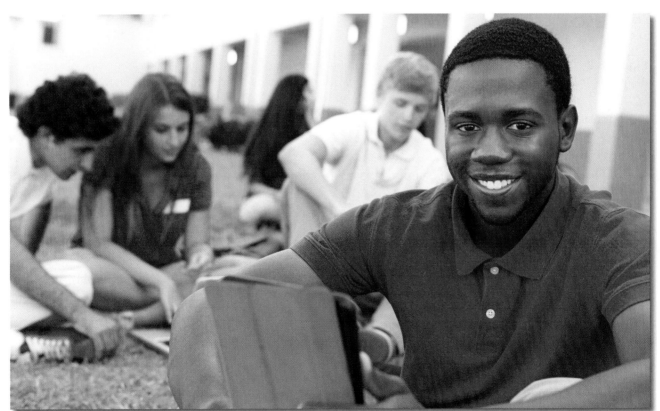

Monkey Business Images/Shutterstock.com

Figure 6.9 Personal calendars, either paper or digital, can help you keep track of important appointments, activities, and tasks. *What tools do you find most effective for managing time?*

to expand your knowledge and skills. Some allow students to fit their learning easily into their schedule.

- *Financial management.* Many people use technology to track their personal finances, balance their checkbook, and pay bills. Some financial management programs can be used to create budgets, track spending, and prepare reports for filing income taxes. By making these tasks automatic, technology can save users a great deal of time.

- *Filing and record keeping.* What types of records and files do you need to keep? addresses and phone numbers? medical costs? Data can be easily entered and sorted using spreadsheets and databases.

- *Speeding household tasks.* Some electronic programs are designed to store recipes and menus and generate shopping lists.

The tools you use to manage your time can be as simple as paper and pencil and a calendar or as advanced as the latest technology. Select the tools readily available to you and ones you feel comfortable with. That way, the tools will help you manage your time effectively (**Figure 6.10**). As new technologies are developed, consider implementing new tools to manage your time.

Think About Your Reading

What technology tools do you or your friends use? In what ways do they help you save time?

Assess

LESSON 6.2

COMPREHENSION CHECK

1. List four steps to follow in creating a time management plan.
2. What are the five categories of goals that can be included in a time management plan?
3. List the information that should be included in a weekly time management plan.
4. Name four ways to avoid time wasters.
5. Name two time management tools. How can each tool help a person manage time?

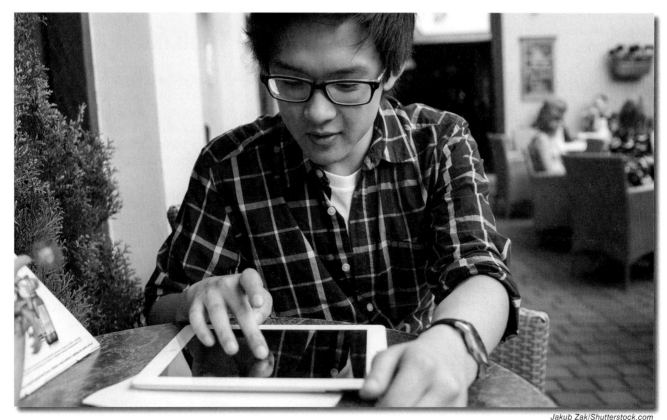

Figure 6.10 Feelings of satisfaction and success can result when you manage your time using technology.

CHAPTER SUMMARY

Everyone has the same number of hours in a day, yet most people wish they had more. Since time is limited, managing it is important. *Time management* means controlling the use of time by making a plan and following it.

Time management skills are essential in the workplace in order to meet the goals and priorities of an employer. Identifying priorities, breaking a project down into manageable subgoals, working to meet those goals, and avoiding time wasters are essential in meeting workplace goals and deadlines.

Two key aspects of planning are values and goals. A person's activities should reflect their values and goals in all areas: personal, work, relationship, service, and leisure activities. When people do what is important to them, their values are influencing their actions and helping them reach their goals.

Planning use of time needs to be done weekly and daily. A weekly plan should include all the tasks that a person wants to get done and a deadline for each. A weekly plan should include small goals that lead toward reaching a long-term goal. A daily plan breaks the weekly plan down into related tasks for a single day.

By avoiding time wasters, individuals can save time and turn it to good use. Time management tools, such as calendars and computers or mobile devices, can help people plan and organize their time.

VOCABULARY ACTIVITIES

1. Write a paragraph telling the story of a fictional teen and use all of the following terms correctly. Trade stories with a partner and read each other's stories. Provide feedback about grammar, spelling, and organization. Revise your story based on your partner's feedback.

Content Terms

deadline (6.1)	service activity (6.2)
inventory (6.2)	time management (6.1)
procrastinate (6.2)	

2. Write an explanation of each of the following terms that would make the terms' meanings clear to a middle school student.

Academic Terms

commitment (6.2)	organization (6.2)
estimate (6.2)	reputation (6.1)
leisure (6.1)	

ASSESS

Your Knowledge

3. What are the benefits of managing time?
4. What are the steps in developing a time management plan?
5. What are five ways that technology can be used to save time?

Your Understanding

6. Why is it important to set deadlines for tasks?
7. How does a person's use of time reflect his or her values?
8. How could a person's use of time impact the ability to reach goals?

Your Skills

9. Develop a time management plan for yourself. Include weekly and daily goals, appointments and activities, and deadlines for projects and assignments.
10. Make a recommendation to an employer regarding the use of a mobile device as a time management tool in the workplace. Include in your report an analysis of the advantages and disadvantages that you considered in making your recommendation.

CRITICAL THINKING

11. **Make Inferences.** Create a chart or table listing the five categories of activities. For each category, list some goals that are common to teens and young adults. In a paragraph, explain how time management could help achieve each goal. *Choice*: Draw pictures that represent each category. *Group option*: Create the list with a partner.

12. **Develop a Hypothesis.** Analyze two time management tools for their value in helping you manage your time. Gather information on their cost, ease of use, and features that could help manage time. Weigh these features and make a judgment about whether they would be good tools for your personal time management needs. Write a paragraph summarizing your findings. Also analyze whether your chosen time management tools would be good for your workplace time management needs. Compare the effectiveness of the time management tools in personal and in workplace applications. *Choice*: Present your information to the class in an oral presentation.

13. **Categorize and Compare Results.** Conduct a survey to determine how at least ten students in your grade use time. Calculate the average number of hours spent on personal, work, relationship, service, and leisure activities. Then in a one-page paper, compare your use of time with the class averages. Discuss how your use of time helps (or does not help) you reach your life goals. *Choice*: Include one or more graphs showing your findings.

14. **Categorize and Summarize Results.** Keep a daily diary for a week. Record everything you do and how much time you spend at it. At the end of the week, analyze your use of time. Record the number of hours you spent in personal, work, relationship, service, and leisure activities. Show your use of time in a pie chart or a bar graph. Write a paragraph summarizing your use of time. *Group option*: Work with a partner and compare your results. Calculate the average amount of time you spent in each activity area. Create a pie chart or bar graph that shows your averages.

CORE SKILLS

15. **Social Studies, Writing.** Interview a young adult who works full time. Ask questions about how he or she uses time in various areas. In a paragraph, compare that person's use of time to a student's use of time. Cite evidence from the interview to support your comparison. *Group option:* Lead a class discussion about young adults' and students' uses of time. What factors do you think affect how these people use their time? What time management suggestions would you give to students and working young adults based on your findings?

16. **Research, Writing.** Take a field trip to a department store or an office supply store. Identify as many time management tools as you can. Prepare a list of these tools along with a description of how they could help you use your time more wisely. *Choice*: Instead of taking a field trip, use the Internet to visit office supply store websites.

17. **Research, Writing.** Research a career of your choice. Write a paper on the importance of time management for success in that career. Cite evidence from your research to support your point of view.

18. **Writing, Speaking.** Using a digital device, design a one-page weekly time management calendar. Include slots for high-priority items, medium-priority items, low-priority items, daily goals, daily lists, and an hourly schedule. Create your own time management plan for one week using your calendar. *Group option*: Exchange calendars with a partner. Complete your plan on your partner's calendar. Then provide feedback to your partner regarding the effectiveness of the plan.

19. **Speech, Writing.** Research an electronic program that could be used for home management tasks (for example, cleaning, maintenance tasks, or other chores around the home). Prepare a report for the class and a demonstration of how that program works.

20. **Research, Speaking.** Research a tool that could be used for personal time management. Identify the strengths of the tool and weaknesses. Prepare a demonstration of the tool's use to present to the class along with your findings. *Group option*: Work with a partner to research and prepare the presentation. *Choice*: Present the demonstration to a small group versus the whole class.

CAREER READINESS

21. **Evaluating Software.** Your employer has given you the task of evaluating time management software for the company to use. Visit a computer store to ask about what software is available and find out what the software is designed to do. Prepare a report describing what you learned and recommend one or two pieces of software that you think would be used for assisting with time management in the home. *Group option*: Work with two or three other students and visit several stores. Include recommendations for use in time management in the workplace.

22. **Communicating Importance.** Suppose you are the owner of a sandwich shop and have just hired a new worker who is a high school student. Write out the talk that you would give to your new employee about the importance of time management and how you expect him to manage his time on the job. Use communication skills and techniques appropriate for the workplace in your talk. Also explain how time management is essential to effective collaboration in the workplace. After writing your talk, deliver it to the class.

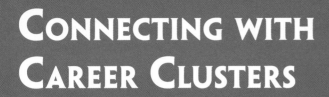

CONNECTING WITH CAREER CLUSTERS

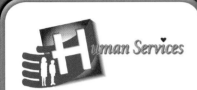

PATHWAYS

Early Childhood
 Development & Services

**Counseling and Mental
 Health Services**

Family and Community
 Services

Personal Care Services

Consumer Services

SCHOOL COUNSELING SERVICES

Professionals in counseling services are commonly known as *counselors*. Many counselors work in school settings. School counselors help students identify school and career goals that match their interests, abilities, and personality traits. They also help students learn to resolve conflicts, make good decisions, and develop healthful life habits. They work with individual students, small groups, and entire classes.

At the elementary and middle school levels, counselors help students identify strengths, weaknesses, or special needs. Working with parents, school personnel, and social workers, they help students handle various social, behavioral, and personal problems. They also try to identify cases involving abuse and assist student clubs that oppose drinking and driving, drug use, and tobacco use. They begin the career exploration process as middle school students plan and prepare for high school.

In high school, counselors advise students on career planning, educational and training options, and job-search skills such as résumé writing and interviewing techniques. At the college level, counselors focus on job placement and career development.

School counselors are usually required to have a master's degree and the appropriate certification. Some states also require a teaching certificate.

CAREER OUTLOOK

A job in a counseling field requires high physical and emotional energy; a strong interest in helping others grow and reach their potential; the ability to inspire respect, trust, and confidence; and good communication, listening, problem-solving, and conflict-resolution skills. Expertise is required in the area in which counseling services are offered and is usually obtained through an advanced degree. For example, a counselor who works with children may have an advanced degree in child psychology.

Employment for school counselors is expected to grow faster than average through 2022, but job opportunities may be affected by school budget constraints. Median earnings of school counselors averaged $53,400 in 2014. Overall, salaries for school counselors ranged from $32,000 to $86,600.

EXPLORE

Internet Research

Research the requirements in your state for a school counselor. Identify the coursework needed, schools that offer the training, requirements for practical experience, and the total length of the educational and training period. Contact one of the schools and learn what job opportunities exist in your area. *Alternative*: Expand your research to include another area of counseling that would require specialization in an area of interest to you (for example, child psychology or business psychology) and then gather similar information.

Job Shadowing

Spend a day with your guidance counselor. Observe the different areas in which your guidance counselor assists students. Identify various resources your counselor uses to guide students in their career choices. Summarize your experiences and findings in a report.

Community Service/Volunteer

Research opportunities in your school and community to participate in peer conflict resolution, peer-to-peer counseling, or peer justice programs. See your guidance counselor about becoming involved in one of these programs, take the required training, and then volunteer your services. Keep a journal of your experiences.

Project

Assist your school counselor with a student club that opposes drinking and driving, drug use, or tobacco use. Become a member of the club and help carry out a project. Complete a report describing the club, its mission, the involvement of the student body, and the goals and effectiveness of the project.

Interview

Interview a counselor for advice regarding choosing a career in the counseling field. Consider counseling professions in various settings, such as educational settings, health care settings, and business settings. Find out the counselor's recommendations for good schools to attend, valuable internship opportunities, and the jobs offering the most prospects for someone eager to work hard and get ahead. Summarize your interview in a report.

Part-Time Job

Seek a part-time job assisting the camp counselor in a youth summer camp or recreation program. Identify the responsibilities of the counselor and the effectiveness of the role you played.

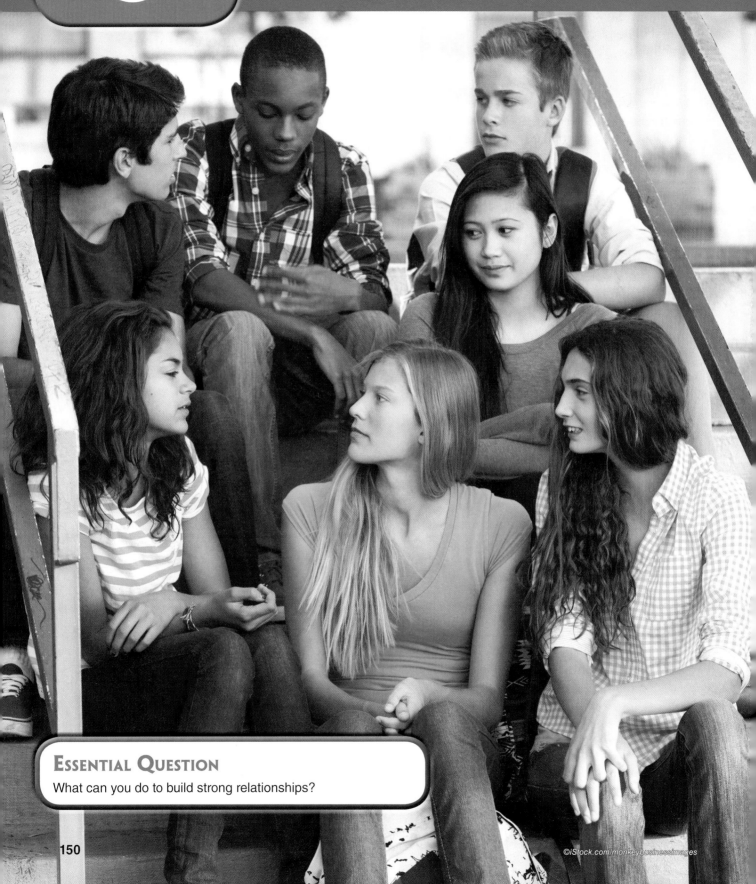

UNIT 3

RELATING TO OTHER PEOPLE

ESSENTIAL QUESTION

What can you do to build strong relationships?

CASE STUDY

How Do You Relate to Others at Work?

Read the case study and discuss the questions that follow. After finishing the chapters in this unit, discuss the questions again and identify any answers you would change based on information you learned.

Arik hurried to his after-school job. His school in Germany allowed him to work half the day for an employer in his field of interest. For him, it had been a real eye-opener. He loved computer programming and was willing to sit and work on his computer half the night, if needed. His supervisor at work, however, required that he spend half of his working hours talking through his plans for the program he was creating. At first, Arik felt this was such a waste of time. Why should he spend so much time sharing his ideas with others? Wouldn't they steal his ideas? But it did not turn out that way at all. His coworkers provided insight into his programs. Their input saved him hours of work. As he hurried to the team meeting room, he was excited. He had some new ideas and wanted to get their thoughts right away. This teamwork approach was turning out great.

Victoria settled into her position behind the machine, ready to start as soon as the beginning bell sounded. At the sound of the bell, she quickly unwrapped her bundle of pieces and started sewing them together. She worked quickly, as her wage depended on how many shirts she completed. She had some ideas about how the process could be made faster, but there really was no chance to talk about anything at work. She commented to a supervisor once about one of her ideas, but the supervisor just laughed. She told Victoria she had been working there 25 years, and changes did not happen very often. Plus, time was money, and she should keep working. Victoria wondered if all the factories in her city in Belize operated the same way. She had heard from one of her classmates that some of the factories were starting work teams, where groups worked together on projects. She liked the idea of being able to offer improvements and make things better.

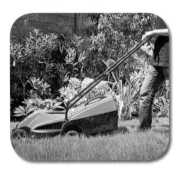

Andrew knocked on one of his client's doors in his Chicago suburb, as he had scheduled an appointment to discuss making some changes in the client's lawn care program. He had found a new fertilizer that matched the soil type and light exposure for his client's lawn. He loved the small business he had started a couple of years ago, first mowing lawns, then proceeding to full lawn care programs. It did require that he be organized to keep up with the work, have the knowledge about what would work well for his clients, and be able to communicate with his clients. The results were worth the effort, for he was well on the way to saving for his college tuition. He checked over his notes, making sure he had all the information he would need to share with his client.

Successful relationships can contribute to positive attitudes with peers, with families, in communities, and in the workplace. Think about the relationships in these three work environments and answer the following questions.

For Discussion

1. What characteristics did Arik's work relationships have that contributed to his success?
2. How did the relationships in Victoria's work environment limit her ability to grow as a person or reach personal goals?
3. How did Andrew use relationship skills to build his own business?

Delpixel/Shutterstock.com

DEVELOPING COMMUNICATION SKILLS

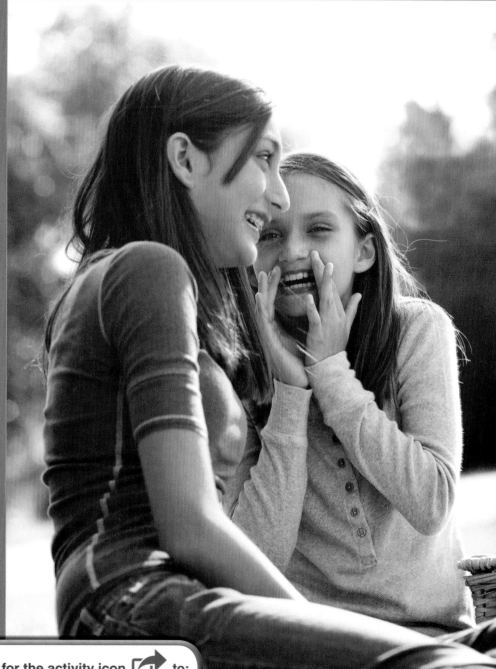

Reading Prep

Before reading the chapter, make a chart with the headings *Things to Know* and *Skills to Learn*. As you read, fill in important points from the text under the appropriate heading.

Key Questions

Questions to answer as you study this chapter:

- How can a person develop good communication skills?
- What factors can prevent good communication from taking place?
- How can good communication skills help resolve conflicts and solve problems?

While studying this chapter, look for the activity icon   to:

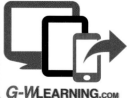

- **build** vocabulary with e-flash cards, matching activities, and vocabulary games; and
- **assess** what you learn by completing the lesson comprehension checks online.
  www.g-wlearning.com/humanservices/

AFTER STUDYING THIS CHAPTER, YOU WILL

KNOW:

- Types of messages that promote good communication.
- Factors that affect communication.
- Steps for resolving conflict and solving problems.

UNDERSTAND:

- How the written communication process can result in shared meanings.
- How verbal and nonverbal messages can impact the meaning of communications.
- How communication can break down and hurt relationships.

BE ABLE TO DO:

- Demonstrate effective speaking and listening skills.
- Identify how technology can be used to make interpersonal communication effective.
- Apply the steps of conflict resolution to solve a problem.

GETTING STARTED

"Do you know what happened with Sam today?" Ariana asked her friend Emma. "He was upset because I said that I didn't want to go see the new superhero movie with him. I mean, I don't—I'm really tired of all those guys making poses and acting tough and all the buildings blowing up. But that's all I meant. He thought I didn't want to go out with him anymore. Can you imagine that? Now he's really hurt, and I don't know what to do. How can I fix this?"

People communicate all the time, but communicating clearly is not always easy. It is important to be clear. Poor communication can cause serious misunderstandings. Somehow, the message that is sent can differ from the message that is received. A poorly presented message conveys the wrong information or gives the wrong impression. It can hurt someone's feelings or harm relationships.

Learning to communicate well is an important interpersonal skill. Effective communication is vital for developing rewarding relationships with family, friends, coworkers, and other people. Besides helping you get along with others, good communication skills can help you express yourself. Stating your thoughts and ideas clearly will help others understand you. These skills can also help you work through problems and resolve differences with other people. The end result will be improved relationships with others.

You communicate with others every day. Speaking, listening, reading, and writing are all forms of communication. Understanding the communication process will help you improve your skills in all these areas.

THE COMMUNICATION PROCESS

Content Terms Build Vocab

communication
sender
encoding
channel
receiver
decoding
nonverbal communication
verbal communication
body language
context
direct eye contact
communication style
I-statement
you-statement
active listening
clarifying
paraphrasing
reflecting
passive listening

Academic Terms

feedback
monitor
personal space
assertive
point of view
aggressive

Objectives

After studying this lesson, you will be able to
- **describe** the communication process.
- **identify** different forms of nonverbal and verbal communication.
- **demonstrate** effective speaking and listening skills.

Focus Your Reading

1. As you read, develop a profile of a good communicator. Create a graphic organizer with the heading *A Good Communicator* and two columns underneath. As you read, write qualities of a good communicator in the first column. In the second column, write what skills a good communicator uses.

2. Share an example with a partner (through words or actions) of how each content term can promote good communication.

Although it may seem simple, communication is a complex process. **Communication** is an exchange of information among two or more people. It is a two-way process that involves encoding, sending, receiving, and decoding messages (**Figure 7.1**).

The **sender** is the person who is the source of the message. **Encoding** a message is the process of thinking about what you want to say and how to say it and then transmitting or sending it through a **channel**. The channel may be the air, if the message is sent in person, or some form of technology or print, if the message is spoken on a phone or written on a digital device or piece of paper. The **receiver** is the person who hears or reads the message and interprets its meaning, a process known as **decoding**. *Feedback* is a signal the receiver gives back to the sender to indicate how the message was understood. Each part of the communication process is needed to make sure that good, clear communication takes place.

Both sender and receiver need to use certain skills to communicate effectively. The sender needs *encoding skills*—skills in sending clear and accurate messages. The receiver needs *decoding skills*—skills in listening to the message and interpreting it correctly. The receiver also needs to provide feedback that allows the sender to know that the message was understood.

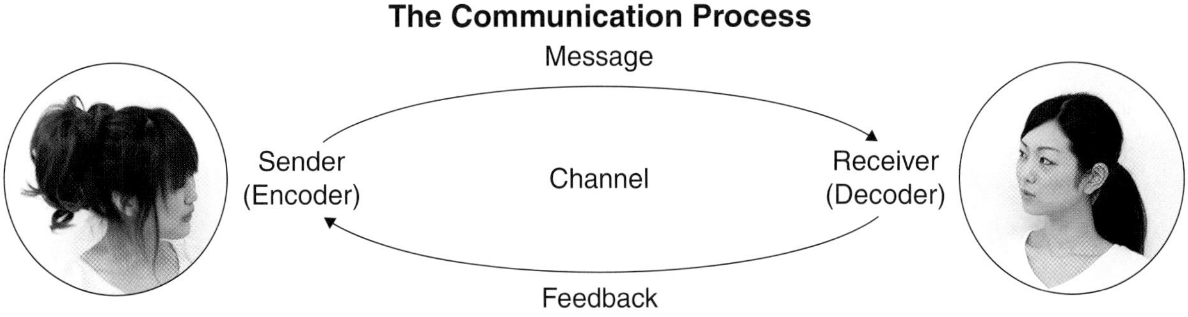

The Communication Process

takayuki/Shutterstock.com

Figure 7.1 Communicating effectively means sending and receiving messages clearly. *How would a sender know if a message was understood without any feedback from the receiver?*

Good communication occurs when the sender and receiver understand a shared meaning about the message. The receiver signals this understanding back to the sender by using feedback, such as a nod, smile, or comment. Many messages need a more complex or detailed kind of feedback, however. A receiver who states his or her understanding of the sender's message provides very effective feedback. This approach gives the sender a chance to *monitor* (observe) the way the message was understood and clarify the receiver's understanding if needed.

Think About Your Reading
Why is feedback an important part of making sure that someone understands your full message?

Good communication skills are critical for success in all types of relationships. In the family, in friendships, in romantic relationships, in workplace relationships, in your community interactions—all relationships will benefit as you develop good communication skills.

Types of Communication

Two types of communication are used in sending and receiving messages. The first is nonverbal communication. **Nonverbal communication** is a way of sending and receiving messages without using words. This includes body language such as facial expressions, body gestures, eye contact, and tone of voice. The second type is

verbal communication, which is the use of words to send and receive messages. Speaking and writing are forms of verbal communication.

The way you use both nonverbal and verbal communication affects the messages that you send and receive. As you become aware of how you encode and send messages to others and match your intention to the actual message, you develop better communication skills.

Nonverbal Communication Skills

People communicate without speaking. You often know when family members or close friends are feeling happy or sad without a word being spoken. You can tell by their facial expressions or the way they walk. You decode their nonverbal communication to help you understand their emotions (**Figure 7.2**).

Developing your own skills at encoding and decoding nonverbal communication is important in two ways. First, you become aware of the nonverbal messages you send and receive. Second, you can learn to encode and send clearer nonverbal messages so that they support the words you say. Overall, you will improve your ability to send and receive clear and accurate messages.

Think About Your Reading
When people are talking on the phone or communicating online, how could the absence of nonverbal communication affect their understanding of the message?

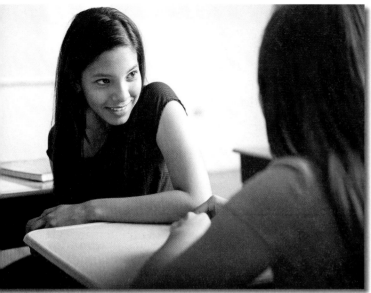

Figure 7.2 *What nonverbal messages are being communicated in this figure?*

antoniodiaz/Shutterstock.com

Body Language

Much of our nonverbal communication comes through body language. **Body language** involves sending messages through body movements and position. Through body language, people express their thoughts, feelings, and emotions. People's cultures, backgrounds, and past experiences influence how they decode or interpret body language. Considering how others may interpret your facial expressions, gestures, and body motions as a sender or a receiver can help you communicate more effectively.

Facial Expressions

A person's facial expressions can communicate a wide range of emotions to others (**Figure 7.3**). For the sender, a smile says that the sender's message is a pleasant one, and for the receiver, it encourages others to continue to share their thoughts and feelings. A dull, bored expression tells others that either the sender or listener is not interested in what is being said. A frown or furrowed brow shows that someone is worried or disagrees with what someone else has said. Think about the messages you are sending with your expressions to make sure they are in line with what you want to communicate.

Gestures

People also use gestures to help communicate their messages more clearly. Perhaps you have seen people who wave their arms or shake their fists when they speak. The use of gestures helps them emphasize their spoken words so others understand their meaning. Gestures can also be used in place of words in some cases. Someone who shrugs when asked "What do you want to do?" is saying that he or she does not have a strong preference. A vigorous nod in response to the question "Want to see a movie?" communicates "yes."

The use of gestures can vary according to people's cultural backgrounds (**Figure 7.4**). The amount of movement, the meaning a gesture may have, and the acceptability of certain gestures can vary. It is helpful to understand cultural differences in your community to help you communicate clearly. Watching how people from different groups respond to different gestures made by others can help you learn how they will interpret gestures. If you are not sure if the meaning of a gesture will be clear—or possibly be offensive—use words.

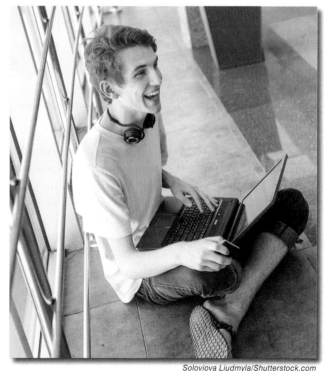

Soloviova Liudmyla/Shutterstock.com

Figure 7.3 Facial expressions are forms of body language that send messages to others. *What message is being sent by this teen's body language?*

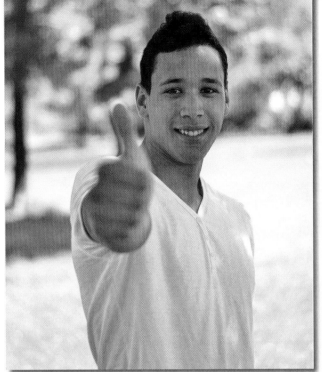

Aleksandar Mijatovic/Shutterstock.com

Figure 7.4 A simple hand gesture is a form of body language that sends a message to others. *In what different ways might this hand gesture be interpreted?*

Body Movements and Position

The way you sit, stand, or walk while communicating also sends messages to others. Good posture or a relaxed stride shows self-confidence. Sitting forward in a chair shows you are alert and care about the message, whether you are the sender or receiver. Crossing arms can seem like a barrier to open communication. Turning away or stepping back during a conversation can suggest that the sender is unsure of the message, the receiver is becoming less interested in the conversation, or either person is ready for the conversation to end.

The space that you keep between your body and another person also impacts the message being sent. *Personal space* is the amount of space that you need between yourself and another person for both of you to feel comfortable. If people back away when you are talking to them, you may have been too close for their personal comfort. The amount of personal space that people prefer is affected by the **context**, or the situation in which communication is taking place. Examples of different contexts for communication include personal settings, family, friends, business, and work environments. The amount of personal space that

people prefer in public is often influenced by their culture and family background. In a professional or work setting, more space is generally needed between two people when communicating than is needed among friends or family members. The increased space indicates that the focus of the conversation is on business. In a private setting, you will likely feel comfortable sitting closer to someone who is a good friend. Less space between two speakers indicates that a message is more confidential.

A person's touch conveys different meanings as well. A firm handshake sends a message of friendliness. A light touch on the forearm can add emphasis to a message or encourage the receiver to pay close attention. Again, cultural differences in interpreting forms of touch can affect the message that is sent or received when communicating.

Think About Your Reading

What are some examples of body language that could be interpreted in different ways, depending on the sender's and receiver's cultural backgrounds?

Direct Eye Contact

Direct eye contact means looking directly at a person when you are speaking to them and again when they respond (**Figure 7.5**). This does not mean staring. It means that you connect eye-to-eye, then maybe look away for a second, then look at them, connecting with their eyes again.

Looking in a different direction while you talk sends a message that you do not care that much about the person you are talking to. It might also suggest that what you are saying is untrue or that you do not have much confidence in what you are saying. Using direct eye contact when receiving a message conveys that you care and are interested in what the person has to say. Looking at a mobile device or out a window while the other person is talking says you do not care about the message—and perhaps about the person. For good communication, maintaining eye contact throughout the conversation is important. Using direct eye contact when you communicate will benefit your relationships in all areas.

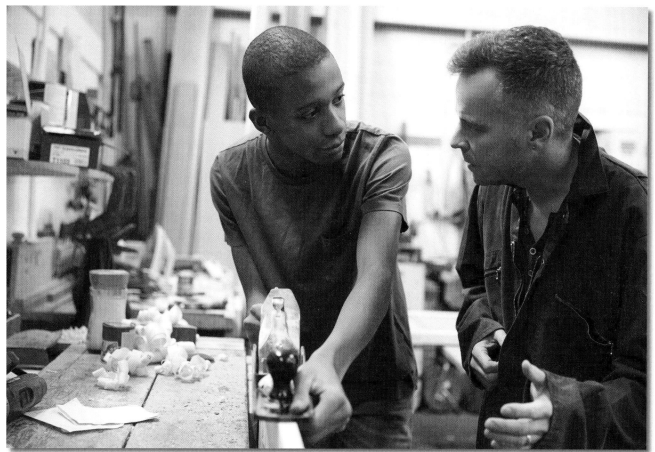

Monkey Business Images/Shutterstock.com

Figure 7.5 *Why would it be important to use direct eye contact and look at someone in authority when being given directions?*

Think About Your Reading

Why is it sometimes hard to use direct eye contact when you communicate? Is it more difficult in some situations than others?

Tone—How You Say It

Even your tone of voice can change the meaning of what you say. A strong voice conveys confidence. Too loud or strong a voice, however, can come across as bullying. A soft, quiet voice can make you seem timid, reserved, or unsure of what you are saying.

The emphasis you place on words can also affect the meaning, as in these two examples: "I said I want to go now" versus "I *said* I want to go *now.*" Thus, senders and receivers need to make sure that their tones of voice match the content of what they are saying.

Learning how nonverbal messages are sent and interpreted can help you encode and decode communications more effectively. Practicing accurate nonverbal messages will help you clearly communicate your message as well as interpret others' messages. Your nonverbal messages, however, are only one part of the communication process. To convey precise meanings, you need to understand and develop your verbal communication skills.

Verbal Communication Skills

Your verbal communications are influenced by your family, your school, your community, your communication style, and the skills you have

developed to express yourself. Even so, you can develop verbal skills to help you communicate clearly in any relationship.

The Words You Use

Your family, friends, schoolmates, and other people in your life influence the words you use to express yourself and the messages you encode. From your family, you learned certain languages. When you are with your friends, you probably use more informal language. School influences the way you speak, read, and write. Listening to others adds to your vocabulary. Even the region where you live influences the way you speak. All these factors produce differences in verbal communication.

Your Communication Style

The way you express yourself comfortably is your **communication style**. As you learned in Chapter 2, the social and emotional patterns you use to express yourself are related to your temperament and are part of your personality. Some people are reserved and do not share their thoughts or feelings readily. Others are outgoing and talk easily with anyone they meet. Because of these differences, people vary in the ease with which they learn speaking skills. Whatever your temperament or communication style, you can learn to express yourself clearly and effectively.

Skills for Expressing Yourself

Do you ever have a hard time telling someone how you really feel? Maybe a friend asked to borrow your car. You were not sure how to say "no" without hurting his or her feelings. You let your friend use your car, but you worried the whole time it was gone.

Skills for expressing your own thoughts, ideas, feelings, and intentions can be learned. Communicating well with others begins with you. By developing your skills in expressing yourself, you will send clearer messages. Others will more accurately interpret what you say and will understand you better. This skill is important no matter what context your conversation takes place in—at home with family, with friends, at school, in the community, or at work.

Use I-Statements

How can you express yourself so others understand what you are thinking and feeling? You can start by using I-statements to send clear messages. **I-statements** are words that directly express your thoughts, feelings, and ideas. They state your *point of view*, or way of seeing things. Learning to use I-statements can help you be an *assertive* communicator. An assertive communicator clearly expresses thoughts, needs, and wants in a way that is considerate of others. Five types of I-statements are outlined in **Figure 7.6** to help you express yourself clearly in different situations.

Suppose you do not want to lend your car to the friend asking to borrow it, but you do not know how to say so. The self-awareness circle in **Figure 7.7** can help you deal with this situation. It helps you use I-statements to express your point of view in a logical way. The circle is a tool to help you think through the action you want to take and express yourself more clearly.

You can start with the *observation*, which is a descriptive statement: "I gather that you want to borrow my car." This is just a fact, something you are observing. Because you are stating a fact, no emotion is included in this message.

Then add the thought, "I've worked hard to make the car look nice." This thought statement clearly reveals your thinking to help your listener see your point of view. It also gives you a little time to expand on your observation and to be thinking where you want to go with this conversation.

Then state how you feel about someone borrowing your car. "I feel worried when someone uses my car. I'm afraid that the person may have an accident with it." By this time in the conversation, your listener should be gaining some understanding of your position.

Next, you can state what you want to do about the situation: "I really don't want to lend my car." Finally, you end with an action statement: "I plan to stick to my policy of not lending my car to anyone."

These statements can help you speak honestly and openly. Your friend now has a clear picture of

Types of I-Statements

Type	Characteristics	Examples
Description	• Reports what you have seen or heard. • Describes information taken in through your senses.	"I smell smoke." "I heard you say that you are going to the concert." "I can taste a lot of sugar in these cookies."
Thought	• Starts with statements such as "I think," "I wonder," or "I believe." • Tells others how you interpret what you have seen or heard.	"I think Mr. Obley should use a different grading system." "I wonder if it will rain today." "I think I am gaining weight."
Feeling	• Lets others know how you feel.	"I feel good because I passed the test." "I feel upset with Mr. Obley's grading system." "I feel worried that it will rain during the ball game."
Intention	• Lets others know what you want to do. • Starts with statements such as "I want" or "I wish."	"I want to pass this course." "I want to play ball in the sunshine." "I wish I could lose some weight."
Action	• Lets others know what you are doing now, have done in the past, or will do in the future. • Uses action verbs.	"I studied two hours last night." "I am going to study two hours tonight and again tomorrow." "I'm going to memorize that information before the test."

Figure 7.6 *How could using I-statements like these help you be a more assertive communicator?*

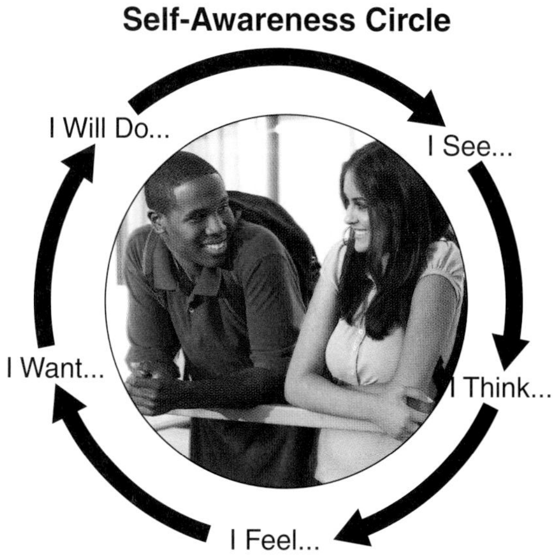

Self-Awareness Circle

I Will Do...

I See...

I Want...

I Think...

I Feel...

Monkey Business Images/Shutterstock.com

Figure 7.7 Your personal observations, thoughts, awareness, feelings, desires, and actions make up the self-awareness circle. *How could you use the self-awareness circle to express your point of view?*

your thoughts, feelings, and desired actions. Because you have explained your point of view, your message is clear. Because you spoke in an unemotional way, your friend might be disappointed in your decision, but is not likely to feel hurt.

You should encourage others to make I-statements themselves. This process of sharing and listening to I-statements helps people understand each other and accept that another's point of view is valid (**Figure 7.8**).

Think About Your Reading

Choose a sensitive situation in which you could apply the self-awareness circle. Practice the I-statements that you could use, starting with "I see..." and working around to "I will...."

Avoid You-Statements

Verbal communication is most effective when you speak from a personal point of view. Starting a sentence with "I see," "I think," "I feel," or "I want" lets the receiver know that you are expressing your own perspective.

Although I-statements send clearer messages, many people use **you-statements** instead. You-statements try to dictate another person's thoughts, feelings, or intentions. Examples are "You are so dumb," "You should apologize to me," and "You should really tell her how you feel!" This kind of speech can result in the person being an *aggressive* communicator, expressing thoughts, needs, and wants in a way that hurts others. You-statements attack the other person, not the problem. They send messages that judge, command, or blame the other person. Some people use them to vent their personal feelings or give solutions.

You-statements attack the receiver's self-esteem. The listener may feel that the sender is saying that his or her thoughts, opinions, or plans are unimportant. As a result, the receiver responds in a defensive manner, which gets in the way of effective communication.

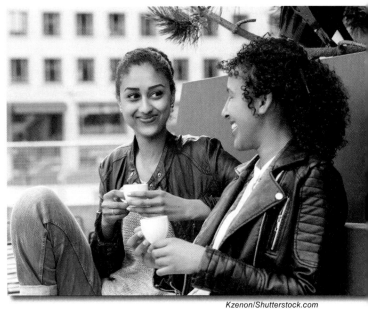
Kzenon/Shutterstock.com

Figure 7.8 Using I-statements makes communication smoother and helps people accept other viewpoints.

to clearly understand the message. You maintain eye contact in order to observe and understand the feelings the sender is sending nonverbally. You provide feedback to the speaker, which lets the sender know if the message was clearly and accurately received. These steps for being a good listener let the speaker know you care about what he or she is saying.

Think About Your Reading

Think of situations in which others give you advice using a you-statement. Is there an I-statement that could give the same advice without risk of offending the listener?

Receiving Messages

Communication is a two-way process. For good communication to occur, people need to encode a clear message and decode accurately. Your listening skills are an important part of this process. You will need to use those skills in the two parts of receiving a message—taking in the message and decoding or interpreting it.

If you are a good listener, you do more than just hear the words. You decode the message accurately. You pay close attention to what the person is saying and how he or she is saying it. You make an effort

Active Listening

You can be more certain that you are interpreting a message clearly when you use **active listening**. This means you give the sender some type of sign that you are listening. Giving feedback shows you are listening and encourages the sender to keep talking. The feedback may be a short verbal response such as "yes." Active listeners also use other verbal responses, such as clarifying, paraphrasing, and reflecting.

- *Clarifying.* **Clarifying** means using questions to make sure you understand a message. Examples include asking "Did you say that his car was wrecked?" or "Where did you say this happened?" This form of active listening encourages the sender to restate or expand the message to make it clearer. As the conversation continues, both of you can use questions to clarify each other's responses.

- *Paraphrasing.* **Paraphrasing** means repeating in your own words what you think has been said. As the listener, you might say, "What I hear you saying is that you are uncomfortable with other people driving your car." When you paraphrase a message, the sender can tell whether you correctly understood the information he or she shared.

- *Reflecting.* **Reflecting** means you act like a mirror and reflect back the sender's feelings as well as thoughts, using your own words. Reflecting is a lot like paraphrasing, but you also include feelings when reflecting. Reflecting can be useful when the receiver wants to help the sender identify certain feelings. For example, you might say, "It seems this situation really frustrates you and is making you angry. You have really worked hard to find a solution." Reflecting is a way to show others that you care about them and to express empathy.

When you use active listening, you give the sender a chance to see what you heard and understood and to correct any pieces of the message that were decoded incorrectly and misunderstood. Thus, good listening skills are a vital part of effective communication. The chart in **Figure 7.9** lists seven ways to practice good listening. These skills are important for relationship success in all areas of life.

Passive Listening

When people just take in messages, they use **passive listening**. This means they are hearing words without always listening for meaning. How do you feel when the person you are talking to does not respond to what you have said? The person does not smile, nod, or comment. You get no feedback at all. The silence can be frustrating or even annoying. You do not know if your message is being received accurately. People who often use passive listening are not trying to understand the sender's message. In these cases, good communication will not take place.

Think About Your Reading

What are some ways that good listening skills could help you succeed on the job?

Keys to Good Listening

- Show interest in what the other person is saying by sitting forward and using eye contact.
- Try to block out interruptions.
- Let the sender complete his or her thoughts before saying anything. Accept the sender's ideas and feelings.
- Use good verbal skills in giving feedback. Ask questions, reflect feelings, or restate an idea when appropriate.
- Control your nonverbal messages. Make sure that they are positive and reinforce your comments.
- Be aware of strong emotions. Understand that they can affect a message's clarity and your response to it.
- Do not let silence make you nervous and compel you to speak. Silence can be helpful by providing time for both people to think about what was said.

Figure 7.9 Being an active listener helps you get involved in the communication process. *How could your active listening skills affect a speaker's self-esteem?*

LESSON 7.1 Assess

COMPREHENSION CHECK

1. Briefly explain the communication process.
2. Explain the difference between nonverbal and verbal communication.
3. Provide two examples of each: facial expression, gesture, and body motion. Describe how each can impact a message.
4. List five different types of I-statements that can be used to express your point of view and illustrate each with an example.
5. Explain the difference between active and passive listening. How does active listening promote good communication?
6. Imagine you are listening to a friend describe how a close relationship ended. List three different forms of active listening and provide an example of a response for each.

Objectives

After studying this lesson, you will be able to

- **describe** several factors that affect communication.
- **identify** negative communication patterns.
- **explain** how communication barriers impact messages.

Focus Your Reading

1. Draw a chart with two columns. Label one column *Factors That Affect Communication Positively* and the other *Factors That Affect Communication Negatively*. As you read the lesson, write key concepts in the appropriate column.

2. Pick one of the communication patterns and write a short skit in which the characters use that pattern. Share your skit with a classmate.

Content Terms

Build Vocab

blaming
placating
distracting

Academic Terms

sensitive
prejudice

Certain factors aid good communication, while others hinder it. Your self-esteem, emotional state, and environment can influence the messages you communicate to others. In addition, communication barriers, such as closed minds and prejudice, can prevent good communication. Understanding how these factors help or hurt communication can help you improve your communication skills.

Your Self-Esteem

Self-esteem is an important factor in the way messages are sent or received (**Figure 7.10**). It affects how likely people are to communicate clearly and to listen actively.

High Self-Esteem and Positive Communication Patterns

People with high self-esteem are usually more willing to express their thoughts, opinions, and desires. It is easier for them to use I-statements to express themselves with confidence. They believe that others are interested in what they have to say.

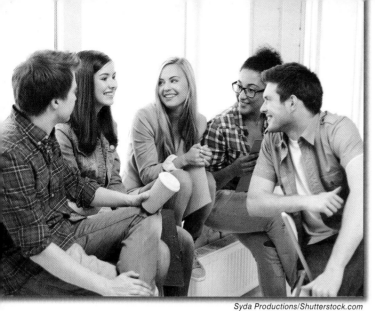

Syda Productions/Shutterstock.com

Figure 7.10 Positive self-esteem can help you communicate clearly without the use of hidden messages. *What personal thoughts and feelings could keep you from understanding a message accurately?*

People with high self-esteem also find it easier to focus their full attention on the message another person is sending. They are less sidetracked by nervous thoughts or worries about hidden messages. As a result, they are more successful at reaching a shared meaning when communicating.

Low Self-Esteem and Negative Communication Patterns

People with low self-esteem send and interpret messages differently from those with high self-esteem. They tend to have more problems encoding clearly and decoding accurately. They may not be sure of their own feelings. They often avoid direct eye contact, which prevents them from accurately sending and receiving messages.

People with low self-esteem tend to communicate in negative patterns. They may use avoiding, lying, blaming, placating, and distracting rather than say how they really think or feel. Negative communication patterns result in even lower self-esteem and cause feelings of worthlessness to increase.

People with low self-esteem may fear that others will reject them and their ideas. Therefore, they are afraid to let others know what they really think and feel. To avoid rejection, they may be passive, meaning they withdraw and say little or nothing.

- *Lying.* *Lying* is a negative communication pattern in which people are not honest. They do not share observations, thoughts, and feelings in an accurate way. Lying prevents people from building healthy relationships.
- *Blaming.* **Blaming** is a pattern in which people accuse others for everything that goes wrong. They find fault with others in order to cover up their low self-esteem. You-statements often signal that blaming is taking place.
- *Placating.* **Placating** is a pattern of communication in which people will say or do something just to please others or to keep them from getting upset. Going along with the crowd is easier for people with low self-esteem. They are afraid to do or say anything that might call negative attention to themselves.
- *Distracting.* **Distracting** is another poor communication pattern in which people just ignore unpleasant situations. They may put the issue aside as not really being important. This is easier than risking an attack on their low self-esteem.

Changing Negative Communication Patterns

Communication is a skill that anyone can learn. A person with these negative communication patterns can take steps to build good communication skills. Practicing making I-statements is one approach. Using the I-statements to work around the self-awareness circle can help build confidence in self-expression. Using I-statements with family members or good friends helps a person with low self-esteem realize that his or her thoughts and feelings are accepted and even valued. As that person gains confidence from these interactions, he or she is more likely to use I-statements with other people.

Making encouraging comments and giving positive feedback can improve your communication with someone who has low self-esteem (**Figure 7.11**). As communication skills get stronger, relationships will grow and develop. The other person's self-esteem will increase. As self-esteem increases, so does the ability to communicate clearly.

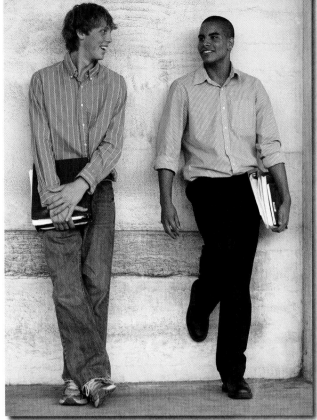

Figure 7.11 Giving positive feedback that shows you are listening will encourage a person with low self-esteem. *What kind of feedback would discourage a person with low self-esteem?*

Huntstock.com/Shutterstock.com

Think About Your Reading

When a friend is using a negative communication pattern, how could you respond to help improve your friend's self-esteem?

Your Emotional State

Your emotional state is another factor that can affect communication. Before trying to communicate, you need to recognize what your current emotional state is. Intense emotions get in the way of encoding and decoding accurate messages. If your emotions are intense, use an I-statement and let the other person know you need time to sort out your feelings before discussing the issue. For example, you can say, "I am really upset about this. I need some time to think. I'd like to take a break and talk about this later."

Go for a walk or wait before trying to communicate. By doing this, you can think about your feelings, what caused them, and how to control them. You can also avoid upsetting the other person. After you feel calmer, you are more likely to have success communicating a message that others can understand.

Your Environment

Along with your emotional state, the environment in which you communicate can affect the communication process. The time of day or the amount of time you have can make a difference in whether a shared meaning is reached. A relaxed environment helps good communication take place. A quiet place, where it is easy to talk without interruptions, will promote the sharing of thoughts and feelings and allow feedback to flow between speakers (**Figure 7.12**).

A busy or noisy environment or being rushed makes good communication more difficult. Fatigue or illness can keep a person from showing interest. Distance between the people who are communicating makes it harder to interpret body language and nonverbal signals. Communicating over the Internet or even by phone makes it hard to get a complete picture of the sender's total message.

Whether you are sending or receiving a message, choose the best environment possible. The choice of time and place is important, especially when communicating *sensitive* or personal information.

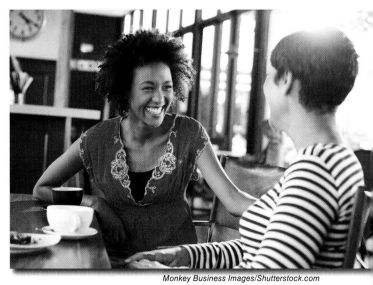

Monkey Business Images/Shutterstock.com

Figure 7.12 Communicating in a place where you will not be interrupted can help you reach a shared meaning with another person.

An environment that allows direct eye contact and a chance to read nonverbal signals will promote the most accurate interpretation of the sender's message. If the issue being communicated is very serious or emotional, make sure to allow enough time to discuss it fully.

Your Cultural Background

Different cultures can result in people seeing things from different points of view. There may be different rules for acceptable behaviors and for showing emotions. These are all part of communication, and differences can make it hard to reach a shared meaning.

Your cultural background influences the words you use and the way you use them to express yourself. The meanings of words may vary from one culture to another. You can send clearer messages by using the language, pronunciation, and words other people will understand. Slang, for instance, can be difficult to understand for someone who is not part of the group that uses that slang regularly.

Different cultures have their own values and beliefs about how people should live and behave. Such expectations will affect the messages they send and how they receive others' messages. Some cultures avoid eye contact as a rule of politeness. Other cultures see avoiding eye contact as a weakness. Some use hand gestures freely, and these may have different meanings from one culture to another. Some cultures share emotions openly; some are more reserved. When communicating with people from a different culture, it is important to learn what their rules of proper behavior include so your communication can be effective.

Think About Your Reading

What cultural differences exist in your community that could affect people's abilities to communicate well and reach a shared meaning?

Communication Barriers

In addition to low self-esteem, intense emotions, difficult environments, and cultural differences, there are other barriers that get in the way of good communication.

People with closed minds shut out or ignore opinions and beliefs that are different from their own. As receivers, they may filter out information they do not want to hear. They tune out the message the sender is trying to share (**Figure 7.13**). *Prejudice* is another communication barrier. Prejudice occurs when a person forms opinions about others without complete knowledge or facts.

How can you overcome these barriers to communication? First, understand that they do exist and can interfere with communication. Only then can you try to avoid them. Practicing the following methods will help you develop skills to become a better speaker and listener:

- *Avoid sending mixed messages.* Think before you speak and say what you mean. Use body language that supports your words.

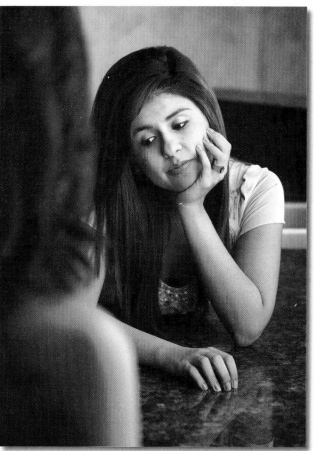

CREATISTA/Shutterstock.com

Figure 7.13 People with closed minds prevent good communication by ignoring messages they do not want to hear. *What body language indicates that a communication barrier exists?*

A Breakdown in Communication

It was late Saturday afternoon, and Shayla was sitting at the kitchen table, working on her laptop computer. She had a big research paper due on Monday for her history class. She was hurrying to get it done so she could go out with friends that night.

She was annoyed because her brother had friends over, and they had just started playing a loud video game in the next room. It was distracting her from focusing on her paper, but she was almost finished, so she did not bother to move to another room. Shayla's dad came into the kitchen and started taking vegetables out of the refrigerator.

"Shayla, would you please set the kitchen table when you finish your homework?" he asked.

"Sure, dad," Shayla replied, half-listening as she continued typing. "I'll be done in a few minutes."

"Thanks," her dad replied. "All the dishes in the dishwasher are clean. I'm going to run up to the store to get some green peppers for the dish I'm making. If your mother gets home, let her know where I am and tell her I'm making dinner."

Shayla was absorbed in typing and did not respond. She did not even hear the door shut as her dad left. She had just finished her paper when the phone rang. It was Shayla's mom.

"I'm on my way home from the mall and thought I would pick up a pizza for dinner," she said. "What kind of pizza should I get?"

Shayla told her mom what she wanted, and then hung up the phone. She cleared away her schoolwork and started setting the table. However, there was not enough clean silverware or plates to finish. Just as she was wondering what to do, her mom arrived with the pizza. A few minutes later, her dad arrived with groceries. He noticed only half of the table was set and then he saw the pizza box on the counter.

"Shayla, I told you there were clean dishes in the dishwasher," he said. "I also told you that I was making dinner. You should have told your mom she didn't need to pick up a pizza. You need to pay attention and listen better."

Shayla became upset and stalked out of the kitchen.

"All I heard you say was that I should set the table," she muttered as she left the room. "Couldn't you see that I was busy?"

For Discussion

1. At what point in the conversation did the breakdown in communication occur?
2. What factors contributed to the breakdown?
3. What caused the miscommunication to escalate into a conflict?
4. What could Shayla and her dad have done to make sure they communicated accurately?

- *Keep an open mind.* When communicating, listen to others' opinions and beliefs and try to understand their points of view. Using the active listening skills will help you in this area.

- *Overcome your own prejudices.* Ask questions and get all the facts before forming an opinion. Try to understand and accept others' differences, including cultural differences.

- *Practice active listening when others speak.* Do not let your mind wander. Pay attention to the speaker and do not interrupt. Respond only when the speaker is finished and it is your turn.

LESSON 7.2

Assess

COMPREHENSION CHECK

1. Describe three negative communication patterns that are commonly used by people with low self-esteem.
2. Explain how intense emotions affect the communication process and how to address this problem.
3. How can your environment affect your ability to communicate?
4. Name and describe two barriers that hinder good communication.

THE WRITTEN COMMUNICATION PROCESS

Content Terms

Build Vocab

texting
social media
digital footprint
cyberbullying

Academic Terms

author
face-to-face interaction
anonymous

Objectives

After studying this lesson, you will be able to

- **describe** the written communication process.
- **identify** skills for effectively expressing a point of view in writing.
- **list** strategies for understanding and interpreting written messages.
- **explain** benefits and disadvantages of using communication technologies.

Focus Your Reading

1. Create three columns, one for each of the three main headings of this lesson. As you read each section, list the specific skills that can make your communication more effective.

2. Identify various forms of social media familiar to you and your friends.

The written communication process is different from the spoken communication process. You need distinct skills for clear written communication to take place. In written communication, the sender is an *author*, one who creates and writes the message. The receiver reads the message. In written communications, there are typically no nonverbal signals involved that can help clarify the meaning of the message. Feedback may or may not take place, depending on the situation. Thus, reaching a shared meaning between author and reader can be difficult.

Despite these difficulties, gaining skills for communicating successfully in writing is very important. You will use these skills at school, on the job, and in personal relationships. At school, you are asked to read and write as you gather information and share with others what you have learned (**Figure 7.14**). At work, you may be asked to read and follow instructions, read and act on a new company policy, or read and research information related to a project. Modern communication technologies make it easy to send and receive written messages to those with whom you have

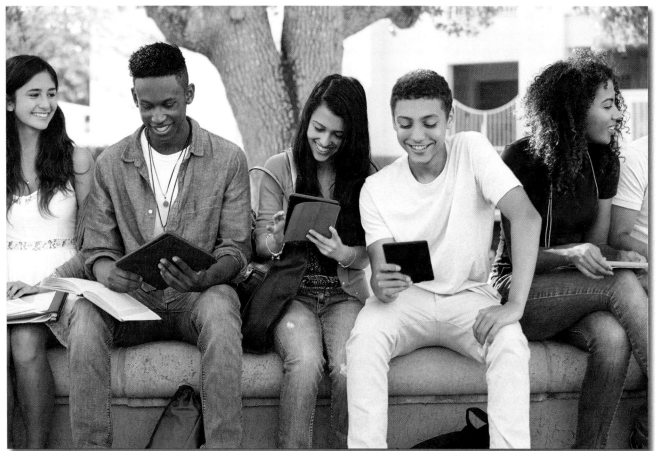

Figure 7.14 *How many different ways do you use reading and writing skills daily? What strategies do you use to make sure you have a shared meaning with the sender of a written message?*

Monkey Business Images/Shutterstock.com

relationships. These messages are transmitted instantly, so being able to send accurate and clear messages is important for good communication to take place.

Written Communication Skills

It is important to develop skills for writing clear and accurate messages. Then your written communications will more likely fulfill their intended purposes.

Depending on the message you are sending, different skills are needed. If you are writing a message expressing your point of view—that is, your observations, thoughts, ideas, desires, or intentions—then using the self-awareness circle and I-statements will help you organize and express yourself clearly. This will help you send an assertive message, expressing yourself while also being sensitive to the thoughts and feelings of others. You-statements will appear

aggressive to the reader and will send the message that you are telling others what to do. That is likely to result in your message being received poorly. Since you will not be seeing receivers' responses when they read your message, you cannot respond to clarify your intentions. Thus, even if you did not mean to be bossy or aggressive, receivers may think that was your attitude.

At school or at work, you may be writing different kinds of messages. You may need to report on something that happened or analyze a problem and propose a solution. Skills for sharing information clearly with others will benefit you throughout life (**Figure 7.15**). The following approaches will help you communicate these messages effectively:

- *Outline.* In school and work communications, you need to be able to organize your thoughts and write them down in a logical sequence for others to understand your message. A good way to approach one of these more

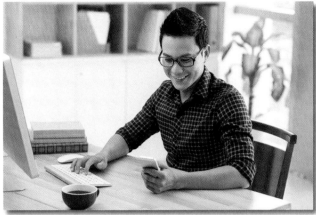

Dragon Images/Shutterstock.com

Figure 7.15 Written communication skills are transferable skills that will benefit you in any job you may have. *How could skills for using communications technologies help you present a clear written message?*

formal pieces of writing is to begin with an *outline* where you set out your ideas in order. As you think through the outline, you may find it makes more sense to move some ideas from one place to another.

- *Provide evidence.* If you are writing a report, it is important to document your findings or results so others are more likely to accept your view of the situation. Providing evidence to support your claims will help make them convincing.

- *Reread.* School and work communications are important. To make sure that you communicate effectively, read through the message and revise it to fix any statements that are unclear or not what you intended to say.

- *Proofread.* Many written communications today take place electronically. Having strong keyboarding skills can help you communicate quickly and accurately. You cannot rely on spell-check programs to guarantee that a written message is error free, however. The program may accept a word that is incorrect because it is a real word and spelled correctly. For instance, it could accept *there* in place of *their.* Be sure to proofread your written messages carefully to look for such errors.

- *Present.* Gaining presentation skills will help you present information clearly using pictures, diagrams, and charts.

Reading and Comprehension Skills

Just as you need writing skills for sending written messages, you also need skills for reading and understanding written messages that you receive. When you read a message, you should be able to interpret what the writer said well enough to understand the author's meaning. This is important in school, where you need to understand a teacher's instructions for an assignment. It is also important at work, where you need to carry out the tasks that an employer gives you. It is important in written communications with friends and family to make sure that you understand others' intentions and plans.

As you read messages, check for your own understanding. Write down questions that arise as you read. You may find the answers to your questions as you continue reading. If not, you may need to find additional information. After reading, summarize what you read in your own words. This is a way of reflecting the message back to yourself, to clarify your understanding. If necessary, read a confusing or unclear passage more than once to see if you can better understand what is being said (**Figure 7.16**).

If you have any question about a written communication, it is important to clarify the message by responding as you would with active listening. Use the active listening skill of clarifying by asking, "Could you please clarify the directions for step 2 on this project?" Another approach is to talk to others who have read the same communication. To make sure you understand something you have read, you could paraphrase your understanding of the message to a friend or coworker and compare their understanding with your interpretation.

Communication Technology and Social Media

Much of our communication today takes place electronically. People use mobile devices, e-mail, and social media to connect with friends, family, businesses, employers, teachers, fellow students,

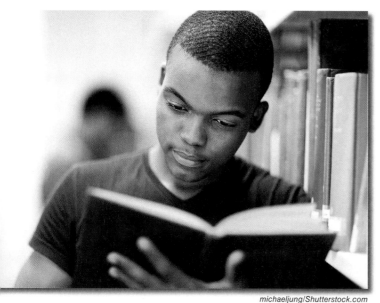

Figure 7.16 Reading carefully and rereading confusing passages can help you understand written communications.

michaeljung/Shutterstock.com

When you receive an electronic message, provide feedback as close in time as you can to when you received the message to make sure you have a shared meaning. Use active listening electronically to clarify, paraphrase, or reflect your understanding.

Texting

Texting, or text messaging, is the practice of sending a short message through mobile phones. Texting offers many advantages. Senders have the benefit of quick and frequent communications, often with immediate feedback if your receiver is available. As a receiver of text messages, you can read the message when you have time, at your convenience. Because texting requires having someone's phone number, the communications are more controlled than social media.

Social Media

Social media are media used for interacting with many people at once. It is made possible through online technologies and includes websites such as Facebook and Twitter; video websites like YouTube; gaming websites; blogs; and other websites. Using social media, you can create and share messages instantly that can be received and read by many others. The great reach that these sites provide is one of their attractions. This reach also adds to the potential for miscommunication multiplied by everyone who reads the message (**Figure 7.17**). Making sure that everyone who reads a message has the same shared meaning as you can be difficult. Thus, your choice of words is very important when you post something on a social media site.

The positive aspects of social media include the speed at which you can reach many people. You can keep in touch with many friends quickly and easily. Social media can be used to promote ideas or a way of looking at things, as in political races. In the business world, many use social media to advertise their products or business.

and others. Your skills for using this technology effectively will be a personal resource that can help you reach your life goals.

Electronic communication is fast. You can communicate with people who are far from you with no delay. You can gather ideas or advice from friends or family, find information to help you make a decision, check on homework with classmates, keep up-to-date with news from friends, submit homework to your teacher, and even take a class online. You can use electronic communications to build friendships, keeping current with what is happening in others' lives and sharing what is happening in yours. In the workplace, you can share information quickly and work collaboratively on projects.

Electronic communication lacks two components of good communication: *face-to-face interaction*, with which you can read the other person's nonverbal signals, and the immediate opportunity to make sure that you have a shared meaning. Thus, it is important to choose your words carefully to make sure the message is clear, easy to interpret, and free from communication barriers.

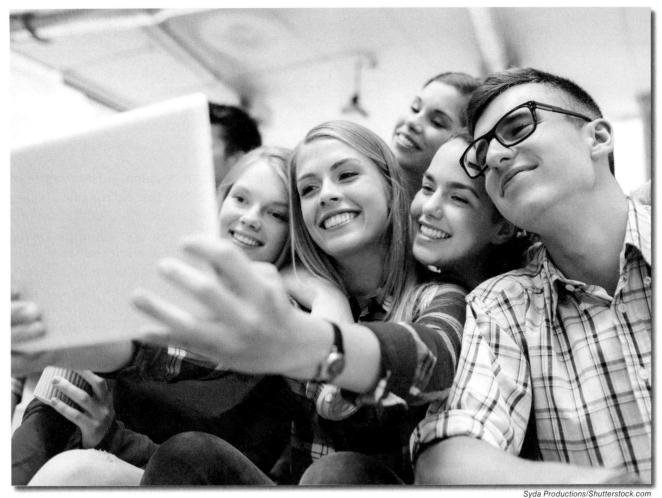

Syda Productions/Shutterstock.com

Figure 7.17 Social media has the advantage of fast communication with several people at once. *In what ways could this also be a disadvantage?*

Your Digital Footprint

As you use various types of communication technology, you are creating a digital footprint. Your **digital footprint** is a collection of information about you and the various websites that you visit over time. When you visit various websites, you can leave behind evidence that you visited that site. When you leave messages that are not appropriate or post pictures or videos that you think are private, realize that *everything* you ever put online can become part of your digital footprint.

The danger of social media is that others may access personal information about you that you do not want shared. Even a close friend might accidentally allow someone to access information you shared online with them. It is safest not to put on your social networking site any personal pictures

or personal information that you would not want made public. Once a message or image is put on social media, it is no longer private. Some colleges and employers check common social media sites for inside information about potential students or future hires. Posts that have inappropriate words or pictures can cost someone admission to a college or a job offer.

Scammers, predators, hackers, and business competitors look through social networking sites for information or people to target. The more information you share, the more likely it will be that someone could try to steal your identity, trick one of your friends into sharing some personal information, or hack into your personal or private accounts. Predators look at your digital footprint and gather so much information that it seems they know you well, care about you, and deserve your

respect and trust. They do not really want to help you, though. They want to take advantage of you.

Using social media with success requires you to use good judgment about whom you communicate with and to limit personal information. For personal sites, you can set privacy settings to limit those who can read your social media messages. Remember, though, that once the information is posted, it is no longer private.

Cyberbullying

Cyberbullying is using technology, such as the Internet or mobile devices, to send hurtful or threatening messages to another person. Cyberbullying can include the following actions:

- spreading lies or rumors through e-mail or instant messaging
- pretending to be someone else online
- registering another person for something online without their permission
- posting pictures of others without their permission

Social media can make it easy for people to be cyberbullies. Through social media, hurtful messages are sent to many people at once, making it difficult to defend yourself from them. Because there is no face-to-face contact, the tendency to not say something hurtful is gone. In addition, cyberbullies can take advantage of the possibility of being *anonymous*, which means that their true identity may not be known. These messages are also stored in your digital footprint and could surface in the future at a time when your ability to achieve life goals could be hurt by them. If you are a victim of cyberbullying, report it to someone in authority. Your parents, school authorities, and law enforcement can help address cyberbullying (**Figure 7.18**).

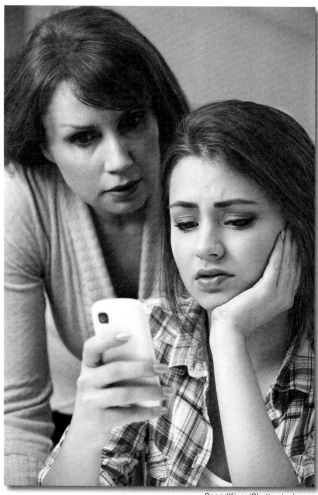

SpeedKingz/Shutterstock.com

Figure 7.18 If you are being cyberbullied, you should tell an adult in authority.

Assess

LESSON 7.3

COMPREHENSION CHECK

1. Why is it difficult to make sure a shared meaning is reached through the written communication process?
2. What skills can help persons effectively communicate their points of view in writing?
3. What strategies can you use to make your school and work written communications effective?
4. List two strategies you can use to make sure you understand written communications.
5. Identify two skills for communicating electronically.

Think About Your Reading

What communication skills could you use to clear up a misunderstanding or an inaccurate message sent through social media?

SKILLS FOR RESOLVING CONFLICTS

Content Terms
Build Vocab

conflict resolution
problem ownership
consensus building
negotiation
compromise

Academic Terms

conflict
escalate

Objectives

After studying this lesson, you will be able to

- **apply** the steps of conflict resolution to a problem.
- **identify** skills used in negotiation and consensus building.
- **explain** the meaning of ethical communication.

Focus Your Reading

1. As you read, list the steps for resolving conflicts and summarize the key concepts under each step.
2. Brainstorm a list of words that are related to each content term. Choose one term and write a paragraph using the content term and the related words you identified.

Many problems occur in relationships because of poor communication. Someone may not send a message clearly. Someone else might not receive a message accurately or may misinterpret it. As a result, people disagree or argue. Feelings get hurt.

When conflict occurs, it is important to restore good communication and positive feelings (**Figure 7.19**). Conflicts that are left unresolved can threaten the health and survival of relationships.

Conflict occurs when any two people disagree on some issue. Some conflict is a normal part of most relationships. Even when people attempt to communicate clearly, conflict can occur. Although conflict occurs for many reasons, it is often due to differences among the persons involved. Friends may argue over where to eat. Family members may disagree over where to vacation. An employer may feel that an employee is spending too much time talking to friends. Because people have different personalities, wants, needs, and values, conflict is common.

People often respond to a disagreement by arguing. They generally use this negative form of communication to protect their self-esteem. Arguing attacks the other person, not the problem. You-statements are commonly used in arguments, and they often include name-calling or blaming. "You are so stupid!" or "You never help out!" are examples. Both are aggressive communication

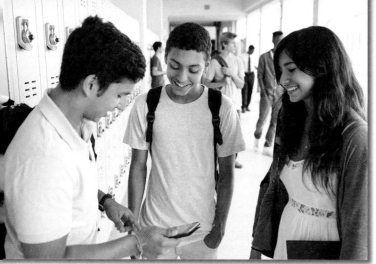
Monkey Business Images/Shutterstock.com

Figure 7.19 Learning conflict resolution skills will help maintain positive relationships. *Why would both speaking and listening skills be important in resolving conflicts?*

because someone is expressing his or her own thoughts without giving any thought to the feelings of others. These statements are destructive to a relationship, as they create more hostility and the real issue underlying the conflict is left unresolved. In fact, these kinds of statements often lead to the argument *escalating*, or getting worse, because the person being addressed often responds in the same way.

Think About Your Reading

In what ways can conflict be harmful to a relationship?

Steps to Resolving Conflicts

Conflicts cannot always be eliminated from close relationships, but they can be controlled—and resolved or settled. How can you successfully solve problems and disagreements in your relationships?

Conflict resolution is one skill that can help you resolve conflicts in a positive way. Using this skill builds relationships. It encourages a better understanding of the other person's point of view. Overall, it helps you and whoever else is involved in the conflict deal with an issue and together reach a fair solution.

The chart in **Figure 7.20** lists some important guidelines to follow when resolving conflicts. These guidelines can set the stage for people to resolve their conflict. Once the stage is set, those involved have to take the following steps to resolve a conflict successfully:

- Identify the problem.
- Identify who owns the problem.
- Accept ownership of the problem.
- Solve the problem.

Identify the Problem

The first step in resolving a conflict is to identify the real issue. Using good communication skills, such as I-statements and active listening, can help identify the problem. These skills need to be used in an assertive manner, where you make observations and express your thoughts and

---

Guidelines for Resolving Conflicts

- Bring the conflict into the open as soon as possible.
- Find the right time and place to discuss the issues.
- Stay calm. Speak with a moderate tone and at a moderate pace.
- Use I-statements to communicate your thoughts, feelings, and ideas.
- Stick to the subject. Do not bring up other issues.
- Be specific in stating the facts that relate to the problem.
- Avoid you-statements. Name-calling, blaming, or accusing messages will not solve the problem.
- Do not walk away from the discussion.
- Recognize and accept the other person's feelings, ideas, and opinions.
- Keep your emotions under control.
- Be an active listener when the other person speaks.
- Try to compromise in reaching a solution.

Figure 7.20 Practicing these guidelines for resolving conflicts promotes positive feelings.

feelings and desires in a way that is considerate of others. It is important to take time to analyze and identify the real problem before taking any action. See **Figure 7.21** for an example of how this can be done.

Identifying the problem does not always involve talking first with another person involved in a problem situation. A person might benefit by talking through an issue with a third party—someone not involved in the situation. That person can listen and perhaps provide some perspective on what is going on in the situation. In the end, though, the people who are involved in the problem situation have to address it together.

Identify Who Owns the Problem

The next step is to identify **problem ownership**. The person bothered by the situation is the one who owns the problem, and that is the person who must be satisfied with the solution.

In Deon's situation, described in Figure 7.21, does the problem affect him, his teacher, or his employer? Is Deon's teacher bothered by Deon's low grades or shortened time schedule? Probably not, so the problem does not belong to her.

Is Deon's employer bothered by his grades or assignments? Probably not, so the employer does not own the problem. Deon is the only one upset over his grades and not getting his assignments done, so he owns the problem. Therefore, Deon is responsible for solving the problem.

If the problem affects or disturbs more than one person, both people share ownership jointly. If Deon chooses to work fewer hours on the job so he can get his assignments done, his employer may get upset. Then Deon's work hours become his employer's problem, too. That could present a joint problem for Deon and his employer.

Accept Ownership of the Problem

Accepting ownership of the problem is the next step in resolving the situation (**Figure 7.22**). Accepting ownership means recognizing that the problem is yours and that the responsibility to solve it is yours. In the example in Figure 7.21, if Deon owns the problem, he can work to change the situation. If he and his employer jointly own the problem, they must work together to find a solution.

You cannot solve another person's problem. If you are bothered by a situation, but the problem

---

Identifying the Problem

Deon has gotten low grades on his most recent English assignments. He thinks this is because his teacher is assigning too much homework. He decides to confront his teacher, which begins the conflict.

"I am upset because you give us so many assignments," Deon begins. He has identified his feelings and given one possible reason for them.

The teacher reflects his message by saying, "I see that you are upset with the amount of work you have in this class." Then the teacher asks Deon a question to help Deon identify his real problem: "Do you think that the work is the problem?" Deon's teacher continues to help him identify the problem: "Is it your low grades? Is it my high expectations? Is it your time schedule? You mentioned that your boss recently gave you two additional hours of work each day."

After thinking about each issue, Deon identifies his time schedule as the basic problem. He does not have time to get all his work done.

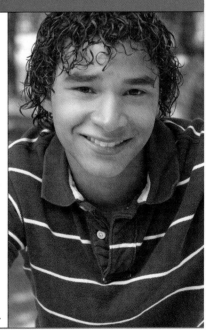

Volt Collection/Shutterstock.com

Figure 7.21 *What could Deon have done on his own to better identify his problem?*

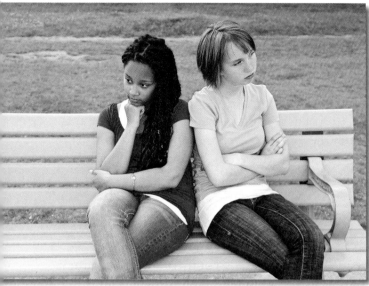
Elena Elisseeva/Shutterstock.com

Figure 7.22 People need to own a problem in order to solve it. *What defense mechanisms might a person use to avoid taking ownership of a problem?*

belongs to another person, that person needs to accept ownership of the problem in order to solve it. For example, if Deon's parents are upset by his low grade in the English class, they still cannot solve the problem. They can put pressure on Deon, though, to own the problem and take steps to solve it.

If two people own the problem, they must work together to find a solution. Sometimes only one person accepts the responsibility for a joint problem. In this case, reaching a solution that is fair to both people is often difficult.

Think About Your Reading

Why might it be hard for a person to accept ownership of a problem?

Solve the Problem

Once you take ownership of a problem, you can take steps to solve it. The decision-making process detailed in **Figure 7.23** can be applied to solving problems. If you are solving the problem by yourself, meaning you are the only one owning it, you will identify and evaluate your options, choose a solution, and carry it out. If a problem

is owned by two people, they can work together through each step.

In Deon's case, he identified his time schedule as his major problem. What are his alternatives? He could work fewer hours so he could study more. He could drop the English class and try to add a class with fewer assignments. Finally, he could ask his teacher to give him an extension on the class. Then he could finish it in summer school.

How beneficial would each alternative be for Deon? He must carefully consider his choices. If he chooses to work fewer hours, he will have less money. He also will have to discuss his work hours with his employer. His employer may get upset, and Deon may lose his job.

The second choice could give him a little more time. Switching classes, however, would be difficult this late in the semester. English is a required course, so Deon must complete it successfully at some time.

The third alternative would enable him to keep working now and continue with the class. It would take him longer to complete the course if he went to summer school. Also, taking summer school would make it impossible for him to work full time during the summer.

After thinking about each alternative, Deon decides the first one is best for him. He wants to finish the English course now. He feels he can get along without the extra money. He then takes steps to carry out his decision.

Deon knows he must discuss his work hours with his employer to carry out his solution. If he is going to work fewer hours, his employer will be affected. If his employer gets upset, Deon will have to work with his employer to find a solution

Solving a Problem
1. Identify the problem.
2. Identify the alternative solutions.
3. Evaluate the alternatives.
4. Choose the best solution.
5. Implement the solution.
6. Evaluate the solution. Was it effective in solving the problem?

Figure 7.23 The steps of the decision-making process can be used to work out a solution to a conflict.

satisfactory to both. If he can find a coworker who can pick up some of the additional hours, he might offer to work some of the extra hours, but not every day.

Solving a Problem as a Group

If a problem is owned by several persons, such as a work team, then they all need to use teamwork and work together to solve the problem. The team may identify several alternatives and have each person research an option. Then the team comes together to share their information and discuss the pros and cons of each alternative.

When a team or group is choosing an alternative, the best solution is sometimes identified through consensus building. **Consensus building** is a process in which a group works together to find a solution that is acceptable to all involved. It may not meet everyone's top priorities, but the solution is one that all can accept (**Figure 7.24**). To carry out consensus building, the group discusses each option as a group, identifying all the pros and cons of each choice. If group members agree that one choice has the most positives, it is chosen. If there is a question about which choice is the best, then the team narrows down the options by eliminating ones that do not work for all participants. Then the members reevaluate the list of pros versus cons until they come up with an option that works for everyone.

Negotiating a Solution

When a problem is jointly owned and cannot be readily solved, those involved may need to use negotiation to resolve the situation. **Negotiation** is a communication process in which people take turns sending and receiving messages with the goal of reaching an agreeable solution. To do this, all people involved need to send clear and accurate I-statements. When they are receivers of

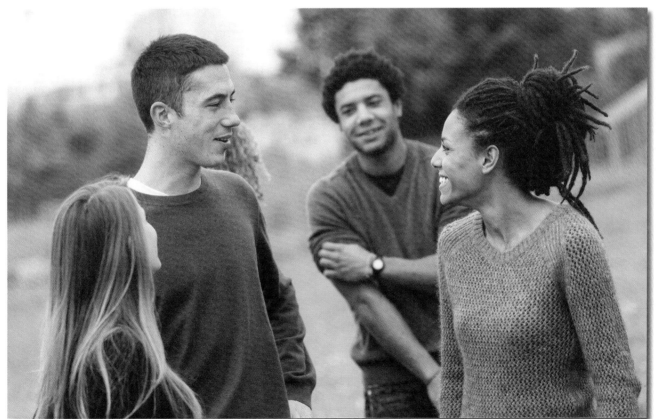

Figure 7.24 When members of a team work together to solve a problem, several steps are needed to evaluate all the alternatives and identify a solution that works for everyone. *Why would solving a problem through consensus building result in positive attitudes from a work team?*

messages, they both need to understand and consider the messages others are sending before they respond. When more than one person owns a problem, they may need to negotiate in each stage of the problem-solving process. Maintaining open communication in each stage is critical for success.

Sometimes an impartial person can step in and help with negotiations. A couple may ask a counselor to help them negotiate. Friends may help with negotiating a solution. The negotiator acts as a middle person, helping each person express thoughts and feelings clearly and making sure the other person uses active listening skills. The negotiator in effect encourages each person to use good communication skills as each side presents its point of view related to each step in the problem-solving process.

Think About Your Reading

What attitudes would make it difficult for two people to negotiate effectively?

Reaching an agreeable solution is not always easy. One-sided thinking can hinder negotiation. Sometimes one person takes a stand and refuses to recognize the other's point of view. When that happens, a solution that is satisfactory to both cannot be reached.

People can overcome obstacles that arise during the negotiation process through compromise. **Compromise** is a give-and-take method that allows all people involved to express themselves. It is an effective way to resolve conflicts. No one person wins or loses. Everyone gives in a little to reach a solution that is workable to all. Compromise protects and helps maintain each person's self-esteem. Each person recognizes the worth of others' opinions, feelings, and desires. People who feel accepted are more likely to work toward an agreeable solution.

Using Ethical Communication

Many problems that occur in relationships can be avoided when all concerned use ethical communication. In ethical communications, your interactions with other people show evidence of personal ethics. Your communication can be counted on to be truthful. Your words and actions show you are dependable, responsible, and caring. Others will be more open to sharing with you when they feel they can trust you to recognize and be willing to accept their best interest, not just your own (**Figure 7.25**). Ethical communication helps promote compromise and find solutions acceptable to all involved.

LESSON 7.4

Assess

COMPREHENSION CHECK

1. Explain why conflict resolution can help people handle conflict in a positive way.
2. In a conflict situation, what three steps must occur before the problem can be solved?
3. In conflict resolution, who must own the problem for negotiation to take place?
4. What takes place during the negotiation process?
5. How does consensus building increase a group's ability to solve a joint problem?
6. Explain how compromise can help resolve conflicts.

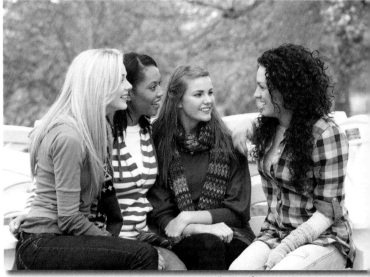

oliveromg/Shutterstock.com

Figure 7.25 Ethical communication fosters positive relationships between people.

CHAPTER 7 REVIEW AND ASSESSMENT

CHAPTER SUMMARY

The communication process involves sending and receiving messages. As a sender, you need skills in sending clear, accurate messages. As a receiver, you need to listen well and interpret messages correctly. In nonverbal communication, you send messages without using words. Through body language, you express your thoughts, feelings, and emotions to others. In verbal communication, you use words. You can improve your ability to express yourself clearly by using I-statements. Besides sending clear messages, you need skills in receiving messages. Active listening is a skill that helps you interpret and understand messages clearly.

Your self-esteem, emotional state, and environment can affect the way messages are communicated. In addition, certain factors can get in the way of good communication, such as a closed mind, mixed messages, prejudice, and cultural differences.

Good written communication skills, including reading, writing, and electronic communications, are important for success in relationships throughout life. Because there is no face-to-face interaction, you will need to choose your words carefully to make sure your message is clear, easy to interpret, and free from communication barriers. Social media makes it possible to share messages with many people at once, thus increasing the possibility of mass miscommunication.

Good communication skills are needed to resolve conflicts in a positive way. Conflict resolution is a step-by-step skill you can develop to resolve conflicts successfully and build relationships. First, identify the problem. Next, identify and accept problem ownership. Finally, reach an agreeable solution to the problem through negotiation and compromise.

VOCABULARY ACTIVITIES

1. Create a Venn diagram and label the two outer areas *Good Communication* and *Bad Communication*. Label the middle area, where the two circles overlap, *Either*. Place the following terms in the appropriate area.

Content Terms

active listening (7.1)
blaming (7.2)
body language (7.1)
channel (7.1)
clarifying (7.1)
communication (7.1)
communication
  style (7.1)
compromise (7.4)
conflict resolution (7.4)
consensus
  building (7.4)
context (7.1)
cyberbullying (7.3)
decoding (7.1)
digital footprint (7.3)
direct eye contact (7.1)
distracting (7.2)
encoding (7.1)
I-statement (7.1)
negotiation (7.4)
nonverbal
  communication (7.1)
paraphrasing (7.1)
passive listening (7.1)
placating (7.2)
problem
  ownership (7.4)
receiver (7.1)
reflecting (7.1)
sender (7.1)
social media (7.3)
texting (7.3)
verbal
  communication (7.1)
you-statement (7.1)

2. Write one sentence about communication using each of the terms, but leave a blank where the term goes. Exchange your sentences with a partner and fill in the correct terms in your partner's sentences. Review each other's work.

Academic Terms

aggressive (7.1)
anonymous (7.3)
assertive (7.1)
author (7.3)
conflict (7.4)
escalate (7.4)
face-to-face
  interaction (7.3)
feedback (7.1)
monitor (7.1)
personal space (7.1)
point of view (7.1)
prejudice (7.2)
sensitive (7.2)

ASSESS

Your Knowledge

3. What types of nonverbal and verbal messages help a sender and receiver have the same understanding of the message?
4. What are four factors that could interfere with or prevent good communication?
5. What are the steps for resolving conflict?

Your Understanding

6. How does the written communication process produce shared meanings?
7. How could you-statements affect the communication between two people?
8. How could low self-esteem affect a person's verbal and nonverbal communication?
9. How do negative communication patterns affect relationships?

Your Skills

10. Express your own thoughts, feelings, and intentions by using five different types of I-statements.
11. Give an example of how you could employ active listening skills when using a communications technology to help a friend make a decision.

12. What steps would you take to solve a problem of failing grades in a class?

CRITICAL THINKING

13. **Make Inferences.** Record the various nonverbal techniques that your teachers use during a typical day. Using a spreadsheet, list the teachers and the different types of nonverbal techniques. Tally the total number of different techniques used by each teacher (not the total number of times each technique was used). Summarize your findings in a short paragraph, comparing the techniques with your opinions of each teacher's effectiveness.

14. **Evaluate Findings.** As a class, identify several conflict situations (consider personal experiences, current events, or historical references). Choose one of the conflicts and describe how it was resolved. Evaluate the techniques used to handle the conflict, citing information from the text. Explain how the steps in conflict resolution and negotiation did or could have enhanced the process. *Group option*: In small groups, create a role-play to illustrate how the steps of conflict resolution and negotiation could be applied to solve this problem in a team setting.

15. **Compare Results.** Assess your ability to be an active listener. Try an experiment in which you use the active listening skills of clarifying, paraphrasing, and reflecting when someone is trying to share a confidential message with you. Compare this conversation to one in which you deliberately avoid looking at the speaker and remain passive as he or she talks. In a paragraph, describe the differences in how these two conversations arrived or did not arrive at shared meanings. In your paragraph, do not reveal the confidential information you were given. Just analyze the differences, if any, in results.

16. **Categorize Findings.** Attend a school event or activity and make a list of the different types of body language you observe. Beside each type, identify the nonverbal messages that were communicated. Put each message and your interpretation on a small card. Hand it to the person who sent the nonverbal message. Explain that you are doing a research project, and ask the person to respond to the accuracy of the message. Identify the gaps between the message you received and the message that was sent. Write a paragraph explaining your experiment and the results of your research.

CORE SKILLS

17. **Writing.** Identify and summarize a situation that upset you. Using the self-awareness circle, write I-statements to express your personal observations, thoughts, feelings, intentions, and actions related to this situation.

18. **Writing.** Pretend your report card lists your grade in a class as one level lower than what you understood it would be. Using the self-awareness circle, write five different I-statements that you could use to express yourself positively to your teacher.

19. **Social Studies, Writing, Speaking.** Write a paragraph explaining how different cultural backgrounds in your community could result in different patterns of communication and difficulty in communicating a shared meaning. Discuss how these difficulties could affect stereotypes and prejudice in your community. Suggest ways community leaders could help build healthy relationships between members of different cultural groups.

20. **Writing.** Use a digital device to design and print a poster illustrating the importance of good electronic communication techniques. *Choice*: Choose a target audience: students, families in counseling, workers on the job, or another. Design a poster for your target audience and present using good verbal, nonverbal, written, and electronic communication.

21. **Research, Writing.** Search online to research the communication skills that are used by a counselor. In a paragraph, identify the skills that you feel are most important for a counselor to be effective on the job.

22. **Social Studies, Writing.** Working in small groups, research words or expressions that are unique to your particular culture, community, or geographic area. Use online resources to identify other possible meanings for these expressions. Present your findings to the class in a skit.

CAREER READINESS

23. **Communicating Information.** Choose an on-the-job situation in which communication barriers result in problems between employees or between an employee and a customer. Write a short scene to illustrate the problem, ways to overcome such barriers, and strategies for improving communication on the job. *Choice*: Work with one or more partners and role-play the problem and solution for your class.

CHAPTER 8

DEVELOPING RELATIONSHIP SKILLS

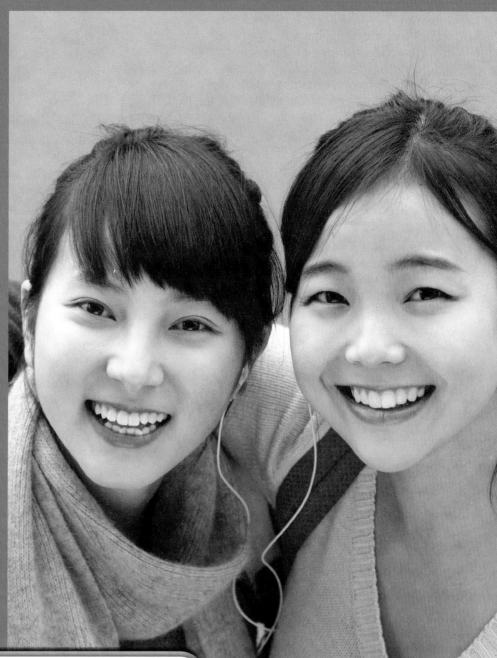

Reading Prep

Arrange a study session to read the chapter aloud with a classmate. At the end of each lesson, discuss any concepts you wish to discuss further. Take notes of words you would like to discuss in class.

Key Questions

Questions to answer as you study this chapter:

- How can you develop good friendships?
- How can you develop strong, meaningful family relationships?
- How can you develop positive, healthy relationships with others in your community?

While studying this chapter, look for the activity icon to:

- **build** vocabulary with e-flash cards, matching activities, and vocabulary games; and
- **assess** what you learn by completing the lesson comprehension checks online.

www.g-wlearning.com/humanservices/

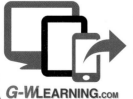

©iStock.com/bo1982

Lesson 8.1 Developing Friendships
Lesson 8.2 Relationships in the Family
Lesson 8.3 Relationships in the Community

AFTER STUDYING THIS CHAPTER, YOU WILL

KNOW:

- Qualities of a good friend.
- Steps in developing good friendships.
- Factors that can affect different relationships.

UNDERSTAND:

- How good friendships can help a person grow to maturity.
- How negative peer pressure can hinder the growth of close friendships.
- How diversity can contribute to a strong community.

BE ABLE TO DO:

- Analyze a relationship for the qualities needed to develop it into a close friendship.
- Respond with assertiveness to negative peer pressure.
- Negotiate a solution to a family problem.

GETTING STARTED

Everyone was having a great time at the party except Dee. She had recently moved to the area and did not know anyone well. Her only friend at school, Cary, had invited her to the party, but then got sick at the last minute. Dee sat alone, embarrassed and wondering, How will I ever get through this? No one wants to talk to me.

As she gazed across the room, Dee recognized Tosha from her biology class. She was standing alone, too. Dee smiled and Tosha waved back. She probably doesn't like being alone either. What can I lose by trying? Dee thought. She took a deep breath and decided to start a conversation.

As it turned out, Dee and Tosha had much in common and became close friends. Dee was glad she had taken the first step in starting a new friendship.

Everyone needs a friend—including you. A friendship is one type of personal relationship that can help you grow as a person. Friends help you learn and understand more about yourself and others. Friendships usually grow between people who have much in common, but other qualities also matter. Your peers will most likely be the source of your closest friendships.

Families are also an important source of close, lifetime relationships. The shared backgrounds, common views, and similar interests help family members form special bonds. With so much in common, family members often become close friends.

The way you relate to other people in your community and at work will affect your quality of life, too. Understanding this importance will help you develop successful relationships with others.

Skills for developing personal relationships can be learned with practice. Developing these skills will benefit you in many ways. Relationship skills will help you get along with other people, no matter where you are: at home, at school, at work, or in your community. They will help you choose friends who can help you grow. You will feel more in control of yourself and the direction your life path is going. Your ability to develop long-lasting relationships will increase. Your future relationships in your family, with your friends, and in the community will be affected in a positive way.

DEVELOPING FRIENDSHIPS

Content Terms
Build Vocab

acquaintance
code of conduct
icebreaker
blind spot
cyber-acquaintance
bullying

Academic Terms

empathy
rapport
conform

Objectives

After studying this lesson, you will be able to

- **describe** the qualities of a friend.
- **recognize** ways that friendships can help a person grow.
- **explain** how to develop a close friendship.
- **distinguish** between positive and negative effects of peer pressure.

Focus Your Reading

1. Create a chart with three columns. In the first column, write down what you already know about developing friendships. In the second column, write down what you want to know about the topic. As you read, write ideas that you learn about the topic in the third column.

2. Identify a person or situation that exhibits or reflects the meaning of each content term. Explain how that person or situation fits the term.

Throughout your life, you will probably experience many different types of relationships. You will have relationships with your family, teachers, peers, coworkers, and acquaintances. You will have friendships ranging from casual to close. All relationships can affect your personal growth and development.

Friendships usually grow between people who share common interests, goals, and outlooks on life. Developing close friendships takes more than just sharing similarities and interests, though. Close friends have certain qualities in common that contribute to the growth of the friendship.

Types of Friendships

Think of all the people you know. Some you may have just met, while others are your closest friends. You will likely have many different friendships in your lifetime; friendships can be grouped into a few types.

Acquaintances are people you know, but who are not your close friends. Some acquaintances are casual, such as students you say hello to when passing in the hall. You may see other acquaintances more frequently. Questions such as "What are you doing now?" or "What classes are you taking?" inspire a more involved conversation. Communication with acquaintances typically remains brief.

Good friends are people whom you see often and spend enough time with to know quite well. Good friends share common interests and experiences (**Figure 8.1**). They also share personal thoughts and feelings. This mutual sharing shows that some trust exists between them.

Usually, only a few people in your life are considered *close friends*. A close friend may also be considered your *best friend*. You know that close friends will not make fun of you or laugh at your ideas. You can trust these friends to care about what is best for you. You probably have many acquaintances, but only a few close friends.

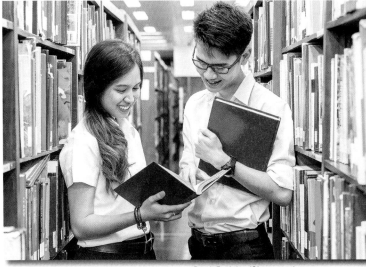

Figure 8.1 Discussing homework assignments and school sports are examples of information you might share with a good friend. *What are your favorite topics to talk about?*

of a friend are described in **Figure 8.2**. The more these qualities exist in a friendship, the closer that friendship will be.

Think About Your Reading

Think about your relationships and classify people as acquaintances, good friends, or close friends. Which group is the largest? Why do you think that is?

Think About Your Reading

What qualities do your friends have that you would like to see in yourself?

What Is a Friend?

What qualities do you look for in a friend? Do you look for someone who understands and accepts you? Do you look for someone who is open and honest with you, someone who makes you feel good, or someone you can trust? Each of your friends is likely to have some of these qualities. These qualities define a **code of conduct**, or a pattern of behaving and acting that you expect from people who are your friends.

For a friendship to develop, you need to have certain qualities as well. Think about it; if you are looking for these traits in a friend, other people are, too. Both people need to develop similar traits for a friendship to grow. The important characteristics

Why Do You Need Friends?

Friendships take time and commitment to develop. Friends care for, encourage, and support each other. People need to contribute to the relationship for a friendship to grow.

The reward makes the effort worthwhile; friendships offer lifetime benefits. Good friendships help you mature intellectually, emotionally, and socially in the following ways:

- *Friendships can help you know and understand your own thoughts and feelings.* With friends, you share ideas, dreams, and plans for the future. Friends try to provide open and honest feedback. They can help you think through decisions and solve your personal problems. In this way, they help you

grow intellectually. Sometimes a friend can help you interpret your feelings. "You seem hurt. She really offended you, didn't she?" Such feedback shows active listening by your friend and can help you grow emotionally as you identify and then deal with your real feelings.

A Friend Is...
Someone with whom you can talk. You can share your thoughts and feelings and know you are understood. Because you have much in common, you both communicate clearly and with ease. You understand each other's nonverbal messages. You interpret each other's meanings in a similar way.
Someone who accepts you. A friend accepts you just as you are and accepts the real you. You do not have to act like someone you are not. You feel comfortable when you are together. A friend does not put you down, laugh at you, or make fun of you when you make a mistake. Instead, a friend makes you feel good about being you.
Someone who supports you. When you need support, a friend gives you the help you need. A friend may encourage you to grow and to do your best by helping yourself. If you have a personal problem, you can count on a friend to help you through it.
Someone you can trust. When you share your inner thoughts and feelings, you know a friend will be reliable and honest. A friend will not use what you said in a negative way. A friend will keep your thoughts in confidence. You can count on that person to look out for your well-being.
Someone who is open. For a friendship to grow, both people must take the risk to share their thoughts and feelings. A friend is someone you can count on to be sincere and to share his or her concerns with you.

Figure 8.2 Friendships develop and grow between people who share many of the same personal qualities. *Could a person be a close friend without having all of these traits?*

- ***Friendships can help you accept yourself as a person and increase your self-esteem.*** Everyone needs to feel important and worthwhile. Good friends will listen to you, accept your ideas, and include you in activities. They like you for who you are. You, in turn, feel comfortable and relaxed with them. By accepting you and helping you feel loved, they help you grow emotionally.

- ***Friendships can help you develop empathy.*** What is empathy? *Empathy* is an emotion in which you feel what another person is feeling. You feel as though you are having the same experience as that person. Empathy helps you appreciate others and their different perspectives. You become more sensitive to the thoughts and feelings of others. You can develop empathy as you listen to how others think, learn how they feel, and respond with a caring attitude. Thus, having friends and feeling empathy helps you grow intellectually, emotionally, and socially (**Figure 8.3**).

- ***Friendships can help you increase your communication skills.*** Friends usually spend a great deal of time talking to each other.

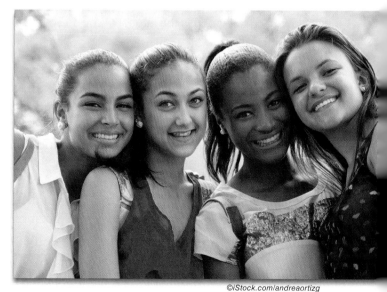
©iStock.com/andreaortizg

Figure 8.3 Friendships help people develop social and emotional skills while meeting needs for companionship. *How could spending time with a group of friends with different perspectives impact your growth and development?*

They share and listen to each other's personal thoughts. They try to understand each other, listen to each other's point of view, and share feedback that helps both people grow. Learning to communicate clearly with friends is an important skill that helps you get along with others and grow socially.

- *Friendships can help you learn to work cooperatively.* When friends cooperate, they share their ideas and resolve their differences. They consider each other's opinions and viewpoints before choosing a solution or plan of action that is agreeable to all concerned. In a friendship, reaching an agreement is easier because friends develop a *rapport*—a feeling of connectedness—with each other. They like each other, have much in common, and accept and respect each other. These qualities make it easier to cooperate. Concern for friends' welfare also makes cooperation easier. A friendship makes a good environment for growing socially and learning to work with others.

- *Friendships can satisfy the need for companionship.* Most people have a need for others with whom they can spend time. They need to feel close to other people, to care for others and feel cared for by others, and to love and be loved. These needs continue throughout the life cycle. Close friends can meet many of these needs and help you grow socially and emotionally as a result.

- *Friendships can help you prepare for future long-term relationships.* Your close friendships will serve as a guide in future relationships. As you mature, you develop more caring, sharing relationships. You appreciate and accept your friends for their unique qualities. You care about them, their growth, and their well-being. You expect them to treat you the same way. These mature qualities contribute to close long-lasting adult relationships, even marriage. Who helps you grow as a person? Who encourages you to be the best you can be? Who makes you feel confident, secure, and supported? Many of the same qualities found in a close friendship will help create a lasting marriage.

Think About Your Reading

How do your friends help you grow intellectually? emotionally? socially? How do you help them grow in these ways?

Skills for Developing Friendships

How can you develop a friendship? What qualities do you have for building friendships? Knowing how to develop a friendship is a skill you will always use. You can help a friendship grow in several ways (**Figure 8.4**).

Qualities for Developing Close Friendships
I am friendly.
I can accept others.
I can accept others' viewpoints even if they are different from mine.
I can reveal myself to others.
I have rapport with others.
I like most people.
I feel that most people like me.
I am honest with others.
I have trust in others.
I can keep information a secret.
I can relate person to person.
I like to benefit others.
I like to make other people feel good about themselves.
I enjoy rewarding others.
I am dependable.
I like to learn from others.
I am willing to share power with others.

Figure 8.4 Each of these personal qualities can help people develop close friendships with others. *Are there areas listed above that you need to work at and develop?*

Be Friendly

"He who has friends must show himself friendly." This old proverb still applies. To make friends, you must interact with other people in a friendly way. Smile and make direct eye contact when you talk to people. Being friendly shows other people that you believe they are worth getting to know. It shows respect for them.

How can you start a conversation? First, introduce yourself, "Hi, I'm James." The other person probably will respond with his or her name. Then follow up with an **icebreaker**, a short interaction that helps you connect with another person. What you use for an icebreaker will depend on the situation. The weather is a topic used for an icebreaker just about anywhere and anytime: "Sure is a nice day today." If you are at school or at an event, you can talk about what is going on. The point is to choose something that invites the other person to respond to get the conversation going.

Think About Your Reading

What are some common icebreakers that you have used or heard other people use?

Develop Rapport

After a friendly greeting, try to develop rapport. Work to create an atmosphere in which the other person feels comfortable and wants to talk. For rapport to exist, both people need to sense each other's friendliness, warmth, and interest in each other (**Figure 8.5**).

Saying something interesting can start the conversation and engage the other person. A basic

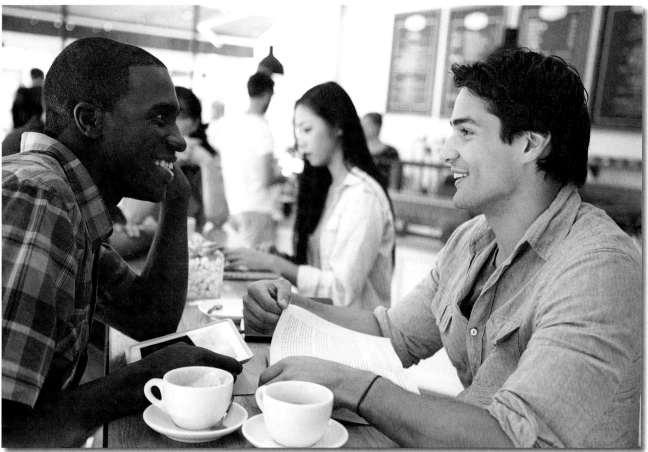

Monkey Business Images/Shutterstock.com

Figure 8.5 To develop rapport, information needs to be shared back and forth as you try to identify what you have in common. *What type of feedback will encourage the other person to keep talking? What feedback might end the conversation?*

knowledge of several topics can help you move the conversation forward. Start with some easy-to-answer questions: "Where do you go to school?", "What classes are you taking this semester?", or "Where do you live?" Questions that require more than a "yes" or "no" response encourage the other person to talk. Use active listening so you can respond to the person's comments and give feedback that will encourage the person to keep talking with you.

The other part of developing rapport is sharing some information about yourself, such as where you live, how your classes are going, or your interest in a sport. Another way to develop rapport is to use direct eye contact. A warm smile shows the person that you are interested in becoming friends. Appropriate gestures can be helpful, too—think of what you know about body language.

The goal of developing rapport is to promote conversation and sharing, so you can learn what you have in common. Most of the sharing at this stage is informational, as you get to know each other. The more you have in common, the easier it will be to share feelings and thoughts and develop a deeper friendship.

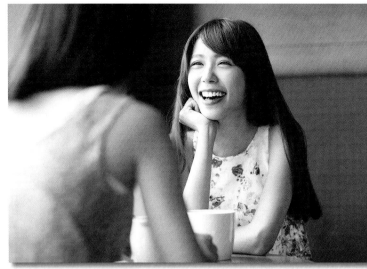
Tom Wang/Shutterstock.com

Figure 8.6 Topics that you and another person have in common are good starting points for developing a friendship.

and feelings. This sharing goes beyond the general information that you used to start the relationship and develop rapport. To be open with someone, you risk being accepted or rejected. A fear of rejection may cause reluctance to speak. You may feel safer by hiding your inner thoughts. To develop a close relationship, however, you must take the risk of sharing your inner self. The benefit comes when others accept what you say and choose to share personal information with you in return. From that point, your friendship can grow deeper.

Think About Your Reading

How does paying close attention to a person when he or she is talking help build rapport?

Share Yourself

To develop a deeper friendship, you will need to spend time together. Areas of common interest will help you find activities to do together. You may have classes together in school, similar leisure activities, similar passions for sports teams, similar religious beliefs, similar goals for your neighborhood, similar career goals, or the same employer (**Figure 8.6**).

Common interests or experiences can provide activities that bring you together, but you will need to find time for personal sharing to take the friendship further. For relationships to grow, you need to share your personal opinions, thoughts,

Build Trust

Honesty and reliability are important parts of trust—and of making a friendship grow. Most people are not willing to trust a person who says one thing and does another. Trust between people develops in stages over time. You can start building trust by sharing information that is not threatening or too personal. In the next stage, you can check for the other person's response. Does he or she show a caring attitude and concern for how you are feeling? Does your friend share similar thoughts with you? In being trustworthy, your friend is helping to build the relationship.

Finally, you evaluate what your friend does with the shared information. Trust takes time to develop, but it can easily be destroyed. If the

information is used in a negative way, trust is broken. If a friend makes fun of a secret you share or embarrasses you, the trust is broken. Similarly, if you violate your word to keep a friend's secret, you will destroy that friend's trust in you.

Respond with Empathy

Learning to respond with empathy can help you develop closer relationships. Try to identify with the other person's feelings. Show that you are sensitive to the other person's concerns and are interested in his or her well-being. Your empathy will encourage the other person to continue sharing personal thoughts and feelings with you. The other person will feel accepted. You will build esteem in the other person. You will develop trust and feelings of closeness.

You can develop your skills for showing empathy with practice. Use good active listening skills. Using eye contact, focus on the speaker. Show a genuine interest in what the speaker is saying through your body language. A smile, a nod of the head, or a raised eyebrow—all can show that you are interested and concerned. A touch on the hand, an arm around the shoulder, or a hug can also send messages of caring and concern when the situation suggests they are needed (**Figure 8.7**).

Verbal feedback can also show empathy. Phrases like "Tell me about it," "Go ahead, I'm listening," or "Let me hear the whole story" tell another person you are really interested in what he or she has to say. Phrases such as "I see," "I understand," and "good idea" assure the sender that you are listening with concern.

Be Open to Growth

In a close relationship, you can learn more about yourself as well as the other person. As you share personal information with each other, you may become aware of **blind spots**. Your blind spots are limits to your knowledge or understanding. As a relationship grows closer, each person can point out the other's blind spots without fear of rejection. Both grow from the experience.

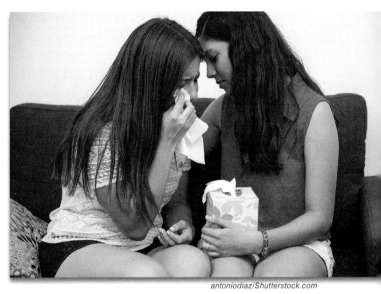

Figure 8.7 Showing empathy to a friend will help you develop closer relationships. *What communication skills will help you send a message that you care about the other person's well-being?*

Think About Your Reading

Why might a person become defensive when you point out a blind spot to him or her?

The Goal of a Close Relationship

Not all friendships become close. The goal of a close relationship is to experience fulfillment through sharing. Sometimes the sharing is intellectual, emotional, spiritual, or physical. A marital relationship can provide closeness in all these areas. Other types of relationships may provide closeness in one or two areas.

Developing a close relationship requires a commitment from both people. That means taking time to get to know each other. Both participants need to share openly and to respond with empathy. Both need to be committed to helping each other grow.

Some relationships may grow in closeness over a period of time but eventually end. Sometimes trust is broken and, as a result, one person feels hurt. If the conflict is not resolved in an acceptable way, the relationship may end.

Some close relationships may change over time as people grow and mature. People who were very close may grow apart later as their lives change. They may have less time to spend together. Their emotional needs may be met through other relationships. Relationships sometimes end or change to a different level.

Think About Your Reading

In what ways would it be more difficult to develop rapport with someone through a long-distance relationship? In what ways would it be easier?

Developing Friendships with Communication Technology

Some of your acquaintances may be **cyber-acquaintances**, people you have met online. Sharing information online is a quick way of finding out if you have something in common. The relationship may seem to develop quickly, and the level of sharing may deepen faster than if you were meeting face-to-face.

The skills of being friendly, developing rapport, sharing, building trust, and responding with empathy can all develop through electronic communication. The downside of electronic communication is the absence of the face-to-face contact. Is either person lying? How can you tell?

In day-to-day living situations, you can see what the other person does with information you have shared. You can see how they respond in a class, how they relate to their parents, or how they work on the job. You can identify whether they are *ethical communicators*—that is, whether their communications are truthful and match their actions.

While the speed, frequency, and ease of using communication technology make it attractive for developing a relationship into a friendship, it is important to be aware of the dangers involved. Meeting people through mutual friends or through shared interactions at work or school provides the safest source for starting relationships.

Peer Relationships

You will most likely develop your closest friendships with others in your peer group. Your peers are at the same stage of their life paths as you. They often have similar needs, concerns, interests, and goals. Peers can both positively and negatively affect each other.

Peer Pressure

Peers often affect the way others in the same age group think or act (**Figure 8.8**). People—particularly teens—want to feel part of the group, which often has its own code of conduct for those who belong to the group. In order to belong, they must often *conform*, or adapt to certain standards of appearance, dress, and behavior in their peer group. Sometimes you will agree with these standards and what the group wants to do. In fact, when the group's standards and conduct are positive, peer pressure can have beneficial effects on your behavior. For example, if most students in a class are taking part in a community service project, their participation can persuade one or two more hesitant students to join in.

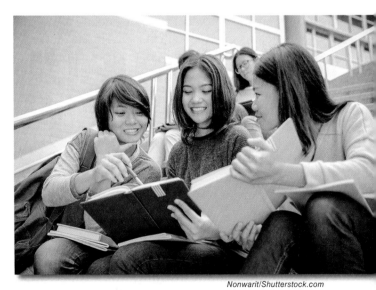

Nonwarit/Shutterstock.com

Figure 8.8 Peers can influence each other to act like the entire group. *What evidence of peer pressure can you identify in this group? What evidence is there that shows these peers think and act independently?*

Think About Your Reading

What examples can you think of where peer pressure is positive?

At other times, however, peer pressure may be negative. Peers may pressure a teen to do something that goes against his or her values or goals. They may want a teen to join in activities that could be harmful to health and well-being or to that of others. Sometimes people want friendships so badly that they give in to negative peer pressure. In truth, close friendships are hindered by negative peer pressure. Such pressure does not encourage the open, honest sharing or acceptance of individual differences that is central to close friendships. In addition, negative peer pressure threatens the personal growth of all concerned. If friendship is based on conformity, then when the person stops conforming, the friendship will be disrupted. That is not the way true friends behave.

Resisting Negative Peer Pressure

The *passive* way to handle negative peer pressure is to give in to it. Teens who take that approach may be violating their principles and harming their well-being—and they are certainly not building strong friendships. The best way to respond to negative peer pressure is to use *assertive* behavior. In assertive behavior, you let peers know what you think and feel by using good

REAL-LIFE SCENARIO

Peer Pressure

The telephone rang and Marc's dad picked it up. "Would you please come down to the police station?" an officer asked. "Your son has been picked up for stealing a car."

Marc's dad turned pale and swallowed hard as he responded, "Yes, we'll be there." His mind raced as he wondered how this all came about.

Marc was outgoing and friendly. He liked to be with people. He wanted his peers to like him and to include him in their groups. He especially wanted to belong to a certain popular group. To try to get the popular group to notice him, Marc would pick on others in his classes. He would break a pencil or rip a notebook. He would poke others in the back or push them in the hall. He would laugh at them, tease and make fun of them, and call them names. Instead of making friends, Marc was becoming a bully. Few people liked him.

Rebelling against authority was Marc's next attempt at getting the attention and friendship he wanted. He ignored his parents' requests and did not carry out his chores at home. He did not bother with homework. Marc's parents were frustrated with his lack of responsibility. They pleaded with him to do better. They ordered him to do what they asked. They yelled at him for getting poor grades, telling him all the consequences of failing in school.

Marc tuned them out. He also ignored his teachers and talked constantly in class. He proudly served his detentions, which brought him more attention. The attention he was getting, though, was from other students who were also serving detention. They started to hang out together, looking for new excitement and activities to try. This time Marc and his friends had gone too far—and had ended up at the police station.

For Discussion

1. Why did Marc's attempt to build friendships fail? What factors did he not consider?
2. How did Marc respond to not being part of the popular peer group? What other responses might a young person make when important relationships fall apart?
3. What effect did Marc's bullying activities have on his self-esteem?
4. What characteristics drew Marc to his new friends? What aspect of the relationship provided evidence that these friends did not have the qualities of real friendship?
5. What communication techniques did Marc's family use to try and solve Marc's problem? Identify some examples of ways they could have responded with empathy.

communication skills. You use I-statements to explain what you think, how you feel, what you desire, and what you intend to do without putting others down. You use eye contact and look directly at the person to whom you are talking. You speak clearly with even tones. If necessary, you walk away.

People who are assertive do not let others take advantage of them. They are not afraid to disagree, say "no," or express what they believe. They are not afraid to ask questions to make sure they understand a message. They communicate clearly, yet show respect for others' thoughts and feelings.

If peers pressure you to do something you really do not want to do, try an assertive response. Tell them, "No, I'm not interested." Stand firm for what you think is right for you. The more you assert your own thoughts and say what you believe, the easier it will become.

Handling Bullying

Sometimes negative peer pressure takes the form of **bullying**, or using *aggressive* behavior to intentionally harm or intimidate another person. People may bully in several ways (**Figure 8.9**). Any form of bullying or aggressive behavior harms the growth of a relationship. It destroys feelings of caring, nurturing, and safety in the relationship.

Types of Bullying	
Type	**Examples of Behavior**
Physical bullying	Punching, poking, hair pulling, beating
Emotional bullying	Rejecting, defaming, humiliating, blackmailing, manipulating friends, isolating, pressuring peers
Sexual bullying	Exhibitionism, requests for sexual activities, sexual harassment, abuse involving physical contact and assault
Verbal bullying	Name-calling, teasing, gossip

Figure 8.9 Bullying appears in many different forms. *Which types of bullying do you think are most often reported?*

Bullying can cause the person being bullied to feel depressed, anxious, isolated, and even suicidal. It tears down self-esteem. Demonstrating behavior that respects yourself and others will help you stand up to a bully and develop healthy and long-lasting friendships.

An assertive response can help you stand up for yourself when around a bully. Being assertive is not always easy, especially if you are unsure of yourself. Using the self-awareness circle (as described in Chapter 7) with responses such as "I see," "I think," "I feel," and "I want" can help you be assertive. The first time you stand up for yourself may be difficult, but with practice, it will become easier. If you stand up to a bully and he or she does not stop the bullying, tell a person in authority what is going on.

What should you do when someone else is being bullied? Of course, anyone who joins the bully is on the same level as the bully. Being passive and doing nothing may not be much better—someone is still being victimized by the bully. Helping the person get out of the situation or standing up to the bully shows maturity and character and gives needed relief to an innocent person. This can be difficult. Sometimes it just takes labeling the action as bullying and telling the person to stop being a bully. Getting others to support you in confronting the bully also helps. In that case, you are using positive peer pressure against the bullying.

Sometimes it is necessary to get help from an adult authority figure. All states have antibullying laws that address bullying in schools, on school-provided transportation, through school-owned technology, or at school-sponsored events. When you report bullying that occurs in any of these situations, school officials are required to address the bullying and take measures to stop it. In some states, bullying appears in the criminal code.

Think About Your Reading

Why might a person tolerate bullying in a relationship? What effect could constant bullying have on a person's growth and development?

Healthy Versus Unhealthy Friendships

Remember the characteristics of a good friendship? Those qualities should remain true of friendships you have at any level, from a casual acquaintance to the closest friendship. Healthy relationships with others should help you grow as a person intellectually, socially, and emotionally.

Relationships are abusive and unhealthy when one person takes advantage of the other. For example, if a person tries to control you, places extreme demands on your time and space, or tries to limit your interactions with others, these are signs of an unhealthy relationship. If a relationship is one-sided, with one person giving all the time, it is unhealthy. If a person demands favors from you—physical or other—the relationship is abusive. Your growth and development are being hurt by these ways of treating you. These are not good friendships, but are abusive relationships.

Ending unhealthy relationships is important. Following the steps in the self-awareness circle can help a person use I-statements to let the other person know the observations, thoughts, feelings, desires, and actions he or she will be taking to end the relationship. "*I see* you are telling me what to do again (observation). *I don't think* you value my thoughts and feelings (thought). *I don't like* it when you tell me what to do. *I feel hurt* and used (feelings). *I really don't want to* spend time with you anymore (desire). *I won't* be meeting with you anymore. It's over (action)."

You may find that you need some help in ending an unhealthy friendship. Seek support from parents, other positive friends, or counselors at school (**Figure 8.10**). The sooner you end an unhealthy relationship, the healthier your situation will be. Remember that in ending such a relationship, you are protecting your own growth and development.

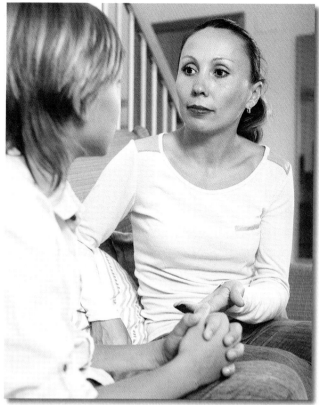

Iakov Filimonov/Shutterstock.com

Figure 8.10 Talking with a parent or other trusted adult can help you end an unhealthy relationship.

LESSON 8.1

Assess

COMPREHENSION CHECK

1. What are the different types of friendships? In your own words, briefly describe each and give an example.
2. What are five characteristics of a good friend?
3. Describe six skills that can be used to develop a positive friendship.
4. Explain how peers may influence a person's choices. Include a positive example and a negative example.
5. List three characteristics of an unhealthy or abusive relationship.

RELATIONSHIPS IN THE FAMILY

Objectives

After studying this lesson, you will be able to

- **identify** factors that affect family relationships.
- **analyze** ways to improve parent-teen relationships.
- **explain** the benefits of developing strong relationships with siblings, grandparents, and extended family.

Focus Your Reading

1. As you read, list each key factor affecting family relationships. For each factor, identify skills your family members could use to contribute to growth in the relationships between your family members.

2. Define your support network by listing the people you can rely on to help you with a problem.

Content Terms
Build Vocab

support network
extended family

Academic Terms

consistent
scope

The family can be a source of strong, meaningful relationships. Relationships with parents, siblings, and other family members help people learn about themselves and others. Lifelong relationships often provide love, affection, sharing, acceptance, support, and trust. Such family relationships can provide a model for you to develop your own long-lasting adult relationships.

Several factors influence the development of close family relationships. Even the closest families experience some conflicts as each person grows and develops. Learning to handle these conflicts in a positive way can strengthen family relationships. It can also help you learn how to resolve conflicts in your future adult relationships.

Factors Influencing Family Relationships

Family members get to know one another as a result of living together. How well they know each other depends on how involved they are in one another's lives. Family members' skills for developing relationships will impact the quality of family interactions. Also, patterns of relating within the family may be influenced by

the family's cultural background. The communication, decision-making, problem-solving, and group interaction skills modeled and taught in the family can influence family members' abilities to develop close relationships outside the family. The closeness of family relationships depends on several factors:

- *How well do family members understand each other?* Each family member is a unique individual with personal likes, dislikes, needs, and goals. Each person also changes over time as he or she grows and matures. For close relationships to develop in the family, members need to know and understand each other.

- *How much time do family members spend together?* The type of sharing that helps family members really get to know each other takes time and effort. Quality time is needed for closeness to develop (**Figure 8.11**). Different cultural backgrounds and social and economic circumstances may affect the amount of time adults spend with children. Family members must make an effort to contribute to family relationships, or those relationships will not grow.

- *What common interests do family members share?* If family members develop shared interests, finding time for building closer relationships is easier. Whatever the activity,

doing activities together can provide time for sharing. This will help members build their communication skills and develop long-lasting future relationships. It can also be enjoyable for everyone who takes part.

- *What kind of communication occurs in the family?* Communicating clearly and accurately is very important between family members. Using I-statements lets others know how a family member feels without destroying self-esteem. Remember that you-statements can hurt others and lead to conflict and fighting. I-statements can be used to help identify problem ownership so families can resolve conflicts. Practicing active listening skills helps members clarify the messages they receive when other members speak.

- *Does consistent support and care exist in the family?* The family environment needs to meet the needs of its members as they grow and develop. When children are loved and cared for and their needs are met on a *consistent* (regular) basis, they can grow to social and emotional maturity. This will help them develop strong, healthy adult relationships. Chapter 1 discusses the impact of family environment on development. Strong family support can help members succeed.

- *Does love and acceptance exist in the family?* Close relationships are developed in an atmosphere of love and acceptance. The family environment needs to be secure and nurturing. Saying "I love you," being helpful to one another, or doing small favors for one another shows love and concern. A warm hug or a pat on the arm can also make each member feel secure in the family. Listening and caring about what each member says and does build feelings of worth and acceptance in the family (**Figure 8.12**).

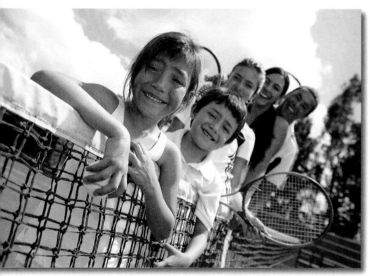

Andresr/Shutterstock.com

Figure 8.11 Spending time together is necessary to develop close relationships within the family. *How might families fulfill this need in different ways?*

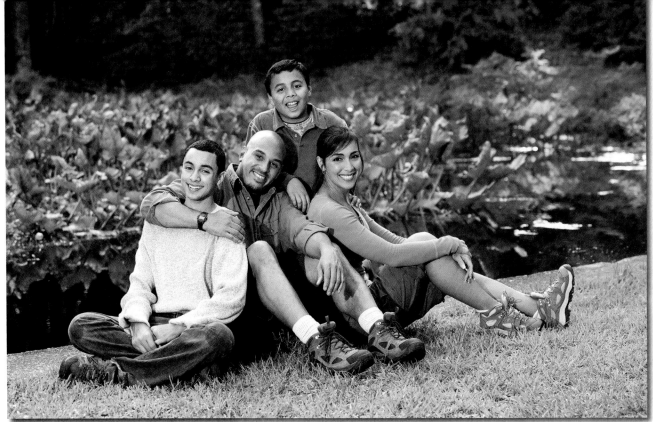

Figure 8.12 *How might families differ in the ways they help each other feel loved and accepted?*

Relationships with Parents and Guardians

The factors outlined in the previous section help build strong, meaningful relationships between family members. Even so, relationships between parents or guardians and teens often become strained. Understanding the parent-teen relationship can help you manage the changes that occur during the teen years.

Understanding Parents' Points of View

Mutual understanding between teens and their parents or guardians can lead to a strong relationship. To have that mutual understanding, teens need to try and look at things from their parents' or guardians' points of view. They need to consider how the issues parents face impact their thinking, their feelings, and their responses. To help that mutual understanding develop, teens also need to share their own thoughts, feelings, and goals with their parents, using good communication skills to speak for themselves. The give-and-take of speaking and listening helps teens and parents understand each other.

In raising their children, parents and guardians are influenced by societal role expectations. In U.S. society, many parents feel pressured to raise perfect children. Meeting such expectations is unrealistic, but parents may still feel the pressure from teachers, friends, or their own parents. Few parents have been trained to help children grow to physical, intellectual, social, and emotional maturity. For the most part, parents and guardians are simply trying to do their best. Most parents rely on their past family experiences to help them raise their children. Knowing what parents or guardians experienced as they grew up can help teens understand how their parents relate to them.

Parents' cultural backgrounds can affect their points of view about parenting and their expectations of their children. Parents' and guardians' backgrounds can impact the way they relate to each other, the roles they take, the way they relate to and care for children, and their personal and work priorities. Teens who discuss cultural influences with their parents gain a better understanding of those parents and some of the reasoning behind their choices and decisions.

Think About Your Reading

Talk to a parent or guardian and ask him or her what it was like when he or she was a teen. What issues did he or she struggle with?

Most parents and guardians put considerable time and effort into providing for their families. Living expenses are high in today's world. Many people are competing for the same jobs and are expected to perform at their best during the workday, work overtime, take work home at night, or travel. Some parents have to work at more than one job to meet the family's financial needs. These responsibilities leave less time to spend with the family. A parent may need to relocate to get a promotion or to take a new job. That means the whole family must move, which puts stress on every member. Too much pressure from work can place a strain on relationships between family members

(**Figure 8.13**). Talking with parents or guardians about their work can help teens understand these pressures.

In today's mobile society, many families have moved away from the **support network** provided by close relatives. In past generations, grandparents, aunts, uncles, and other relatives lived nearby and were available to help parents with daily problems. They assisted with child care and discussed common questions about parenting. Many families today do not have that support group nearby. As a result, they have fewer resources in emergencies, and children have fewer family role models. These developments add more pressure on parents.

Parents must make decisions that protect the well-being of all family members. As teens recognize the *scope*, or the amount and variety, of their parents' or guardians' responsibilities, they begin to see why their parents make certain decisions. They will recognize their concerns for their children's health, safety, and development. Efforts to

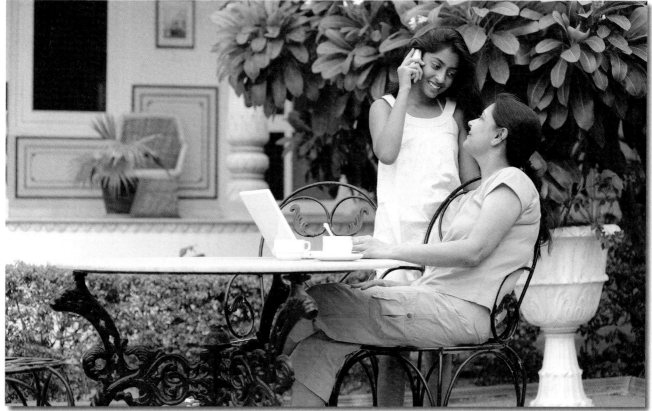

absolute-india/Shutterstock.com

Figure 8.13 Work demands can reduce the amount of time parents have to spend with their families. *How could you learn more about the issues facing your parents or guardians?*

understand this will help teens resolve conflicts that may arise.

Using Technology to Connect with Family Members

Good communication skills can help parents or guardians and teens understand one another's viewpoints, and modern technology can promote that communication. It helps if family members know what is happening in each other's lives so they know what to expect. What time is each family member expected home? Have schedules changed during the day? Does one member need a ride to get to an appointment or event? Using communication technology can help family members keep current with each other's lives. A quick text or e-mail can remind family members of an agreed-upon plan or alert them to sudden changes that impact those plans or expectations. Good and frequent communication can prevent many potential conflicts.

Parent-Teen Conflicts

Both teens and their parents or guardians are adjusting to changes. As teens grow to maturity, they become more independent. Teens' abilities to think for themselves increase. Teens have strong opinions and ideas they want to express. They develop their own friendships and want to choose their own social activities. As teens become young adults, they emotionally separate from the close, dependent bond with the family. This separation process enables them to develop other personal relationships in the future.

Most parents and guardians desire this growth and independence for their children. The actual process, however, forces parents to change as well, and change can be difficult. They must learn to gradually let go and allow teens to become independent (**Figure 8.14**).

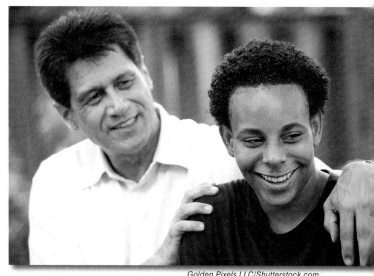
Golden Pixels LLC/Shutterstock.com

Figure 8.14 As teens grow more independent, parents and guardians must adjust to these changes.

Parents and teens often have different views on how much independence is appropriate for a maturing teen. Maturity occurs gradually, but some teens want total independence as soon as possible, whether they are ready for it or not. Sometimes parents or guardians do not want to recognize their teen is maturing. They may keep a tight control even when the teen is able to handle more responsibility. These differences can lead to conflict.

Negotiating Solutions

When parents and teens desire to keep family relationships close and healthy, they make the effort to negotiate solutions to their conflicts. A willingness to negotiate shows respect and concern for the thoughts and desires of all parties involved. To negotiate a solution, both parties need to accept some give-and-take. Everyone needs to benefit from the solution for it to be workable and satisfactory to everyone.

How can teens plan ahead for negotiating with their parents or guardians? These steps can help teens prepare:

- Set a time to talk about an issue.
- Think about exactly what you want to say and how you can express yourself most clearly.
- Think about what end result you desire.

Think About Your Reading
Why might it be hard for parents to give teens more independence?

- Consider what aspects of the solution you can negotiate.
- Determine which aspects of the situation are more important to you and which ones you are willing to compromise on.

Family meetings can provide a time and place to talk, share feelings, set goals, or make plans related to family living. Good communication and decision-making skills will help these family meetings be effective.

Think About Your Reading

Why would families who hold weekly family meetings demonstrate stronger communication skills in stressful situations?

One-on-one interactions between parents or guardians and teens can also keep the door open for good communication. Personal time allows family members to know one another better and develop a close relationship (**Figure 8.15**). Some parents and their adult children become close friends. Siblings, grandparents, aunts, and uncles can also be a source of close friendships.

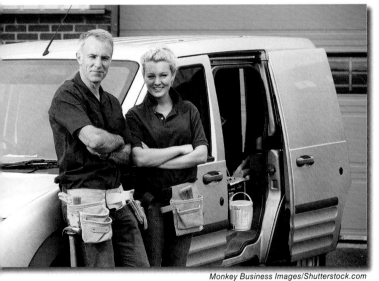
Monkey Business Images/Shutterstock.com

Figure 8.15 Doing tasks together is an opportunity for teens to develop a close relationship with their parents.

Relationships with Siblings

At times, siblings may have a close relationship. They learn from and encourage one another. At other stages of life, they may spend less time with each other, and each sibling spends more time with peers.

Just as siblings can be close friends, they can also be rivals. Sibling rivalry is common between brothers and sisters if they are growing through different stages or even if they are going through the same stage. Some siblings struggle with self-esteem, peer pressure, new roles, or new responsibilities, and those struggles can affect their relationships with brothers and sisters. Siblings may be trying to compete with one another or for their parents' attention. Parents can help siblings work out difficulties in their relationships in a positive way, but the siblings have to be willing to work at it, too.

Some siblings do not maintain the close relationship they had earlier in their lives. The breakdown may occur just as it would in other relationships—due to a violation of trust, unwillingness to work together, or an attack on personal value and worth. Sometimes, it can simply happen because the siblings move in different directions. Some siblings who lose closeness for a period of time find later that they can regain it and that doing so restores something they value.

Most siblings have the chance to spend time together and share many experiences. Sibling relationships can become strong and close, lasting a lifetime. Older siblings who have experienced moving into young adulthood can help their younger siblings meet the challenges that arise as they do so. Siblings can become the core of a strong support group.

Relationships with Grandparents

Relationships with extended family members can be a source of good friendships, role models, and mentors. **Extended family** includes grandparents, aunts, uncles, cousins, and other relatives.

Because they may be retired, grandparents often have the benefit of being able to spend focused time talking and listening with their grandchildren. This interaction benefits both generations.

Children benefit from the love and support provided by grandparents. Grandparents who care for children, listen to them, and pay attention to their ideas and activities help build the child's positive self-esteem. As children get older, they will be more willing to confide in a caring, listening grandparent who has built a relationship with them. At times when teen-parent conflicts may be tense, a grandparent may be able to lend a listening ear and provide helpful insight. Grandparents also benefit from their interactions with grandchildren. Family relationships provide an aging adult with feelings of worth and value (**Figure 8.16**).

As time goes on, grandparents may need support and help from their own children and grandchildren. Sometimes grandparents move in with the family, and they may need help with personal care, preparing meals, or finances. Such changes in the family impact the relationships between family members. Strong, supportive relationships over the years can help family members make adjustments to such changes.

LESSON 8.2

Assess

COMPREHENSION CHECK

1. Identify five factors that can help build close relationships within the family.
2. Name three topics teens could talk about with parents or guardians to increase their understanding of their parents' or guardians' perspectives.
3. List five activities a teen can do when planning to resolve a conflict with parents and negotiate a solution.
4. Identify ways that relationships with siblings and grandparents can add to the quality of life for family members.

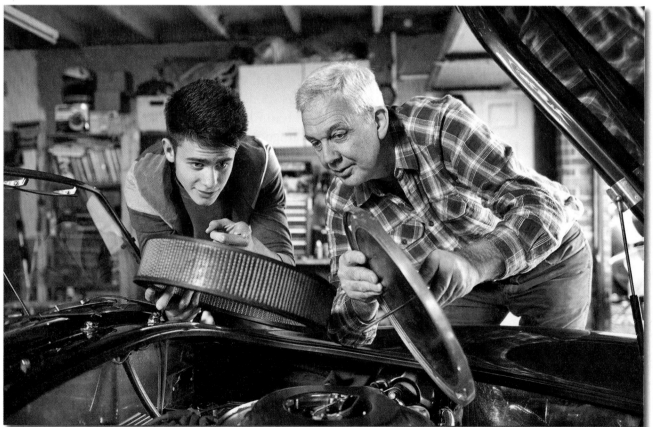

CWA Studio/Shutterstock.com

Figure 8.16 Grandparents often have the time to share their knowledge and resources with grandchildren. *How does a strong relationship with your grandparents benefit both generations?*

Content Terms
Build Vocab

significant adults
professional relationships
multiculturalism

Academic Terms

detached
perspective

Objectives

After studying this lesson, you will be able to
- **relate** appropriate communication skills to different types of relationships in the community.
- **analyze** the impact of diversity on relationships in the community.

Focus Your Reading

1. For each community topic, summarize how positive, healthy relationships could impact quality of life.
2. Identify specific groups who add diversity to your community and describe the ways in which they contribute to multiculturalism in your area.

Having good relationship skills will help you interact with people and develop friendships in your community, as well as among friends and family members. Knowing how to relate to people who are younger and older than you is a valuable skill and can lead to rewarding friendships. In today's global society, it is important to know how to build relationships with people of other cultures. Building positive relationships with people in all areas of your life will help you experience personal growth and success.

Building Friendships in Your Community

The social skills used in building good friendships apply to building relationships in your community. These relationships may develop into close friendships, but most will remain at a more casual level. Still, the skills of being friendly and developing rapport will help you get to know others around you where you live and work. You can use these skills whether you are getting to know your neighbors or coworkers, participating in a parent-school organization, working on a common goal in a community group, or taking part in other community activities.

Sharing with others in your community will likely focus on areas of common interests and goals (**Figure 8.17**). Whether the group you are involved in is recreational or focused on improving conditions in the community, participating in a group gives you an opportunity to make friends with peers and with people of different ages. Since those participating in the group have common interests or goals, participating in groups like these makes it somewhat easier to make friends. After all, group members have something they know they share.

As you move through different stages in your life span, it is likely that you will move into new communities. Your family may move as you grow up, or you may join a new community when you go to college. When you graduate and go to work full time, you may move to a new community to find a job. Wherever you live, using good relationship-building skills and becoming involved in your community will help you develop good friendships.

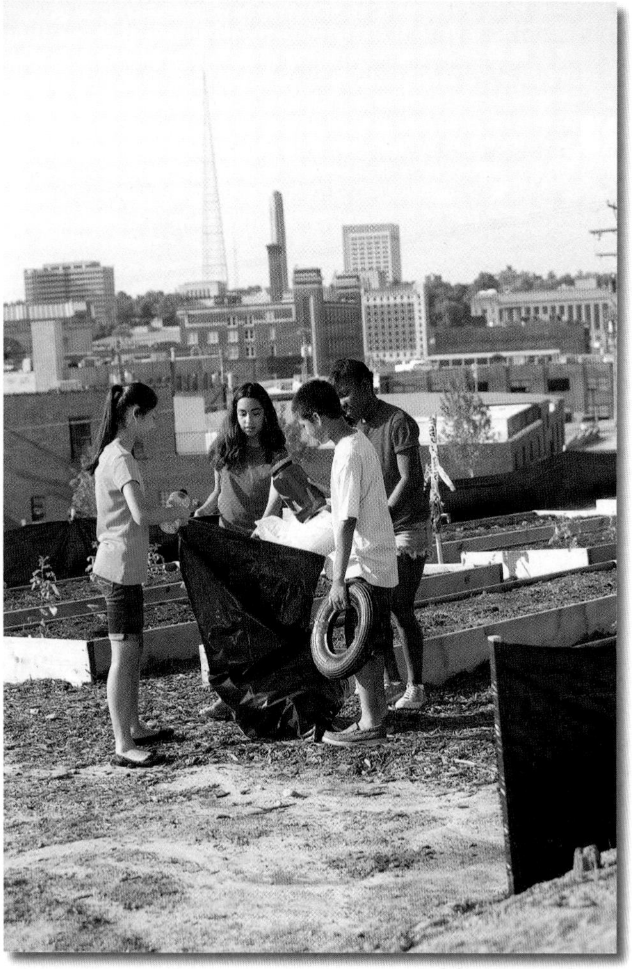

Figure 8.17 Volunteering in a community activity can make your community a better place to live. *In what ways could volunteering benefit your growth as an individual?*

©iStock.com/Jani Bryson

Think About Your Reading
Where in your community have you met the most people who have become your good friends?

Community Involvement

The community activities you choose to take part in will depend on your goals and values. Since your goals and values will probably change somewhat over time, the activities you focus on will also change over time. As a teen, many of your community activities will be focused on your school. You may be involved in an athletic team, a volunteer organization that supports young children (for example, before- and after-school clubs), or recreational groups that provide summer programs for children and families. As a young adult, you may play on an athletic team, participate in a theater or music group, or join a group that enjoys hiking or some other activity that interests you. As a young parent, you may take part in a parent-school organization to support your child's school. There are many clubs and programs that welcome volunteers to assist in providing services to members in your community.

In these community activities, sharing takes place at different levels. Some relationships will be strictly professional; others may grow more personal. The fact that you are involved in an activity with others will create some common ground. Trust develops as others see you as being dependable and responsible. As you develop skills for showing empathy and caring about others, others will be more likely to care about you. Involvement in your community will help you develop good friendships where you live.

Relationships with Significant Adults

Adults other than parents who play an important part in your life can be called **significant adults**. They may be relatives, teachers, youth leaders, religious leaders, coaches, or neighbors. Whatever their exact role, they are people who take the time to get to know you. They care about you and what happens to you in life (**Figure 8.18**). A good friendship can develop with a significant adult even if that person is much older than you.

Relationships between significant adults and teens usually are less stressful than those between teens and their parents or guardians. Parents feel responsible for what their teens do. Significant adults also feel responsible for the well-being of the children they interact with, but they do not have the same kind of pressure that parents feel. Thus, they often relate to teens with more empathy.

Sometimes you may find that important relationships in your family are damaged. Talking to a significant adult in your life may be helpful. You may find it easier to share your point of view as well as listen to what they have to say. Those adults might be parents themselves and be able to provide some insight into how your parents might see the situation.

While relationships with significant adults can be enjoyable and rewarding, you should always be alert for any unhealthy patterns in these relationships, even with people you trust. Remember that unhealthy relationships are demanding and controlling and prevent you from growing intellectually, socially, and emotionally. If someone makes you feel uncomfortable, talk about it with a parent or other close friend. They may see

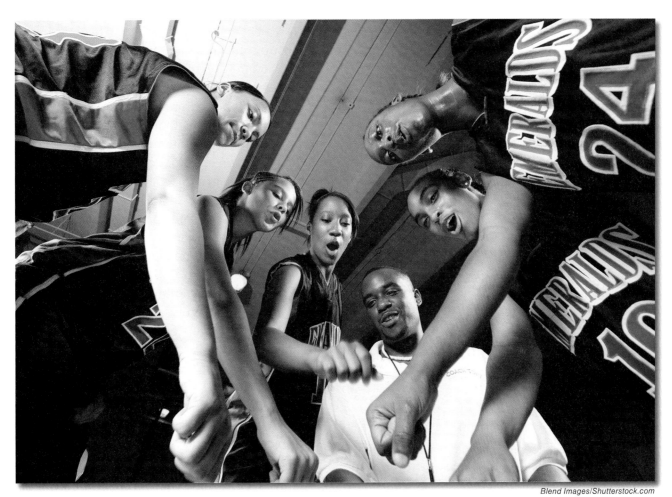

Blend Images/Shutterstock.com

Figure 8.18 Significant adults can offer encouragement to teens as they grow and develop to maturity. *What life skills does participating in a team sport help a person develop?*

things that you do not see. They can help you take steps to protect your safety and personal growth, if necessary.

Professional Relationships in the Community

Some relationships need to be maintained at a professional level (**Figure 8.19**). Relationships with teachers, principals, counselors, a family doctor, a dentist, and a religious leader are all examples. **Professional relationships** exist between two or more people when services are provided by the professional. These services must be provided using a professional code of conduct, one that is safe and appropriate for all involved. Conversation with the professional should focus on the specific task, service, or work at hand. A professional relationship is not necessarily a cold or *detached* (distant) one, however. People can relate to these figures in a friendly, caring way, and when one is seeking the advice of a counselor, teacher, or religious leader, it is certainly acceptable—and perhaps even necessary—to speak of one's inner thoughts and feelings. The professional must always be careful to remain in a respectful position physically, however, especially with young people.

Skills for being friendly and developing some rapport are still needed in a professional relationship. These skills help people develop mutual respect so they can work together to address the concerns at hand. Remember that you show respect when you use active listening skills and speak with clear verbal and nonverbal communication. You also deserve respect from professionals as they listen to what you have to say and make sure that your message has been understood.

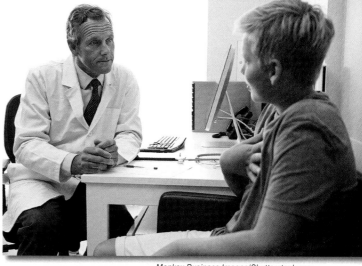

Monkey Business Images/Shutterstock.com

Figure 8.19 When you talk with your doctor or dentist, the focus of communication will be on the information and issues related to your health. *What are some other examples of professional relationships you might have in a community?*

Ethical communication is needed in a professional relationship. Both parties need to be honest in their communication, providing information that contributes to the task at hand. Lying benefits no one; it solves no problems. The professional should not pressure the other person to provide intimate information, although he or she can try to build trust for the other person to discuss relevant details in a situation when providing counseling. Ethical communication sticks to the common focus of the meeting.

The following skills will help you maintain a professional relationship.

- Share input using I-statements to state your point of view clearly.
- Listen closely.
- Use clarifying, paraphrasing, or reflecting to make sure you understand instructions or directions.
- Use eye contact when speaking and listening.
- Keep personal sharing to a minimum. If someone asks for more information than you want to share, ask them how that is relevant.
- Focus on the common task at hand.

Think About Your Reading

What factors might make it difficult to speak openly in a professional relationship?

Relationships with People of Other Cultures

Over your life span, you will encounter people from many different cultures, reflecting the diversity of U.S. society. U.S. society is marked by **multiculturalism**, which is the influence of many different cultures on society. Some of the individuals you meet at school, at work, or in your community probably have a cultural background different from yours (**Figure 8.20**). This difference may be apparent in their customs, language, traditions, or racial background. They may have different beliefs, personal and family values, or religious practices. All these factors reflect a person's unique cultural heritage.

Getting to know people who are different from you can have a positive effect on your personal growth. Through such a relationship, you will gain knowledge of human nature. You

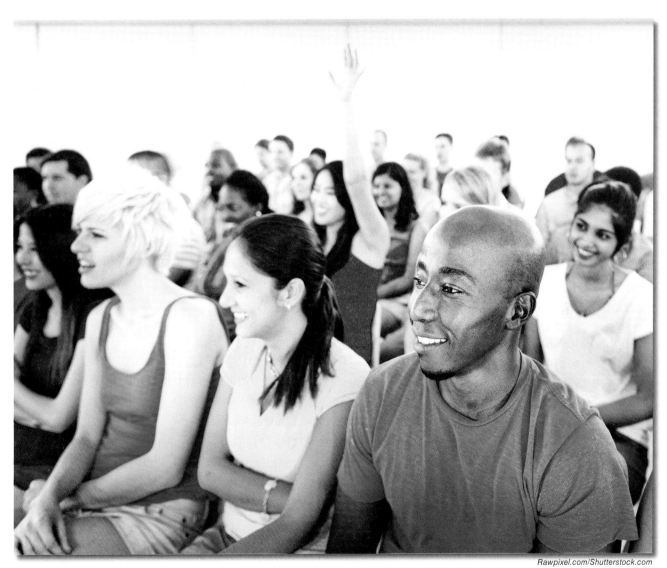

Rawpixel.com/Shutterstock.com

Figure 8.20 Communities are made up of diverse people with many different backgrounds. *What are some examples of things community members might have in common?*

will understand both the uniqueness of other cultures and the qualities that all people share. Through these experiences, you will gain a new *perspective*, or point of view, on life.

Meeting people of other cultures may seem challenging at first. In fact, you may feel uncomfortable associating with someone who seems to have no common ground with you (**Figure 8.21**). Remember that the other person feels just as uncomfortable as you. Try to consider how that person feels and thinks and respond with empathy.

Take the initiative to introduce yourself and be friendly. Use an icebreaker to begin a conversation and help the other person feel at ease. Reach out and try to develop rapport. Listen to his or her ideas. Show respect for the person's cultural background with polite questions and active listening to the answers. If the individual is new to the school, the workplace, or the neighborhood, offer to help him or her become acquainted with the location of key features and the expected ways of acting. Building positive relationships with people of other cultures will strengthen you, your school, and your community and will promote an appreciation of diversity.

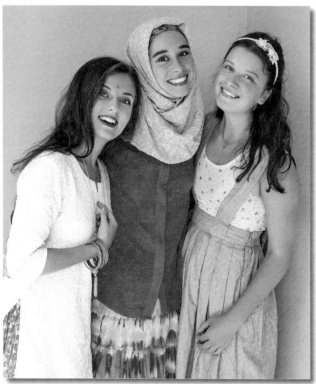

Mila Supinskaya/Shutterstock.com

Figure 8.21 At first, it may seem like you have little common ground with a person of another culture. With time, however, you are likely to find common interests and experiences that can help you build a friendship.

> ## Think About Your Reading
> In what ways could a friendship with a person from another culture help you grow?

Lesson 8.3

Assess

COMPREHENSION CHECK

1. Give two examples of significant adults in your life outside your family and state what role they play in your life.
2. What relationship skills can help you become involved in a community?
3. What ways should a professional relationship differ from a personal relationship?
4. List three steps teens can take to develop relationships with people of different cultural backgrounds.
5. Explain how relationships with people of diverse cultures can help you grow as a person.
6. How does developing relationships with people of other cultures promote an appreciation of diversity within the community?

CHAPTER SUMMARY

Friendships often develop between people who have common interests and share their personal thoughts and feelings. Sharing with openness, trust, acceptance, understanding, support, and encouragement creates this special bond. Close friendships help people grow intellectually, emotionally, and socially. The experience helps them prepare for future long-term relationships.

Friendships often develop between peers, as they tend to have much in common. Peers also may pressure each other to make certain choices in order to identify with a peer group. When teens feel pressured by their peer group, thinking about and asserting their own priorities and goals is important.

The family is an important source of close relationships. Several factors affect these relationships. Family members who develop common interests are likely to spend more time together sharing, having fun, and building friendships that can last a lifetime. Even healthy family relationships experience parent-teen conflicts. Empathy and understanding are the keys to resolving these conflicts in a positive way.

Skills for developing both personal and professional relationships are important in building strong ties within communities. Community members can provide support groups for family members and contribute to a family's quality of life.

VOCABULARY ACTIVITIES

1. Write five sentences, each of which uses two of the terms correctly. Each sentence should describe how to build healthy relationships. Use each term once.

Content Terms

acquaintance (8.1)
blind spot (8.1)
bullying (8.1)
code of conduct (8.1)
cyber-acquaintance (8.1)
extended family (8.2)

icebreaker (8.1)
multiculturalism (8.3)
professional relationships (8.3)
significant adults (8.3)
support network (8.2)

2. Create a crossword puzzle that uses all of the terms, writing definitions that show how each term is connected to relationships. Exchange your puzzle with a partner and solve each other's puzzles. Discuss any different understandings you have of the terms until you can reach a consensus on the correct meaning.

Academic Terms

conform (8.1)
consistent (8.2)
detached (8.3)
empathy (8.1)

perspective (8.3)
rapport (8.1)
scope (8.2)

ASSESS

Your Knowledge

3. What are the characteristics of a good friend?
4. Examine the development of relationships. What can a person do to develop a close friendship?
5. What are three steps families can take to build strong relationships within the family?

Your Understanding

6. How can friendships help a person grow to maturity?
7. How does negative peer pressure hinder the growth of close friendships?
8. What are some ways that diversity benefits a community? How can you promote an appreciation of diversity?

Your Skills

9. Analyze a friendship and determine the qualities needed for the relationship to develop into a close friendship.
10. Write an assertive response to a situation in which a peer pressures you to steal money from another student's locker.
11. Write a scenario in which you negotiate a solution to the following problem: your family cannot agree on where to go out for a family dinner.

CRITICAL THINKING

12. **Make Inferences.** Keep a daily journal for one week to note the times you could have been, but were not, assertive when you were in a social situation. For each instance, write down some I-statements you could have said. What differences in the outcome of each situation might have occurred with an assertive response?

13. **Compare Findings.** Evaluate your own opinion of what constitutes an ideal friend. List the personal qualities, desirable interests and goals, and priorities you would like to see in an ideal friend. Compare your list to the qualities described in Figure 8.2 of the text. Write a paragraph describing how the lists are similar or different, citing evidence from the text to support your analysis and explaining any differences in your

list compared to that list. *Choice*: Present your comparisons in a chart, but be sure to include a column where you explain differences.

14. **Illustrate a Concept.** Write a scene portraying a real or fictional teen-parent conflict. Evaluate the conflict for types of communication used. What listening skills were used? What items were negotiated? Explain how this conflict is related to parents letting go and teens becoming independent. *Group option*: Work with a partner on the scene and the analysis. Then act the scene out for the class, using expressions and body language appropriate to the characters and their thoughts and emotions. Then answer classmates' questions about the different parts of the scene and your analysis.

15. **Develop a Hypothesis.** Observe and then write a list of all the ways your peers meet each other in the school halls. Include their verbal greetings, gestures, facial expressions, and other body language. Can you identify differences based on cultural backgrounds? Can you identify differences in how your peers communicate versus how adults in your community communicate? Write a paragraph describing the similarities and differences you discover through your observations, as well as any conclusions you can make about peer and adult communication.

CORE SKILLS

16. **Writing.** Observe and take notes on what is done and said in various peer pressure situations in your school for one day. In a paragraph, describe one example of giving in to negative peer pressure and one example of successfully resisting it. Did each response cause you to feel more or less respect toward the person who responded? Summarize by explaining how attitudes are shaped by the responses people make. *Group option*: Share your observations with a partner, analyze them together, and report your summary to the class in an oral report.

17. **Social Studies, Writing.** Describe in one paragraph a method you use to develop rapport when meeting someone you do not know very well. Compare it to the method presented in the text. Then interview a person in the community who is outgoing and well known. Ask this person what methods he or she uses to get to know a new person. Summarize this person's responses and compare his or her methods with the method you use. What changes could you make to

improve your rapport-building skills? Present your findings in a one-page paper.

18. **Writing.** Use a computer program to create a poster that depicts the qualities of a good friend and display it in the classroom.

19. **Research, Writing.** Observe three television programs that emphasize friendships. Rate them according to how well they illustrate the qualities of a friend described in Figure 8.2. Prepare a checklist of the qualities to use in rating the programs. Summarize your findings in a paragraph.

20. **Writing.** Interview a guidance counselor in your school and ask questions about the strategies used in your school to help new students become acquainted and promote positive friendships. Compare these strategies with the text strategies for developing friendships. Identify any additional strategies that you think would be beneficial for your school to use. Summarize your findings and recommendations in a report.

21. **Technology.** Work with a small group and create a multimedia presentation that could be used to teach friendship-building skills to an elementary class. Identify a specific elementary classroom you could present your multimedia presentation to and talk to the teacher or guidance counselor about the level at which you should present the information. Refer to the text for strategies to use in developing friendships and create your presentation. *Choice*: Create a colorful handout to leave with students to remind them of your key points.

22. **Research.** Research all the groups that meet in your school around a common interest. Create a flyer that lists all of the groups and identifies the common interests that each group is built around. Share the flyer with your school guidance counselor. *Choice*: Post your flyer on the school website. *Group option*: Work with a small group and also research various groups in your community that are built around a common interest. Prepare a combined report that includes both school and community groups and post on the school website.

CAREER READINESS

23. **Connecting with Careers.** Interview a social worker, juvenile police officer, or psychologist to identify the relationship between young people's feelings and social problems, such as bullying, alcohol and drug abuse, and crime. Identify what training the professional has had in working with young people struggling with these social issues. Write a report summarizing your findings.

CHAPTER 9

DEVELOPING GROUP INTERACTION SKILLS

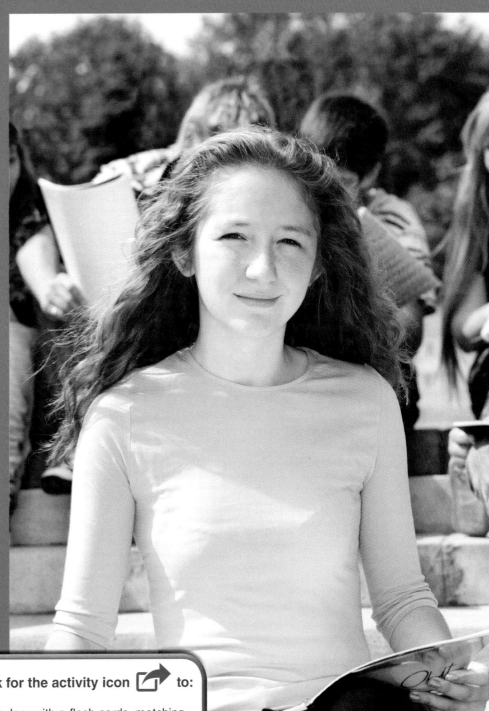

Reading Prep

Before reading the chapter, skim the headings and subheadings and charts in each lesson. On a sheet of paper, write down three facts you want to learn or skills you want to gain from reading each lesson. After you read each lesson, note what you learned under each statement.

Key Questions

Questions to answer as you study this chapter:

- What traits and skills do effective leaders demonstrate?
- What does it take for a group to be successful?
- How are leadership and group skills effectively used in the workplace?

While studying this chapter, look for the activity icon 📲 to:

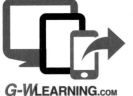

- **build** vocabulary with e-flash cards, matching activities, and vocabulary games; and
- **assess** what you learn by completing the lesson comprehension checks online.

www.g-wlearning.com/humanservices/

G-WLEARNING.com

AFTER STUDYING THIS CHAPTER, YOU WILL

KNOW:

- The responsibilities, traits, and skills of effective leaders.
- The characteristics of an effective group member.
- The qualities of an effective employee.

UNDERSTAND:

- How different styles of leadership can be used effectively.
- How responsible group members contribute to the effectiveness of a work group.
- How leadership and group interaction skills contribute to an effective workplace.

BE ABLE TO DO:

- Analyze a situation for the style of leadership needed to solve a problem.
- Evaluate a discussion technique for its potential effectiveness in meeting a group's need for information.
- Plan, organize, and evaluate a group meeting.

GETTING STARTED

"Why don't you join FCCLA this year?" Amy asked.

"What 's that?" responded Julia.

"The Family, Career and Community Leaders of America," Amy replied. "It's a great club! We have a lot of fun. We learn about different careers, take field trips, do community projects, and take part in state competitions. You can meet so many people who share the same interests as you—it's really a terrific opportunity."

"Well, it sounds interesting, but I'm not sure I have time," Julia said.

"Why don't you come with me to the meeting after school today and see what you think? We're looking for new members," Amy said.

Julia nodded. Amy's enthusiasm had sparked her interest. "I guess that's the best way for me to decide. I'll call home to let them know I'm staying after school."

"Great!" Amy said. "I'll introduce you to some of the other members at lunch today."

Participating in student organizations will help you develop both your leadership skills and your skills for working in groups. Both of these skills can help you at work, at home, and in your community—anywhere you work together with other people. In this chapter, you will learn how group members and group leaders can make a difference in the ability of group members to work together, get along, and succeed in getting tasks done.

The skills you learn now can help you in your future. Learning leadership and group interaction skills can help you contribute to an effective workplace. Skills for relating to customers, coworkers, supervisors, and others in authority on the job can help you be successful in your career.

LESSON 9.1

EFFECTIVE LEADERSHIP

Content Terms

Build Vocab

leader
group
task-oriented leadership
relationship-oriented
    leadership

Academic Terms

coordinate
enthused
authoritarian
democratic
collaborate

Objectives

After studying this lesson, you will be able to
- **identify** the roles and responsibilities of group leaders.
- **distinguish** between various leadership styles.
- **match** leadership styles to appropriate settings.

Focus Your Reading

1. Create a graphic organizer to chart and describe the qualities of a good leader.
2. For each style of leadership, identify a person you know who uses that style and summarize how that person provides leadership for a group of people.

A **leader** is the person who is placed in charge or takes charge of a group. A **group** consists of two or more people interacting in ways that affect each other. The leader of a group strongly influences the thoughts and behaviors of the other members (**Figure 9.1**). He or she is responsible for helping the group succeed.

There are, of course, many kinds of groups. Some—like a collection of students who meet regularly for lunch or a few friends who get together to go to a movie—are informally organized and not really focused on accomplishing a task. This lesson is about groups oriented toward getting a job done. That job could be academic, such as for a class project; social, such as for planning a school event; or community-driven, such as for volunteering to clean up a community park. Whatever the task, the members of the group come together to get something done.

Responsibilities of Group Leaders

Effective leaders possess the traits and skills described in **Figure 9.2**. The first step in developing effective leadership skills is understanding and fulfilling the responsibilities of leadership.

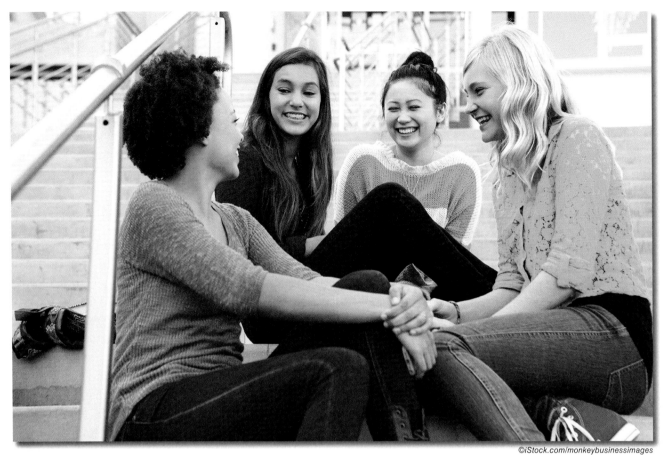
©iStock.com/monkeybusinessimages

Figure 9.1 A positive attitude can motivate group members to participate. *What other qualities would you like to see from leaders in a group?*

Leadership Traits and Skills

- Has positive self-esteem.
- Shows enthusiasm.
- Sets a good example for others.
- Shows empathy. Listens to group members and recognizes their needs and opinions.
- Motivates the group to work toward its goals.
- Makes decisions and stands behind them.
- Handles problems diplomatically.
- Takes a stand on issues.
- Manages group resources by delegating responsibilities.
- Does a fair share of work; carries out assigned duties.
- Gives credit where due to group members. Praises them for their efforts.

Figure 9.2 These skills and traits are needed for a person to assume a leadership role. *Which of these do you possess? Which of these traits would you like to see in a boss or supervisor?*

Effective leaders have four main responsibilities. Their commitment to and skill in meeting these responsibilities can motivate the group to succeed. The confidence they show in themselves and in the group contributes to the group's success as well. The four main responsibilities of effective leaders are the following:

- *Identify the group's goals.* Effective leaders answer the questions: Why is the group together? What needs motivated individuals to join the group? What does the group expect to accomplish?

- *Develop a plan that will help the group reach its goals.* Effective leaders develop a plan. What steps need to be accomplished to reach the identified goals? What talents and skills can group members contribute to achieving those steps? What resources does the group need and have available to carry out those steps? How can all these resources be managed so the group reaches its goal?

- *Carry out the plan.* Effective leaders help the group carry out the plan. Who is going to do what task, and in what order? What do members need to do to **coordinate** (organize their combined efforts in) their work?
- *Evaluate the group's performance.* Effective leaders help the group evaluate its performance. Did the group reach its goals? How could the group work together more effectively in the future when facing new tasks?

> ## Think About Your Reading
> Have you ever been in a group where the leader did not carry out his or her responsibilities? What effect does this have on the way a group functions?

Leadership Roles

As a group leader, you will have several different roles to fulfill. Since your main responsibility is leading the group to reach its goals, you will need to be a good communicator. You will need to direct discussions to find out what your group members are thinking. You will also need to be a motivator to get people *enthused* (excited) and involved. Finally, because problems often come up as you try to meet the group's goals, you will need to be a problem solver.

The Leader as a Communicator

All leaders need to practice good communication skills. Skills for sending, receiving, and interpreting messages are necessary so everyone in the group shares the same meaning. If not, group members might duplicate work that is being done by others or neglect sharing information. Nonverbal messages need to support what is said.

A leader can help others express their ideas by using active listening skills. As a leader, you can show interest in what each team member has to say. Your comments can encourage people to participate. Clarifying, paraphrasing, or reflecting can be used to help make sure all members

understand what a person has said. In this way, leaders can make sure the meaning is clear.

> ## Think About Your Reading
> What are some examples of comments a leader could say that would encourage people to share their ideas?

The Leader as a Director of Discussion

A leader can help team members contribute to the group through discussion. This method can be used to identify a problem, gather information, or get input from group members. Discussion can be used to make group decisions. A good leader tries to encourage everyone's participation and may need to make a point of asking for input from quiet group members or persons who are new to a group. Different techniques can be used to inspire members to share ideas (**Figure 9.3**).

Effective discussion is directed toward a goal identified by the leader. Others may want to add their ideas about the goal, expanding it beyond the group's original purpose. At times, the leader may need to redirect the group to keep it on track and focused on the correct goal.

The Leader as a Motivator

One of the main roles of the leader is to get all members of a group involved. When group members are involved, they have better attitudes toward the group and are more supportive in carrying out group activities. The following techniques can help motivate a group.

- *Be persuasive.* People prefer being asked to help instead of being told what to do.
- *Include all members in discussions.* Group members are more likely to have a better attitude when their opinions and feelings are considered. People like to be asked for their opinions, even if another form of action is taken.
- *Include friendly competition in group activities.* Competition can encourage members to work together to reach goals.

Discussion Techniques	
Small-Group Discussion Techniques	
Brainstorming	Members contribute whatever ideas come to mind. All ideas are accepted. No comments are made while discussion is in progress.
Buzz session	Large group is divided into smaller groups of four to ten people. Each, led by a chairperson, briefly discusses one view of a problem or a situation. Following the discussion, the chairpersons report each group's opinion to the entire group.
Role-playing	Individuals are given fictional, real-life situations to act out in short drama. After the role-play, the group discusses the main objective.
Large-Group Discussion Techniques	
Roundtable	Members sit in a circle or around a table to discuss a topic. A chairperson opens the discussion and summarizes throughout.
Panel	Four to six people form a panel to discuss various aspects of a chosen topic. A moderator introduces the topic and panel members and draws them into conversation. The panel discusses the topic back and forth for the audience's benefit. The audience participates during or after the discussion.
Colloquium	One or more resource people respond to questions from an interviewer and from the audience.
Symposium	Several speakers give a presentation. Each presents information on a different aspect of a topic.
Forum	Speakers present their opinions or points of view on a topic or issue. Members of the larger group may ask questions after all speakers have finished their presentation.
Debate	Two speakers or teams present two opposing sides of a controversial issue. After the speakers present their views, the opposing speaker may offer a rebuttal. That speaker tries to point out flaws in the other person's argument. A moderator helps maintain control.

Figure 9.3 An effective leader uses these discussion techniques to encourage group participation. *Are any of these techniques new to you? Which techniques would be most useful for gathering information on a topic?*

- *Show recognition.* Find ways to recognize the contributions that group members are making to the group's efforts. Feeling that their efforts are noticed and valued helps convince people to continue making an effort.
- *Look successful.* People like to succeed. If group members believe they are part of a successful group, their enthusiasm for the task and for working together will increase. In addition, others will want to join.

The Leader as a Problem Solver

A fourth role of a group leader is seeing that problems get solved. In any group project,

unplanned situations will arise. Someone gets sick and cannot complete a task. One part of the project does not come together as quickly as planned or does not turn out quite the way it was expected to. Group members may disagree on how to carry out part of the plan.

Begin by identifying the problem. In doing so, remember that different people are impacted by a problem in different ways. Getting input from many group members will help a leader make sure that all aspects of the problem are understood and can be addressed. Encourage group members to discuss their concerns. Listen to and observe the verbal and nonverbal messages that members—including yourself—are sending to make sure that messages are encoded and decoded accurately, and

you understand people's meanings and their feelings about the situation (**Figure 9.4**). Then make sure the group determines ownership of the problem. Finally, guide the group using the steps of the decision-making process to work out a solution.

Think About Your Reading

How could a leader's communication skills either help solve a problem or make the problem worse?

Leadership Styles

All leaders will need to carry out the aforementioned responsibilities and roles to some extent. The style of leadership that leaders use, however, can vary with the situation and the structure of the group. Different groups require different kinds of leadership.

Task-Oriented Leadership

One style of leadership focuses on the job that needs to be done. This style, known as **task-oriented leadership**, is the appropriate style when a specific task needs to be accomplished. In this case, the leader's emphasis is not on how each person feels or thinks about the task. The emphasis is on the job that needs to be completed.

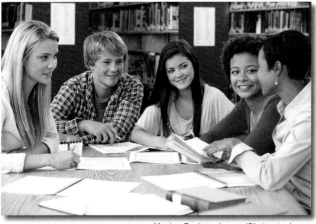

Monkey Business Images/Shutterstock.com

Figure 9.4 As a group leader, pay attention to the verbal and nonverbal messages your group members send.

With task-oriented leadership, the leader makes sure that the larger task is broken down into smaller units that individual members can carry out. He or she makes sure that the group is aware of the skills and abilities of each team member and that the appropriate people are assigned to each individual job. A task-oriented leader also has to make sure that each part of the job is completed. After the task is done, the leader guides the effort to evaluate the progress of the group. This style of leadership is important when groups are trying to meet certain standards.

Someone using task-oriented leadership may use an *authoritarian* approach to leadership in which he or she dictate how the group operates. An authoritarian leader likes to be in control of the situation and makes most of the decisions. This kind of leader assigns tasks and monitors members as they do their work to make sure the group is on schedule and that tasks are being done correctly. Sometimes the authoritarian approach to completing a task is most effective. A group of firefighters would not sit down and discuss how to put out the fire. Instead, each person would follow the leader's instructions to complete the task.

Relationship-Oriented Leadership

Some groups need a more *democratic* or *collaborative* style of leadership. In **democratic** leadership, group members are asked to **collaborate**, or work together, as decisions are made and carried out. **Relationship-oriented leadership** recognizes this need for collaboration. This style of leadership places greater emphasis on the feelings, thoughts, and needs of each group member (**Figure 9.5**). Of course, a relationship-oriented leader still has to make sure that the group accomplishes its goals.

How would you use this style of leadership if you were the leader of a group planning a class party? You would see your role as guiding the group and getting everyone involved in the planning. With this kind of leadership style, you guide rather than direct group discussions. You listen as members share their ideas. Knowing that everyone's opinion is important, you make sure that all members contribute and that all members show

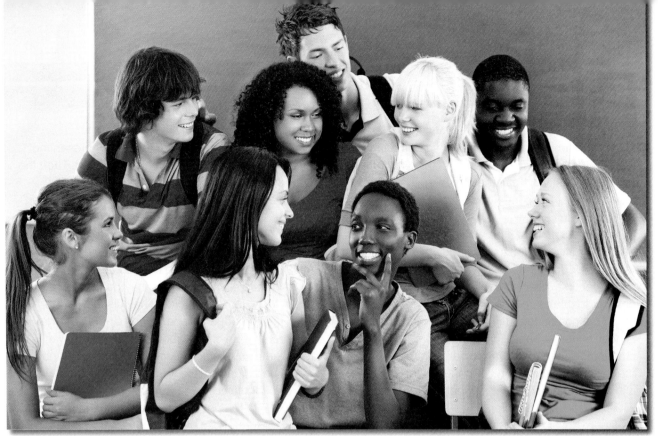

Figure 9.5 A relationship-oriented leader is willing to consider each group member's ideas. *What strategies could a leader use to do this if the group is large?*

©iStock.com/skynesher

respect for each other's ideas. Once you understand how each group member feels, you can ask for suggestions on setting a work schedule. Then you can ask for volunteers to carry out specific tasks. Using this approach gets everyone involved and motivates the group to reach its goal.

After the class party, evaluate your group's success. Ask the group members to share what they think worked and what did not work and why they think so. You lead the group to discuss and decide what could be done better next time.

Developing Your Leadership Style

Most people are more comfortable with one leadership style or the other. Many strong leaders use both, depending on the needs of the situation. Developing leadership skills takes time and practice. Your effectiveness in a leadership role will depend on your personality, the situation, and the other group members.

Examine Your Personality

Considering your personality is an important part of determining your leadership style. If you need to get tasks done or see a job carried out, you are most likely a task-oriented leader. If you are a person who can guide people to work together, you have a relationship-oriented style. You are able to help a group come up with its own ideas and solutions. Someone who enjoys discussion and give-and-take is also probably more of a relationship-oriented leader.

How much control do you need? If you are task-oriented, you may want to supervise each phase of a project. On the other hand, you may want others to be responsible for various parts of the project.

> ### Think About Your Reading
> Analyze your own personality, personal preferences, and leadership skills to identify whether you would prefer to lead with a task-oriented or relationship-oriented style.

Using Leadership Skills

A community group has formed a committee of five with the task of finding a band for an upcoming community festival. Kayla has been appointed the chairperson of the committee.

Kayla's first step was to call each of her committee members to ask what time would be convenient for them to meet. She also asked if they had any specific concerns or questions they wanted to talk about at the meeting. Then she asked each committee member to think about some possibilities for a band.

At the committee's first meeting, Kayla stated its goal: finding a band. Then she asked the group to brainstorm the qualities the band should have. The next step was to think of bands in the area that fit these qualities. This helped them determine the suitable choices available.

Then, Kayla guided the group in evaluating the alternatives. They identified both positive and negative factors for each band. At that point, the committee members felt they needed more information to make a decision. They needed to know which bands were available that night, what kind of music each could play, and what they charged. The committee members agreed to research one band each, and Kayla assigned one band to each person. They agreed on the date for the next meeting, when they would discuss what they learned.

At the next meeting, the members presented the information they had gathered about the bands. The group as a whole discussed all the alternatives. Kayla could tell that two committee members favored one band and two favored another. She wondered if she should call for a vote. She did not want to have the committee divided. Instead, she suggested the committee present a report to the larger community group without recommending a specific band. All the members of the committee agreed. As chairperson,

Kayla drew up the report for the group, presenting all the factors the committee had identified. Then the large group voted for the band it wanted.

After the large group voted, Kayla implemented a plan. She asked the committee member who had supported the band that was chosen to make the contact and confirm the date. Arrangements were made, and the band came for the community festival.

After the event was over, the committee met again to evaluate its choice. They discussed the qualities and performance of the band. They shared comments from others about how the band was received. They also discussed whether the band would be a good choice for another event that was going to take place two months later. This evaluation was put into a report and presented to the entire group for future reference.

For Discussion

1. In leading the group through the decision-making process, when did Kayla use a relationship-oriented style of leadership?
2. Why do you think she used a relationship-oriented style of leadership in this situation?
3. When did Kayla use a task-oriented style of leadership?
4. Why do you think she used the task-oriented approach?
5. Do you think one style would be more effective than the other? Explain your reasoning.
6. What technique did Kayla use to develop rapport in her group?
7. What technique did she use to get the group members involved?
8. How did she encourage unity and avoid division in her small group?
9. Explain why you think Kayla was or was not an effective group leader?

Examine the Situation

Before you agree to lead a group, it is helpful to evaluate the situation (**Figure 9.6**). What type of situation needs leadership? If you are a task-oriented leader, is it a structured situation? Can the different parts of the task be identified? Will there

be specific guidelines to follow? Will you be able to exercise the kind of control you desire?

If you are a relationship-oriented leader, will the situation be challenging? Will you be able to use your creativity, as well as that of group members'? Are you willing to lead the group in forming its goals?

Guidelines for Evaluating a Leadership Situation	
1. Know your leadership style.	
Task-Oriented	**Relationship-Oriented**
• Focus on getting a job done. • Emphasize parts of the task. • Identify the expected outcome. • Set specific guidelines. • Exercise control over group.	• Focus on feelings and needs. • Emphasize people. • Leave some goals open to discussion. • Allow for creativity. • Encourage members to share responsibilities.
2. Evaluate the leadership style needed for the situation. 3. Compare your personal preferences with the requirements of the situation. 4. Evaluate whether the group members will support you.	

Figure 9.6 Deciding whether to take a leadership position with a group requires careful thought. *What other factors might you consider before agreeing to lead a group?*

Most situations require a flexible leader. To be flexible, you may need to use parts of each leadership style. Part of the time, you may need to focus on group relationships. You may need to encourage group members to add their opinions and ideas. You may need to help the group relax and work as a unit. Then, as the ideas are put together into a plan, you may need to become more task-oriented. You may need to exercise more control to get the job completed. In these situations, you use skills for both styles of leadership.

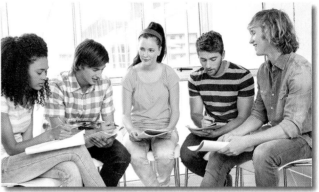
©iStock.com/Wavebreakmedia

Figure 9.7 Determining group members' expectations of you can help you choose the correct leadership style.

Examine the Group Members

In thinking about the most effective leadership style for a particular group, you also need to consider whether you will be able to get the group members to work together. If they elect you, you probably will have their support. If you are appointed for a position, you may need to determine the group's expectations of you (**Figure 9.7**). Whatever the case, you need the confidence and support of the group members to succeed. Think about the task to be completed and the relationship that exists between you and group members.

Developing skills for both styles of leadership is helpful for all leaders. The key is to be flexible and use the style that is needed for the situation and the makeup of the group. Whatever the situation, all leaders need to practice their skills as they work to fulfill their leadership roles.

LESSON 9.1

Assess

COMPREHENSION CHECK

1. List the four main responsibilities of a group leader.
2. Explain why effective leaders need good communication skills.
3. Describe two small-group discussion techniques and two large-group discussion techniques.
4. Give an example of a situation in which you would use A) a task-oriented leadership style and B) a relationship-oriented leadership style.
5. Which style of leadership would you prefer to work under? Describe the characteristics of that style of leadership.

Content Terms

Build
Vocab

teamwork
chairperson
secretary
minutes
parliamentary procedure
Robert's Rules of Order
constitution
bylaws
agenda
constructive feedback

Academic Terms

disbanded
expertise
cohesive
etiquette

Objectives

After studying this lesson, you will be able to

- **describe** the characteristics of a successful group.
- **identify** responsibilities of effective group members.
- **plan**, **organize**, and **evaluate** a group meeting.

Focus Your Reading

1. As you read, write a list of the qualities of an effective group member. Underline the qualities that you already demonstrate and circle the qualities that you need to develop.

2. Find an example of a constitution for a group. Look at the constitution and identify the people required to make this group function.

People take part in groups for different reasons, and these reasons may change over time. Some people join a group so they can take part in a worthwhile project related to a cause they value or that meets their needs. Others join a group to make friends by meeting people who share similar interests (**Figure 9.8**). Some join a group so they can learn a new skill from an experienced person willing to share his or her expertise with other group members.

In your school and work life, you will most likely belong to several different groups. You may work on a project with a team of people that is *disbanded*, or broken up, when the project is completed. You may be part of a training group that takes part in classroom and hands-on instruction to learn a new set of skills or procedures. Employers form work groups because no one employee is likely to have all the *expertise*, or specialized knowledge, that a situation requires. By drawing on people from different departments or areas of the organization, a team can take advantage of many individuals' skills and knowledge.

Groups are important because a collection of people can accomplish what no single member can do in the same amount of time. Whatever the type of group you take part in, you can help

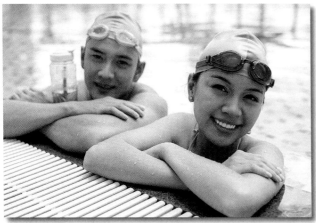
©iStock.com/DragonImages

Figure 9.8 People join groups for many reasons. *What are some interests that would attract you to join a group?*

that group succeed by gaining a set of skills that will help make you an effective group member.

Think About Your Reading

What are some examples of groups you were in as a child? in the teen years? In what groups do your parents or other family members take part? How do these groups meet different needs?

Qualities of Successful Groups

Successful groups demonstrate **teamwork**, which means everyone does his or her part to help the group accomplish its goals. For teamwork to take place, all members of a group must be recognized as important. Everyone must feel they contribute equally to the group's common goals. In addition, all members of the group must do their part, carrying out their work responsibly and correctly.

Group Goals

Goals give a group a sense of purpose and direction. Group members know what they are expected to accomplish as a team. An effective group will have clearly defined goals to which group members can relate. Members can see that their personal goals will be met through the

group goals. As the team members work together to fulfill group goals, their personal needs are met as well. If a group has no purpose or direction, members will have no clear idea of where to direct their efforts or what is expected of them.

Leaders guide the group to reach its goals. At the same time, leaders listen to and include the ideas of the team. Active team members participate in reaching goals by attending meetings, contributing ideas, working on committees, and taking part in group activities.

Think About Your Reading

What are some goals that you could accomplish by joining a group?

Cohesiveness

Successful groups are *cohesive*. They stick together because group members feel they belong to the group. Groups members feel their input is important and, in turn, accept other members' contributions. All members feel that they can express their ideas and opinions and take part in setting goals and making plans to meet those goals. The group as a whole cooperates and takes responsibility in carrying out tasks. Support within the group brings feelings of satisfaction and keeps the group intact.

Group Setting

Groups are more productive when the setting for the group's activities matches its plans and goals (**Figure 9.9**). If the group is large, breaking into small teams can promote a good exchange of ideas. Small teams work best at round tables, which allow members to look directly at one another as they talk.

Group Structure

Every group needs some type of structure. Group members need to know what is expected of them so they can work to reach goals. Leaders guide and motivate the group. Group members support their leaders to help make the group

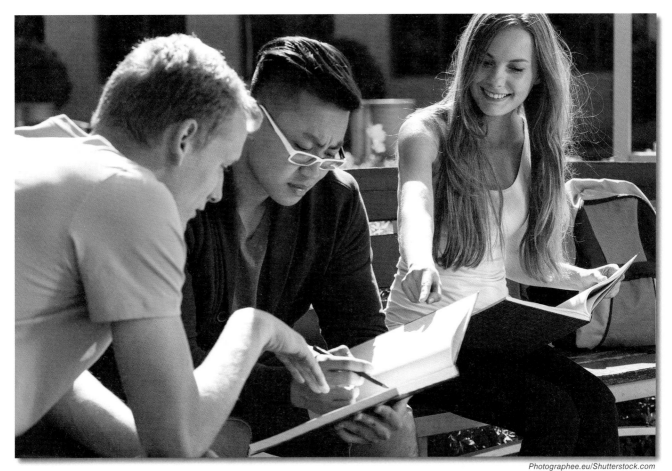

Photographee.eu/Shutterstock.com

Figure 9.9 This casual setting is effective for informal discussion, but could slow serious decision making. *What might be some distractions that would hinder productive work in such a setting?*

successful. This structure helps the group effectively meet its goals.

Roles and Responsibilities of Group Members

Group members are just as important as group leaders. Group members are the ones who complete tasks and reach goals. You can be an effective group member by fulfilling the following roles and responsibilities:

- *Be a clear communicator.* When you talk, make clear and simple statements to help others in the group understand your comments and point of view. Use active listening to make sure you understand what others share. Show respect for other members by commenting only on ideas, not on the person who gave them.

- *Be cooperative.* You may need to give up your personal desires in order to help the group reach its goal. When all members cooperate, they will be more willing to work together for the benefit of the whole group.

- *Be willing to participate.* You need to be willing to express your ideas, even if your suggestions are not carried through in the plan of action. Most group plans have several steps to carry out. As a team member, you need to be willing to help carry out the plan.

- *Control your participation.* Communication in a group first involves paying attention to others. Listen carefully so that you understand the purpose and direction of each discussion. Decide whether you have something to contribute (**Figure 9.10**). If you do not, wait until the discussion moves to a point where you can offer useful information or ideas.

Think About Your Reading

If one or two group members talk all the time, what effect will it have on the group's success?

- *Be an informed participant.* Prepare for group meetings. Knowing what issues will be discussed, what information is needed, and what can be expected will help you contribute to the group.

- *Control your emotions.* Intense emotions lower the chance of sending clear and accurate messages. If you feel your emotions are getting too strong to make your thoughts constructive to a discussion or task, you may want to be quiet until you feel calm again.

- *Be empathetic to others' emotions.* If another group member becomes upset or angry, suggest that the group take a break. Then that person can go for a walk, get some exercise, or find some other way to calm down and collect his or her thoughts. If necessary, talk to the person to try to help him or her resolve the issue causing the upset. Try to be respectful of group members and their feelings.

- *Support the leader and the group.* Team leaders need the support of the team. Let your leaders know they are doing a good job. They appreciate constructive input that team members have to offer. Be supportive of other members as well, especially new members who may need encouragement as they are welcomed into the group. If someone contributes a good idea or does a particularly good job on a task, show you recognize and appreciate it.

  Developing the skills of an effective group member is an important task for all workers. You will need these skills on the job. They are an important part of the professional *etiquette* or appropriate behaviors that will help you succeed in the world of work.

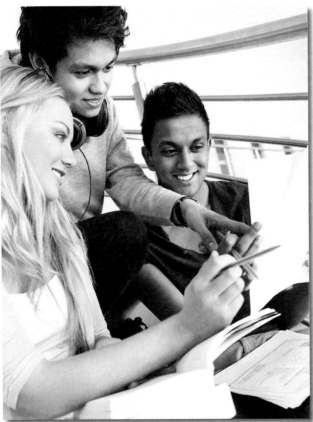

©iStock.com/Dean Mitchell

Figure 9.10 Knowing when to speak and when to keep quiet can help members contribute to the effectiveness of the whole group. *What are some examples of I-statements that a leader could use to open the door for others to share their ideas?*

How to Plan, Organize, and Evaluate a Group

Groups provide opportunities for people to learn together (**Figure 9.11**). Many of these experiences provide opportunities for group interaction, helping members develop their group skills. Some experiences build leadership skills. Still other experiences are related to the specific tasks or goals of the group.

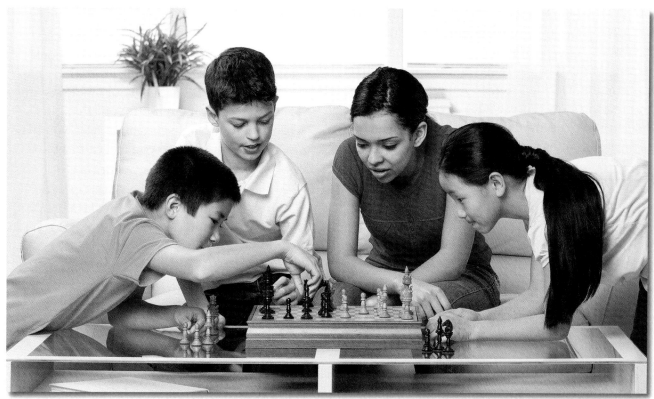

AVAVA/Shutterstock.com

Figure 9.11 Groups may be formed with a few people or many people. *What interests could you share with younger-aged children that could help them grow and develop?*

Student organizations provide many opportunities to meet all these needs. Family, Career and Community Leaders of America, Inc. (FCCLA), for instance, is open to students in family and consumer sciences classes. The group's purpose is to prepare students to be leaders in their families, careers, and communities. It does this work by providing educational experiences in such areas as financial management, career planning, balancing family and careers, leadership development, and community service.

Think About Your Reading

Describe a need in your school or community that a group could possibly meet if members worked together and explain how their combined efforts could make a difference.

Planning a Group

Have you ever thought about organizing a club or group? Perhaps you share a common interest with others. You may have identified a personal need you feel could be met in a group. For example, if you enjoy running as a form of exercise, you might like some companions to run with you. Whatever prompts the decision, you alone or you and one or two other interested individuals can easily start a group. Begin by planning the purpose of the group and writing down what you want to accomplish. Contact others who might be interested in joining. Use e-mails, newspaper articles, bulletin board notices, or announcements to let other people know that you want to start the group (**Figure 9.12**).

Organizing the Group

If the group will be a local chapter in a national organization, contact the headquarters for information. People there will help you get started with step-by-step procedures to follow so that your local chapter meets any requirements the national organization has. If you are organizing a stand-alone group, you need to appoint someone to lead the first meeting when the group organizes itself.

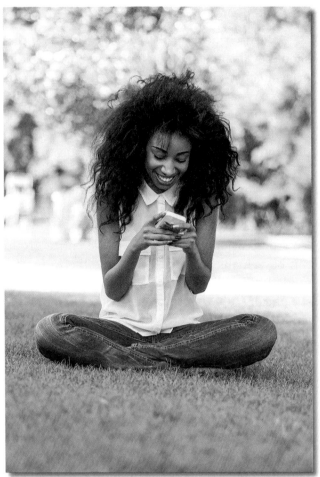
Samuel Borges Photography/Shutterstock.com

Figure 9.12 You can use communication technologies to help get people interested in your group.

You or one of the other individuals who started the group would be a logical choice. You can also ask someone to keep a record of the meeting until a secretary is elected.

Elect Officers

Typically, groups have *officers*, or people who fill specific functions. Most clubs or groups have at least a *president* or **chairperson**, who leads the other members. Also, most groups have a **secretary**, who records the minutes of each meeting. The **minutes** are a record of what happens at the group meetings. There may be other officers that you feel will be needed as well. There may be a vice president, who leads the meeting when the president is absent, a treasurer, or various committee members. Officers are usually nominated

and elected for a one-year term by a majority vote of all group members present.

Identify Rules and Procedures

Many organizations follow **parliamentary procedure**. This is an orderly way of conducting a meeting and discussing business. The procedure is detailed in the book **Robert's Rules of Order**.

Following a set procedure helps a meeting progress smoothly. The leader has a format to follow so that items of business are brought up, discussed, and decided with nothing important neglected. Following procedures also helps ensure that discussions are orderly. Group members know when they can speak and when to complete business. Voting procedures give members input in making group decisions.

A newly formed group will need to develop a constitution and bylaws. A **constitution** is a formal written statement that governs how the group functions. It usually states the purpose and broad goals of the group. It also outlines specific benefits that members will gain from being in the group. **Bylaws** state when meetings are held and how often, when elections are held, and what procedures are used. Any other information important to the group's organization can be included in the bylaws as well.

Think About Your Reading
What problems might develop if a group does not follow rules or procedures?

Prepare for Meetings

Successful groups have an agenda for every meeting. An **agenda** is a list of what the group will be doing and discussing at a meeting (**Figure 9.13**). The group leader—the chair or president—should prepare the agenda and distribute it to the group members in advance of the meeting. The leader's copy may be more detailed with specific ideas or questions to guide the members' participation or the discussion.

Group Meeting Agenda
1. Call to order
2. Reading and approval of minutes
3. Officers' reports
4. Committee reports
5. Unfinished business
6. New business
7. Program
8. Announcements
9. Adjournment

Figure 9.13 Most meetings follow this order of business, which is based on parliamentary procedure. *How could using a structured agenda help a group meet its goals?*

The leader or officers can also plan the amount of time needed for the group to work through the agenda (**Figure 9.14**). By keeping the agenda concise, most items can be completed during the meeting. No more than one item should be left unfinished. Group members will feel discouraged if they see that too much is left undone.

Physical arrangements for the meeting should be made in advance. Tables and seats can be arranged in the most effective way for the work that needs to be done. Any needed supplies should be gathered before the meeting. If the meeting is long enough, a break should be planned at a logical stopping point in the agenda.

The leader also needs to consider what type of leadership style to use so that the meeting will be successful. In some parts of the meeting, a relationship style may be required. Group members may need to express personal opinions and feelings related to an issue being discussed. At other points in the agenda, the leader may need to be more task-oriented to organize getting a task done.

Think About Your Reading
What problems could develop when a meeting is not well planned?

Evaluate the Group

After each meeting, the leader and other officers should evaluate what took place. A short checklist of evaluation questions works well to guide this process: What parts of the meeting went smoothly? Which did not? Were there any problems that surfaced in the meeting? If so, how can these be handled in future meetings? What techniques seemed to encourage group members to engage in the discussions and decision making? If there was a lack of involvement, how can the group members be encouraged to participate in the future?

An occasional evaluation by the entire group can be valuable, too. This can take the form of a guided discussion during a special meeting held specifically for the purpose, with all members answering evaluation questions. Small-group discussion techniques can be used to bring out members' opinions. At the opening of an evaluation meeting, the purpose and goals of the group should be stated. This reminder can help the members evaluate the various meetings and activities to see if they are truly meeting the group's goals.

Evaluations provide the opportunity for officers and members to give constructive feedback. **Constructive feedback** is information that can be used to identify processes that worked or improve ones that need to be changed. Constructive feedback can be positive or negative. An example of positive feedback is praising the way a project or task was carried out because it was well organized, with good communication among those doing the project. Feedback that says nothing more than "the car wash team did a great job" is not constructive feedback because it does not provide any specifics about how or why they worked well together. Constructive feedback can be negative as long as the comments can be used to address problems. Complaining about confusion or blaming the leader for poor leadership is not constructive feedback. Saying "having written instructions might make the process easier and smoother to carry out" is constructive even though it points to problems. This type of feedback is valuable and will help any group work toward meeting its goals.

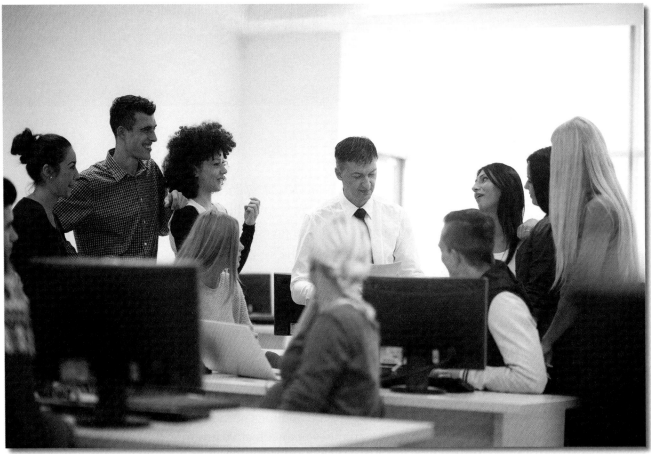

dotshock/Shutterstock.com

Figure 9.14 *What would be the benefit of a leadership team reviewing agenda items before a large group meeting?*

Think About Your Reading

What are some ways that you could provide constructive feedback on a project if no formal evaluation was held?

The groups you are part of and the role you play in them will change over your life span, as your needs and interests change. Not all groups will be organized and run as formally as the steps just described. The basic steps in planning, organizing, and running a group, however, will help any group you are a part of be successful in reaching its goals.

LESSON 9.2

Assess

COMPREHENSION CHECK

1. List two characteristics of a successful group.
2. Explain how group goals can help a group stay together.
3. List six responsibilities of a group member.
4. Why should a group have clearly defined rules and procedures?
5. Explain the purposes of a group's constitution and bylaws.
6. Suppose you are interested in forming a new group. In your own words, briefly describe how you would plan and organize a group meeting.

EFFECTIVE WORKPLACES

Content Terms

Build Vocab

work team
supervisor
customer relations
customer service

Academic Terms

workplace
designated

Objectives

After studying this lesson, you will be able to

- **describe** relationship skills needed by effective employees.
- **identify** skills of an effective member of a work team.
- **explain** how skills for relating to customers can impact a business.

Focus Your Reading

1. As you read about each type of workplace relationship, identify specific skills that will help you be successful in your work relationships.
2. Compare the qualities needed by members of a work team to the qualities of an effective group member.

A *workplace* is a large group in which all the employees are members of the group. Over your life span, you are likely to work in many different workplaces and have several different roles in them, including varying roles for leadership. Thus, your group interaction skills will impact your success in the workplace and affect your quality of life.

An effective workplace is one in which the goals of an employer are met. For this to happen, all members of the group need to collaborate toward those goals. Having and using good relationship skills will help employers and employees work together to create an effective workplace. Leaders need to exercise appropriate leadership skills, matching their styles of leadership with the tasks being completed by the group. Group members need to exercise effective group member skills.

Relationships in the workplace need to be professional. They need to focus on the work being completed, whether it is a service being provided to a customer or a product being made. Skills for developing good relationships still apply in order for people to feel satisfied with their experiences in the workplace.

Relating to Fellow Employees

Using good communication and relationship skills will help you contribute to a positive work environment. Skills of being friendly and developing rapport will help you get to know others in business or industry settings and build positive attitudes between colleagues.

Effective employees benefit the company they work for. Develop these communication and relationship skills to help you be an effective employee in business and industry settings (**Figure 9.15**):

- Use active listening to make sure you have a shared meaning.
- Listen to directions carefully and follow them.
- Ask questions about anything you do not understand.
- Speak clearly and distinctly so that others can easily understand what you are saying.
- Practice being friendly so you can get along with everyone.
- Show respect for others' ideas, positions, and perspectives as you collaborate with coworkers to carry out assigned work.
- Keep a positive attitude as you solve problems and work together toward goals, recognizing that diverse opinions and positions can help a work team identify good alternatives.
- Keep all communication on the job at the professional level.
- Use communication tools capably and responsibly. Taking personal calls at work takes time away from the job you are doing. Personal calls, e-mails, or messages should be returned during breaks or after work, not during job time.

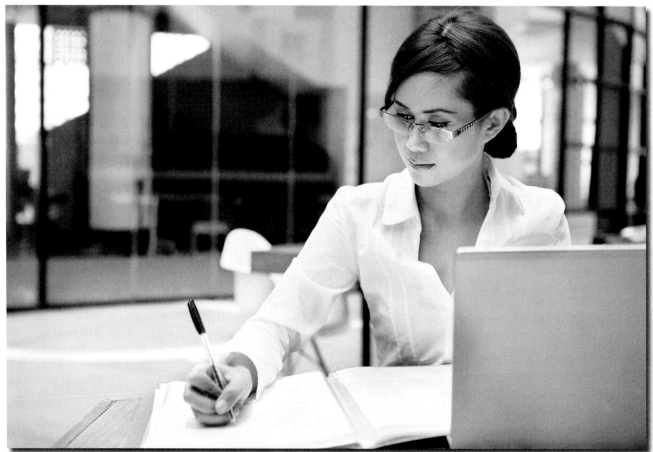

Creativa Images/Shutterstock.com

Figure 9.15 Good communication skills can help you be an effective employee. *Why would speaking and listening skills be important even if you are providing services online?*

Think About Your Reading

How could personal relationships at work interfere with good job performance?

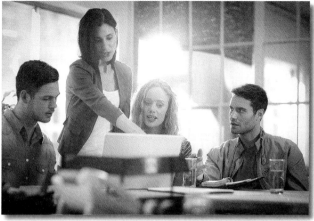

wavebreakmedia/Shutterstock.com

Figure 9.16 In many jobs, people work together in a work team to produce products, provide services, set goals, or solve problems. *What group interaction skills are needed for a work team to be effective?*

Because friendships develop between people who have much in common, you may develop some close friendships with your coworkers. If you do, remember that the work you are doing is the only activity that should take place during the workday. Activities that you and those coworkers do as friends need to take place outside of the workplace. In addition, you need to interact with each other in a professional manner at the workplace.

It is not often that you will like everyone with whom you work. You may have nothing in common with your coworkers. You may have different personalities, interests, points of view, and ways of communicating. You will still need to find a way to work together positively and contribute to an effective workplace. Your skills for being an effective employee can help you work with others in diverse situations to reach the goals of your employer.

Being Part of a Work Team

Your employer will expect you to work cooperatively with others to meet the goals of the workplace. This means you will need to be an effective member of a work team (**Figure 9.16**). A **work team** is a group that is brought together to complete a task as a result of the jobs that members do. An effective work team requires both effective leadership and effective group participation. Depending on the work setting, you may have different roles in different work teams and need to use good leadership skills and group interaction skills.

The leader of a work team is the person who takes charge in the group. In many work teams, one of the members has more responsibility and is *designated*, or assigned, to be the leader when the team is formed. An effective leader needs skills for communicating, directing discussion, motivating all team members, and solving problems as the team identifies its goals, develops a

plan to reach the goals, and carries out the plan. In some settings, the work team shares the leadership responsibilities. The whole team collaborates as they work together to identify goals and plans to reach those goals. Team members also work together to solve problems that arise as they progress toward their goals.

Group members are usually assigned to a work team based on their skills and knowledge of a particular area of the organization's activities. That means that others will depend on each member to contribute what he or she knows and to complete his or her share of the work. If a team member fails to go to work, others will have to pick up the slack, which is not fair to them and is potentially destructive to the work team's goals. Teams also need people to do different parts of the work. The team's success will be greater if the jobs each person does match each person's personal strengths. When you are on a work team, being honest and open with other members about your skills will help your team be successful.

Think About Your Reading

What would be the benefits of working in a work team under a designated leader? What could be some benefits of sharing leadership in a work team?

Group Problem Solving

Any time you work toward a goal, various obstacles are likely to arise that need to be overcome so the group can move forward. A work team can use the steps in problem solving when it encounters challenges in carrying out group plans (**Figure 9.17**). In step 1, the team identifies the problem and the challenges the team is facing. Brainstorming is a good discussion technique to gather input from all team members. All ideas are put on the table as the team tries to identify the root cause of their problem and then move to step 2, in which they identify possible alternative

Applying the Steps of Problem Solving in a Work Setting		
Goal: The team has a goal of increasing production by 10 percent by the end of the month. Two weeks have gone by, and production has increased by only 3 percent.		
Step 1 Identify the problem.		
The team first tried to identify the root cause of their problem by *brainstorming*. John suggested that illness has kept some of the team from contributing, and thus they were behind in reaching their goals. Mia suggested that time was lost while they waited for materials to arrive from vendors. Raul thought some time was lost when the Internet access was interrupted. The team agreed that their production was slowed due to several outside interruptions. How could they control the impact of these interruptions?		
Step 2 Identify alternative solutions.		
Alternative 1: Raul suggested the team look at some of their projects to see if information could be shared, thus saving individual team members some time in being ready for the sales team.	*Alternative 2*: Mia suggested that team members who were sick find some way of increasing their production when they returned.	*Alternative 3*: John suggested they seek an alternative Internet provider.
Step 3 Evaluate the alternatives.		
Alternative 1: The team's projects all have some similar resources that could be used by everyone on the team. Sharing could save time.	*Alternative 2*: People returning to work from being sick would find it difficult to work harder than they already were.	*Alternative 3*: Seeking an alternative Internet provider would take time and require input from more people than just their team.
Step 4 Choose the best solution.		
The team looked at the three options and decided that alternative #1 had the best promise of helping them reach their team goal without requiring any one person make up for lost time.		
Step 5 Implement the solution.		
John, Mia, and Raul identified all the projects they would need to complete in order to reach their goal. They identified which resources they could share to save time on individual research, and split those research tasks between the three of them. Saving individual time would ultimately help all three increase production and reach the team goal.		
Step 6 Evaluate the solution.		
After one week, the team reviewed their progress. Their total production had increased to 7 percent, and they were on target to make their goal of 10 percent by the end of the month.		

Figure 9.17   The steps of the problem-solving process can be applied to work settings.

solutions. Input from all team members helps ensure that all aspects of the problem and all possible solutions are identified in this step.

In step 3, the team analyzes the solutions, looking to find the one that is most effective in helping the team reach their goal. Again, input from all members helps the team clarify possible consequences of each option.

In step 4, the team chooses an option. Whatever option is chosen, all team members need to agree that it is the best possible choice for the team. This is where *consensus building* can be used so that the choice is acceptable to everyone on the team. One alternative may benefit some team members, but not others. That alternative will be discarded in the consensus-building process. Team members need to compromise, giving up some aspects they value so that the entire team benefits. The alternative chosen is one that everyone agrees will benefit the team as a whole.

In step 5, the team carries out the agreed-upon solution. Each member of the team must work to implement his or her part of the solution. In step 6, the team members need to provide *constructive feedback* as part of the evaluation process. What worked well? What could have been done differently? The goal is to create an even more effective work team.

Relationships with Supervisors and Authority Figures

As an employee, you will work for an employer who may be an individual, a group of partners in a small company, or a larger organization with several tiers of managers and supervisors. In most work situations, you will be required to report to someone who is in authority over you. A **supervisor** is the person who serves as a leader for a permanent work team. Your supervisor will be responsible for the work assigned to and completed by your regular team (**Figure 9.18**). If your team is not reaching its goals, your supervisor will take steps to correct the problem. He or she may ask your team to work harder or faster, assign different team members to different tasks, or have the team collaborate and come up with their own solution.

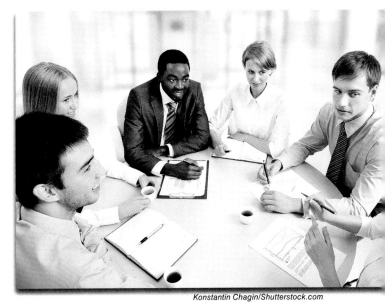

Konstantin Chagin/Shutterstock.com

Figure 9.18 A supervisor may be responsible for assigning work to a team and making sure that it is completed in a timely manner. *What leadership skills will help a supervisor be successful?*

Remember the different leadership styles that people may use to lead. Your supervisor may use a style of leadership that you really do not like. It is important, however, to work effectively under any leadership style. The skills used by an effective employee will help you be a contributing team member no matter which style of leadership your supervisor uses.

Your supervisor will report to his or her own supervisor or manager. Thus, the work you and your team members do impacts the success of your supervisor, as well as that of the entire company. At all levels of management, different teams will make decisions that will impact others in the company. The work atmosphere will be more positive if you are friendly, show interest in your work, and do your very best. Show respect for your supervisors and other authority figures when you interact with them. Showing respect to them will help you gain their respect. Mutual respect promotes clear communication and reaching common goals.

You are not likely to become close friends with your supervisor; you should not expect to do so or be disappointed if it does not happen. Your relationships with supervisors and authority figures should be on a professional level. Your

supervisor's main focus is getting the job done well. Consequently, you will be valued to the degree that you contribute to this goal.

Customer Relations

Customer relations refer to all the interactions that take place when you are providing services to the people who are your employer's customers. Customers may be members of the public or individuals who represent other businesses that are interested in the products or services your employer provides. These interactions with customers are critical to the success of a business. If customers are satisfied, they are more likely to return. If they feel offended or unappreciated, they will likely go elsewhere for their business. Your communication style can make a big difference in the success of your employer.

Friendly service is the key to good customer relations. A smile along with some general conversation can make customers feel comfortable and welcome. **Customer service** means you meet the customer's needs in an efficient, effective, and courteous manner. It is your desire to please and help customers. That will likely require you to ask some questions like, "Can I help you? Are you finding what you are looking for? Do you have any questions?" You also need to have knowledge of the product or service your employer provides and understand how it can meet your customer's needs.

Your interactions with customers may take place in person, on the phone, or online. Whatever the communication method, expressing a desire to help and please the customer will help the interaction go smoothly. On the phone, use a friendly, pleasant voice when talking to customers. You need to use good communication skills, both speaking and active listening, as you ask questions, listen to the answers, and try to match the customer's needs and your employer's products or services. Remember to keep the conversation related to the task at hand. Working with customers is an occasion when a professional relationship is needed (**Figure 9.19**).

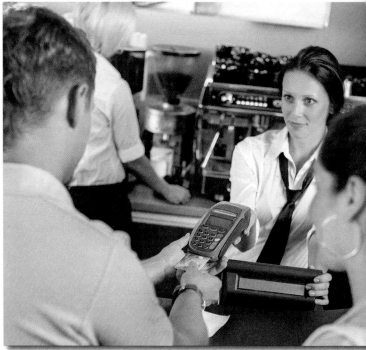

CandyBox Images/Shutterstock.com

Figure 9.19 A friendly and courteous approach is key to making customers feel comfortable and willing to return to your place of business in the future. *What other skills might you need in order for a customer to be happy with your service?*

Think About Your Reading

How do you like to be treated when you are shopping for a purchase? What type of service helps you make an informed purchase?

LESSON 9.3
Assess

COMPREHENSION CHECK

1. List the relationship skills an effective employee will demonstrate.
2. Explain what it means to be an effective group member in a work team.
3. How should you respond to an authority figure in the workplace?
4. Why are relationships with customers so important to the success of a company?
5. What are the characteristics of good customer relations?

CHAPTER SUMMARY

Groups are important because they can accomplish what no single person can do in the same amount of time. Many opportunities exist in which people become involved in a group, either as leaders or group members. Skills for leadership and group interaction can be learned and can contribute to success throughout the life span.

Effective leadership is needed for a group to be successful. A leader is responsible for seeing that goals are identified, plans are made to carry out the needed tasks, and the work is done so that goals are met. Leaders may use a task-oriented style or a relationship-oriented style to meet their responsibilities. The role of leader also requires skills for communicating, directing discussions, motivating members, and problem solving.

Being an effective member of a group requires skills for speaking and listening, a willingness to relate to and work with other people as a team, and the ability to work toward group goals. An organized group will benefit from having a structure with defined leadership and procedures.

Effective workplaces are examples of groups working together to reach the goals of the employer. Effective employees will utilize communication and relationship skills to successfully carry out the work assigned to them. They will fulfill roles of leader or group member as needed in work teams and share in group problem solving through consensus building and compromise. They will relate professionally to supervisors and customers and contribute to the goals of the employer as they carry out their responsibilities at work.

VOCABULARY ACTIVITIES

1. Working with a partner, create flash cards with the following terms and brief definitions. Take turns with your partner quizzing each other to ensure that you both know the definition of each term.

Content Terms

agenda (9.2)	customer service (9.3)
bylaws (9.2)	group (9.1)
chairperson (9.2)	leader (9.1)
constitution (9.2)	minutes (9.2)
constructive feedback (9.2)	parliamentary procedure (9.2)
customer relations (9.3)	relationship-oriented leadership (9.1)

Robert's Rules of Order (9.2)	task-oriented leadership (9.1)
secretary (9.2)	teamwork (9.2)
supervisor (9.3)	work team (9.3)

2. Write sentences using each of these terms correctly. Write two sentences for each term, one applying it in a workplace setting and another, different sentence applying it to a setting outside the workplace.

Academic Terms

authoritarian (9.1)	disbanded (9.2)
cohesive (9.2)	enthused (9.1)
collaborate (9.1)	etiquette (9.2)
coordinate (9.1)	expertise (9.2)
democratic (9.1)	workplace (9.3)
designated (9.3)	

ASSESS

Your Knowledge

3. What responsibilities and roles does an effective leader carry out?
4. What are the characteristics of a successful group member?
5. Describe the qualities of an effective employee.

Your Understanding

6. Explain how each style of leadership can be used effectively.
7. Describe the characteristics of a person you would like to have in a work group with you and explain why these characteristics could help the group be effective.
8. What steps could a leader take to lead a work group in solving a team problem? How could this process contribute to an effective workplace?

Your Skills

9. Explain what style of leadership you would use to lead a group to clean up a local park. Explain why you would use that style in this situation.
10. Choose two discussion techniques to use to gather information for your club's next meeting on the topic, "Why Our School Should Have an Open Campus." Explain how you would use each choice.
11. What steps would you take to plan and organize a chapter of a national career and technical student organization at your school?

CRITICAL THINKING

12. **Support a Judgment.** Choose one of the following topics and identify which large-group discussion technique you would use to promote that topic. In a paragraph, explain your choice. Cite evidence from the text to support your choice.
    - changing the legal drinking age
    - choosing a new technology to use at work
    - developing effective parenting skills

13. **Propose a Solution.** Identify a need in your school that could be addressed by forming a new school club. Write a statement of purpose and goals for the club. Identify a style of leadership you would recommend for the club, citing evidence from the text to support that recommendation. *Group option*: Work with a partner to create the club and identify five possible bylaws for it.

14. **Make Inferences.** Think about three different group problem-solving situations in which you have been involved. In a one-page paper, describe each situation and identify and analyze the leadership style used, making a judgment regarding the effectiveness of the match between the situation and the style. Cite evidence from the text to support your judgment. If appropriate, make suggestions for and role-play improved leadership skills based on your judgment. *Group option*: Work with a partner who has been in similar group situations.

15. **Analyze Observations.** Attend a school board meeting and observe that group in action. In a paragraph, describe the way the meeting was organized and run, the group's setting, the styles of leadership used, members' involvement in discussions and decisions, and techniques of control that you observed. Cite evidence from the text to support your analysis of the style of leadership used.

CORE SKILLS

16. **Research.** Interview an employer and ask about his or her idea of an ideal employee. In a paragraph, summarize how the employer's list is similar to or different from the list of the qualities of an effective employee listed in the text. *Group option*: Work as a team, using teamwork skills, with each member interviewing a different employer. Compare each person's findings and develop a joint list of an ideal employee from this group of employers.

17. **Research.** Create a spreadsheet listing the clubs in your school. For each club, identify its purpose, goals, and organizational structure. Include a summary of the activities of the group and identify the needs it meets in group members' lives. (Do not include the school's athletic teams.) Publish your findings on the school website where extracurricular or student activities are listed.

18. **Writing.** Create an agenda for a class meeting in which you will be leading the group in identifying problems and desired changes in the hot lunch menu. Identify what items you need on the agenda, what sources of information you will need, and what types of discussion you will use to further your agenda. Put your agenda into an electronic slide format to use in leading the class. As a class, use teamwork skills to solve the problems.

CAREER READINESS

19. **Analyzing Teams in the Workplace.** Interview a person whose job requires him or her to participate in a work team on a regular basis. Ask questions about the value of collaboration; how the team functions; who serves as the leader in the group; what style of leadership is used; what roles team members take; and what strategies they use to gather information, make decisions, and solve problems. Write a report summarizing your findings and make a judgment as to whether this work group functions effectively. Explain the value of this team's collaboration in the workplace. Cite evidence from the text and from your interview to support your analysis and judgment.

20. **Creating a Workplace Leadership Manual.** Develop a leader's manual that could help you in future leadership situations in a career of your choice. Include one or two pages for each of the following sections: *Communication Tips for Leaders*, *Guiding Group Discussions*, *Techniques for Motivating Work Teams*, and *Solving Problems as a Group*. Be creative as you develop each section. Include diagrams, guidelines, lists, pictures, posters, and sample displays. Be sure to cite your sources of information. Using interpersonal communication skills, role-play presenting your manual in a business or industry setting. *Group option*: Work in groups of four to develop and complete the manual and prepare your finished product for posting on a website.

CONNECTING WITH CAREER CLUSTERS

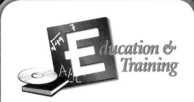

PATHWAYS

Administration and
  Administrative Support

Professional Support
  Services

Teaching/Training

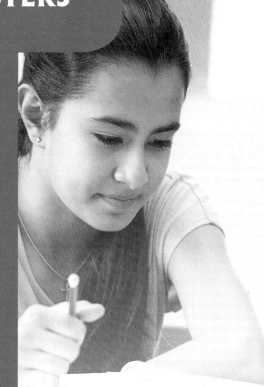

TEACHING/TRAINING

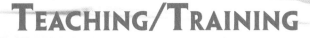

Professionals in teaching and training can be teachers at many levels. Secondary teachers work with high school students from varied backgrounds and promote learning through a variety of techniques. They focus on a specific subject area, such as family and consumer sciences, mathematics, English, Spanish, or biology.

Most teachers work in a classroom five days per week during the school year. Classrooms for some subjects have labs in which teachers facilitate practical learning. This requires constant interaction with each student as well as continual supervision of the entire class. Some teachers may also offer online courses, which require additional skills in online teaching and learning.

A bachelor's degree and completion of an approved teacher education program are needed for a teaching license in most public schools. Most states require teachers to pass competency tests in basic skills.

Jobs requiring teaching skills are also found in industry and business settings where employees need to learn new skills or updated information about products or processes used or sold by companies. In these positions, the trainer may develop a training program that meets the specific needs of a company. Trainers themselves need to be skilled in the area they teach and should have an understanding of how to teach and how adults learn.

CAREER OUTLOOK

A teaching or training career requires an ability to guide, encourage, and promote learning in others; skill in assessing student needs and designing classroom activities; a capacity for presenting information creatively; and enthusiasm for helping others develop.

Job opportunities in teaching are expected to grow about as fast as average for all occupations. There continues to be a high demand for specific subject areas, such as science, math, foreign languages, bilingual education, and some career and technical areas. Median annual earnings for all teachers in 2014 was $55,050, with a range from $39,000 to $92,000 depending on the degree level, experience, and location.

Job opportunities in training and development are expected to increase at an average rate of growth, offering in 2014 a median wage of $49 per hour and an annual salary of about $101,930. The top industries offering jobs in training and development are management companies, finance, and insurance. As technologies change, the need for training and development specialists is likely to increase.

EXPLORE

Internet Research

Search the Internet for information on a secondary teaching career in your state. Research entry and top salaries of teachers in your area. Identify two postsecondary schools that offer a program for aspiring teachers. Compare their requirements for entry, the courses of study offered, and the costs of obtaining a degree from each. Prepare a report of your findings.

Community Research

Investigate the training needs of a business or company in your community. What new changes are expected in the company's mode of operation, safety procedures, technology use, materials available, energy use, impact on the environment, or other changes you can identify? How does the company meet the training needs of its employees? Write a report summarizing your findings.

Job Shadowing

Choose a subject area that interests you and follow a teacher in your school and one in another school. Write a report on the various activities of each teacher, including before-, during-, and after-school responsibilities. Compare the jobs of the two teachers and the programs offered by each school.

Community Service/Volunteer

Spend time tutoring a subject area that you know well. Write a paragraph describing the teaching techniques you will use to help students understand the subject.

Project

Help teach in a boys' or girls' club. Plan several lessons, and for each, write lesson plans identifying the activities to use. Afterward, describe how the activities helped the children grow and develop.

Part-Time Job

Explore a teaching career by working as an aide in summer school, summer camp, a youth program, or a child care center. Develop a journal with daily entries describing the work you do, your interactions with students, the positive aspects of the job, and the frustrations you experience.

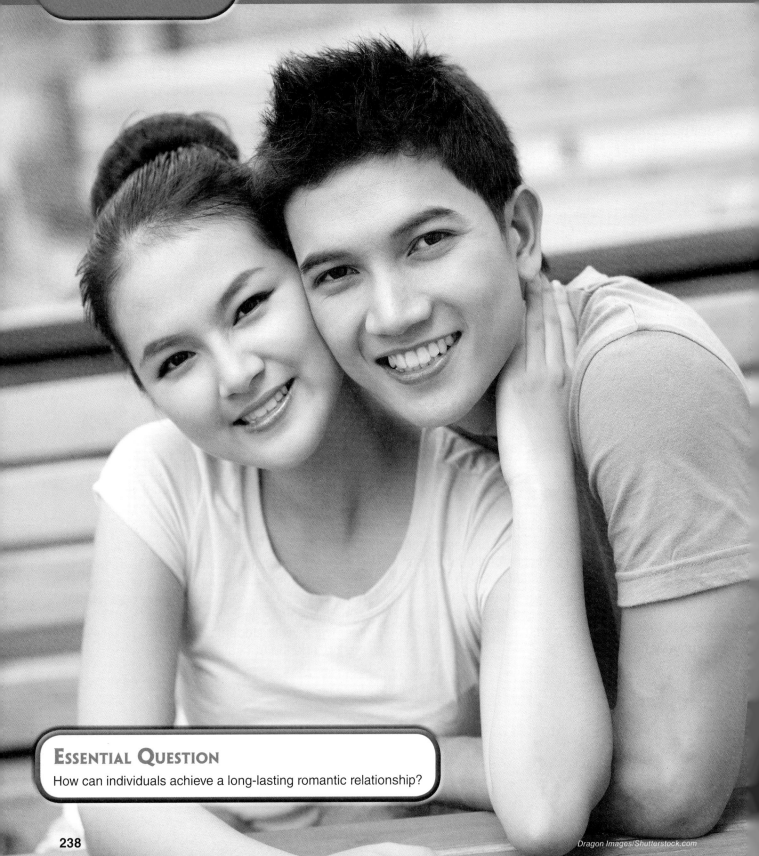

UNIT 4

ROMANTIC RELATIONSHIPS

ESSENTIAL QUESTION

How can individuals achieve a long-lasting romantic relationship?

238

Dragon Images/Shutterstock.com

CASE STUDY

Many Paths to Marriage

Read the case study and discuss the questions that follow. After finishing the chapters in this unit, discuss the questions again and identify any answers you would change based on information you learned.

Jean-Patrick knew as a young teen whom he would marry. His father had arranged a marriage for him and Monique with her father five years earlier. Their families lived close to each other in Mali, West Africa, sharing cropland, working together to dig a well, and sharing the produce from their crops. Soon they would be joining their two families through the marriage. Jean-Patrick and Monique were excited to become husband and wife. They had known each other all their lives. Their wedding was being planned by their parents, and as soon as Monique was 15, she would be married. Jean-Patrick was working hard in the family fields, as he knew the land would need to support his family as well.

Belinda enjoyed dating Immanuel. He was good-looking, strong, motivated, and knew what he wanted. He could be demanding and sometimes seemed controlling, but she knew that he loved her. He just wanted her to spend all her time with him instead of her friends. While they were in college in London, England, that was more of an issue, but now both had graduated and most of her college friends had moved away. She liked spending her time with Immanuel. Most of the time when they were together they got along well. But then there were the times when they got together with Immanuel's family. He acted very different around his family. The men all were served dinner together, and they ate first. After the men finished eating, the women and children were allowed to eat. The men and women did not interact socially. The men made decisions and went off by themselves, not even discussing their plans with the women. One weekend with his family, Belinda felt like she did not even exist to Immanuel. When she asked him about it later, he responded that it was just his family's way of doing things. Belinda began to wonder, *Would he*

be that way in our own home if we got married? How strong are these traditions that impact the way men and women relate to each other?

Shari looked around her at the little house where she and Raja lived. It was a house by Fiji standards, although she thought it really looked more like a hut. And it was not just the two of them 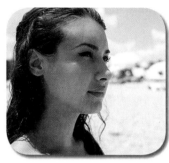 living there. His mother, five sisters and brothers, two aunts, and a grandparent also lived with them. Shari knew that Raja came from a different culture, and she thought she would be able to adjust, but this was a little much! Raja and Shari had married in Canada, where they had met in college. When Raja finished college, he persuaded Shari to move to the Fiji Islands, where he had grown up. Shari agreed, willing to adventure out into the world with the man she loved. But this situation was no longer adjusting to the man she loved, but adjusting to his whole family. She wondered if he would consider moving back to Canada.

For Discussion

1. What qualities do all three of these relationships have in common that could potentially contribute to a long-lasting marriage relationship?

2. What characteristics in each relationship could be red flags that could hinder the development of a healthy, long-lasting romantic relationship?

3. What qualities or characteristics might you look for in a spouse? Why?

Fotoluminate LLC/Shutterstock.com

DATING RELATIONSHIPS

Reading Prep

Divide the chapter among yourself and two partners. Each of you should take responsibility for preparing a study guide for one lesson and distribute that guide to your partners.

Key Questions

Questions to answer as you study this chapter:

- How does the dating process contribute to long-lasting romantic relationships?
- What are the signs of mature love?
- What are the key components of a healthy dating relationship?

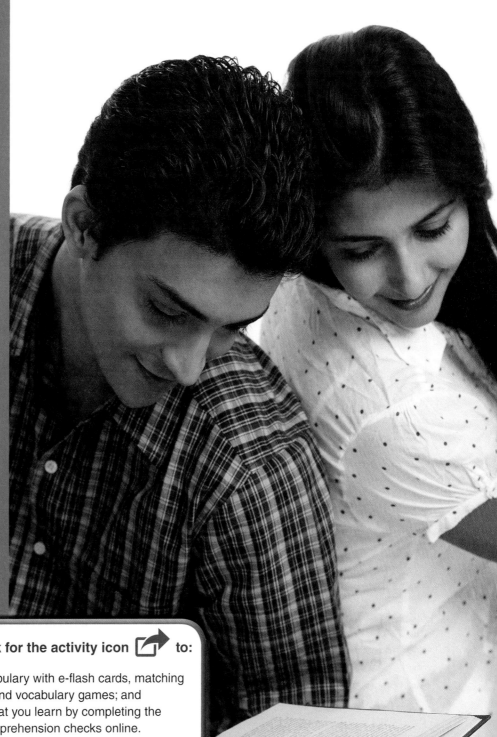

 While studying this chapter, look for the activity icon ⤴ **to:**

- **build** vocabulary with e-flash cards, matching activities, and vocabulary games; and
- **assess** what you learn by completing the lesson comprehension checks online.
  www.g-wlearning.com/humanservices/

G-WLEARNING.com

imaged.com/Shutterstock.com

AFTER STUDYING THIS CHAPTER, YOU WILL

KNOW:

- The purpose and functions of dating.
- The signs and symptoms of common sexually transmitted infections.
- The types of abuse that occur in relationships.

UNDERSTAND:

- How mature love grows and develops.
- How to evaluate a dating relationship.
- How abstinence can contribute to a person's overall well-being.

BE ABLE TO DO:

- Analyze a relationship for evidence of mature love.
- Analyze a relationship for healthy or unhealthy behavior.
- Develop assertiveness skills to say "no" to unwanted dating pressures.

GETTING STARTED

The students silently waited for their next assignment. As the teacher began to explain it, Sandy glanced at Nathan. Their eyes met, and he raised an eyebrow and smiled. He is so cute! Sandy thought as she smiled back.

The teacher suggested that students work in pairs on the new material. Nathan moved closer to Sandy. "Want to work together?" he asked.

"Sure," she calmly replied, but her heart was pounding fast.

At the same time, Dan slid over by Kyla. "Hi, Kyla! Need a partner?"

"No thanks. I think I'll work with Jed," she replied as she moved closer to Jed's desk.

Dan's smile faded. His stomach felt like lead. He wished that the ground would open up and swallow him.

You have probably experienced feelings similar to those felt by Sandy and Dan. These feelings can be both exciting and discouraging. Most teens spend a lot of time thinking, talking, and dreaming about dating. They feel elated when their attempts to develop romantic relationships are successful. They feel hurt when their attempts are rejected.

In U.S. society, young people generally make their own dating choices. They often decide whom they will date, where they will go, and what they will do on a date. Parents and peers do have some influence on these dating decisions. During the early dating years, parents often set guidelines and limits. Both parents and peers may influence a young person's decisions by their approval or disapproval. In many cases, the final decision is left to the young person. As you face these types of decisions and think about your future, it is helpful to understand the purpose and process of dating in U.S. society and the characteristics of a healthy romantic relationship.

THE DATING PROCESS

Objectives

After studying this lesson, you will be able to

- **explain** the functions of dating in U.S. society.
- **recognize** the changes that take place in relationships during the dating process.

Focus Your Reading

1. Develop a concept web with the word *Dating* at the center. Use the headings *Functions of Dating* and *Stages of the Dating Process* as main lines off the center topic. As you read, add key ideas connected to each of those ideas.

2. Before reading, work with a partner to brainstorm examples of activities that could be part of each dating stage. As you read about each dating stage, see if your examples are appropriate.

Dating is the process that leads to the development of romantic relationships. Romantic relationships are those relationships in which people are attracted to each other and which potentially could lead to an ***intimate*** (close and honest) marriage relationship. It is likely that you will have several romantic relationships before you identify one specific person with whom you think you want a relationship that will last your lifetime. The dating process can help people sort through initial feelings of attraction; find out the kind of person they want to have a long-term relationship with; and develop a deeper relationship in which two people know, love, and care for each other. These characteristics are needed for the relationship to last.

Understanding the purpose and process of dating can help you in the following ways:

- ***You keep a positive attitude about yourself.*** Dating relationships include both positive and negative experiences. Your overall attitude toward yourself can remain positive because you realize that all these experiences, even the negative ones,

are part of growing (**Figure 10.1**). You may fall in and out of love several times before finding the right partner of a lifetime.

- *You avoid a long-term commitment too early in life.* Since feelings come and go, they are not a good basis for making lifetime choices. Maturing takes time—time to learn about yourself and what you like and dislike in dating partners. It takes time to go beyond the initial attraction and develop a strong, intimate relationship that will last.

- *You make decisions that are consistent with your long-term goals.* You may have goals to finish a college education, develop a career, or save some money before marriage. Your efforts to reach these goals can be hindered by the long-term consequences of some dating decisions. By being prepared for risky situations before they arise, you can ensure that you make decisions that reflect your values and your future goals.

Think About Your Reading
What examples can you identify in which a poor dating choice affected a person's life goals?

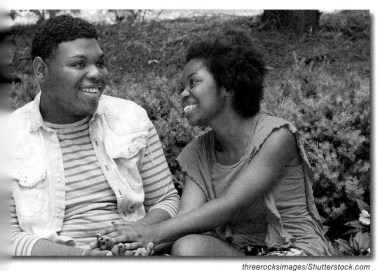
threerocksimages/Shutterstock.com

Figure 10.1 The positive and negative experiences of dating are all part of growing toward maturity.

Reasons for Dating

Dating can be a fun activity, but it also serves several different functions. Your dating years should provide experiences in which you learn about others and yourself, intellectually, socially, and emotionally. Dating also provides enjoyable companionship and gives you opportunities to develop your communication and negotiating skills and your ability to act responsibly. Finally, dating serves the function of helping you know what qualities you want in a dating partner and helping you identify whether qualities exist that will lead to a satisfying lifelong relationship.

Understanding Others

As you spend time in a dating relationship, you should learn how the other person thinks and feels. What does he or she like to do? What do the two of you have in common? What are his or her values and goals in life? It takes time to really get to know someone. You need to see a person in various situations, with different people and in different circumstances, to really learn what that person is like. How does he or she make decisions? What makes him or her upset? How does he or she work with other people to solve shared problems? Does he or she behave differently with some people than with others? What do you think causes those differences? As you observe the person in different life settings, you will get to know that person at a deeper level. It takes time— several months of time—to really know someone. If the dating process does not lead to this kind of understanding, the relationship will not last.

Understanding Yourself

As you date and get to know others, you get to know yourself better. Developing a relationship requires that you also share your ideas and feelings. As you share, and the other person reflects back what you say, you will learn more about yourself (**Figure 10.2**). It is important to be honest with yourself during the dating process. Do a self-check to make sure that you are expressing your ideas and feelings and that your input is valued in

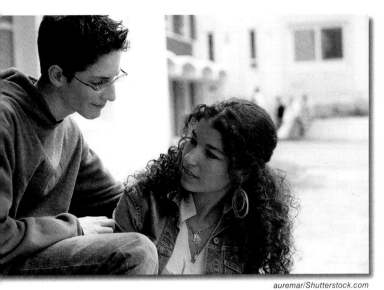

Figure 10.2 The communication that takes place in dating should help you get to know each other's thoughts, ideas, feelings, and perspectives. *How does such sharing help you grow as a person?*

the relationship. You should grow and develop as a person in the dating process.

Think About Your Reading
What are some things you might learn about yourself through dating?

Providing Companionship

Dating gives you the opportunity to spend time with someone who shares your interests. It is important to have interests in common so you will have activities you can enjoy doing together. By doing things together, you learn more about each other in various settings. Common interests, common values, and common goals are important for relationships to last over time. If you do not have activities you like to do together, the relationship will not likely last.

Improving Communication Skills

Dating provides opportunities to talk and listen to your dating partner. These skills are critical for the relationship to develop intellectually, socially, and emotionally. As a relationship grows,

deeper sharing will take place. Sharing your thoughts and ideas about various topics, including controversial ones, is important in getting to know someone well. Active listening skills will help develop the relationship and show that you are interested in what the other person thinks and feels, that you care about him or her, and that you want to reach shared understandings as you talk.

Learning to Negotiate

Dating requires that young people consider others' opinions when decisions need to be made, and thus can give you opportunities to learn how to negotiate. Neither person in a dating relationship should make all the decisions about what to do, where to go, or what to talk about. This give-and-take process requires that each person be sensitive to the other's ideas and feelings, making sure he or she feels accepted, appreciated, and validated. To feel *validated*, you will need to feel that your input has been considered to be just as important as the other person's. As you date over time, you should have several opportunities to discover how well you make decisions together, how you discuss options, how you think through alternatives, and how you make good choices. In fact, the longer you date someone, the more likely you will have a chance to practice solving problems together. When difficult situations arise, you have the opportunity to see how both of you function under pressure, such as whether you take ownership of a problem when a solution is needed. Dating experiences should help you both grow as individuals and as a couple (**Figure 10.3**).

Think About Your Reading
If one person always gives in when making decisions about where to go on a date, what effect will this have on each person's growth in the relationship?

Learning to Be Responsible

Dating provides opportunities to take responsibility for your decisions. At first, the commitments are small. Promising to meet at 4:00 is a

commitment to be reliable and to meet your date on time.

In dating, you will also need to take actions that show responsibility for other commitments you have made. Some of these commitments will be to yourself, based on your values. For instance, taking the responsibility to say no to drugs, alcohol, and sex can help you fulfill a commitment to your health. Other commitments will be to your parents.

Dating also provides experience in showing another person that you can take responsibility to care for them. You are willing to help them grow, solve a problem, or meet a need. You show that you can put aside your selfish interests. For instance, you show you are willing to put aside your own concerns when the other person is troubled and needs comfort, reassurance, or help solving problems. You may show your commitment by dropping what you are doing to meet with the person you are dating when he or she has an immediate need. Such actions help keep a relationship growing.

Evaluating Personality Traits

One of the main benefits of dating is the chance to find out what personality traits you most like in a partner. If you have dated only a few people, you do not have much information to use in making comparisons. If you have dated several people, however, you have more experience to make judgments. You learn to evaluate qualities and find those that do or do not appeal to you. You become more aware of what it takes to get along with your dating partner. The qualities you would like to find in your ideal mate for marriage become easier to identify as a result.

Stages of the Dating Process

Most dating relationships pass through several stages. They often begin informally in group situations. In **group dating**, a group of people spends time together doing activities and developing friendships. As teens get older, a couple will usually separate from the group and spend time as a pair. In **pair dating**, a couple develops a relationship with each other. Pair dating may lead

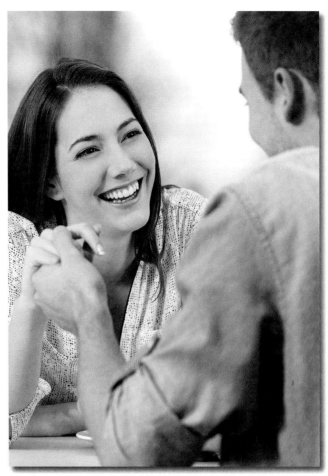

Antonio Guillem/Shutterstock.com

Figure 10.3 Dating provides opportunities for you and the other person to practice communication and problem-solving skills.

to **exclusive dating**, which is a commitment to date only one person. Eventually, a couple that is dating exclusively may make a serious, long-term commitment. Of course, many exclusive dating relationships end with a breakup.

Group Dating

Most teens develop their first dating relationship during informal group dating. It may not even be called a date, but the group hangs out together. *Hanging out* gives you a chance to interact with potential dating partners without making a commitment to one person. The entire group plans activities, so everyone can socialize, enjoy the friendship of others, and have fun (**Figure 10.4**). Group dating can provide positive growing experiences. You can get to know several of your peers. You can gain experience communicating with

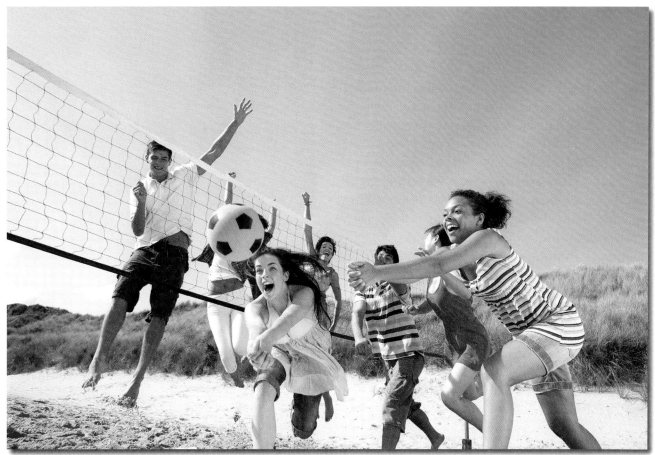

Figure 10.4 Group dates often include fun activities in a relaxed atmosphere. *How could this setting help people get to know each other?*

many different people, sharing your ideas, and listening to theirs. In these ways, you can improve your social skills.

Think About Your Reading

In what ways can dating as a group provide more opportunities for growth than pair dating?

Pair Dating

Young people usually pair off when they are attracted to one particular person. In pair dating, two people spend time as a couple building their friendship. They may go on a **formal date**, in which they attend a planned event together. At other times, they may just meet and spend time together on an informal basis.

Sometimes couples attend a **double date**, which is when another couple joins them on the date. Double dating can be a good transition from group dating to pair dating. It can help reduce the nervous feelings a new couple may feel at first over how to get to know someone and what they will talk about. Since the date is usually planned around some type of activity, the atmosphere is more relaxed. In fact, many activities are more fun when several people are involved (**Figure 10.5**).

The Advantages and Disadvantages of Exclusive Dating

Exclusive dating occurs when two people make a commitment to date only each other. Exclusive dating, sometimes called *going out*, is a statement to others that the couple has spent time getting to know each other and are not interested in pursuing an intimate relationship with other

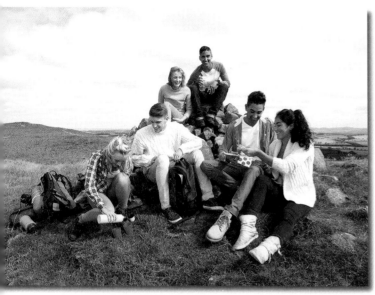
oliveromg/Shutterstock.com

Figure 10.5 Pair dating with other couples provides benefits of being in a group, yet time to get to know your specific partner. *What could you learn about your partner in a setting like this?*

peers. They have discovered each other's interests, attitudes, ideas, values, and goals in life and found a match. They both feel committed to building a close relationship exclusively with each other.

Exclusive dating does have some advantages. Besides knowing that they care for each other, the couple feels secure with each other. They feel comfortable in knowing what to expect from each other. In building the relationship, they can develop trust, openness, and respect for each other. They can relax and be themselves when they are together. As a couple, they may feel more committed to resolving and handling conflicts in a positive way.

Exclusive dating can have some disadvantages as well, however. Some young people narrow their dating to only one person for reasons other than building a long-term relationship. Some date exclusively to increase their sense of self-esteem—being special to one person makes them feel important. They may date exclusively to keep up with peers. The desire to have a steady and committed companion before you are really ready can hinder growth. It can limit your experiences with other friends and, thereby, hurt those friendships. It can limit your opportunities to meet new people who can help you learn more about yourself.

Think About Your Reading
What are the reasons that young people you know choose to date one person exclusively?

Another disadvantage is that ending an exclusive dating relationship can be difficult. Someone else has begun to count on you. If you decide that the relationship no longer works for you, you may feel trapped. You may want to avoid hurting your partner, or you may be afraid of what he or she will say to others about you. (Lesson 10.3 discusses ending a relationship.) These are the risks that go with making a commitment to one person too early in life.

Social Media and the Dating Stages

In today's world, as teens and young adults get to know each other through social media, some aspects of the dating process may take place online. A major benefit of social media is that information can be shared with many people at once. As you express your interests, ideas, values, and goals through social media, others who think and feel as you do may connect with you. It is a way of quickly narrowing down your pool of eligible dates to those who have something in common with you (**Figure 10.6**).

One major issue with meeting people through social media or dating websites, however, is that people often exaggerate their positive points and completely ignore their weaknesses. In fact, some people do not tell the truth about themselves in presenting their online personality. In other words, it is very difficult to verify honesty and truthfulness online. You need to develop trust and confidence in the real person, not the online presentation of that person, before the relationship can go far.

When developing a relationship with someone online, it is important to meet the person in a safe place before you become attached. In fact, meeting the person in a public setting in the company of friends you know and trust is a very good way to proceed safely. Predators are skilled at knowing about people from their online presence

Social media can contribute to the development of a romantic relationship, but face-to-face interaction is essential for a relationship to grow. Spending time in different settings is required to really see how mature a person is in different areas of life: how he or she acts, thinks, talks, responds to others, makes decisions, solves problems, upholds values, and works toward reaching goals.

Commitment to Marry

Although relationships vary among couples, most people follow the dating process through to an engagement to marry someone. This formal commitment is the final stage before marriage. At this point in your life, in high school, do not be surprised if you feel you are not ready to consider marriage. That feeling is very common. Marriage takes much preparation and a total commitment to the relationship.

In many relationships, the magnetism that draws two people together does not last. Exclusive dating leading to engagement and marriage should be approached slowly. It takes time for a couple to develop a relationship and identify whether the attraction they feel will be long-term or if it is best to end the relationship and begin the dating process again.

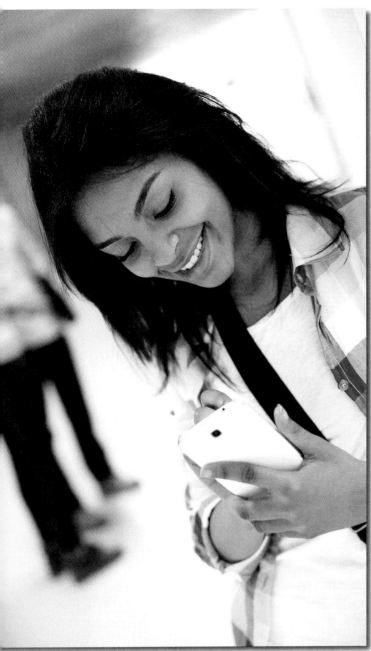

Goodluz/Shutterstock.com

Figure 10.6 Social media can help you find people with interests similar to yours. *What are some risks of dating through social media?*

and communicating messages they know those individuals want to hear. Once they have built an emotional connection with someone, they may ask that person for money or ask him or her to travel someplace to meet them alone. Either of these requests is a red flag, a clear warning that a predator is on the prowl. You should stay away from predators, for your safety's sake.

LESSON 10.1

Assess

COMPREHENSION CHECK

1. What is dating? What does the process of dating lead to?
2. Describe three ways that understanding the process of dating can help you.
3. List four reasons for dating.
4. List three reasons why group dating can provide positive growing experiences for young teens.
5. List two advantages and two disadvantages of exclusive dating.
6. Why is it important to be cautious when meeting someone that you know only through social media?

LESSON 10.2

Objectives

After studying this lesson, you will be able to

- **distinguish** between mature love, romantic feelings, and infatuation.
- **explain** how mature love grows in a relationship.
- **develop** personal boundaries that will help you reach your goals.
- **identify** benefits of choosing abstinence.

Focus Your Reading

1. Compare the similarities and differences between infatuation and mature love.
2. Research one sexually transmitted infection and summarize your findings in a paragraph.

H ow would you define *love*? A simple definition separates love into two main categories. One is the exhilarating feeling that can be called **romantic love**. The other is the long-lasting, caring, and giving type of love that can be called **mature love**. Sometimes romantic love sparks a relationship that grows into mature love. Sometimes a caring and giving friendship grows into a romantic relationship as well. Romantic love alone, however, is not enough to build a long-lasting relationship. At times, these feelings increase, then decrease. Mature love is the type of love that can keep a relationship together over a long period of time. Consequently, it is important to determine whether or not mature love exists in a relationship.

Romantic Love

The outward signs of romantic love are easy to recognize. You may have seen couples walking hand in hand, staring into each other's eyes. They are so focused on each other, they tune out the rest of the world.

Content Terms

Build Vocab

romantic love
mature love
infatuation
abstinence
personal boundaries
sexually transmitted infections (STIs)
human papillomavirus (HPV)
genital warts
gonorrhea
sterility
chlamydia
genital herpes
syphilis
hepatitis B
acquired immunodeficiency syndrome (AIDS)
human immunodeficiency virus (HIV)

Academic Terms

phenomenon
assessment
complication

Romantic Attraction

When two people are romantically attracted to each other, they feel a type of magnetism or chemistry between them. Scientists have studied this *phenomenon*, or notable occurrence. They have found that when you are attracted to someone, chemicals are released in the brain similar to those released in the stress response. These chemicals cause your heart rate to increase, make you feel sweaty and clammy, and give you a dry mouth. The stress response normally prepares the mind to make a quick *assessment*, or evaluation, of a potentially dangerous situation and prepares the body to quickly respond. This means that a lot of the reflection and logical thinking that should take place when making a decision about a dating partner will not happen when romantic attraction is driving the relationship.

What specifically attracts two people to each other has also been studied. Researchers have found that nonverbal messages appear to have more impact on romantic attraction than what people actually say (**Figure 10.7**). How someone looks, moves, stands, smiles, and makes eye contact—all these nonverbal cues contribute to how people are attracted to each other. That means you may be romantically attracted to someone you do not really know, someone you have nothing in common with, or someone who has different values and goals in life. For those reasons, it is important to build a relationship on more than romantic attraction.

Infatuation

Sometimes the strong feeling of attraction between two people is only an infatuation. **Infatuation** is a romantic attraction that tends to be self-centered or one-sided. A person may think, *This is the greatest thing that ever happened to me.* Such feelings focus on the self, rather than on the well-being of the other person. In fact, the other person may not even share the same feelings as the one who is infatuated.

Feelings of infatuation begin and often end quickly. Statements like "I loved her as soon as I saw her" or "It was love at first sight" refer to the strong attraction that one person can feel very quickly for another. Such feelings may be based on a few attractive traits in the other person. If those feelings are merely an infatuation, they may leave as quickly as they came when someone more attractive comes along.

Sometimes a couple will base their relationship on infatuation and move ahead quickly to marriage. Then they are hurt and disappointed when reality sets in. Their first disagreement may produce some unkind thoughts, words, or actions. They start to see character flaws in the other person. The feelings of infatuation start to fade. One may say, "I thought you loved me" or "I thought I knew you." Infatuations are fleeting. They are not the basis for a strong, long-term relationship.

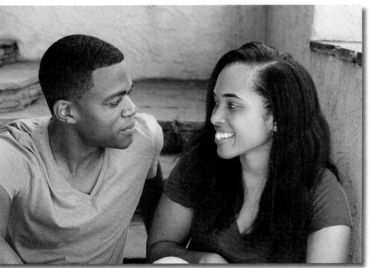
©iStock.com/lighttheway

Figure 10.7 Eye contact is a nonverbal communication technique that often is part of the initial attraction between two people. *What other nonverbal signals do you find attractive? Are there any nonverbal signals that you think could turn interest away?*

> ## Think About Your Reading
> Why might it be hard to tell if a relationship is based only on romantic attraction and infatuation?

Mature Love

Mature love is different from infatuation (**Figure 10.8**). Mature love is characterized by each partner having a giving, unselfish attitude

Infatuation Versus Mature Love	
Infatuation	**Mature Love**
Based on an instant desire for each other	Based on sharing interests and ideas
Decreases over time	Deepens and grows as a friendship grows
Self-centered, with attitudes like, "I don't want to lose you," "You're the best thing that ever happened to me," or "Let's hurry up and get married"	Others-centered, giving of the self to benefit the other person
Possessive and one-sided	Encourages growth in the other person
Leaves nagging doubts, unanswered questions, or areas that you do not want to question	Accepting of each other, even with imperfections
Lacks confidence and trust in each other's commitment	Trusting and secure
Often involves pressure to be sexually involved	Patient, kind, and willing to take time to make wise decisions

Figure 10.8 This chart shows how you can tell the difference between mature love and infatuation. *Why is it important to be able to identify whether your attraction is infatuation?*

and caring about the well-being of the other. People who have mature love for each other like to do things that please each other. They are committed to finding and doing what is best for each other. They may give up personal desires to bring benefits to the partner or to both of them as a couple.

You cannot "fall" into mature love—mature love grows as a relationship grows. It takes time and effort to develop mature love.

The growth of mature love can be described in four stages. Each stage stimulates the growth of the next (**Figure 10.9**).

- *Rapport.* First, the two individuals develop rapport. They care about each other and enjoy being together. They want to spend more time getting to know each other.

- *Personal sharing.* As rapport grows, the couple enters the second stage, in which they share more personal thoughts, ideas, and feelings. Through this sharing, each person exposes his or her inner self and finds acceptance by the other. That acceptance builds a deep sense of trust. If one or the other does not feel accepted, mutual sharing and the growth of love stop and the relationship will not develop further.

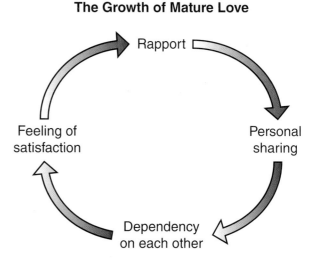

The Growth of Mature Love

Figure 10.9 The growth of mature love can be described as a cycle, with each stage stimulating the growth of the next stage. *Why would this cycle need to continue over time?*

- *Dependency on each other.* In the third stage, the two people become attached to each other and grow to depend on each other for support and encouragement. They miss each other when they are apart and look forward to being together. They both contribute to the relationship to meet each other's needs.

- *Feeling of satisfaction.* In the fourth stage, both individuals feel their personal needs are being met in the relationship. They each feel important and valuable to the other. As their needs are fulfilled in the relationship, their love grows deeper.

How does the cycle continue? As needs are met, the couple is motivated to spend more time together. Times of deep personal sharing increase. They share empathy, feeling what the other is feeling. They become more attached to each other. They depend on each other to meet more and more of their emotional needs. As these needs are met, more interaction is encouraged. In this way, the cycle continues, and mature love grows deeper.

As couples grow in mature love, they become committed to each other's happiness and well-being. This commitment remains strong, even if romantic feelings decrease. To keep love growing, couples must continue giving to the relationship throughout life. They must continue to spend time together, share, depend on each other, and meet each other's needs (**Figure 10.10**).

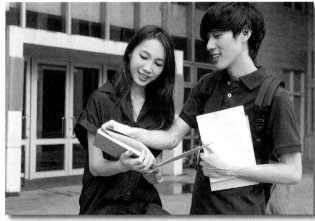
East/Shutterstock.com

Figure 10.10 A couple needs to spend quality time together to keep mature love growing in their relationship. *How could the growth of mature love help keep romantic love alive?*

Think About Your Reading

Could the growth of mature love develop in a couple of weeks? in a month? Why might it take more time for one couple to develop mature love than for another couple?

Expressing Affection

As feelings between two people grow, a couple may find themselves drawn into a desire to give physical expression to their love. Physical expressions such as close hugs and affectionate kisses are normal. As a relationship grows, however, sexual feelings may grow more intense. Teens may feel confused and even pressured to yield to their desires. There are many personal benefits in making a decision to practice **abstinence**, choosing to not have sex.

Abstinence gives a couple time to grow the relationship. Once a relationship begins to focus on sexual activity, it is difficult to slow down the relationship and spend more time talking and getting to know each other intellectually, socially, and emotionally. Without the chance to develop the relationship in that way, mature love cannot grow, and the relationship will end. In addition, there are both psychological and physical consequences of being sexually involved before entering a committed marriage.

It is difficult for a person to make a logical, good decision when his or her body is flooded with the brain chemicals that go with being attracted to another person. Thus, it is very important to think through this decision ahead of time and set personal boundaries. **Personal boundaries** are limits for behavior that you will accept in your relationships. With regard to sex outside of marriage, a personal boundary of abstinence will help you reach your personal potential and develop strong, intimate relationships.

Making a Decision to Wait

Though the physical desire to be sexually involved may increase, this does not mean you have to give in to your desires. Thinking about your choices, considering the consequences, and making a logical decision based on your standards is important (**Figure 10.11**). Think through this decision ahead of time, before you find yourself

---

Consequences of Sexual Decisions	
Consequences of Not Waiting to Have Sex	**Consequences of Waiting until Marriage to Have Sex**
Increased fear that the relationship may end	Allows time to build the relationship
Increased doubts about the relationship	Growing trust
Increased feelings of guilt	Freedom from guilt
Decrease in self-esteem and self-respect	Increased self-respect and respect for partner
Decrease in verbal communication	Contributes to sexual freedom in marriage
Slows growth of mature love	Allows growth of mature love
Possible pregnancy and early parenting	Avoids unwanted pregnancy
May contract a sexually transmitted infection	Avoids sexually transmitted infections
May affect physical ability to have children in the future	Safeguards health and ability to have children in the future

Figure 10.11 Consider the consequences of having a sexual relationship before marriage. *How could thinking about these consequences help you set personal boundaries?*

under emotional pressure. Your response to this decision can have lifelong effects.

Decide now what is acceptable to you. Set your personal boundaries. If you become involved in a serious relationship, be honest with your partner ahead of time. Use your I-statements to speak for yourself—stating your thoughts, feelings, desires, and intentions—and let your partner know what your limits are concerning sex.

Teens sometimes feel pressured by their dating partners. They are made to feel that they must prove their love by having sex. Such demands are not a part of a true loving relationship. Mature love will be willing to wait. If a partner pressures you, let that partner know that you need to be respected for your personal standards. If the partner truly cares for you, he or she will respect your decisions. If the pressure continues, that means the partner cares more about his or her own feelings than about yours. In that case, it may be time to end the relationship.

Teens sometimes feel pressure from peers to have sex. They may feel that "everyone is doing it." Some teens may worry about what their friends will think of them if they are not having sex. Statistics show, however, that many young adults choose abstinence during their dating years, and some who say they are having sex are not really doing so.

Some teens also feel pressured by the constant reference to sex in the media. Advertisements, television shows, movies, videos, and music all suggest that sex is a casual activity between any two people who have the desire. This constant reference to sexuality makes it difficult for teens to play down the role of sex in their lives. Unfortunately, the media seldom show the true consequences of such activity—the negative emotional consequences as well as pregnancy and disease that can result.

There are several good reasons for choosing abstinence. The negative consequences of premarital sexual activity are both psychological and physical. They affect not just the persons involved, but also their family members, future spouses, and the community as a whole.

Psychological Consequences

Having a sexual relationship does not signify commitment. Only marriage signifies commitment. Without the commitment that being married represents, a partner could be gone tomorrow. The fear of that happening and doubts about the other's love can eventually destroy a relationship. Either partner could be left feeling used, unwanted, or worthless. Trust is vital to a fulfilling relationship. Complete trust is only possible within the commitment of marriage.

Feelings of being used, abused, and devalued are common consequences of early sexual involvement in a relationship (**Figure 10.12**). Such feelings can keep a person from reaching his or her full potential. These feelings are painful, and they are hard to overcome. It can take years of being in a positive relationship in which a person feels appreciated, cared for, loved, and valued to overcome these early feelings.

Many people are brought up to believe that sexual intimacy belongs in marriage. Values learned from family, friends, and religious beliefs concerning this issue may be very strong. Going against these values can cause intense feelings of guilt, regret, and anxiety. A person may sacrifice feelings of self-esteem if strongly held family and personal values are disregarded.

The negative consequences of self-doubt, feeling used or abused, fear, lack of trust, and guilt are psychological. These can hurt the growth of mature love in a relationship. There are also physical consequences of sexual activity in a relationship.

Think About Your Reading

How could setting personal boundaries early in a relationship help avoid the experience of feeling used, abused, or devalued?

An Unwanted Pregnancy

One of the physical consequences of sexual activity is pregnancy. There is no contraceptive that is 100 percent effective in preventing pregnancy. Some are more effective than others. Some have various side effects. *Abstinence*, not having sexual relations, is the only 100-percent effective method to avoid pregnancy.

If pregnancy occurs, the couple may face the decision of whether or not to marry. Marriage is

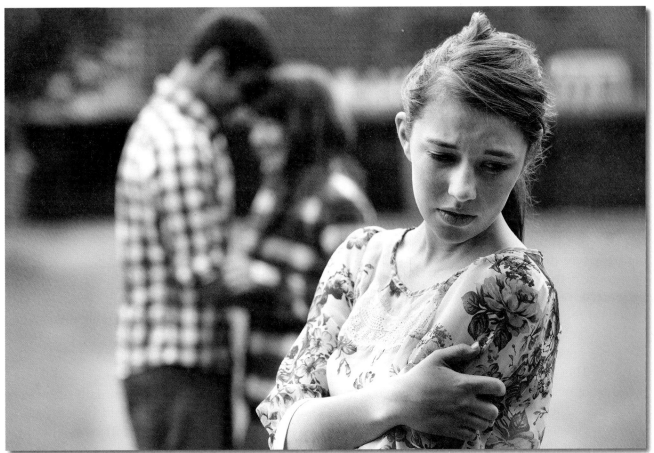

SpeedKingz/Shutterstock.com

Figure 10.12   Often, teens who are sexually involved feel devalued or used once a relationship ends.

a long-term commitment and needs the full participation of two mature people. Most teens are not socially and emotionally ready to commit themselves to a marriage or to raising a child (**Figure 10.13**).

Sometimes parenting looks attractive to teens who are looking for someone to love them, care about them, and make them feel important. This approach sometimes is glamorized in the media, without consideration of the host of real-life problems and issues that go with teen parenting. When a baby comes into a teen relationship, the adjustment is extremely difficult. One or both parents may have to leave school to care for the child. Most teens are not able to make it financially.

What if the partners do not marry and the young mother decides to keep the baby? If she does not finish her education, her income will be limited. Even if she finishes high school, having a baby can make it a challenge to enter a postsecondary program. That means her job prospects and future income will still not be as great as they would have been if she had gotten that schooling. Either way, her social growth will also be affected since much of her time will be spent caring for the baby (**Figure 10.14**).

The young father is also affected by the birth of a child, as all states require that parents take care of and support their children until they reach a certain age, usually 18 or when the child graduates from high school. Unless the child born to a

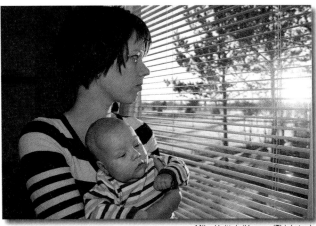
Mika Heittola/Hemera/Thinkstock
Figure 10.14 Teen mothers often experience feelings of isolation as their social worlds change to accommodate a baby.

teen couple is adopted by other parents, the young father will be required to pay child support.

Teenage pregnancy also poses health risks for both the mother and her baby. Because a teen mother's body is not yet fully developed, the strain of pregnancy creates health risks for her. Many pregnant teens ignore or deny their condition. As a result, they do not always receive proper *prenatal* (before birth) care. Pregnant teens are more likely to experience **complications** such as *anemia*, which is an iron deficiency that leaves a person weak and tired. Babies born to teen mothers are often premature or have low birthweight. These factors can lead to increased health risks at birth and throughout childhood.

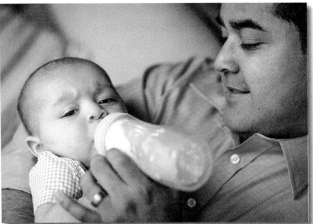
Andy Dean Photography/Shutterstock.com
Figure 10.13 Caring for a new baby is a 24-hour responsibility that requires social, emotional, and intellectual maturity. *How could parental immaturity affect the baby's growth?*

Think About Your Reading

Statistics indicate that many teen parents are single and struggle with poverty. Why is it so hard to break the cycle and change this statistic?

Sexually Transmitted Infections

Another very serious negative physical consequence of sexual activity is the risk of disease. **Sexually transmitted infections (STIs)** are passed from one person to another by sexual contact. They are also referred to as *sexually transmitted diseases (STDs)*. In many cases, there are

no obvious, outward signs of the infections, yet these infections can still be spread from one partner to another. Many STIs have a harmful effect on a person's reproductive organs, and some can result in early death. The most common STIs are human papillomavirus (HPV), gonorrhea, chlamydia, genital herpes, syphilis, hepatitis B, and acquired immunodeficiency syndrome (AIDS).

The **human papillomavirus (HPV)** is the most common sexually transmitted infection in the United States. The virus infects the skin and mucous membranes. Most people who become infected with HPV do not even know they have it. Certain types of HPV cause **genital warts**, or small bumps or clusters of bumps in the genital area. Some types of HPV can cause cervical cancer, other types of cancer of the sexual organs, and throat cancer. A vaccine is available that can protect both males and females against some types of HPV, but the only sure way to prevent all types of HPV is to avoid sexual activity.

Gonorrhea is a bacterial infection that can damage the male and female organs, resulting in **sterility**, or the inability to have a child. Gonorrhea grows in the warm, moist areas of the reproductive tract, and also in the rectum, mouth, or throat. The infection can be treated with antibiotics. Some strains of the bacteria, however, are becoming resistant to these medications, making them more difficult to treat. Also, medications cannot undo any permanent damage that has resulted from the infection before treatment began.

Chlamydia is a bacterial infection that can damage a woman's reproductive organs. It is one of the most common bacterial STIs in the United States. Detecting the infection may be difficult because many men and women have no obvious symptoms. Chlamydia can be treated and cured with antibiotics, but if it is left untreated, it can cause sterility. In addition, an infected mother can pass the disease to her unborn child, giving the child an increased risk of developing serious infections.

Genital herpes is a widespread, incurable virus. It stays in the body and reappears periodically, producing painful sores or blisters. A person with the disease may experience repeated outbreaks of blisters. Genital herpes can be spread

even when sores are not present. It can also be passed from an infected woman to her newborn infant at birth.

Syphilis, caused by bacteria, can be treated with an antibiotic. The early stages of the disease are not easily recognized. A sore, called a *chancre*, appears ten days to three months after infection has occurred. Because this sore heals, however, the disease is not suspected. Ignored, the disease then spreads to other parts of the body. Rash, fever, sore throat, and headache are common symptoms. The later stages of the disease damage other parts of the body, including the liver, skin, heart, or nervous system. If left untreated, it may result in death.

Hepatitis B is caused by a virus that attacks the liver. It is spread by sexual contact with an infected person or by exposure to infected blood.

Acquired immunodeficiency syndrome (AIDS) is a disease that is caused by the **human immunodeficiency virus (HIV)**. This virus attacks the body's cells that normally fight infection and disease. HIV is passed from one person to another through body fluids such as blood, vaginal secretions, and semen. The virus can be spread from an infected person in two main ways: through sexual activity or by sharing intravenous needles. During pregnancy, at childbirth, and while breastfeeding, an infected woman can pass the virus to her child.

HIV can live in the body for many years before symptoms appear. An infected person can still spread the virus in that time. Some people with HIV do not experience early symptoms; others experience severe flulike symptoms, including fever, sore throat, rash, and rapid weight loss. Once a person contracts HIV, he or she remains infected for life, and symptoms may recur. That person's immune system continues to weaken until it can no longer fight disease, resulting in the progression to AIDS. At present, most AIDS patients die from serious infections or cancer.

When young people are sexually active prior to marriage, the chance of becoming exposed to an STI is great. The only way to fully prevent a sexually transmitted infection is to avoid all vaginal, anal, or oral sexual activity. Even one such event may be the source of an STI. Sexual activity

with more than one partner is especially risky. Blood tests can identify the presence of STIs, but the best way to avoid them is to abstain from any sexual activity.

Think About Your Reading

Do you think many teens fully understand the health risks associated with having more than one sex partner?

Ways to Say No to Sexual Pressures

"No, I don't want to."

"If you really loved me, you wouldn't ask."

"I respect myself too much."

"I believe in waiting for marriage."

"AIDS is forever."

"I make lifelong decisions."

Figure 10.15 Practicing these responses can help teens stick to their decision to say "no" to sexual pressures. *How can your communication skills help you stick to your personal boundaries?*

Responding to Pressures

If you have made a decision to avoid sexual relations before marriage, how can you stick to your decision? Waiting until marriage is sometimes difficult, especially when others around you seem not to be doing so. How can you respond to such pressure? There are several ways (**Figure 10.15**).

The most important step is to set your *personal boundaries* ahead of time. What do you think is acceptable behavior? What is not? Think through the consequences of various behaviors. Make choices that will help you stick to your decision and reach your life goals.

Talk to your partner before you become sexually involved. Plan what you will say. Do not give

REAL-LIFE SCENARIO

A Dating Relationship

Al and Marietta have been dating for six months. They believe they are in love with each other. When they first started dating, they planned ahead and went to many different places. They had fun being together as they went to the museum, on biking trips, and on picnics. Now they find themselves spending a lot of unplanned time together. They meet after school and spend evenings in one or the other's home. They do not spend much time with their friends either.

When they are alone, it is hard to control the passionate kissing and hugging. The pressure to become more and more sexually involved gets greater. Marietta finds herself feeling angry and confused. She does not want to give in to the sexual pressures. She misses the times they spent just having fun, laughing, and doing things together. In fact, she almost dreads the evening dates because the same problem occurs over and over. Marietta is not sure how to deal with it.

For Discussion

1. In what situations do the sexual pressures become the greatest for Al and Marietta? What could they do to decrease these pressures on themselves? How could discussing the problem help them find solutions?

2. When one dating partner pressures the other to become sexually involved, does it mean that he or she really cares for the other person? Why or why not? How can you tell if a dating partner is considering the happiness of both people rather than personal or selfish interests?

3. Are Al and Marietta feeling romantic love for each other or mature love? What actions and feelings suggest that their love is romantic love? What evidence is there that this could be mature love?

4. Using I-statements, write a script in which Marietta confronts Al about her desire for less pressure to be sexually involved.

mixed messages by dressing or acting in a way that contradicts the decision you made.

Avoid situations that may cause you to be tempted, such as parking a car in a quiet area or going home with your partner when no one is there. Try not to spend as much time alone. Instead, find alternative activities that involve other people. Go out with friends or participate in sports activities. Also avoid alcohol and drugs, which decrease your ability to think and to say no.

It is never too late to make a decision to wait. Even if you cannot change past actions, a decision to wait can help you avoid continued psychological and physical risks. Saying no *now* can help you develop a future relationship based on sharing, caring, mutual respect, and trust (**Figure 10.16**).

Think About Your Reading

How could a future marriage relationship be affected by the sexual choices you make now?

COMPREHENSION CHECK

1. Identify four differences between mature love and infatuation.
2. Describe how mature love grows through a four-stage cycle.
3. State two negative psychological consequences of sexual activity outside the commitment of marriage.
4. Describe the negative effects of pregnancy on a teen couple's life.
5. Describe two long-term consequences of STIs.
6. Identify the two main ways that the AIDS virus is spread.
7. Explain how setting personal boundaries for dating can help teens reach their life goals.
8. List three statements teens can use to respond to sexual pressures.

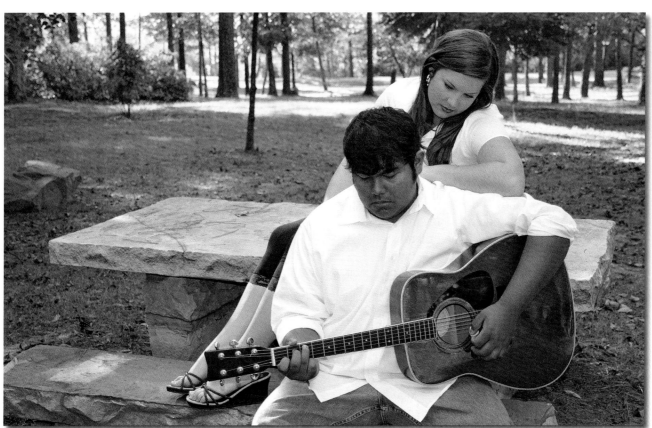

Darryl Vest/Shutterstock.com

Figure 10.16 Many choices during the dating years can affect the rest of your life. *What are some choices facing you that could have long-term impacts on your ability to achieve future goals?*

Objectives

After studying this lesson, you will be able to

- **evaluate** a dating relationship for healthy qualities.
- **describe** various forms of abuse that may occur in a relationship.
- **identify** personal boundaries that can help deter abuse in a relationship.

Focus Your Reading

1. As you read, think of a romantic relationship you have seen in action and evaluate it for healthy qualities in all four of the areas described in the text.
2. For each type of abuse, list some behaviors that would describe it and explain why those behaviors are hurtful.

Content Terms

Build Vocab

abuse
emotional abuse
social abuse
physical abuse
sexual abuse
rape
date rape

Academic Terms

evidence
automatic

Good relationships sometimes just happen, but in most cases, people need to invest time and effort to make sure that their relationships are leading them toward their life goals. That means taking time to evaluate dating relationships as they develop.

Components of a Healthy Dating Relationship

Romantic relationships that last show *evidence*, or signs, of strength in four areas: close friendship, mature love, romance, and the use of healthy relationship skills. These four qualities can be pictured as the four legs of a stool (**Figure 10.17**). Both partners need to be committed to helping the relationship grow in all four areas. That commitment means each partner dedicates himself or herself to making this exclusive relationship work. That personal decision needs to be renewed often for the relationship to last.

If a relationship is strong in all four areas, it will be solid. If a relationship is weak in even one area, the stool will be wobbly. If one area is completely missing, the couple might still be able to

How Sturdy Is Your Relationship Stool?

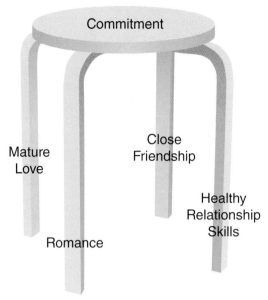

Commitment

Mature Love

Close Friendship

Healthy Relationship Skills

Romance

Constantine Pankin/Shutterstock.com

Figure 10.17 If you liken a strong, healthy relationship to a sturdy stool, each leg on the stool could represent certain characteristics. *Why would both persons need to be committed in all four areas for the relationship to be strong and long-lasting?*

stay on top of the relationship if they lean heavily on the strong side. If anything comes along that rocks the relationship, however, the stool could topple over and result in a broken relationship and two unhappy people.

You can evaluate your romantic relationships for these qualities. If any leg of the relationship is weak, you need to think about whether that can change and be strengthened, or whether you should end the relationship because that characteristic will always be weak or missing.

> ## Think About Your Reading
>
> Do you think any one of the four legs is more important than the others in keeping a relationship stable and long-lasting?

Checkpoint 1: A Close Friendship Is Growing

The qualities of a close friendship include sharing thoughts and feelings openly, giving and receiving acceptance and support, trusting each other, and promoting each other to grow and be the best each person can be. Evaluating this leg of your relationship is critical in order to identify areas where personal growth is needed for the relationship to be healthy. **Figure 10.18** lists points that can be considered in making this evaluation. A lot of personal immaturity results in unhealthy relationships. A developing friendship usually focuses around common interests. It is important that you have activities you like to do together to help promote growth in all areas of your life.

Checkpoint 2: Mature Love Is Growing

Mature love takes time to develop as two people share, depend on each other, meet each other's needs, feel secure with each other, accept each other, and earn the trust that develops as you give of yourselves to benefit each other. Rate your relationship for the growth of these qualities using the points listed in **Figure 10.19**. If mature love is not growing, a couple needs to talk about the relationship. Do they want to work at growing the relationship, or should they end it?

Checkpoint 3: Romance Is Alive

Some people are very good at keeping the romance alive in their relationship. Others have to work harder at it. Whether it is a conscious decision or an *automatic* behavior, keeping the romance alive in the relationship helps make the relationship last.

What does it take to keep two people attracted to each other? The nonverbal messages that first cause two people to be attracted to each other need to be emphasized. Appearance and good grooming are always important, even when you have been in a relationship a long time.

People are affirmed in their love for each other in different ways. Some respond to praise and positive comments. Others feel really loved and appreciated when they are given a gift, even if it is small. Others like to have their partners do something special for them, some little act of kindness that makes them feel uniquely special.

Checkpoint 1: A Close Friendship Is Growing	
Healthy Relationship	**Unhealthy Relationship**
Both partners have common interests, goals, and values.	Couple does not have much in common. Relationship focuses on physical attraction.
Both feel that they can trust the other person, and this has been proven over time.	One person does not really trust the other; always keeps his/her guard up.
Both persons are growing intellectually. Both think logically about new ideas. Both can think ahead and plan for the future.	One person only sees his/her own point of view, is closed-minded, is prejudiced, makes choices on the present versus long-term consequences.
Both persons are growing emotionally. They know who they are and accept themselves. They can control the actions that go with their emotions. They can identify their emotions and feel love and empathy.	One person has low self-esteem, does not feel accepted, has issues with anger, does not trust others, uses defense mechanisms, does not believe that others can love him/her; may be violent in outbursts of anger.
Both persons are growing socially. Both have developed strong character traits and are responsible, dependable, caring, and trustworthy. Both can give and take as they interact and cooperate with others.	One person is self-centered, not considerate of others, lies and is dishonest, lacks ethics or standards, insists on his/her own way, will not compromise, may disregard the law.
Both persons are making healthy choices that promote physical growth.	One person makes some poor decisions; uses alcohol, tobacco, or drugs; takes part in risky behaviors; uses physical violence.

Figure 10.18 In a healthy relationship, both persons need to show evidence of growth to maturity and enjoy being together. *How could several elements of an unhealthy relationship at this checkpoint affect a relationship long-term?*

Checkpoint 2: Mature Love Is Growing	
Healthy Relationship	**Unhealthy Relationship**
Both partners share equally.	One partner holds back, is reserved, or is not open.
Both persons depend on each other for needs to be met.	One person can "take it or leave it," does not really depend on the other, is not willing to be vulnerable.
Both persons are attached to each other.	One person remains somewhat detached.
Both partners like to spend time together.	The couple struggles to find time to do things together.
Both feel satisfied with the relationship. Both feel their needs are met.	One does not feel satisfied, feels some needs are not met.
Both care about the other's well-being, even more than their own.	Caring is lopsided; one cares about the relationship more than the other. One person is more focused on him- or herself than the other's well-being.

Figure 10.19 If any one of the unhealthy characteristics exists in a relationship, it is not likely that mature love is growing. *How could the existence of these unhealthy qualities make so much difference in a relationship?*

Others really need a physical touch, such as a hug, holding their hand, or warm embrace. Some people really feel special when their partner sets time aside to just focus on the two of them, without interruptions. It takes time in a relationship to discover what it is that makes the other person feel especially loved. You can use the points in **Figure 10.20** to guide you in thinking about this aspect of a relationship.

All of these ways of affirming each other can help keep the romantic spark alive in a relationship. It usually does not take all of them, though. There is usually one action that speaks love loudly to your partner—and it is probably different from the action that speaks most to you.

| **Think About Your Reading** |
| Why is it important to know what *romantic* means to your partner? How could this knowledge impact romantic attraction? |

Checkpoint 4: Healthy Relationship Skills Are Used

A couple's patterns for speaking, listening, making joint decisions, and solving problems together have a critical impact on their

Checkpoint 3: How Is Romance Seen in Action?

- I feel loved when praised, thanked, and appreciated verbally, through words.
- I feel loved when I get a small gift.
- I feel loved when he or she does some thoughtful act of kindness, such as helping me with some chore I need to get done.
- I feel loved when holding hands, getting a hug, and being close to each other.
- I feel loved when we spend quiet time together just by ourselves.

Figure 10.20 Several actions can help keep the romance in a relationship. *How could people's different expectations impact their view of romance in their relationship?*

relationship. Good relationship skills will contribute to healthy, long-lasting relationships.

It takes time in a relationship to really discover how another person will respond to different situations. People can be quite good at covering up some of their inner issues, and when you are romantically attracted to someone, your ability to see those behaviors is hindered. "Love is blind," is often stated when others see an obvious flaw in one person in a relationship and the other person does not.

To check on this aspect of your relationship, set some goals and then work together toward them to see how each of you thinks, plans, and works through obstacles. Complete some projects together to learn how you as a couple make decisions and handle disagreements. In doing so, both partners need to be fully honest about their view of the situation. If you always agree on everything now, one of you is probably not thinking or not expressing his or her true opinions. That pattern of behavior could result in unexpected disagreements in the future, when the partner becomes tired of giving in. Evaluating your relationship skills in action can help you identify whether the relationship is healthy. Use the points in **Figure 10.21** to make that evaluation.

As you evaluate a dating relationship using these checkpoints, you may discover that your relationship has a lot of the qualities of a healthy relationship, but some unhealthy qualities still exist. You then must ask yourself whether these qualities can or will change over time. Are they areas in which either person is growing? More time growing the relationship will help give you some answers. You may find that most of the time the healthy qualities prevail, but sometimes unhealthy ones appear. The question to answer will be how much or how often. Do the healthy qualities outweigh the unhealthy ones?

Recognizing Abuse in a Relationship

Some qualities of an unhealthy relationship are *red flags*, clear warning signs that the relationship must end. Safety is of critical importance in a relationship. A safe environment is one in which

Checkpoint 4: Healthy Relationship Skills Are Used	
Healthy Relationship	**Unhealthy Relationship**
Both persons speak with I-statements and clearly convey their own thoughts, feelings, desires, and intended actions.	Persons use you-messages, put-downs, name-calling.
Both speak in a way that shows respect for others, even when talking about difficult topics.	One or both speak aggressively, telling the other what to do, what to think, or what to say. One or both puts down the other's opinions as stupid or dumb.
Both listen to each other, giving feedback to make sure they understand the other's total message.	One (or both) does not listen or does not try to understand; may be passive-aggressive, causing hurt by doing nothing.
Both give undivided attention to their communication, making sure they have a shared meaning.	One tunes the other out, such as playing computer games or sending text messages to others when communicating.
Both use good decision-making skills, considering alternatives, thinking through options, considering each other's opinions, and evaluating final choices.	One or both makes quick decisions, does not take time to research solutions, does not listen to input from others, or blames others when things go wrong.
Both are willing to accept problem ownership.	One or both never accepts responsibility for a problem.
Both are willing to compromise.	One or both has to have his or her own way.

Figure 10.21 Evaluating your relationship skills in action is critical to a long-lasting healthy relationship. *How could the presence of any of the above unhealthy practices affect a relationship?*

you can grow and reach your potential. **Abuse** is behavior used in a relationship to exert power and control over another person, and it endangers the safety of the person being abused. Abuse may be carried out by both males and females. Thus, it is important to be able to recognize abuse in a relationship (**Figure 10.22**). The sooner an abusive relationship is ended, the better it is for your personal growth and development.

Abusive behavior in a relationship can destroy a person emotionally, socially, and physically. Learning to recognize the signs of an abusive relationship can help you take steps to end the relationship and to move toward healing and personal growth. Several of the characteristics of abuse are evident in the unhealthy practices identified in Figure 10.21.

Emotional Abuse

Emotional abuse is any behavior that tears at a person's core being or sense of self and destroys

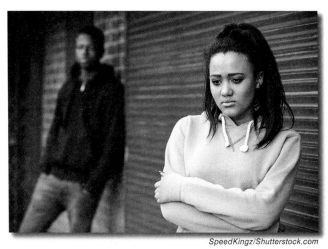

SpeedKingz/Shutterstock.com

Figure 10.22 Abuse occurs when one partner tries to control the other. *Why is it sometimes hard to identify when abuse is occurring in a relationship?*

self-esteem. Words that are cutting, humiliating, or degrading—anything that tears the other person down—is emotionally abusive. That includes name-calling, making the person feel guilty, or

making him or her feel stupid. If one partner heaps such verbal abuse on the other partner regularly, the person being abused suffers deeply.

Social Abuse

Social abuse is any behavior that destroys the ability of a person to develop healthy relationships with others. When one person tries to control whom a partner talks to or spends time with, where the partner goes, what the partner reads or does, that is abusive and shows a lack of trust.

Some abusers treat their partners like slaves; they expect their partners to meet their every desire, jump to meet their needs, and do their bidding. These abusers act like a dictator, making all the decisions. They try to define the roles both persons in the relationship should carry out. Sometimes a partner may use social threats to stay in control of the relationship. These may be threats to tell secrets that the other person has shared. It may even be threats to spread outright lies that the person knows would be destructive to his or her partner's life. These are all kinds of social abuse, and the person being abused needs to leave that relationship.

Physical Abuse

Physical abuse includes causing actual physical harm as well as making threats to cause harm. These threats may be toward the partner in the relationship or toward other people the partner loves and cares for. Any form of physical violence is unacceptable in a relationship.

Violence can be in the form of an angry look, yelling and swearing, hitting, holding the other person down, or preventing the other person from moving. Violence is any action that causes fear in a person (**Figure 10.23**).

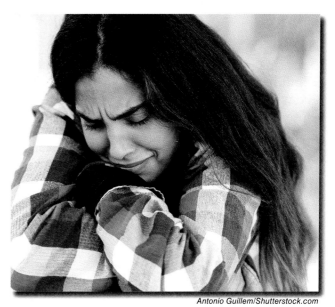
Antonio Guillem/Shutterstock.com

Figure 10.23 Physical abuse harms a person's health and emotional well-being.

Sexual Abuse

Sexual abuse is forcing another person to be sexually involved in any way. If someone has said "no" to sex and his or her partner continues to pressure that person to have sex, that is abusive. Sending sexual pictures and texting sexual messages can be sexual abuse, too.

Sometimes people find themselves in situations in which a "no" reply is disregarded. Forced sexual intercourse is called **rape**. Sexual intercourse with a dating partner against one person's will is called **date rape**. The use of force or the threat of force is often involved. Acquaintance rape can occur between friends, classmates, or coworkers. It is the most common form of rape.

Studies show that alcohol and drugs are often involved when date rape or acquaintance rape takes place. When alcohol or drug use is involved, people's judgment is impaired. Some people become more aggressive. Those who become victims may not be able to fight off an aggressor or flee a potential rape situation. The best way to avoid becoming a victim of rape is to avoid alcohol and drugs while dating or attending parties. If others around are using these substances, ask to

---

Think About Your Reading

What are the fears that keep people in unhealthy relationships? How can they overcome those fears?

---

be taken home or leave the party. Call a parent or friend if you need a ride home.

Date rape drugs cause victims to become physically helpless and unable to remember forced sexual intercourse. These drugs often have no color, smell, or taste, and are usually slipped into a beverage. To protect yourself when you are on a date or in a group, never trust anyone with your drink. Open your own beverages and do not drink out of a large punch bowl or other open container if you are at an unsupervised party. If a beverage seems suspicious, throw it out.

Teenagers sometimes have a hard time interpreting the nonverbal messages that are given by a dating partner or acquaintance. Be careful that your nonverbal messages and your spoken messages match. Use clear words to state what activities you want to avoid. Clarify that your "no" means *no*, and watch out for your own safety and well-being. If necessary, get help from a friend or an adult or get out of the situation.

Setting Personal Boundaries

Personal boundaries are the limits to behavior that you will accept in your relationships. These limits apply to what you are willing to say, think, or do in your relationships with other people. They also apply to what you are willing to allow others to say or do to you. Personal boundaries can help you know when a relationship has crossed the line.

Knowing the qualities of a healthy relationship can help you set personal boundaries that include those qualities and exclude the unhealthy behaviors. When you have identified these unhealthy behaviors ahead of time as being outside of your personal boundaries, it will help you make the decision to end a relationship when those unhealthy behaviors develop (**Figure 10.24**). Abusive behavior should never be acceptable behavior.

Think About Your Reading
What are some personal boundaries that a person could list to help them recognize an unhealthy relationship?

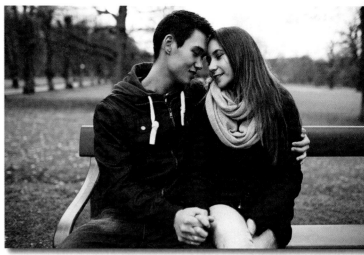
©iStock.com/Jacob Ammentorp

Figure 10.24 Knowing your personal boundaries can help you identify and act on unhealthy or abusive behaviors.

Confronting Abuse in a Relationship

Signs of abuse in a relationship are a warning that the relationship is not healthy, the interactions will not get better, and violence may increase. If abuse exists in a relationship, it is difficult to change the direction of the interactions. Ending the relationship is often the only way to protect oneself and to recover from the abuse and move forward toward one's own life goals. You may find that you need help ending an abusive relationship. A parent, a guidance counselor, a religious leader, a close friend, or law enforcement can all be sources of help ending an abusive relationship (**Figure 10.25**).

Letting your dating partner know that you will not accept abuse is the first step in changing the direction of the relationship. I-statements can help you make this message clear. "I see you yelling at me again (description). I think this relationship is not healthy (thoughts). I feel afraid and put down when you yell at me (feelings). I do not want to continue in a relationship like this (desires). We are over (intentions)."

A common response from an abusive partner is to blame the other person. "It's your fault that I end up yelling. You just don't listen to what I have to say." Another common response is to downplay the abuse. "It's really not abusive. That's just in your mind. Everyone acts like that in our neighborhood. It's normal."

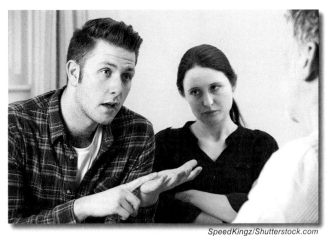
Figure 10.25 Ending an abusive relationship can be a fearful process. *Who could assist you in getting safely through ending an abusive relationship?*

SpeedKingz/Shutterstock.com

Another typical response of an abusive person is to claim strong feelings. He or she might say something like, "I'm just so jealous. I care about you so much." Even more extreme are threats like, "If you leave me, I'll kill myself. I just can't go on without you." These threats continue the emotional abuse, making the person being abused feel guilty.

All of these responses continue the abuse and are simply more red flags that the relationship should end. Remember the steps of problem-solving in Chapter 4. A person must accept ownership of the problem in order to take steps to solve it. Only the abuser can change his or her personal responses, and that process will take time and personal growth.

It can be difficult to end an abusive relationship. Thus, it is very helpful to have someone be with you when you break the relationship off. A friend can help ensure your protection and your success. If your partner has been abusive, he or she will try to exert power and control over you. He or she may be persistent in trying to start the relationship again. A complete separation without any contact is important to end a relationship with an abusive person. Remember that it is the abuser's responsibility to accept ownership of the problem. You cannot fix an abuser, but you do need to protect yourself. Counselors can help an abuser work through problems and change. They can also help you find ways to heal from the abusive relationship and grow.

Accepting Problem Ownership

If you find yourself using some of these abusive behaviors in a relationship, you need to accept ownership of the problem and take steps to change. Seek to identify the root causes of your behaviors. Are you insecure yourself? Why do you cut down someone you care about? Why do you need to control the other person? These are all signs that personal growth toward maturity needs to take place. *Self-discipline*, or the ability to control your own personal responses, both words and actions, is a character trait that should develop as part of social and emotional maturity. Chapter 2 discusses these aspects of maturity in depth. These are areas in which you need to grow before you continue in any romantic relationship.

Ending a Dating Relationship

Dating relationships end in many ways. Sometimes a couple will date a few times, and then one person just never hears from the other again. That person may have decided that the two of them did not have enough in common. In other cases, the couple simply drifts apart. They date less and less. One or both may become interested in someone else. If a relationship ends in either of these ways, you may feel hurt and disappointed. You probably, however, will not be devastated by the experience.

If you have been exclusively dating, ending the relationship can be painful. Close relationships rarely end by mutual consent. Usually one person wants to break up, but the other does not. The least interested partner may have found someone else or thinks the relationship is not growing closer.

Breaking up is most difficult for the person who wants to keep the relationship going. Breaking up is not easy for either partner, however. When dating relationships do end, the adjustment can be made easier by focusing on growth. Making the best of the situation is a positive approach. The following suggestions may help.

- *Realize your partner will feel hurt.* If you are breaking off the relationship, be sensitive to the other person's feelings. Show empathy. Explain why you feel the relationship needs to end. If you continue the relationship to

avoid hurting your partner, you are not being honest. The relationship will suffer, and your partner will be hurt anyway.

- *Change your dating patterns.* Once a relationship is over, it is difficult to keep on seeing each other. After the pain of the breakup has lessened, you may be able to be friends with your former partner. Being friends will be easier if you both have developed new relationships.

- *Recognize that your feelings are normal.* Feelings of pain and loneliness do not mean that you made a wrong decision when you went into the relationship or when it ended. They are part of the grief that goes with ending a close relationship. These feelings are a sign that the relationship was valuable to you, not that you made a mistake. Allow yourself to grieve for a while—and then move on with your life.

- *Emphasize other aspects of your life.* If you are the person who wanted the relationship to continue, you may feel lonely or depressed for a while when it ends. Doing something

that you enjoy can help you get over that sadness (**Figure 10.26**). The pain will pass, and you will be able to put your energy into building a new relationship.

Think About Your Reading

What are some reasons it is difficult to maintain a friendship with a former dating partner?

LESSON 10.3

Assess

COMPREHENSION CHECK

1. List four areas that contribute to a long-lasting, healthy romantic relationship.
2. Describe the qualities of a healthy relationship.
3. List four types of abuse that occur in relationships and give an example of each.
4. Identify personal boundaries that will help avoid an abusive relationship.

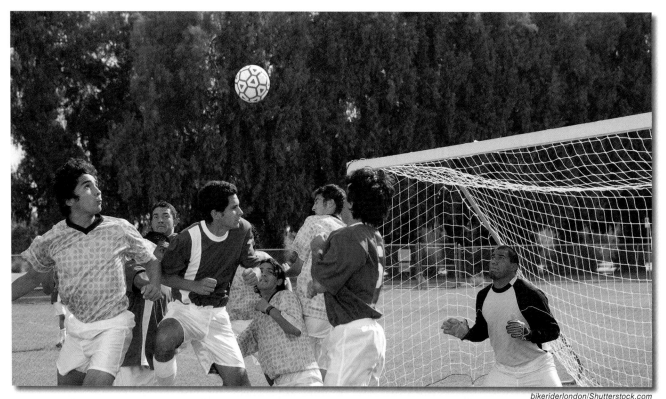

bikeriderlondon/Shutterstock.com

Figure 10.26 Playing sports, exercising, or talking to a friend are examples of activities that can help you adjust to feelings of loss that are normal when a close relationship ends. *What activities do you enjoy that help you focus on personal growth?*

CHAPTER SUMMARY

In U.S. society, formal and informal dating serves many important functions. Dating is a way for young people to learn more about other people, themselves, and the qualities they desire in a marriage partner.

Dating usually proceeds through several stages. Group dating gives teens the chance to develop their first relationships. Pair dating lets teens get to know another person better. Some dating relationships develop into friendships; some move to the stage of exclusive dating; others may end after one or a few dates.

As a couple becomes more attracted to each other, they focus on building their relationship. Their attraction may be short-lived if it is based only on romantic feelings. Mature love grows as the couple spends time together, shares, depends on each other, and meets each other's needs. As dating relationships become more serious, young couples may feel pressured to deal with sexual feelings. Learning to control these feelings can help them avoid serious psychological and physical risks.

Evaluating a romantic relationship in four areas can help couples identify whether they have the potential of developing a long-lasting, healthy relationship. Those areas are friendship, mature love, romance, and use of relationship skills. Abuse in a relationship may occur when one person tries to exert power and control over the other partner. Setting personal boundaries can help individuals identify when a relationship crosses the line of acceptable healthy behaviors. Someone in an abusive relationship has to get out of it for his or her safety. A person who is abusing another individual needs to get help to address the underlying issues that lead him or her to be abusive.

VOCABULARY ACTIVITIES

1. Make a chart that uses and explains all the relevant vocabulary terms to identify the negative consequences of sexual activity.

Content Terms

abstinence (10.2)
abuse (10.3)
acquired
  immunodeficiency
  syndrome (AIDS)
  (10.2)
chlamydia (10.2)
date rape (10.3)
double date (10.1)

emotional abuse (10.3)
exclusive dating (10.1)
formal date (10.1)
genital herpes (10.2)
genital warts (10.2)
gonorrhea (10.2)
group dating (10.1)
hepatitis B (10.2)

human
  immunodeficiency
  virus (HIV) (10.2)
human papilloma virus
  (HPV) (10.2)
infatuation (10.2)
mature love (10.2)
pair dating (10.1)
personal boundaries
  (10.2)

physical abuse (10.3)
rape (10.3)
romantic love (10.2)
sexual abuse (10.3)
sexually transmitted
  infections (STIs)
  (10.2)
social abuse (10.3)
sterility (10.2)
syphilis (10.2)

2. Use each of the following terms in a sentence that describes a healthy dating or romantic relationship or a way to build such a relationship.

Academic Terms

assessment (10.2)
automatic (10.3)
complication (10.2)
evidence (10.3)

intimate (10.1)
phenomenon (10.2)
validated (10.1)

ASSESS

Your Knowledge

3. Discuss the functions of and reasons for the dating process.
4. Name five different sexually transmitted infections.
5. Identify four types of abuse that take place in some relationships.

Your Understanding

6. Explain how mature love grows and develops.
7. How can a person identify whether a dating relationship is healthy?
8. How can waiting until marriage to become sexually involved contribute to your overall well-being?

Your Skills

9. Evaluate a dating relationship for the growth that should be taking place in a healthy dating relationship. Write a paragraph about why you think this relationship is healthy or unhealthy.
10. Who do you know who thinks he or she is in love? Analyze that person's relationship for evidence of mature love.
11. Create a list of three assertive responses you could use to say "no" to unwanted sexual pressures.

CRITICAL THINKING

12. **Make Inferences.** Plan a group dating activity. Analyze the activity and identify the various ways it would fulfill the functions of dating. Also analyze

how social media might affect the activity and the dating stages. Cite evidence from the text to support your analysis and summary.

13. **Evaluate Observations.** Watch a television sitcom in which marital or dating relationships are portrayed and identify the relationship qualities you observe. Evaluate those qualities for characteristics of mature love or infatuation. Discuss your observations with an adult or a classmate. In a paragraph, summarize your evaluation of the type of love depicted in this show, citing evidence from the chapter and from the show to support your ideas.

14. **Develop Generalizations.** Work with a group to gather various definitions of love and gather some clues to identify when couples are really in love. Interview different people from different age groups (teens, young adults, married couples, older adults) to get their opinions on the issue. Analyze your data as a group, look for similarities in responses, and create some generalizations about what love is and how you can know you are in love. *Choice:* Analyze your group's work and evaluate whether you think the generalizations have merit or not. Cite evidence from the text to support your analysis.

15. **Solve Problems.** Write scenarios of various dating concerns in your community. Analyze the scenarios for the root problem behind each concern. Working with three or four classmates, consider some healthy ways to handle each of the concerns. Identify healthy responses that partners in each scenario could make to help them grow as people. Share your work by posting your scenarios and solutions on your class website.

CORE SKILLS

16. **Reading, Writing.** Clip articles related to dating and love from an advice column in a newspaper or teen magazine. Analyze each column. Are they talking about mature love or feelings of infatuation? Cite evidence from the text and use specifics from the columns to support your analysis.

17. **Research, Writing.** Research issues related to teen sexuality and sexually transmitted infections. Identify some personal boundaries that could help teens avoid these issues. Write a summary of your research and explain how your recommendations for personal boundaries could be effective.

18. **Research, Writing.** Survey your community for opportunities for healthy dating activities. Refer to websites, a telephone directory, community bulletin boards, or event calendars for ideas. Create a

report listing the options that promote healthy dating activities in your community. In your report, explain why these are healthy options. *Group option:* Divide the community into areas and have one group member prepare a list for each area.

19. **Writing.** Use a digital program to design a flyer or poster illustrating creative ways to say "no" to unwanted dating pressures. Post the flyers and posters on a bulletin board by the school office or on the school website.

20. **Writing, Speaking.** Assemble a collage showing healthy dating activities in your community. Summarize how these activities can help persons grow and mature.

21. **Research.** Search online to learn more about one of the sexually transmitted infections. Prepare a digital report, and include a graph showing the incidence rate of this disease over the last five years. Cite the sources for your information and for the data used in the graph in your report.

22. **Research, Math, Writing.** Survey parents to gather data about what expectations they have concerning responsible dating by teens. Include questions related to the appropriate age for dating, activities to do or places to go, ideal hours for dates, and opinions related to group or pair dating. Compile the information on a digital spreadsheet, analyze the data, and prepare a report on parents' attitudes toward dating. Use charts or graphs to illustrate your findings.

CAREER READINESS

23. **Researching Helping Careers.** Interview a school counselor, psychologist, police officer, mental health counselor, or drug abuse counselor to learn how these professionals work with both abusers and victims of abuse in their careers. Develop questions to ask in your interview and write a summary of your findings in a one-page report. Identify resources that the professional uses to help abusers grow and develop healthy skills and to help victims recover from the experiences of abuse.

24. **Researching Sexual Harassment in the Workplace.** One issue that some working people confront is sexual harassment, which involves unwanted words or actions of a sexual nature in the workplace. Sexual harassment is illegal. Research and report on the issue. Include estimates on the extent of the problem, the incidents that have been defined as harassment, and the steps that can be taken by workers who have been harassed to end the unfair treatment.

CHAPTER 11

CHOOSING TO MARRY

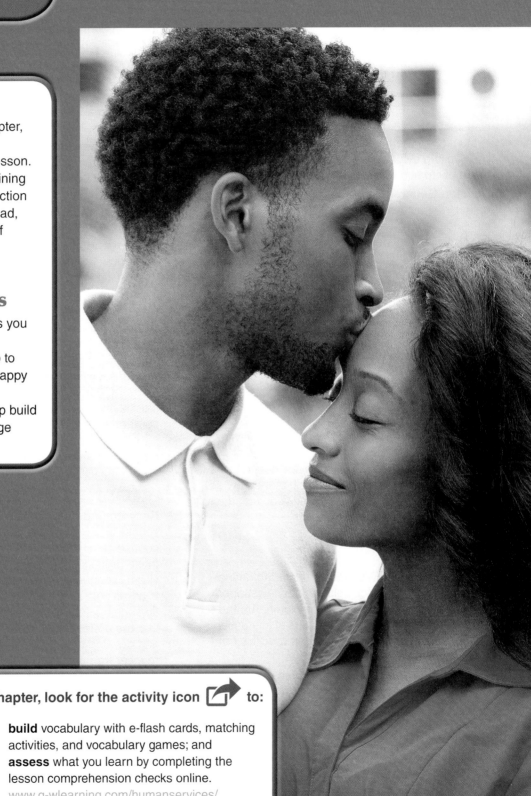

Reading Prep

Before reading the chapter, skim the headings and subheadings in each lesson. Write a sentence explaining what you think each section will be about. As you read, revise your sentences if necessary.

Key Questions

Questions to answer as you study this chapter:

- What qualities help to make a marriage happy and long-lasting?
- What skills can help build a satisfying marriage relationship?

While studying this chapter, look for the activity icon 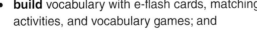 to:

- **build** vocabulary with e-flash cards, matching activities, and vocabulary games; and
- **assess** what you learn by completing the lesson comprehension checks online.

  www.g-wlearning.com/humanservices/

G-WLEARNING.com

A and N photography/Shutterstock.com

Lesson 11.1 Qualities of a Long-Lasting Marriage
Lesson 11.2 Evaluating Readiness for Marriage
Lesson 11.3 Preparing for a Long-Lasting Marriage

AFTER STUDYING THIS CHAPTER, YOU WILL

KNOW:

- The personal qualities that contribute to a happy and healthy marriage.
- Factors to evaluate when considering readiness for marriage.
- Issues couples should discuss and make plans about before getting married.

UNDERSTAND:

- How personal qualities and skills affect the quality of a marriage relationship.
- How similarities and differences between a couple affect their marital relationship.
- How planning for married living improves a couple's marriage relationship.

BE ABLE TO DO:

- Assess personal characteristics for the qualities needed to develop a long-lasting marriage.
- Evaluate personal skills for communicating, decision making, and solving problems with another person.

GETTING STARTED

"Did you hear about Jason getting married?" Ethan asked.

"Are you kidding?" Matthew replied. "He always seemed so focused on helping his dad run the family business. I didn't think he had time to date."

"I ran into him yesterday," Ethan said. "That's when he invited me to his wedding. His future wife has worked for their business for two years, and last spring they got engaged. You'll probably get an invitation, too."

"What's the bride's name?" Matthew asked.

"Laurie," Ethan replied. "Jason said he didn't think he would ever find the girl of his dreams until he met Laurie."

Many young people are concerned about how to prepare for a happy marriage. They may know some broken marriages or may have lived in unhappy family situations. They have seen conflict in marital relationships and want to know how to avoid similar problems.

In a happy marriage, both partners feel satisfied. Many factors can influence happiness in a marriage. Some are personal qualities that relate to a couple's maturity. Some factors relate to similarities and differences between the two people in the couple. Others relate to how close the relationship has developed and what skills the two married people possess.

In this chapter, you will learn more about the positive qualities needed to build a strong marriage. You will also learn about ways a couple can honestly evaluate their relationship before becoming engaged to see if they are ready for marriage. You will learn more about the important issues an engaged couple needs to identify and discuss to evaluate their relationship and prepare themselves for a successful marriage. Finally, you will learn how a wedding satisfies legal requirements and symbolizes the beginning of the couple's new life together.

QUALITIES OF A LONG-LASTING MARRIAGE

Objectives

After studying this lesson, you will be able to

- **identify** personal qualities that contribute to a happy and stable marriage.
- **explain** how emotional stability impacts communication.
- **compare** the effects of sensitivity and empathy on a relationship.
- **explain** how mature thinking skills impact a marriage relationship.

Focus Your Reading

1. As you read this lesson, write a description of a person who demonstrates the qualities needed for a strong and stable marriage.
2. Give an example of how a couple could demonstrate each personal quality listed in Figure 11.1.

Think of a marriage like a house built of bricks. Each *factor,* or feature, in a marriage relationship is like a brick in a wall (**Figure 11.1**). Combined together, these components strengthen the relationship and make it stable and successful. If a marriage is missing too many of these factors, however, the relationship may become weak and break apart.

Your personal qualities, skills, and resources all accompany you into a marriage relationship. Some qualities can make married living quite difficult because they make it hard to build a satisfying relationship. These include being self-centered, insensitive, rigid, unwilling to change, and unreasonable. These qualities hinder a couple's ability to communicate clearly or solve problems fairly. They are signs that more time is needed for personal growth to maturity.

Some personal qualities make it easier for a couple to build and strengthen a satisfying relationship. Many of these qualities tend to increase with maturity. You can use the questions listed in **Figure 11.2** to evaluate the growth of these qualities in your own life. As two people mature and develop these qualities, they will experience greater happiness and satisfaction in their relationship.

Building a Marriage

Personal Qualities	Homogamous Factors	Relationship Skills/Abilities	Other Factors
Sensitive	Similar interests	To disclose inner thoughts and feelings	Complementary qualities
Empathic	Similar goals and values	To communicate clearly	Support of family and friends
Loving	Similar backgrounds	To actively listen	Positive reasons for wanting to marry
Emotionally stable	Similar role expectations	To accept each other	Preparation for marriage
Positive	Logical	To give for each other's best interest	To negotiate
Trustworthy	Reasonable	To build mutual respect	To make joint decisions
Caring	Thoughtful	To build trust	
Giving	Dependable	To give and receive mature love	To solve problems together
Flexible	Responsible		

☐ Personal Qualities ☐ Homogamous Factors ☐ Relationship Skills/Abilities ☐ Other Factors

Figure 11.1 The combined effect of these factors helps make the structure of a marriage strong and stable. *Do you think some of these factors have more impact than others on the strength of a marriage?*

Think About Your Reading

Think about a couple you know who struggle to get along in their relationship. What qualities do they have that make it hard to develop a strong marriage?

The Ability to Give and Receive Love

The ability to give and receive love is vital to a happy marriage. Expressing love and showing that one cares for one's spouse strengthens a marriage relationship. A spouse needs to be willing to commit to helping meet a partner's needs. He or she also needs to be willing to do what is best for the other person. That means taking time to share and listen to what the other person has to say, which builds trust and mutual respect and helps develop mature love.

Accepting love includes being willing to let a partner meet one's own needs. It means allowing oneself to depend on another person, to be open to that person, and to be vulnerable. For some, this step is difficult. Taking this step requires self-acceptance and the belief that another person will accept and love one for who one really is. It also means accepting a partner as he or she is. The ability to give and receive mature love in these ways will strengthen the marriage and add to marital happiness.

Are You Ready for Marriage?

Am I able to unselfishly give love?

Am I able to receive love?

Am I sensitive to the hurts and needs of others?

Am I willing to try to see and experience the world from the other person's point of view?

Can I recognize my own emotions?

Can I accept my emotions and control them?

Can I express my emotions without hurting another?

Am I able and willing to adjust to change?

Can I accept differences in a partner?

Can I give and take in resolving differences?

Do I usually respond logically?

Am I able to define issues?

Do I think through the alternatives when making a decision?

Am I reasonable when evaluating alternatives?

Figure 11.2 A person's honest responses to these questions can help determine his or her readiness for marriage. A mature person would answer "yes" most of the time. *What might cause a person to self-evaluate in a way that does not reflect true personal qualities?*

The Ability to Express Empathy

Both sensitivity and empathy are important qualities for the growth of a satisfying relationship. **Sensitivity** requires being aware of how the other person thinks and feels and taking those thoughts and feelings into consideration when responding with words or actions. For two people to share in each other's lives, they must be sensitive to each other's thoughts and feelings. Being sensitive to each other requires sharing inner thoughts and feelings openly and being willing to see a situation from the other's point of view.

Empathy also keeps a relationship close. In empathy, the couple goes beyond awareness of the other person's inner thoughts and feelings to actually identifying with them (**Figure 11.3**). Each partner feels what the other feels. They know how to respond and meet each other's needs as a result. As their needs are met, they become more attached to each other. In this way, empathy helps mature love grow.

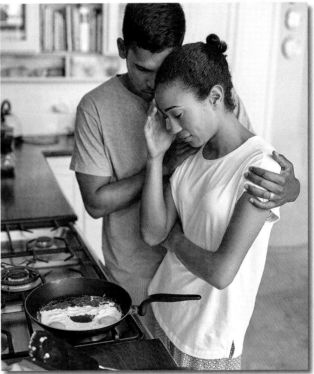

Daxiao Productions/Shutterstock.com

Figure 11.3 Empathy goes beyond sensitivity. In empathy, two people experience each other's emotions and can anticipate each other's needs.

Think About Your Reading

What are some examples of situations in which a couple would show empathy for each other?

Emotional Stability

Emotional stability is an important personal quality in marriage. An emotionally stable person is able to withstand common minor stressors in life without becoming upset, angry, nervous, or anxious (**Figure 11.4**). In the event of a major stressor, the person is able to control behaviors and return to an even emotional state in a short period of time. High self-esteem, positive life attitudes, and skills for handling stress can help a person be emotionally stable.

People who are not emotionally stable experience extreme swings in their emotions. These swings may occur often, without warning, and the behaviors that follow from the emotional extremes are often uncontrolled. Small stressors may suddenly cause these people to show flashes of extreme anger or violent outbursts. Without emotional stability, good communication is difficult. Unclear verbal and nonverbal messages may be sent and received. Intense emotions shown by one partner may cause the other to respond defensively. Both partners may then resort to name-calling, using defense mechanisms, or making irrational statements. These kinds of speech attack another person's self-esteem and break down trust in a relationship. The ability to control emotions can help couples avoid such negative communication patterns.

Emotional stability comes with growth and maturity. In any relationship, a person is likely to feel a variety of emotions. With maturity, individuals feel more positive about themselves and who they are. Their self-esteem increases, and their skills for handling emotional responses improve. The ability to handle emotions helps people keep a positive attitude in a relationship.

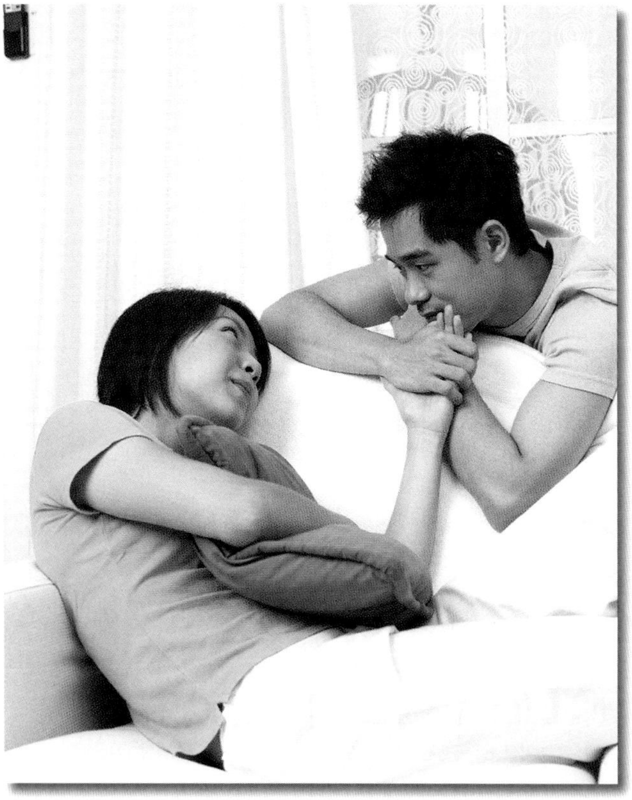

focal point/Shutterstock.com

Figure 11.4 A person who is emotionally stable copes effectively with the everyday stressors of life.

Think About Your Reading

How could developing empathy help you maintain emotional stability?

Flexibility

Many problems in marriage arise because a couple has difficulty adjusting to each other's needs and wants. The partners in the marriage may be unwilling to change. Each may insist on having his or her own way. Such *rigid* (inflexible) attitudes make it almost impossible to keep a relationship healthy and growing.

Flexibility means being willing to change. In a strong marriage, a spouse does not always need to have his or her way. Instead, each partner is willing to negotiate differences with the other. Spouses can agree to a decision that benefits both people, rather than just themselves. If both partners are flexible, they can resolve their differences. Each of them can reach a compromise that is satisfying to both (**Figure 11.5**).

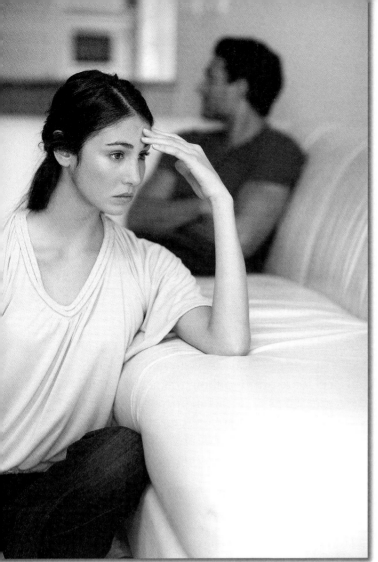
wavebreakmedia/Shutterstock.com

Figure 11.5 Being flexible often involves compromise. Both partners show they are willing to adjust to satisfy each other. *What messages are being sent by the body language between this couple related to flexibility in their relationship?*

Flexibility also means accepting and learning to tolerate certain personality traits or habits that one does not like in the other person. A spouse cannot expect the partner to change to suit him or her, but must be willing to accept the partner as he or she is.

Think About Your Reading

How does being self-centered affect a person's flexibility?

Mature Thinking Skills

Thinking skills have an impact on a person's ability to make good decisions. Many decisions have long-term effects on a relationship. Some decisions will relate to one person, and some will involve the relationship with the partner. Other decisions will relate to the person's family, children, career, or community.

Being able to apply mature thinking skills in decision making is an important skill to bring to a marriage. First, a spouse needs to have the self-control to gather the facts before making a decision. Then, he or she needs to think logically and connect accurate pieces of information together to draw a reasonable conclusion. Mature thinking also involves being able to analyze information and project likely outcomes of a decision. These skills are vital to making good decisions. Without these skills, people jump to conclusions, take actions that are not reasonable, and make poor choices.

In marriage, spouses make many decisions together. Applying mature thinking skills to shared decision making will help a couple make decisions that match their priorities and help them reach their goals. This adds to a satisfying relationship.

Assess

LESSON 11.1

COMPREHENSION CHECK

1. List four personal qualities that make it easier for couples to build satisfying and lasting marriages.
2. Explain how both sensitivity and empathy strengthen a marriage.
3. Describe the characteristics of an emotionally stable person.
4. Give one example of how emotional stability or the lack of it could impact a marriage.
5. Describe three qualities of a flexible person.
6. Explain how a lack of mature thinking skills could affect the decisions a couple makes.

Objectives

After studying this lesson, you will be able to

- **identify** factors that should be evaluated when considering marriage.
- **explain** how certain similarities and differences between spouses can affect a marital relationship.
- **analyze** how skills for communicating, making decisions, and solving problems impact readiness for marriage.
- **explain** how commitment applies to multiple areas in a marriage relationship.

Focus Your Reading

1. For each heading in this lesson, predict how that factor could impact a marriage relationship. As you read, evaluate the accuracy of your predictions.

2. Build a concept web for the term *homogamy* as it applies to developing close relationships.

Two young adults may bring many mature qualities into a relationship. At the same time, however, they will still need time to build a successful marriage.

Many factors affect a couple's marital relationship. Some of these factors relate to the couple's age, financial status, and common interests. Others relate to how well the two people communicate, make decisions, and resolve their differences. The thoughts and feelings of family and other friends can also affect a relationship. Evaluating a relationship before marriage to see if these qualities are present in a way that will contribute to a strong marriage is an important first step.

Age at Marriage

The link between age and marital success is related to emotional, intellectual, and social maturity. A young couple's ability to

Content Terms

Build Vocab

homogamy
complementary quality

Academic Terms

principle
contention

meet their financial needs is also a factor. Generally, a person is better prepared to make the lifetime commitment that marriage represents after the teen years.

During the late teen years, much personal growth is still occurring. You continue to learn more about yourself and to accept yourself for who you are. You learn more about what you like and dislike in others. You decide what qualities you desire in a person with whom you want a long-term relationship. You begin to see your life goals more clearly and to make plans to reach them. You begin to choose a job or career and make plans to become financially independent. This period of growth is important in a young person's life.

Marrying during the teen years adds more stress to a relationship. Many teens are not mature enough to handle the responsibilities and make the adjustments required in the early years of marriage. Developing into a mature person takes time. It also takes time to develop your skills and resources for living on your own. As you plan for a successful future, give yourself the time you need for personal growth by waiting to marry until you have matured and are better prepared.

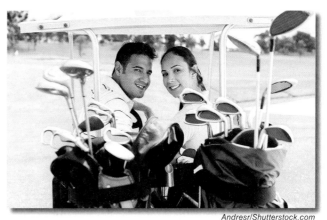

Andresr/Shutterstock.com

Figure 11.6 Couples with similar interests and backgrounds enjoy their time together. *What personal interests do you have that take a lot of time and would be valuable to share with your life partner?*

or the center of joint activities. Couples who are about the same age are more likely to have similar interests than those who are far apart in age. They will find it easier to develop leisure activities they both enjoy. Their friends will likely be similar to them in age and interests as well. Similar interests are not only helpful early in a marriage, but also help enrich relationships through the years.

> ## Think About Your Reading
> What do you think the ideal age range would be for marriage? Why?

Similarities Between Partners

Researchers who have studied marriage relationships have developed a *principle*, or idea, called **homogamy**. That principle suggests that people who have similarities in certain areas are more likely to have a satisfying marriage (**Figure 11.6**). You can see these homogamous factors in Figure 11.1. They include similar interests, similar goals and values, and similar backgrounds.

Similar Interests

Common interests can help a relationship grow. They can be a source of topics for discussion

Similar Goals and Values

People are often attracted to those who have similar life goals. A person's values affect what he or she does and the way he or she does it. They affect the goals a person sets, the choices that person considers, and the decisions he or she makes. Choosing a partner with similar goals and values can reduce the possibility of future areas of conflict developing in the relationship.

This does not mean marriage partners need to think alike on every issue. In many areas of their lives, partners can have their own values and goals. Some issues may be more important to one partner; some will be more important to the other partner. Some will be equally important to both as a couple.

Top priority areas for many couples include children and parenting, family roles, education, work expectations, and religious beliefs. A marriage is more likely to succeed if the couple agrees on values, goals, and expectations in these areas (**Figure 11.7**).

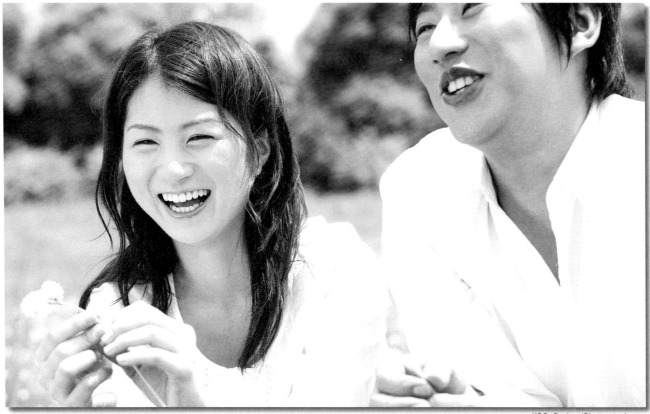

KPG_Payless/Shutterstock.com

Figure 11.7 A marriage is more likely to succeed when couples talk about their goals, values, and priority areas before making the decision to marry.

Think About Your Reading

What goals and values do you hold that are essential for you to have in common with your partner?

Similar Backgrounds

People are often attracted to others with a similar cultural and social background. They usually feel comfortable around each other and are likely to accept each other more quickly. This shared background may be a source of similar interests, values, and goals.

Similar backgrounds can make it easier for the couple to establish good relationships with each other's families as well. Because family customs may be similar and social and economic expectations may be alike, acceptance of the spouse by in-laws may come more quickly.

When couples from different backgrounds choose to marry, they will have more adjustments to make. Adjusting to differences in family attitudes, customs, and expectations takes time. Having common interests, values, and goals help a couple to have a strong marriage despite such differences.

Racial Differences

Couples in an interracial marriage may face additional challenges. Even if the two people love each other deeply, the differences between the spouses may cause conflict. Family members and friends may not support an interracial relationship—they may even object to it. They may not extend their friendship and include the spouse. Interracial couples need to consider these factors in-depth before marriage.

These challenges can cause a couple to think through their decisions more thoroughly. Their differences can cause them to evaluate their interests, priorities, and goals even more closely. Similarities in these areas can help them work through the challenges they will face. Also, many

interracial couples find that each family and their friends accept the relationship and the new spouse. That support can help them build a strong marriage.

Differences in Religious Views

When young people date, differences in religious views may not seem important. Religious views, however, are an important factor to consider before marriage. A person's faith can strongly influence his or her beliefs and practices. Marrying someone of a different faith can cause problems unless the couple discusses the issue first.

Differences in religious views usually become more important to a marriage when children are born. Dealing with the question of raising a child in a certain religious faith is the biggest problem that interfaith couples may face. If each partner wishes to raise children to follow his or her beliefs, conflict between spouses can result. Discussing

this issue before marriage and reaching a mutually satisfying decision can help a couple make decisions that will avoid the issue becoming a point of *contention* (disagreement) in the future.

Think About Your Reading

Consider all the areas of homogamy and identify which are most important to you in a relationship.

Complementary Qualities

Sometimes a person is attracted to another person who is quite different. When these differences benefit the relationship, they are called **complementary qualities**. That means the strengths of one person make up for the weaknesses of the other. The couple's qualities balance each other, and the relationship benefits (**Figure 11.8**).

Paula and Marco's relationship is a good example of this. Paula is outgoing and sociable.

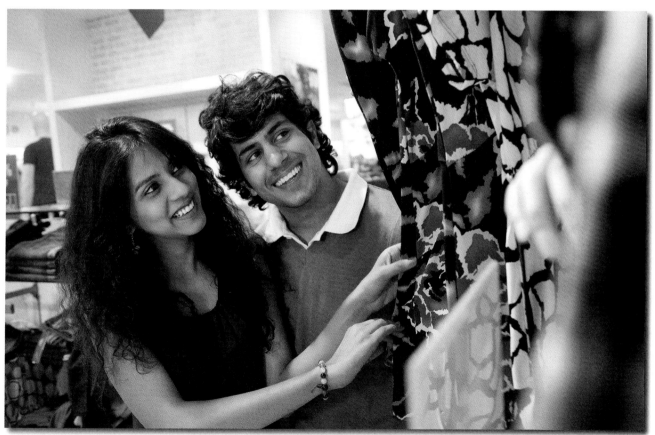

India Picture/Shutterstock.com

Figure 11.8 Complementary qualities can benefit a relationship if both people are open to growth and willing to make adjustments. *In what areas could you benefit from a partner's strengths?*

She is so involved in various clubs that she has little time to herself. At one of her club meetings, she met Marco. Marco is quiet and calm, yet friendly. Even though he is different from her, she is strongly attracted to him. His steadiness meets a need for her life to slow down a little. Marco also likes being with Paula, as her outgoing personality motivates him to become more socially involved. In this case, their differences benefit the relationship in a positive way.

Couples who have major differences that are not complementary qualities may find it difficult to work together as a team. For instance, what if Marco preferred to stay home and read quietly? He may not want to be more outgoing and sociable. Paula may not want to slow down, but may expect Marco to keep up with her social life. If they cannot balance their differences, they will not find agreeable solutions to conflicts.

Think About Your Reading

What are some examples of complementary qualities?

Communication Skills

The strength of a marriage relationship will be related to the quality of communication that takes place in it (**Figure 11.9**). Good communication means that messages are sent, received, and understood. Verbal messages are clear. Nonverbal messages, such as facial expressions and body language, support what is said. Both participants in a conversation use active listening skills to be sure a shared meaning is reached. If misunderstandings occur often in a relationship, one or both partners needs to work to develop better communication skills.

For communication to be satisfying in a long-lasting relationship, it also needs to be personal. A couple needs communication skills for sharing their personal thoughts, feelings, and inner desires. Both partners need to feel their views are accepted and valued by the other. If either feels ignored or unaccepted, the relationship will not grow.

How Do We Communicate?

- I feel free to share my personal thoughts and feelings.
- My partner freely shares deep and personal thoughts with me.
- I feel that my ideas are accepted.
- I accept my partner's point of view.
- I listen actively, making sure I understand what is shared.
- My partner listens actively to me.
- I trust my partner.
- I do not spread what my partner has shared confidentially with me.
- Our communication helps us know each other intimately.
- We communicate clearly, with few misunderstandings.

Figure 11.9 Couples can use this checklist for evaluating how well they communicate with each other. If they answer "no" to most questions, they need to spend more time developing their relationship before considering marriage.

Quality communication in a marriage relationship is based on trust. Each member of the couple can trust the other with intimate thoughts and feelings. Both know the other will respond with each other's best interests in mind. There is no fear of being hurt or rejected. Trust leads to freedom and acceptance in a relationship. In this way, high-quality communication helps mature love grow.

Skills that foster such growth can help a relationship continue to be satisfying. That does not mean there may not be some misunderstandings. These occasions, however, should become rare. Good communication skills can help a couple clear up misunderstandings, make joint decisions, and solve problems in a marriage.

Decision-Making Skills

Within a marriage, many decisions must be made, both small and large. For the marriage to last, those decisions must be shared. Using decision-making skills as a couple improves with

practice. Over time, spouses become skilled at working together to identify an issue and talk about various alternatives. They learn how to cooperate in choosing an alternative that satisfies both of them and in developing a plan to carry it out. They also become skilled at evaluating decisions together and giving each other constructive feedback to improve their joint decision-making skills.

This process helps both partners feel they have contributed to making the decision. In that case, they will more likely support each other in carrying it out. They will also have greater success in carrying out their plans and in reaching the goals they have set for their marriage.

Think About Your Reading

How will a relationship be affected if one person makes all the decisions or makes decisions without consulting the other person?

Problem-Solving Skills

It is important for a couple to evaluate their skills for solving problems and settling differences before they consider marriage (**Figure 11.10**). These skills will affect their satisfaction with the relationship.

Problem-solving steps are much like those used for decision making. The difference is that greater self-control is needed in communication when solving problems. When issues become problems, emotions tend to rise. For problem solving to occur, problems need to be identified in a mature and thoughtful way. For a couple, that often means waiting until emotions cool down before beginning to work at resolving differences. Using I-statements to express observations, thoughts, and feelings will help a couple reach a solution without damaging the relationship.

Disagreements are normal in a relationship. In a growing relationship, the couple's skills for solving problems together should improve. There should be fewer occasions when they argue or fight. Attitudes of respect and sensitivity to each other should increase, as should their skills for negotiating acceptable solutions.

Evaluate Your Decision-Making and Problem-Solving Skills

- We disagree about little things.
- We both like to make our own decisions.
- We make decisions on impulse.
- We go by our gut-level feelings when we make decisions.
- We both want to prove our point when we disagree.
- We expect each other to keep quiet when we disagree about personal matters.
- We use comments such as, "You should ..." when we disagree.
- We get angry when we do not get our own way.
- We yell and call each other names when we get upset.
- We try to figure out who is at fault to take the blame for a problem.

Figure 11.10 A couple who responds "yes" to these questions will have difficulty resolving problems in a marriage. *What areas of immaturity do you see in these responses?*

The Views of Families and Friends

A couple's chances for a successful marriage increase when family and friends approve of each marriage partner. The partners may have evaluated their relationship in all the areas discussed in this lesson and agree that they are ready for marriage. When family and friends also agree, the partners are more likely to feel confident about that decision and to receive support from the other people they care about.

Receiving love and acceptance from both families is another benefit. Each spouse's family loves and cares for him or her. When they extend love and acceptance to that person's partner, his or her feelings of self-esteem and confidence will increase. When both families express love, the couple's relationship will be strengthened.

Family support can also be a great help to a couple through the adjustments of the early years of marriage (**Figure 11.11**). Family members can

be a source of friendship, counseling, or financial help. A good relationship with both families can help a couple make satisfying choices about how to manage the relationships with each family, such as decisions about which holiday to spend with each family.

Think About Your Reading

What are some activities that you enjoy doing with your family that you would like your spouse to enjoy as well?

The approval of friends can also increase a couple's satisfaction with their relationship. If each person's friends extend that friendship to include the partner, good feelings surround the couple. Also, friends' acceptance will probably result in fewer conflicts arising over the time that one partner or the other spends with friends.

Couples who choose to marry without the approval of family and friends face more challenges than do those who have that approval. In this situation, their relationship must be strong. Developing new mutual friendships will help.

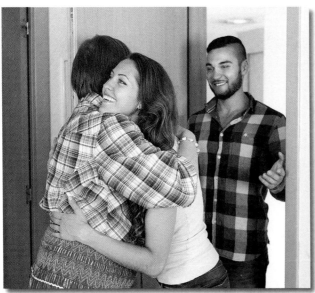

Iakov Filimonov/Shutterstock.com

Figure 11.11 Friendships with family members strengthen relationships. *What are some areas that would benefit if your family reached out and supported you in a relationship?*

The couple will need well-developed skills for resolving conflicts with each other, old friends, and family members. In addition, the couple will need greater flexibility to find solutions that are satisfying to both. They will need to encourage each other often so that their self-esteem and confidence remain high. With good communication skills, positive attitudes, and a willingness to work out problems, these couples can still have a strong marriage. They may also find that their relationships with family and friends improve over time.

Reasons the Couple Wants to Marry

People decide to marry for many different reasons. Infatuation and other one-sided emotional needs are negative reasons. To be successful, a marriage must be based on positive reasons.

Negative Reasons

Some couples want to marry because they like being together. Wanting their romantic feelings to last for a lifetime, they decide to marry. This infatuation can cloud a couple's judgment of their relationship. They may be overlooking personal differences. One may often give in to make the other happy or keep quiet, rather than express personal opinions. When the infatuation fades, they begin to feel dissatisfied with the relationship. Even minor differences soon become major issues. If the couple cannot resolve those issues, the relationship may fall apart.

Some people marry to avoid loneliness. Others marry for the financial security that a partner may bring. To some, marriage may seem to be a way to achieve adult status or to escape from problems at home. Sometimes, young people marry because of a pregnancy. All of these are poor reasons for marriage.

Positive Reasons

Mature love, intimacy, companionship, and a desire to grow together throughout life are

healthy reasons for marriage. They contribute to a satisfying relationship. As satisfaction increases, the couple's desire to stay together does, too.

A relationship based on mature love is a good foundation for a successful marriage. Keeping a relationship strong and healthy over time takes a commitment in all four areas described in Chapter 10: continued growth of mature love, ongoing romance, continued growth in friendship, and continual commitment to using good relationship skills (**Figure 11.12**).

For a relationship to last, both partners need to be committed to this one relationship. Both partners need to be willing to turn aside from all other possible romantic relationships. They need to be committed to keeping this relationship growing and satisfying for both. This commitment begins with the engagement.

Assess

LESSON 11.2

COMPREHENSION CHECK

1. Explain why marrying as a teen may add more stress to a relationship.
2. Couples who have many similarities are more likely to have a strong marriage. List and briefly describe three possible areas of similarities.
3. Give two examples of complementary qualities in a couple's relationship.
4. Explain how skills for communicating, making decisions, and solving problems can be evidence of whether one is ready for marriage.
5. Briefly describe two ways in which a family's support can help a couple's relationship.
6. Explain how a commitment in the four areas of a romantic relationship will help make a long-lasting, healthy marriage.

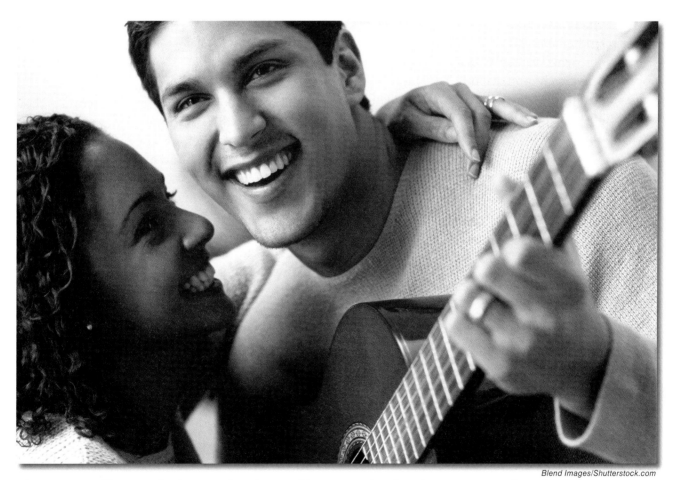

Blend Images/Shutterstock.com

Figure 11.12 The growth of mature love is a positive reason for choosing to marry and can lead to a long-lasting and satisfying relationship.

Objectives

After studying this lesson, you will be able to

- **identify** important decisions to be discussed during the engagement period.
- **compare** different expectations for fulfilling roles in a marriage.
- **recognize** the legal aspects of beginning a marriage.

Focus Your Reading

1. Create a checklist of questions that a couple could use to evaluate if they are ready for marriage.
2. Define and give at least three examples of role sharing and identify the benefits of sharing roles.

Content Terms

Build Vocab

engagement
complementary role
role sharing
lease
ceremonial wedding
civil ceremony
vow

Academic Terms

harmonize
institution

As a couple prepares for marriage, they will need to continue evaluating and growing in their relationship. They will need to communicate clearly, set goals, make decisions, discuss expectations, resolve problems, and continue to build a loving relationship. These experiences will help prepare them for the adjustments they will have to make in the early years of marriage.

Engagement

The **engagement** is the final stage in the dating process leading to marriage. The engagement period signifies the start of a couple's plans for married life. It usually begins with a formal announcement to family and friends that the couple intend to marry. A partner may either give or receive a ring to identify this commitment to marry.

Most marriage counselors recommend an engagement period of six months to two years. The length of time depends on several factors. These include how well the couple know each other, whether they are ready to handle the responsibilities of marriage, and whether they can support themselves financially.

The engagement period provides time for a couple to discuss important issues and expectations. Both will have expectations for each other, for children, for relating to their families, and for other areas of their shared life.

Role Expectations

Roles are particular patterns for daily living. Some common roles of a marriage partner include being a friend, lover, companion, wage earner, cook, housekeeper, bill payer, or nurse. The expectations that partners have for the roles both they and their spouse should fill are strongly influenced by the roles their parents took in their families (**Figure 11.13**). These expectations are also impacted by each partner's cultural background. Cultures can have strong expectations for marital roles. Thus, if a couple has similar backgrounds, many role expectations will be similar.

It is necessary for the couple to discuss each other's role expectations, and the engagement period offers an excellent opportunity to do so. Sometimes persons in love think they can overlook differences in role expectations or put off decisions about roles that will not impact them until later. They may overlook that living out their day-to-day roles will occupy much of their time throughout the various stages of life. For a marriage to be successful, a couple needs to determine what roles make sense for each of them. Both partners need to fully support this decision.

If not, there will be constant friction and irritation between the two. Those negative feelings can do serious damage to a relationship. Roles will change over time, especially as children become part of a family, and expectations about these changes also need to be discussed. Living up to personal roles is easier if a couple knows what is expected. Thus, communication about roles is important.

Some couples choose to adopt **complementary roles**. That is, each person takes on roles that *harmonize* with or support the roles the other person takes. For example, if one partner has mechanical skills, he or she carries out roles related to maintenance of the home and cars, while the partner with skills in food preparation may carry out the role of preparing most of the meals. Some couples choose **role sharing** as a way of handling some responsibilities. Through role sharing, they work together to carry out a task. For example, a couple may choose to prepare meals and clean up the kitchen together. Role sharing allows couples to keep in touch with one another's thoughts and feelings while sharing responsibilities.

> ## Think About Your Reading
> How are roles divided in your family? Give some examples of how family members carry out different roles and identify whether these are complementary roles or shared roles.

Planning Finances

Couples need to discuss finances during the engagement period. Future income, expenses, paying bills, saving for desired purchases—all these areas of money management should be discussed before marriage. Couples also need to decide who will actually pay the bills and who will make certain purchases. Most important, they need to agree on their overall financial goals (**Figure 11.14**).

Basic steps for developing a spending and savings plan are discussed in Chapter 22. Meeting with a financial planner is also a way a couple can define their financial goals and make plans to meet them. That professional can help identify

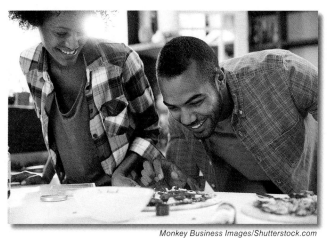

Monkey Business Images/Shutterstock.com

Figure 11.13 Roles are certain patterns that each family member identifies and shares. *What roles do you expect to fulfill in your marriage?*

potential areas of conflict that could arise in the future so that the couple is sure to address them.

Think About Your Reading

What are your expectations for your first home? What kind of income will it take to establish and maintain such a home?

Planning for Housing Needs

A couple's housing options and their choice of where to live will depend on the money they have to spend and on other factors. Most young couples rent housing, since a large sum of money is needed to buy a home. Apartments, which are available in a range of prices, are the most popular choice. A couple should consider the cost of utilities, furnishings, and rental insurance in addition to the cost of the rent before signing a **lease**, or rental agreement.

Other housing factors that a couple must consider include the location, which needs to give both spouses access to work or school. They may also think about the character of the neighborhood, its closeness to child care facilities, and its closeness to family and friends.

Planning for Career Goals

As they plan for the future, couples need to discuss their career goals. Each person's career will affect family life. The demands of work will influence the amount of time a couple has together. Work schedules may affect the way they divide or share roles in the home (**Figure 11.15**). Their incomes from work will influence the amount of money they have to spend. Other career issues that will affect the family include promotions, pay raises, job relocations, or future educational expenses.

A couple should discuss their expectations for each other and their top-priority issues. If their commitment to their relationship is a top priority,

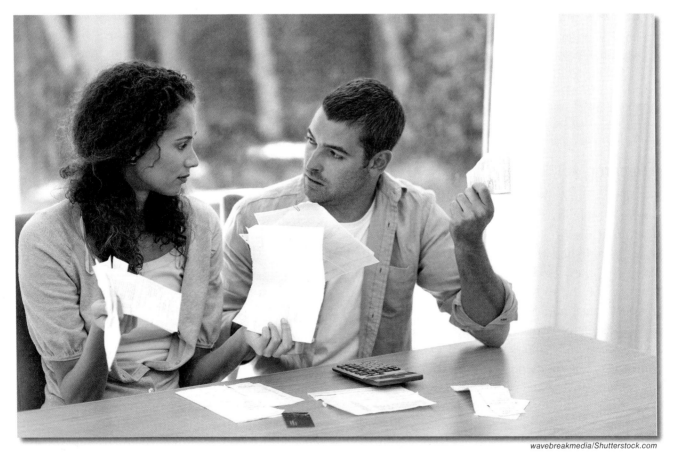

wavebreakmedia/Shutterstock.com

Figure 11.14 Before marriage, it is important that a couple discusses financial goals. *What financial goals might a new couple have?*

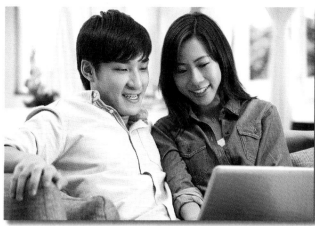
Monkey Business Images/Shutterstock.com

Figure 11.15 Discussing career goals and work schedules can help couples plan for time together.

their marriage can be healthy. They both can grow individually, and they will work to balance the pressures of their lifestyle. If either partner puts personal goals ahead of the relationship or family goals, the marriage will likely suffer.

Think About Your Reading

How important is it to you to complete your education before getting married? What would be the advantages? Why might it be more advantageous for some people to finish school after they get married?

Planning for Intimacy

The security of marriage allows a couple to express their love in physical intimacy. They are confident their relationship will last because they have established trust and are totally committed to each other. Sexual satisfaction in a relationship goes hand in hand with love, caring, mutual respect, trust, and commitment to each other.

An engaged couple should make sure they are informed about sexual roles and expectations in marriage. This does not mean that either partner must have any sexual experience before marriage. Experiences during the engagement period are often not satisfying because the security and commitment of marriage are missing. Premarital relations may be accompanied by fear, doubts, or guilt.

The couple may feel disappointed because they do not experience the satisfaction they expected.

To make the adjustment to intimacy in marriage easier to carry out, the couple should use the engagement period to discuss any concerns and anxieties about the sexual aspects of marriage. Sensitivity to each other's physical and emotional needs can help them make the needed adjustments once they are married.

Planning for Children

Another area that needs to be discussed before marriage is the issue of children. This issue raises many, many questions. Does each partner want to be a parent? How many children does each one want? When do they want to have them, and how far apart do they prefer that the children be born? How will children affect their income, expenses, roles, and careers? What will they do if they want children, but learn they cannot have them?

In addition to planning for children, a couple should discuss their viewpoints on how to raise children. Who will have major responsibility for child care? What expectations does each spouse have for the other's involvement in child care? What are their attitudes toward child guidance and discipline? These need to be discussed before marriage so that the couple is united in their approach to parenting.

Think About Your Reading

Do you want to become a parent some day? How many children would you like to have? How important is it that your spouse has similar feelings about parenthood?

Planning Relationships with Families and Friends

Families and friends are both important areas to be discussed during engagement. What family obligations does each spouse have? Will the couple celebrate birthdays, anniversaries, and holidays with family members? Which holidays will be spent with which family? Good relationships

A Growing Relationship

Jennifer and Samuel felt they were ready for marriage. They were deeply in love, and they had grown very close. They shared many common interests and were truly committed to each other. They knew they had some differences, but they believed they could work them out.

Both of them had promising careers. Jennifer worked as a manager for a local restaurant chain. She was organized and efficient, as well as friendly and outgoing. She enjoyed her work, but she knew she would have to relocate if she ever wanted to get a promotion. Samuel was also an organized person and very attentive to detail. He was less social than Jennifer, preferring to spend time alone with her. He worked as a computer technician for a large company. This company had employees throughout the United States and in other countries as well. Jennifer and Samuel realized their jobs could pull them in different directions.

Jennifer and Samuel both wanted to have children, but they were not sure when. They were not sure how children would affect their career choices. That seemed like a decision they would make later.

For Discussion

1. What personal qualities can you identify for Jennifer and for Samuel that could contribute to their having a successful marriage?
2. What similarities could have attracted them to each other? In what ways might their personality differences cause conflicts?
3. In what ways could Jennifer's and Samuel's careers pull them in different directions? How could this affect their marriage? How important would it be to agree on a potential solution before they marry?
4. What are some questions that Jennifer and Samuel should discuss about parenting? If they do not agree in these areas, how could having children increase conflict in their relationship?

with families can strengthen a couple's relationship. A couple needs to make decisions about relating to other family members that both families will accept and support.

Couples also need to discuss their personal friendships and joint friendships. Engaged couples may find that as they spend more time together, their friendships with others change. They may spend less time with their present friends. Some friendships will remain strong, while others just drift apart. Mutual friends of the couple may take the place of individual friends (**Figure 11.16**). Discussing expectations about friendships before marriage can decrease the possibility of future conflict in this area.

Premarital Counseling

Some couples choose to talk to a counselor before marriage. This person may be a licensed marriage and family counselor, a religious leader, or the person who will be performing the marriage ceremony (**Figure 11.17**). The counselor may discuss such topics as personal readiness for marriage, expectations for each other, skills for communicating, skills for making decisions and problem solving, and even money management. The counselor may spend some time with the

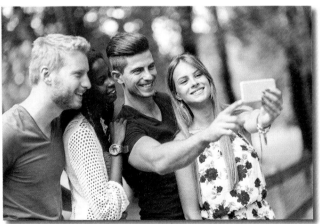

Andor Bujdoso/Shutterstock.com

Figure 11.16 Married or engaged couples are likely to spend time with mutual friends. *What do you think are reasonable expectations for seeing friends that are not mutual to the relationship?*

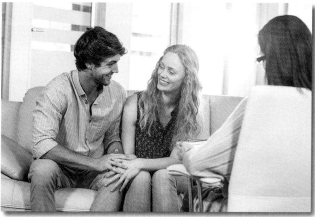

wavebreakmedia/Shutterstock.com

Figure 11.17 Many couples seek premarital counseling to help them evaluate their relationship and their plans for the future. *Which areas of a relationship do you think would be most difficult to evaluate by yourself?*

couple together and some time with each partner alone. There may be more than one meeting.

In some cases, the counseling process reveals that one or both partners has a "me-oriented" rather than "we-oriented" attitude. Such a strong focus on personal wants and desires may be evidence of immaturity. In this case, it may be a sign the couple should wait before marrying.

Think About Your Reading

What are some reasons that a couple may hesitate to pursue premarital counseling?

Breaking an Engagement

The engagement period is a time of preparation for marriage. For most couples, it is a happy time as partners prepare for a new life together. In the course of this planning, however, some couples discover they are not ready for marriage.

A couple may decide to break the engagement for various reasons. One person may sense a need to grow personally. The two may recognize poor communication patterns or an inability to make decisions together. They may discover they are not suited for each other. If either partner doubts the relationship will be successful, the couple would be wise to break the engagement. Ending

a relationship is difficult at any time, but a broken engagement is better than an unhappy marriage.

Planning the Wedding

The engagement period also provides time for a couple to complete their wedding plans. The customs and traditions of the couple's families often influence the details of the wedding. The couple's personal desires and social and economic status may also influence these plans. In the midst of all the planning, the partners need to continue developing their relationship as a couple.

Marriage

Marriage is a legal contract involving the couple and the state. The state sets minimum standards for that contract. These standards are designed to establish some order and stability in marriage as an *institution*, or important part of society. Once these standards are met, the couple can proceed with the wedding ceremony.

Marriage Laws

All states have certain requirements concerning the marriage contract. They require that both parties must be competent and eligible to enter the contract. Also, both parties must enter the marriage contract willingly, or by mutual consent. The contract cannot be legally dissolved without state action.

Although all states have marriage laws, particular details may differ. A couple planning to get married should check the laws in their particular state. Many couples seek this information from the licensed official who will perform their marriage ceremony. Most marriage laws specify certain requirements, minimum ages, licensing necessities, and the legal standards for those who officiate.

The Wedding Ceremony

The wedding ceremony serves two purposes. First, it meets a requirement that a couple be legally joined by a licensed official. Secondly, the ceremony symbolizes to themselves and to others the couple's commitment to their relationship.

Some couples choose a **ceremonial wedding** performed by a religious official. Typically, family members and friends share in such a ceremony and witness the couple's vows of commitment to each other. Family and friends celebrate this commitment by sharing gifts to help the couple establish a new home. **Vows** are statements that specifically express the couple's commitment to each other, and they are a traditional part of the marriage ceremony (**Figure 11.18**). The marriage official will have a copy of the marriage ceremony, including the vows, and will discuss this with the couple in advance. Sometimes couples like to write their own vows as a way of making the ceremony unique for them. This needs to be discussed with the marriage official.

Some couples choose a **civil ceremony**. For this type of ceremony, family members and a few friends witness the couple's vows taken before a judicial or public official.

Sometimes exceptions exist in the laws associated with certain weddings, as in the Quaker community. Instead of having a legal official, the couple marry themselves. The members of the congregation sign the marriage license as witnesses.

The Honeymoon

A honeymoon allows time for the couple to relax after the wedding and adjust to their new life. Some couples use this time to travel. Others may just spend some time alone, away from the pressures of work and other responsibilities. The length of the honeymoon may vary, depending on the couple's finances and schedules.

LESSON 11.3

Assess

COMPREHENSION CHECK

1. What is the purpose of the engagement period?
2. Identify three important issues a couple needs to discuss during their engagement.
3. Describe two ways of dividing roles in a marriage relationship.
4. List three reasons why a premarital counselor may suggest that a couple make their engagement longer.

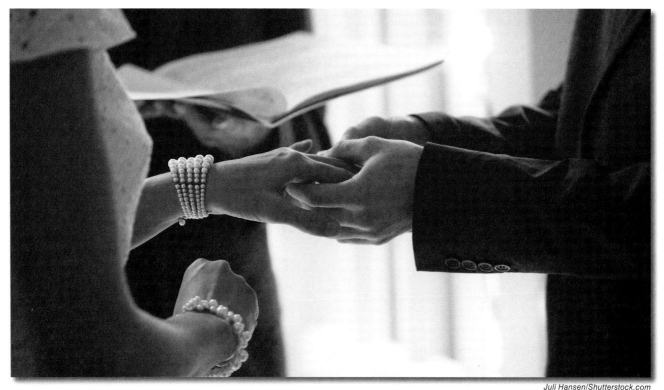

Juli Hansen/Shutterstock.com

Figure 11.18 During a wedding ceremony, couples exchange vows by stating their commitment to each other. *How do you think vows relate to the four areas of commitment for a long-lasting relationship?*

CHAPTER SUMMARY

Certain personal qualities can help couples build a stable marriage. Many of these are qualities that tend to increase with maturity, one reason that it is best for teens not to marry. Couples who develop these qualities in their relationship will experience greater satisfaction in married life and have a greater likelihood of a successful marriage.

Couples should honestly evaluate their relationship before becoming engaged. Since certain factors affect marital happiness, this evaluation can help a couple determine their readiness for marriage. Some factors are related to similarities and differences between the two people. Other factors include a couple's ability to communicate, make decisions, and solve problems together. Each of these factors will affect the way the relationship grows.

An engagement period provides time for continued evaluation and growth in the relationship. It also allows time for planning future needs and role expectations. Deciding whether to have children and assessing family relationships are other issues in this planning process. A premarital counselor can assist couples in evaluating their relationship. After evaluating their relationship, some couples may discover they have doubts about the upcoming marriage and break the engagement. The engagement period also includes planning the wedding.

Marriage is bound by a legal contract and is a commitment to give fully to one relationship. A couple must accept the responsibility of following certain laws to fulfill the marriage contract. The wedding ceremony legally joins a couple.

VOCABULARY ACTIVITIES

1. Write a sentence relating how each term contributes to a strong, lasting marriage, but leave the term blank. Give your sentences to a partner and have him or her fill in the missing terms. Fill in your partner's sentences. When you have both completed the sentences, discuss any differences and revise the sentences as needed to reflect the correct meaning.

Content Terms

ceremonial wedding (11.3)
civil ceremony (11.3)
complementary quality (11.2)
complementary role (11.3)
emotional stability (11.1)
engagement (11.3)
flexibility (11.1)
homogamy (11.2)
lease (11.3)
role sharing (11.3)
sensitivity (11.1)
vow (11.3)

2. Write two sentences for each term. In the first, relate the term to marriage. In the second, relate the term to some other aspect of life.

Academic Terms

contention (11.2)
factor (11.1)
harmonize (11.3)
institution (11.3)
principle (11.2)
rigid (11.1)

ASSESS

Your Knowledge

3. What are the personal qualities that contribute to a happy and healthy marriage?
4. What factors should be evaluated when considering readiness for marriage?
5. What issues should couples discuss and make plans about before getting married?

Your Understanding

6. Identify five different personal qualities and three different personal skills and explain how each of those qualities and skills can affect the quality of a marriage relationship.
7. How can similarities and differences between a couple affect their marital relationship?
8. Explain how planning for married living can benefit a couple's relationship.

Your Skills

9. Write a paragraph in which you evaluate your development of the personal qualities needed for a long-lasting marriage.
10. Identify a problem in your school that you can address. Work with a partner to solve this problem and present your solution to the class. Before working through the solution with your partner, develop a checklist to evaluate your personal skills for communicating, decision making, and solving problems with your partner. After working through the solution, evaluate each other's skills using your checklist.

CRITICAL THINKING

11. **Make Inferences.** Write a paragraph describing a person who could be a homogamous partner for you. What qualities would this person have in common with you? Explain how these qualities could add to a long-lasting marriage relationship, citing evidence from the text to support your explanation.
12. **Analyze Data and Summarize Findings.** Make a list of the general and specific qualities

you desire in your ideal mate. Compare your list with those of other classmates. Are there any differences between the qualities desired in males or females? Are there qualities that are desired in all spouses? Summarize your conclusions about the class lists in a paragraph. Then add a paragraph analyzing your own summary for qualities that will contribute to a long-lasting marriage, citing evidence from the text to support your analysis.

13. **Support a Point of View.** Analyze the following statement: "If your family and friends do not approve of your potential marriage partner, you should not get married." Write a paper either agreeing or disagreeing with the statement. Use specific arguments to support your position, citing at least two sources to support your point of view.

14. **Make Generalizations.** Compare the family roles of both spouses in two different married couples you know. What differences are there in the two couples? What similarities are there in the ways the two couples fulfill roles in their families? Discuss your findings with two other classmates. Look for differences and similarities between the two families you analyzed and the families they studied. Then work with the class to prepare a class list of roles most commonly taken by spouses in your community. Write a paper summarizing your findings, compare your own findings with the class list, and conclude with generalizations that are supported by your data.

CORE SKILLS

15. **Research.** Interview a person who can legally officiate at a wedding in your state. Ask him or her to explain the marriage laws in your state. What type of ceremony does the official generally use? What vows does the official recommend? Have him or her describe any symbolism related to the traditional wedding ceremony. Prepare a one-page report summarizing your findings from the interview.

16. **Writing.** Invite someone from the community to join a panel to discuss recommendations for preparing for marriage. (Your classmates will invite other guests who will join with your person to form the panel.) Guests may include a religious leader, marriage counselor, wedding planner, or parent who recently had a child marry. Prepare questions to ask the panel. Summarize the presentation in a report. *Group option*: Work in a group of four to prepare the report and post on the class website.

17. **Writing.** Write a marriage contract listing the expectations you have for yourself and for your spouse. Include your ideas about the roles you both should take in marriage. Try to be specific. Submit a printed copy of the contract to your teacher.

18. **Research, Writing.** Use the Internet to research wedding customs in two different cultures. Write a report comparing each culture's wedding customs to those you have observed in your own culture.

19. **Research, Using Data from Multiple Sources.** Use a spreadsheet program to prepare a checklist to evaluate a relationship. Include the factors affecting the quality of a marital relationship, rating them as very important, somewhat important, and not very important. Survey three married couples, asking them about their views of the importance of each item on your list and using the same three ratings you used. Gather their responses and compile the totals. Summarize your findings, comparing their responses with your list. *Group option*: Work in a group of four to prepare the lists, gather data from married couples, and then compile the data. Prepare a graph showing the number of persons rating each factor as very important, somewhat important, and not very important.

20. **Writing, Reading.** Identify a television sitcom or a movie that has a married couple as main characters. Analyze the personal qualities and skills, including communication skills and behaviors, that are modeled in the relationships between the characters and evaluate them for their contribution to a healthy, long-lasting marriage relationship. In a one-page paper, describe the qualities and skills you saw modeled and present your conclusion, citing evidence from the text to support your evaluation. *Choice*: Use your checklist from the previous activity to evaluate the relationships you observe.

CAREER READINESS

21. **Researching Careers.** Form teams of four to five students and research a career area that focuses on helping couples build strong marriage relationships. Have each team prepare a summary of the services provided by professionals in that career area. Appoint one person on each team to present their findings in a symposium on "Local Services for Building Strong Marriages in Our Community." *Choice*: Present your findings in a digital format on your school website.

Reading Prep

Before reading the chapter, copy the headings down on a piece of paper in outline form. As you read, list the main ideas of each section under the appropriate heading.

Key Questions

Questions to answer as you study this chapter:

- What patterns of adjustment to conflict contribute to a high-quality marriage relationship?
- What personal adjustments do spouses need to make to build a strong marriage?
- What other adjustments are common in the early years of marriage?

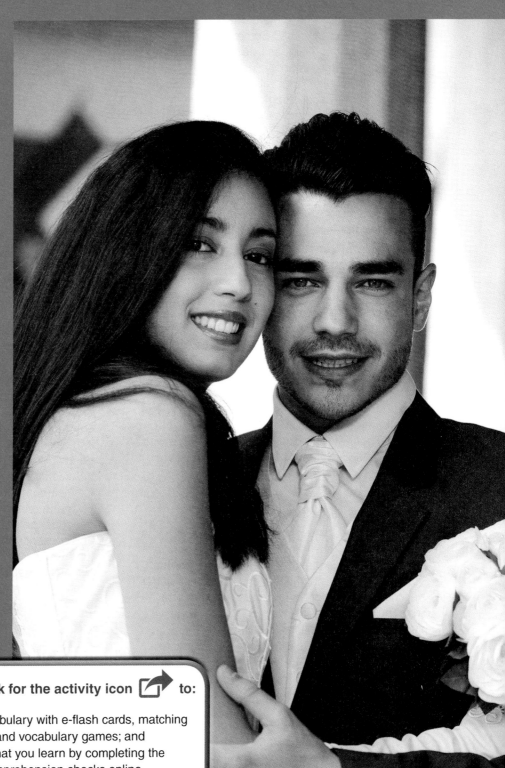

Jean-Philippe WALLET/Shutterstock.com

While studying this chapter, look for the activity icon 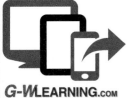 to:

- **build** vocabulary with e-flash cards, matching activities, and vocabulary games; and
- **assess** what you learn by completing the lesson comprehension checks online.
  www.g-wlearning.com/humanservices/

G-WLEARNING.com

AFTER STUDYING THIS CHAPTER, YOU WILL

KNOW:

- The basic patterns that people follow in handling conflict.
- Common areas of adjustment in the early years of marriage.
- Sources of help for couples as they adjust to marriage.

UNDERSTAND:

- How a couple can handle differences in a way that strengthens a relationship.
- How a couple can increase the quality of their marriage relationship.
- How marriage counseling can help a couple improve their relationship.

BE ABLE TO DO:

- Create a plan that provides accountability for money within a marriage.
- Develop skills for settling disagreements in a way that promotes a positive relationship.

GETTING STARTED

Carey and her cousin Sasha were watching Sasha's brother and his new wife cut the cake at their wedding reception.

"I can't wait to get married," said Carey. "Your brother and his wife seem so in love, and she looks like a fairy tale princess in that beautiful dress."

"Well, this is just the beginning of their life together as a married couple," Sasha replied. "They are really happy now, but marriage certainly isn't a fairy tale."

Sasha's older sister had been married for several years, and Sasha knew that marriage was not always easy. Her sister and her sister's husband worked hard to maintain their healthy, happy marriage. In addition, Sasha had observed many arguments between her mother and father before they decided to divorce. Sasha knew there was a lot to consider before getting married.

You have probably observed a variety of marriage relationships in your family and community. Some marriages probably seem more successful than others, with qualities you admire.

These couples seem to thrive. They are able to work together and be happy. You have probably seen other marriages in which couples do not get along well. Their relationships seem to be divided, unstable, and unhappy. You may wonder why some marriages succeed and others fail.

No one formula will guarantee a perfect marriage for every couple. Couples can, however, develop a quality relationship in the following ways:

- dealing effectively with conflicts in their day-to-day living
- learning to balance interpersonal relations
- adapting to financial and social changes

As you will see in this chapter, all couples must make some adjustments in their marriage relationship. As they grow and change over time, they will continue to make adjustments to keep the quality of their relationship high.

PATTERNS OF ADJUSTMENT TO CONFLICT

Content Terms
Build Vocab

marital adjustment
hostility
concession
accommodation

Academic Terms

method
quarrel

Objectives

After studying this lesson, you will be able to
- **identify** patterns a couple may use to handle conflict.
- **relate** these patterns to the quality of a marriage relationship.

Focus Your Reading

1. As you read this lesson, summarize how a person would deal with conflict with a spouse using each pattern of adjustment.
2. Write a scenario in which a person uses one of the patterns of adjustment. Role-play the scenario with a partner.

All married couples experience some conflict in their relationship. Whenever two people live together on a day-to-day basis, some disagreements will arise. Couples deal with these conflicts by making adjustments. **Marital adjustment** is the process couples use to modify their relationship as needed throughout their married life. The goal of making these adjustments is to develop and maintain a high level of quality in the relationship. As the quality of the relationship goes up, that relationship is more likely to last.

The quality of most marriage relationships is somewhere on a continuum that represents the feelings and attitudes a couple has about their relationship. At one end of the continuum, the relationship is happy, satisfying, and fulfilling. At the other end, the relationship is unhappy, dissatisfying, and unfulfilling. Most marriage relationships move back and forth somewhere in the middle of the continuum, shifting with the changes that couples experience in daily life.

When conflicts occur, couples make adjustments in their marriage by using certain *methods*, or ways of doing things. These basic patterns of adjustment include hostility, concession, accommodation, and compromise (**Figure 12.1**). The method they choose may depend on the situation. A couple's success in making adjustments that are constructive and fair to both partners will determine the degree of happiness in their marriage.

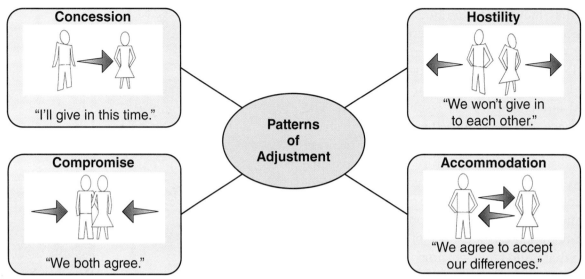

Figure 12.1 A couple's choice of a pattern of adjustment will depend on the situation they are trying to resolve. *Which pattern do you find yourself using often in your relationships?*

Hostility

Sometimes couples handle their differences with **hostility**. They never really settle conflicts and do not agree on solutions. Instead, they continually *quarrel* (argue) about the conflicts that arise. Sometimes they may hit or physically abuse one another in their anger and frustration. Unresolved hostility has negative effects on a relationship. If it begins in one area of the relationship, it will gradually spread to other parts.

This method of handling differences produces the lowest quality in a relationship. Because the couple does not find any satisfactory solutions to the conflict, the marriage relationship typically weakens over time.

Think About Your Reading

Where do you think a relationship would fall on the continuum if all conflicts are handled with hostility?

Concession

There will be times in a marriage relationship that one spouse just gives in to the partner. Rather than work to reach a joint agreement, one simply agrees with the other person. This method

is known as **concession**. If both spouses give in some of the time, the quality of the relationship can be quite high (**Figure 12.2**). If one spouse feels that he or she is giving in *all* the time, however, dissatisfaction will grow. The quality of the relationship will then decrease.

Accommodation

Sometimes spouses may not be able to find an agreeable solution to a particular conflict. In these

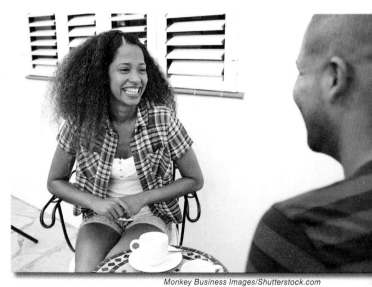

Figure 12.2 Concession can lead to a quality relationship, as long as one person is not giving in the majority of the time.

cases, they may use **accommodation**. This means they accept each other's differences and agree to live with them. Each puts up with the other's behavior or opinion, even though neither particularly likes what he or she is putting up with. No mutual agreement on the issue is reached. The differences still exist, but they do not obstruct the relationship. This method does not increase the quality of the relationship, but it helps couples work around their differences. It can be a workable pattern if the issues or behaviors being accommodated are not too important. Even then, accommodation has a chance of promoting frustration that builds up over time.

Compromise

Compromise tends to be the most satisfying and lasting way to resolve differences in a marriage. When couples compromise, they find a solution to which they both agree. Both must be willing to give and take to reach an agreeable solution.

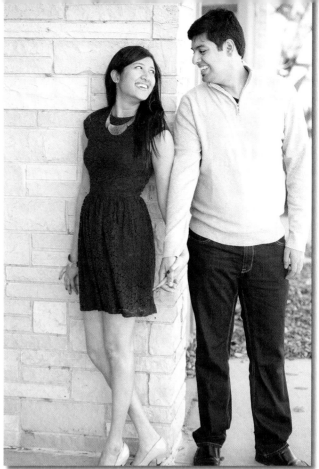

FeyginFoto/Shutterstock.com

Figure 12.3 *Why do you think compromise is the most satisfying pattern of adjustment for married couples?*

> ## Think About Your Reading
>
> Think about a time when you had to compromise with someone. How did you feel about the solution?

Of all the patterns described, resolving differences through compromise will bring the greatest satisfaction to a relationship. With this approach, both members of the couple feel their ideas have been expressed and accepted (**Figure 12.3**). Both feel they have taken part in finding a positive solution. Neither feels that there was a winner or a loser.

Of these four strategies, hostility is the most destructive to relationships and should be avoided. Most couples use each of the other three methods at some time in their marriage. No one method can be used all the time since conflicts vary. Looking at the pros and cons of each possible solution will enable a couple to choose the best method for handling a particular problem. The

better they become at choosing the best method for each situation, the more satisfying their relationship will become.

LESSON 12.1
Assess

COMPREHENSION CHECK

1. In your own words, briefly explain how the quality of marriage can be judged on a continuum.
2. List and define four ways of resolving differences.
3. Identify some examples that indicate hostility is being used to solve a problem.
4. Describe how repeated use of concession could affect a relationship.
5. Explain the difference between *accommodation* and *compromise*.
6. Give an example of how a couple can compromise to resolve their differences.

Objectives

After studying this lesson, you will be able to

- **identify** strategies for making interpersonal adjustments in a marriage.
- **describe** characteristics of pair adjustment.
- **explain** how to use the sandwich approach in communication.
- **compare** active and passive interactions.
- **identify** common marital roles.

Focus Your Reading

1. Imagine you are a marriage counselor. As you read the lesson, develop questions that you could ask a couple you were counseling related to each area of interpersonal adjustment.

2. Give four examples of what a person might say if using the sandwich approach to express an opinion in a sensitive situation.

Content Terms

Build Vocab

interpersonal adjustment
pair adjustment
sandwich approach
active interaction
passive interaction
self-actualization
marital role

Academic Terms

trivial
appreciation
balance

Marriage is the joining of two unique individuals. Each person has his or her own personal preferences and opinions. These unique features of their personalities do not change after marriage. To live together successfully, the couple must learn to adjust to each other. The changes they make as they learn to live with each other are called **interpersonal adjustments**.

Thinking of *We* Instead of *Me*

When couples adjust their individual lifestyles to have a satisfying life together, it is called **pair adjustment**. This kind of adjustment starts during dating as partners seek to find similarities in interests, values, goals, and expectations.

Once two people marry, the day-to-day adjustments of being a couple continue. Prior to marriage, each person has a great deal of independence. Each decides when and how to eat, exercise, relax, and sleep. After marriage, all these matters make a difference

to another person (**Figure 12.4**). Even *trivial*, or minor, habits can become subjects for joint discussion and decision making. For a relationship to last, both partners need to think of themselves as "we" together, rather than as "me," the individual.

Sometimes consideration for the other's desires and feelings is enough to settle a difference. If either spouse sticks with self-centered "me" attitudes, however, hostility can increase. If hostility expands and spreads to other areas of the relationship, the couple will find it more difficult to resolve any issues.

Think About Your Reading

Why do you think pair adjustment is an ongoing task for a couple?

Accepting Habits

No one is perfect. You are not, and your spouse will not be. Two people may overlook each other's irritating habits while dating. Each may even think the other person will change these habits once they are married. After marriage, however, habits do not change or go away. Instead, habits often become more irritating because the person who does not like the habit sees it repeated often.

When people first marry, they are learning new behaviors and establishing new routines. Many everyday behaviors can cause friction as two people adjust to living with someone else. It is normal that a few of each person's habits will irritate the other spouse. In a marriage, accepting these minor irritations is easier when both people focus on the positive aspects of their relationship.

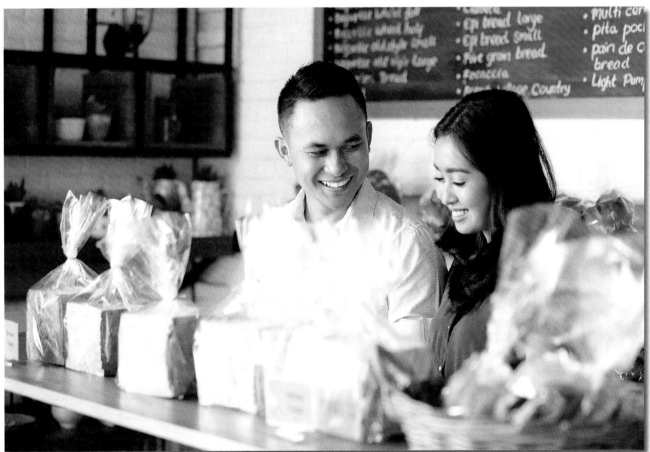

Odua Images/Shutterstock.com

Figure 12.4 After marriage, a couple must learn to adjust to changes in their daily routine. *What personal qualities will help couples make these adjustments?*

Showing Appreciation

Praise, sincere compliments, and thoughtfulness are ways one spouse can show appreciation for the other. Both verbal and nonverbal expressions of *appreciation*, or approval, can keep a positive atmosphere in the relationship. These positive responses along with warm affection help keep the romantic spark alive as well (**Figure 12.5**). When spouses show appreciation for each other, the quality of their relationship increases.

Think About Your Reading

Why do you think couples might fail to keep the romantic spark alive through positive feedback? What adjustment patterns might contribute to this?

Keeping Communication Lines Open

Open and honest communication needs to take place regularly in a marriage. Daily sharing of events, situations, frustrations, or successes can help spouses keep these communication lines open. Planning a set time each day just to talk can help make communication a priority. Deep, interpersonal sharing is important as well, so couples also need to plan for longer periods to talk. A relaxed environment free of distractions and away from interruptions is best for this kind of meaningful sharing to take place.

Sometimes a spouse may need to say something to the partner about a sensitive topic—something that may upset the other person, but that needs to be said. Planning what to say before discussing sensitive issues can help avoid an argument. If you have a criticism to make, use the **sandwich approach** by putting a negative comment between two positive comments. The positive messages help the other person accept the negative (**Figure 12.6**). For example, how could you share with your spouse that you do not like vegetables with cream sauce when he or she has prepared some? First, a positive comment could be made, such as, "This is a delicious meal." Then say, "I do prefer vegetables without a cream sauce, though." Then another positive message follows. "I really appreciate the work you put into cooking." Using I-statements helps in talking about sensitive issues.

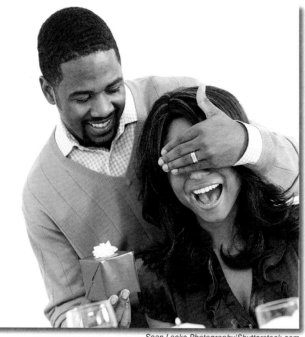

Sean Locke Photography/Shutterstock.com

Figure 12.5 Spouses can also show appreciation by giving small gifts or other tokens to express their love.

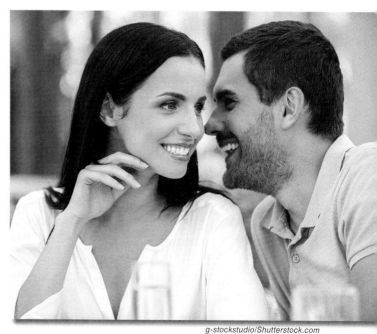

g-stockstudio/Shutterstock.com

Figure 12.6 The sandwich approach is effective for giving criticism in a way that keeps healthy lines of communication open.

Think About Your Reading

What elements of communication are missing when a couple tries to carry on a conversation while one person is focused on another task?

Resolving Conflicts

If spouses are in the habit of taking time daily to share their thoughts and feelings, it will be easier to resolve differences when they come up. Some differences can become major disagreements. They will weaken the relationship if they are not resolved. If disagreements build on each other, hostile feelings are more likely to grow. Hostility may result in anger and blame being placed on each other. Using the problem-solving process is difficult when the couple is tense and emotions run high.

When one spouse is very upset, he or she needs to take time to calm down. The couple will have greater success in reaching a compromise if they both stay calm. Using empathy and trying to see the issue from the partner's point of view helps as well. When working to resolve conflicts, spouses should keep their voices even and use good listening skills. Respect and acceptance of each other's opinions help both persons maintain positive self-esteem throughout the discussion.

Using Problem-Solving Skills

If conflict is handled right away, the source of the problem is easier to identify. The couple must think about the real cause of the disagreement. They may discover that the issue that brings on the conflict may not be the real, underlying cause of the problem. Once the real problem is identified, the spouses need to stick to that issue and resolve it. They should avoid bringing up past arguments as they work to find a solution to the current problem.

Next, the couple needs to continue using their problem-solving skills and identify possible solutions, discuss them, choose one solution they both agree with, and develop a plan to carry it out. One advantage of working to solve problems as a couple is that two people are putting their brains and skills to the task.

In each stage of the problem-solving process, the spouses may need to negotiate. That includes listening to each other's opinions and considering both points of views. Give-and-take is needed to compromise and come to a solution agreeable to both.

When a couple successfully resolves differences, no one person wins or loses. In fact, both partners win if they can resolve the difference in a way that benefits their relationship (**Figure 12.7**).

Asking for Forgiveness

There will be many times that each person in a relationship needs to ask for forgiveness. No one is perfect. It is quite likely that one partner's words or actions may at some time hurt or offend the spouse. It takes maturity to admit mistakes and ask for forgiveness. Sometimes a spouse will not even realize what he or she said or did that caused the problem. In these situations, it is important for the hurt spouse to use I-statements to let the other person know what was so bothersome and why.

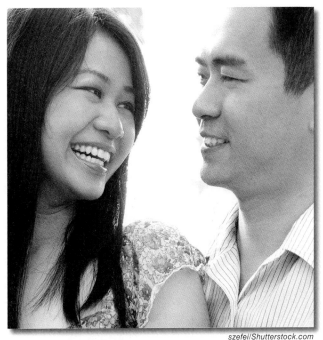

szefei/Shutterstock.com

Figure 12.7 *What is the advantage of neither partner winning nor losing when a couple solves a problem?*

Asking forgiveness is not the only step. The words "Please forgive me—I didn't mean to hurt you" need to be backed up with actions. The person at fault needs to take whatever actions are needed to help the partner feel loved. That might mean giving a small gift, doing a favor, doing some thoughtful act of kindness, giving an embrace, or setting aside some quiet time alone. Whatever the appropriate action, the spouse needs to convey true remorse for what was done or said and the sincere desire to restore the relationship.

Extending Forgiveness

Forgiving each other and moving on is part of reducing anxiety and anger in a relationship. Forgiving means not bringing up an upsetting incident the next time the spouses have a disagreement. Once they are resolved and forgiven, past offenses need to stay in the past.

Couples need to communicate honestly about an issue in order to leave it in the past. Both spouses need to feel that the issue was resolved. They need to share I-statements expressing personal observations, thoughts, feelings, and desires about whatever was said or done.

Staying Actively Involved with Each Other

Spouses continue to grow and change individually throughout life. Time spent together will help them keep in touch with each other's thoughts and feelings. Sharing their lives will help maintain their friendship with each other and keep their relationship strong.

Active interaction involves two people who are doing something together and are engaging in physical and verbal exchanges about what they are doing. When people actively do activities together, they learn more about what their spouse is thinking and feeling. The marriage relationship

Real-Life Scenario

Adjusting to Marriage

Salvador and Isela have been married for a year. Their first few months of married life seemed so exciting. They spent most of their time together. They would shop together, meet each other for lunch, watch a movie, or have friends in for dinner.

As the weeks passed, however, they found themselves spending less time together. Isela had to work late at the office a few evenings. She also accepted a position on the board of a volunteer organization, which involved evening and weekend events. Salvador joined a bowling league and was gone a few evenings with his friends. He also enrolled in a weekend class at the local community college. Isela and Salvador found they were together less and less. Both were feeling hurt that the romantic spark was disappearing from their relationship.

Arguments became frequent, and they usually ended with each blaming the other for the situation. Salvador thought Isela should work fewer hours so she could be home earlier. Isela thought Salvador should quit bowling so they could at least have those evenings together. They did not invite their mutual friends over anymore. They did not feel very romantic toward each other as their relationship gradually got worse. Sometimes they wondered why they ever got married.

For Discussion
1. What are some of the areas in which Salvador and Isela are having difficulty adjusting?
2. What adjustment patterns are they using to resolve their differences?
3. How are their patterns of adjustment affecting the following areas: trust, communication, cooperation, the growth of mature love, and the quality of their relationship?
4. How could they use compromise to improve the quality of their relationship?
5. In what areas could Salvador and Isela's relationship benefit from marriage counseling? Why?

will be strengthened if spouses spend time in active interaction (**Figure 12.8**).

In **passive interaction**, people are involved only as an observer or listener. Watching television or reading books are passive interactions. These activities can become active if spouses discuss the programs they watch or the books they read. Active interaction produces more growth in a relationship than passive interaction.

Think About Your Reading

What family activities would fit the category of active interaction? passive interaction?

Meeting Emotional Needs

People's satisfaction in marriage will increase as their emotional needs are met. The need to love and be loved, to have respect, and to achieve self-actualization are some of these emotional needs.

The Need to Love and Be Loved

The primary emotional need met in marriage is the need to love and to be loved. In a strong relationship, mature love continues to grow as two people spend time together and share personal thoughts, ideas, and feelings. Such sharing cultivates feelings of acceptance, belonging, and importance. Through deep, intimate sharing, spouses become more attached to each other. They depend on each other and meet each other's needs.

Think About Your Reading

How could failure to share thoughts, feelings, and ideas result in the loss of love in a relationship?

The Needs for Respect and Self-Actualization

As mature love grows, other emotional needs are being met. The need for respect is met when someone makes a spouse feel that he or she is an important part of the person's life. Once this need is met, the spouse feels better able to grow and reach his or her full potential in other areas of life.

Each spouse needs to find some emotional satisfaction in personal accomplishments. **Self-actualization** is the experience of reaching your potential and feeling fulfilled. The person who continues to develop in other areas of life, who continues growing as a person, adds vitality to the relationship. In this way, the quality of a relationship is strengthened (**Figure 12.9**).

Experiencing Physical Intimacy

An important aspect of sharing love in a marriage is physical intimacy. Trust and commitment to each other can help the couple experience a more meaningful sexual relationship. Mutual respect and appreciation can build positive self-esteem

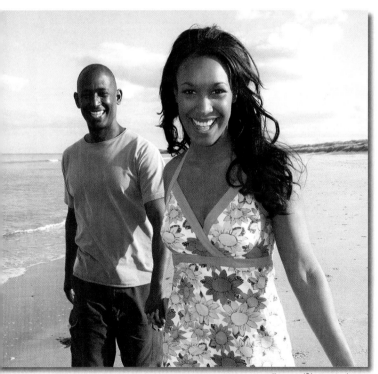

oliveromg/Shutterstock.com

Figure 12.8 A couple can actively interact as they do activities together where they can talk and share. *What interests do you have that you could enjoy with a partner to promote active interaction?*

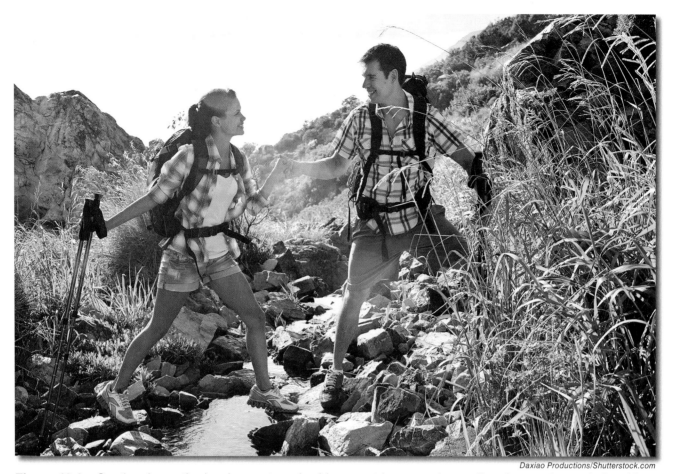

Daxiao Productions/Shutterstock.com

Figure 12.9 Continual growth, development, and achievement increase the quality of a marriage relationship.

through the sexual experience. Showing sensitivity to each other's thoughts and desires can also help a couple experience sexual fulfillment. As a couple continues to bond emotionally and commit to each other's well-being and enjoyment, they will experience satisfaction in physical intimacy.

For most couples, sexual satisfaction increases as the relationship develops. Love grows, and trust builds. Respect and empathy are shared. As a result, the couple solidifies their commitment to each other.

Keeping Balance in the Relationship

Balance in the relationship is maintained when both spouses work to contribute fully to the relationship. Both are committed 100 percent to making the relationship work and work well. Both are fully committed to making adjustments

that need to be made in order for each spouse to feel satisfied with the relationship.

In a balanced relationship, both partners feel important to the relationship and to each other. There is no need to compete since both partners know that the other will make choices to benefit their well-being. There is no need to control the other spouse, because both partners contribute equally to the relationship.

When one spouse is more committed to the relationship than the other, the relationship becomes unbalanced. The less committed person actually appears to have more power, may take advantage of the other, may make demands on the other person's time and resources, may cross over personal boundaries, and appears to focus on personal wants and desires.

A relationship could also become unbalanced if one spouse has expectations that the other cannot meet. For instance, some people count on having all their emotional needs met by their spouse.

It is difficult for a spouse to meet this expectation. Some of an individual's needs can be met through personal accomplishments at work or in the community; some can be met through good friends or family members who can empathize with the feelings a spouse might have. Expecting a spouse to meet all of a person's needs can put too much stress on a relationship.

Mutual respect for each other helps a couple keep balance in their relationship. Through good communication, they can identify areas of imbalance that develop and work to solve the issue before it becomes a problem. They focus on cooperating for the benefit of their relationship.

Adjusting to Marital Roles

Many of the roles a person has before marriage will continue after marrying. After marriage, however, these roles change somewhat. A person becomes a married son or daughter, living independently of his or her family perhaps for the first time. He or she will also be a son-in-law or daughter-in-law, new roles with different expectations.

The **marital roles** a person may be expected to fulfill after marriage include spouse, friend, wage earner, cook, caregiver, or housekeeper. If a couple has children, each also acquires the role of mother or father. Each of these roles carries certain responsibilities and expectations.

Think About Your Reading

What type of interactions might take place in an unbalanced relationship?

Keeping a Cooperative Attitude

Adjusting to new roles is easier when a couple cooperates and works together (**Figure 12.10**). Before a couple marries, they usually discuss their expectations for each other. When partners are able to live up to each other's expectations, their relationship is enhanced. They are happier with themselves and each other. Living out

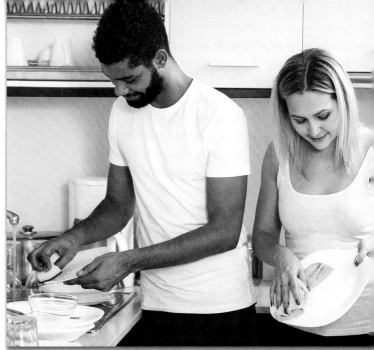

Iakov Filimonov/Shutterstock.com

Figure 12.10 Cooperating to carry out a task shows teamwork in the relationship. *What are the benefits of working together on common household chores?*

these expectations will be easier if the couple has a cooperative attitude, is sensitive to each other's needs, and is willing to adjust.

Periodic Evaluation

Roles do not stay the same as the marriage continues. Sometimes new roles are added, such as the role of parent. With new roles come new responsibilities. For this reason, couples need to talk about their roles often. Taking time to communicate openly and reevaluate expectations can help couples adjust to changing roles.

LESSON 12.2

Assess

COMPREHENSION CHECK

1. List eight ways a couple can improve the quality of their relationship in interpersonal areas.
2. Explain how pair adjustment affects a couple's relationship.
3. Describe what is meant by the sandwich approach.
4. Explain how active interaction improves the quality of a relationship more than passive interaction does.
5. Give three examples of common marital roles.

ADAPTING TO FINANCIAL AND SOCIAL CHANGES

Objectives

After studying this lesson, you will be able to

- **determine** financial and social adjustments that add quality to a relationship.
- **identify** outside sources of help for strengthening a marriage.

Focus Your Reading

1. List the financial and social changes a person experiences when getting married. As you read, identify strategies that would help that person adjust to these changes.
2. List people that a couple might consider substitute family after moving into a new community.

Content Terms

Build Vocab

substitute family

marriage enrichment program

marriage counseling

Academic Terms

accountability

qualified

As a couple adjusts to married life, different views about money management and social commitments may surface. The couple will need to agree on how to handle these issues. Discussing financial and social issues before marriage can help a couple adjust more easily. The true test, though, is in living through these issues day by day. Participating in marriage enrichment programs or counseling can also help a couple maintain their marriage relationship and resolve conflict.

Financial Adjustments

Different views about money management can be a major source of conflict in a marriage, and lifestyle adjustments may be needed in order to live on the income available. Couples need to develop a financial plan. Both partners need to know the basics of this financial plan and be willing to follow it and share responsibility for it. Both need to know where money is spent, how much is spent, and why it needs to be spent or saved (**Figure 12.11**).

Couples also have to address the issue of *accountability* (responsibility) to each other. Instead of spending what they want, when they want, married persons are responsible to each other for

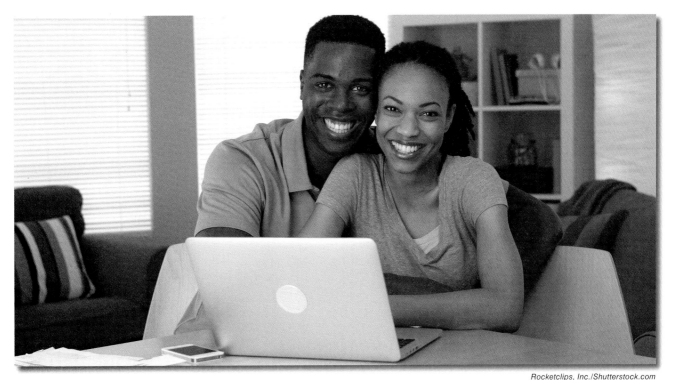

Rocketclips, Inc./Shutterstock.com

Figure 12.11 Both partners in a marriage should be in tune with the couple's financial plans and status.

how money is handled. Couples address this issue in different ways. Some couples set aside a certain amount of money that each spouse may spend freely, without accountability. This can reduce the possibility of conflict over small purchases. Some couples put all their finances into one pot, paying bills and setting money aside for savings from that shared pool of funds. Others divide up the bills, and each person pays certain expenses.

If a couple manages money jointly, they have accountability to each other. Each spouse can help the other keep track of the family funds. They will need to review their financial plan often to make sure they are on track with their spending and savings plans. When both partners know the plan, they will have greater success in carrying it out.

During the engagement period, a couple may have identified who would carry out different roles involved with managing family finances. Once these roles are put into action, they may need some adjustments. Are the bills getting paid on time? Is either person spending too much without accountability? Good communication and problem-solving skills will be critical to handle such money-related issues without arguing or fighting.

A financial advisor can help a couple identify adjustments that need to be made in their finances and some possible solutions. This can help reduce conflicts related to money and make it easier for a couple to compromise and find a solution that both can follow.

Think About Your Reading

Why do you think money issues are the number one source of arguments in marriages?

Social Adjustments

Throughout dating and engagement, a couple becomes identified as a pair. After marriage, they need to establish their pair identity and grow as an independent unit. They need to make their own family decisions and be responsible for their own lives.

A couple establishes their own identity as an independent unit by living on their own (**Figure 12.12**). They make their own decisions based on discussion between the two of them.

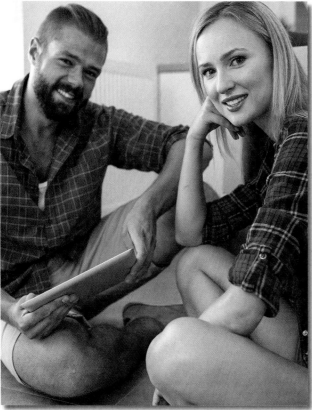

Jakub Zak/Shutterstock.com

Figure 12.12 Choosing an apartment and living on their own can help newlyweds develop their own identity as a couple. *What strategies could a couple use to develop their own identity if they find themselves sharing living spaces with other people?*

Setting up a joint living agreement can help newlyweds in this situation establish boundaries that will help them grow as an independent unit. This agreement should specify dollar amounts for rent and other costs, expectations for sharing in household work or other maintenance chores, and identification of personal and private spaces.

Think About Your Reading

How could a couple's growth in pair identity be affected if parents interfere too often?

Relating to Family

A marriage joins two families. Each spouse's family is a very integral part of him or her, as are the family ties the spouse feels. These strong attachments, which are formed during infancy, continue throughout life. In the marriage relationship, the partners seek to develop a similar type of attachment with each other. At the same time, some feelings of attachment to family members continue. The marital relationship improves when good relationships are maintained with family members.

Keeping a Balance

Good relationships with family members are balanced. Spending too much time with family members takes away from the pair relationship. On the other hand, too little contact with family members causes hurt feelings. Parents can feel ignored, and conflict may develop as a result. As explained in Chapter 11, a couple should discuss in advance how they will handle family occasions, such as holidays and vacations. After they have come to a joint decision, they can share that decision with both spouses' families.

Keeping Family Counsel in Perspective

Good family relationships occur if the couple can show respect for both sets of parents. This does not mean the couple does whatever the parents ask. Instead, they can listen to family members' suggestions and advice. They can be courteous and thank parents for their concern.

They take responsibility for the consequences of their decisions. If they make a mistake, they learn from it together and move on. At this time, family and friends can be supportive and offer encouragement. Newlywed couples need this independence for their relationship to grow.

Sometimes a newly married couple lives with others, most often parents, to help them transition to living independently. They may not have enough money to be fully independent, yet they still need to establish their identity as a pair. Taking steps toward being independent can help couples reach that goal. Paying some rent, paying for food, contributing toward utilities—these can help couples feel like a separate unit. Taking their turn as a couple and sharing in meal preparation and housekeeping tasks can also help them learn to function as a pair. These steps not only help a couple develop their pair identity, they also will help the joint living arrangement work smoothly.

The couple needs to be firm, however, in making their own decisions, and both sets of parents need to accept they have the right to do so.

Think About Your Reading

What communication skills will help you speak for yourselves as a couple when handling pressures from parents and family members?

Supporting Parents in Their Adjustment

Parents also have adjustments to make when their children marry. Their new role is one of encouragement and emotional support. When asked, parents can share their opinions, but they should offer them as suggestions, not commands. Sometimes this new role is hard for parents. They may be accustomed to giving guidance and being heavily involved in their children's decisions. It takes time for them to adjust to their new role. The married couple can help them do so by showing patience and giving gentle reminders if parents push too hard on a particular issue (**Figure 12.13**).

Adjusting Friendships

A strong network of mutual friends can strengthen and add to the quality of a marriage. As a couple builds their identity as a pair, they may find their friends will change. They will more

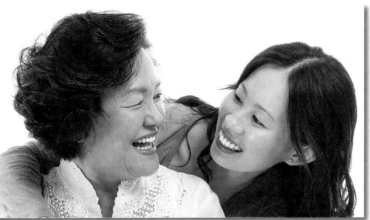

wong sze yuen/Shutterstock.com

Figure 12.13 It is important for couples to be understanding of their parents' adjustments. *How do you think parents feel about the adjustments they make when an adult child is married?*

likely spend time together with joint friends. Sincere friends can listen with empathy and provide constructive advice. They can share with a couple in both easy and tough times. In addition, both spouses will have personal friendships they will want to maintain. Each spouse should recognize the importance of these long-standing friendships to their partner.

Adjusting to a New Community

Young married couples sometimes move from their home community into a new one. If relatives then live far away, they may develop substitute family relationships. A **substitute family** is a group of nonrelatives who encourage or help a married couple in a way that family members would if they were present. Most communities have several organizations where people can meet others with similar interests. Clubs or recreational programs provide opportunities to share common goals and work together for the community's benefit. Through these activities, a couple can find new friends and adjust to their new community (**Figure 12.14**).

Sources for Help

A stable and happy marriage does not automatically happen. Some couples have more success than others in adjusting to their relationships. Others do not adjust well or resolve conflicts easily. Their marriage may be troubled. Couples may seek to strengthen or improve their marriage by attending marital enrichment programs or marriage counseling.

Marriage Enrichment Programs

Organized programs designed to help couples maintain or improve their marriage relationships are called **marriage enrichment programs**. Their main purpose is to keep marriages strong and help them grow. These programs are usually sponsored by community service agencies, religious groups, or educational groups. They usually seek to help couples in the areas of personal growth, growth as a couple, and financial planning.

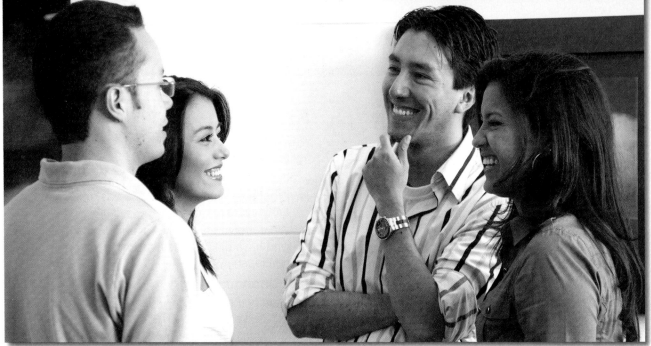

Andresr/Shutterstock.com

Figure 12.14 Getting involved in neighborhood events is one way for a couple to adjust to a new community. *How could couples learn about events happening in their new neighborhood?*

Think About Your Reading

What would be the advantage of taking part in marriage enrichment programs on a regular basis?

Couples should seek a marital enrichment program designed for their particular need. Couples should also check to be sure the program leader is a *qualified*, or trained and experienced, professional in the field of family counseling. Recommendations from past participants may be helpful in choosing an enrichment program.

Marriage Counseling

Marriage counseling is somewhat different from marriage enrichment. **Marriage counseling** also seeks to improve marriages, but usually focuses on helping couples identify and resolve existing problems. Marital enrichment programs may be used as part of counseling to strengthen various areas of the relationship.

When looking for a marriage counselor, couples should seek a qualified, licensed marriage counselor. Since many states do not require marriage counselors to be licensed, some counselors may be practicing without professional training. Couples interested in finding a qualified

counselor in their area can contact the American Association for Marriage and Family Therapy for a list of accredited marriage counselors.

Many religious institutions also provide family and marriage counseling and enrichment programs. Couples can also check the Internet or local directories for listings of government or private social service agencies that offer marriage counseling. In every case, it is important to check the program's purpose and cost as well as the counselor's qualifications.

LESSON 12.3

Assess

COMPREHENSION CHECK

1. How should a couple adjust to financial changes after marriage?
2. Explain why a couple needs to establish pair identity when relating to others.
3. Name two issues a couple should discuss to help keep family relationships balanced.
4. Describe how parents can help a young couple establish their pair identity.
5. List three ways in which marriage enrichment programs may increase the quality of a marriage relationship.
6. Explain how marriage counseling is different from marriage enrichment.

CHAPTER SUMMARY

A marriage that is high in quality is happy, satisfying, and fulfilling. The quality of most marriage relationships varies from time to time. The goal of making adjustments in married life is to try and maintain a high level of quality.

Marriage partners will differ in many aspects of their lives because they are two unique people. The way they handle their differences will affect their relationship. When they can settle their differences and find agreeable solutions, the quality of their relationship will be higher.

As a couple adjusts to living together, they will need to resolve differences in many interpersonal, financial, and social areas. Sometimes they may seek marriage counseling or marriage enrichment programs to help them make adjustments and improve their relationship.

VOCABULARY ACTIVITIES

1. Write the description of a marriage enrichment program. In that description, use as many of the content terms as you can.

Content Terms

accommodation (12.1)
active interaction (12.2)
concession (12.1)
hostility (12.1)
interpersonal adjustment (12.2)
marital adjustment (12.1)
marital role (12.2)
marriage counseling (12.3)

marriage enrichment program (12.3)
pair adjustment (12.2)
passive interaction (12.2)
sandwich approach (12.2)
self-actualization (12.2)
substitute family (12.3)

2. Make a flash card with each term on one side and the definition on the other. Work with a partner, quizzing each other on the meaning of each term until each of you has gotten all of them correct.

Academic Terms

accountability (12.3)
appreciation (12.2)
balance (12.2)
method (12.1)
qualified (12.3)

quarrel (12.1)
trivial (12.2)

ASSESS

Your Knowledge

3. What are four different methods that couples can use to handle conflict?
4. What are common areas of adjustment in the early years of marriage?
5. What are some sources of help for couples who have difficulty adjusting to a marriage relationship?

Your Understanding

6. Identify a scenario in which you used concession to resolve a conflict. Then give an example of how you could have used accommodation or compromise to resolve the same conflict and explain how these methods could benefit the relationship.
7. How can a couple make day-to-day choices that will increase the quality of their marriage?
8. How can marriage counseling help a couple improve their relationship?

Your Skills

9. Create two scenarios that depict two different ways couples may choose to manage their finances in a marriage. Evaluate which scenario provides the most accountability between spouses.
10. Explain how you would resolve the following dilemma in a way that builds relationships: You have been looking forward to attending a play-off game with your close friend. A week before the game, your spouse asks you to attend an important event at the same time as the game.

CRITICAL THINKING

11. **Draw Conclusions.** Interview a marriage counselor or religious leader. Ask about the major conflicts and difficulties couples typically experience in the early years of marriage. Summarize the counselor's responses. Then identify steps that couples could take to avoid or handle these conflicts or difficulties to strengthen their marriage.
12. **Make Inferences.** Watch a television sitcom that depicts interactions between a married couple. In a paragraph, describe the interactions that you observe. Analyze those interactions for patterns of communicating, making decisions, and solving problems, citing references from the text to support your analysis. Then evaluate

the interactions for their potential impact on the quality of the marriage relationship. *Group option*: Work with a group to watch the same television program. Analyze the interactions together and prepare a group report to share with the class.

13. **Solve a Problem.** Write a scenario depicting a problem in the early years of marriage. Share your scenario with a classmate. Read and analyze the other's scenarios and write a paragraph identifying some steps the couple could take to improve the quality of their relationship. *Choice*: Read your scenario aloud and have your partner share the improvement steps with the class.

CORE SKILLS

14. **Writing.** Reflect on your personal feelings and desires about spending quality time with your and your spouse's families after you are married. Identify specific occasions for which it is important for you to be with one family or the other. Summarize your thoughts in a paragraph, expressing how you expect to carry out your personal desires for family involvement after you are married.

15. **Writing.** Identify a problem that could develop in a marriage for each interpersonal area of adjustment. Invite a marriage counselor to be a guest speaker and respond to these scenarios that you have written. In a paper, summarize the counselor's responses and compare those recommendations to those provided in the text. *Group option*: Divide up the areas, with each person in your group writing scenarios covering the topics in one area.

16. **Reading, Writing.** Clip an advice column from a newspaper, or copy one from an online paper, that deals with marital problems. In a paragraph, evaluate the situation and identify what type of adjustment pattern is being used by the couple. Identify what type of adjustment pattern the columnist is suggesting. Do you agree with the column writer's advice? Cite evidence from the text to indicate what impact the columnist's suggestion could have on the relationship and why you agree or disagree with the advice.

17. **Research.** Over a one-week period, analyze how students in your school use the four patterns of adjustment in their day-to-day relationships. First, create a chart with the four patterns of adjustment listed down the left side. Then add columns for five days. Record a short description each

time you observe students using a pattern of adjustment. At the end of your observation period, write a paragraph describing which pattern you observed being used most often and explaining why you think that was the case.

18. **Research.** Using the Internet, research marital enrichment programs and marriage counseling services. Locate a minimum of three different programs, and identify the purposes of each program and the credentials required for the leaders. Identify specific services that are available in your community.

19. **Math.** Survey three married couples: (A) a young couple, (B) a couple with young children, and (C) an older, retired couple. Ask each couple to list the top five issues likely to cause conflict or irritation with their spouse. Compile your responses with those of four classmates. Use a digital program to create a bar graph showing the results for each age group.

20. **Social Studies.** Search online to identify different role expectations for married couples in other cultures. Choose one culture and imagine what your life would be as a spouse of a person from that culture. In a paragraph, describe the role expectations that would exist for you if you lived in that culture.

21. **Writing.** Create a questionnaire to identify how couples make decisions related to money management. Interview each partner of a couple separately, using your questions. Create a table showing their responses. Compare the responses of each partner. Write a paragraph summarizing your findings. Then describe how you would like to handle money management when you are married. *Group option*: Work in a small group, compare your findings, and combine your data into one table.

CAREER READINESS

22. **Researching a Career in Counseling.** Research the career of marriage counselor or financial planner. Find out what education and experience a person in either career needs and what steps someone must take to meet whatever licensing requirements there are for such a career in your state. Learn what you can about the kind of work people in that profession do, the setting in which the work is done, and the average income of people in that profession in your state. Prepare a report summarizing your findings.

CONNECTING WITH CAREER CLUSTERS

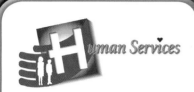

PATHWAYS

Early Childhood Development & Services

Counseling and Mental Health Services

Family and Community Services

Personal Care Services

Consumer Services

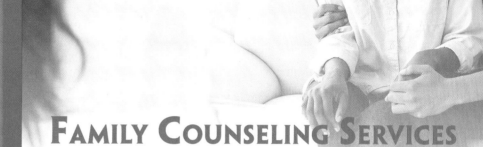

FAMILY COUNSELING SERVICES

Many professionals in counseling services work with couples and families. *Marriage and family counselors* work with individuals, couples, and families to resolve conflicts and prevent potential breakdowns in family functioning. The goal is to improve communication among members of the family, change individual perceptions of one another, modify behavior, and thereby help families and individuals avoid crises in their lives.

Marriage and family therapists diagnose and treat mental and emotional disorders within the context of the family. The goal of therapy is to treat the disorders and improve the functioning of individuals within the family system, so that the needs of all family members can be met.

These specialists work with clients to set goals and carry out therapy plans, often collaborating with other professionals. Many are *self-employed*, working out of their homes or private offices.

Marriage and family therapists and counselors often work flexible hours so that those in crisis can obtain help when needed. Evening or weekend counseling sessions are common.

A master's degree is usually required to enter the field. Supervised field experience plus a license or certificate may also be required.

CAREER OUTLOOK

A job in family counseling or family therapy requires high levels of physical and emotional energy; an ability to work under stress and maintain the confidentiality of clients; and a desire to help people improve their lives.

As families experience increased changes in society—economic downturns, increased health issues, increased aging population, increased substance abuse—these major changes, which can occur simultaneously, will cause crises in families, and increase the need for family counselors and therapists. Faster-than-average job growth is expected for marriage and family therapists and counselors. Social service agencies employ the largest number of marriage and family therapists. Median annual earnings in 2014 were about $48,000 with a range from $30,500 to $78,900.

EXPLORE

Internet Research

Research your state's requirements for credentialing marriage and family therapists or counselors. Locate an accredited university that offers marriage and family therapist or counselor training and identify the courses required. Visit the university's website for its school placement data. Identify what percentage of students find jobs in the area of their degree. Search for information on jobs that are available in marriage and family counseling and therapy. Who employs persons with this degree in your community? in your state? Prepare a report summarizing this career information.

Job Shadowing

Ask your school counselor to recommend a counseling open house or workshop that would present a clear picture of a typical day for a marriage and family therapist. Write a report describing what you learned about the profession and whether such a career might suit you. An alternative assignment would be to interview a family counselor or therapist about his or her job, the demands and stressors of the job, the rewards of the job, the personal qualities needed by a person who carries out the job, and sources of information that could help a person decide whether this career area might a good fit.

Community Service/Volunteer

Connect with the local office of United Way and volunteer your services to work with children whose families are in crisis. Keep a journal of your activities and analyze your conversations with the children. Remember to keep confidentiality.

Project

Conduct a case study for experience in gathering information as you maintain utmost confidentiality throughout the project. Research what data should go into a case study. Choose a friend (someone willing to talk to you openly) who has a family-related conflict. List the questions you could ask to help identify the root of the problem. Identify some skills that could help resolve this problem. Also identify some resources that families with such a problem or conflict could utilize to resolve their problem and build healthy relationships within the family. Write up your case study.

Interview

Interview a local religious leader who provides marriage and family counseling for congregation members. Inquire about the frustrations, challenges, and rewards of the job. Ask for information about what topics are covered in the counseling sessions, what skills the leader tries to help families develop, and what resources are used to help families build healthy relationships. Ask what the leader thinks are the greatest issues that exist in families today. Summarize your findings in a report.

Part-Time Job

Apply for a part-time job as a receptionist for a social services agency or clinic that provides family counseling. Keep a journal of your work experiences and record any relevant career information you learn from the job.

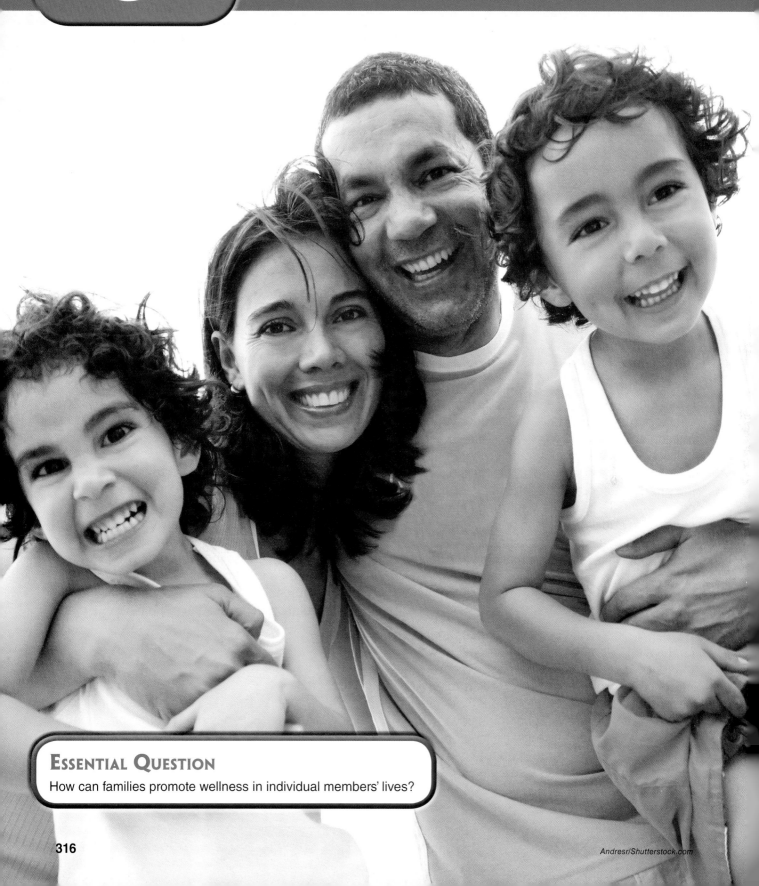

ESSENTIAL QUESTION
How can families promote wellness in individual members' lives?

Andresr/Shutterstock.com

CASE STUDY

Strong Families Adjust to Crises

Read the case study and discuss the questions that follow. After finishing the chapters in this unit, discuss the questions again and identify any answers you would change based on information you learned.

The storm blew through the night, casting huge waves up on the shore and flooding the streets in front of Mesing's home in Taiwan. She had helped her parents board up the windows of the house when they got the news that the storm was coming and had carried jugs of fresh water up the stairs. Mesing, her brothers and sisters, her parents, and several neighbors were all on the top floor of the house, hoping to stay above the floodwaters. Not everyone had a second story in their house where they could stay dry. It seemed these storms arrived every year about this time, and Mesing's family had made preparations ahead of time. They had a large supply of rice and vegetables upstairs, so there was food for everyone. They had flashlights so they could see and a small battery-run stove so they could cook. The storm could last several days, and they were all prepared to stay there until the storm ended and water subsided. Mesing felt cozy and safe, even though the winds howled outside as she sat and listened to the adults retell stories from previous years' storms.

Ayana hurried into work for the afternoon shift at the gas station in her small hometown in Alaska. She had to keep this job, as it was the only way she could pay restitution for the items she had stolen. The judge told her she had to finish school as well. That was part of her probation. Ayana's parents were shocked when they got the call that Ayana had been picked up with her boyfriend for theft. They had been strict about Ayana's dating, as she had goals to be a nurse and they knew she had to do well in school. Once Ayana started dating Mani, however, she had been missing her curfew and lying about where she had been. When Ayana and Mani were caught for stealing, it seemed all her future plans had fallen apart. Still, Ayana's parents had hired a lawyer, and now Ayana had a second chance. Ayana knew it would take hard work to pay her restitution, get her grades up, and finish school. She was determined she could make good choices from now on.

Joe was excited. His parents were returning from a weeklong counseling event for military couples. They had texted him about the good that had come out of the sessions, and he was anxious 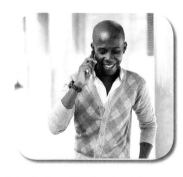 to see them. His parents' relationship had not been good in a long time. Months ago, his parents had quit communicating, and when they did, they ended up yelling at each other. His dad had become more and more silent and withdrawn, drinking heavily. Joe's dad had been injured on his last tour in Afghanistan and struggled with walking on his prosthetic foot. *There has to be some way to help*, thought Joe, so he had contacted a group called Heal Our Patriots. Joe was able to get his mom and dad into a weeklong getaway for military couples. From what their text messages said, it seemed that the experience had been a good one.

For Discussion

1. How did each crisis affect each family?
2. What different strategies did each family use to respond to the crisis?
3. What common characteristics helped the families in each situation adjust to meet the different needs of family members?

MickyWiswedel/Shutterstock.com

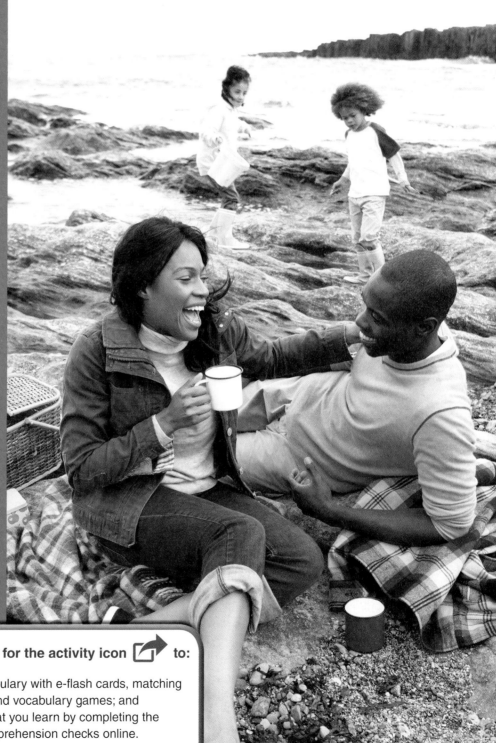

CHAPTER
13

TODAY'S FAMILY

Reading Prep

Preview the chapter by skimming the lessons and noting the headings and subheadings. For each lesson, write down one question that you want to have answered by studying the content.

Key Questions

Questions to answer as you study this chapter:

- How have families changed over time?
- What are the benefits of family living?
- How can families meet their members' needs through different family structures?

While studying this chapter, look for the activity icon 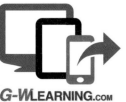 to:

- **build** vocabulary with e-flash cards, matching activities, and vocabulary games; and
- **assess** what you learn by completing the lesson comprehension checks online.
  www.g-wlearning.com/humanservices/

G-WLEARNING.com

AFTER STUDYING THIS CHAPTER, YOU WILL

KNOW:

- Key terms related to family structures and roles.
- The functions a family fulfills in U.S. society.

UNDERSTAND:

- How families have adjusted throughout history to meet the needs of family members.
- How different family structures can fulfill the functions of the family.
- How each family structure offers certain advantages and disadvantages.
- Why some people choose to remain single.

BE ABLE TO DO:

- Apply successful adjustment strategies from past generations to possible future changes for the family.
- Locate resources to help families carry out their functions.

GETTING STARTED

Anita looked around the classroom at her many friends. There was Rosalee, who lived with her mom and younger brother. They did not have much money, and Rosalee had to spend most of her time babysitting her brother while her mom worked her night job. The three of them seemed very close, though.

Anita then glanced over at her friend Britta. Britta always had the best clothes and extra money to spend. Anita thought it was because both her parents worked so hard. They were often gone on business trips. Britta's grandmother, who lived with the family and helped care for Britta, always made Anita feel special whenever she visited.

Josh had become a close friend, too. Anita was glad that her parents had moved next door to Josh, his dad, and his stepmother and two stepsisters. Josh had moved to the neighborhood three years ago and knew how it felt to try to make new friends. He had helped Anita adjust to the neighborhood and her new school.

Families live differently now than they did years ago. Economic, social, and cultural changes have brought about transformations in family roles and structures. Today's family structures are more complex and less traditional than those of the past, yet families fulfill many of the same functions. In spite of the many challenges a family faces, the family remains a strong institution, meeting needs in the lives of family members, impacting communities, and affecting society as a whole. While most people live in families, some choose to remain single, either for a period of time or for their entire lives.

TRENDS IN AMERICAN FAMILY LIFE

Content Terms

Build Vocab

family
household

Academic Terms

demographic
self-sufficient
lifelong learning

Objectives

After studying this lesson, you will be able to

- **define** the term *family*.
- **describe** how societal, demographic, and economic changes have affected the family and individuals.
- **explain** the benefits of living in a family.

Focus Your Reading

1. As you read each section, use a chart to identify key features of family life during the era discussed and compare the features to family life today.
2. Use examples from relatives or neighbors to explain the differences between a family and a household.

The family unit has changed over time and continues to do so. Thus, different individuals may define family in different ways. Their own definition may depend on who all is involved in fulfilling the functions of family in their own life (**Figure 13.1**).

The U.S. Census Bureau defines a **family** as two or more people, related by birth, marriage, or adoption, living in the same household. The Census Bureau defines a **household** as all the persons occupying a living unit. A family, a single person living alone, unrelated persons living in the same apartment, and one or more family units living together all make up a household. By these definitions, three people in their early twenties who are unrelated by birth, marriage, or adoption and who are living together to share expenses would be a household, but not a family.

You will likely find yourself in various forms of households over your life span. Now, you may live with a parent, stepparent, adoptive parent, grandparent, foster parent, or some other relative in a family household. Many young adults continue to live in their family households during college and their first years on a job as they work to save money for their own place. You may at some time live alone as a single or share housing with one or more roommates. You may marry and live with your spouse and add

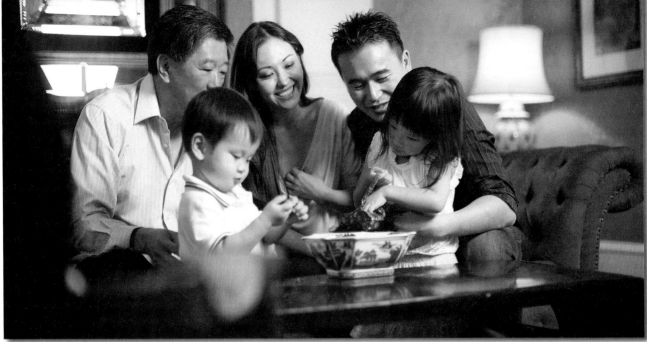

merzzie/Shutterstock.com

Figure 13.1 The word *family* may mean something different to different individuals, but whatever the definition, the family needs to meet the needs of members in the family group. *How might your definition of family be different from other definitions around the world?*

children to this family. As you age, you may find yourself in different situations, perhaps returning to your original family household for support in meeting your needs or your own family's needs. Late in your life, your elderly parents may leave their own household to live in yours.

Think About Your Reading

How would you define *family*? Does your definition include characteristics other than those used by the U.S. Census Bureau?

However families are defined, they have functioned throughout history to meet the various needs of the members in their household. Every period in history has presented challenges to families trying to make lives for themselves. To survive, families have learned to adjust to these challenges and to adapt to societal and demographic trends. They have survived by learning to change as the economic and social needs of their societies changed (**Figure 13.2**). By studying the effects of societal, demographic, and economic trends, you can predict how future trends will impact families and the individuals in them.

The Colonial Family

Ole and Martha were a typical young family of the early 1700s, ready to face the hardships of colonial life. They grew up together in the same community. Their families farmed land near each other. Ole visited Martha's home often, helping the men in her family put up a new building or

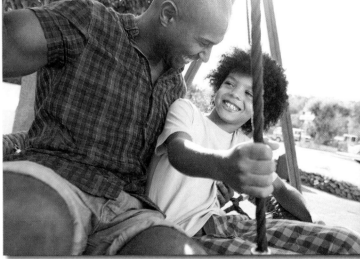

Monkey Business Images/Shutterstock.com

Figure 13.2 Social and economic changes have contributed to the transformation of the family. *What social and economic conditions impact families today?*

harvest crops. Martha went with her mother to help Ole's mother sew quilts and preserve food. When Ole was old enough to get his own farm, he asked Martha's parents for permission to marry her. After all, he needed a wife and family to help him survive colonial life.

Ole owned a small plot of land when he married Martha, his bride of 16 years. Martha had learned many skills while growing up and was prepared for her new role as wife. She knew how to grow fruit and vegetables in the garden and preserve some for the long winter months. She could spin yarn, weave cloth, and sew garments for every family member. She could make candles and soap. She had helped care for younger brothers and sisters at home, so she knew about child care. She was ready when her first baby arrived.

Ole and Martha worked on the farm from sunrise to long past sunset. Ole hunted turkey and deer, and Martha cleaned and prepared the meat for meals. They plowed the fields, planted seeds, and tended and harvested crops. Eventually, they acquired a few farm animals to provide labor, food, hides, and wool for clothing, and they had children who helped with various chores.

As Ole and Martha's life shows, the work of most families in colonial times—and for many generations to follow—centered on agriculture. Families worked to obtain and own land for farming. All family members worked together to provide for the family's needs.

The work done by both spouses was important and necessary for the family's survival. Their roles were similar to those they saw their parents fulfill. Children were valuable because many chores needed to be done. For that reason, large families were the norm, and children began helping with farm chores at a very young age (**Figure 13.3**). Relatives lived nearby. They worked together, helped one another in times of trouble, and celebrated special events together.

Think About Your Reading

What are some characteristics of families today that are similar to those of the colonial family?

The Family During the Industrial Revolution

The invention of technologies in the 1800s made it possible for machines to complete jobs that were previously done by hand. This societal change resulted in economic changes. New jobs required different skills, which in turn impacted the *demographics* (population characteristics) of families and the ways they lived.

Fritz, living in the 1870s, knew that his ancestors had farmed his land for years. His parents wanted him to continue farming, but Fritz had heard about good jobs in factories in a nearby city. Fritz and his wife, Maria, moved to the city for a job.

Life in the city was very different from what they had expected. Fritz did find a job in a factory, but it paid less than he had hoped. They found an apartment, but the rent took much of his pay. They had to buy food, as they no longer had land to raise it. Maria stayed at home and cared for their two small children. Maria's homemaking skills stretched the money Fritz made. She spent most of her time cooking, washing, and ironing. The children's care was almost totally hers. Fritz had little time to spend with the children because he worked long hours six days a week.

Maria missed the times when they worked together on the farm. She missed being able to

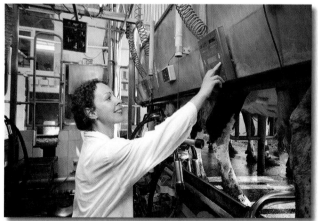
Pavel L Photo and Video/Shutterstock.com
Figure 13.3 Before farming machinery was available, large families were needed to do the work. *In what other ways has technology changed family living over time?*

walk over to her parents' place to talk while she and her mother knitted or mended clothes. She missed her sister, who was always eager to help her take care of the children. City life had brought many changes to her family.

As you can see, during the Industrial Revolution, many families moved from rural areas to large cities and found work in factories (**Figure 13.4**). This change in demographic meant that families were no longer *self-sufficient*, meeting their own needs. They no longer worked the land for their survival—they worked for someone else. Families became dependent on others to produce food and clothing, as they adopted the role of consumers. Now that their lives were free of farm chores, large families were no longer an advantage. Parents began to have fewer children, resulting in another demographic change.

Parenting roles changed, too. A man worked long hours away from his family and became the main provider. Because he was gone from the home so much, his role in parenting decreased. Raising the children became a major part of the mother's role, since she was the one whose full-time job was homemaking. Women worked long hours alone in the home. The stress on the marriage relationship was high. Support from other family members was not available, since many families no longer had relatives living nearby.

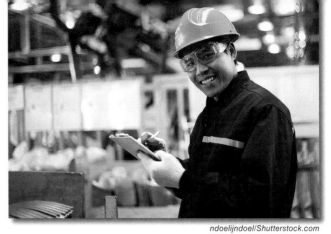
ndoelijndoel/Shutterstock.com

Figure 13.4 As in the Industrial Revolution, some family members today are involved in producing manufactured goods. *How has technology changed the way people mass-produce goods today?*

Think About Your Reading

In what ways was family life during the Industrial Revolution similar to family life today?

The Family in the Technological Age

The growth of new technologies exploded in the 1900s, continuing to change societies and the ways people worked and provided for families, but also changing every aspect of the ways people communicated (radio waves, televisions, and then computers) and traveled (cars, airplanes, and rockets). The late 1900s brought about continued inventions with the Internet, which then led to the inventions of multiple personal electronic devices, all impacting the daily lives of individuals and families.

Monique finished college in 1985 and was teaching when she met Andre. They dated for a year before they decided to marry. They both continued to work, saving enough for a down payment on their own home. Their careers kept them both quite busy. They managed their busy schedules by sharing household tasks while working full time.

When Jackie was born, Monique and Andre were excited to become parents. Monique wanted to spend more time with her newborn, so she took leave for one semester. Not wanting to give up her teaching position, Monique returned to work when Jackie was only six months old. It took some time to adjust to the new schedule, but Andre and Monique shared both household chores and parenting tasks. Andre's mother was delighted to babysit while Monique taught school.

Monique and Andre's story highlights some of the changes in family life brought on by societal trends in the age of technology. As industries grew, so did the production of goods. Families bought appliances and cars to make life more comfortable. Housekeeping became easier with these new conveniences, but the demand on family income increased. With this economic change, many women joined the workforce.

When mothers went to work outside the home, this change in demographic resulted in a change of their role in childrearing. Women now had to share that role with child care workers, other

family members, babysitters, and teachers. Many husbands became more active in parenting.

The marriage relationship changed as a result. It became based on mutual love and affection, rather than on the need for one person to provide and care for another. Higher education was no longer a goal just for men. More women obtained college degrees and higher-paying jobs. A shared wage-earner role led to both spouses sharing the work at home. More couples divided parenting, child care, and housekeeping tasks to balance work and home responsibilities.

With the advance of technology, economics and the job market changed. Workers were replaced by machines. Many jobs required less physical labor, but more technical skills (**Figure 13.5**). Computers made complex jobs simpler, and new jobs emerged in service and information industries. Time and energy for leisure activities became more common.

Because legal changes made divorces easier to obtain, couples who were not happy with their marriages separated, and the divorce rate

increased. As a result, many families became headed by a single mother or father. New family structures emerged as divorced persons remarried and merged their families.

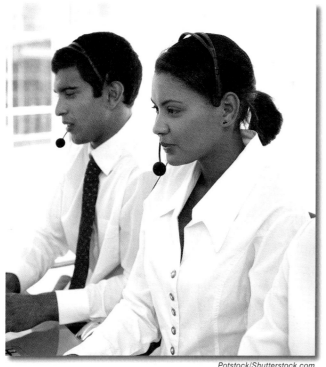

Figure 13.5 In this technological age, many work at providing services for others. *In what ways has technology impacted the way services are provided today?*

Potstock/Shutterstock.com

The Changing Family

History demonstrates how the demographics of families (their locations, their makeups, marital status, employment, income, health, and roles) change in response to economic and social pressures. Trends in societal and economic changes will continue to impact families and individuals, and families will continue to adjust. They will face some old challenges, such as balancing work and family responsibilities. They also will face some new challenges, such as caring for older parents. Another challenge is the need for workers to practice *lifelong learning*, or education and training throughout their work lives, to be able to keep a job in an era of ever-changing technology and a global economy. Throughout these challenges, the family has adjusted to meet the needs of its members. Skills for adjusting to change can help families and individuals maintain a strong family unit in a changing society.

The family will continue to transform according to societal, demographic, and economic trends. You can examine and analyze these trends to predict how families and individuals might change in future years.

Benefits of Family Living

Family living offers several benefits to its members. These benefits help to keep the family unit strong, even through many changes. A family can do the following for its members:

- *Satisfy physical needs.* These include providing food to eat, clothes to wear, medical care when needed, and a place to live.

- *Be a source of protection.* Parents, siblings, and extended family can protect other members from experiences that could bring harm or danger. This is particularly important for children.

- *Be a source of love and affection.* Whether shown outwardly or in quieter ways, family members can be a source of love and caring for one another. Such bonds of affection can remain strong throughout a lifetime and meet emotional needs of family members (**Figure 13.6**). They also teach family members how to care about and for others.

- *Provide long-lasting relationships.* Even though many changes occur in the outside world, the family can provide lifelong friendships and a sense of belonging throughout a person's life span.

- *Provide support and encouragement.* Family members can provide needed emotional support and encouragement when others feel down or face challenges. Those with more experience can also offer good advice in new or difficult situations. Even being there to provide a sympathetic ear can help a family member in times of trouble.

- *Provide companionship.* Family members have similar backgrounds and may enjoy similar interests, hobbies, or leisure activities. Sharing experiences enriches members' lives and helps build ties that remain strong even through change.

LESSON 13.1

Assess

COMPREHENSION CHECK

1. Explain the difference in the definitions used by the U.S. Census Bureau for family and household.
2. Briefly describe two major societal, demographic, or economic changes before the technological age that affected families and individuals.
3. Name six benefits of family living.

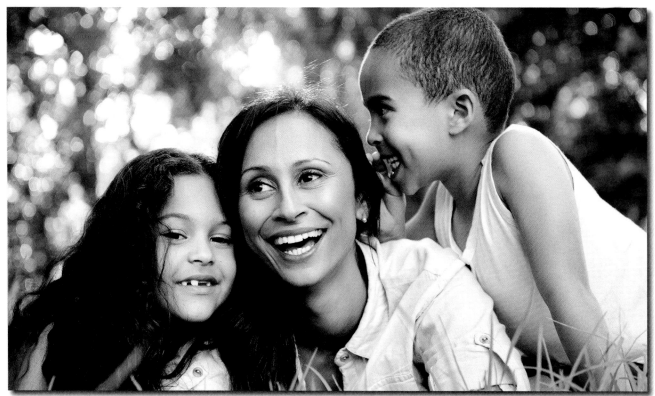

Daxiao Productions/Shutterstock.com

Figure 13.6 *How do families help meet the emotional needs of their members?*

LESSON 13.2

FUNCTIONS OF THE FAMILY

Content Terms

Build Vocab

cultural identity
custom

Academic Terms

function
helpless

Objectives

After studying this lesson, you will be able to

- **describe** the functions of the family.
- **explain** how technology can impact family functions.
- **relate** cultural identity to family functions.

Focus Your Reading

1. Develop a graphic organizer for functions of the family, listing the ways families carry out each function.
2. Identify the elements of your own cultural identity.

The family has been the basic unit of society throughout history. As such, it carries out four important social *functions*, or purposes. In most cultures, the family is the main unit for the reproduction and the socialization of children. It is through the family that the various basic physical needs of family members are met. Families also meet members' emotional and social needs. Finally, families influence the roles that people play in families and in society. Technology and culture both influence the ways families carry out these functions.

Reproducing and Socializing Children

When parents have children, they make it possible for a society to extend into a new generation (**Figure 13.7**). Giving birth, however, is only the beginning. Children are born *helpless*, needing others to provide and care for them as they grow to maturity. The family fulfills a major role in meeting children's needs as they grow and develop by socializing them to understand the ways of their society.

Children need to learn skills that will help them become productive members of society. The family reinforces those skills and provides the nurturing environment in which those skills can be developed.

326

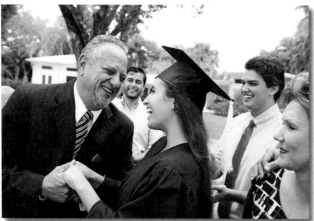

Monkey Business Images/Shutterstock.com

Figure 13.7 Families reproduce and socialize children, extending their family tree into a new generation. *How has your family impacted the goals you have established?*

In another part of socialization, the family also interprets and transmits the standards of the society to children. Children need to learn what is and is not acceptable behavior. Families teach, train, and provide examples of how these standards apply to individual lives. Society as a whole benefits, and communities become safer, better places to live as families carry out the function of socializing children.

What children see and hear impacts their views of the world, their communities, themselves, and life in general. In this way, technology also contributes to socializing children. Parents play an important role. They need to monitor their children's use of technology to ensure that the socializing effect of technology is positive. There are many technological tools that can promote learning, growth, and good communication when used with parental involvement and supervision. That involvement and supervision is very important in modern life, when technology makes it possible for children to be exposed to harmful, negative messages.

Think About Your Reading

What other influences in society socialize children?

Meeting Physical Needs

The family is responsible for providing care and protection for family members. This includes providing food; clothing; shelter; and protection from harm, injury, and disease (**Figure 13.8**). Usually, one or more family members hold a job to earn the income that ensures these needs can be met.

While income provides the financial resources families need, physical needs are satisfied by accomplishing certain tasks, such as cooking, cleaning, providing transportation, shopping, and more. Usually, these tasks are shared by various family members. Families may divide these tasks in different ways. With the cooperation of all members, families will have greater success in fulfilling this function.

Over time, technology has impacted the way families meet physical needs. Labor-saving appliances make cleaning easier to do today than in the past. Microwave ovens allow adults to prepare meals quickly after a day of work or for children to reheat meals. Technology also makes it possible for some people to work from home. This allows adults to be present when children come home from school, even while they are working to earn their income. Information on almost every subject is available through the Internet in minutes. Family members can use that information to shop

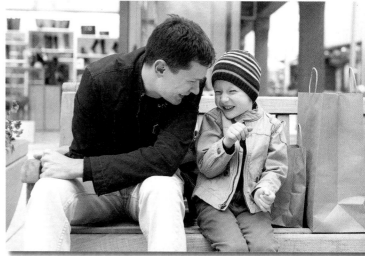

Aleksei Potov/Shutterstock.com

Figure 13.8 Parents are responsible for meeting children's physical needs, such as clothing and protection.

wisely in order to conserve resources or to gain expert information on health issues.

Meeting Emotional and Social Needs

The family can be a source of close relationships in which people live together and love and care for one another. Family members provide companionship for one another and can build lifelong friendships. These close, intimate relationships help meet each member's emotional and social needs.

Family members can work together to develop strong family ties. This takes spending time together, talking, listening, working at resolving disagreements, and taking part in family activities. Family members need to show love and affection for each other while they are working and playing together. Enjoying activities together in a caring atmosphere fosters the growth of close relationships between family members (**Figure 13.9**). Children need to experience the love and acceptance of such nurturing relationships to mature.

Close relationships require frequent and positive communication. Technology makes it possible for family members to keep in frequent contact, even over distances. This aspect of technology is positive. Text messaging and e-mail allow family members to check in on one another or to pass on news quickly and conveniently without needing to travel. Much technology, however, is used in "alone time." Children or parents often play or work on a computer without interacting with each other. Families may send a lot of text messages, but not take the time to communicate well—with direct eye contact, in close proximity, making sure that messages are clearly and accurately sent and interpreted. If technology fills too much of any family member's time, quality family relationships will not develop.

Think About Your Reading

How could work in the technological age impact the development of close, intimate relationships in the family?

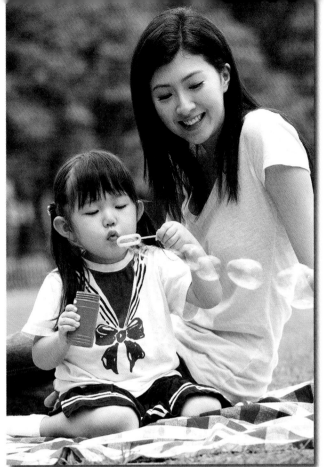

Monkey Business Images/Shutterstock.com

Figure 13.9 Family activities foster the growth of close, quality family relationships. *What activities does your family do to grow closer?*

Influencing Roles in Society and Community

Family can influence the place that its members take in society. For instance, your family may influence the educational path you choose and the career you eventually select. In this way, the family affects your role as a future adult in the workforce.

Your family gives you your **cultural identity**. This is the way you see yourself as a member of your specific cultural group. Through your biological parents, you inherit physical traits unique to their cultural backgrounds. As you grow up in a family, you learn expected functions of the family. You also learn expected roles of family members as well as of other adults in the society around you. Your family influences the values and religious beliefs you have. In addition, it can influence the **customs**, or accepted ways of acting, you observe and the traditions you will continue in your own family (**Figure 13.10**).

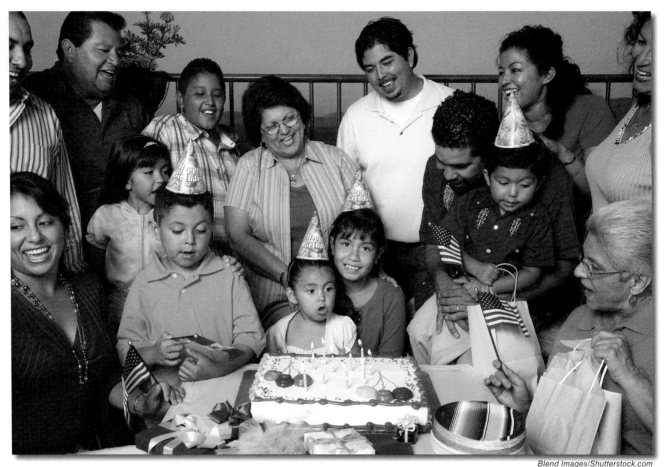

Blend Images/Shutterstock.com

Figure 13.10 Families pass on their beliefs, traditions, and expectations to the next generation. *What traditions would you like to pass on to your own family?*

Your family also influences the personal roles you have and the expectations that go with them. Currently, you have the role of a son or daughter. The expectations that come with this role changed as you grew from infancy through childhood into adolescence. They will continue to change as you become an adult. Should you marry, you will acquire a new role as husband or wife. If you become a parent, you will acquire another role. The expectations for each of these roles are influenced by your family as well as by the society in which you live.

Technology, especially through media and the Internet, makes it possible to observe people all over the world carrying out their roles in different ways. Talking about differences in families and the roles that people take can help members understand choices that their family has made to meet the needs of members.

Think About Your Reading

What expectation do you have for your own personal roles of the future?

LESSON 13.2

Assess

COMPREHENSION CHECK

1. List four functions of the family. Then briefly explain how the family carries them out.
2. Explain how technology can impact family relationships and family functions.
3. What is *cultural identity*? How does it relate to the functions of family?
4. How does effective family functioning impact community and society?

FAMILY STRUCTURES

Objectives

After studying this lesson, you will be able to
- **distinguish** among the various family structures.
- **identify** challenges each family structure faces in fulfilling the functions of the family.
- **list** various public policies that impact families and their abilities to carry out their functions.

Focus Your Reading

1. Create a chart with three columns labeled *What I Already Know, What I Want to Know,* and *What I Learned*. On the left side of the chart, record each type of family structure. Before you read, fill in the first column with what you already know about each family structure. If some questions come to your mind, write them in the second column. As you read, write what you learn about each structure in the third column.

2. For each family structure, draw a diagram showing whom you would find in a household with that family structure.

Families can take different family structures. A **family structure** is the form that the family takes in terms of the makeup of parents, children, and other family members. Six common family structures are nuclear, single-parent, stepfamily, extended, childless, and adoptive. These common groupings can include several variations, as structures can reflect different circumstances and even change over time. Even though families have different structures, they try to fulfill the same functions for family members. Each structure has unique challenges in fulfilling family functions.

The Nuclear Family

The **nuclear family** includes a married couple and their biological children. In a nuclear family, neither parent has children from a previous marriage.

A nuclear family can be a very supportive family structure for children, with two parents present to encourage growth and development and provide support (**Figure 13.11**). Both parents can contribute to socializing children and providing resources focused on the family's needs. Children have the opportunity to develop interpersonal skills interacting with both males and females. Parents also provide *models* for both male and female roles that children can learn.

Parents also benefit from living in a nuclear family structure. They have the advantage of an adult partner to help with the many tasks of parenting and providing for a family. The two parents can support and help each other in times of stress. They can meet each other's needs for love and intimacy. A nuclear family has experienced fewer stressful life events, such as divorce or the death of a spouse, that deplete social, emotional, and financial resources needed to meet family members' needs.

Parents may take different roles in a nuclear family depending on their skills, time available, careers, and personal preferences. A benefit of the nuclear family is that these families have multiple resources to use to provide a quality environment in which children can grow and develop.

The Single-Parent Family

A **single-parent family** includes one parent and one or more children. The parent may be a mother or father. A single-parent family may result from divorce, separation, or death that dissolves a nuclear family. It can also be formed when a single person adopts a child or an unmarried woman gives birth.

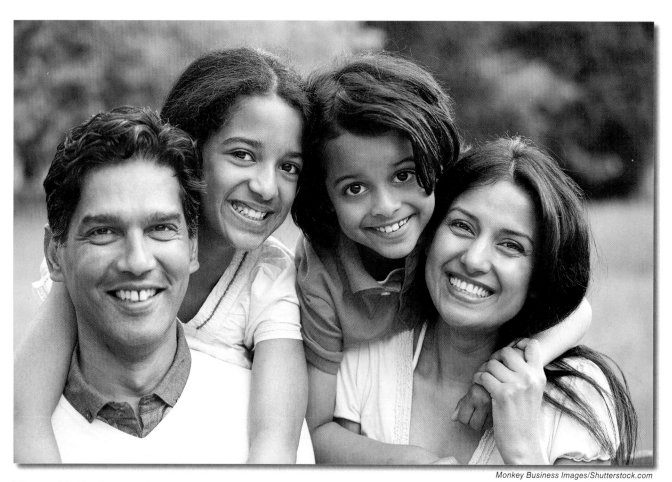

Monkey Business Images/Shutterstock.com

Figure 13.11 In a nuclear family, children have the benefit of frequent interaction with both parents. *How can this interaction impact the growth of all family members?*

In this family structure, the single parent is responsible for all the adult roles in the family. The role of provider is a major role. Along with this role come other financial responsibilities, such as budgeting and paying the bills. In addition, the single parent must be a caregiver, housekeeper, cook, shopper, nurse, and decision maker. Because he or she has so many roles to fill, a single parent may sometimes feel overwhelmed. Often, there is not enough time, energy, or money to handle all these roles. Lack of money is often an issue when the single parent is female, as women generally earn less than men.

Because a single parent has so many demands on his or her time and energy, children in these families are often given more responsibility than they have in two-parent families (**Figure 13.12**). They may be required at a young age to get themselves up, dressed, and off to school on time. They may cook for the family, care for younger siblings, or help with household tasks. Older children may have a job and contribute to the family financially. With such responsibilities, children learn quite early to be independent.

Children in a single-parent family may have fewer resources than those in two-parent families to help them handle the stresses of daily living. Only one parent is there to meet their emotional needs for love and affection. Children have only one role model to help them learn acceptable social roles. Money may be in short supply with only one parent providing an income.

Nonetheless, a single-parent family fulfills the same functions as other family structures. It can provide a warm, positive setting so children feel love and security. As physical needs are met and activities are shared, children learn to become responsible individuals, just as they do in other family structures.

Many single parents turn to outside sources to seek help in managing all their responsibilities. Assistance and support is often available from social service organizations, businesses, and religious organizations. Community resources, such as a local food shelf or pantry, gift-box programs, adopt-a-brother or adopt-a-sister clubs, or before- and after-school programs, can assist single parents in meeting the physical, social, and emotional needs of the family.

In some single-parent families, the absent parent helps with finances and continues to be a role model in the child's life. For instance, some divorced fathers pay child-support payments or have custody of the children for part of the time. You will learn more about parental and financial responsibilities of both parents after a divorce in Chapter 16.

Other family members or friends can help provide role models and assist with child care, too. They can spend time with the children, listening to them, giving love and affection, and encouraging them in their achievements. Such assistance can make the single parent's workday easier to manage or give him or her time to enjoy other interests, improve job skills, and develop new relationships.

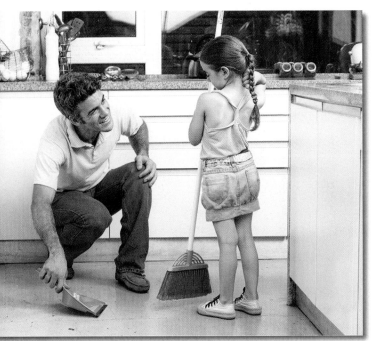
ProStockStudio/Shutterstock.com

Figure 13.12 In a single-parent family, children learn to be independent by taking responsibility earlier for helping with family tasks. *How can such responsibility impact growth and development?*

Think About Your Reading

What strategies can a single parent use to help carry out the functions of a family?

The Stepfamily

The challenges of living and parenting alone often lead single parents to seek out a new partner. When they join in marriage, they form a stepfamily. A **stepfamily**, also known as a *blended family*, includes two spouses, one or both of whom have been married before and have children from one or more previous marriages.

The stepfamily, like the nuclear family, has the advantage of two parents working together to fill the parenting role and maintain the home. With two parents contributing, there is less strain on each parent's time and energy. The couple has their marriage relationship to meet their own emotional needs for intimacy.

The children in a stepfamily have access to more resources because they have the benefit of two parents in the home. They have both male and female role models. Relationships with stepparents take time to develop, but can be a source of love, affection, encouragement, and understanding (**Figure 13.13**).

The stepfamily can be a complex structure. When two different family groups combine to make a new family unit, the new structure creates new family roles. These include the roles of newly married spouses as well as stepparent and stepchild. The absent parents, grandparents, and other relatives also have roles in the life of a blended family. Working out the role expectations to meet family needs takes time. You will learn more about this adjustment in Chapter 16.

Think About Your Reading

In what ways does the combining of two families help parents fulfill the functions of the family?

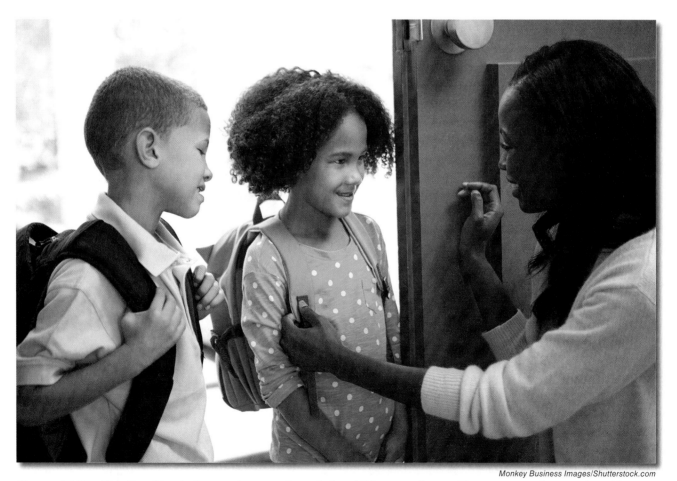

Monkey Business Images/Shutterstock.com

Figure 13.13 Relationships between stepparents and stepchildren can be positive sources of support and love.

The Extended Family

In an **extended family**, several generations of one family live together, sharing the home and family activities. In such a family, parents and their children share the same household with grandparents, aunts, uncles, or cousins (**Figure 13.14**). Depending on the ages of the family members, this structure creates different benefits and challenges.

The extended family structure can benefit family members. There are more individuals to help carry out the functions of the family and meet members' various needs. When children are young, grandparents or aunts and uncles can help with the demands of balancing child care, the work of the home, and work outside of the home.

As children interact with older family members, they learn to trust and appreciate them. This interaction can also help those older family members feel needed and loved. As grandparents age, children can help meet their needs in return.

Unique challenges also exist in the extended family. Older family members usually gain a respected position in the family. They can offer experience in childrearing and other aspects of family living. Having several adults living in a household, however, can increase stress levels. Different generations may have different ideas about parenting, different approaches to managing money, and different expectations for each other. A challenge of the extended family is to identify boundaries for various members' roles

Real-Life Scenario

Different Family Structures

Trista hurried home as soon as school was out. Her mother worked the late afternoon shift at an assisted-living facility, and she had to babysit her little sister, Tara. Ever since her parents separated three years before, Trista had the responsibility of caring for Tara while their mother worked. After Tara went to bed, Trista would do her homework and then talk to friends or watch TV. She usually fell asleep on the couch waiting for her mother to come home. She liked to wait up so she and her mother could talk before they went to bed.

Noah rushed to his locker as soon as the bell rang. He had to hurry to his after-school job. He worked at the local supermarket from the time school was out until 9:00 each night. He stocked shelves and sometimes bagged groceries at the checkout. With his schedule, Noah found it hard to get his homework done. He knew that the money he made really helped his family, however. After Noah's dad was laid off from his job, he found work at a much lower pay. Noah's mom looked for a job, too, but could only find work paying minimum wage. The cost of a babysitter for Noah's little brother was so high that she decided to stay home and care for him herself. Noah's grandmother lived with them, but her health was poor. Sometimes she needed care as well. Noah's income was a real help to the family, but

his parents insisted that he save some each week. They were determined that Noah go to college.

Dominique and his brother lived with their parents, who worked until 6:00 each night. Both boys were responsible for getting their homework done by the time their parents came home. Then they both had to do household chores. Sometimes Dominique helped cook supper. At other times, it was his turn to clean the kitchen or do laundry. They all had to work until the chores were done.

For Discussion

1. Identify the type of family structure in each situation. List the family members who make up the structure of each.
2. What roles did family members take in each of these families?
3. In each family, were the roles affected by the structure of the family or by other changes in the society? Explain your answer.
4. What are the differences in the ways each family fulfills its functions?
5. What are the similarities between these families?
6. How are these families similar to the early American families of colonial times? How are they different from the colonial families?

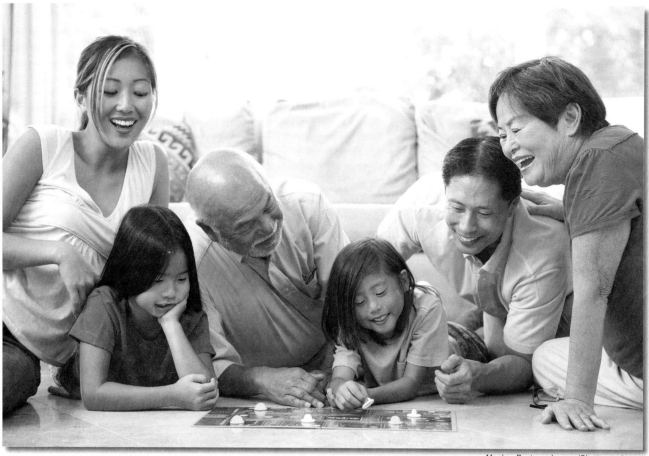
Monkey Business Images/Shutterstock.com

Figure 13.14 In this extended family, three generations live in the same house. *What are some benefits of having extended family live in the same home or nearby?*

so that the needs of all family members are met. In addition, very elderly family members might themselves need care to meet their physical needs. This places demands on parents, who feel caught between a responsibility to care for both their children and their parents. Family resources often become strained in these situations.

Extended families can be formed in different ways. One common form is the modified-extended family. Relatives live near one another, but do not share the same household. They are involved in each other's lives, helping out when needed with needs like child care and housekeeping tasks. They may work together on large projects and celebrate social events together. Such cooperation and support strengthens the relationships within the family.

Think About Your Reading

How could an extended family structure help the family fulfill its functions?

The Childless Family

Some families do not include children, just adults. The adults' reasons for remaining childless can vary. They may be delaying having children, be unable to have children, or plan to never have children.

The childless family may have more financial resources than one with children, since the couple does not have the expenses that go with

childrearing. Both adults often work. They may pursue challenging career goals because they can give more attention to their jobs. The spouses in childless families tend to share their roles in the home, working together to reach their goals (**Figure 13.15**).

The Adoptive Family

An **adoptive family** consists of one or more parents and an adopted child or children. Depending on the structure of the adopting family, various functions of the family can be impacted. Outside resources and support from family members may be needed to help meet the needs of both parents and children.

An adoptive family faces unique challenges. The first is for parents to adjust to the parenting role. The second is talking to the child about the adoption. Usually, adoptive parents must adjust to the new role of parenting quite suddenly. In many cases, they must wait for the child for quite a long time, sometimes years, before the adoption is completed. The date of arrival is often uncertain and may occur suddenly. Parents can turn to groups of adoptive parents or counselors to help them adapt to their new roles.

A related adjustment has to do with the age of the adopted child. Many adopted children are not infants. In that case, the parents need to adjust to raising a child that has grown up in other another setting and already developed his or her ways of relating to adults. The child, too, has to adapt to having parents who want to provide guidance and direction in ways that he or she is not accustomed to.

Another challenge is deciding how to talk about the adoption to the children. Most experts today think that children should be told early that they were adopted. Parents can emphasize the child was wanted, specially chosen, and brought into their family. Children will have questions

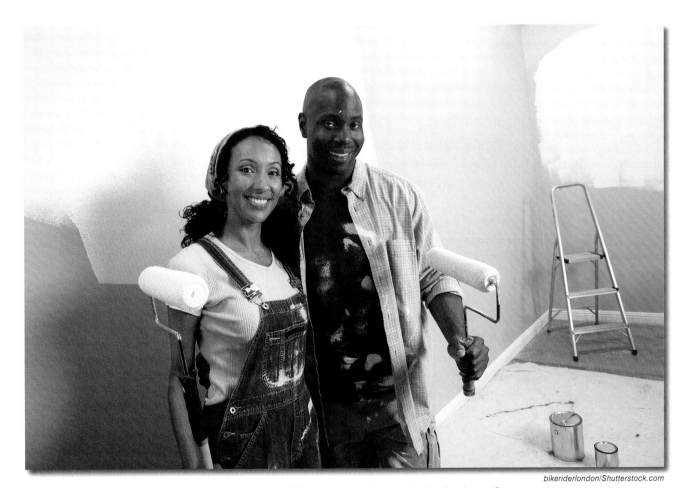

Figure 13.15 *Why do you think childless families tend to share roles in the home?*

about their birth parents, especially as they get older. They may want to find out who their birth parents are and even meet them. There may be times when they feel insecure or uncertain about their identity.

Close relationships within the adoptive family can help meet these challenges (**Figure 13.16**). As a couple models a strong marital relationship, adopted children will feel more secure. Then parents can build the child's self-esteem and affirm that the child is loved and wanted. Honest and open communication about the child's feelings can build trust between the adoptive parents and child as well.

Think About Your Reading

What challenges might an adoptive family have in fulfilling the functions of the family?

Public Policies and Laws Supporting Families

Public policies, or government actions meant to achieve certain goals, that support families include those that bring about better living conditions for all families, respecting their diversity and cultures. No matter what their structure, families benefit from opportunities that help them carry out their functions. Access to good jobs, housing, and transportation help families meet their economic needs and feel secure in their ability to do so. Access to health care benefits everyone in the family. Public policies that provide strong school systems help children learn and reach their potential.

All states have laws designed to protect families and their members' rights to assume roles and functions within the family and society. Some of these laws relate to different events that occur in the family, such as marriage, divorce, child custody, child support, child abuse and neglect, adoption, *compulsory* (required by law) education, and family medical leave. These changes can impact both family structure and family functions. Public policies and laws need to protect

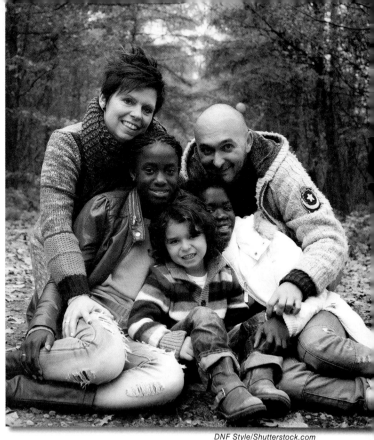

DNF Style/Shutterstock.com

Figure 13.16 As the adopting family freely shows love, affection, and acceptance, the child's feelings of security increase. *What might be some challenges that go with a multiracial adoptive family?*

human dignity and promote better life conditions for all.

LESSON 13.3

Assess

COMPREHENSION CHECK

1. Identify two benefits of living in a nuclear family.
2. List five ways a single-parent family may be formed.
3. Describe some challenges that single parents may have meeting the needs of their family members.
4. Explain the difference between an extended family and a modified-extended family.
5. Describe one benefit and one challenge unique to an extended family.
6. Identify two challenges faced by adoptive families.
7. Summarize how public policies and laws that impact family life could affect the family's ability to carry out its functions.

LESSON 13.4

SINGLE LIVING

Content Terms

Build Vocab

single living
nonfamily household

Academic Terms

transition
independence

Objectives

After studying this lesson, you will be able to

- **identify** reasons people choose single living.
- **describe** some advantages of single living.
- **explain** some challenges of single living.

Focus Your Reading

1. Outline the reasons for and advantages of not marrying. Add common concerns of those who do not marry.
2. Create a sentence which uses three of the four vocabulary terms in a connected thought.

A lifestyle in which a person lives alone is referred to as **single living**. The household consists only of one person. At some time in their lives, most people experience single living (**Figure 13.17**). For some, the period of single living may be temporary. For many young people, single living is a *transition* period, a stage between two others. In this case, the two other stages are living with parents and living with a spouse. Others choose to remain single throughout their lives.

The U.S. Census Bureau has identified a type of single living category called **nonfamily household**. This category includes a one-person household, a person living alone, and a household in which unrelated people share the home—*roommates*, as college students would say. Being a part of a nonfamily household can give young people time to save money, share living expenses, and plan for their future, without making a commitment to any one person. It also gives them an opportunity to adjust to living with someone who is not a family member, which requires them to adapt to the habits and preferences of someone who grew up with different family customs. This aspect of living in a nonfamily household can be a useful preparation for becoming part of a two-person family later.

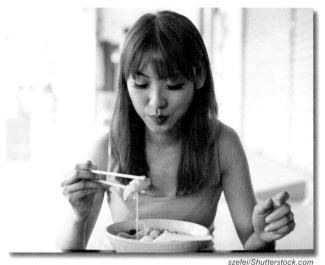

Figure 13.17 More young people remain single for a longer period of time than in the past. *In what different life transitions might persons find themselves living as single adults?*

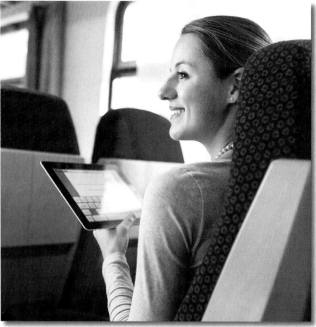

l i g h t p o e t/Shutterstock.com

Figure 13.18 Single living can give young people time and freedom to pursue personal goals, such as travel.

Reasons for Single Living

Sometimes living alone is the chosen lifestyle. Often, this choice is short-term, pursued only until the person is ready for marriage. Living single may also be a long-term choice to never marry. On the other hand, single living may not result from a decision, but be a result of circumstances in life.

Delaying Marriage

More young people today are postponing marriage until they are older. Some choose to finish their education before they get married. Others wait even longer, wanting to establish themselves in a good job or become financially stable. Some want to fulfill lifelong dreams, such as extensive traveling, before making a commitment to another person (**Figure 13.18**).

When older singles do marry, their maturity helps them to work harder at developing a good marriage relationship. They may have determined that friendship and companionship are more important than anything else they might want in life. Since they are older when they marry, they tend to have children at an older age. This situation can be beneficial in some ways, as older couples may be more able to handle the emotional

demands of parenting. Delaying having children carries risks as well. When the mother is over age 35, the health risks of pregnancy increase. Older couples sometimes remain childless, have only one child, or attempt to adopt a child. Older couples tend to be more financially established, which helps them succeed in reaching their goals.

Think About Your Reading

What are some of the benefits of delaying marriage until you are older? What are some of the concerns of marrying at an older age?

Choosing Not to Marry

Some people prefer single living because it offers flexibility and *independence*, or the chance to live alone as one wishes. These singles never seek a marriage partner. Since social pressures to marry have lessened, they are probably less likely than people in earlier generations to feel they must get married.

People choose the single life for many different reasons. Some people are intensively involved

in their careers and do not want to commit to a relationship. They may not want the responsibility of marriage or parenting to take time away from their work goals. Some people have been deeply hurt in previous relationships. To avoid being hurt again, they decide to remain single. Yet other single people have a dependent family member who is ill, is older, or has a disability. Because they devote so much time tending to the needs of that person, they may not want to burden a spouse with the responsibility.

Changes Leading to Single Living

Divorce and a spouse's death are leading reasons for an increase in the number of singles. Many divorced people who do not have children or custody of their children return to single living. The loss of a spouse also forces many people to live their remaining years alone. Although circumstances make them single, they may choose to remain that way.

In addition to these life circumstances, there is one more that can cause a person to be permanently single—never finding a suitable marriage partner. Some people who want to marry may never find a person they want to commit to. As a result, they live alone even though their intention was to marry.

Advantages of Single Living

For many people, single living is an attractive lifestyle for the following reasons:

- Singles may have more freedom, independence, and time to do whatever they want than married people (**Figure 13.19**).
- Singles usually have fewer living expenses than a person with a family.
- Singles often have more mobility than married people. They can easily make career changes or move to another city, since they do not need to take into account the career opportunities or wishes of another person.
- Many singles gain self-confidence in knowing they can take care of themselves emotionally and financially.

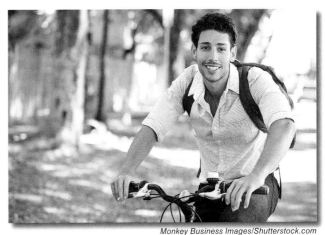
Monkey Business Images/Shutterstock.com

Figure 13.19 Some adults view the freedom of single living as attractive and desirable. *How could single living impact the way a person spends time?*

Many singles work to build a strong support network of family and friends. They meet others through friends, work, or other social activities. Their social life can be structured as they wish, either busy or relaxed.

> **Think About Your Reading**
>
> In what ways are the roles of singles different from the roles of married couples?

Concerns of Single People

For some singles, living alone may have disadvantages. Social relationships or dealing with stereotyped images of their lifestyles are two concerns.

Social Relationships

Some singles may need to make more of an effort to develop social relationships. Demanding careers can make it difficult to meet others. The field of dating partners may shrink as one grows older. Some singles may feel uncomfortable trying to fit into society and social occasions, especially when many events are geared toward couples. The single person may feel increasing loneliness as others the same age marry and develop lives around their children.

Some singles may feel they are missing out on part of life. They may desire the closeness and sharing of married life. They may want to have a child, but not as a single parent. These factors may draw the single person toward marriage.

Stereotyped Images

Many singles must also deal with the stereotypes associated with single living. Singles are sometimes viewed as being self-centered because they pursue their own interests. They may be considered irresponsible and unstable.

Some people believe that a person must be married to be happy. As a result, a single person may feel pressure from family members and friends to marry. Some parents believe that single living is not an acceptable lifestyle. Friends may want the single person to experience the fulfillment they have found in marriage.

Singles have the same needs as others for friendships and emotional support (**Figure 13.20**). If they develop these, they can be happy and experience personal fulfillment. Singles who are self-confident believe they can make a worthwhile contribution to society. If they remain single, such positive attitudes will help them live a complete life. If they eventually marry, they will have a rich background to bring to the relationship.

LESSON 13.4
Assess

COMPREHENSION CHECK

1. List four reasons why some people choose to remain single.
2. Identify four advantages of choosing single living as a lifestyle.
3. Describe two challenges of single living.

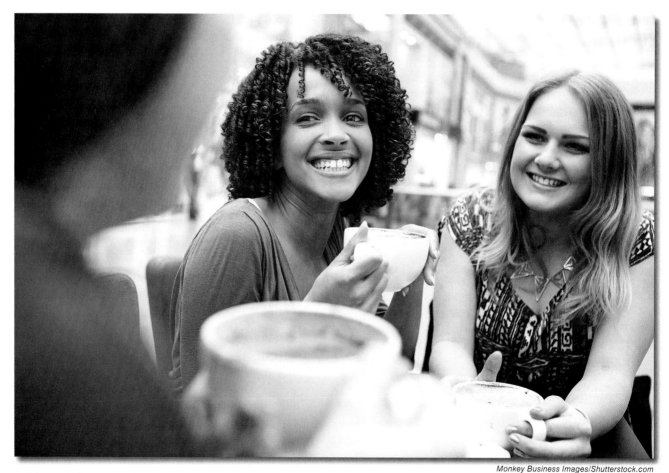

Monkey Business Images/Shutterstock.com

Figure 13.20 Getting involved in social activities is one way for singles to develop friendships. *How could involvement in a community group help meet the needs of a single person?*

CHAPTER SUMMARY

The family is a flexible institution that constantly adjusts to economic and social changes. Throughout the history of the United States, the types of work and roles of family members have changed. Through all these changes, the family continues to be an important unit in society.

The family fulfills several important functions. It is the main societal unit for the reproduction and socialization of children. Families meet the physical and emotional needs of family members. Families also influence the personal roles of their members.

Several types of family structures are common in the United States. Though today's family structures vary, most families try to fulfill the needs of family members. There are several public policies and laws that impact families and how they fulfill their functions.

Although many people marry and form their own families, single living is more common today. For many singles, this lifestyle offers more advantages than disadvantages.

VOCABULARY ACTIVITIES

1. Working with a partner, create flash cards with the following terms and brief definitions. Take turns with your partner quizzing each other to ensure that you both know the definition of each term.

Content Terms

adoptive family (13.3)
cultural identity (13.2)
custom (13.2)
extended family (13.3)
family (13.1)
family structure (13.3)
household (13.1)
nonfamily household (13.4)
nuclear family (13.3)
single living (13.4)
single-parent family (13.3)
stepfamily (13.3)

2. Create a crossword puzzle that includes all of the following terms, with their definitions. Exchange puzzles with a partner and complete the one you receive. Discuss with your partner any disagreements you have on the meaning of a term. Consult a dictionary to find the correct definition.

Academic Terms

compulsory (13.3)
demographic (13.1)
function (13.2)
helpless (13.2)
independence (13.4)
lifelong learning (13.1)
model (13.3)
public policy (13.3)
self-sufficient (13.1)
transition (13.4)

ASSESS

Your Knowledge

3. Describe five different family structures.
4. Identify and describe four different functions the family fulfills in U.S. society.

Your Understanding

5. How are changes in family size an example of how families have adjusted over time?
6. Do you think that families in colonial times and during the Industrial Revolution had as many varieties of family structures as are found today? Why or why not?
7. Explain the different challenges each type of family structure has in fulfilling the functions of the family.
8. How can living as a single prepare a person for marriage and family life?

Your Skills

9. Identify some of the successful adjustment strategies that past generations made in the family as technologies and careers changed. Which of these strategies could be helpful for families adjusting to a global economy?
10. What resources are available in your community to help single-parent families fulfill their functions?

CRITICAL THINKING

11. **Predict Outcomes**. Write a paragraph or two that describes the family of the future. Think about current societal, demographic, and economic trends and how they might impact families and the individuals in them. Include ideas about how the family will fulfill its functions in the society of the future.

12. **Compare and Contrast.** Interview a grandparent or other older adult about the early years of his or her married life. Include questions about the type of work he or she did, the family's structure, and the roles carried out by members of the extended family. Then interview a parent and ask the same questions. Record answers for both interviews. In a paragraph, compare and contrast the responses from the two generations. How are they similar? How are they different? *Choice*: Present your findings orally to the class.

13. **Make Generalizations.** Work in a group of four and create a survey to discover who carries out which roles in different families. List various roles in the left column and various possible family

member titles across the top. Have each group member survey a family that he or she knows about, such as a friend's family or your own. Tally the results from all four surveys. Choose one family member that is common to all four surveys (mother, father, teen, younger child, grandparent) and identify similarities and differences in the roles taken by this person in the four different families. Write a paragraph describing your findings and identify any generalizations you can make about the roles taken by such persons in families in your community.

14. **Make Inferences.** Compare two television shows that emphasize family living. Identify the family structure each family illustrates. List the family members in each show, identify their roles, and describe the relationships between members in each family. Present your findings in a report. *Choice*: Evaluate how well each family fulfills its functions, citing evidence from the text to support your evaluation. Summarize your findings in a paper.

CORE SKILLS

15. **Research, Writing.** Search online to identify the types of jobs common in your community in the past. Write a report that compares past trends in your community to the trends described in the text. *Group option*: Work in small groups to research several nearby communities and prepare your report as a digital presentation to present to the class.

16. **Interviewing, Writing.** Interview a farm family in or near your community. Write a one-page report comparing the roles of these family members with the roles of family members in the colonial years. Describe ways they are similar and ways they are different. *Choice*: Complete your report as a digital presentation.

17. **Writing.** Prepare a chart on the functions of the family. Create four columns for the chart. List one main function of the family as the heading for each column. Under each, list five examples of what families do to fulfill that function. Then write a paper describing a family that fulfills its functions, including your examples.

18. **Writing.** Take the role of an online advice columnist. Write a letter to the columnist from the member of a family that is having difficulty meeting all its functions. Specify in the letter what areas or issue is problematic. Then write a response that identifies ways to approach the

issue and lists resources in the community that can provide help.

19. **Interviewing, Writing.** Interview a single person and ask questions about the advantages and disadvantages of single living as he or she sees them. Work with a small group of classmates to identify common responses in each area. Create a spreadsheet listing the advantages and disadvantages identified and the number of singles reporting each. Create a graph showing your findings. *Choice*: Write a paragraph summarizing your findings.

20. **Interpreting and Communicating Information.** Search online to identify the types of jobs common in your community today. Choose one of those jobs and read about the type of work involved, the typical working conditions, and the level of income and types of benefits these workers receive. Present your findings in a chart. Then write a paragraph analyzing how you think having this job would impact a single parent. What aspects of single parenting would be helped by this job? Which aspects would be challenged by this job?

21. **Using Quantitative Information.** Compiling, analyzing, and presenting quantitative information is a key workplace skill. To develop that skill, find the U.S. Census Bureau information on families in your community. Using a computer and spreadsheet software, prepare a graph showing the percentage of families of different structures. Look at social and economic information for your community as well. Include that information in accompanying graphs and write a paragraph explaining how the social and economic data influences families of different structures in your community.

CAREER READINESS

22. **Identifying Resources.** Prepare a list of questions to ask a social worker about services available in your community to help families fulfill their basic functions. Interview the social worker, asking your questions and recording the responses. Write a report identifying these services. *Choice*: Search the Internet to identify additional information on local family services. Create a table or chart that lists the name, address, and contact information of each organization that provides the services and list the services that each provides. Post your findings on your school website.

CHAPTER 14

STRENGTHENING FAMILY INTERACTIONS

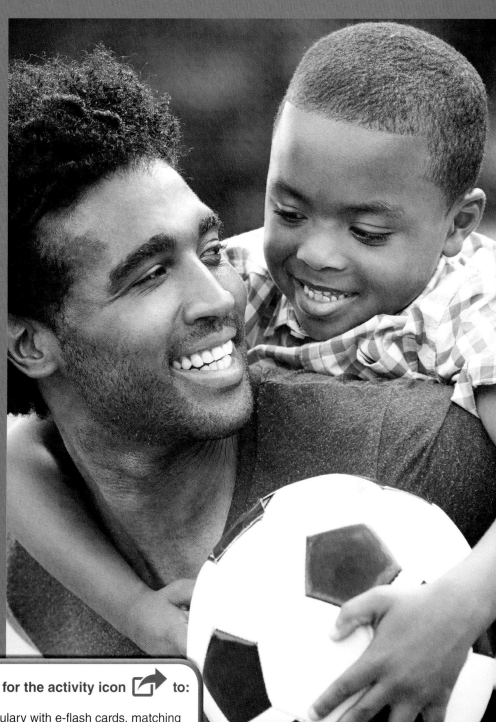

Reading Prep

Before reading the chapter, skim the headings, subheadings, and charts in each lesson. On a sheet of paper, write down three facts you want to learn or skills you want to gain from reading each lesson. After you read each lesson, write down what you learned under each statement.

Key Questions

Questions to answer as you study this chapter:

- How do family interactions affect the family system?
- What patterns of interaction lead to strong, healthy families?
- How can families deal with negative interactions and strengthen the family system?

While studying this chapter, look for the activity icon to:

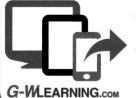

- **build** vocabulary with e-flash cards, matching activities, and vocabulary games; and
- **assess** what you learn by completing the lesson comprehension checks online.
  www.g-wlearning.com/humanservices/

G-WLEARNING.com

344

©iStock.com/Cathy Yeulet

Lesson 14.1 The Family as a System
Lesson 14.2 Positive Patterns of Interaction in Families
Lesson 14.3 Dealing with Conflict, Violence, and Abuse in the Family

AFTER STUDYING THIS CHAPTER, YOU WILL

KNOW:

- The rights and responsibilities of family members.
- The skills that are essential for building strong families.
- The signs of abuse in the family.

UNDERSTAND:

- How the family functions as a system.
- How family interactions affect the family system.
- How to deal with conflict in the family.

BE ABLE TO DO:

- Apply democratic decision-making skills in the family system.
- Make choices that could restore balance to a family system.
- Develop strategies that could be used to build a strong family system.

GETTING STARTED

Rowena's dad opened the door leading to the auditorium as Rowena and her mother hurried inside. He helped them remove their coats and quickly took them to the coat check. Once their coats were checked, the three politely smiled and thanked the usher, who escorted them to their seats. They sat side by side through the play, laughing and clapping with the rest of the audience.

Afterward, they chatted with friends, neighbors, Rowena's classmates, and teachers. No one could tell that the three had been involved in a big argument before hurriedly leaving home. Only Rowena and her family knew about the heated words that were exchanged over Rowena's late date the night before. This was a matter that the family members intended to keep private. To

everyone in the auditorium, this family appeared happy and content.

What goes on inside a family is usually private. Others may not know how family members treat one another when no one else is around. Many families have private patterns for communicating, solving problems, or making decisions.

Family interactions affect the self-confidence and self-esteem of family members. They can influence the development of members' personal skills for communicating, making decisions, and resolving conflicts. They can affect the way members of the family handle stress. Finally, they can influence the interactions members will experience in the families that they form in the future.

THE FAMILY AS A SYSTEM

Content Terms

Build Vocab

family system
free society

Academic Terms

interrelated
absorb

Objectives

After studying this lesson, you will be able to

- **identify** various rights and responsibilities of family members.
- **explain** how interactions within a family system work.
- **describe** how families can achieve and restore balance in a family system.

Focus Your Reading

1. Draw a diagram of a balance scale. As you read this lesson, list the two parts that need to balance in the family system (one on each side of the scale) and examples of each part.
2. Draw a diagram that includes all the members of your family system and list their chief roles and responsibilities.

The family is a system because all family members interact with one another. In a **family system**, the words and actions of every family member have an effect on every other family member. In an effective family system, members work together and manage their various resources to meet the needs of all family members. Families have an impact on the community where they live. Strong families contribute to healthy communities where groups of people can work together to help meet the needs of all. Healthy communities contribute to a **free society**, where policies and actions are promoted to bring about better living conditions for all people.

Family Systems Are Complex

The more people there are in the family, the more complex the family system. When a family system is composed of two people, interactions occur in only two directions—between the two members. As families add members, the number of relationships multiplies. In a family of four, there are 12 different relationships (**Figure 14.1**). When the extended family enters the picture, even more relationships exist.

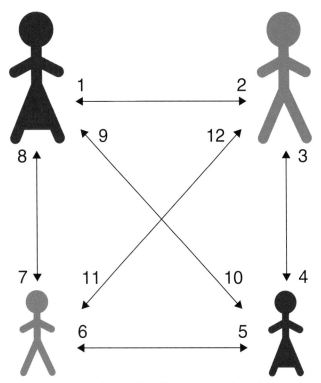

Figure 14.1 In larger families, interactions become very complex. Each arrow in the diagram represents two relationships in the family. *How many additional relationships are created by adding one more family member?*

Family relationships tend to have their own distinct patterns of interaction. These patterns are often based on the roles within the family. For instance, your mother is likely to relate to your father differently than how she relates to you and your siblings. Learning more about these interactions is one way to help you understand and strengthen your family relationships.

Rights and Responsibilities

Being a member of a family usually involves both rights and responsibilities. These rights and responsibilities are *interrelated*, meaning that one cannot exist without the other. Those rights and responsibilities fit into four areas:

- *Satisfying physical needs.* Family members have the right to eat the family's food, live in the family home, and share other family resources. They may be expected to meet their responsibilities by helping with

household chores and contributing to the family income.
- *Promoting emotional support.* Giving and receiving love tend to go hand in hand. For members to receive love and affection, others must provide it. Members will feel better about providing love if they receive it in return.
- *Speaking and being heard.* Family members have the right to voice their feelings and be heard by others. Such a right also means that each member has the responsibility to willingly listen to others in the family.
- *Supporting and encouraging.* Family members provide support and encouragement to other members. In return, each family member is responsible for offering encouragement and support to the others.

Managing Family Resources to Meet Needs

Families can balance members' rights and responsibilities by making sure all members have chances to grow to their potential. This includes managing family resources, such as time and money, so the needs of all individuals in the family are being met. Children need opportunities to learn new skills, *absorb* (take in) new information, be creative, express themselves, develop relationships with family members and friends, and mature. Parents also need opportunities to keep on learning and growing. They need time to enhance their relationships with others, improve old skills, and learn new skills.

> ## Think About Your Reading
> What might happen in a family if everyone claimed to have rights, but no one was willing to fulfill any responsibilities?

Balancing Roles

Family members have various roles. Families balance their family system by identifying and defining each member's roles. Each member

needs to know what the expectations are for his or her role and what fulfilling that role involves. These expectations are based on family needs and the members' stages of life and should be clear and realistic. For instance, if a parent has to work late, a teenager may be asked to provide care for a brother or sister until the parent gets home. All members may be expected to work and contribute to help the family fulfill its functions and meet its goals (**Figure 14.2**). Members should have responsibilities that match their skills and abilities. Then they will have greater success fulfilling them. As family members fulfill their roles, they help keep the family balanced.

Think About Your Reading

How might the family be affected if members do not fulfill their expected roles? Are there any family needs that might be left unmet?

Adjusting to Changes Inside and Outside the Family

The expectations for family roles may change as the needs of family members change. For instance, both children's and parents' roles change as children grow older (**Figure 14.3**). Children take on more responsibilities and contribute to the functioning of the family. Parents provide less direct supervision of children's actions. Adjusting to these changes helps keep the family system balanced.

Sometimes changes inside or outside the family affect a member's ability to carry out expected roles. For example, illness or an accident may prevent a person from accomplishing some aspects of his or her role well.

Sometimes family members do not fulfill their roles or carry out their responsibilities. For instance, a parent may abandon the family, or a teenager may rebel against parents' expectations.

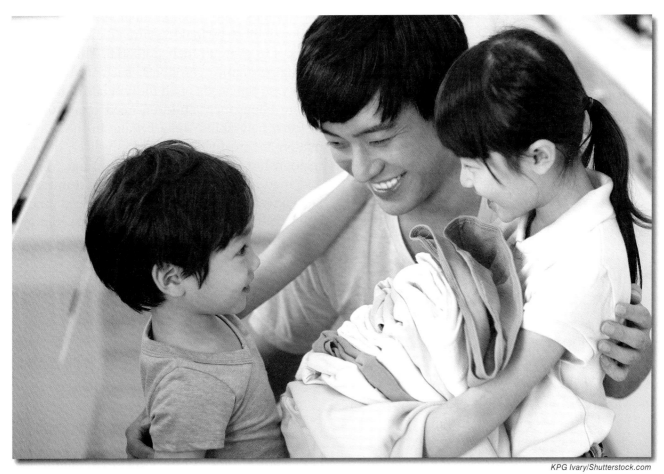

KPG Ivary/Shutterstock.com

Figure 14.2 In a family system, all members should take on roles to contribute to the family's goals.

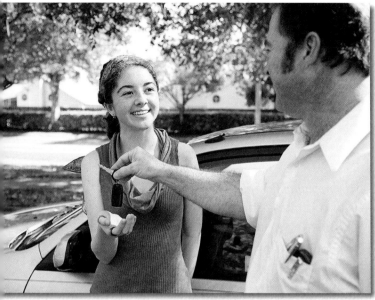
Lisa F. Young/Shutterstock.com

Figure 14.3 When children enter the teen years, the roles of both parent and child change. *What qualities could help families adjust to these changes in roles?*

By neglecting their responsibilities, one family member affects every other family member in a negative way.

Think About Your Reading

What resources could help a family adjust to the loss of a job and help meet the needs of family members?

Restoring Balance in the Family System

When the family becomes unbalanced, it is not able to function effectively. Then the family system must adjust. This is done in one of two ways. Either the members not fulfilling their roles are helped so that they can, or other members must handle the neglected role, either alone or by working together. Sometimes outside resources may be needed to help the family restore balance and function effectively.

In the first way, family members provide help for the member who is not fulfilling his or her roles. For instance, a father may develop an alcohol abuse problem. This problem may reduce his ability to carry out his role as an income provider. Family members may provide support to the father so he can return to fulfilling his roles. They may need to seek outside resources, such as medical help or counseling, to provide this help. By giving such support, they are helping return the family to balance.

In the second way, family members work together to carry out the unfulfilled roles. For instance, if family income is reduced by the father's problem, another family member may get a job. The family tries to return to a balance so the needs of family members are met.

Impact of Families on Communities

The impacts of family interactions are far-reaching. Families make up communities; communities combine to make up a society. If families cannot fulfill their functions and meet the needs of their members, society suffers. Broken relationships, emotional problems, child abuse, family violence, and poverty can result when the family cannot fulfill its functions. These issues all have an impact on other families and on society as a whole. Therefore, the family's ability to fulfill its functions should be a primary concern to communities and society.

LESSON 14.1

Assess

COMPREHENSION CHECK

1. Describe how a family functions like a system.
2. Briefly explain why expectations for family members need to include both rights and responsibilities.
3. Describe how a family can restore balance to the family system.
4. How does effective family functioning impact communities and society?

Content Terms

Build Vocab

democratic decision making
family routines
family traditions

Academic Terms

impending
consider

Objectives

After studying this lesson, you will be able to

- **describe** patterns of communication and decision making that increase positive family interactions.
- **relate** how family activities can strengthen the family.

Focus Your Reading

1. Outline the key skills needed in each area of family interaction in order to build strong families.
2. Describe an example of each content term.

As the needs of family members change, expectations and roles change. The overall goal of keeping the family strong, however, remains the same.

Strong families have a family *code of conduct* that includes expectations for specific behaviors. They have good communication skills. They make decisions, deal with conflict, and resolve their problems together. They avoid family violence and focus on activities they can do together that build strong family bonds. Patterns of interactions like this are positive and build strong, united families in which members show affection, respect, and trust for one another.

Maintaining Good Family Communication

Open, honest communication among family members is key to developing close relationships. Family members need to use active listening skills and show respect for each other's viewpoints. Such positive communication builds strong feelings of self-esteem and a sense of self-worth in family members and also builds attachment between family members (**Figure 14.4**). Techniques for building good communication skills were discussed in Chapter 7. The techniques discussed there apply to family communication as well.

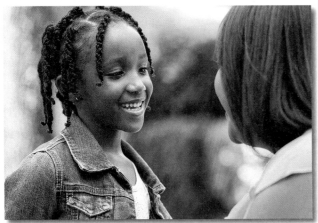

pixelheadphoto/Shutterstock.com

Figure 14.4 When a family member cares enough to listen, positive feelings grow. *How important is it to have direct eye contact when sharing personal thoughts and feelings about a sensitive topic?*

Sometimes family members may feel that their input is not valued or that others do not respect their thoughts or ideas. When they feel this way, they should use I-statements to express their thoughts and feelings. For instance, they could say, "I don't feel respected when you roll your eyes when I'm talking," or "I feel hurt when you ignore my opinion." Using I-statements keeps communication open and honest in the family. Such messages should be communicated as close as possible to the action or remark that caused the feeling. Other family members need to know right away when their words or actions hurt the relationships in the family. It is much easier to fix the problem in that case.

Setting Aside Time to Talk

Families need time to communicate often to promote the growth of family relationships. The evening meal is a good time for families to share the day's events. Work schedules, however, do not always allow all members to eat together at the same time. In that case, the family must set aside other times when they can share their thoughts, ideas, feelings, and activities.

Family meetings are one way to plan for family communication. These can be times to gather input from the members on current decisions, *impending* (upcoming) problems, or future plans.

One advantage of having family meetings regularly is that small issues can be handled while they are still small. If families wait until a problem is large and the need to address it is obvious, the conflict may be more difficult to resolve.

Maintaining a Sense of Trust

Having a strong sense of trust within the family helps keep communication lines open. When members trust each other, they are more likely to share personal thoughts because they know their private thoughts will be kept confidential. They may be more willing to look for advice or counsel from each other. They know others in the family can be trusted to make suggestions that have their own well-being in mind.

Loyalty grows in the family when members have proven themselves to be trustworthy. They can be counted on to tell the truth and carry out their duties and can be relied on to act responsibly. They have shown genuine concern for others in the family and respect for members' privacy. These experiences contribute to building trust further (**Figure 14.5**).

Sometimes family members fail to be positive communicators. Instead, they communicate in ways that are critical, cutting, or controlling of each other. Such messages show a lack of

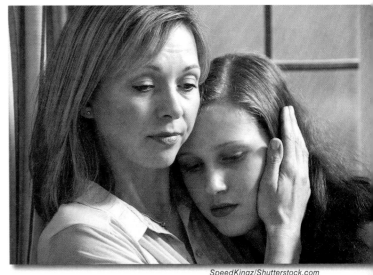

SpeedKingz/Shutterstock.com

Figure 14.5 *How does showing genuine concern help family members trust and rely on one another?*

understanding and a lack of empathy for other members' situations. In these instances, too, the member who is the subject of this negative communication should respond with I-statements to let the other family member know the behavior is not acceptable. The family member who communicated in the negative way should then apologize and change his or her behavior.

When negative communications occur often and become a pattern, trust is broken, and the relationship suffers. Individuals begin to withdraw instead of share; they protect themselves and are no longer willing to take the risk of saying how they really feel. To rebuild the relationship, trust needs to be restored. I-statements can help others know how the injured family member feels, express forgiveness, accept forgiveness, and reestablish good sharing and listening. Restoring trust will take time, though, because feelings have been hurt. Individuals must work at being dependable, responsible, and caring in their relationships with each other over time to restore that trust.

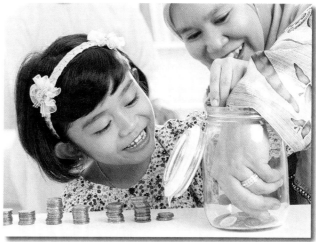

szefei/Shutterstock.com

Figure 14.6 All family members benefit when they share in decision making within the family. *What skills could you learn by helping to make decisions related to family finances?*

Think About Your Reading

What happens to the family system when a member breaks trust and does not look out for the well-being of other family members? How can trust be rebuilt?

Taking Part in Family Decision Making

In healthy families, everyone contributes to making decisions (**Figure 14.6**). When everyone in a family collaborates and takes part in making decisions, all members feel important. Each member's self-esteem increases. The basic steps for making good decisions detailed in Chapter 4 are also used in family situations.

A family can be *considered*, or viewed as, an organization. Every organization needs a system for carrying out decisions. In a business, the president is responsible for the whole system. That does not mean the president makes all the decisions or carries out all the tasks; however, the president is the one held responsible.

A family operates in a similar manner. Ultimately, someone must take responsibility for what is done; however, all members can take part in the decision. They can provide information, ideas, feelings, and different points of view. Each family should identify its own plan for sharing decision-making responsibilities. Once this is decided, members know what is expected of them regarding planning and carrying out family decisions. That plan could differ from one decision to another, depending on the issues involved.

Democratic Decision Making

Some decisions can be made by all family members together through **democratic decision making**. In this approach, members offer suggestions for alternatives and even take part in gathering information. They discuss the advantages and disadvantages of each choice. They jointly select the best choice and help carry out the plan of action (**Figure 14.7**). All members can be involved in the evaluation of the decision, too. Was it a good choice for the family? Why or why not?

Collaborating in decision making in this way is a learning process for younger family members. Through these experiences, members can learn

how to use the decision-making process to make choices that will help them reach their goals.

Selective Decision Making

Sometimes it is best to involve just certain family members in making a decision. For example, it may be appropriate that the responsibility for some decisions be given directly to the individual member best able to handle it. Also, parents may divide responsibilities according to each family member's interests or expertise.

Parents can have children make decisions on small matters to help them develop decision-making skills. Young children may be given a choice between two simple items, such as "Do you want to wear this outfit today, or this other outfit?" Deciding between two acceptable choices can help a child develop skills to make difficult choices later. It also helps the child feel that he or she has some control over his or her life.

Think About Your Reading

What can families do to increase a young teen's success with making decisions?

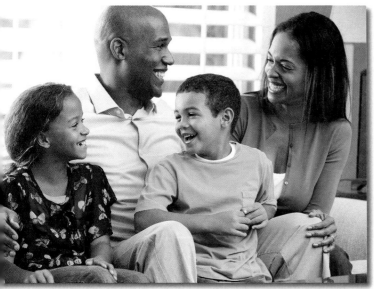

Monkey Business Images/Shutterstock.com

Figure 14.7 *What are the advantages of democratic decision making?*

The Impact of Cultural Differences

Sometimes a family's relationships, functions, communication, and decision-making patterns are influenced by cultural background. For instance, it may not be common to listen to the input of children in some cultures. In others, the input of men and women may vary in importance. In yet others, the voice of an older adult carries great weight in family decisions. Knowing the influence of your cultural background can help you understand the communication and decision-making patterns in your family.

Once you understand your parents' or guardians' point of view, you can take steps to encourage them to include you more in decision making. Let them know you want to hear them thinking about alternatives; you want to learn from them. Ask them to involve you in family decision making so they can teach you to make good decisions. Then show them you can make good decisions and take responsibility for your actions.

Sharing in the Family

Busy schedules tend to make family leisure time scarce in today's families. Nonetheless, the benefits of spending time together are greater than the disadvantages. For most families, the desire to strengthen the family unit through family activities is important (**Figure 14.8**).

Time for Having Fun

Sharing enjoyable activities together helps build family relationships. The fun that members have is in itself a good way to bond. In addition, memories of good times spent together draw the family closer. Family outings can be educational as well as fun. Family hobbies, such as camping or fishing, give members something to do together. Through these activities, members learn to cooperate to carry out a joint task. They have increased opportunities to communicate with one another and to build their communication skills. Even chores can be fun when members find creative ways to get a job done.

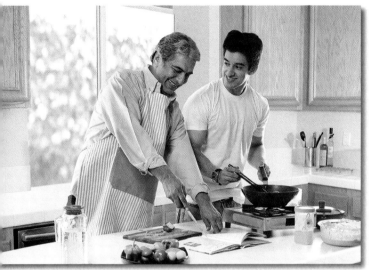

Figure 14.8 Spending time in family activities helps build long-lasting relationships among family members. *What activities do you like to participate in with family members?*

India Picture/Shutterstock.com

Time for Meaningful Family Routines

Family routines are small events or activities that are repeated on a regular basis. Meaningful routines strengthen the family and provide opportunities for sharing and showing affection. Mealtime routines are an example. These may involve preparing the food, eating the meal, and cleaning up afterward. Bedtime routines are especially common in families with small children. In many families, parents read to small children once they are in bed. The quiet activity helps settle the children and gives the parent and child time together.

These regular events in the family add security to the family environment. Children know what to expect and when to expect it. They know they can count on a time to talk and a time when others will listen to them.

Traditions in the Family

Most families enjoy celebrating special events and holidays together. The particular way the family observes these occasions become family traditions. **Family traditions** are established patterns of behavior or customs handed down through generations. Most families have their own religious and cultural traditions. Other repeated activities can also become family

traditions. For instance, the family may plan a special camping, shopping, hunting, or fishing trip every year. These annual events can help members develop their common interests and provide quality time for family members to communicate.

Family traditions can also build a sense of family identity. Often, they are celebrated with grandparents and other relatives. Such celebrations can provide a link with the past. Through these traditions, younger family members feel connected to their roots, and older members feel that the family identity will continue in the future.

Family traditions are a source of strength and unity for all family members during all stages of the family life cycle (**Figure 14.9**). Meaningful traditions bring family members together, strengthening the bonds that exist. These patterns of interaction are part of a strong and healthy family.

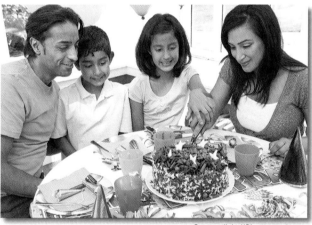

Spotmatik Ltd/Shutterstock.com

Figure 14.9 A family's traditions are often passed from one generation to another. *How does taking part in family traditions strengthen the family unit?*

LESSON 14.2

Assess

COMPREHENSION CHECK

1. Explain how positive communication can strengthen the family.
2. Describe how being dependable, responsible, and honest impacts trust in the family.
3. Explain what is meant by democratic decision making.
4. Identify the difference between family routines and family traditions.

DEALING WITH CONFLICT, VIOLENCE, AND ABUSE IN THE FAMILY

Objectives

After studying this lesson, you will be able to

- **identify** strategies for handling conflict in the family.
- **list** various forms of violence and abuse that occur in the family.
- **determine** measures for preventing violence and abuse in the family.

Focus Your Reading

1. Create two columns with the headings *Skills That Strengthen the Family* and *Negative Family Interactions*. As you read, identify skills that families can use to become stronger in the first column and list the behaviors that are negative in the second column. For each behavior in the negative column, draw a line to one or more skills in the first column that could help families handle that negative behavior.
2. Locate one example of each source of emergency help for abused family members in your community.

Whenever two or more people live together, there are disagreements. How those disagreements are handled can affect family members' growth. It can make a difference in whether the family atmosphere is positive or negative. It can affect family unity and the degree to which family members stick together and support each other. Finally, how the family handles disagreements impacts the family system and its ability to restore balance when needed.

Dealing with Problems

Effective family systems deal with problems. Individuals own their own problems, seek help in reviewing options and solutions as needed, solve issues, ask forgiveness when they make mistakes, reconnect with one another, and move on. When mistakes are made, others need to show understanding and love. Everyone makes mistakes. Learning from them can help people grow.

Content Terms

Build Vocab

codependent
scapegoating
assault
battery
child abuse
child sexual abuse
Shaken Baby Syndrome
neglect
crisis-care center
shelter
group home
foster care
independent living
victimhood

Academic Terms

resent
regress

Who Owns the Problem?

Conflicts can arise when one family member tries to solve a problem that belongs to someone else (**Figure 14.10**). Such help is often given with a you-statement: "You shouldn't let her go out before her homework is done."

Such comments often do not help a situation, but do just the opposite. Children may feel that parents do not trust them to solve problems on their own. A parent hearing a you-statement from his or her partner may *resent* (be angry about) the hidden message that he or she is not capable of solving a problem without help. Taking steps to help family members own their own problems works to restore balance in the family system when needed.

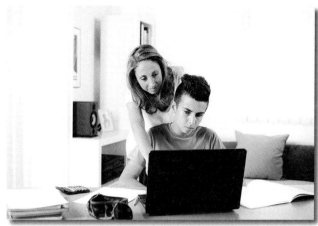

Jean-Philippe WALLET/Shutterstock.com

Figure 14.10   Solving other family members' problems for them does not help them to grow. *How is self-esteem affected when others try to solve your problems?*

Real-Life Scenario

Family Interaction

Cameron was nervous all through supper. He knew his math teacher had called his parents about his failing grade. His parents did not say a word until after supper.

Cameron's brother was already in bed when his parents called Cameron to come in the study. "I hear you are having some trouble with math," Cameron's dad said. "Would you like to talk about it?"

Cameron really did not know what to say. "I'm trying, Dad. It's just a hard subject for me."

"What do you think would help?" his mom asked.

"Well, I could use some extra help with my homework assignments."

"Do you think your teacher could give you some help?" Cameron's dad asked.

"Maybe, but she's pretty busy."

"When she called, she said that she would be willing to stay tomorrow after school. Would you be willing to talk to her then?" Cameron's dad asked.

"I guess so," said Cameron. "What time?"

"She said 3:30 would be fine. Why don't you give me a call when you're done, and I'll pick you up?"

Randy's mother also received a call from the teacher that day. As Randy walked in the house, his mom called to him. "Your teacher called today, and you are in trouble! You're failing math! How can you do that? Don't you know you have to pass math to graduate?"

Randy threw his books on the table. "That dumb teacher! She never explains anything. Besides, I hate math. I don't care if I never graduate!"

"Well, I have to go in to talk to her tomorrow. You'll just have to work harder. I don't have time to keep going in to see the teachers."

For Discussion

1. How did Cameron's parents control the environment for their family discussion?
2. What types of messages were used to communicate in Cameron's family? What types were used in Randy's family?
3. In Randy's family, who took ownership of the problem with the math class?
4. How did Cameron's parents help him take ownership of his problem?
5. What solutions did each family find? Who will likely be most successful in solving his problem?

Using Active Listening and I-Statements

Encouraging the person with the problem to work through it is the best way to help family members grow (**Figure 14.11**). This takes active listening skills and requires giving feedback using I-statements. By showing understanding and empathy, family members can encourage each other to solve their own problems.

As family members become better at handling conflict, their self-esteem increases. So do their skills for solving problems. Negative feelings are expressed in words instead of being bottled up, where they can explode in the future. A deeper sense of caring and understanding grows between family members. They begin to trust each other. It becomes easier for family members to accept and respect one another as individuals who can handle their own problems.

Think About Your Reading

How can I-statements help family members identify who owns a problem?

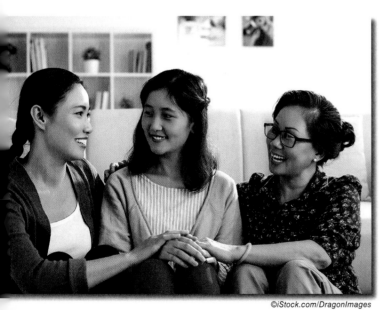

©iStock.com/DragonImages

Figure 14.11 Using active listening can help family members identify steps they need to take to solve their own problems. *What other skills can be used to encourage individuals to solve their own problems?*

Learning to Compromise

When family members use compromise to resolve arguments, both sides benefit because no one loses. If you fight for your point of view and win the argument, then the other person loses. That person may feel defeated, worthless, and ill-treated. You may win the argument, but you hurt the relationship. When people refuse to compromise, the issue may never be resolved fairly.

To compromise, you may need to admit to a misunderstanding or to accept that you both see the issue from a different point of view. You may even need to admit that you could be partly wrong. If both people give a little to reach a compromise, all will feel better about the solution (**Figure 14.12**). The fear of failing or being wrong is reduced for all involved.

Accepting Differences

Sometimes family members do not reach a compromise, but just accept their differences and move on. Using accommodation in this way can help families make a decision or settle an issue, although it does not build unity or a spirit of working together. If good communication skills are used in the process, though, and all members have a chance to provide input and express their own viewpoints, a positive family environment can be maintained. Sometimes just knowing that others have heard what they have to say makes it easier for members to go along with an overall family decision. Listening shows respect, and respect can help family members feel valued and accepted.

The Problem with Solving Others' Problems

A **codependent** relationship exists between family members when one person tries to rescue and enable others to continue with problematic behaviors instead of letting others take responsibility for their own choices. The rescuer may act in this way because it helps him or her feel needed. The rescued person benefits because his or her problem is solved, at least temporarily.

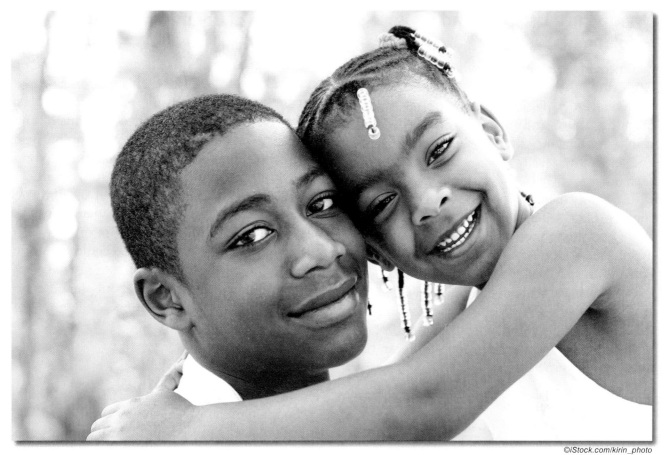
©iStock.com/kirin_photo

Figure 14.12 Siblings learn to compromise when interacting during playtime. *How could shared decision making in the family help members learn the skills of compromise?*

Codependence is destructive, however. When family members try to solve problems that really belong to others, everyone is hurt. The person who really should own the problem suffers because he or she will not learn to recognize and solve his or her own problems. As a result, this person will not grow and learn from the issue at hand. For example, if Simone fails a test, and her mother goes in to the school and makes excuses to the teacher, her mother is owning the problem, and it really is not solved. Only Simone can solve Simone's problem. She is the one who has to change her studying habits and improve. The person who should own the problem suffers in another way. He or she is likely to feel inferior and incapable. This promotes low self-esteem and even less motivation to confront issues and solve problems.

The person trying to solve others' problems also suffers. If that person acts in the codependent way often, he or she will eventually feel exhausted and burnt out. That family member will feel that he or she is always giving to others while no one is stepping up to help meet his or her needs. In addition, the problem solver will feel angry because no real change in behavior is taking place in the person with the problem. That means the problem is never really solved.

Reviewing Personal Boundaries

If you are the person who has dominating family members trying to solve your problems, you need to put an end to it and take ownership of your problem. Remind family members of your personal boundaries and that solving the problem is something *you* need to do. Use I-statements to express your own boundaries. For example, you could say, "I feel dumb when you try to solve my problems. I want to take care of this myself."

If you are the person bothered by another family member's issue and it is not a problem that you can solve, you need to review your own

personal boundaries. What is acceptable for you to do and what is not? You can also use I-statements to express your boundaries. For example, in the event of a child failing an exam, a parent can respond, "I am upset that you failed your exam, but I cannot pass the exam for you. Is there anything you would like from me to help you as you work on this problem?" You are reviewing your own boundaries, recognizing that you cannot solve the problem, and then offering support for the person as he or she solves his or her own problem.

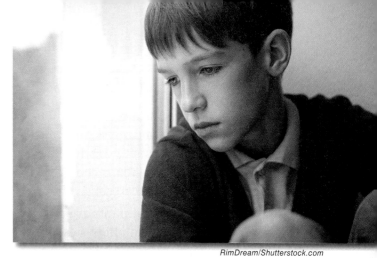
RimDream/Shutterstock.com

Figure 14.13 Scapegoating within the family can lead to low self-esteem.

The Problem with Scapegoating

Sometimes family members will not take ownership of a problem that is theirs, but will blame others instead. This practice is known as **scapegoating**. The person who gets blamed for the problem is the *scapegoat*. Family members accuse that person and at the same time defend their own actions. Because they do not claim ownership of the problem, they do not take action to change the behavior at the root of the problem.

If the same person always becomes the scapegoat, it may seem that he or she is responsible for all the family problems. If that is a family member, he or she will suffer lowered self-esteem. He or she will feel unloved and unaccepted by the family. Failures, real or imagined, cause that person to believe he or she cannot do anything right (**Figure 14.13**).

> ### Think About Your Reading
> How could learning to solve problems together help reduce family violence?

Preventing Family Violence and Abuse

Sometimes a family conflict becomes more than a disagreement. Family members become angry and lash out at each other. They may abuse each other verbally or physically. *Violence* is any physical act intended to harm another person.

Assault and Battery

The terms *assault* and *battery* are often used together to describe violent acts, but they are different. **Assault** is the threat to cause physical harm to a person. For instance, threatening someone with a weapon is assault. **Battery** is the use of force resulting in physical contact with a person that the individual did not permit. This includes physical acts of violence, such as slapping, choking, hitting, punching, kicking, and stabbing. Millions of women suffer battery from spouses or boyfriends each year. Cases of battering a husband have also been reported.

> ### Think About Your Reading
> Think of a recent news story involving family violence. How were the family relationships described?

Child Abuse

Child abuse is a serious form of family violence. **Child abuse** is any physical or mental threat or injury to a child who is under the age of 18. Thousands of children die every year from abuse, and the number of reported cases is increasing. Often, the abuse is part of a cycle. People who were abused as children often become the abusers themselves. It is important to identify what abuse is, who abuses, why they do so, and what characteristics can break the cycle. All forms of abuse have long-term effects on children.

Forms of Child Abuse

Abuse can take different forms:

- *Physical abuse.* *Physical abuse* is the intentional hurting of someone physically, causing injury. For example, punishing a child by hitting him or her with a belt is considered physical abuse because it can cause injury.

- *Shaken Baby Syndrome.* Infants are particularly vulnerable to a form of physical abuse called **Shaken Baby Syndrome**. This is brain damage caused by fast and forceful shaking, blows to the head, or dropping or throwing a child. Caregivers sometimes shake an infant in anger or because they mistakenly think shaking will stop the infant from crying. The shaking whips the infant's brain around within the skull, causing damage to the nerves because the protective tissue within the brain has not yet developed. This condition can leave an infant deaf, blind, or intellectually disabled.

- *Emotional abuse.* *Emotional abuse* includes actions by a parent or caregiver that interfere with a child's development and damage self-esteem. Emotional abuse occurs when parents constantly make demands that a child cannot meet. When parents continue to criticize a child for not meeting their expectations, the child will feel inferior and guilty.

- *Child sexual abuse.* **Child sexual abuse** includes any sexual contact or interaction between an adult and a child or teenager. This sexual interaction can be physical or nonphysical. Physical sexual abuse includes rape, as well as all forms of sexual touching. Nonphysical sexual abuse refers to actions such as exposing oneself, taking pornographic pictures of children, and using obscene language.

- *Neglect.* **Neglect** is failing to give a child proper shelter, clothing, food, medical care, supervision, love, or affection. Neglect can be either physical or emotional.

Millions of American children suffer from abuse each year. Violence at the hands of parents is a leading cause of death for children under three years of age. Many cases of neglect or abuse are not easily identified.

Signs of Child Abuse

Signs of possible physical abuse are unexplained bruises, welts, burns, fractures, joint injuries, cuts, or scrapes that repeatedly occur (**Figure 14.14**). Signs of possible emotional abuse are more varied and difficult to detect than those of physical abuse. A child who is being abused may *regress*, or go backward, in development. A child who is hostile and aggressive, or an extremely compliant child—one who does everything that is asked without any response—may be showing signs of abuse. Also, a child who is dependent, withdrawn, and portrays a poor self-image may be emotionally abused.

Signs of neglect include such behaviors as begging or stealing food, constant fatigue, or failing to attend school. A child who always arrives early at school or leaves late may have no place to go and thus be suffering from neglect. Older

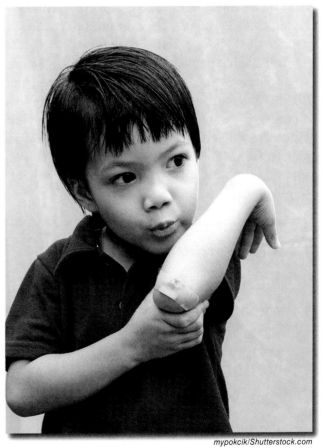

mypokcik/Shutterstock.com

Figure 14.14 An occasional mishap occurs to all growing children and does not signal physical abuse. An uncommon number or frequency of injuries may signal abuse.

children, such as teens, who are sexually involved with many partners or in trouble with the law may not be receiving needed supervision at home, indicating neglect.

Signs of sexual abuse include bedwetting, torn or stained underclothing, or difficulty walking or sitting. Frequent urinary infections or sore throats may be signs of sexual abuse as well. Along with these physical signs, children who have been sexually abused may suffer from poor self-esteem. They may withdraw socially or show a lack of emotional control. Some show fear of closeness, and others regress to childlike behaviors.

Reporting Child Abuse

All states have passed laws that require teachers, child care workers, and medical staff to report child abuse if they suspect it is happening. People are often afraid to report suspected child abuse. They may be anxious about possibly sending the abuser to jail. They may be concerned that the child will be taken away from the parents. That action does sometimes happen, especially in cases of sexual abuse. It is important to remember that *not* reporting abuse results in problems for the child because the abuser will continue to abuse. The abuse will likely get worse, and the child may be permanently harmed or even die. Abuse almost never stops on its own. The only way to really help the child is to report the suspected abuse.

Sources of Help for Child Abuse

Cases of suspected child abuse should be reported to the local police or a social service agency. During a crisis, call a hotline number or the police emergency number (**Figure 14.15**). The National Child Abuse Hotline or the website Childhelp can help a person locate the local child protective services reporting line. Help can be

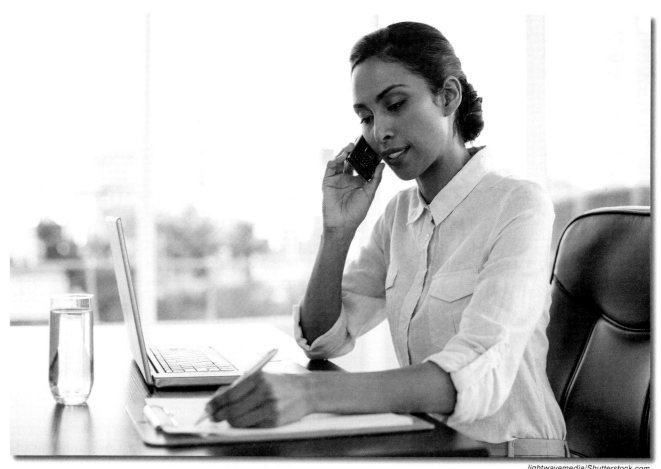

lightwavemedia/Shutterstock.com

Figure 14.15 Trained hotline personnel offer support 24 hours a day. *What skills would such personnel need in order to provide services to family members in need of help?*

obtained for the abuse victims to get away from the immediate danger of a crisis situation. The care options include the following:

- **Crisis-care centers** are safe shelters for abused children and are short-term care resources. Children may be placed in these centers for two to four days. Crisis nurseries are usually open 24 hours a day. Social workers and the courts attempt to protect abused children. State agencies provide medical care, child care services, and foster care.

- **Shelters** provide short-term safety to escape from a family crisis. The most common shelters are for women and children in abusive families.

- **Group homes**, also called *residential care*, may be available for teens or children who live in abusive families. In this arrangement, abused teens or children live in these homes along with counselors, who provide them with care and counseling.

- **Foster care** is temporary care for children under 18 years of age. A child or teen is placed with foster parents who meet state requirements. Social service agencies have to review the children's situation frequently to be sure their needs are being met.

- **Independent living** is sometimes an option for teens whose parents agree to give up legal control. This option is only suitable for mature and emotionally stable teens who can provide for themselves financially.

Think About Your Reading

Children become emotionally attached to their main caregiver, even if that person is an abusive parent. How does this make it harder to identify child abuse?

Families at Risk

Some families are more likely to suffer violence and abuse than others. Research indicates that having an abusive childhood can lead to being abusive as a parent. Unfortunately, these adults then teach their children to respond to the next generation in an abusive way.

Immaturity contributes to abusive situations as well. Adults who have not developed mature emotional and social traits may respond to problems by yelling and hitting. Parents who have low self-esteem may feel they and their children are not worth much.

Poor parenting skills are another factor. A parent may not know what behavior to expect from a child or how to guide the child properly into showing acceptable behavior. The parent may lash out in anger or frustration when a child is simply acting his or her age.

Poverty, job loss, and marriage problems increase stress in a family. Higher stress can decrease parents' abilities to handle situations calmly. Single parenthood increases stress since the parent must handle the child's guidance alone. Such situations have a higher risk of being abusive.

Substance abuse in families increases the risk. Alcohol is a depressant, and adults under the influence of alcohol may respond in ways they would not normally.

The factors just described do not *cause* child abuse; they are risk factors. The more risk factors present in a family, the greater the risk that a caregiver might lose control and engage in abusive behavior.

Think About Your Reading

What resources are available to help families who are at risk of family violence?

Breaking the Cycle

One effective deterrent to violence and abuse in the family is to strengthen the family unit (**Figure 14.16**). Good communication, decision-making, and conflict-resolution skills help break the cycle of violence from one generation to the next. Experiences that encourage family members to mature can help develop self-esteem, self-acceptance, and self-control.

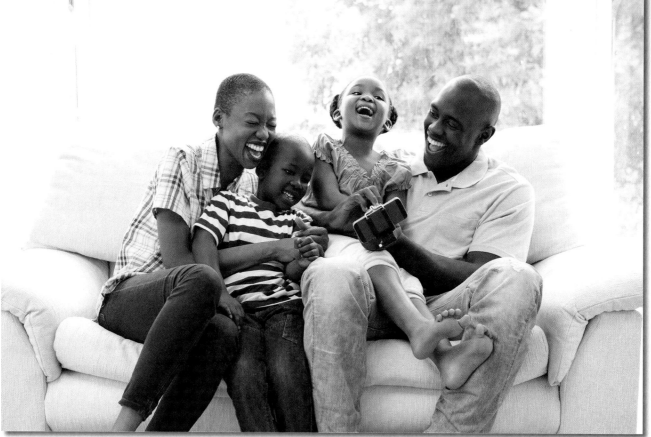

Figure 14.16 A strong family system includes several members who can help meet members' needs. *What are some skills and resources that families can use to help protect against possible family violence and abuse?*

wavebreakmedia/Shutterstock.com

Sometimes families need professional help to understand and learn from their past and work out their current problems. A professional family counselor can help families identify steps for changing patterns of violence and abuse. They can help families develop skills for resolving their problems in a nonviolent way. Other resources such as therapy programs are also available. These are sponsored by private, community, religious, or government groups. With help, the cycle can be broken.

Overcoming Victimhood

Victimhood is living as a *victim*, or a person who has been wronged, harmed, or hurt by others. Living as victims causes people to feel powerless, overcome by circumstances around them. They may struggle with anger because they do not feel they have any control over life. They may take the passive approach and avoid all possible situations in which they could get hurt.

When you have been hurt, it is important to connect with people who can help you heal.

You need to receive care and support. The people who provide support may be professional counselors, or they can be good friends or family members who are able to listen and encourage you to learn from the past, grow as a person, and move forward. Their support should help you regain confidence, build self-esteem, focus on growth, and renew feelings that you can make a difference, you do have choices, and you can take responsibility for what lies ahead.

Lesson 14.3

Assess

Comprehension Check

1. List four strategies that will help families deal with conflict.
2. Name one benefit of family members using compromise to resolve their arguments.
3. List two negative effects of scapegoating on family members.
4. Identify four common forms of child abuse.

CHAPTER SUMMARY

Families are systems because interactions within them are multiple and complex. Family interactions tend to be private and long-lasting in their effects on individual family members. The family identifies expectations for each member's roles and the rights and responsibilities that go with each role. The family balances various roles to carry out its functions. When something causes a member's role to change, families need to adapt to make the family system balanced again.

Throughout the family life cycle, the needs of family members and expectations for their roles will change. Skills for communicating clearly, making decisions together, and resolving their conflicts will help families adjust to these changes. Family leisure activities help bring family members together. The family unit will be strengthened as bonds between members grow and a sense of family identity increases.

Healthy interpersonal skills can help families avoid violence and abuse among family members. When signs of abuse exist, families need help changing patterns of interaction so that the needs of family members can be met.

VOCABULARY ACTIVITIES

1. Categorize each of the following terms except *family system*. After you have categorized them, explain what all the terms in each category have in common in terms of the family system.

Content Terms

assault (14.3)
battery (14.3)
child abuse (14.3)
child sexual abuse (14.3)
codependent (14.3)
crisis-care center (14.3)
democratic decision making (14.2)
family routine (14.2)
family system (14.1)

family tradition (14.2)
foster care (14.3)
free society (14.1)
group home (14.3)
independent living (14.3)
neglect (14.3)
scapegoating (14.3)
Shaken Baby Syndrome (14.3)
shelter (14.3)
victimhood (14.3)

2. Write a brief paragraph about the family system that includes each of the following terms, used correctly.

Academic Terms

absorb (14.1)
consider (14.2)
impending (14.2)

interrelated (14.1)
regress (14.3)
resent (14.3)

ASSESS

Your Knowledge

3. List two rights and two corresponding responsibilities of family members. What role does each family member fulfill?
4. Name three skills that can help a family break a cycle of violence.
5. Describe some signs in children of physical abuse, emotional abuse, sexual abuse, and neglect.

Your Understanding

6. Describe what it means when we say the family functions as a system and give an example.
7. How would scapegoating affect the family system?
8. Explain the key steps in resolving conflicts among family members.

Your Skills

9. What are some steps you could take to help your family plan a vacation using democratic decision-making skills?
10. Write a scenario in which a family member uses active listening to help diffuse anger and restore balance to a family system.
11. Prepare a plan, following the example in Figure 4.5 earlier in this text, that could help a family with teens build strong relationships in the family.

CRITICAL THINKING

12. **Compare and Contrast.** Prepare a set of survey questions to ask teens and adults about the rights of a child, parent, and grandparent in a family. Prepare another set of questions to ask about teens' views on the responsibilities of various family members. Survey five teens and five adults and record their answers. Write a paragraph describing the similarities and differences between the teens' and adults' views. *Group option*: Complete the activity with a partner or in a small group. *Choice*: Present your findings in a skit or rap.
13. **Make Inferences.** Write a paragraph describing and identifying how your family balances the rights, responsibilities, and roles of various family members to maintain balance in the family system. *Choice*: Present your information in an alternative format, such as a song, rap, poem, drawing, picture, video, or presentation.
14. **Make Inferences.** Working in a team with three or four classmates from families of different cultures, discuss the relationships that exist in each teammate's family. How do your teammates

relate to their parents and siblings? How do the other members in your teammates' families relate? As a group, write a two-page paper comparing your family relationships. Make inferences about what family relationships might be typical in your respective cultures. Provide specific examples from your findings to support those inferences and analyze how cultural backgrounds influence family relationships and functions.

CORE SKILLS

15. **Reading, Writing.** Read three articles that describe strategies for dealing with conflict in the family. Summarize the recommendations from these articles and compare them with strategies in the text. Make a judgment on the potential success of the strategies, citing evidence to support your evaluation. Remember to cite all sources used. *Group option*: Work with a team of three, each person reviewing one article, and collaborate on your final summary. *Choice*: Present your findings in a digital presentation to the class or post on your class website.

16. **Research, Writing.** Using the Internet, research and prepare a report on one area of violence and abuse in the family. Describe the methods of communication, decision making, and conflict handling related to this area of violence. Identify resources available in your community for victims of violence and abuse. *Choice*: Present your information in a flyer or poster for your classmates' reference.

17. **Writing.** Interview a counselor who works with family members in abusive situations. Ask questions to identify the challenges that people have to overcome when exposed to abuse in their family. Write a scenario describing a person dealing with some of these challenges and their strategies for building positive family relationships.

18. **Research, Writing.** Contact a crisis-care center in your community. Find out what its policies are, whom it serves, what services it provides, and when and how it refers calls to other sources of help. Present this information in a report to the class.

19. **Writing.** Using digital tools, draw a diagram with a different block representing each person in your family. Use arrows to indicate all the possible interaction patterns that could exist between family members. Count the arrows to determine the total number of interactions. Analyze how this number could affect the relationships among your family members. Write a paragraph describing your

findings and cite evidence from the text to support your analysis. *Choice*: Compare your findings with a partner for similarities and differences.

20. **Research, Math, Writing.** Using a spreadsheet, prepare a checklist of at least 20 leisure activities in which families might participate. Survey your class to identify how many families participate in each activity. Write a paragraph describing your findings. *Choice*: Use software to prepare a bar graph, indicating what percentage of your class participates in each leisure activity.

21. **Math, Writing.** Gather data from 10 classmates regarding the total number of interaction patterns that exist in their families. Using a digital device, develop a scatter plot to present the number of classmates with each number of interaction patterns. Write a summary of your information, including the average number of interaction patterns existing in the families of the students surveyed. *Choice*: Explain how increased interaction patterns affect the family system.

22. **Research, Writing.** Use the Internet to locate a technology-based game that family members can play together to build communication, decision-making, or problem-solving skills. Create a report describing how this game could build these skills and what specific age levels the game targets.

CAREER READINESS

23. **Investigating Career Requirements.** Research a career related to providing support to children who have experienced abuse (for example, pediatric psychiatrist, child psychiatrist, child psychologist, and child and family therapist). Find out what education and training a person needs to pursue this career. Research the kinds of work done by someone with that career and explain how this work can help stop the cycle of abuse in families. Prepare a report that presents your findings. *Choice*: Compile a list of organizations in your community that employ people with this career. Present those findings along with your report.

24. **Planning Programs for Families.** Assume you are an employee of an organization that provides leisure programs for families. You have been assigned the task of researching the needs in your community for additional leisure programs that could be offered. Complete the research and prepare a report for your employer indicating what programs you would recommend and the rationale for why those programs would benefit the families in your community.

Reading Prep

Arrange a study session to read the chapter aloud with a classmate. At the end of each lesson, discuss any words you do not know. Take notes of words you would like to discuss in class.

Key Questions

Questions to answer as you study this chapter:

- What are the effects of a crisis on individuals and families?
- How can a crisis be prevented?
- How can crises be managed?
- How can a family in crisis restore balance to the family system?

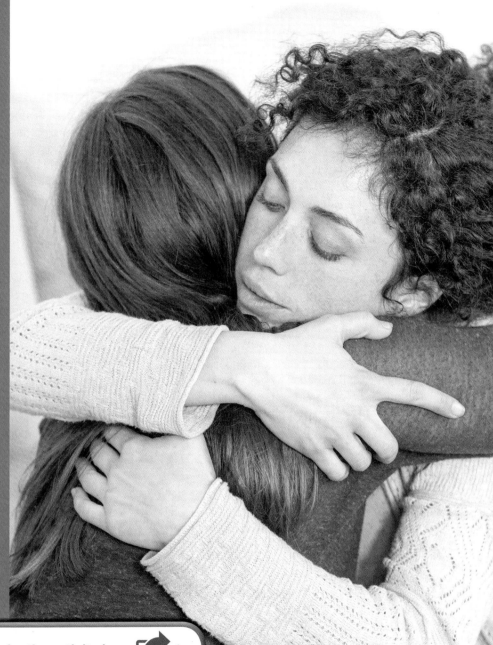

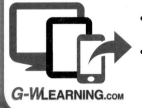 While studying this chapter, look for the activity icon to:

- **build** vocabulary with e-flash cards, matching activities, and vocabulary games; and
- **assess** what you learn by completing the lesson comprehension checks online.
  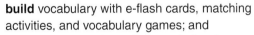 www.g-wlearning.com/humanservices/

Adam Gregor/Shutterstock.com

AFTER STUDYING THIS CHAPTER, YOU WILL

KNOW:

- What can cause a crisis.
- The stages of the grieving process.
- What resources can help individuals and families handle stress and avoid a potential crisis.

UNDERSTAND:

- How crises affect the family system.
- How individuals and families can prevent crises.
- How individuals and families can cope with crises.

BE ABLE TO DO:

- Manage stress in your life.
- Locate resources to help families cope with crises.

GETTING STARTED

Glenda put her hand to her head as she tried to sit up in bed. Where was she? She started to call out, but feelings of nausea overtook her. As Glenda's body started to shake, a nurse hurried over and lowered her back onto the bed. Glenda's parents stood by her bedside, too nervous to talk.

Glenda's family was in a crisis. Glenda had nearly died from a drug overdose. Fortunately, she had been saved. When the police were called to break up a loud party, they found Glenda unconscious and rushed her to the hospital. She was not merely sleeping, as her friends had thought.

When Glenda's parents were called, they were shocked. This really isn't happening, is it? they thought. For a few hours, they feared Glenda might die. Now that she had finally regained consciousness, they had mixed emotions. They were relieved, yet angry and hurt. Why did she do it? Were they somehow to blame? Even worse, would she do this again?

Families experience many changes in life. Most of them are minor enough for family members to deal with them. These changes are only stressful enough to motivate family members to take action. A crisis can happen, however, when individuals and families experience so much stress that members are unable to carry out regular functions. These crises can be very disruptive to family life and disturbing to family members. Families can learn ways to come together to handle these crises and the resulting effects. Sometimes those approaches include getting outside help.

LESSON 15.1

THE IMPACT OF CRISES ON INDIVIDUALS AND FAMILIES

Content Terms

Build Vocab

crisis
stressor
pileup effect
grief
alienated

Academic Terms

state
stage

Objectives

After studying this lesson, you will be able to

- **identify** four categories of life events that might lead to a crisis.
- **explain** how a crisis affects individuals and families.
- **relate** feelings during a loss to the grieving process.

Focus Your Reading

1. As you read, list and categorize the ways that a crisis affects individuals and families.
2. List events that currently are stressors in your life. Then analyze Figure 15.2 to see if any of the items on your list are in the diagram.

A **crisis** is a life experience or event affecting an individual, family, community, or society that could lead to an unstable or dangerous situation (**Figure 15.1**). Examples are a loss of a job, a fire in the family home, a major illness, or a divorce. Such events usually require people to make major changes in their lives to return to a healthful, balanced *state*, or condition. Life events that cause stress and might lead to a crisis are called **stressors**. Whether these stressors lead to a crisis depends on four factors:

- the nature of the event itself
- the number of stressful events experienced at the same time
- how people identify and interpret the event
- the resources available to manage the stressful event

Events That Cause Crises

The following four categories of major events often cause crises for individuals and families:

- *Devastating events that cause a great loss.* Events that cause great losses, such as the death of a family member, are

368

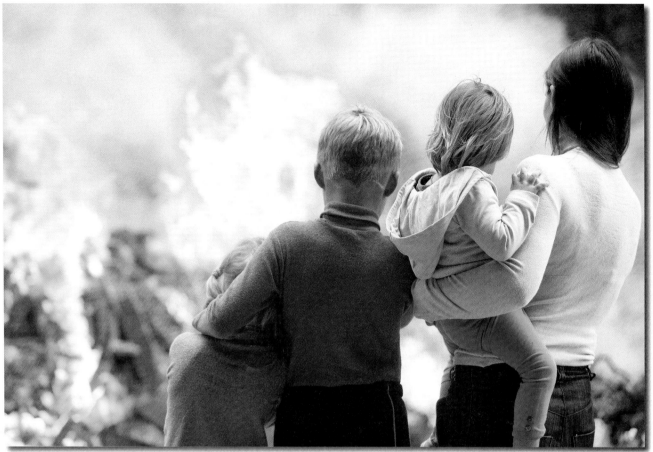

Figure 15.1 Some crises-producing events are life threatening and affect all the members in the family. *What other major events do you think could result in a family crisis?*

Vadim Ratnikov/Shutterstock.com

more likely to lead to crises than are those that cause small losses.

- *Very stressful events that impact many family members.* A stressful event that affects several or all the members in a family, such as a divorce, is very likely to produce a crisis.

- *Sudden, important events.* When an event is unexpected, such as a car accident that leaves a family member seriously injured, individuals and families have no time to prepare for the change. That can turn the event into a crisis if the event also causes serious problems. If the individuals and family also have no previous experience with such a change, they often feel the situation is out of control.

- *Events requiring major adjustments.* Events that require little or no change are less likely to result in crises than those that require

major adjustments, such as the destruction of the family home in a natural disaster.

Think About Your Reading

Why can hurricane damage to the family home be a crisis-producing event in a family?

Crises can also result when several changes occur at the same time or very close in time to each other (**Figure 15.2**). Each of these events may in itself be too small to produce a significant loss, but the stress from each event continues to build, producing a **pileup effect**. The end result is a crisis. For example, the stress from poor grades on a test, an argument with a friend, conflict with parents, and pressure from peers can all pile up and lead to an unstable situation for the teen involved.

The Pileup Effect

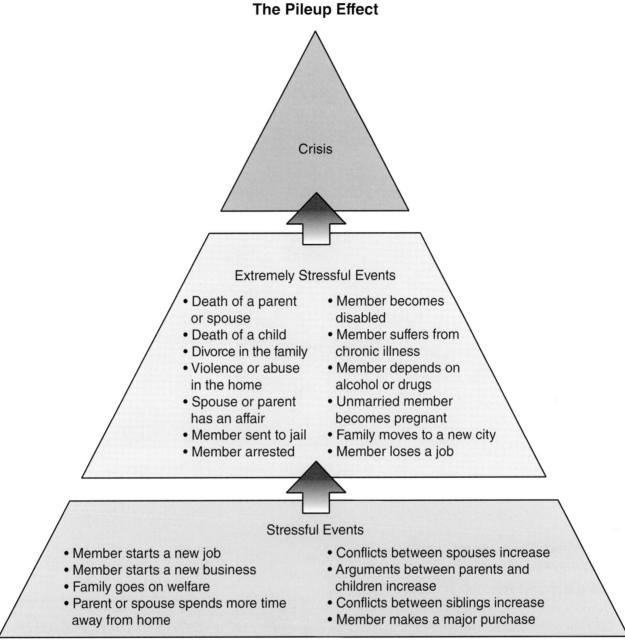

Crisis

Extremely Stressful Events

- Death of a parent or spouse
- Death of a child
- Divorce in the family
- Violence or abuse in the home
- Spouse or parent has an affair
- Member sent to jail
- Member arrested

- Member becomes disabled
- Member suffers from chronic illness
- Member depends on alcohol or drugs
- Unmarried member becomes pregnant
- Family moves to a new city
- Member loses a job

Stressful Events

- Member starts a new job
- Member starts a new business
- Family goes on welfare
- Parent or spouse spends more time away from home

- Conflicts between spouses increase
- Arguments between parents and children increase
- Conflicts between siblings increase
- Member makes a major purchase

Figure 15.2 Many life events bring changes and increase stress for individuals and families. The combined stress of several events at the same time can lead to a crisis.

How Crises Affect Individuals and Families

A crisis that chiefly affects one individual can also be a crisis for the family. Every member in a family affects every other member. While the effects of a crisis depend on the type of event, effects of crises can be grouped into two categories: imbalance in the family system and loss of family functions.

Systems Become Unbalanced

Remember that when the family is functioning smoothly, it is *balanced*. Each member carries out his or her roles. The family works together to meet the needs of each member, fulfilling its functions in each member's life.

When individuals are functioning in a healthy state, they are able to fulfill their individual roles, provide self-care, and meet their own needs and the needs of others who might depend on them.

Their physical, intellectual, social, and emotional needs are balanced with the resources available to meet them.

In a crisis, one or more changes disrupt balance in a system. Individual family members are unable to fill their roles. Suddenly, the family is not functioning smoothly as a unit. Needs are not being met. Individuals and families need time, resources, and support to adjust to the changes that produced the crisis and restore balance.

A Loss Affects Individual and Family Functions

Most crises situations involve some type of loss. The loss may be the permanent or temporary removal of a family member from the family, the loss of an individual's skills or abilities, the loss of a job, lost or reduced income, or loss of or damage to a home. Whatever the loss, individuals and family members need to cope with it, adjust to it, and return to normal functioning as quickly as possible.

A loss usually hinders an individual's or family's ability to fulfill normal functions, at least for a period of time. For example, the function of reproducing and socializing children is hindered by illness, divorce, hospitalization, or loss of a family member. A job loss could hinder an individual's ability to take care of his or her responsibilities, such as paying rent or making car payments. A natural disaster could affect the family's ability to meet all members' physical needs. The function of assigning roles in a family may be hampered by any crisis that prevents members from carrying out their roles. Finally, the family's ability to carry out the function of providing close relationships and intimacy may be hindered by a death, divorce, or a move away from relatives (**Figure 15.3**).

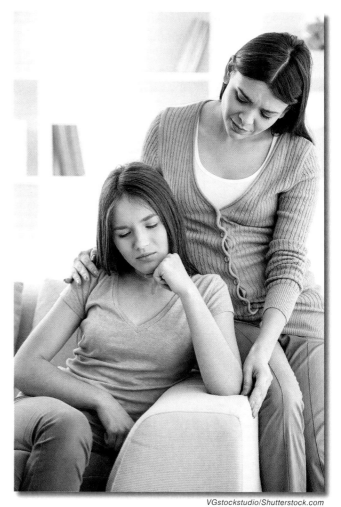

VGstockstudio/Shutterstock.com

Figure 15.3 Crises can hinder family members' abilities to meet one another's social and emotional needs.

The Grieving Process

When individuals and families experience a loss, they typically go through a grieving process. When they reach the end of that process and can identify and accept the loss, they will be able to handle the changes resulting from the loss and go on with their lives.

When experiencing **grief**, individuals may pass through certain emotional *stages*, or steps in a process. First, they may deny the loss, with an attitude that says, "This isn't really happening." Next, they often experience feelings of anger, expressed by statements such as "Why is this happening to me?" This may be followed by feelings of guilt, as they think, *What did I do to cause this?* To try and get rid of these feelings, they may blame

---

Think About Your Reading

In a crisis, why is it important that individuals and families have access to resources that can help them return to a balanced individual state or family system?

---

others for the problem, thinking ideas such as *If his boss were nicer, he wouldn't have been fired.* At this point, they may feel sorry for themselves, thinking, *I'm miserable about this.* These feelings may lead to depression, with an attitude of "I can't do anything to fix this."

All these feelings are normal responses when grieving. It is important, however, that individuals and families move on to the final stage of the grieving process. That is, they have to accept the reality of the loss. Acceptance is reflected in an attitude that says, "This has happened to our family, and we are sad, but we can and will move on." Acceptance is needed so individuals and families can take steps to adjust to the changes brought about by the loss. Families need to work so individual needs are met and the functions of the family can once again be carried out. Roles may need to be adjusted. Financial resources or help from others may be needed. Acceptance enables the family to take action to restore balance in the family system.

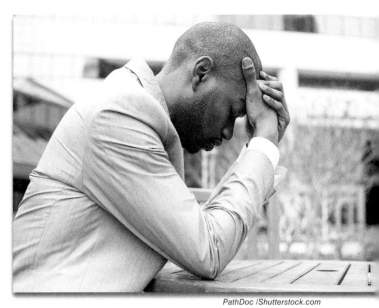

PathDoc /Shutterstock.com

Figure 15.4   When individuals cannot adjust to a loss, they often find it difficult to carry out daily tasks. *How could this lead to additional crises in the family?*

Think About Your Reading

What strengths can help individuals and family members move through the grieving process to acceptance?

Unhealthy Adjustment Patterns

If individuals and families do not adjust, they may develop unhealthy behavior patterns (**Figure 15.4**). Feelings of anger, blame, and guilt will continue. Individuals may feel depressed. They may stop eating, withdraw from others, or fail to show up at work. They may abuse alcohol or other drugs to cover up their feelings or dull the pain. In anger, they may lash out and abuse family members, friends, coworkers, and others they see on a daily basis.

When the family does not function normally, the physical and mental health of members may suffer. Parents may ignore their parental responsibilities. As a result, children may be neglected,

malnourished, or abused. Children's emotional development will suffer if they do not experience love and acceptance. They may feel **alienated**—alone, without hope, or cut off from others who care. Feeling alienated is a major factor in teen suicide. Responding to crises with unhealthy behavior patterns may hinder the growth and development of family members and cause serious long-term results. Developing skills for preventing and adjusting to crises is important for all family members.

Lesson 15.1

Assess

Comprehension Check

1. Explain how stressors can bring on a crisis for individuals and families.
2. List four types of crisis-producing events.
3. Briefly describe how the pileup effect may result in a crisis.
4. Briefly explain how a loss can hinder individuals and families in their ability to fulfill normal functions.
5. Identify four emotional stages that are experienced during the grieving process.

Objectives

After studying this lesson, you will be able to

- **determine** if sources of stress are internal or external.
- **identify** strategies for managing family stress.
- **recognize** factors that help individuals and families prevent crises.

Focus Your Reading

1. Outline ways individuals and families can prevent a crisis.
2. List examples of internal and external stress in your own life.

Content Terms

Build Vocab

internal stress
external stress

Academic Terms

hectic
optimistic
reserve

Individuals who are prepared to adjust to and handle stress-producing life events are more likely to be resilient and bounce back from the impacts of stressors. Strategies for managing individual stress and building positive attitudes are discussed in Chapter 3. Strategies for solving problems are discussed in Chapter 7.

Handling Stress in Group Situations

Stress can occur in any setting where change occurs and individuals and families are required to adapt to the change. Individuals and families who practice skills for managing personal stress and building positive attitudes will be more able to solve problems and manage stress in group situations as well. They use the following strategies to help prevent problems and crises:

- Identify sources of the stress.
- Foster good interaction skills with others in the group and collaborate to find solutions to manage the stress.
- Reduce the amount of stress or the effects of the stress.
- Use outside resources to help handle the stress and its effects.

Various groups will have different resources for managing stress and preventing a crisis. On the job, work groups will have

team members with different areas of expertise for assisting the team, identifying and managing stress, and adjusting to changes. Work groups also will have a supervisor or boss who may provide additional resources to help the team meet its goals.

Family groups also need to use the above steps to prevent stress from producing a crisis situation. In this process, families experience additional pressure, as they are responsible for the health and well-being of individual family members. The techniques that are discussed in this lesson apply both to families and to other interpersonal groups in a community.

Identifying the Source of Stress

Identifying the exact source of stress can be hard for a family or group. Sometimes the stress comes from within the family or group.

At other times, the stress is from outside sources (**Figure 15.5**).

Internal Stress

Stress that comes from inside a family or group is called **internal stress**. There are two main sources of this type of stress:

- *Normal growth and development.* Internal stress from normal growth and development takes place slowly over time. For example, adolescents may continually ask for a little more independence. Parents may then feel frustrated by these demands, but not recognize the exact cause of their frustration. Because the cause of the stress is not identified and addressed, each new request for independence puts more strain on a family.

- *Unresolved conflicts.* Internal stress resulting from unresolved conflicts continues to

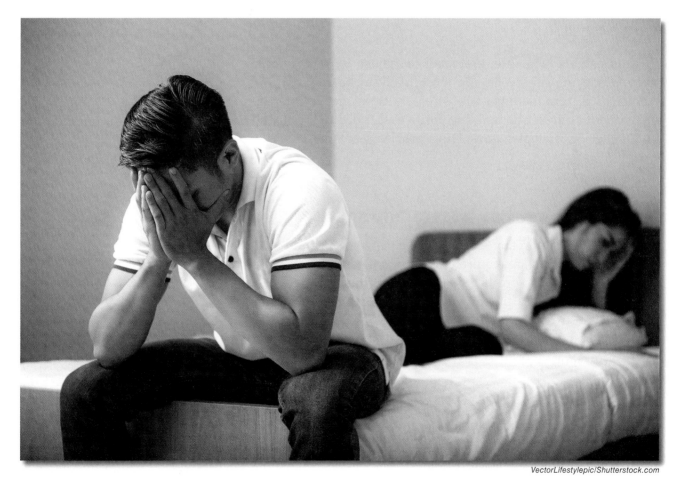

VectorLifestylepic/Shutterstock.com

Figure 15.5 Stress from outside sources may increase tension in the family. *How could the closing of a local factory result in a crisis for a community?*

374 Unit 5 Family Relationships

Copyright Goodheart-Willcox Co., Inc.

build tension in a family or group. When old conflicts are not resolved, new problems add to the already existing stress.

Internal sources of stress are more likely to cause the pileup effect, building into a crisis situation. Arguments and fighting then become more frequent. The good communication that could help group members identify and decrease the stress does not take place. One or more members of a family may experience headaches, colds, sleeplessness, and other physical problems because of the stressful situation. Family members may take more medication to try to handle their problems. The source of the stress then becomes even harder to identify. Sometimes families need to seek help from a professional counselor to identify the real source of internal stress.

External Stress

Stress caused by factors outside the family is known as **external stress**. Pressures from work, a natural disaster, or war are all examples of external sources of stress. External stressors that produce crises usually come quickly and without notice. They are likely to affect the whole family and sometimes whole communities.

External stressors are usually easier for family and group members to identify than internal stressors. In external stress, family members can see the stress-producing event as a threat to the family unit (**Figure 15.6**). Finding a solution to

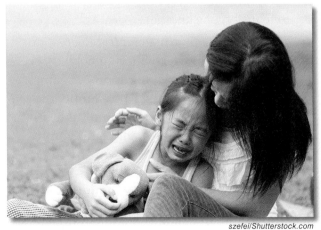

szefei/Shutterstock.com

Figure 15.6 When stress can be readily identified, it can be easier to address and resolve.

which all family members agree can be easier when the source of stress is outside the family, too. Some external stressors, such as a natural disaster that destroys a home, can be very significant, and the family may take a long time to recover.

Think About Your Reading

What are some normal sources of internal stress during adolescence?

Managing Stress

Families and groups learn to manage stress in two ways. First, they may reduce the amount of stress they experience at one time. Second, they may reduce the effects that stress has on them. By managing stress and its effects, individuals and families can help prevent problems and crises.

Reducing the Amount of Stress

Living in a busy society makes it hard for families and groups to reduce the amount of stress they experience. Nevertheless, choosing to reduce the stress in your life will contribute to the health and well-being of you and your family. There are several ways to reduce the amount of stress in your life:

- *Remove the source of stress.* Sometimes it is hard to identify any one cause of the increasing stress in a family group. Families may need to make several small changes to reduce the total stress. Members may change their schedules so they are less *hectic* (busy or chaotic). They may choose to work different hours or attend fewer meetings. They may buy a tool or appliance to make tasks faster and easier or hire outside help. They may shop online rather than go from store to store. By making several small changes, they can reduce the total amount of stress.

- *Remove members from the source of the stress.* Sometimes a family chooses to remove all the members from a stressful source affecting one or a few members

(**Figure 15.7**). For example, a family might move away from a dangerous neighborhood.

- *Break down the stressor into smaller parts.* Sometimes a family or group is able to break down the source of stress into smaller, easier-to-handle parts. For instance, a strain on family finances can be stressful for all members. Breaking financial needs into smaller categories makes it easier for the family to identify ways to handle each area of needs. As each area is addressed, the progress contributes toward reducing the larger stressor. Responsibilities for addressing smaller parts of the problem may be divided among members as well.

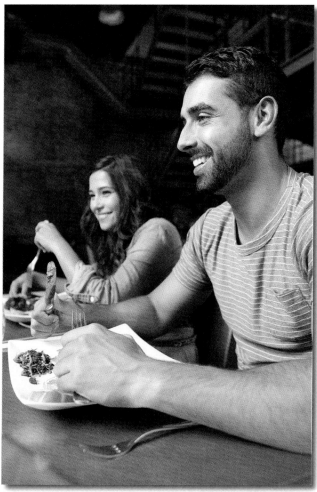

Joana Lopes/Shutterstock.com

Figure 15.7 Taking the family to a favorite restaurant to eat could remove family members from a source of stress. *What might be some examples of stressors family members are avoiding by eating out together?*

Think About Your Reading

Is it easier to reduce the amount of stress from some sources more than others?

Reducing the Effects of Stress

At times, families and groups are not able to reduce stress. Instead, interactions increase the stress. Communication breaks down. Members do not share their thoughts and feelings as readily as before. They respond with less sensitivity to others' feelings and worries or react more quickly with anger. Stressful events lead to more stress in the family unless steps are taken to change such responses. There are several strategies for reducing the effects of stress:

- *Change responses to stressful events to positive, healthful ones.* A little humor may help lighten a tense situation. Laughter can help everyone relax. Another way to change the response is to make sure that everyone is eating a healthful meal. A positive approach can help everyone feel reassured that the family or group can handle the stressful event.

- *Set aside time to communicate.* Finding a quiet place away from a normal setting to talk can help members speak honestly, listen to one another, and answer questions. Finding this quiet place may mean turning off all phones for a short time. Eliminating the possibility of interruptions allows members to focus on one another.

- *Take part in a family activity.* Recreation can help reduce stress. Sharing hobbies, exercising together, or playing sports or games are all activities that the whole family can enjoy. These provide an outlet for reducing the effects of stress and build family unity (**Figure 15.8**).

Many of these responses are not what people normally do when under stress, but they can be very helpful. Such responses help families and groups manage the effects of stress and maintain balance.

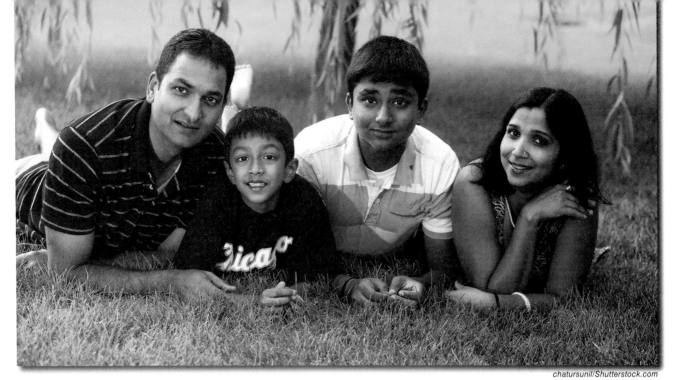

Figure 15.8 Time spent together can build family unity and help reduce the effects of stress on the family.

Copyright Goodheart-Willcox Co., Inc.

Think About Your Reading
What routines would you recommend for a family with a lot of stress?

Developing Individual and Family Resources

What resources can help individuals, families, and groups handle stress with resilience and avoid a potential crisis? A positive view of life, financial resources, personal characteristics, interpersonal skills, strong family support, and the help of friends or community groups all aid individuals and families in times of crisis.

An Optimistic Viewpoint

Your viewpoint can make a difference in whether life experiences, however difficult, become crises or are seen as manageable problems. Sometimes the difference can be the way individuals and families look at the situation. An *optimistic* view of life, in which you look at events positively, can help individuals and families handle change. With a positive attitude, even extreme changes and big problems look like challenges that can be met rather than like problems that are insurmountable.

Financial Resources

Financial resources can help individuals, families, and groups handle crisis events (**Figure 15.9**). Having and following a savings plan can build a financial *reserve*, or emergency fund, that will help during times of disaster or loss of income. Insurance plans can protect against large losses of income or property. Financial resources can be used to obtain counseling to help with internal stresses as well.

Personal Characteristics

The personal characteristics of flexibility and commitment help people manage stress. Individuals and families will handle stress better and avoid a crisis if they are flexible and able to adjust. *Flexibility* is a personal characteristic that is seen when people are willing and able to adapt to change. That willingness helps individuals and families be resilient as they adjust to changing roles and find new ways to balance personal and family needs. Flexibility can also help people adapt to new demands being placed on them, whether individually or as a group.

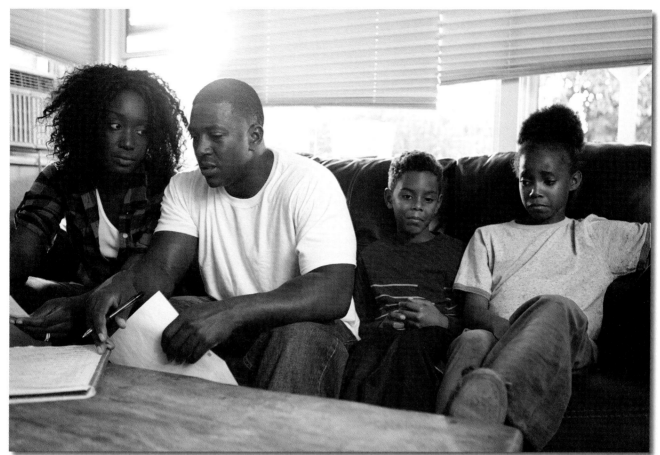

Monkey Business Images/Shutterstock.com

Figure 15.9 Having adequate financial resources can relieve the stress from events like unemployment. *What other situations can you think of where money in savings could help reduce stress in your life?*

Family members need to be committed to meeting one another's needs and showing support and encouragement. They need to show love and affection for one another, thus fulfilling emotional needs in the family. In fact, showing love and affection can be particularly important in a stressful situation, when family members may feel alone or afraid. Finally, family members need to be willing to make choices that consider the well-being of others in the family. Such commitment will maintain family members' self-esteem and help them stick together to find solutions to family problems.

Think About Your Reading

Why is it hard for families with a lot of internal stressors to consider the well-being of others around them?

Interpersonal Skills

Three types of skills are important to handling stress: communication skills, decision-making skills, and negotiation skills. Good communication skills need to be practiced all the time. Then, when changes occur, individuals and families will be able to share personal thoughts and feelings without offending or hurting others. They will use good listening skills to make sure that clear and accurate messages are being sent and received.

Positive communication between family members can maintain self-esteem in each member and a sense of family unity. When stress occurs, family members can use these skills to encourage and support each other. Hearing the support from loved ones will increase each family member's confidence in the family's ability to adjust.

By regularly making decisions together in situations that are not crises, families and groups set good patterns for decision making under stress.

As they take time to listen to each other, they encourage input from each other. They know how to identify and evaluate their alternatives and can use this skill to solve a problem. They know how to develop a plan of action and divide tasks among the members to carry it out. As a result of working together on making the decision, each member feels important and more willing to help the group handle the stressful life event.

As families and groups resolve conflicts through negotiation and compromise, they build mutual respect among members. They learn to take ownership of their problems. They learn to work together to reach solutions that benefit all concerned. They learn to be group-oriented rather than self-oriented. In times of stress, they can use these skills to resolve problems that could build into crises situations.

Family Support

Family members can build strong support for each other. They do this by spending time together, taking part in leisure activities, celebrating special events, and starting their own traditions (**Figure 15.10**). They create their own history together. Strong bonds between the members can help a family work together to handle stressful life events. The family members are committed to helping one another grow and succeed. They build one another's self-esteem and help one another feel capable of handling problems. They

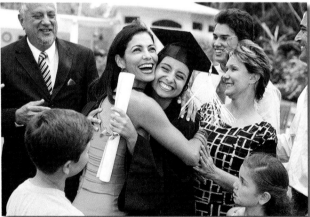

Monkey Business Images/Shutterstock.com

Figure 15.10 Celebrating special events helps family members build strong bonds that serve as a resource in times of stress. *What other activities can families do to strengthen bonds between family members?*

stick together, providing love and affection, companionship, and emotional support to one another.

Think About Your Reading

Why is it that strong and healthy families have the best chance of restoring balance to their family system in a crisis?

Friendships and Community Support Groups

Involvement in a community can result in strong support from friends and neighbors. In times of stressful life events, friends can offer encouragement and understanding. Some can provide direct assistance, such as help with child care.

Community support groups are especially helpful because the people in these groups often have experienced similar situations. Such support groups can help individuals and family members understand their feelings and identify their needs. Support groups can offer a listening ear and provide someone to talk to about the changes individuals and family members are undergoing and how to handle them. With the support these groups provide, individuals and families are encouraged to believe they can handle the problems facing them. Sometimes a community group includes professionals who are qualified to provide information specific to a family's situation. In addition, they can help individuals and family members develop skills for handling the changes they are experiencing.

LESSON 15.2

Assess

COMPREHENSION CHECK

1. Explain the difference between internal and external stress.
2. List three ways families can reduce the amount of stress they experience.
3. List three ways that family members can reduce the effects of stress.
4. Explain how five different resources can help individuals and families prevent stress from leading to a crisis.

LESSON 15.3

MANAGING CRISES

Content Terms

Build Vocab

coping behavior
chronic illness
disability
mental disorder
learning disorder
autism spectrum disorder
assistive technology
substance abuse

Academic Terms

inconvenient
implement
phobia

Objectives

After studying this lesson, you will be able to

- **identify** strategies to manage a crisis or problem.
- **evaluate** individual and family coping skills.
- **identify** community resources that aid individuals and families in crisis situations.

Focus Your Reading

1. Prepare a chart with two columns. In the first column, list four behaviors that families can use to cope with a crisis. In the other column, give an example of each behavior being applied in a family coping with a drug-abuse crisis.
2. List examples of coping behaviors that would strengthen the family unit. Contrast with examples of behaviors that harm the family unit.

Even the most well-prepared individuals and families will experience some crisis-producing events during their lives. Chronic illness, the death of a loved one, drug or alcohol abuse, and unemployment are examples of crises that many individuals and families face. Often, these events occur suddenly, without time for preparation. They will be unexpected and *inconvenient*, or coming at a bad time. Most likely, the family will not have prior experience dealing with them. As you will recall from Lesson 15.1, all those factors mean that these events are likely to cause a crisis.

Responding to a Crisis or Problem

When a crisis or problem occurs, individuals and families need to use coping behavior to manage the situation. **Coping behavior** is planned behavior that helps persons adjust as quickly as possible to changes that have taken place. Notice the word *planned*. Planning for coping behavior requires a logical process. This is the key to useful individual and family responses. The chart in

Figure 15.11 lists four strategies that individuals and families can use to cope with and manage a crisis or problem. These include understanding the situation, seeking solutions to the problem, strengthening the family unit, and emphasizing personal growth.

Coping Behaviors to Manage a Crisis
Understand the situation.
• Ask what changes have taken or will take place. • Identify how individuals and the family are affected. • Use good communication skills. • Seek professionals who can provide information.
Seek solutions to the problem.
• Ask what can be done to handle the changes. • Keep a tolerant attitude. • Do not blame others for the problem. • Avoid the use of drugs and alcohol as coping aids. • Be open and flexible. • Look for a solution that benefits all involved. • Identify available resources in the family and community.
Strengthen relationships and the family unit.
• Set aside quiet, uninterrupted times to talk. • Share thoughts and feelings openly. • Accept each other's thoughts and feelings. • Encourage each other. • Take time for friend and family leisure activities.
Emphasize personal growth for all involved.
• Encourage all members to pursue individual interests. • Keep involved with friends and community. • Set goals for the future. • Make plans to reach personal and family goals.

Figure 15.11 Coping behaviors are positive steps that family members can take to manage a crisis. *What interpersonal skills are used in all four of these steps?*

Personal Coping Behavior

High self-esteem, positive self-concept, and positive life attitudes can help you believe in your own ability to adjust. These qualities will help you be resilient and look for ways to achieve personal growth with each experience. Flexibility can help you make the needed adjustments.

Your skills for communicating with others can help you build and maintain friendships. Friends will encourage you through hard times. They can help you relax as you spend leisure time with them. They can also encourage you to stay active in your community.

Your personal management skills are also important resources. You can learn to manage both your time and your money. Your problem-solving skills can help you find solutions when problems arise. They may lead you to community and government resources that are available in times of crises. All these resources can strengthen you to cope with changes that will affect you and your family.

Family Coping Behaviors

Coping behavior helps the family stabilize so it can again fulfill its functions within the lives of family members. As family members take steps to identify and *implement*, or carry out, a solution, they need an attitude of tolerance for one another. This requires them to keep open lines of communication and flexibility and do whatever needs to be done to cope with a crisis. Coping behavior also takes a commitment from members to find a solution that benefits everyone in the family.

In a crisis, the family's own interactions can be the most valuable resource for coping. Actions that encourage the growth of family members and strengthen the family unit are important. Healthy, growing family members are more likely to succeed at working together to solve problems.

Think About Your Reading

Why is it important to practice the behaviors that you will need in a crisis situation before a crisis occurs?

Using an Emergency Plan

All families should develop an emergency plan they can use in the event of a sudden disaster that threatens the home or that can occur when family members are in different locations. The plan should include steps for communicating with each other, a safe place for meeting, and a plan for getting all members together. Sample emergency plans are available at the Ready website run by the U.S. Department of Homeland Security.

Technology can greatly enhance a family's ability to communicate in an emergency or a family crisis. It can do this in the following ways:

- Phone calls, text messages, e-mail, and social media can all be used to let family and friends know that you are in a crisis situation. To be prepared, you need to have your contacts up-to-date (**Figure 15.12**). You might want to make a family list serve so you can send a quick message to everyone at once, saving time.

- Program into your phone a number to use in case of an emergency and clearly label the number as such. This might be the number of a parent or guardian. First responders will then know whom to contact quickly if you are not conscious or cannot respond.

The emergency plan should include an emergency preparedness kit. Include spare batteries or a hand crank charger so you can keep your phone and radio operating if electricity fails. Consider what your family's immediate needs would be in an emergency situation to identify what you need in your kit.

The Internet can be a good source of information during a crisis that affects a whole community, such as a natural disaster. Look for government websites or sites you know will have valid information related to the situation. In a crisis, these sites will have up-to-date information that can help you understand the situation and seek help. Local government websites may list community resources that are available, such as shelters and supplies of food and water.

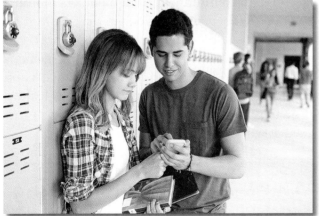

Monkey Business Images/Shutterstock.com

Figure 15.12 Keeping your phone and contacts up-to-date with important numbers can enable you to make important calls in a time of emergency.

Think About Your Reading

What items would your family need in an emergency preparedness kit?

Managing Chronic Illness and Disabilities

Many families experience the chronic illness of a family member or have a member with a disability. A **chronic illness** is a medical problem that cannot be cured. Some illnesses require changes in the person's eating or activity patterns. Some may require ongoing use of medication to manage the symptoms and effects of the illness. Some chronic illnesses end in death. All these issues place a lot of stress on the individual with the illness and on the family system as a whole.

A **disability** describes a condition that interferes with certain abilities. A physical disability may result in a problem with a person's vision, hearing, speech, or motor skills. An intellectual disability may result in a delay in intellectual skills.

A disability or chronic illness may affect a family member of any age. A chronic illness is a permanent condition; a disability may be temporary or permanent.

Mental Disorder and the Family

One type of disability that impacts families is a **mental disorder**, also called a *mental illness*. Mental disorders include a wide range of problems, such

---

as anxiety disorders and *phobias* (intense fears), bipolar disorder, depression, mood disorders, and personality disorders. Family members who have a mental disorder may act like they can contribute to healthy family functioning, but in reality, they may struggle. This makes it hard for families to recognize the illness and then seek treatment.

Mental disorders have many causes. Genetics may be a factor. Life experiences, such as a brain injury, exposure to stress, or substance abuse, can have an impact on mental disorders. Prenatal exposure during pregnancy to toxins, viruses, alcohol or drug use, and abuse can also result in mental disorders. Because people often feel a sense of shame or embarrassment when a family member has a mental disorder, many families do not seek treatment or help in these situations. Nonetheless, many people with mental disorders can be helped through medications, counseling, or both (**Figure 15.13**). Such help can benefit the family system as the person again contributes to helping the family fulfill its functions.

Children with Disabilities

Some children are born with a physical or intellectual disability. Their physical activities or cognitive functioning is impaired in some way. A child with a **learning disorder** has difficulty learning to carry out certain skills, even though his or her intelligence is average. Some children struggle with behavioral disorders, such as

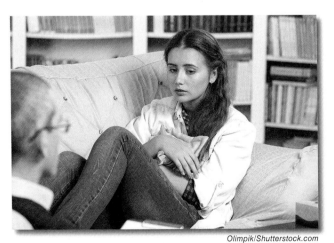

Figure 15.13 Many people who have mental disorders are helped through therapy sessions. *Why might therapy help people with mental disorders?*

hyperactivity. Autism spectrum disorders have increased in children over the last few years. **Autism spectrum disorder** is a developmental disorder that results in children having difficulty with social interactions.

Children with disabilities need special help to reach their full potential for development. A pediatrician, family doctor, or school psychologist can recommend tests to determine the exact nature of the child's disability. They can also recommend specialists who can advise the family on ways to help the child.

Coping with Chronic Illness and Disability

Learning to live with chronic illness or a disability can be difficult. It is emotionally stressful for the family. The person with the disability may feel anger or frustration over the loss of abilities or guilt about putting new burdens on the family. One family member may have to stay home to provide care for the person with a disability. Conflicts over extra demands on time and money for medical care may occur. Other family members' needs may be put aside. All these factors can result in tensions increasing and sometimes in family members withdrawing from one another.

In order to cope with these challenges, family members must continue showing love, support, and affection for one another. They need to listen to each other with active listening skills and with empathy. Doing so can help members accept the illness or disability and the effect it will have on the family. Attitudes of cooperativeness and flexibility are important, too. Each family member should be sure to see to his or her own needs and keep involved in activities that promote personal growth (**Figure 15.14**).

There may be some technological resources to help a family meet the needs of members with a chronic illness or disability. **Assistive technologies** are devices that assist people who have disabilities with hearing, vision, or mobility tasks. There are many computer applications that can help children with disabilities learn in ways that address their specific needs. Information

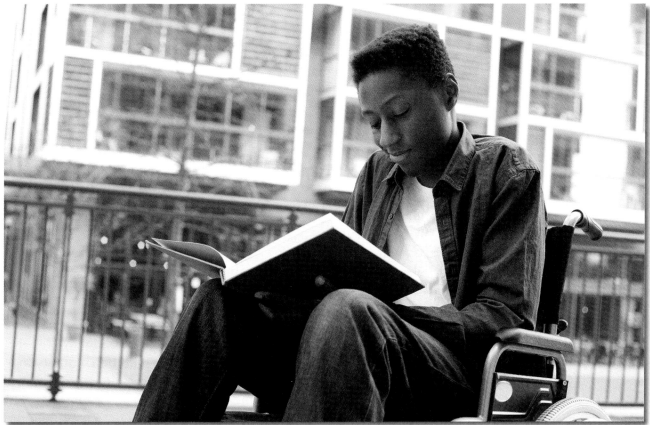
©iStock.com/michaelpuche

Figure 15.14 Family members with disabilities should be encouraged to engage in hobbies and explore personal interests. *In what ways can technology help family members with disabilities be more independent?*

related to technologies available for various illnesses or disabilities can be found on reliable websites.

Understanding an illness or disability and its long-term effects is an important part of adjusting to it. Community resource people are available to make this process easier. Medical professionals are key resources in providing basic information. They can educate family members about the situation and related medical procedures, concerns, and treatments. Counselors and religious leaders can help family members adjust emotionally to the stress of chronic conditions. Educators and school psychologists can also help a person with a chronic illness or disability develop to his or her full potential.

Think About Your Reading

How might a severe illness affect the functioning of a family? What coping behaviors could help the family manage such a crisis?

Coping with Drug and Alcohol Abuse

Some families experience a crisis when a member uses illegal drugs or abuses prescription drugs or alcohol. Drug or alcohol abuse is also called **substance abuse**.

Drug and alcohol abuse tend to be used as coping mechanisms to hide from problems. Substance abuse tends to occur more in families when spouses or parents and teens do not resolve conflicts. Another trigger of substance abuse is a lack of parental involvement in children's lives at a young age.

The Effects of Substance Abuse on the Family

Drug and alcohol abuse lead to increased stress in a family. One major area of stress is the constant concern for the health and safety

of the abuser. The person's physical health is in danger. Brain cells are destroyed by the substance abuse, and body organs may be damaged as well. There is also danger of accidents resulting from the choices the person makes due to his or her impaired judgment.

Another concern for the family is the person's influence on others. The use of drugs or alcohol by parents may influence their children to do the same. Teens who abuse substances may influence the choices of younger siblings.

When a family member abuses drugs or alcohol, others in the family may feel they are to blame. Rather than seek information or help, family members may try to cover up the user's problems. They may feel embarrassed and ashamed when contacted by law-enforcement or hospital officials about the member's abuse.

Community Resources for Coping with Substance Abuse

Interaction patterns that strengthen families—good communication, joint decision making, and problem solving—usually break down before substance abuse develops. In such situations, families have a hard time coping with the problem. In addition, substance abuse can be very difficult to treat and requires the knowledge and skills of specialists. For these reasons, outside programs are important resources for coping with drug and alcohol abuse (**Figure 15.15**).

Neighborhood groups, schools, and government agencies want to help families avoid and cope effectively with drug and alcohol abuse. Professionals in health, education, social services, and law enforcement work together nationwide to provide solutions for these problems. Families experiencing substance abuse can seek help from these agencies. These agencies often provide immediate help with food, clothing, shelter, and medical assistance. Such steps may be necessary to help the family restore its functions.

Long-term family therapy may be needed to handle the stress and resolve the underlying problems that contributed to the drug or alcohol abuse. Drug counseling centers, religious organizations, health care systems, psychologists, and other

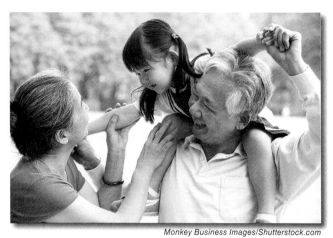

Monkey Business Images/Shutterstock.com

Figure 15.15 A serious alcohol or drug problem often requires the assistance of a professional to help the abuser and his or her family return to a normal life. This arrangement often reshuffles roles in the family. *What roles might have to be reassigned in the family to balance the family system during treatment?*

community programs are all potential sources of therapy. In an effort to help everyone affected by the problem, counselors often work with all family members (**Figure 15.16**). Doing so helps family members learn to support one another, enabling individuals to fulfill their roles in the family again.

Prevention is the best resource a family has for coping with alcohol and drug abuse. Educational programs that address four different goals help families deal with these issues. These programs do the following:

- *Focus on growth and development.* This approach helps families provide the type of

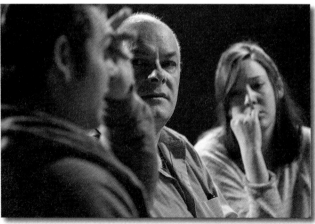

Burlingham/Shutterstock.com

Figure 15.16 Substance abuse affects the entire family. For this reason, counselors often treat substance-abuse problems with family therapy.

environment that children need to develop positive attitudes and become emotionally mature, feeling loved, secure, and competent. Such programs promote emotional health and reduce the likelihood of substance abuse.

- *Help families handle problems that could lead to future abuse.* Some programs are designed to help families handle problems arising from lack of education, health care, housing, and child care. By helping families manage these problems, community agencies can reduce the amount of stress that family members experience and reduce the likelihood that a member will develop a substance abuse problem.

- *Educate people about the serious consequences of drug and alcohol abuse.* In this approach, professionals in education, health, and law enforcement detail the effects of substance abuse and the factors that influence people to make such decisions.

- *Help people develop skills that serve as personal resources during times of stress.* In addition to learning decision-making and communication skills, people learn assertiveness skills to stop others from using or abusing them. Assertiveness skills can help young people withstand the peer pressure to join in drug and alcohol use.

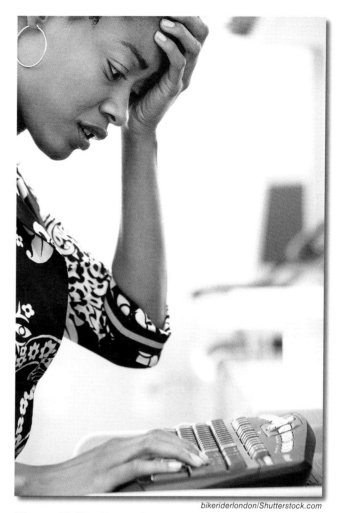

bikeriderlondon/Shutterstock.com

Figure 15.17 Unemployment and searching for a new job can cause stress for all family members. *What family functions are threatened when a parent loses a job?*

Think About Your Reading

What services are provided to families with drug or alcohol problems through your local community?

Managing Unemployment and Financial Crises

The loss of a job can occur anytime. No matter what the reason is, joblessness can be stressful for individuals and families and result in a crisis. This is especially true if income is sharply decreased or stopped. Emotional stress may cause the unemployed person to feel a sense of failure, isolation, and despair (**Figure 15.17**).

Resources During Financial Crises

Most financial advisors recommend having enough money in an emergency savings account so bills can be paid for at least three months. Such a savings account can make the difference between a job loss becoming a crisis situation or not. It enables the individual or family to continue meeting needs while the unemployed person searches for a new job. A job loss can occur at any time, however, and individuals and families may not have their emergency savings established.

In the family, members' skills and abilities are important resources in adjusting to the stress of lost income. The family needs to stick together and believe that they can find ways to cope with and handle the problem. Some family members

Facing Unemployment

Carlos's family knew that the construction season was almost over. Soon, Carlos's dad would be out of work. Thinking about another long winter with no income was causing everyone in the Sandoz family to be edgy. One Saturday evening, Carlos asked for a family meeting.

"Isn't there something we can do to help Dad keep his job?" Carlos asked.

His dad shook his head. "I don't think so, son. I'm a road builder, and not too many roads are built in the winter."

"But you have so many other skills, Dad," Carlos said. "You know how to drive those big road-building machines. Couldn't you drive trucks in the winter?"

Carlos's dad thought quietly for a minute. "That might be worth a try, Carlos. You may have a good idea. I thought I was too old to try something new, but maybe that wouldn't be too difficult for me to try."

"They offer truck-driving courses at the technical college. I saw it on a bulletin posted at school. Do you want me to find out about it?" Carlos asked.

Mr. Sandoz was beginning to catch Carlos's excitement. "Yes, I'd be willing to look into it," he said.

For Discussion

1. Explain how the upcoming layoff could be a potential crisis-producing event for the Sandoz family.
2. Was the source of stress for the Sandoz family external or internal?
3. What factors made it seem difficult for the Sandoz family to handle the stress and prevent the potential crisis?
4. What family resources did the Sandoz family use to help them prevent a crisis?
5. List four actions Carlos took to cope with the potential crisis.
6. What could Carlos have done if his father had been less willing to adjust and consider something new? What other alternatives could they have considered to avoid a crisis?

---

may be able to find work or work extra hours at an existing job to help make up some of the lost income. All can cooperate to cut expenses by avoiding unnecessary items and activities.

Social support from family members, friends, and relatives is an important resource during a financial crisis. These people can offer encouragement and aid until a new job is found, which helps individuals meet their needs and helps the family system become balanced.

Outside Resources During Financial Crises

Help with obtaining basic food, shelter, clothing, and medical services is available locally through government and social service agencies to some individuals and families. Community and religious organizations in the area may also provide similar help.

Unemployed workers may be able to get unemployment compensation from the state labor or employment department. This is a portion of previous earnings that the government pays to workers who have lost their jobs through no fault of their own. If a financial crisis affects an entire community, in the case of a natural disaster or the closing of a leading employer, for example, state and federal aid programs are often available.

LESSON 15.3

Assess

COMPREHENSION CHECK

1. List four strategies that families and individuals can use to manage a problem or crisis.
2. Describe a family that has strong coping skills.
3. Describe an individual who has qualities needed to cope with crises.
4. Identify three ways in which educational programs are designed to prevent drug and alcohol abuse.
5. List three ways that communities may offer help to families in crisis situations.

CHAPTER SUMMARY

A *crisis* is an experience or event that causes a person to make a change in his or her life. A single life event or combination of events can cause a crisis in the family. When a crisis occurs, the entire family is affected. As a result, the family may not be able to carry out its functions for some time. This situation can hinder the growth and development of family members. Developing coping skills enables individuals and families to adjust to the crisis and handle family functions again.

Families can take steps to prevent a crisis. First, they can learn to identify sources of stress. Then they can learn to manage stress before a crisis develops. Developing and using family resources can help them return balance to the family system and avoid the negative effects of a crisis.

When a crisis does occur, individuals and families need to use good coping skills. These skills can help families adjust to changes so that the family can return to normal, meeting the needs of its members. Many resources are available, both within the family and in the community, to help families and individuals manage problems and crises. Specialized resources may help families cope with chronic illness, disability, drug and alcohol abuse, unemployment, and financial crises.

VOCABULARY ACTIVITIES

1. Create a concept web that shows how all of these terms relate to crises. In addition to listing each term, define it.

Content Terms

alienated (15.1)	external stress (15.2)
assistive technology (15.3)	grief (15.1)
autism spectrum disorder (15.3)	internal stress (15.2)
	learning disorder (15.3)
chronic illness (15.3)	mental disorder (15.3)
coping behavior (15.3)	pileup effect (15.1)
crises (15.1)	stressor (15.1)
disability (15.3)	substance abuse (15.3)

2. Write a paragraph that uses all the terms to describe how families may face crises.

Academic Terms

hectic (15.2)	phobia (15.3)
implement (15.3)	reserve (15.2)
inconvenient (15.3)	stage (15.1)
optimistic (15.2)	state (15.1)

ASSESS

Your Knowledge

3. What four factors determine if stressors lead to a crisis?
4. Identify five common emotions that people experience in the grieving process.
5. Identify six resources individuals and families can use to handle stress and thereby avoid a crisis.

Your Understanding

6. How do crises affect the family system?
7. What strategies can individuals and families use to prevent problems and crises?
8. Explain how families can manage and meet special needs in the family. What technologies are available to help meet these needs? Use the four steps for coping with crisis in your response.

Your Skills

9. What steps could you take to reduce stress in your life before a big exam?
10. What resources and support systems are available in your community to help families through the crisis of a major illness?

CRITICAL THINKING

11. **Find Solutions to a Problem.** Locate a news article describing a crisis or problem in an individual's or family's life. Analyze the article to identify sources of stress that could have led to this crisis. Determine strategies for managing the crisis or problem and identify resources and support systems both inside and outside the family that could be used to help handle it. Write a paper summarizing your analysis and your solutions. *Group option*: Work in a small group to complete the analysis and recommendations. Present to the class and ask for feedback about the strategies you recommend. What other ideas did your classmates have? After the presentation, meet with your small group to discuss the class's feedback.

12. **Make Inferences.** Write a one-page scenario illustrating how several normal events could contribute to the pileup effect, resulting in a crisis for a family. Include a description of coping strategies that could help the family handle the crisis, citing evidence from the text to support your suggestions. *Group option*: Work with a partner to create the scenario. *Choice*: Present your scenario as a rap or a play.

13. **Apply Concepts.** Create a scenario in which a family learns of a child's addiction to drugs. Describe the feelings the family may experience, citing evidence from the cycle of the grieving process. Explain how the feelings in each stage could affect a family's ability to adjust and cope with the crisis. Then identify four steps individuals and the family could take to manage the crisis, citing evidence from the text to support your recommendation. *Choice*: Describe what resources are available to help the family at each stage of the grieving cycle. *Group option*: Create the scenario with a partner.

CORE SKILLS

14. **Writing.** Interview a school counselor or nurse and ask questions about how to reduce stress in your life. In a one-page paper, summarize the interview and compare the counselor's suggestions with strategies from the text.

15. **Research, Writing.** Contact your local emergency center and interview workers about the guidelines for handling a major emergency in your community. List possible external sources of stress that could contribute to such an emergency for families in your neighborhood. What community resources are available to help handle these sources of stress? Write a report on your findings. *Choice*: Deliver your report to the class using presentation software.

16. **Research, Social Studies.** Form a small group and research information on drug or alcohol abuse in your community. Have each person in your group present information from the perspective of a different community service worker, including a law-enforcement officer, a social worker, a school counselor, and a hospital employee. Present what you have learned to the class as a panel.

17. **Reading, Writing, Social Studies.** Choose a situation or event that can cause a crisis for a family. Use online resources to research and prepare a report on government and community resources available for families in such a crisis. *Choice*: Post your report to your school website as a resource for families.

18. **Writing.** Using technology, prepare a flyer with tips for reducing stress in the family when undergoing a crisis in your community. Categorize the crisis by type and by its effects on individuals and families. *Choice*: Post your flyer to your class website.

19. **Research, Social Studies, Writing.** Using the Internet, research the effects of drug or alcohol use and abuse on individuals and the family. Prepare a paper describing these effects and relate them to crises that may arise in a family as a result. Cite the references you found in your research. *Choice*: Present your information in multimedia segments to be used on your school public address announcements or on the school website.

20. **Research, Science.** Use online resources to research a chronic illness or disability and identify treatments or technological resources for managing the illness or disability. Write a report describing the illness and treatments, as well as the impact that such a condition could have on balance in a family system. *Group option*: Form groups based on the illness or disability chosen. Compile your information and present it to the class.

CAREER READINESS

21. **Researching Careers.** Many people with physical disabilities are helped by physical therapists. Use online and print sources to investigate this career. Find out what knowledge and skills a physical therapist needs, any licensing or certification requirements needed to get a job, the settings in which they work, the kind of work they do, the average salary of these workers, and the outlook for this career in the future. Present your findings in an electronic report. *Choice*: Interview a physical therapist and include his or her comments about the work in your report.

22. **Developing an Informative Community Website.** You work for the local government. The town council has given you and three coworkers (who will be your classmates) the task of developing a website with resources in case a natural or civic disaster strikes the community. You should include information on the types of disaster that might occur in your area and how to respond to each type, advice to families on how to develop an emergency plan, resources that can provide help to families in an emergency, phone numbers and websites to consult for information, and any other information you think important. Work with your team to develop the content of your website. Make sure it is logically and clearly organized. *Choice*: Present the information electronically.

CHAPTER 16

DIVORCE AND REMARRIAGE

Reading Prep

Preview the chapter by scanning the text headings and images. Write a paragraph predicting what you think you will learn in the chapter.

Key Questions

Questions to answer as you study this chapter:

- What are some causes of divorce?
- How does a breakdown in a marital relationship affect the family?
- What can families do to adjust to divorce and strengthen the family system?

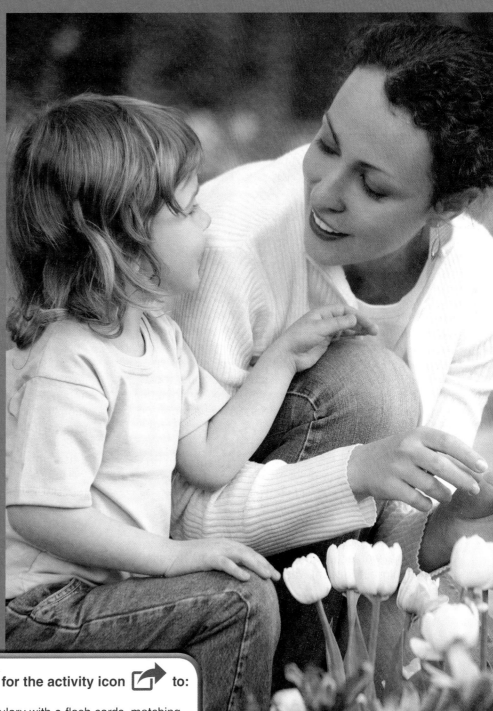

While studying this chapter, look for the activity icon 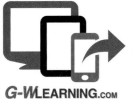 to:

- **build** vocabulary with e-flash cards, matching activities, and vocabulary games; and
- **assess** what you learn by completing the lesson comprehension checks online.

www.g-wlearning.com/humanservices/

G-WLEARNING.COM

Pavel L Photo and Video/Shutterstock.com

AFTER STUDYING THIS CHAPTER, YOU WILL

KNOW:

- The stages in the breakdown of a relationship.
- The effects of divorce on all members in the family system.

UNDERSTAND:

- How the needs of children and adults can be met when experiencing a divorce.
- How intimate relationships can be developed within a stepfamily.

BE ABLE TO DO:

- Analyze life situations for factors that could contribute to a breakdown in a family.
- Project possible strategies for rebuilding strong relationships within a family.

GETTING STARTED

Four-year-old Marcia sat on the steps by the door of the child care center. Her eyes were shut tight as she tried to hold back her tears. The lump in her throat just would not go away.

Seeing Marcia sitting alone, her child care teacher walked over and sat beside her. She put her arm around Marcia and gave her a warm hug. Trying to sense Marcia's feelings, she said, "You're feeling pretty sad, aren't you?"

Marcia nodded her head, and the tears began to flow. "Daddy packed his suitcase last night and left," she sobbed. "He even took his winter coat. He said he would be gone for a long time."

A child's understanding of what happens when parents separate is often dim. What children see is a dearly loved parent leaving. Children feel hurt, rejected, insecure, and uncertain of the future. They may wonder if the remaining parent will leave, too. They often feel at fault for the problems in the family.

Separation, divorce, and remarriage bring about major changes in families. Changes occur in the family structure and in members' roles. Close relationships within the family change. Financial changes take place, too. Studying the effects of separation and divorce may seem like a negative way to build strong marriages. Learning about these effects, however, points out the importance of making careful, mature choices in dating and in choosing a marriage partner. People who are aware of the causes and effects of divorce may think more carefully about the commitment of marriage.

This chapter will also help you understand the issues of single parenting, a common result of divorce. Single parents face many challenges as they try to reorganize their lives to meet the needs of family members. Sometimes single parents remarry, which brings more adjustments as families work to build a strong stepfamily unit.

Content Terms

Build Vocab

divorce
barrier to divorce

Academic Terms

inevitable
constructive

Objectives

After studying this lesson, you will be able to

- **describe** the effects of divorce on the family system.
- **identify** barriers to divorce.
- **recognize** the factors that contribute to divorce.

Focus Your Reading

1. Divide a piece of paper into three columns, one column for each main heading in this lesson. Identify what you already know about each topic. After you read, fill in key concepts for each topic.

2. Draw a picture of what you think could be a barrier to divorce. Write a brief explanation of why you think so.

The ending of a marriage is called **divorce**. Statistics clearly show that divorce is common. Young people have a 50 percent chance of living in a family that has experienced divorce at some point in their lives. Divorce may affect young people's parents. It may happen to young people personally, if they have a marriage that ends in divorce or if they marry someone who has been divorced.

This does not mean that divorce is *inevitable*, or bound to occur, in every marriage. What it does mean is that there are many factors that can lead to a divorce. Couples need to be alert to these factors and take steps to nurture and strengthen their relationships. A close, intimate marriage is the best protection against the hurt that divorce brings to a family and the challenges that result from divorce (**Figure 16.1**).

The Effects of Divorce

A divorce affects many people: the two adults, children, relatives, friends, and others in the community. Remember that people are interdependent. What happens in one family affects everyone in that family and other people around them.

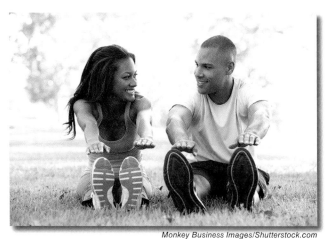
Monkey Business Images/Shutterstock.com

Figure 16.1 If you plan to marry in the future, making mature relationship choices during the dating years is important. *What are some qualities that will contribute to a long-lasting, intimate marriage?*

Think About Your Reading
How does divorce affect different people?

Children often suffer in a divorce. Divorce does not end parent-child relationships if the spouses have children. It only changes the relationship. An ex-spouse is still a parent. Parents still need to work together to fulfill the functions of the family and meet the needs of their children.

Divorce brings about an imbalance in the family system. After parents split, there are fewer resources to meet the needs of the family. In fact, since a divorce splits the family between two households, the needs of the family actually increase. The adjustments required as a result of divorce can be very difficult for adults and children. Adjustments are needed in physical living arrangements, emotional ties, finances, social ties, and parenting arrangements.

Most often, divorce results in poor communication between family members. Making any type of adjustment is easier when family members understand the changes taking place. Good communication skills can help family members work out all the details. In the case of separation and divorce, however, understanding and good communication are often missing (**Figure 16.2**). This lack of communication often spills over into the community. When parents do not send the same messages in communicating with teachers, school officials, coaches, day care providers, and others who provide services to children, problems result for all involved.

Ending a marriage relationship is a legal matter. Obtaining a divorce can be a long, stressful process. Recognizing that divorce is not a quick and easy way to end a relationship is important. Spouses who are considering divorce need to understand the negative impact of the length of this process. The process can cause a great deal of stress in all members of the family system.

On the other hand, continuing to live in a difficult or abusive situation is not healthy either, and separating without divorcing causes stress and complications as well. In separation without divorce, care and responsibility for any children is split, but not in a clear or legally enforceable way. In addition, this may mean that the two spouses have legal claims on each other's financial resources, and that if no divorce takes place, neither spouse can legally remarry.

Barriers to Divorce

Many people feel the pressure to stay married, even when their relationships are not growing or are not healthy. People may feel they cannot break

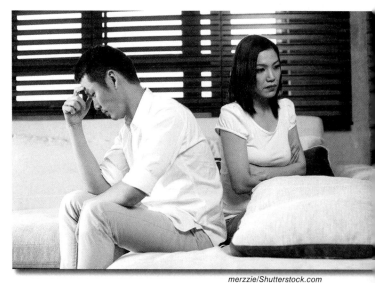
merzzie/Shutterstock.com

Figure 16.2 Good communication, which is vital for healthy family adjustments, is often absent in situations where parents divorce or separate.

the commitment to stay together "until death do us part." They may stay married for the sake of children or to avoid the disapproval of family and friends. Some victims of abuse do not pursue a divorce because they fear that the abuser may carry out threats to harm them. Others fear the loneliness of being single or fear they cannot afford to live alone. Some hope the happiness of an earlier time in the marriage will return.

These fears or pressures serve as barriers to divorce. A **barrier to divorce** is any factor that keeps a couple from moving ahead with a divorce. Such barriers can result in a person living in a situation of abuse for a lifetime. That barrier is destructive, but some barriers can be *constructive*, or have a positive impact. They may influence a couple to try and rebuild their relationship.

Most people who divorce do remarry. This fact indicates that many people do hope to find an intimate and fulfilling marital relationship, even if they have seen such hopes dashed (**Figure 16.3**). The key to the problem of divorce, then, is the breakdown in the marriage relationship.

Think About Your Reading

How might living in an abusive situation be more harmful to the development of a child than divorce?

Factors Contributing to Divorce

Researchers have identified several factors that often contribute to divorce. Background

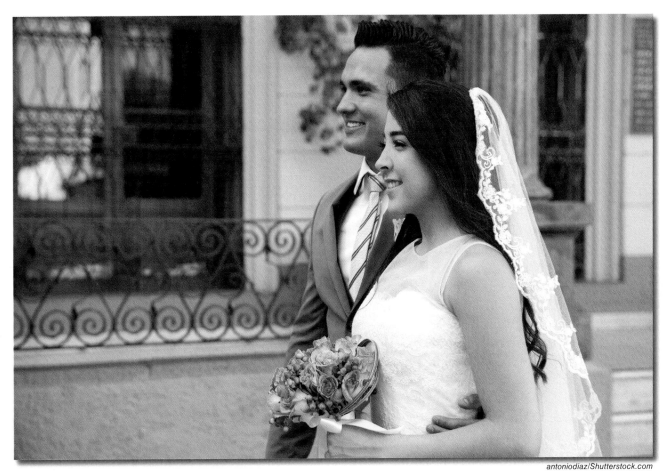

antoniodiaz/Shutterstock.com

Figure 16.3 The desire for companionship and a close relationship often leads a divorced person to remarry. *Why is it important to evaluate a relationship prior to a second marriage for qualities that would lead to a long-lasting relationship?*

differences between spouses, issues arising from maturity, and a lack of relationship skills can lead to divorce. Marrying into problem situations and marrying to escape problems at home are other significant factors. Frequent financial conflicts may also increase the chances of divorce. Finally, many marriages involving a teen end in divorce.

Differences in Backgrounds

Major differences in backgrounds can result in differing views and expectations for marriage. These differences can increase conflict in the relationship and then be hard to resolve. If a couple disagrees on most aspects of the relationship, divorce is quite likely to result. As discussed in Chapter 11, a couple does not have to have a similar background for a marriage to succeed. Having similar and realistic expectations for marriage, however, can help a marriage stay intact. Having complementary qualities can be the basis of a strong, successful marriage as well.

Issues with Maturity

Immaturity can also lead to a marital breakdown. Some individuals never do grow to intellectual, emotional, or social maturity. Their immature traits contribute to faulty thinking and poor choices; self-centeredness and a lack of strong character traits such as responsibility, dependability, and honesty; and uncontrolled emotions such as anger and anxiety. These immature traits result in unhealthy relationships and contribute to a breakdown in a marriage relationship over time (**Figure 16.4**).

In other marriages, one or both spouses may develop maturity that was not there before. This can be a problem, too, if it results in changes in the spouse's thoughts, feelings, and goals. If this growth takes place in the marriage, a couple may find they do not have as much in common with each other as they once did. Their lack of readiness for marriage affects the stability of their relationship.

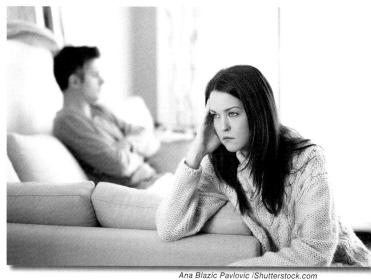

Figure 16.4 Lack of maturity harms the marriage relationship over time. *What are some signs of immaturity?*

Think About Your Reading
How might intellectual immaturity affect a couple's relationship?

Poor Relationship Skills

A lack of relationship skills makes it difficult for a couple to adjust to each other during the early years of marriage. Couples need to communicate clearly, make decisions together, and solve problems in a way that leaves both partners satisfied. These skills are important for living together as a pair. If a couple does not develop these skills, the chance that they will divorce increases.

Problem Situations

Marrying into problem situations also increases the chance of divorce. For instance, a premarital pregnancy may influence a couple to marry even if they are not ready. Then they must adjust to parenting as well as to each other during the early years of marriage. This puts a lot of stress on the relationship. Marrying to escape problems

at home does not help a marriage, either. Past conflicts with parents may be brought into the marital relationship. Even if they are not, the spouse who is looking for an escape may not be ready for marriage.

Financial Conflicts

Finances tend to be a major source of conflict in a marriage. Financial problems increase if one spouse is unemployed or lacks the training or education to get a good job. Such problems can increase the chance that a marriage will end in divorce.

Even if both spouses have good jobs, they may have strong differences regarding money matters. Personal habits related to spending and saving money may differ sharply. How the household budget is handled may cause additional conflict (**Figure 16.5**). If one spouse brings money or property to the marriage, arguments may arise over "his car" or "her bank account." Divorce often results from disagreements over how to handle money and other valuables in the marriage.

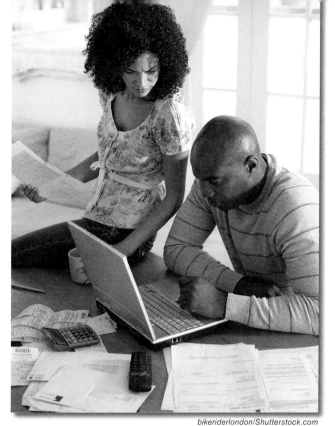
bikeriderlondon/Shutterstock.com

Figure 16.5 Arguments about finances can cause ongoing conflict between spouses. *What interpersonal skills are critical for a marriage relationship to succeed?*

Think About Your Reading

How would good communication and decision-making skills help couples handle financial conflicts?

Teen Marriages

Many teen marriages end in divorce. This is closely related to several of the factors already discussed. During the teen years, much personal growth takes place. Personal views and goals are still developing. Relationship skills are developing, too. Career goals and steps to reach them are being identified. Financial independence is not likely. As a result, many teen marriages do not survive.

Each of the factors described in this lesson attacks a healthy romantic relationship. Personal differences, issues with maturity, and poor communication skills can topple the friendship leg of the relationship stool (as described

in Chapter 10) and impact the growth of mature love, a second leg in the relationship stool. A lack of caring and giving breaks the romantic leg of the relationship. Without good decision-making and problem-solving skills, the fourth leg of a sturdy relationship, healthy relationship skills, can wobble and break when problems arise in the marriage. Along with breaks in the four legs, these factors can also result in a lack of personal boundaries and a broken commitment to the relationship. Such a broken relationship often ends in divorce.

LESSON 16.1

Assess

COMPREHENSION CHECK

1. Briefly describe the effects of divorce on a family system.
2. What are two barriers that might keep a couple from getting a divorce?
3. List six factors that may contribute to divorce.

Objectives

After studying this lesson, you will be able to

- **describe** how the emotional stage of divorce impacts the family system.
- **explain** how enforcing boundaries may end a relationship.
- **define** the legal terms associated with divorce.
- **list** various arrangements that can be made for children in a divorce settlement.

Focus Your Reading

1. As you read, develop a graphic organizer that follows the path from the breakdown of a relationship to a divorce. Include key concepts for each stage of divorce.
2. Identify and define terms used in divorce court proceedings that you have heard in the news or on television shows.

How can a loving, caring relationship change so much that it ends in divorce? A couple may ask themselves that question and wonder how it happened. When did it start to fall apart? A breakdown in the marriage relationship can be caused by many factors and goes through several stages.

Failure to Nurture a Relationship

Failing to *nurture*, or care for, a relationship is one cause of a breakdown. A marriage relationship needs regular, loving care and the commitment from both partners to provide that care. To keep the relationship alive and growing, couples need to spend time together. They need to share their thoughts and feelings and do activities together. In these ways, spouses build mature love and strengthen their marital relationship.

Content Terms

Build Vocab

emotional divorce
legal separation
legal divorce
petitioner
respondent
mediator
no-fault divorce
legal custody
physical custody
sole custody
visitation rights
joint custody
alimony
child support

Academic Terms

nurture
procedure
ground

When a relationship is not nurtured, couples grow apart. One or both partners find themselves with a different focus. This focus may be work, hobbies, or other relationships with friends or family that occupy most of either person's time.

Sometimes a relationship does not grow because a couple moved into marriage too quickly, and they failed to see each other clearly. They did not take the time to really get to know each other, or one was not honest and open enough to let the other person know and see his or her true inner self. Then, after being married, the real traits that had been hidden became evident and resulted in problems.

Sometimes when a relationship does not grow, the couple develops destructive behavior patterns. Some marriage relationships become abusive, with either spouse hurting or threatening to cause harm to the other in order to exert control. This behavior may be due to a lack of maturity. In this case, the abusive spouse is unable to learn about caring for the well-being of others or being respectful of others' rights, thoughts, and feelings. When the couple was first in love, these flaws may have been overlooked, or perhaps one spouse believed the other would change (**Figure 16.6**).

Alcohol and drug use and abuse can also destroy a marriage relationship. Chemical effects on the brain and body cause individuals to make irresponsible choices. These individuals often cease to carry out their roles in the family. They may fail to meet the needs of their spouses or children. In many cases, they become mean and violent under the influence of excessive alcohol or illegal drugs.

Enforcement of Boundaries

When individuals in a relationship decide that they cannot continue as they are, they begin to

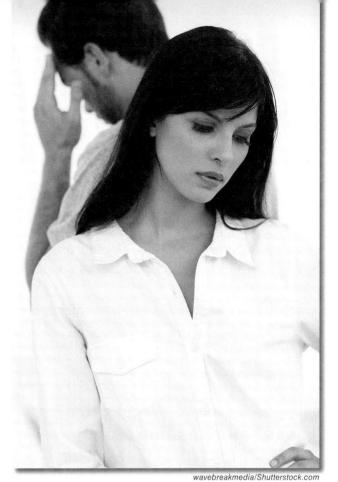

wavebreakmedia/Shutterstock.com

Figure 16.6 Flaws that were overlooked during dating can lead to a breakdown in the marriage relationship.

revisit their personal boundaries and think about what they will and will not accept in the relationship. Enforcing these boundaries may bring about a change in a partner's behavior. The action may open his or her eyes to the value of the relationship and the need to change. That is a positive result of setting boundaries. When a partner is making an effort to change, the spouse may revise those boundaries as progress is made. This positive result of setting boundaries is most likely to occur if the partner who changed the boundaries explains why and makes clear that the marriage is in trouble.

Setting new boundaries can result in a breakdown of the marriage if the spouse does not change, however. For example, Bill was upset because his wife frequently left for several days without telling him where she was going. She would spend large amounts of money while she was gone, draining their finances. This behavior had not changed, even though Bill had tried to resolve their problems and sought counseling.

They no longer had a relationship where love and concern for each other was shared. Bill finally set a boundary and told his wife that if she left again, she should not plan to return. Their relationship would be over. He identified the problem, named the behavior that had to change, and created a consequence of her not responding. She still walked out the door, and Bill moved forward with a divorce.

Think About Your Reading

What boundary could a person set who deals with a spouse who abuses alcohol or drugs?

It is very important that a spouse who is abused sets boundaries to protect himself or herself. These limits need to be identified in words and carried out with actions. A spouse might say, "I need you to stop being disrespectful to me when we have a discussion, or I will leave the room and not return until you are calm." For the boundary to work, the person setting it must be willing to carry out the stated consequence. That was the case with Bill. It can be helpful to have others who provide support as the abused spouse acts to protect himself or herself.

Stages of a Marriage Breakdown

When marriages break down, they typically go through several stages. These stages last different periods of time from one marriage to another, but most breakdowns go through the three stages of emotional divorce, separation, and formal divorce.

Emotional Divorce

Factors both inside and outside the marriage can attack the relationship. Spouses who cover up their hurts and do not share their inner feelings build walls between themselves and their partners. Their emotional needs are not met. In this situation, one or both spouses may withdraw from the relationship. They may seek to fulfill emotional needs outside the marriage. Such responses attack and tear apart the relationship from the inside. This first stage in the breakdown of the marriage relationship is called **emotional divorce**.

During this time, both partners often go through emotions similar to the stages of grief (as described in Chapter 15). At first, they may deny that the relationship is really failing; then they may express anger over the loss of their dream of a happy marriage. There may be some feelings of guilt, but most often both partners blame the other for the breakdown in their relationship. Feelings of depression are common as individuals struggle with the feelings that accompany emotional divorce (**Figure 16.7**).

Skills for communicating and resolving conflicts can help couples renew and strengthen the relationship. Couples may seek marriage counseling or a family therapist to help them identify areas of their relationship that need to improve. With effort, many couples do work out their problems. They rebuild their marriage into a healthy and growing relationship. Often, though, the breakdown in the close marital relationship makes it difficult to rebuild the marriage.

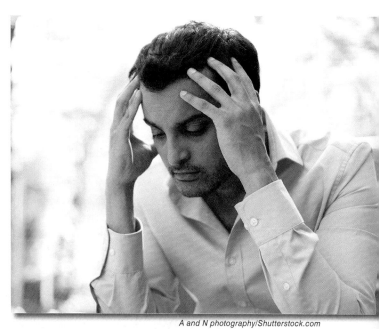

A and N photography/Shutterstock.com

Figure 16.7 During emotional divorce, many couples experience feelings of depression as they grieve the deteriorating relationship.

Separation

Couples may struggle with their relationship for some time before they decide to separate. Separation is often the next stage of the breakdown. Exactly what causes couples to stop trying to hold the relationship together varies. The stage of separation usually moves couples closer to acceptance of the end of the relationship.

The Effects of Separation

In a separation, the spouses set up different households. One partner usually moves out of the home while the other stays in it. The partner who leaves may seek separate living quarters or move in with family or friends. For parents with children, a separation produces a divided family structure. The children may live with one parent or the other (**Figure 16.8**), or they may be moved back and forth between the parents. In some cases, the children may be split up, so that some live with the mother and some with the father.

One partner may file papers for a legal separation. A **legal separation** is a legal agreement for the couple to live apart, divide their property, and provide for their children but remain legally married. A couple may use this approach if they do not believe in divorce.

Sometimes the spouses move back together after a period of separation. The reasons for doing this vary. They may be lonely. They may remember the warm, close times they shared together. Professional counseling may have helped them resolve their differences. They may decide their

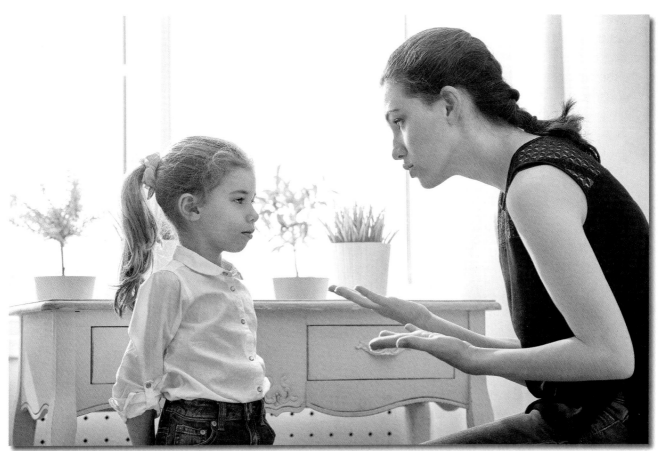

Yuganov Konstantin/Shutterstock.com

Figure 16.8 When parents decide to separate, they need to discuss this with their children honestly. Children need to be reassured that the parents will still love them and take care of them.

differences were not as great as they thought. Sometimes couples do work out their differences and reunite the family. In many cases, however, separation ends in divorce.

Think About Your Reading

Why do you think that separation usually ends in divorce?

Divorce Counseling

For many couples, the thought of divorce brings fear and uncertainty. Sometimes couples seek a divorce counselor who acts as a third party. Divorce counseling is aimed at resolving differences with a goal of saving the marriage. The counseling may be obtained through the court system, from social workers, or through private counselors.

When a couple decides to divorce, the divorce counselor assists. This person can help the spouses understand the legal procedures and the alternatives they have. The counselor also can help the couple cope with the feelings that tend to surface in a divorce. After the divorce is final, the counselor can help each person adjust to the changes created by the divorce.

The Legal Divorce

The final stage of a divorce can be a lengthy legal process. In each state, certain laws and *procedures*, or set steps in a process, govern a legal divorce. A **legal divorce** is the ending of a marriage through the legal process. Legal divorces are often handled in a type of court called *family court*. These courts handle issues like divorce, separation of spouses, child custody and support, and violence in the family. Information on family court services in your community can be obtained at the local courthouse.

Divorce Proceedings

Although the exact laws differ somewhat from state to state, divorce proceedings follow a general pattern. First, the couple must show they meet the state's residency requirement. That is, they must have lived in the state for a certain length of time

before they can apply for a divorce. The length of time varies from three months to one year, depending on the state.

In divorce proceedings, there are two parties. The person who files for divorce is called the **petitioner**. The other spouse is the **respondent**. Most persons filing for divorce seek legal counsel (**Figure 16.9**). Legal services may be available to some families at low or no cost.

A common and less expensive solution to divorce lawyers is use of a divorce **mediator**. A mediator is a third party who works with both spouses to help them negotiate and reach a solution that both accept. A mediator can help a couple work out how they will divide property, what will happen to the family home, and how they will share childrearing responsibilities. Once the agreement is reached, the mediator or one of the attorneys writes up the agreement. If children are involved, a parenting plan or schedule is included. These papers become part of the divorce judgment by the court.

No-Fault Divorce

A **no-fault divorce** is a legal term used to identify a divorce in which neither spouse is being blamed for the divorce. If both spouses agree to the divorce, the court does not inquire into their reasons. Instead, the spouses must make a statement that their marriage has broken down and

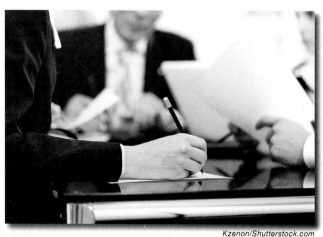

Kzenon/Shutterstock.com

Figure 16.9 Ending a marriage is a legal matter, and requires meeting the laws or requirements in your state. *What would be the benefit of having a lawyer involved with settling a divorce?*

cannot be saved. If they agree to a fairly even division of their property, most courts do not interfere.

Think About Your Reading

How could no-fault divorce benefit families? Can you think of any negatives of having no-fault divorce laws?

Grounds for Divorce

The *grounds*, or legally acceptable reasons, for divorce differ in each state. In many states that do not allow no-fault divorce, the couple can still simply state that their marriage is *irretrievably broken*. This means the relationship cannot be restored. If one spouse does not want the divorce, he or she contests or fights it. Then a battle may develop over determining the grounds for divorce. If one partner requests certain child care arrangements or a money settlement, the grounds for divorce are very important. They can affect the *judgment*, or the court's final decision. Adultery is considered grounds for divorce in all states. Cruelty, desertion, alcohol or drug addiction, inability to have sexual relations, or insanity have also been accepted as grounds for divorce.

Custody Settlements

The court is responsible for awarding legal custody of children in a divorce settlement. **Legal custody** refers to having the rights and responsibilities of providing for each child's care until he or she reaches age 18. People with legal custody have the authority to make important decisions in matters affecting the life and development of a child (**Figure 16.10**). Legal custody can be

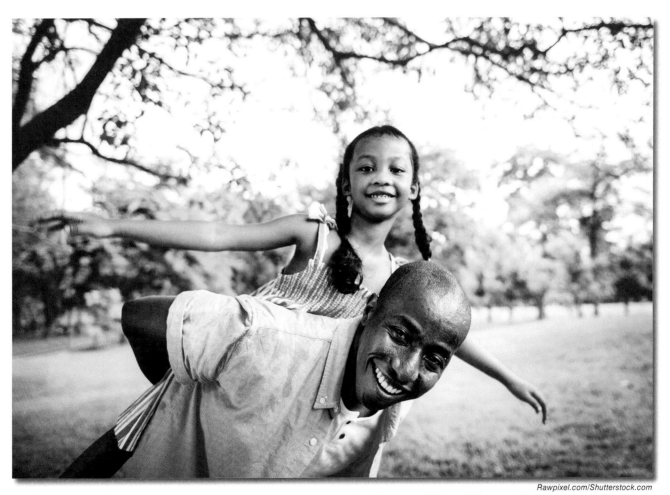

Rawpixel.com/Shutterstock.com

Figure 16.10 Custody settlements determine with whom the children will live. *What could be the benefit of children having both parents involved in making important decisions that affect their life and development?*

assigned to one parent or shared between both parents. Depending on the situation, the court tries to set up fair custody arrangements.

Physical custody refers to where the children live and which parent provides the routine daily care and control of the children. Physical custody can also be assigned to one parent or shared between both parents.

Sole Custody

In **sole custody**, one parent is assigned the legal and physical custody of children. In most cases, the person who provided the major share of child care before the divorce is given sole custody. The mother is often granted sole custody of the children. That means the children live with their mother, and she has the major responsibility for them. The father may be required to help pay for their support. Today, however, more fathers are being granted sole custody of their children than was true in the past.

The court also establishes **visitation rights**. These are specific arrangements for the noncustodial parent to visit the children. They spell out how often that parent can see the children and for how long. They also state what rights the noncustodial parent will have during holidays and school vacations. Changes to this arrangement must be sought through the court. It is a felony—a serious crime—for either parent to interfere with the custody and visitation rights that are established by the courts. If a child is in danger of physical harm, those rights can be suspended.

Joint Custody

If both parents want to be involved in the children's lives, they may request and receive **joint custody**. With joint legal custody, both parents share the rights and responsibilities of raising the children and making decisions that impact their lives. With joint physical custody, children spend equal amounts of time at each parent's residence.

For joint custody to be granted, both parents must be judged as fit and proper people to have legal care, custody, and control of the children. They both must agree to have a full and active role in parenting. They are required to consult with each other in major areas, such as religious upbringing, education, and health care. They must agree to work cooperatively for the best interests of the children in all decisions.

Joint custody keeps both parents involved in their children's lives in their parenting roles. It also forces the parents to continue relating to each other. For couples who have had problems relating in the past, this arrangement may not work very well. They may continue to argue and fight, but do so through the children.

When parents can develop an agreeable plan that considers the well-being of the children, often with the help of a mediator, joint custody is usually more accepted by both parties. Good communication regarding children's well-being and the involvement of both parents is beneficial for children in the divorced family.

> ### Think About Your Reading
> Which custody arrangement do you think is the best environment for children in a divorced family? Why?

Financial Settlements

Divorce proceedings often include financial settlements. Two types of financial settlements commonly found are alimony and child support.

Alimony

One spouse may request alimony as part of the divorce settlement. **Alimony** is a financial settlement paid to a spouse (**Figure 16.11**). These settlements are also sometimes called *maintenance* or *spousal support agreements*.

Judgments for alimony are based on need. Need is determined by factors such as income, assets, debts, previous standard of living, and a person's ability to be self-supporting. In some settlements, the spouse receives a lump sum. That is, he or she gets a set amount of money one time and does not receive any payment afterward. Some alimony settlements are monthly payments given for a period of time or for specific purposes, such as for going to college.

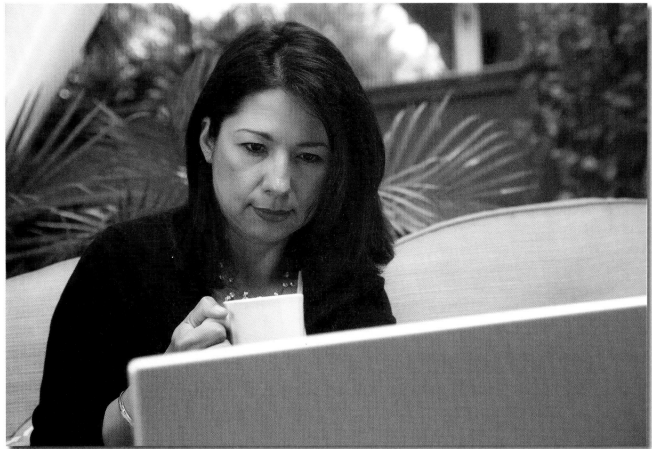

Andy Dean Photography/Shutterstock.com

Figure 16.11 Finances to pay for more education may be part of an alimony settlement. *How could alimony payments be important for the well-being of children in the family?*

Think About Your Reading

How would alimony payments benefit children living with the custodial parent?

Child Support

The court also sets **child support** payments. These are payments that a noncustodial parent is legally required to pay toward the expense of raising children under age 18. These payments end when the child—or the youngest child, if there are multiple children—reaches age 18. The court assumes that the custodial parent shares his or her income directly with the children. Child support payments are required to maintain the child's standard of living. The court considers the

parents' incomes and other factors in determining the amount of this payment. By federal law, not paying child support is a felony. Parents who do not meet child support payments can be sent to jail.

LESSON 16.2

Assess

COMPREHENSION CHECK

1. Identify two possible outcomes of enforcing boundaries in a difficult relationship.
2. Briefly explain how emotional divorce affects a marriage relationship.
3. Explain the difference between a legal separation and a legal divorce.
4. Describe a no-fault divorce.
5. List and describe two types of custody settlements.

Objectives

After studying this lesson, you will be able to

- **apply** the steps for managing a crisis to a divorce.
- **describe** how divorce affects the lives of family members.
- **determine** the challenges facing single-parent families and stepfamilies.

Focus Your Reading

1. Draw a graphic organizer with branches going to at least three family members: parent 1, parent 2, and children. As you read, list the adjustments each family member goes through as a result of a divorce.

2. Draw a cartoon strip that depicts a single parent experiencing role overload.

Content Terms

Build Vocab

role overload
stepparent

Academic Terms

intentional
circumstance

Strengthening the family is important after a divorce. After a divorce, parents and children must adjust to the new arrangements. Some parents may become single parents, which adds new responsibilities to their lives. After divorce, some parents may remarry, forming stepfamilies. Relationships in these stepfamilies should be strengthened as well.

Adjusting to Divorce

Divorce is a traumatic experience for all involved. Many changes result, and these have a lifelong effect on parents and children. Adjusting to these changes takes time. People who experience a divorce struggle with emotional trauma, new parenting arrangements, new living arrangements, and lower family income (**Figure 16.12**).

Applying the Steps for Managing a Crisis

The steps for managing a crisis in the family can apply to adjusting to a divorce. Helping all members understand the

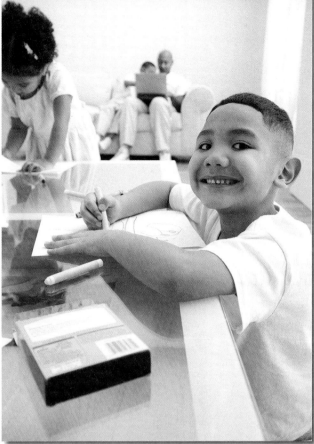
Blend Images/Shutterstock.com

Figure 16.12 Divorce requires adjustments from both parents and children. *Why is good communication so difficult for divorced parents, yet so critical for children's benefits?*

situation is the first step. At the center of that understanding should always be the principle that the divorce is not any one person's fault. This is important because of the need to keep cooperative relationships between all parties. Children adjust more readily if their parents can cooperate in carrying out parenting tasks. They also benefit when both parents continue to be involved in their lives. Thus, it is important to avoid scapegoating against any family member.

The second step for managing a crisis is to seek solutions to the problem. When all the needs of all family members are considered, a divorced family must address multiple problems. Many of these problems will not have an easy solution, and community resources may be needed to assist with some of them. Adults adjust to a divorce more easily if they can be reasonable as they work out the details of their new relationship as ex-spouses.

The third step in managing a crisis is to strengthen the family unit. This is hard in the case of a divorce, as the family is separated into two units. As with other family crises, setting aside quiet, uninterrupted times to talk; sharing thoughts and feelings openly; accepting each other's thoughts and feelings; and encouraging each other are all critical pieces for healing in individuals' lives. It is likely to be very difficult for the two ex-spouses to follow through on all these actions together. Still, they need to make an effort to be open and accepting when discussing such issues as decisions involving their children. Each parent can follow all these steps individually with their children. Taking time for family leisure activities will also help reduce the effects of stress and build positive feelings in each of the two new family groups.

The fourth step in managing a crisis is to emphasize personal growth for individual family members. All members need this positive experience. Children in the family need encouragement to grow toward maturity intellectually, socially, emotionally, and physically. To review strategies for reaching maximum growth and development, see Chapter 2. It is hard to focus on growth experiences when all family members are feeling drained and emotionally exhausted by a divorce. Parents have to take *intentional*, or purposeful, steps to promote growth in the family and celebrate the successes of individual family members. Continued involvement with friends, community, and extended family can help families emphasize personal growth.

Emotional Adjustments

When a divorce occurs, parents and children often struggle with many feelings, particularly hurt. A common reaction to being emotionally hurt is withdrawal. Individuals build walls around themselves, trying to protect themselves from more hurt in the future. To others, this response may appear as an uncaring attitude. Instead, it is a sign that healing needs to take place. All family members will need supportive relationships in which they feel cared for, understood, loved, and accepted. Over time, these relationships will promote social and emotional well-being.

The ex-spouses can get this support from their parents, other relatives, spiritual leaders,

counselors, and close friends. Parents should be careful not to burden children, especially young ones, with being their main source of support. Parents, however, need to work at meeting this need for children (**Figure 16.13**). Grandparents and other family members can also be a loving, secure source of support for children.

Think About Your Reading

How is the loss of a relationship from divorce different from the loss of a relationship due to some other outside factor?

The Divorced Adult

Mixed feelings are common for the ex-spouses after a divorce. Feelings of loneliness may be combined with feelings of rejection and hurt. A divorced person may wonder if anyone will ever want to marry him or her again. The desire for a close friend and close relationship is strong. Such emotions often influence people who have been recently divorced to jump into a new relationship too soon. Before getting involved in a new relationship, however, this person needs to take time to heal and reevaluate the qualities he or she desires in a partner.

Rebuilding self-esteem and self-confidence is an important part of the adjustment process. This adjustment is helped by looking for ways to grow and learn through the divorce experience. A person may need to learn more about himself or herself and develop personal skills. Thinking about life goals and perhaps training for a new occupation are other needs to consider.

Identifying the qualities desired in a new partner is important before the divorced adult returns to the dating scene. The fact is, second and later marriages have an even greater statistical chance

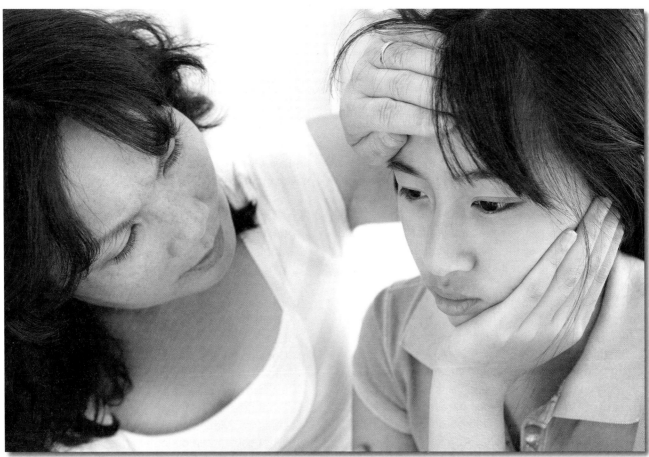

Monkey Business Images/Shutterstock.com

Figure 16.13 It is important that parents are main sources of support for their children as children deal with feelings of being hurt.

of ending in divorce than first marriages. That fact makes it clear that this step is very important. A divorced adult should carefully think about all the qualities of a healthy dating relationship discussed in Chapter 10 and consider the traits that were present in the marriage but not evident to him or her before the marriage. Learning from the past can help a person grow in the future.

Children of Divorced Parents

Children must deal with mixed emotions as well. They may feel angry that their parents have divorced. They may feel hurt and rejected by the parent who does not have custody. They may blame one of the parents or themselves for the divorce. Feelings of insecurity are common among children since the family unit has been broken and their source of love and nurturing is divided.

The children's emotional adjustment can be made easier if both parents continue to be actively involved in children's lives. They both need to spend time with each child, showing love and affection. They both can show interest in the child's friends, achievements, and activities. Also, grandparents and other extended family members may be able to offer security and affection at this time (**Figure 16.14**).

Think About Your Reading

Why do you think it is important that children have someone they can maintain a strong, close attachment to during a breakup in the family?

New Parenting Arrangements

Parents and children need to adjust to new parenting arrangements. The parent with sole custody takes on the new role of single parent. The noncustodial parent must adjust to the new role of being a visiting or part-time parent.

Children often have less access to both parents after a divorce. The custodial parent may be gone more due to work, school, or dating. The noncustodial parent is no longer in the home every day. He or she may visit often at first, but less often as time goes on.

REAL-LIFE SCENARIO

Adjusting to Divorce

"Mommy, look what Tara did to the coloring book!" Joel exclaimed as he turned the pages. Tara had marked a big black X across the father's face in each picture.

Katie looked across the table at her five-year-old daughter. She knew the divorce had been hard on all of them, but she had thought they were adjusting well.

Tom had paid for her to complete an accounting course at the technical college. Since she had found a job at the bank, she felt life had improved for her and the children. Now this!

Katie wondered what she should do. She also wondered if Tom's decreasing visits had anything to do with Tara's anger. Since meeting his new girlfriend, Tom had not visited his children even once.

Katie decided to talk to Tara's kindergarten teacher. Perhaps she had shown some unusual behavior there as well. She hoped the teacher might have some suggestions.

For Discussion

1. Identify and describe the custody arrangements in this family.
2. What evidence is there of an alimony settlement?
3. What steps has Katie taken to adjust to the problem of lower income in single-parent families?
4. Considering the stages of grieving over a loss, what do you think might have been the reason for Tara's action?
5. What other behaviors might a child use that could be evidence of the grieving process?
6. What could Katie do to help her daughter with the emotional adjustment to a divorce?

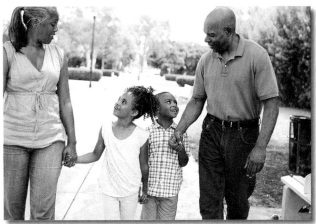

Figure 16.14 Close relationships with grandparents and other relatives can help children adjust emotionally to the parents' decision to divorce. *What interpersonal skills could help grandparents relate to both parents in a divorce?*

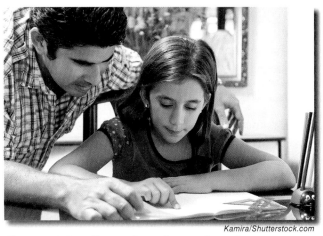

Kamira/Shutterstock.com

Figure 16.15 Even when divorced, each parent should continue to be involved in a child's life. *What are some ways that a child benefits from such involvement?*

Parenting roles must be adjusted, too. Questions of how to relate to the children, what to do with them, and what needs should be met may arise. It is not uncommon for the noncustodial parent to plan fun activities, buy extravagant gifts, or spoil children to try and win their favor when he or she has visitation. That leaves the custodial parent as the one who enforces rules on a daily basis, appearing to be the "bad guy."

Communicating about children's needs is an important part of co-parenting (**Figure 16.15**). Differences need to be set aside to focus on how children's needs can best be met. Consistency in rules for behavior will benefit the children. Expectations for daily tasks, such as homework and helping with household chores, can be similar at both parents' homes. Differences in guidance between one parent and the other must be discussed and settled. Parents should show respect even if they do not like each other, in order to benefit the children's daily lives. Counseling can be helpful for parents as they work to identify good parenting solutions after a divorce.

Think About Your Reading

What are some ways family members could reduce the stress that goes with adjusting to a divorce?

New Living Arrangements

Along with handling emotional stress, family members must adjust to new living arrangements. A family house may need to be sold so the money can be split between the divorced couple. The family may need to move to a new neighborhood and find new friends. Children must adjust to living with one parent and visiting the other. Adults must adjust to managing a household alone, without help from the ex-spouse.

The divorce court usually identifies an area within which the children with the custodial parent must live, thus making visitation with the noncustodial parent realistic. Any living arrangements that reduce the number of changes will also help to reduce the stress in the children's lives. For example, if children can stay in the same school, they will have their same teachers and same friends—people who can help them handle the emotional adjustments of the divorce. If grandparents or other relatives live nearby, they can help a single parent with some of the challenges of adjusting to new living arrangements.

The *McKinney-Vento Education of Homeless Children and Youth Assistance Act* is a federal law that ensures educational stability for homeless children and youth. Living with grandparents on a temporary basis is an example of being homeless under this law. If a parent with children moves in with family or friends on a temporary basis, this

law requires that school districts help children continue in the school they were attending before they had to leave their home.

Lower Income

For most families, both spouses have less income after a divorce. This shortage of money can be a major source of stress. Since women tend to earn less than men, female-headed families tend to have less household income than male-headed ones. These households cannot always count on child support payments, either. Many fathers do not fulfill their responsibilities to pay child support, even though it is a crime not to do so. Some fathers ignore their obligation; some have such low incomes that they cannot pay.

Whatever the extent of the change in income, everyone in the two new households has to adapt to the changes. New *circumstances*, or conditions, typically require changes in lifestyle. The families may need to cut back on luxuries or treats. They may have to wait longer to make major purchases or to take vacations. It can help children adapt to these changes if their parents communicate honestly and openly about them.

Think About Your Reading

How could family members work together to help restore balance to the family system after a divorce?

Single-Parent Families

Usually the parent who has legal custody also has physical custody of a child. This means the child lives with that parent most of the time. Most single parents struggle to meet financial and parenting responsibilities, and many cope with loneliness.

Role Overload from Added Responsibilities

Most of the time, the single parent alone carries the responsibility for child care. Although

there is only one parent now, many parenting decisions remain to be made (**Figure 16.16**). What should the parent do when the child is sick, grades are poor, or the child misbehaves? Even when the parent is tired or angry, reasonable parenting decisions still need to be made. No one else is there to fill in while the parent calms down or thinks over the situation.

Working, parenting, and managing the household alone often result in role overload for the single parent. **Role overload** means the single parent has too many roles and responsibilities to carry them all out well. As discussed in Chapter 13, grandparents, other family members, and friends may help a single parent with child care responsibilities. Such support can help the single-parent family fulfill its functions and meet the needs of each family member. Government aid programs can help in some cases as well.

Think About Your Reading

What are some ways that a single-parent family can restore balance to the family system so the needs of family members are met?

Coping with Loneliness

Loneliness is often a problem for single parents. Because they are alone, single parents tend to focus more on their children than on themselves. They

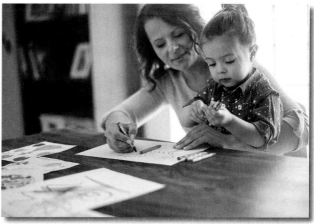
gpointstudio/Shutterstock.com

Figure 16.16 Single parents are responsible for the entirety of child care; there is not another parent to fill in if the single parent is stressed.

feel it is important to succeed at parenting. They devote most of their time to providing for the family and caring for their children. As a result, little time is left to spend building other relationships.

Supportive Friendships

Friendships are especially important for single parents. They need friends who accept them and help them believe in their own abilities. Friends can encourage them to take steps that will help them grow as people. This support increases the single parent's self-esteem and confidence. An attitude of personal growth can lead to the development of new skills. Personal accomplishments will bring feelings of success (**Figure 16.17**).

Remarriage and the Stepfamily

Many divorced people remarry within a few years after their divorce. The reasons for this decision vary. They may desire the closeness of a marriage relationship or more financial security. The desire to share parenting tasks with a spouse may be another reason.

When either spouse has children from a previous marriage, they then form a *stepfamily* or *blended family*. The newly married parent becomes a **stepparent** to the children of his or her new spouse. The stepfamily brings more resources together to meet the needs of family members. It also brings more challenges.

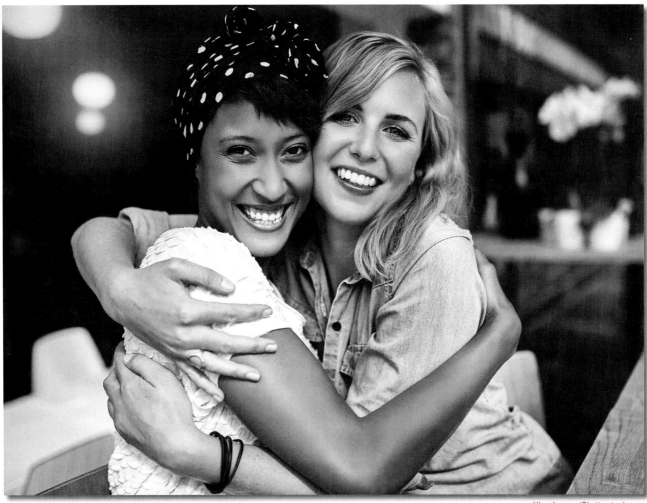

Uber Images/Shutterstock.com

Figure 16.17 Friendships are important for the single parent. *How can good friends promote personal growth and healthy future relationships for a divorced person?*

Adjusting to the Marriage

The early years of a second marriage are full of adjustments, just as they were in the first marriage. The adjustments in a second marriage can be even more complicated.

One reason for these difficulties is that feelings of hurt and rejection that carry over from the divorce may still exist. To deal with this, both spouses need to experience acceptance and unconditional love. They need each other's full support and encouragement. They need to build each other's self-esteem. Fulfilling their own emotional needs will help them meet their children's needs for love, affection, and security.

In addition, the new couple is adjusting to a new parenting arrangement. They will have less time for each other than a newlywed couple with no children. They have less time to communicate with each other, resolve conflicts privately, and develop mutual interests. Making sure they set aside time to develop their personal relationship is an important step to ensure that the marriage is strong.

Stepparenting

The most challenging role in a stepfamily is that of stepparent. The relationship between a stepparent and stepchild can be fulfilling, but it can also be strained. Building this relationship takes time. A stepchild may feel fears, doubt, mistrust, and insecurity. He or she may still feel anger and rejection toward the parents from the first family. The child may resent the stepparent trying to take the place of the absent parent. The child may purposely misbehave as a way of expressing these feelings or may withdraw from the stepparent, treating him or her coldly. Both the parent and stepparent need to treat these responses with patience and understanding.

Although stepparents cannot take the place of absent parents, they can fill the gap the absent parents leave. The stepparent can provide a listening ear. Listening with empathy is important. Messages such as "I understand" can encourage the child to talk about feelings. Responding by reflecting can help the child identify feelings. Saying to the child, "It hurts when things like that happen, doesn't it?" help the child identify the feelings that are deep inside.

As more experiences are shared, feelings of love between stepchild and stepparent will grow, especially when acceptance and affection are shown (**Figure 16.18**). All this takes time, however.

It is important that the parent and stepparent support each other in parenting decisions. They can work out rules ahead of time and support each other in enforcing them.

Life in a stepfamily can be complicated further if both parents in the remarriage have children, creating two sets of stepchildren. Creating new traditions that bring both parents and all the children together can help strengthen the new family. Encouraging open communication between the stepchildren helps, too. The stepparents also need to work to treat all the children relatively equally so that none of them feels ignored or overlooked.

Needs of the Stepfamily

First and foremost, a stepfamily must adjust to a new marriage, family structure, and parenting situation. These adjustments take time. Besides these adjustments, the stepfamily must also do the following:

- *Allow time for family unity to grow.* Stepfamilies need time to develop bonds that build a sense of togetherness. They also need time for love to grow between family members.

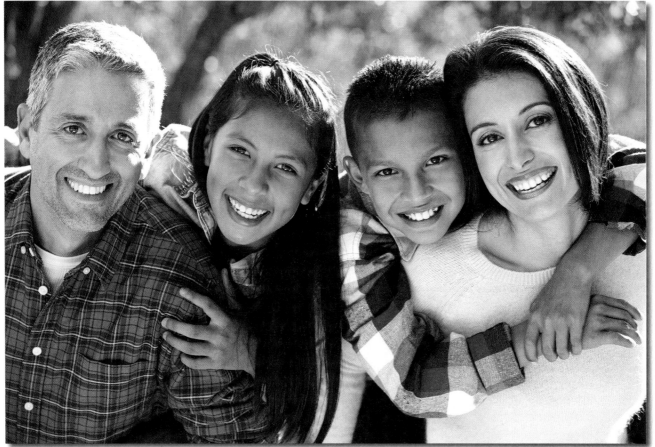

Monkey Business Images/Shutterstock.com

Figure 16.18 Given time, members of the stepfamily can build close bonds of affection. *What interpersonal skills can help make this goal become a reality?*

- *Provide personal space for each family member.* Children are especially possessive of their space. Establishing some personal space for each member may help each of them feel at home.

- *Make workable visitation arrangements for the absent parent and other people important to the children.* Grandparents and others involved in the lives of the children also need to be included in these arrangements.

- *Accept all family members in the stepfamily structure.* The household members need to accept each other and the reality of the situation. Together, they are a family and can fulfill the functions of a family in each other's lives.

Taking these steps to build healthy relationships within a stepfamily can take considerable time and effort. It can also be rewarding and fulfilling as members find their needs cared for and their goals met.

Assess

LESSON 16.3

COMPREHENSION CHECK

1. How can families use the four steps for managing a crisis to help members adjust to a divorce?

2. Name three common emotional responses to a divorce.

3. Explain how parents can help their children adjust to new parenting arrangements after a divorce.

4. Identify four challenges faced by a single-parent family.

5. List two emotional adjustments that are unique to a couple in a stepfamily.

6. Briefly describe how a stepparent can or cannot fill the gap an absent parent leaves.

7. Give four suggestions to help a stepfamily meet the unique needs of its members.

CHAPTER SUMMARY

A family faces change when a marriage relationship breaks down. Various factors can contribute to this event. Breakdowns that cannot be resolved often result in *divorce*, a legal procedure in which a marriage is legally ended. Divorce does not, however, end the parenting responsibilities of either parent. During the divorce proceedings, certain legal issues must be settled. Custody settlements, visitation rights, and child support payments are determined by the court.

Adjusting to the changes caused by divorce is difficult for both adults and children. Emotional adjustments must be made as well as adaptations to new living arrangements. Often both spouses have less income to live on as a result of maintaining separate households.

When there are children in the family, divorce produces a single-parent family structure. Often a divorced parent remarries, producing the stepfamily or blended family. Both these family structures have unique challenges in fulfilling the functions of a family in the lives of the members.

VOCABULARY ACTIVITIES

1. Divide the terms between you and a partner, with one of you taking the legal terms related to divorce and the other taking the nonlegal terms. Write a quiz using each term on your list in a sentence, but leaving the terms blank. Exchange quizzes with your partner and complete the sentences on the quiz he or she wrote. Check your answers with each other and resolve any disagreements over the meanings of terms until you both agree on the correct definition.

Content Terms

alimony (16.2)
barrier to divorce (16.1)
child support (16.2)
divorce (16.1)
emotional divorce (16.2)
joint custody (16.2)
legal custody (16.2)
legal divorce (16.2)
legal separation (16.2)

mediator (16.2)
no-fault divorce (16.2)
petitioner (16.2)
physical custody (16.2)
respondent (16.2)
role overload (16.3)
sole custody (16.2)
stepparent (16.3)
visitation rights (16.2)

2. Prepare flash cards for each of these terms with the term on one side and the definition on the

other. Quiz a partner on the meaning of each term. Then answer your partner with the correct definition when he or she quizzes you.

Academic Terms

circumstance (16.3)
constructive (16.1)
ground (16.2)
inevitable (16.1)

intentional (16.3)
nurture (16.2)
procedure (16.2)

ASSESS

Your Knowledge

3. What are the stages of a relationship breakdown?
4. What happens to the family system when there is a divorce in the family?

Your Understanding

5. Through all the steps in the breakdown of a marriage and a divorce, how can a family meet the needs of children and adults and restore balance to the family system?
6. How can stepparents develop close relationships with their stepchildren?

Your Skills

7. Reflect on a family you know that has experienced divorce. Which of the factors that can contribute to divorce were evident in that family?
8. What are some skills that could have helped family members from the previous question improve their relationships and strengthen their marriage and family?

CRITICAL THINKING

9. **Make Projections.** Think about families you know. List five actions that you think would contribute to a breakdown in the marriage relationship. Explain why you see the cause-and-effect relationship between each of these actions and such a breakdown, citing evidence from the text to support your analysis.
10. **Draw Conclusions.** Identify a television show that has a stepparent as a main character. Write a paragraph discussing the following questions: Is the stepparent presented from a positive or negative view? How does the stepparent relate to the children in the family? What conclusions could be drawn about stepparent relationships from this show? How realistic do you think those conclusions are? Cite evidence from the text

in support of your answer. *Choice*: Analyze a cartoon, child's story, or novel with a stepparent as a main character. *Group option*: Share your evidence and conclusions with a partner and write a paragraph combining what you both found and thought.

11. **Make Inferences.** Write two scenarios, each one depicting the family interactions that might exist in a divorced family with sole custody and joint custody. *Choice*: Present your scenarios in a video, rap, or song.

12. **Solve a Problem.** Identify a list of concerns that teens may have when their families are going through the stages of divorce. Conduct research through personal interviews, online resources, and consultation with professionals. Research and identify school resources available for teens facing these issues. *Choice*: Start a peer support group for students whose families are going through divorce.

CORE SKILLS

13. **Writing, Social Studies.** Prepare questions related to grounds for divorce, divorce procedures, custody arrangements, or other legal aspects of divorce in your state. Invite a lawyer or legal assistant to speak to your class on the legal considerations of divorce and participate by asking your questions. *Choice*: Summarize the presentation in a written report.

14. **Writing.** Prepare questions about the challenges of parenting in today's families. Help arrange a panel of four or five guest speakers to discuss such challenges. Invite parents of single-parent families and stepfamilies to serve as the guest speakers. *Choice*: Summarize the presentation in a written report.

15. **Research, Writing, Social Studies.** Interview a social worker to identify what resources in the community are available to a single-parent family while the head of the household is going through a divorce. Write a report summarizing your findings. *Choice*: Use the Internet to research available community resources.

16. **Reading, Writing.** Create a flyer that illustrates the stages of divorce. Cite information from the text and from at least one other resource. Identify possible school and community resources that could assist families going through each stage. *Group option*: Work with a team and have each

person on the team research one of the stages for the flyer. *Choice*: Post your flyer to your school's website.

17. **Research, Writing.** Using online resources, research the differences in grounds for divorce in various states and describe them in writing. Include your opinion on why you think there might be variations in grounds for divorce from one state to another.

18. **Research, Writing.** Search online for information about the attitudes toward divorce and patterns of divorce in at least two societies outside North America. Write a paper comparing the two societies' views of divorce to divorce in the United States. Cite evidence to support your conclusions.

19. **Research, Math, Writing.** Survey students in your school to find how many have experienced divorce in their immediate family and in their extended family. Survey your parents or guardians, asking whether they, as teenagers, experienced divorce in their family or extended family. Then create a graph indicating divorce statistics and trends in your community. Write a paragraph analyzing the differences over time, if any.

CAREER READINESS

20. **Writing Employee Materials on Divorce-Related Workplace Issues.** Divorce can be very disruptive to an adult's life, and the effects can spill over into his or her work life. Take the role of a human resources manager who has been asked to write a section of the corporate website providing employees with ideas on how to cope with divorce, resources in the community that can help families going through divorce, and company policies that will help them in this adjustment. Include a section that addresses the company's expectations for workers' job performance during this period.

21. **Solving Problems.** Assume you work at a local social service agency. Your agency works with clients who have limited resources for food, especially single-parent families with young children. For most of your agency's clients, obtaining adequate daily protein is a financial problem. In order to better serve your clients, put together fact sheets about purchasing nutritious food at low cost and preparing healthful meals that do not require a great deal of preparation time.

Connecting with Career Clusters

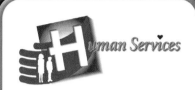

Pathways

Early Childhood Development & Services

Counseling and Mental Health Services

Family and Community Services

Personal Care Services

Consumer Services

Family Services

Workers in family services careers help individuals and families meet their physical, intellectual, social, and emotional needs so that family members can reach their full potential. Jobs in family services include such titles as social worker, case worker, child advocate, and human services specialist. Workers in these areas help families face problems such as disabilities, abuse, or poverty. These professionals often serve as liaisons between students and homes, schools, courts, protective services, doctors, child guidance clinics, and others who provide additional services to families with specific needs.

Workers in family services careers may help families locate assistance from public or private agencies in the community and provide advice regarding food stamps, child care, food purchasing and preparation, money management, or housekeeping and sanitation in the home. Teaching and the modeling of skills may take place in the family home or in an educational setting.

Most jobs in this career area require at least a one- or two-year associate's degree from a technical college or a four-year college degree. Family services workers need knowledge and skills in fostering growth and development in children and youth, healthy eating and nutrition practices, financial planning, home management and sanitation, as well as community services available to help families meet these needs.

CAREER OUTLOOK

Good communication skills for both speaking and listening are needed by family services workers as they help families and individuals develop skills to meet their needs. Workers in this career area need to be dependable, persistent, flexible, and tolerant of stress as they work to help families change old habits and learn new and healthy patterns of interacting and working so that the needs of family members are met.

The role of family services offered through the business community has expanded over the last few years, including positions for social workers. More companies are taking steps to impact the communities where their workers live, helping to solve social problems and identify practices that help their employees succeed both at work and at home. Family services workers in large companies need leadership skills to help develop company policies that benefit both the workers and the company and to build positive relationships within the community.

Job growth in some areas of family services, such as for social work assistants, is expected to be faster than average. Other areas remain average or even a little below average. The median salary for child, family, and school social workers in 2014 was $42,200, with salaries ranging from $27,500 to $72,500. The median salary for other types of social workers was $59,100 in 2014, with a range from $33,000 to $84,600. The higher-paying jobs usually require more education and experience.

EXPLORE

Internet Research

Research the steps involved in becoming a social worker in your community. Try to answer the following questions as you gather your research. Where are people with a social work degree hired in your community? What education is required? Where can postsecondary training in social work be obtained? What jobs are available for people with different degrees of training—associate's, bachelor's, and master's? Summarize your research in a report.

Job Shadowing

Contact your local human services department to identify who might provide educational services for families about family financial planning, planning nutritional meals for the family, caring for young children, or other topics. Ask to sit in and observe one of these training sessions. Write a report identifying the topic that was presented, the strategies used by the presenter, and your observation of how the educational training was accepted by the family members in attendance.

Community Service/Volunteer

Contact your local hospital about health programs they have for parents of young children. Offer to volunteer with their programming. Write a summary of the programming, identifying how parents and children benefit from this program.

Project

Identify specific information that a family in need could use to help solve a problem related to one of the following areas: meal planning and preparing nutritious meals for teens; improving parent-teen relationships; reducing the effects of family stress; meeting the needs of family members in a stepfamily; or another topic you identify. Prepare a brochure that could be used to present the information to families. Offer the brochure to your school counselor or school social worker for use in their offices.

Interview

Locate a social worker in your community, either through your school guidance office or through your county human services office. Set up an appointment to interview the social worker about his or her job, what aspects of his or her career are rewarding, what aspects are difficult to deal with on a daily basis, the types of services that he or she provides to individuals and families, and the training needed to be a social worker. Summarize your findings in a report.

Part-Time Job

Obtain a job working at a local grocery store. Offer to provide educational flyers or posters for the fruit and vegetable aisle that provide ideas for families to incorporate healthy foods into their daily meal plans. These flyers or posters could be created as part of a class project.

UNIT 6

FAMILY RELATIONSHIPS OVER TIME

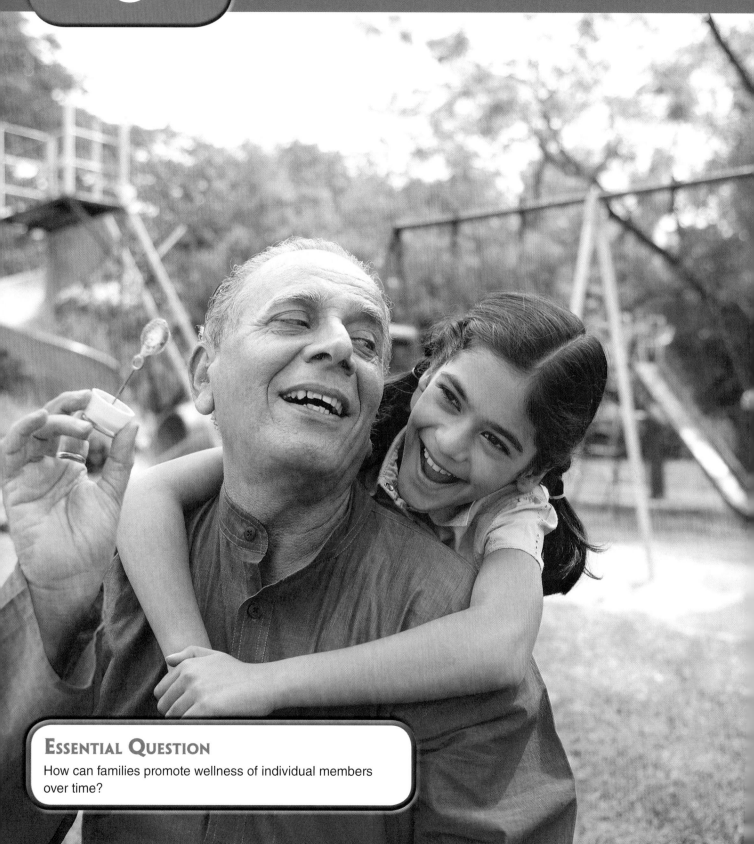

ESSENTIAL QUESTION

How can families promote wellness of individual members over time?

Volt Collection/Shutterstock.com

Chapter 17 The Early Years of the Family Life Cycle
Chapter 18 Relating to and Guiding Children
Chapter 19 The Aging Family

CASE STUDY

How Can Family Members Help One Another?

Read the case study and discuss the questions that follow. After finishing the chapters in this unit, discuss the questions again and identify any answers you would change based on information you learned.

Grandpa Liang walked into the school with his granddaughter Taeko. It was her first day at school, and he had walked her to the door, but that was as far as he was allowed. The teacher welcomed Taeko into the classroom and dismissed Grandpa Liang for the day. He would return later to walk her back home, but only after he helped his son Chen and his wife, Ling, fill some new orders for their product. Chen and Ling were very busy with their growing business. It had grown so much that they had moved into a larger building in Taipei, Taiwan. Chen's parents had moved with them into the city and helped care for Taeko and her brother, Lei, while Chen and Ling worked and promoted their business. Grandma Shu walked to the market each day to buy food for the day's meals. She missed her garden at their old home but did like the choices she found in the daily market.

Gabe looked out over the city lights as he closed the curtains of their high-rise apartment near Penn Station in New York. He turned to help Rachel put the kids to bed, as she had just finished reading them their bedtime story. The children were tired after being in day care since 6:00 that morning. Having three in day care took out a chunk of the family income, but both he and Rachel had good jobs working at the hospital. Managing child care with the long shifts they sometimes had to work was difficult. He wished his or Rachel's family were closer and that they could help out when he or Rachel had to work weekends or a night shift. He wondered if they could afford a nanny or someone

who could come to the house to help out. *I'll have to ask around at work tomorrow*, he thought. *I'll see what solutions others have found*.

Ana hurried home after school, for she knew there was a lot to be done that evening. Her final paper was due in two days, so she had to work on that. She planned to stop at the nursing home

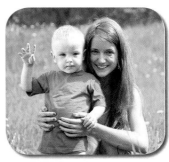

to drop off a new puzzle for Grandma Lena to put together. She knew the days sitting beside Grandpa Lars' bedside became long for Grandma. Then she had to go to her sister Mari's place, where she would babysit for a couple of hours while Mari went to work. She had to do well on her paper, though. It was a final project for her senior class, and her goal was to earn a scholarship at the Malmo University in Sweden. A scholarship would certainly help out the strain on the family budget.

For Discussion

1. How did each family promote wellness for their individual family members?
2. What resources did each family use to help meet the needs of family members at different stages of life?

Iakov Filimonov/Shutterstock.com

CHAPTER 17

THE EARLY YEARS OF THE FAMILY LIFE CYCLE

Reading Prep

Before reading the chapter, look at the three sets of objectives (know, understand, and be able to do) on the next page. Write a question you have about each objective. As you read, look for answers to the questions and record them.

Key Questions

Questions to answer as you study this chapter:

- How can families adjust to the changes in the family life cycle?
- What does it take to be a good parent?

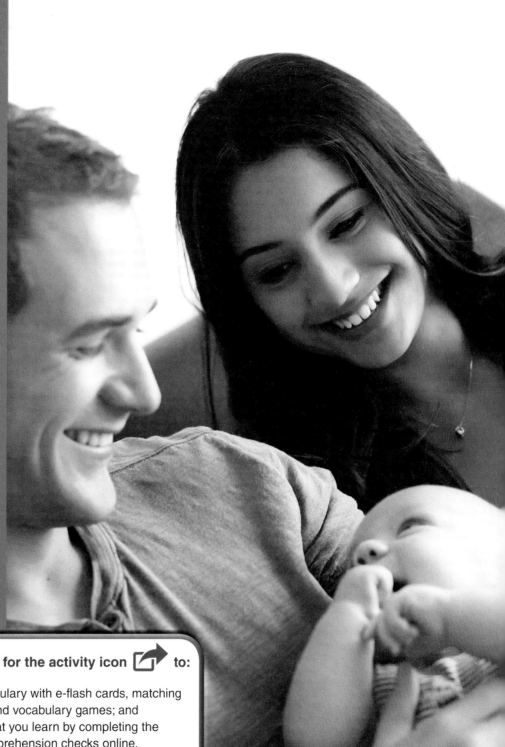

While studying this chapter, look for the activity icon 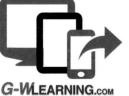 to:

- **build** vocabulary with e-flash cards, matching activities, and vocabulary games; and
- **assess** what you learn by completing the lesson comprehension checks online.

www.g-wlearning.com/humanservices/

G-WLEARNING.com

AFTER STUDYING THIS CHAPTER, YOU WILL

KNOW:

- The stages of the family life cycle.
- The characteristics of responsible parents.
- The risks associated with teen pregnancy.

UNDERSTAND:

- How the family life cycle impacts roles and responsibilities of family members over time.
- How families can manage resources to meet changing needs in the early parenting years.
- How infertility can affect a couple's parenting decisions.

BE ABLE TO DO:

- Apply decision-making skills to parenting choices.
- Analyze personal characteristics for the qualities of responsible parenting.

GETTING STARTED

"Jessica is so cute and fun!" everyone said about Catina's new baby. Catina smiled, but said nothing. She could not let her friends know that sometimes she resented the baby. How could one tiny person require so much work? Jessica had to be fed every three hours around the clock, rocked and held often, bathed, and changed several times a day.

Catina's husband, Roland, spent little time at home. He worked during the days and took college classes in the evenings. He often studied late at the college library because the baby was too noisy.

Roland and Catina had married young. Catina planned to work while Roland finished college, but an unexpected pregnancy had changed their plans. Catina had become ill, missed too much work, and lost her job. The medical bills had wiped out their savings. Now

Catina and Roland argued often. Their relationship was growing tenser by the week.

Families change over time. Each stage that a family goes through produces unique challenges and rewards. These stages make up the *family life cycle.* The early years of the family life cycle typically bring children into the family, and their arrival causes major changes. How would parenthood affect your life? How would your daily schedule and free time change? How would your finances be affected? Would you still have time for your friends? How would your plans for an education or a career be affected? As you will see in this chapter, parenting is an important decision that deserves careful thought. It is a decision that will impact each and every stage of the family life cycle.

Content Terms

Build Vocab

family life cycle
newly married stage
founding family
early parenthood stage
launching stage
empty nest stage
sandwich generation
retirement stage

Academic Terms

vital

extent

Objectives

After studying this lesson, you will be able to

- **identify** the stages of the family life cycle.
- **describe** the changing roles and responsibilities of individuals and family members throughout the family life cycle.
- **recognize** challenges and rewards of each stage of the family life cycle.
- **explain** how families can manage resources to meet members' needs throughout the family life cycle.

Focus Your Reading

1. Create a three-column chart and list each stage of the family life cycle in the first column. As you read each section, write down the changes that occur in each stage in the second column. In the third column, record the adjustments family members must make to maintain balance in the family system in each stage.

2. Draw a picture depicting the family makeup for each stage of the family life cycle.

Just as individuals change throughout their life spans, families change throughout the family life cycle. The **family life cycle** is composed of five stages that include common events and adjustments families go through over time (**Figure 17.1**). Right now, you are a part of your parents' or guardians' family life cycle. If you marry, you will begin your own family life cycle.

Most families go through similar stages in the family life cycle. In each stage, family members have different roles to fill, responsibilities to carry out, and challenges to meet. Along with the challenges, each stage has its own rewards.

Families may experience the stages of the family life cycle in different orders, and they may go through more than one stage at a time. For example, when a divorced parent remarries, he or she simultaneously experiences the newly married stage as well as one of the parenting stages. Some families may skip one or more

Stages of the Family Life Cycle		
Stage	**Key Events**	**Adjustments**
Newly married stage	• Wedding • Living on own	• Adjustments to being a pair • Need to establish a satisfying marriage relationship
Early parenthood stage	• Birth of children • Children in preschool stage • Children in elementary years	• Adjustments to being a parent • Adjustments to caring for children • Stimulating growth of children
Later parenthood stage	• Children in adolescence • Children dating • Children move out	• Parent-teen role adjustments • Need to balance freedom with responsibility • Launching children to college, living on their own, and independence
Empty nest stage	• Last child leaves home • Children marry and become parents • Parents become elderly	• Renewal of spousal relationship • Grandparenting • Caring for elderly parents • Preparing for retirement
Retirement stage	• Retirement from work or job • Death of spouse	• Adjustments to less income • New interests or hobbies • Focus on extended family relationships • Adjustments to physical changes of aging

Figure 17.1 Each stage of the family life cycle is marked by a series of different events. *How could families experience adjustments from more than one stage at the same time?*

stages. For example, a young adult may have a child and move directly into the early parenthood stage. A couple may not have children and may skip the parenting stages.

The steps in preparing for change from Chapter 1 can be applied to adjusting to the changes that go with the family life cycle. Those three steps are (1) gathering information about the changes, (2) developing skills needed to adjust to the changes, and (3) managing the changes using your knowledge and skills. Following these steps can help families meet members' needs as the family goes through the different stages.

It is important to remember that everyone in a family is learning and growing as the family progresses through different stages in the family life cycle. Parents, young children, teens, and grandparents—all are going through new experiences, learning, and changing. As a result, the challenges of each stage increase as the number of family members increases.

The Newly Married Stage

The first stage—the **newly married stage**—begins when two people marry. Sometimes it is called the *beginning stage*. The new family unit is sometimes called the **founding family**, referring to the fact that this stage begins the family life cycle for a newly formed family. In this stage, the couple works at establishing their own family; living on their own; and providing their own housing, food, and clothing. They need to work together to establish their own family of two in a satisfying marriage relationship.

Developing New Roles

During this stage, spouses take on new roles as husband or wife. Responsibilities include making an income, caring for each other's health and well-being, establishing and caring for a home, and managing time and money.

The couple needs to develop good communication patterns and learn to solve problems together. They need to set goals and plan for their future. Their success in these tasks will affect their family through all other stages.

During the early years of marriage, couples often share many responsibilities. They may both work as wage earners and share housekeeping roles (**Figure 17.2**). To build a strong marriage, they should make decisions together. Some of these roles may change when children are added to the family. Financial resources may be strained if one of the partners is pursuing an education during this stage. Time may also be difficult to manage if that partner is working at the same time.

Rewards of the Newly Married Stage

The rewards of the newly married stage come from the satisfaction of building a strong marriage relationship. Each partner in the couple feels loved and trusted by the other. Each feels the satisfaction of being committed to their relationship and knowing that his or her partner is as well.

> ## Think About Your Reading
> How is the family system affected if a newly married couple cannot adjust to their new roles of living on their own?

The Early Parenthood Stage

Pregnancy and the birth of the first child mark the beginning of the **early parenthood stage**. This stage continues through the toddler, preschool, and elementary years of the youngest child in the family.

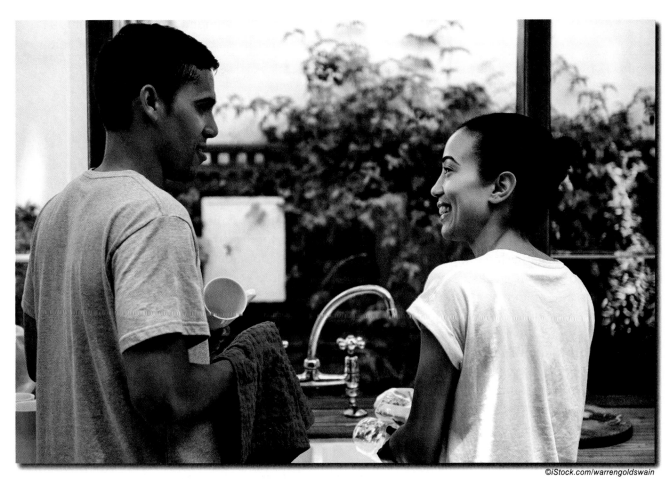

©iStock.com/warrengoldswain

Figure 17.2   The newly married stage is marked by the sharing of responsibilities between the two spouses.

Role Adjustments

Adjusting to the new roles of mother or father can be a challenge. The tasks include caring for young children and meeting their needs. This means that parents need to understand child development and learn how to stimulate the young child's growth.

In many families, two or more children are born during this stage. Relationships become more complex. As children begin school, expectations from teachers, peers, and others in the community also influence family roles.

During the early years of parenting, the family budget often seems stretched to the limit. Financial needs increase as children are born, and the family must find ways to meet those needs by earning more income.

In the young family, there is a need for flexible roles. Often, family tasks are nonstop. Keeping a positive attitude in the family is easier when spouses work together to meet the family's needs.

Parenting and work roles take up much of a couple's time in this stage of the family life cycle. What time is spent together is usually child-centered. Each parent has little time alone, and the same is true of the couple together. This lack of a break from the responsibilities of parenting can be exhausting. Having quiet moments together becomes a major need for a couple with young children. If they are nearby, grandparents and other relatives can help with the heavy load of parenting responsibilities from time to time, giving the couple a chance to have some time together.

Rewards of the Early Parenthood Stage

Although the many tasks of parenting are demanding, this stage of the family life cycle is very rewarding. It is exciting and satisfying to see children grow and learn new skills. Parents feel love for their children—a different kind of love than they feel for each other.

The time spent with children can be rewarding for the family as a whole and can strengthen the love the two parents have for each other. Good patterns of communication lead to trust among family members. Sharing experiences together has the potential for building a strong family bond (**Figure 17.3**). Activities with the parents' families can meet needs in both families and build relationships within the extended family.

Think About Your Reading

What resources can help a young couple handle the heavy demands of parenting during the early parenthood years?

Later Parenthood Stage

As children reach adolescence, major changes take place in the family. These changes mark the beginning of the next stage of the family life cycle: the *later parenthood stage*.

Parent-Teen Role Adjustments

As explained in Chapter 2, the onset of puberty brings about rapid changes in physical growth and sexual development. The adolescent

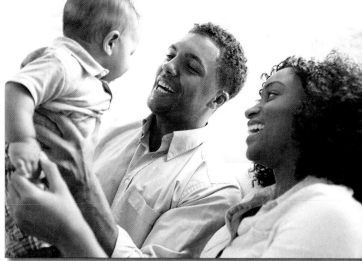

Monkey Business Images/Shutterstock.com

Figure 17.3 In the early parenting years, most parents find the close relationships with their children rewarding. *What skills could help parents and children maintain close relationships during the later parenting years?*

begins to appear more like an adult and less like a child. This time of transition requires parents to let go of some responsibilities while teens take on more responsibilities. This process continues to the completion of the later parenthood stage. Thus, the later parenthood stage is also known as the **launching stage**, the time when parents help young adults complete their education, become financially independent, and move out on their own.

Conflicts may arise when parents and adolescents do not agree on how much responsibility should be given up or taken on. Children often demand more freedom. Other parent-teen issues may also cause conflicts during these years. Teens' dating habits and choices of friends and clothing may become sources of conflict. Performance in school and future goals can be other areas in which teens and parents have disagreements.

Parents are legally responsible for their children until the children reach age 18. Parents often continue in the provider role while their children attend college. The launching stage can extend for several years before children become completely independent. As a result, the strain on a family's financial resources is high at this stage.

Rewards of the Later Parenthood Stage

During the later parenting years, communication skills are important in the family. Patterns of clear and open communication, joint decision making, and conflict resolution are *vital* (very important). These skills can help families manage changes in a way that brings rewards. The goal of these years is to launch a self-sufficient new generation. Seeing children reach that goal is rewarding to parents.

A key to this stage of the life cycle is empathy in communication and decision making. Communicating with empathy can help keep channels open between family members, which can be very important in the parent-teen relationship. Decision making with empathy means maintaining respect for one another's feelings and desires. With empathy underlying parent-teen relationships, family members maintain their strong bonds and eventually become adult friends.

Think About Your Reading

What can young adults do to show empathy to parents at this stage? What can parents do to show empathy to young adults at this stage?

The Empty Nest Stage

When the last child is independent and living on his or her own, the family enters the **empty nest stage**. Parental roles change greatly in this stage. Children no longer depend on their parents for meeting their needs. Instead, they are young adults responsible for meeting those needs themselves. Some marry and begin their own families. When a child marries, parents need to accept the child's mate into the extended family.

Role Adjustments

Parents may still be involved in their adult son's or daughter's life in the empty nest stage, but to a much lesser *extent*, or amount. Parents may still provide some financial help or support young adults in other ways. They may be also involved in grandparenting (**Figure 17.4**). These roles take less time than the full-time parenting responsibilities a couple shouldered in the past. Some parents feel very lonely in this stage. Developing new interests and setting new goals may fill some needs.

The relationships of empty nesters to their own parents may change as well. The older generation may need their children's financial support or help with physical care. This new role of supporting older parents requires adjustments from both spouses. These spouses are the middle generation, between their older parents and their own children. They are sometimes called the **sandwich generation**. This sandwich-like experience of being between two generations, both of which need support, adds stress to family resources, including time and money. In some ways, this experience can feel similar to the high demands on time and energy during the early parenthood stage. The timing of being in a sandwich

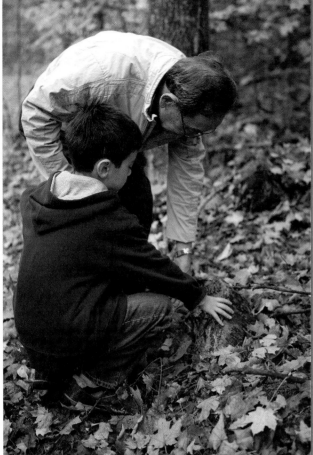

Figure 17.4 In many families, grandparenting is a new role of the empty nest stage. *How could grandparents contribute to healthy relationships in the family?*

©iStock.com/Jill Chen

Retirement Stage

Couples enter the **retirement stage** when one or both spouses retire from their careers. Retirement age varies. Some couples work as long as they are physically able, while some choose an early retirement.

Rewards of the Retirement Stage

Many couples plan ahead while they are still working to prepare financially for the retirement years. They set goals for this time of their life. For some couples, retirement is a time to focus on themselves, hobbies, volunteer work, travel, or leisure activities. Many see it as a chance to devote more time to friendships and grandchildren, too.

Not all people cope well with retirement. Some are unable to adjust to their changed roles. They miss the sense of purpose they felt while working. As a result, their self-esteem may drop. In addition, health problems that come with age and financial difficulties that result from lower income can prevent some retirees from looking at the future with hope.

Death of a Spouse

The family life cycle ends when one spouse dies. The remaining partner then returns to single living. The widow or widower faces two major challenges: dealing emotionally with the loss of a partner and adjusting to a lifestyle change. Personal freedoms may be affected. The loss of income, health, and the ability to live independently are hard to accept. Self-esteem may decline. Fears of being used or abused increase.

Many older adults choose to remain in their own homes as long as possible. Some live with a child, other family members, or a roommate. Others move to communities developed exclusively for older adults. Yet others live in group-care facilities.

Visits with family members and friends are important to the older person (**Figure 17.5**). They can bring joy, meaning, and hope into the person's life. Keeping active in community groups, religious groups, or educational settings also helps older people stay in contact with others.

generation can vary, so these challenges can surface during the later parenthood stage as well.

Rewards of the Empty Nest Stage

Although the empty nest stage can be challenging, it can also be rewarding. When children move out and establish their own households, spouses return to living as a couple. They have more time for each other, which gives them the chance to renew their own close relationship. Strengthening their own relationship is important as they look ahead to the next stage of retirement.

Think About Your Reading

What are some of the challenges of being in the "sandwich generation" between young adults and older adults?

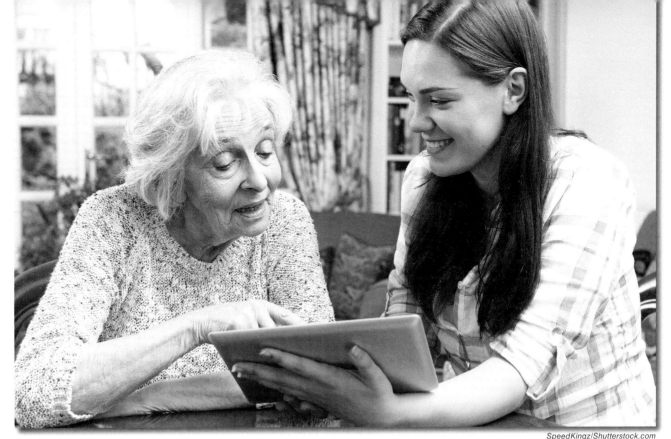

SpeedKingz/Shutterstock.com

Figure 17.5 Older family members can pass on their knowledge and skills to the younger generation. *What skills could young teens offer to assist aging grandparents?*

Technology and the Changing Family Life Cycle

Technology has changed the roles of family members over history, and will probably continue to do so. Families will always need to be alert to the benefits and drawbacks of new technologies and recognize their potential impact on the family's well-being. They will need to develop plans to manage the effects of technology on their lives.

New inventions have made the work of the family easier. Obtaining and storing food, meal preparation, clothing care, transportation, housekeeping tasks, and money management have all been made easier with new technology. Think of chores you do not like to do. It is possible that some future invention will make that chore easier or obsolete.

New technologies have also made it possible to live longer. They are used to diagnose health problems, discover new ways to treat diseases, promote fitness, and assist in medical treatments.

Technology has made communication faster, easier, and available anytime, anywhere. These changes make it much easier for family members at any stage of the life cycle to be in touch with one another. Access to information via the Internet has changed how people learn and their awareness of resources available to them. Family members can use this information to help them adapt to the role changes and meet the challenges of each stage of the family life cycle.

LESSON 17.1

Assess

COMPREHENSION CHECK

1. List the stages of the family life cycle.
2. Identify one particular challenge couples face in each stage.
3. Identify one unique reward for each stage.
4. Explain how the parenting role changes over the stages of the family life cycle.
5. Describe which family resources are stressed in each stage of the family life cycle.

Objectives

After studying this lesson, you will be able to

- **recognize** the importance of the parenting role.
- **evaluate** factors affecting the decision to become parents.
- **identify** personal qualities needed by parents.
- **describe** the characteristics of responsible parenting.
- **identify** the positive effects children have on parents.

Focus Your Reading

1. Review the headings in this lesson and write some questions you have for each topic. Then, as you read, write the answers to your questions.
2. Describe what *parenting* means to you.

Becoming a parent causes major changes in a person's life. These changes result from taking on the responsibilities that go with caring for a child. Parenthood places new demands on a person's time, energy, money, and emotions.

A parent is anyone who is biologically or legally a father or a mother. Once you become a parent, you are always a parent. You cannot reverse that status even if you do not fulfill the parenting role.

The Parenting Role

Parenting means using skills to care for and raise a child to adulthood. Biological parents usually fulfill the parenting role in their children's lives. Sometimes, one parent carries the responsibility alone. In other cases, grandparents, other relatives, stepparents, foster parents, or adoptive parents help with the parenting role.

The role of parent is one that a person can acquire with no preparation. Experience is not required to become a parent, yet parenting may be the most important role you fulfill. Parents

Content Terms

Build Vocab

parenting
miscarriage
anemia
preeclampsia
stillbirth
premature baby
unconditional love
responsible parenting

Academic Terms

temporary
prospective
prestige
conditional

shape the lives of the next generation. Parenting practices have long-term effects on a child's development, happiness, well-being, and future. You can be an effective parent if you are prepared to have children and parent responsibly.

Parents are not the only influence on their children. Other factors also play an important part in a child's life. Family members, teachers, a child's friends, society, and media all have some effect on a child. A child's family and home, however, have the greatest effect on his or her development.

Think About Your Reading

Who in your life has contributed to the parenting role?

Deciding Whether to Become a Parent

As they think about whether or not to have children, couples ask themselves important questions: Are we ready to have children? Do we both want to become parents? As a couple decides whether they are ready for parenthood, they will consider some very personal issues (**Figure 17.6**). Couples are likely to consider the following:

- *Their goals and what they want to accomplish.* How would children fit into their plans?

- *Their relationship as a couple.* Is the relationship strong and growing? Would a child enrich that relationship? If the relationship is fragile, will the added burden of child care destroy it?

- *How they relate to children.* Do they enjoy children and communicate well with them? Do they both want children?

- *Whether they have the financial resources.* Couples will find it easier to adjust to parenting if they feel their income is adequate. Once they feel financially secure, they are more likely to feel ready to be parents.

At some point in your life, you may face decisions about parenthood. Using decision-making skills is one approach you and your spouse can use to make a responsible decision. This process can help you review the alternatives and consequences of each choice. An understanding of the factors that may affect each choice will help you reach a satisfying joint decision.

Parenthood Decisions

What are our life goals?

Do we have a secure and stable relationship?

Do we both want children?

Can we accept changes in our lifestyle?

Do we have any hereditary health problems that our child might inherit?

Are we in good physical health so we can handle the physical and emotional stress of raising children?

At what age should we start having children?

Do we understand how a child grows and develops?

How do we view child care and guidance?

Are we prepared for child-related expenses and lifetime changes in our budget?

How will children affect our career plans?

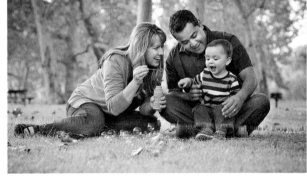

Andy Dean Photography/Shutterstock.com

Figure 17.6 To make wise decisions about parenthood, couples should carefully consider these questions. *How could answering yes to most of these questions help parents have healthy relationships with their children?*

One thing to remember is that if you decide you are not ready to be a parent at one time in life, you may decide you are ready later. The decision not to have children may simply be a decision to postpone having children. Once you do have children, though, you cannot undo that decision.

Think About Your Reading

Why is it important that a couple make a parenting decision jointly?

Reasons for Not Parenting

Some couples choose not to become parents for personal reasons. They may enjoy the freedom of a childless lifestyle. They do not want to commit themselves to raising a child. They may want to invest more time in their careers than in parenting. They may have diseases that they fear would be inherited by their children. They may have had an unhappy childhood and may fear that having children means repeating the cycle in their family.

Other couples may choose not to have children for less personal reasons. They may feel that the world is overpopulated. They may look at the economic problems in the world and feel they could not care for a child. High divorce rates, high crime rates, or an increase in child abuse may be other reasons for their choice.

Sometimes a couple chooses not to have children, but their decision is *temporary*, or short-term. They decide to delay parenting for a short time. They may feel they are not ready to become parents now. Perhaps they have goals they want to reach first. Goals such as a better job, more income or savings, further education, or better housing are common. The decision to delay parenting should be discussed periodically. Couples need to evaluate their progress toward goals or discuss their reasons for waiting to determine if they still apply. Then they should identify when they do want to have a child. Sometimes a couple waits too long. If the wife is older than the safest childbearing years, risks to her health and the baby's health increase (**Figure 17.7**).

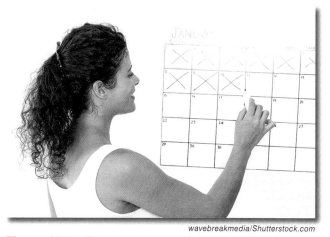

wavebreakmedia/Shutterstock.com

Figure 17.7 Pregnancy poses fewer health risks when a mother is between the ages of 20 and 35. *What impact could this knowledge have on a potential mother trying to establish herself in a career before having a child?*

The Age of the Mother

Age is quite important for the *prospective* mother, or the woman who is likely to become a mother. The health and well-being of mother and child may be at risk if a mother is too young or too old. The safest childbearing years for women are between the ages of 20 and 35.

Although women can bear children before and after this range, the health risks for both mother and child increase. Babies born to women over 35 years of age have an increased risk of complications such as *Down syndrome*. This condition is caused by abnormal chromosome formation.

Teenage girls can have problems with pregnancy because they have not fully developed physically. A pregnancy places an added strain on the young mother's body. Also, pregnant teens do not always receive proper medical care or nutrition. All these factors place pregnant teens at risk for the following problems:

- *Miscarriage.* **Miscarriage** occurs when the fetus (developing baby) dies during the first twenty weeks of development. Pregnant teens are twice as likely as other pregnant women to miscarry during the first few months of pregnancy.

- *Anemia.* **Anemia** is a condition of weakness and fatigue caused by an iron-deficient diet. An anemic mother has too few red blood

cells to carry oxygen to all parts of her body and to the growing baby.

- *Preeclampsia.* **Preeclampsia**, also called *toxemia* or *pregnancy-induced hypertension (PIH)*, is a condition of pregnancy characterized by swelling and high blood pressure. This can cause damage to the mother's organs and can increase the risk of premature delivery or stillbirth. **Stillbirth** is the death of the fetus after 20 weeks of development.

- *Placenta abruptio.* *Placenta abruptio* is the premature separation of the growing baby from the wall of the mother's uterus. Once this separation takes place, the baby cannot survive. Excessive bleeding may result, endangering the mother's life as well.

In addition to the risks to themselves, teen mothers often have *low-birthweight* or *premature* babies. A full-term pregnancy is about 40 weeks. A baby born before the start of the 37th week is considered a **premature baby (Figure 17.8)**. A baby may be born with a low birthweight if it is premature. Low-birthweight babies can also be born as a result of a lack of adequate nutrition for both mother and child. These problems often pose increased health risks for babies at birth. Chances of birth injuries and intellectual disabilities increase. The risk of illness and death within the first year of the baby's life is also higher for babies of teen mothers.

Think About Your Reading

What resources could help pregnant teens overcome some of these risks?

Parenting in the Teen Years

Age is an important factor for potential mothers and fathers when considering parenthood. A couple should be mature enough to handle the roles and responsibilities of parenting. Most teens

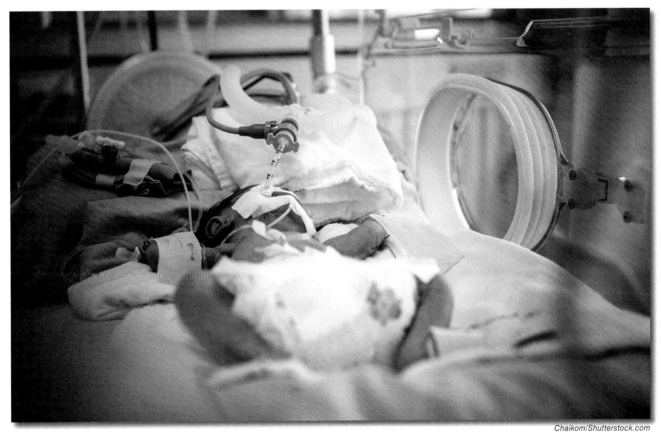

Chaikom/Shutterstock.com

Figure 17.8 Upon birth, premature babies are often kept in neonatal intensive care units (NICUs) to increase their chances of survival.

are not ready to face the emotional, social, and financial challenges involved.

Normally, the teen years are a time of gaining independence, planning a career, and developing close relationships. An unplanned pregnancy can cause emotional stress as each member of the couple tries to cope with new roles. For teen parents, the arrival of a baby greatly limits their social lives. Teen parents soon find out that a baby is a full-time responsibility. They see that their friends have more freedom and are not tied to any major responsibility. As a result, teen parents may find it difficult to fit in with their teen friends and may feel lonely.

Teen parents also face financial difficulties fitting into the adult world. The demands of child care can keep them from completing an education or making future career plans. Teen parents are more likely to be unemployed or have low-paying jobs. Sometimes the teen father accepts no responsibility for the child and offers no financial support, leaving the mother dependent on others. This dependence can put a strain on the teen mother's other relationships, such as with her parents. Stable financial resources can help teens in their adjustment; however, it is difficult for teen parents to acquire such resources.

Think About Your Reading

How would becoming a parent today affect your life?

Reasons for Parenting

One of the most important decisions a couple must make together concerns parenthood. After considering the effect this decision will have on their lives, most couples decide they want to have children.

Healthy Reasons

For many couples, parenting is a means of *personal extension*, a way to pass on a part of themselves and their family into the future. They are excited by being able to share their lives with a new and younger life (**Figure 17.9**).

Some couples want the personal experience of having children. They want to know how it feels

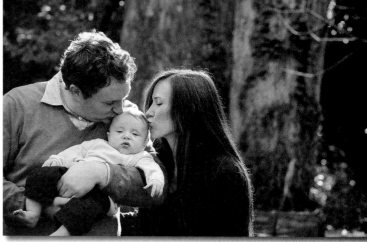

Brocreative/Shutterstock.com

Figure 17.9 The desire to share their life and love with children motivates many couples to become parents. *What additional attitudes and skills are needed in order to be adequately prepared for being a parent?*

to bring a child into the world and help him or her grow. Sharing their love and nurturing and guiding a child to adulthood are important to them. They believe parenting will be a rewarding experience.

These are positive reasons for wanting to parent. Attitudes of sharing and giving to benefit another person will increase a couple's effectiveness as parents. Healthy reasons are evidence of the emotional maturity needed to be responsible parents.

Unhealthy Reasons

Other reasons for parenting are not so positive. Some people may want to parent because they think having children brings them *prestige*, or high status. Others react to outside pressures from family or friends. For example, the couple's parents may want to be grandparents and push them to have children before they are ready.

Some couples choose to become parents to show their physical competence. They want to prove to others that they are adults and can produce children.

For some, parenting is a means of gaining personal power. Having a child depend on them gives them a sense of power. In some cases, they may desire to have power over the child. Sometimes having children gives one parent power over the other.

Some couples want to have children because they want to gain love. They believe that the child

will provide them with the love and affection they deeply need. Some couples believe that having a child will improve their marriage.

Choosing parenthood because of what a child can do for the couple is a sign of immaturity. The needs for esteem, power, and love are best met through the couple's adult relationships and other areas of accomplishment. The truth is, a baby places constant demands for attention and energy on a parent and is not going to give that parent frequent expressions of love. In addition, those demands are more likely to strain a troubled marriage than to improve it.

Think About Your Reading

What are the key differences between the healthy and unhealthy reasons for parenting?

Realistic Expectations

The decision to become a parent needs to be based on realistic expectations. These expectations should be based on facts. If parents have unrealistic expectations, they can hinder the child's development. They may be too protective and not allow the child a chance to learn to do tasks alone. On the other hand, they may not be protective enough, which could result in the child getting hurt.

Suppose a couple decides to have a child because they want power, greater self-esteem, or a fix for a troubled marriage. What happens when a child does not fill those needs? Unrealistic expectations can result in abuse, disappointment, rejection, and unhappiness for all involved.

Preparing for parenthood can help married couples develop realistic expectations for parent-child relationships. It can help them understand how to nurture a child's growth and development. This can lead to healthy relationships within the family.

Qualities Needed by Parents

Besides considering their reasons for wanting to parent, couples should consider the personal qualities needed to be effective parents. Emotional maturity, the readiness to give unconditional love, flexibility, and responsibility are some of these qualities, as well as the readiness to allow children to change their lives forever.

Being Emotionally Mature

As people mature, their emotions become more stable (**Figure 17.10**). They can think before they act, so they control their responses better. This is important in parenting for several reasons.

First, children respond to parents' emotions. If a mother feels tense, a baby will feel tense. If a father feels upset, a baby will feel upset. Emotions are communicated to children even without words.

Second, emotional maturity helps parents identify their own emotions. A parent should be able to say, "I really feel sad when you and your sister fight," or "I'm getting upset with the noise you two are making." Parents should label their emotions so that children, in turn, can learn to identify their own feelings.

Third, emotional maturity helps parents control strong emotional responses. Mature parents take steps to deal with their emotions before those emotions get out of control. Emotional immaturity may be the cause of some abuse to children. Although parents may love their children, some immature adults may respond with violence when emotions are high. Anger over a childish response—which is normal for children—may cause a parent to explode. Parents need to be able to control their emotions and their reactions. They can then teach their children to control their own behaviors.

Think About Your Reading

How do two people share similar feelings without speaking any words?

Being Ready to Give Unconditional Love

Unconditional love is the ability to love another under any circumstance. This is the kind of love parents must have for their children. Children need to know they are loved for who they are.

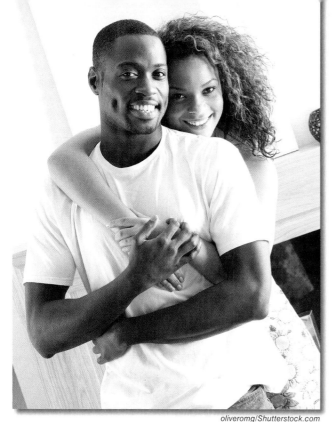

Figure 17.10 Emotional maturity can help prospective parents prepare for their first child. *What behaviors would be considered evidence of emotional maturity?*

They should not feel a need to act in a certain way or pretend they are someone or something else to get love. When children experience unconditional love, they are able to accept themselves as being lovable. Their ability to give love is influenced by the love they have experienced. If they experience love as being *conditional*, or dependent on their

behavior, then they will not learn to give unconditional love themselves.

Being Flexible

Parents need to be flexible because they have to fulfill many roles in raising a child. At different times, they need to be caregiver, teacher, nutritionist, sports coach, mediator of disputes, repairer of broken toys, playmate, and more. They also need to be flexible because they may have to switch from one of these roles to another very quickly. If a toddler who is playing outside falls and scrapes a knee, one of his parents has to stop doing whatever he or she is doing and tend to the child.

Parents need to be flexible in their relationships, too. Parent-child relationships will change throughout the life cycle. During the early years, children are dependent on their parents to provide for all their needs. As children grow, they learn to meet some of their own needs. As teens, they need to take more responsibility for themselves and for their actions. Through all these changes, parents need to be flexible. They must be willing and able to change as the child grows.

Being Responsible

Most parents want to help their children grow to become mature adults. **Responsible parenting** means making choices that will help a child develop fully in all areas of life (**Figure 17.11**).

Responsible Parenting

Responsible parents need to provide

- *guidance* on how people live and act in acceptable, ethical ways
- *a nurturing environment* in which a child feels loved and supported
- *a secure environment* in which a child's physical needs for food, clothing, shelter, medical care, and safety are met
- *a stimulating environment* in which a child learns new skills and concepts by interacting with people and objects

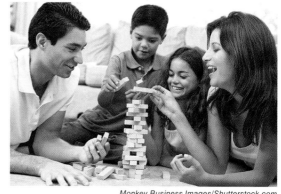

Monkey Business Images/Shutterstock.com

Figure 17.11 Responsible parents provide for their children's growth and development in all these areas. *How could a healthy marriage relationship help parents carry out these responsibilities?*

Responsible parents guide children to learn acceptable and ethical behavior. They provide an environment that is nurturing, secure, and stimulating, thus meeting children's needs and promoting their development.

A couple's effectiveness at responsible parenting will be influenced by several factors. These include personal maturity, a mature relationship, financial resources, and preparation for parenting. Their own personal growth will affect the qualities that they model and that their children see and imitate. Their own relationship should be strong so they can love and support a child, thus providing a nurturing environment. Their financial resources should be adequate to meet a child's needs for food, shelter, clothing, medical care, and a safe environment, thus helping the child feel secure. Their preparation for parenting should help them understand how to encourage a child's growth and development so their child can reach his or her growth potential.

Being Ready for Children to Change Your Life

Parenting requires giving, including the giving of time, energy, money, and skills, to meet a child's needs and encourage development. As parents give, a child receives and responds. These responses can give parents much satisfaction and hope. Children can also help parents grow in the following ways:

- *Children can give parents satisfaction.* For most couples, parenting is a satisfying experience. It is enjoyable to have a child return love and affection. Parents enjoy seeing a child learn new skills, accomplish new feats, and grow as a person. The bond that develops between parent and child can last a lifetime.

- *Children help parents mature.* Parenting is a growth experience. Parents learn to be responsible for the needs of another. The give-and-take of parenting causes love to grow between parent and child. While parents stimulate growth in their child, the child's growth encourages the parents to keep on adjusting. In this way, both parent and child experience growth through their relationship.

- *Children help parents recognize their human weaknesses.* Many times parents are disappointed with what they learn about themselves as they watch themselves interact with their children. They may realize they do not control their emotions as well as they thought. These are times for parents to learn and mature. The parent-child relationship will grow stronger if parents admit their mistakes and learn to adjust.

- *Children can help parents enjoy family leisure time.* Playtime activities involving children help parents have fun. These shared activities can help the parents' relationship as well as the parent-child relationship.

- *Children can give parents hope for the future.* Parents feel pride in seeing their children develop and mature. Sometimes children make mature choices and succeed in reaching a goal. At other times, they respond with more insight than the parents have.

Assess

LESSON 17.2

COMPREHENSION CHECK

1. Explain the difference between the terms *parent* and *parenting*.
2. List three reasons couples give for not wanting to parent.
3. A teen mother and her baby face many health risks. Name two for each.
4. List the safest childbearing years for women.
5. Briefly describe how the responsibilities of teen parenting may hinder the growth and development of a teen.
6. List two healthy reasons and two unhealthy reasons couples give for wanting to parent.
7. Explain why parents' unrealistic expectations for children can be unhealthy for a child.
8. Describe four personal qualities needed by parents.
9. Identify four things that responsible parents provide to a child.
10. List five ways that children can affect parents.

Objectives

After studying this lesson, you will be able to

- **describe** areas of adjustment for young couples planning to become parents.
- **identify** the main causes of infertility.
- **describe** parenting options for infertile couples.
- **examine** technological solutions for infertility.

Focus Your Reading

1. Summarize the key points under each heading. Then choose one of the topics and prepare an oral presentation to give as a community service project.
2. Compare and contrast the terms related to adoption in a three-column table. List the terms in the first column. In the second column, list ways the terms are alike. In the third column, list ways they are different.

Content Terms

Build
Vocab

infertility
endometriosis
ovulation
intrauterine insemination (IUI)
in vitro fertilization (IVF)
surrogate mother
agency adoption
independent adoption
open adoption
closed adoption
home study
international adoption

Academic Terms

substantial
profile

The decision to become parents and have a family is of major importance. Couples who have thought through this decision will take steps to plan and prepare for children.

Some couples are not able to conceive a child. These couples may pursue several options to become parents.

Preparing for Children

Once a couple decides to have children, they need to plan for changes in their lifestyle. They should check their health insurance plan to see what coverage is provided for prenatal and newborn care. The financial costs of having and raising the child should be included in their budget. They should also discuss how parenting could affect their careers, leisure activities, and their own relationship.

Considering Child Care

Child care takes much time and energy. The couple needs to discuss how they will handle child care responsibilities (**Figure 17.12**). How will they adjust their schedules? What does each expect from the other in terms of sharing responsibilities?

Some couples choose to have one parent stay home with the young child. They want to be the young child's main caregiver and role model during these early years. Stable finances can help the young family in this situation.

Often the young family needs the income of both parents. Sometimes these parents are able to adjust their schedules to provide child care themselves. If not, they need to find a caregiver for their children while they are both at work. In some cases, other family members help out with child care. Some families choose to hire in-home child care for their young children. This may take place in the caregiver's home or in the couple's home. Some choose to place the children in licensed child care centers. The couple needs to discuss their options for child care and agree on a solution. Of course, they need to consider their financial resources and the cost of this care as they weigh this decision.

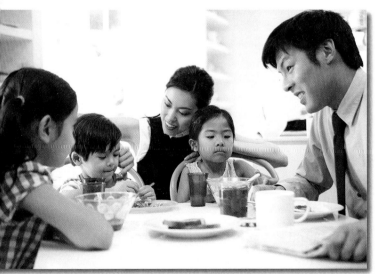

Monkey Business Images/Shutterstock.com

Figure 17.12 Children benefit when both parents are involved in providing their care. *How could good communication skills help parents succeed at sharing parenting responsibilities?*

Think About Your Reading

What resources are needed to provide care for a growing child?

Planning for Financial Changes

Pregnancy and the birth of a child may require adjustments to the family income. One of these changes may involve adjusting to one income. Most women can work up to a few weeks before their due date, depending on the type of work that they do. Sometimes, though, complications occur in pregnancy. In those cases, women may be required to reduce their activity, including their work, and stay home.

The arrival of a child puts increased strain on the family budget. Medical care for pregnancy and childbirth plus doctor's services for the infant are major costs. These should be covered to some extent by a health insurance plan, but there still may be *substantial*, or significant, out-of-pocket expenses. These are the costs that the couple must pay. Couples should consider the costs of providing care for the child for at least the next 18 years. Some experts estimate that families will spend two-and-a-half times their annual income to provide that many years of support. That total is spread out over those years, of course, but the additional yearly expenses for raising a child need to be included in the family budget.

Preparing for Lifestyle Changes

Before children are born, couples devote their time and energy to careers, friendships, or leisure activities. Children place new demands on a parent's time and energy. Parents will have less time to spend with each other or other adults. They will have less money to spend freely. These losses can be very frustrating.

Couples adjust to parenting more readily if they feel they have satisfied their goals for the childless stage of their lives. Perhaps they wanted to complete their education, establish a home, and advance in their careers. If they have accomplished these goals, they will look forward to parenting.

Also, couples who have developed a mature relationship find it easier to adjust to the demands of parenting (**Figure 17.13**). Making adjustments for a child is easier when the couple has learned to adjust to each other and resolve conflicts.

<table>
<tr><td>
Think About Your Reading
How does becoming a parent impact a person's life?
</td></tr>
</table>

Infertility

Most couples look forward to having children when they marry. They hardly consider the possibility that they might not be able to have children. Many couples who want to have children find they are not able to conceive, while others have fewer children than they want. For some, the problem is infertility.

Infertility is a couple's inability to conceive a child. A couple is usually not considered infertile until they have tried to have a child for a year or more. The heartache of not being able to have a child or carry a child to full term affects about 10 percent of all couples.

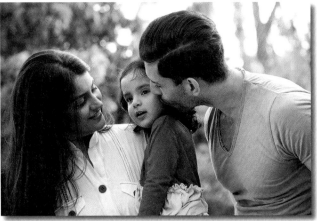

Rehan Qureshi/Shutterstock.com

Figure 17.13 Couples who have developed a solid relationship will find it easier to provide a loving and secure environment for their child. *What characteristics of a well-adjusted marriage relationship could help parents fulfill the role of a responsible parent?*

Causes of Infertility

Infertility problems can affect either males or females. For men, the main causes of infertility are low sperm count or a blockage in one of the tubes that carries sperm. The leading causes in women are hormonal factors or blocked fallopian tubes resulting from disease or infection. Endometriosis is another major cause of infertility in women. **Endometriosis** is a disease in which uterine tissue

---

REAL-LIFE SCENARIO

Parenting Decisions

Eun and Tia had decided they wanted to become parents. Month after month they continued to hope for signs of a pregnancy. They wanted to have a child so much. Even their parents openly talked about the day Eun and Tia would give them grandchildren.

The fear that they would not be able to have children haunted them. They really had not believed that it would be a problem for them. The doctor, however, told them they were one couple in many who had infertility problems.

The doctor suggested a treatment for them, and they had high hopes that treatment would be effective. The doctor told them the success rate for treating fertility was 70 percent. As time continued to go by with no results, however, their hopes dimmed.

For Discussion
1. How might this couple feel pressured into having children?
2. What are some of the feelings a couple may have if they are not able to have children?
3. What are some options that Eun and Tia could consider?
4. There are few babies available for adoption. How might that fact influence Eun and Tia's parenting decisions?

grows outside the uterus. The tissue may appear on the ovaries or block the fallopian tubes. The disease is most commonly diagnosed in women between the ages of 25 and 35.

Other harmful factors contribute to infertility in both sexes. These include exposure to radiation or toxic chemicals, smoking tobacco or marijuana, and sexually transmitted infections.

Emotional Effects of Infertility

Infertility is crushing for many couples. It is common for couples to ask why this is happening to them. They may look for a cause to blame. Feelings of anger, bitterness, and sadness may be overwhelming. They may mourn the loss of the children they will not be able to bear.

Some adjust to infertility and accept childlessness. For others, the desire to have a child becomes even more intense. Some couples consider using expensive reproductive technologies so they can have their own child. Others consider the possibility of adoption.

Think About Your Reading

How might infertility affect a couple's mental attitudes?

Technology and Treatments for Infertility

Most causes of infertility are physical. Males and females are affected equally, so both should be examined by their physician if problems of infertility exist. A doctor may refer the couple to a fertility specialist for further tests to diagnose the precise cause. Once that cause is identified, many couples are successfully treated and able to bear children. Modern medical technology has developed several infertility treatments:

- *Medications and hormones can stimulate or improve ovulation.* To conceive, a woman's ovaries must release a mature egg, in a process called **ovulation**. The egg enters the fallopian tube, where it is most often successfully fertilized. The fertilized egg then travels to the uterus. Hormones are involved in maturing and releasing the egg and in preparing the uterus for a fertilized egg. In some cases, a woman's natural hormone levels are low, and this process does not work normally. These women can be given hormone injections to spur their ovaries to release an egg.

- *Surgical therapies can open blockages.* With new medical technology, blocked fallopian tubes can be opened with minimal discomfort to the patient. A *laparoscopy* is a procedure that allows the doctor to look inside the patient and take pictures internally. With lasers and special equipment, the doctor can then perform surgery to open blocked tubes (**Figure 17.14**).

- *Artificial insemination of sperm can promote conception.* If the problem is a male's low sperm count, a doctor can use a syringe to deposit sperm directly into the uterus. This procedure, known as **intrauterine insemination (IUI)**, makes it more likely that fertilization will take place. It is a painless and relatively inexpensive procedure.

- *Assisted reproductive technology (ART) can increase the rate of conception.* New technologies make it possible for most infertile couples to experience an excellent chance of conception. These technologies may be costly, however, and success is not always certain.

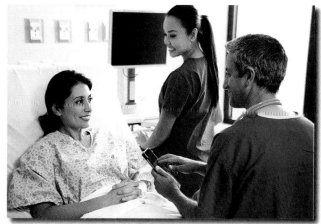
Monkey Business Images/Shutterstock.com
Figure 17.14 When infertility results from a blockage, surgery can correct the problem in most cases. *What other technological resources might couples consider when examining infertility issues?*

ART is used to overcome blocked fallopian tubes and endometriosis. The most commonly performed ART procedure is **in vitro fertilization (IVF)**. This treatment involves stimulating multiple eggs to mature. The mature eggs are removed from the ovaries and fertilized in a laboratory with sperm. After cell division has begun, the fertilized eggs are placed directly into the uterus. More than one fertilized egg is placed to ensure success. All may not implant into the uterine wall, but if they do, multiple births result. Extra fertilized eggs are usually frozen for later use by the couple, should they try again to achieve a pregnancy.

Reproductive technology raises many legal and ethical questions. When the partners involved are married, such technology is generally accepted since it allows infertile couples to have children. Sperm or mature eggs from donor parents can be used, or a fertilized egg can be transplanted into a surrogate mother. A **surrogate mother** is a woman who is hired by the couple to carry the couple's child to birth. Some people have moral objections to the use of surrogate mothers.

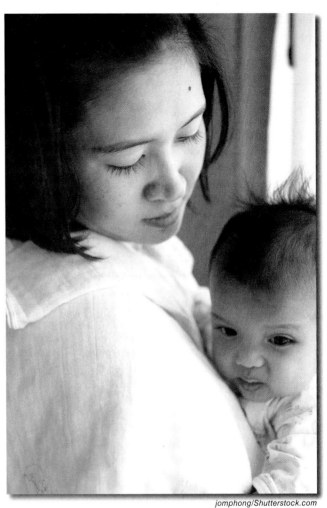

jomphong/Shutterstock.com

Figure 17.15 Many couples seek to adopt infants, but few are available. *How could this issue impact couples' dreams of becoming parents?*

Think About Your Reading

What ethical questions can you identify related to using technology to produce a child?

Adoption

Many people seek to fulfill their dreams for children through adoption. Couples' reasons for adopting vary. Some adopt because they cannot have their own children. Some couples already have children but would like more. Others are single but still want to share their love with a child who needs a family. An emotionally stable adult who can love and provide for a child has a good chance of adopting one.

Because most couples prefer adopting an infant, fewer infants are available for adoption (**Figure 17.15**). The wait for adopting an infant can last up to five years. A couple needs to check with different adoption agencies to determine the waiting time for each.

Rights of Birthparents in an Adoption

Birthparents must consent to the adoption. If the birthparent refuses to consent, the adoption cannot take place. If parental rights are ended due to abandonment or unfitness, this question does not arise. In most states, *abandonment* means the birthparent has not contacted, communicated with, or supported the child for a certain period of time (usually a year).

Sometimes a couple cannot pay for the medical care during pregnancy or will not be able to care for the child after birth. These parents can contact a local human services agency. The agency can arrange for the pregnant woman to receive the

needed medical care. If the expecting parents are interested in having their child adopted, counselors will help them through the steps.

Think About Your Reading

What would be the benefits of receiving counseling if you or your significant other were pregnant and considering finding adoptive parents for your child?

Agency and Independent Adoptions

Most adoptions are arranged through adoption agencies and are called **agency adoptions**. Public adoption agencies usually do not charge for their services since they are tax supported. Private adoption agencies usually have a fee. Legal fees are usually extra. Adoption agencies are licensed by the state. That means they meet certain minimum standards set by the state. They should also provide their clients with psychological counseling and guidance (**Figure 17.16**).

Not all adoptions take place through an agency. **Independent adoptions** are arranged privately. The adopting parents may agree to pay medical expenses for the pregnant mother's care and the birth of the baby. The arrangements are made through a lawyer or doctor. Such adoptions are legal in most states as long as the lawyer's fees are reasonable and no payment is made for the baby. Baby selling is illegal.

Types of Adoption

Adoptions may be open or closed. In an **open adoption**, the adopted child will know the identity of the birthparents. The birthparents may select and meet the adoptive parents. Often technology is used to facilitate this process. The adoption agency can prepare *profiles*, or reports, of potential families that birthparents can review to identify a family they would like their child to join. Birthparents may even be able to meet the family and set up options for future contact if desired. In an open adoption, the child is given information about his or her birthparents.

In a **closed adoption**, the adopted child does not know the identity of the birthparents. Birthparents can specify some of the characteristics they desire in the family selected for their child. The adoption agency, however, will make the final decision.

Some children are adopted through the foster care system. When birthparents cannot care for their children, children sometimes are placed with a family participating in foster care. *Foster care* is 24-hour substitute care for children under the care and responsibility of a state agency. When parental rights for these children end, they remain in foster care while waiting for adoption. Families wishing to adopt children in foster care can contact public or private agencies in their community to identify these children. Often children in foster care are older, but sometimes newborns are available.

All adoptions fall under state regulation. In some states, the birthparents may have the opportunity to change their minds within 30 to 60 days after the adoption consent forms are signed. In other states, the birthparents do not have this opportunity once they sign adoption consent forms. After the court issues a final adoption decree, the adoption is final. Before making a decision, birthparents should receive counseling from social workers who are familiar with the

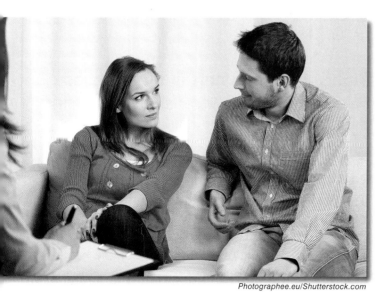

Photographee.eu/Shutterstock.com

Figure 17.16 One advantage of adopting through an agency is that agencies often provide clients with counseling.

legal aspects of adoption so that they fully understand the process and what it means.

Think About Your Reading

What are some benefits of open adoption for a pregnant teen considering finding a family to parent her child? What could be some disadvantages?

Steps in Adoption

The adoption process involves several steps (**Figure 17.17**). These steps help the adoption agency make sure the family is able to provide a warm, secure, and loving home for the child. The agency's goal is to be certain the family will be able to provide the nurturing environment the child needs. The steps in adoption include the following:

- *A couple contacts an adoption agency.* For example, Lin and Sam had many questions about adopting a child when they contacted the agency. The agency worker explained its policies and described the adoption process. Lin and Sam also had an opportunity to say what they expected from the agency.

- *The agency conducts a thorough screening.* All states require that an agency or licensed person thoroughly screen a couple before they are allowed to adopt. Healthy reasons for wanting to have a child are important to determine. In addition to wanting a child, the couple must show they are able to provide for the emotional, physical, intellectual, and social development of the child. Does the couple understand how a child grows and develops? How would they provide child care? What are their views on guidance and discipline? Are they prepared for

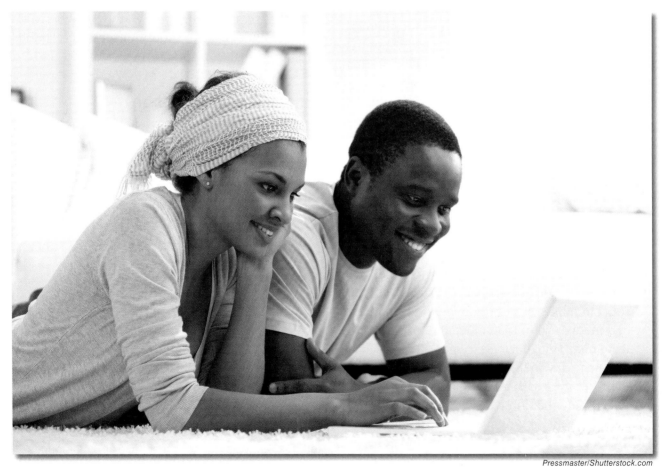

Pressmaster/Shutterstock.com

Figure 17.17 Before proceeding with adoption, both spouses should be certain they want to adopt a child. *What would be the benefit of researching different types of adoption?*

child-related expenses and other changes in their budget?

- *The agency conducts a home study.* Many states require a **home study**. In this process, a social worker visits the home to be sure the parents can provide a safe, roomy environment for a growing child.

- *The agency worker meets with potential parents to discuss possible children.* Lin and Sam were excited when they received notice that they had been accepted to be adoptive parents. They had expressed an interest in an infant with a physical disability. The worker showed them pictures and talked about the history of several different children.

- *Potential parents get acquainted with the child.* Lin and Sam decided they would like to meet one-year-old Jon. The first meeting was arranged in Jon's foster home. More meetings took place afterward, some in the foster home and others in Lin and Sam's home. Usually a child lives with the adoptive family for a while before the adoption is finalized legally. This period lasts six months to a year, depending on the state. During this period, the agency worker visited Lin and Sam often and helped them work through their many questions about Jon. Because Jon had a disability, they were also able to get aid to help with his medical bills. Through the time of adjustment, Jon and his new family became strongly attached to each other. The agency worker was prepared to submit a written recommendation of approval to the court.

- *The adoption becomes legal in court.* The final stage came when Lin, Sam, Jon, the agency worker, and their lawyer went to court to make the adoption legal. The lawyer had made certain that all legal requirements were met. They decided to mark this special day—the day that Jon became a member of their family—with an annual celebration. They knew that Jon would have questions in the future about why his birthparents had found other parents for him. Lin and Sam wanted him to know that he was specially chosen to belong to their family.

Think About Your Reading

How do the steps in the adoption process help secure a good home environment for a child?

Costs of Adoption

Adoptions can cost a lot of time and money (**Figure 17.18**). Agencies are allowed to charge adopting parents certain expenses specified by state law. The adopting parents may be asked to pay for the medical expenses incurred by the birthmother. The costs may also include her living expenses during pregnancy and the costs of counseling she receives. The adoption agency may pay these costs for the pregnant woman, then recover them through the adopting parents.

An agency may charge a set fee for an adoption. Some may add the birthmother's expenses to their own flat rate. Others may charge the adopting parents according to their income. Adoptions may cost the adopting family anywhere between $10,000 and $25,000. Adoption through public programs, including foster care, is less costly.

Single-Parent Adoption

When a single parent wishes to adopt a child, the agency worker will ask the single person the

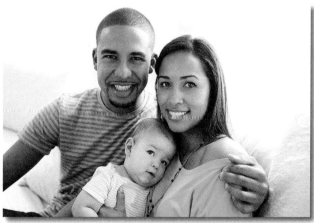

Monkey Business Images/Shutterstock.com

Figure 17.18 Couples who want to adopt a child through a private agency must have sound finances to afford the high costs. *What would be the benefit of researching different types of adoption?*

same questions that are asked of couples. The interview process may be more intense, as the single parent would have to meet all the roles of both parents rather than sharing them with another person. When considering who should be allowed to adopt, all states look to the best interests of the child. Often the social worker or the judge makes that judgment.

International Adoption

The adoption process described to this point is for adopting a child born in the United States, called a *domestic adoption*. Parents can also choose an **international adoption**, where they adopt a child from another country. Some countries have many children living in orphanages. Even so, the costs of international adoptions are high, and legal requirements must be met in both countries. Agencies that specialize in international adoptions will help families meet those requirements and may also provide counseling and support groups. This helps families adjust to raising a child from another culture (**Figure 17.19**).

Whether a child is born into a family or adopted, the responsibilities, challenges, and joys of parenting are similar. Parents need to provide a loving and secure environment in which a child's needs are met and growth is stimulated. In turn, parents can gain satisfaction relating to their children and seeing them grow and mature.

LESSON 17.3
Assess

COMPREHENSION CHECK

1. Name three areas a couple can plan to help them adjust to becoming parents.
2. Identify the main causes of infertility in men and women.
3. Describe how technology can help families address issues related to preparing for parenting.
4. Give three reasons why people adopt children.
5. Briefly describe the steps in the adoption process.
6. Name three ways that an adoption agency might help a pregnant woman during her pregnancy.

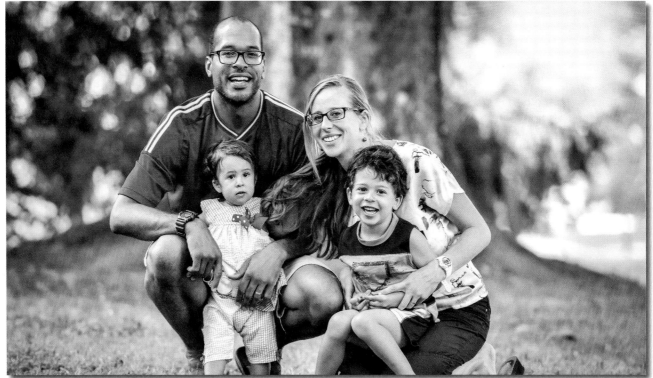

JGA/Shutterstock.com

Figure 17.19 When adopting a child from another country, parents take on the added challenge of helping the child adjust to a new culture. *Why might some families consider adopting siblings in these situations?*

CHAPTER SUMMARY

Parenting is an important role in the lives of many couples. The couple's mutual decision to have children requires careful thought. This decision is based on several factors. A couple may or may not choose to have children for various reasons. Some choose to delay parenting while they develop a career or seek to reach certain goals. As part of their decision, couples should evaluate the personal qualities needed to be effective parents. They must also consider the positive effects children have on parents. Overall, most couples look forward to having children in their family.

Preparing for parenting can help a couple fulfill the roles of responsible parents. Their ability to carry out such roles is increased by planning how they will care for the child. They should also plan how they will adjust to the future financial needs and lifestyle changes.

Some couples who want to have a child are hindered by infertility problems. For many couples, infertility has strong emotional effects, which include feelings of loss and grief. Many adjust to childlessness, while others seek medical help to possibly find a treatment that helps them have a child. Some couples choose to adopt a child. Adoption is a long, complex process typically carried out by adoption agencies that work to ensure that a couple is ready and able to care for, support, and nurture a child.

VOCABULARY ACTIVITIES

1. Working with three partners, organize the terms into four categories: stages of the family life cycle, terms related to infertility, terms related to adoption, and other. Have each group member take one category of terms to study and then review the terms as a group.

Content Terms

agency adoption (17.3)
anemia (17.2)
closed adoption (17.3)
early parenthood stage (17.1)
empty nest stage (17.1)
endometriosis (17.3)
family life cycle (17.1)
founding family (17.1)
home study (17.3)
independent adoption (17.3)
infertility (17.3)
international adoption (17.3)

intrauterine insemination (IUI) (17.3)
in vitro fertilization (IVF) (17.3)
launching stage (17.1)
miscarriage (17.2)
newly married stage (17.1)
open adoption (17.3)
ovulation (17.3)
parenting (17.2)
preeclampsia (17.2)
premature baby (17.2)
responsible parenting (17.2)

retirement stage (17.1)
sandwich generation (17.1)
stillbirth (17.2)
surrogate mother (17.3)
unconditional love (17.2)

2. Make a crossword puzzle using all the terms. Give your puzzle to a partner and complete your partner's puzzle while he or she completes yours.

Academic Terms

conditional (17.2)
extent (17.1)
prestige (17.2)
profile (17.3)
prospective (17.2)
substantial (17.3)
temporary (17.2)
vital (17.1)

ASSESS

Your Knowledge

3. Identify the five stages of the family life cycle and the roles and responsibilities of individuals and family members during each stage.
4. List three risks associated with a teen pregnancy.
5. What are the four ways responsible parents provide for their children?
6. Explain the difference between an open adoption and a closed adoption.

Your Understanding

7. Give one example of how a family may experience the roles and responsibilities of two stages of the family life cycle at the same time.
8. Explain how couples can manage resources to meet the demands of becoming new parents.
9. How can infertility affect parenting decisions?

Your Skills

10. Develop a decision-making tree that could be used for making the decision to start a family. Include alternatives, the pros and cons of each alternative, and a possible plan of action.
11. Write a scenario describing a person who has qualities needed to be a responsible parent.

CRITICAL THINKING

12. **Develop Hypotheses.** Think of the four best parents you know and list the five qualities you think are most important to the high quality of their parenting. Examine these qualities for similarities. From your analysis, create a hypothesis identifying what it takes to be a great parent. Write an essay supporting your point of view, using your data to support your hypothesis. Cite references from the text that also support your hypothesis.

13. **Analyze and Summarize Data**. Assess your peers' attitudes about placing a child in adoption. Develop questions you could ask and then interview 10 of your peers about their attitudes toward adoption. Tally the results in a spreadsheet and create a bar graph showing how many of your peers have the same attitudes. Write a summary of the data you gathered.

14. **Assess and Evaluate Findings**. Analyze current media depictions of attitudes toward children. Choose a television show or movie to critique. List the attitudes that the parents show toward children in the show. Explain what actions, words, or nonverbal messages depicted these attitudes. Then compare your list of attitudes to the list of qualities needed by parents. Write an essay evaluating how the media depicts parent-child relationships, citing your data and evidence from the text to support your evaluation. *Group option*: Gather data with several partners, sharing information from multiple shows or media sources.

CORE SKILLS

15. **Writing.** Interview a grandparent about the ways technology has made a difference in parenting decisions and roles. Summarize your findings in a paragraph.

16. **Writing, Math.** Interview several parents about their parenting experiences. Include questions about what they enjoy most about parenting, what they find most challenging, how prepared they were for parenting, and what preparation they would have found helpful. Discuss your findings in a paper.

17. **Reading, Speaking.** Find an article from your local newspaper or search online for articles illustrating the legal and ethical issues related to the use of reproductive technology. Be prepared to cite your article and discuss its key issues in class.

18. **Social Studies, Research.** Research the procedures for adoption in your state. Present your information in a pamphlet or flyer. *Choice*: Post your information on your class website.

19. **Research, Writing.** Create a flyer providing information on one cause of infertility in either males or females.

20. **Research, Writing.** Gather data from families to identify the biggest challenge each experienced in parenting at this stage of their life. Work in teams of five, with each member of the team interviewing a parent in a different stage of the family life cycle. Write a group report, identifying the biggest challenges, roles, and responsibilities parents face over the family life cycle. *Choice*: Have each team member work with members from other teams to share information on the same topic. Then write your group report summarizing all the data.

21. **Writing.** Develop a checklist entitled "Readiness for Parenting." Include criteria that you think are important for parents to have. Write a paragraph explaining your choice of criteria, citing evidence from the text or other resources to support your point of view.

22. **Research, Writing.** Search online for a list of agencies that serve as a resource for adoption in your community. Identify addresses and phone numbers for each agency as well as a summary of services they provide. Create a poster that presents your findings. *Choice*: Post your findings on your school or class website.

23. **Research, Writing.** Identify sources of information available through different technology, such as print books or magazines, television, radio, and the Internet. Predict how these technologies impact family functions and relationshiops in each stage of the family life cycle. Develop a plan for families in each stage of the family life cycle to use this technology to access information they might need to address the challenges of that stage.

24. **Research, Writing.** Conduct research into current communication technologies. Write a report analyzing how that technology is currently used and how it might change in the future. In discussing the future, consider how families in different stages of the family life cycle might use that technology.

CAREER READINESS

25. **Researching and Writing About Careers.** Gather data online about careers in social work that include working with families during the early years of the family life cycle. Then interview a social worker for an adoption agency. Ask questions about the training for the job, skills for the job, and the rewards and challenges of the work. Write a report summarizing your research and the results of your interview.

RELATING TO AND GUIDING CHILDREN

Reading Prep

Before reading the chapter, make a chart with the headings *Things to Know* and *Skills to Learn*. As you read, fill in important points from the text under the appropriate heading.

Key Questions

Questions to answer as you study this chapter:

- How can parents create nurturing relationships with children?
- How can parents create a stimulating environment for children?
- What methods can parents use to help children learn self-control?

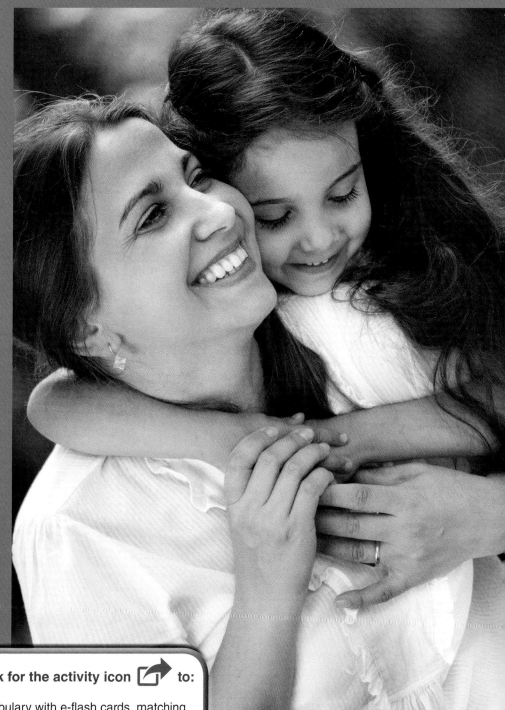

While studying this chapter, look for the activity icon to:

- **build** vocabulary with e-flash cards, matching activities, and vocabulary games; and
- **assess** what you learn by completing the lesson comprehension checks online.
  www.g-wlearning.com/humanservices/

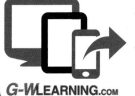
G-WLEARNING.com

spass/Shutterstock.com

AFTER STUDYING THIS CHAPTER, YOU WILL

KNOW:

- The importance of children engaging in different types of play.
- What parenting techniques help a child develop self-control.
- Where to find community resources to help with parenting.

UNDERSTAND:

- How to provide a nurturing environment for children.
- How to create a stimulating environment for children.
- How to choose appropriate guidance techniques for children.

BE ABLE TO DO:

- Relate to children in a nurturing manner.
- Analyze play activities for their impact on a child's growth and development.
- Choose toys that promote growth for children of different ages.

GETTING STARTED

Vanessa struggled out of bed at 5:00 a.m. when her alarm went off. She had to get up early to get herself ready for work and to get all three kids up, dressed, and off to day care. She had to be at work at 7:00 a.m. Her husband Cory worked the night shift and usually returned home at 7:30 in the morning, so Vanessa was on her own getting the kids out the door.

Cory and Vanessa worked hard to provide the best they could for their family. They loved their children, who were ages one, three, and five, but it seemed to Vanessa that providing for the children's care took all her time and energy. There was little time left for her and Cory to spend together, yet she felt they both were very connected in their goal to provide for their family. They had a good routine established. Cory played with the three children while Vanessa made the family meal. Then after supper, they followed a routine of bathing, reading books together, and putting the children to bed before Cory went off to his job.

Vanessa knew that some adjustments in their routines would have to be made when their oldest child started school later this year. Right now, things were rolling smoothly, it seemed. The kids loved their providers at day care and seemed to be growing and learning new things every day. It seemed there were always new challenges and adjustments to be made as the kids changed.

During the first few years of a child's life, parents and guardians tend to be the main influence on a child's physical, emotional, social, and intellectual development. Other family members and perhaps caregivers may also play an important part in a child's growth and development in these early years. Later, teachers and other adults play important roles as they help children attain knowledge and skills developed at different stages. Knowing how to stimulate growth and development is important for parents, as well as for others who work with children and families.

Given the important role they play, many parents feel some anxiety. They want to do a good job of parenting because they know it is a one-time experience for them and is very important to the child's well-being. They also know they cannot take a practice run and then try again. Each child will go through the process of growth and development just once.

Learning how to promote a child's growth and development can help parents make good parenting decisions. Parents will feel more confident as they establish nurturing relationships with their children, provide for their care, stimulate their growth, and provide guidance for their lives.

Content Terms

Build Vocab

nurturing environment
nurturing relationship
mixed messages

Academic Terms

nurturing
modify

Objectives

After studying this lesson, you will be able to

- **identify** characteristics of a nurturing environment for children.
- **describe** techniques parents can use for helping children feel loved.
- **relate** a nurturing environment to the growth of a child's self-concept and self-esteem.

Focus Your Reading

1. Create a graphic organizer for this chapter with the main heading *Relating to and Guiding Children* and with three main branches extending from it. Add the title of this lesson, *Developing a Nurturing Relationship*, to the first main branch. As you read the lesson, list the key ideas from this lesson under that heading.

2. Draw an analogy between nurturing a growing plant and nurturing a growing child.

All children need a *nurturing* (caring and attentive) environment to help them grow and develop. In a **nurturing environment**, children feel secure, protected, and loved. They experience **nurturing relationships** when they are with people who meet these needs.

Helping Children Feel Secure and Protected

Children need to have their basic needs met to feel secure and protected. When children are hungry, they need to be fed. When they are tired, they need an opportunity to sleep. They need shelter and a safe environment to keep them warm and protected. Establishing routines for eating, sleeping, and daily care can help families meet these needs and help children feel secure.

Feeling secure and protected also means meeting children's emotional needs. Little children can sometimes feel overwhelmed in crowds of people. Holding children's hands in a crowded public scene tells them someone is protecting them when they are in the midst of strangers. When children have frights or scares, they feel better if they receive reassuring hugs (**Figure 18.1**).

Helping Children Feel Loved

Children need to feel loved. Children who feel loved will conclude that they are lovable. This idea then becomes part of the child's self-concept. Parents show their children that they love them with both their words and their actions. When these two do not match, children receive **mixed messages** and may not feel loved.

Sending Messages with Love

Children want to hear their parents say, "I love you," but they also need to hear love expressed in nonverbal messages. Children respond to the nonverbal messages of their parents, including tone of voice and the amount of attention given. Even young babies who cannot yet understand words respond differently to different tones of voice.

Some messages show affection, respect, acceptance, or concern for the child as a person. These messages will help the child feel loved. I-statements can help you express your thoughts, feelings, desires, and intentions to a child in a nurturing way. These statements can even be used when children's behavior needs to be *modified*, or changed in some way. For example, you could say, "I see you are having fun, but I need you to go to your room right now and get dressed so we

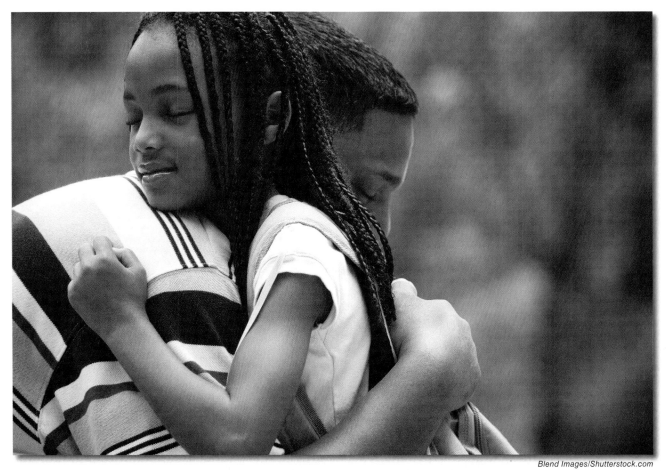

Figure 18.1 Reassuring hugs can help children feel secure, especially when children are experiencing stress or fear. *Why do you think hugs often give people a sense of security?*

can make it to school on time." This approach acknowledges the child's feelings, lets the child know what the expected behavior is, and provides a reason for the expected behavior. This message shows respect for the child and concern about the child's well-being.

As you will learn in Lesson 18.3, statements that recognize and praise children's good behavior or accomplishments are desirable and help children feel lovable and capable. These messages give credit to the child for something he or she did well and contribute to the child's self-esteem. Statements like "I see you shared your toys nicely with your cousin" or "I see you did a good job on that report" help build a child's self-esteem.

Some comments make a child feel worthless or unimportant. Often, tone of voice is what makes these messages demeaning to the child's self-esteem. A person could say, "I *said*, go to your room now and get dressed!" Commands like this can make a child feel like his or her thoughts and feelings are not of value, especially if the command is given in a loud voice. Then the child will feel unlovable.

Think About Your Reading

What are some nonverbal messages that can attack a child's self-esteem?

Making Direct Eye Contact

How often do people look directly at you when they speak to you? How do you feel when they do, and when they do not? Remember that making eye contact is one of the first rules of good communication. When parents speak to a child, especially a young one, it is easy to look down at the child's head. The best way to send a message of care and love, however, is to look directly into the child's eyes (**Figure 18.2**). This may mean lifting

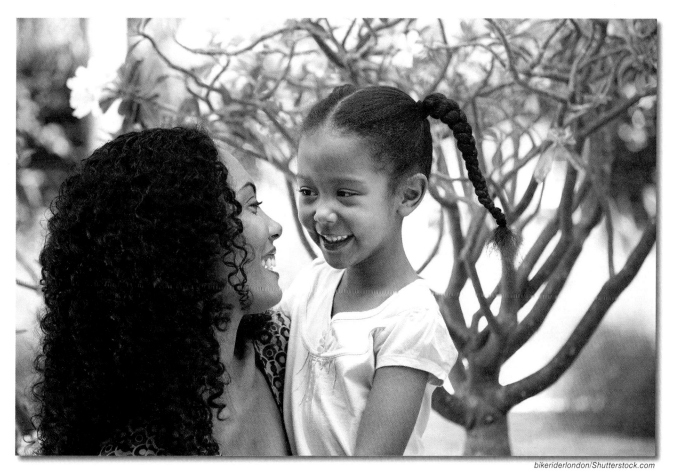

bikeriderlondon/Shutterstock.com

Figure 18.2 Direct eye contact is one way for a parent to send a child a message of love and concern. *What practices could parents use to help them initiate direct eye contact?*

the child up to the adult's eye level or squatting down to the child's eye level before speaking. To talk with older children, it may mean sitting across from them at a table.

Children want to make eye contact with people they care about. Newborns seek to focus on the eyes of the person providing care. Young children try to make their mothers look directly at them. Eye contact meets children's emotional needs and helps them feel they have worth and value, which contributes to their self-esteem. It also helps children learn to make direct eye contact with others as they begin to build relationships with peers.

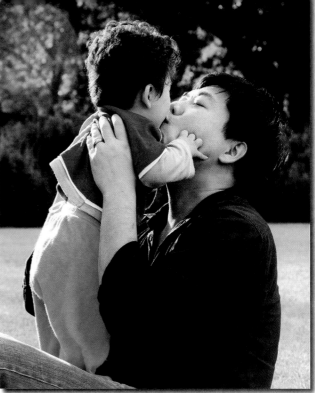
michaeljung/Shutterstock.com

Figure 18.3 Spending quality time with children can help them feel loved and valued. *What are some activities that would fit the category of "quality time"?*

Think About Your Reading

How does direct eye contact contribute to communication with your parents?

Providing Close Physical Contact

The messages sent by close, caring physical contact signal concern, support, and love. Of course, a hug or kiss on the cheek signals a great deal of closeness, but there are other ways of sending this message as well. When someone talks to you, leans over, and touches your arm, there is an immediate message of closeness. Placing an arm around the person's shoulder does the same. Parents can help their children feel loved by using such types of physical contact regularly.

Spending Time Together

An important way for parents to help their children feel loved is to spend time with them (**Figure 18.3**). Doing activities together builds bonds within the family. The kind of time that really conveys love to children, however, is undivided and uninterrupted. This is time that parent and child spend one-on-one with no interruptions from others and with no distractions, such as from a television or radio. When a parent gives a child his or her full attention, the child feels important and valued.

During such focused time, listening to a child is important. By doing so, parents can learn what and how their child thinks and feels. They can learn his or her opinion or what problems the child is having in school or with friends. Sometimes the child just needs someone to listen and show empathy.

To find time, parents may need to consider their values. What is truly most important to them? Even with busy schedules, parents need to set aside time to spend alone with their child. This may be a few minutes at bedtime. As children get older, parents may set aside time on weekends for a special outing together. Even if the undivided, uninterrupted time together is short, it is important for the relationship.

LESSON 18.1

Assess

COMPREHENSION CHECK

1. Identify the characteristics of a nurturing environment.
2. Give examples of four ways a parent can help a child feel loved.
3. Why is making direct eye contact with children important?
4. How does feeling loved impact a child's growth and development?

Content Terms

Build Vocab

newborn
bonding
infant
stranger anxiety
separation anxiety
toddler
autonomy
preschooler
solitary play
onlooker play
parallel play
associative play
cooperative play

Academic Terms

input
appropriate

Objectives

After studying this lesson, you will be able to

- **identify** practices parents can follow to stimulate the development of a newborn.
- **describe** how parents can provide a stimulating learning environment for an infant.
- **explain** how parents can stimulate a sense of autonomy in a toddler.
- **describe** how parents can make a stimulating environment for a preschool child.
- **identify** practices parents can use to help elementary-age children adjust to the school environment.
- **explain** how parents can manage the impact of technology on children.

Focus Your Reading

1. Add this lesson title to the second branch of the graphic organizer you started in Lesson 18.1. Add to your organizer, listing suggestions for developing a stimulating environment for children at each stage of development.
2. Describe the characteristics of a child at each stage of development.

In all children, normal development follows certain patterns. These patterns consist of several changes that take place in a certain order. Children pass through five stages of development before adolescence: newborn, infancy, toddlerhood, preschool, and the elementary-age years. In each of these stages, children learn through different kinds of play. The types of play activities they engage in depend on the developmental needs of their stage.

Stimulating Children's Development

The characteristics of a stimulating environment vary as a child grows and develops. For each stage, there are common characteristics of development that can be stimulated with specific types of play, toys, and types of interaction.

Stimulating the Newborn's Development

The **newborn**, a child between birth and three months, depends on the environment to provide sounds, smells, touch, tastes, and sights to the senses. This sensory *input*, or information, stimulates the development of the newborn's brain. Therefore, it is important that newborns have an interesting and interactive environment.

Bonding begins when children are newborns. **Bonding** is the development of strong feelings of attachment between the parent and the newborn. Parents interact with their newborns by looking into their eyes, talking, smiling, and caressing the skin. These interactions stimulate the neurons in the newborn's brain. The newborn responds to the parent, and this communication creates a close bond of attachment. This attachment is critical in the development of the child.

Crying is the way newborns like Lauren let parents or guardians know their needs. If it is close to feeding time and Lauren starts to fuss, she should be fed before she breaks into a hard cry. Some parents think that responding to a baby's cry right away will spoil him or her. That is not the case. Instead, it will help the baby feel secure and loved (**Figure 18.4**).

If a newborn has a wet or dirty diaper, she needs to be changed. If she is bored, she needs someone to talk, sing, walk, or play with her. If she appears to be in pain, she may need to burp or pass some gas.

Sometimes, Lauren, like other newborns, does not quiet easily. Usually movement and soothing stimulation will quiet her. Her parents may rock her or hold her close while walking with her. They may use a ticking clock or a rhythmic swing to

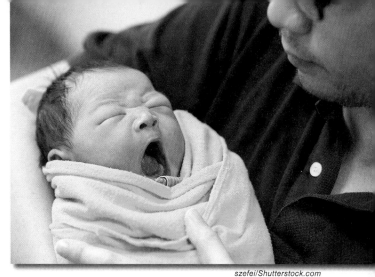

szefei/Shutterstock.com

Figure 18.4 Meeting a newborn's needs helps the child feel secure and loved. *Why is it important to respond quickly to a newborn's cry?*

quiet her. Sometimes they wrap her tightly in a blanket, swaddling her to help her feel secure.

If a newborn is easy to quiet, parents will feel that it is easy to care for the newborn. If he or she is often fussy and difficult to quiet, parents may feel frustrated. Sometimes a fussy newborn causes the parents to become nervous and tense. The newborn can sense this and then becomes even more fussy. Some new parents may find it hard to relax as they adjust to caring for their newborn. They need to take steps to relax by calling someone to talk with or seeking help if necessary. Above all, they need to avoid becoming angry with a crying baby. Shaking a baby or small child can result in *Shaken Baby Syndrome*, a condition that results in brain damage and sometimes in death.

Think About Your Reading

How could a healthy spousal relationship help parents meet the demands of providing a stimulating environment for a newborn?

Stimulating the Infant's Development

Infants—children from three months to one year old—grow rapidly, and their needs continue to change. These changes demand ongoing adjustments by parents (**Figure 18.5**). To meet infants' needs for growth and development, parents must

The Infant: Ages Three Months to One Year	
Characteristics of Development	**Suggestions to Stimulate Development**
• Holds head erect. • Reaches for object. • Recognizes mother. • Rocks like an airplane on tummy. • Rolls over.	• Provide sensory stimuli, such as colorful mobiles; pictures on wall; objects hanging in crib; soft, fuzzy toys to touch, squeeze, and explore; and soft, rhythmic music.
• Grasps objects.	• Provide objects to grasp, bang, drop, or mouth.
• Expresses many emotions: jealousy, sympathy, and affection.	• Display calm and stable emotions in response to child.
• Imitates faces. • Likes to play.	• Play peek-a-boo games. • Talk and sing to child.
• Fears strangers. • Is attached to mother or primary caregiver.	• Show confidence and positive attitude around other people.
• Sits alone, hitches around, creeps on hands and knees, stands alone, and may walk.	• Provide space to move around, objects to crawl on, and objects that allow infant to pull up to a standing position.
• Turns and manipulates objects. • Uncovers toys that have been hidden.	• Provide toys that encourage investigation.
• Points to body parts.	• Play "Where's your nose?" and other games.
• Uses a few words.	• Name objects in the child's environment.
• Holds crayons and makes marks.	• Provide large crayons and large pieces of blank paper to accommodate the infant's large-motor movements.

Figure 18.5 Infants pass through many stages of physical, intellectual, social, and emotional development as they grow. *How many of the suggestions to stimulate development require interaction with others?*

manage the physical environment of the infant and include time for adult-child play and interaction. Having their needs met at this early stage helps the infant develop confidence to separate from the parent and explore his or her world.

Infants quickly learn to recognize those who provide their care. When someone unfamiliar comes near, infants like Damian express **stranger anxiety**. Damian reacts by crying in fear. If he is not secure in his parent-child relationships, this fear will be even greater. As Damian learns that others can be trusted, he will express this fear less and less frequently.

As Damian learns to move about, a new phase of learning begins. At first, he fears moving too far from his mother or caregiver. This fear is called **separation anxiety**. He crawls over to a toy, brings

it back to his mother, and then plays with the toy by her side. As the infant becomes more confident, he moves further and further from his mother to explore the world.

> **Think About Your Reading**
>
> What traits of an infant do you think make parenting enjoyable at this stage? What traits make parenting an infant difficult?

Stimulating the Toddler's Development

Like an infant, a toddler learns by exploring. A **toddler** is a child in the age range from one to three years. A rapid increase in *motor skills* (skills

in movement) opens up a whole new world for the toddler to explore. As a toddler, Andruw will tackle exploring his new world with vigor. As he explores, Andruw is developing a sense of **autonomy**. In other words, he is learning he can do some tasks on his own. He is learning he is a separate person, beginning to develop his own sense of self-identity. Andruw's parents can help him develop autonomy by encouraging him to use self-help skills, such as choosing his own clothing, feeding and dressing himself, and using the toilet.

Stimulating the toddler's development requires providing opportunities to explore and discover the world in which the toddler lives (**Figure 18.6**). At the same time, parents need to make sure that the toddler's environment is safe, so that the child can explore without danger of being hurt. This requires parents to set limits and boundaries. Finding a balance between promoting exploration and setting boundaries can often be frustrating and challenging for parents.

Stimulating the Preschooler's Development

Children in the period from three to five years of age are called **preschoolers**. Much learning takes place during these years, and parents need to manage their children's environment so that children have opportunities to play at their own level. Therefore, knowing what type of experiences a child needs is important.

Preschoolers approach their environment through many different types of play. Eight of these are described in the chart in **Figure 18.7**.

The Toddler: Ages One to Three	
Characteristics of Development	**Suggestions to Stimulate Development**
• Attempts to solve simple problems.	• Provide toys that reward exploration using principles of cause and effect (hop when pulled, squeak when pushed, puzzles, nesting buckets, stacking toys).
• Learns via exploration.	• Take walks or trips to explore surroundings.
• Vocabulary increases.	• Identify objects you can see, hear, smell, touch, or taste.
• Identifies objects by names.	• Read to child and name objects in pictures.
• Enjoys sound patterns and music.	• Teach nursery rhymes and finger plays. • Clap and swing to music.
• Learns to walk well, run, kick, jump, and climb.	• Provide opportunities for gross-motor (large-muscle) development, such as balls to kick and small riding toys.
• Fine-motor (small-muscle) control develops in hands and fingers.	• Provide blocks for stacking, large crayons for coloring, toys to manipulate, finger paints, and clay.
• Becomes interested in self; learns self-identity.	• Talk about gender and sex differences; teach about body parts.
• Learns to feed and dress self.	• Provide opportunities to feed self, choose clothing, and dress self.
• Develops control over sphincter muscles for bladder and bowel control.	• Encourage toilet training for toddlers ages 24 to 30 months.
• Plays alongside friends in parallel play.	• Provide opportunities to play with friends.
• Develops independence.	• Set safe limits to provide a secure place for exploration.

Figure 18.6 The toddler needs opportunities to explore the environment. *Why do you think the toddler years are frustrating for parents?*

Understanding the various types of play will help parents provide *appropriate*, or suitable, activities for their developing children. Each type involves basic developmental skills. The physical skills gained include gross- and fine-motor skills. These encompass large-muscle movements (such as for running) and small-muscle movements (such as for drawing) respectively. Intellectual skills increase

Types of Play for Preschoolers		
Type of Play	**Characteristics in Children**	**Guidelines for Caregivers**
Manipulative play	• Use small muscles. • Put beads on a string. • Run yarn through a sewing card. • Stack, take apart, or put together toys.	• Provide toys that the child can manipulate with success. • Provide toys that offer a new challenge. • Allow the child to repeat skills over and over to master them.
Large-muscle play	• Crawl over objects. • Climb over junglegym. • Walk, run, jump, kick, hop, skip, or pedal.	• Provide opportunities for play, both indoors and outdoors. • Provide adequate space for large-muscle movements. • Provide toys that promote gross-motor skills, such as riding toys, tricycles, and bikes.
Play with art materials	• Explore colors, paints, brushes, and other art materials. • Use play dough, clay, yarn, and other textures.	• Provide opportunities for child to use as many senses as possible while playing. • Allow child to experiment and be creative with materials.
Water and sand play	• Learn science concepts. • Pour, shake, sift, stir, or measure. • Build bridges, plow roads, and navigate boats.	• Allow child to be creative and use his or her imagination. • Provide equipment to measure, pour, shake, stir, and sift. • Include toys such as boats, trucks, diggers, or plows to expand the pretend play.
Block-building play	• Build a tower and knock it down. • Build detailed structures. • Create cities, adding people, cars, and other objects.	• Provide block-building materials that are sturdy and stable. • Allow child to control how a building will be built. • Provide other toys to stimulate pretend play.
Housekeeping play	• Act out home-life experiences. • Imitate different roles. • Pretend to cook, care for a baby, clean house, or wash clothes. • Pretend to go to work, a movie, bowling, a religious service, or other outing.	• Provide child-size equipment, such as kitchen sets, dishes, beds, strollers, and dolls. • Model positive behavior, as children will pretend to do whatever they see parents do.

(Continued)

Figure 18.7 Different types of play involve using different types of skills. *How could using several play centers help a parent stimulate his or her child's growth?*

Types of Play for Preschoolers		
Type of Play	Characteristics in Children	Guidelines for Caregivers
Dramatic play	• Act out real or television events. • Act out stories in books. • Try solving problems. • Express needs or release frustrations.	• Provide props for dramatic play, such as dress-up clothes, hats, umbrellas, briefcases, and books.
Table games	• Learn concepts such as colors, numbers, matching, and counting. • Learn about themselves as they measure their own skills against others. • Learn to play together, take turns, play fairly, work as a team, and follow the rules of the game.	• Play games that use concepts the child can grasp. • Plan child-centered games for the young child. • Allow preschool children to play games in which they can run, chase, and capture one another. • Encourage school-age children to take part in organized games.

Figure 18.7 Continued.

through the processing of information that the child takes in through play and the development of language skills. As children learn to play together, they also develop social and emotional skills.

Stimulating the Elementary-Age Child's Development

The elementary school years—ages 5 through 12—mark significant changes in growth and development (**Figure 18.8**). Most children begin kindergarten at the age of five. This does not mean they magically become ready to learn by sitting at a desk. Learning by experimenting and exploring is still important for children in these years. Children still need to see and touch objects as they grasp new concepts. They also need to practice newly learned skills. The relative freedom children had in earlier years, however, is exchanged for a more structured environment in school.

The school environment brings many changes into a child's life. While many children spent time in preschool or day care settings, school is a new social experience for some children. In school, they may have more contact with other children and adults than ever before. They have new rules to follow and a rigid schedule to keep. Activities

are stopped and started by bells, which children are not used to.

A child like Manasi may have a hard time adjusting to this rigid structure. She may stop along the sidewalk to watch a toad hop in the grass, just as she might have done in the years before she went to school. She is no longer praised for her creativity and exploration, however. Instead, she may be punished for being late for school.

Children need love and understanding as they make the adjustment to the school environment. Manasi's parents can help her by showing an interest in every stage of her development. She needs praise for what she does accomplish. She needs encouragement to believe she can adjust.

All school-age children go through the awkward and sometimes painful stages of social and emotional growth. Parents can help stimulate growth by providing a positive, supportive family environment. Doing so can help children develop feelings of confidence and security.

The Importance of Play

Play is an important activity for all children at all stages because children learn as they play. To children, learning and playing are the same

The Elementary Years: Ages 5 to 12	
Characteristics of Development	**Suggestions to Stimulate Development**
• Learns by experimenting. • Figures out problems.	• Suggest reasons relating to cause and effect; give explanations.
• Needs to see and touch items to understand concepts.	• Provide opportunities to test problems and understand them. • Help child focus on qualities of what is seen.
• Learns systematically through ordering of facts.	• Encourage collections (such as plants, rocks, or stamps).
• Develops skills in reading, writing, and physical dexterity.	• Encourage reading for enjoyment.
• Needs to develop a sense of industry.	• Help child develop skills.
• Develops sense of self from relationships and abilities.	• Relate reasoning to life experiences. • Provide positive feedback. • Encourage friendships.
• Grows physically at rates that vary widely.	• Emphasize positive body image. • Encourage participation in group games.
• Internalizes family rules and values.	• Stress real values and point out what is really important.
• Attaches strongly to adults who model desired behavior.	• Model desired behavior.
• Adjusts moral behavior by what happens to others.	• Keep guidance constant. • Explain rules and consequences.
• Adjusts to school setting.	• Listen to teacher's perception of child. • Be interested in child's work. • Provide praise and acceptance.

Figure 18.8 Parental guidance and support is important as elementary school children make adjustments in their school and home lives. *How could differences in development impact children during the elementary years?*

activity. Play helps children grow in all areas of their development in several ways:

- *Builds self-esteem.* Children develop feelings of control and success when they realize they can make things happen. When children push a truck, it rolls. When they pedal a tricycle, they can make it move.

- *Encourages creativity.* In play, children have the freedom to use their imaginations and to choose the action they desire (**Figure 18.9**). They can use blocks to make a city. Then they can use one of the same blocks and pretend it is a plow.

- *Helps children learn about different roles.* Play gives children a chance to learn about

other people's roles. Through play, children can pretend to be a mother, father, baby, police officer, or mail carrier.

- *Builds relationships.* As they play with others, children learn how to give and take to get a task done. They learn how to share and cooperate. They also learn to follow rules, take turns, and express their feelings.

- *Helps children practice new skills.* Through play, children practice the many new skills they are developing. Changes in physical skills are easy to notice as children learn to run and jump. They also practice new mental skills as they sort out colors or shapes that match or complete jigsaw puzzles. When

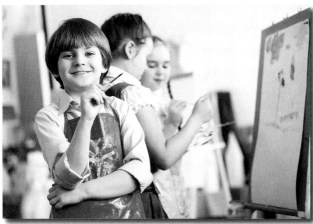
Sergey Nivens/Shutterstock.com

Figure 18.9 Through art or drama, children can express themselves creatively. *Why would a variety of experiences benefit the preschool child's development?*

children begin playing with other children, they develop their social skills.

- *Helps children focus on tasks.* Children often become very involved in their play activities. As they play, they learn to think and reason. Such concentration on a task helps children succeed in the school years.

Think About Your Reading

Think of a leisure activity you enjoy. Identify any area in which this "play" activity helps you grow.

Stages of Play

Children's play reflects the changes taking place in their development. As children grow older, their stages of play change and advance. Each stage builds from the previous one. The five stages of play are based on how children interact with others in a play situation.

- *Solitary play.* In **solitary play**, infants tend to play alone and ignore other children.
- *Onlooker play.* In **onlooker play**, young toddlers watch other children play but will not join in.
- *Parallel play.* In **parallel play**, older toddlers play side by side without interacting with each other.

- *Associative play.* From age three into the elementary years, children enjoy playing with each other. In **associative play**, two or more children play at one activity. They may share toys and ideas, but do not really organize their play.
- *Cooperative play.* Around age 10, children can usually work together in **cooperative play** to reach common goals. The roles they take complement each other. Cooperative play also enables them to play as team members in organized sports.

Think About Your Reading

How could a child's self-concept affect the type of play in which he or she engages?

Guidelines for Toy Selection

Children can be strongly influenced by the media. Many television shows for children are flooded with toy advertisements. With so much competition from the media, how does a parent choose toys wisely?

One point for parents and caregivers to remember is that children do not need expensive toys to make playtime a valuable experience. With a little imagination, parents can provide many play experiences for children at a low cost. Often the simplest toys—blocks, dolls, crayons, paints, or chalk—spark a child's imagination because they can be used in many ways. Many common household items can be recycled to provide hours of imaginative play. Games such as hide-and-seek and hopscotch are fun to play, cost nothing, and provide gross-motor exercise.

When selecting toys for children, parents should consider several factors. Besides being safe, fun, and easy to clean, good toys generally have the following qualities:

- *Are safe to use.* See **Figure 18.10**. Read toy labels carefully. Removable parts such as doll's eyes or buttons are especially dangerous to young children because children can choke on them.

Safety Features for Infant and Toddler Toys	
• Nontoxic paint or finish	• No long cords or strings
• No sharp edges, jagged edges, or points	• No small removable parts that a child could swallow
• Nonbreakable materials	• Nonflammable or flame-resistant materials
• Larger size than the child's two fists	• Washable materials

Figure 18.10 When selecting toys, safety features are important to protect a child's health and well-being. *How could some toys be enriching for one child, but unsafe for another?*

- *Have interesting color, shape, and texture.* Bright colors, textures, and shapes add interest, especially for young children.
- *Stimulate exploration.* Choose toys that have parts to manipulate, sounds to explore, or different options for assembly. For young children, toys that come in a variety of sizes are good choices as well as toys that can be sorted by different parts. Avoid mechanical toys that do all the work for the child.
- *Fit a variety of play settings.* Toys that can be used in many ways will be more interesting to children and will be useful for a longer period of time.
- *Promote creativity.* Toys that promote housekeeping play or dramatic play and encourage the child to practice gross- and fine-motor skills are good choices.
- *Are durable.* Toys need to be sturdy and well constructed.
- *Match the child's stage.* As children develop, their skills increase. Toys that are too complex for the child's stage of development will frustrate him or her. Toys that no longer offer a challenge will bore the growing child.

Think About Your Reading

What are some toys for a preschool child that would meet the criteria described above?

Technology and the Development of Children

Technology is a major part of modern life and can provide a great deal of stimulation for children.

Technology also raises questions. How much television should children watch? How many electronic games should they play? How much time should they spend surfing the Internet or using social media? How much time should they spend texting friends? Such questions plague parents in today's society. When trying to answer these questions, some additional questions need to be asked:

- What are the physical, social, intellectual, and emotional needs of a child at his or her age? If too much time is spent on any one activity, other areas of development do not occur.
- What types of experiences will meet those needs and enhance the child's growth and development?

The American Academy of Pediatrics (AAP) has made general recommendations for parents in managing the effects of technology on their children's development. Both the amount of time spent with media and the content of the media are issues that need to be addressed. The AAP recommends that parents limit entertainment screen time to less than one or two hours per day. It also discourages any media screen exposure for children under two years. While television provides a great deal of stimulation, it offers little opportunity for children to interact, explore, or express their creativity.

The AAP suggests that parents model "media diets," carefully selecting what they view and limiting their own viewing to healthy choices. Parents can actively educate children about media choices by watching programs with them and talking about what they see, the values they observe, and the effects that watching programs can have on their own development.

A media-use plan can be developed by family members, identifying guidelines for when media is used and when it is not appropriate. Family

meetings are good times to discuss a media-use plan. Mealtimes and bedtimes are both opportunities to set aside all media devices, allowing family members to focus on building their relationships at mealtimes and getting sleep at bedtime. No screens should be kept in children's bedrooms.

Media time can have both positive and negative impacts on children's development. Media with appropriate content that promotes development can help children and teens learn as well as develop empathy, tolerance, and other interpersonal skills (**Figure 18.11**). On the other hand, uncontrolled and unsupervised media use can result in exposure to violent images, a decrease in verbal communication with others, a lack of physical activity, and a decrease in healthy interpersonal skills.

As parents plan to stimulate their children's development, they should limit the time children spend on any one activity. A balanced blend of activities is important so children grow in all areas of development.

LESSON 18.2

Assess

COMPREHENSION CHECK

1. What practices can caregivers use to stimulate the development of a newborn?
2. Give three examples of practices that can help stimulate the development of an infant.
3. Describe how caregivers can help a toddler develop a sense of autonomy.
4. Provide three examples of how caregivers can provide appropriate types of play opportunities for preschoolers.
5. Explain how parents can help children adjust to the school environment.
6. Identify three parts of a plan for effectively managing the use of technology in the family.

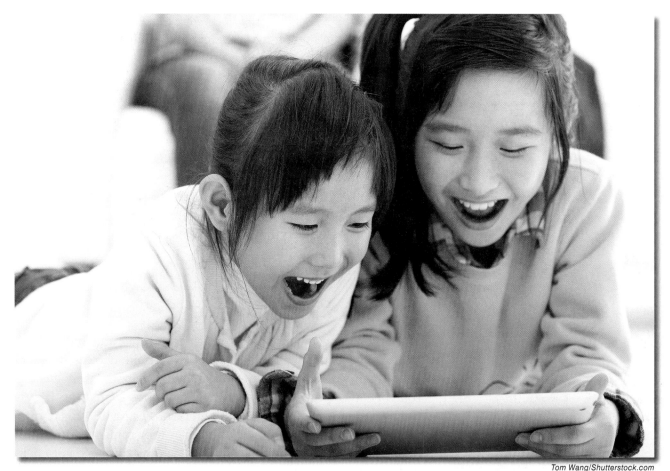

Tom Wang/Shutterstock.com

Figure 18.11   High-quality technologies for children promote education and help children develop skills. *What are some signs of quality in technologies for children?*

PROVIDING GUIDANCE

Content Terms

Build Vocab

guidance
modeling
redirecting
reinforcement
natural consequences
time-out
Individualized Education Plan (IEP)

Academic Terms

diminish
proportionate

Objectives

After studying this lesson, you will be able to

- **explain** how parents use guidance to help children learn appropriate behaviors.
- **identify** principles all guidance methods should meet.
- **describe** different methods of guiding children's behavior.
- **identify** community resources that provide support to parents.

Focus Your Reading

1. Add this lesson title to the third branch of the graphic organizer you created in Lesson 18.1. Add to your organizer, listing the key ideas from this lesson.
2. For each method of guidance, give an example of a parent using this strategy with his or her child.

Children do not automatically know what they should or should not do. They need to be taught what behaviors are appropriate and safe. While busy exploring their world, toddlers may wander into the street, reach out to a fire, or hit a sibling. They do not know which choices may be harmful to them or to others. They have not learned that some actions are acceptable while others are not.

The Need for Guidance

Children need guidance from their parents and others who teach them. Guidance teaches children to make choices that will keep them safe and lead to growth and development. A *guide* is someone who leads the way. Guidance is not something that is done *to* a person. It is done *with* a person (**Figure 18.12**). Parental **guidance** is all that parents do and say as they influence their children's behavior in a positive way. The goal of guidance is to help children grow to be mature adults who respect other people's rights and property and who do not express their emotions aggressively.

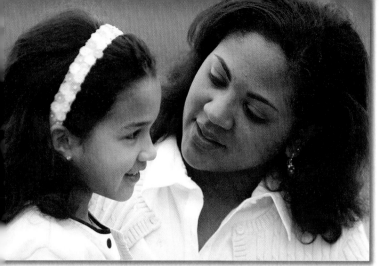
Rob Marmion/Shutterstock.com

Figure 18.12 Parents provide guidance as they lead their child to use acceptable behavior. *How does parental guidance help children learn to control their own behavior?*

With proper guidance, children learn self-discipline. *Self-discipline*, also called *self-control*, is the ability to control your own behavior in a responsible way.

Methods for Guiding Children

Using various methods, parents train their children to use behaviors that are acceptable to them and to society and to avoid unacceptable behaviors. No matter which guidance method is used, it should incorporate these three principles:

- *Love should always be the key ingredient.* Guiding with love helps children develop positive attitudes. Children know their parents care for them and are looking out for their well-being, even if they do not like the immediate consequence.

- *A child's value as a person should always be upheld.* In giving guidance, parents need to communicate that the child's worth as a person is not *diminished*, or lessened. It is the behavior that needs to adjust and change. Feelings of self-worth help children believe they can make appropriate choices.

- *The method used should help the child learn self-discipline.* Different methods are effective for different situations. Helping children understand why certain behaviors are

desirable will help them learn to think about their actions and the potential consequences. Guiding children through this thinking process helps them grow and develop intellectually. As children learn to think about their actions, they develop skills for controlling their behaviors.

Think About Your Reading

How are guidance and self-discipline similar? How are they different?

There are eight guidance methods from which parents can choose. Each follows these three principles.

Modeling

If parents knew that every word they said was being recorded or every action photographed, would they act or speak differently? In truth, the words and actions parents use on a daily basis *are* recorded. They are retained in the mind of the child. Modeling is a method of guidance that takes advantage of that fact. **Modeling** is acting in a way that sets a good example. This approach encourages children to use good behavior. Children learn best by example—they imitate what they see others doing.

Parents are a child's first teachers and first role models. Children love to imitate their parents and pretend to be like them. They imitate their parents' roles in play and imitate their behaviors in their interactions with others.

Through modeling, parents can help their children develop relationships, make decisions, and control emotions. Parents can also help children develop healthful habits and strong character (**Figure 18.13**). The most important and often difficult part of this task for parents is to model the desired behavior. Children will imitate bad behavior as well as good behavior. For this reason, parents have to always be aware of the way they are acting and speaking. They should ensure that their children see and hear good models to follow.

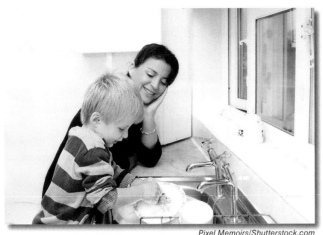
Pixel Memoirs/Shutterstock.com

Figure 18.13 Children imitate the behaviors, good or bad, of their parents or guardians. *What behaviors did you adopt that your parents or guardians modeled?*

Think About Your Reading

What examples can you give of habits you have picked up from people with whom you spend time?

Setting Limits

Parents also guide the child's behavior by setting limits or rules. Limits should be well defined and clearly explained. An example of a limit is a time limit put on daily television viewing. An example of a rule is not taking other children's toys. Children need to know exactly what is expected of them. They should have no doubts about what *is* acceptable behavior and what *is not*. As a child gets older, some limits will need to be changed to match the child's level of development.

Parents may find it helpful to write the limits they have set for children and why they have established those limits. Then it is easier for them to keep in mind what the limits should accomplish.

Setting rules and limits helps parents show parental control, which helps children feel secure. At the same time, children learn to be independent within accepted limits. Once children know what is expected of them, they can learn to control their behavior.

To use this approach to guidance effectively, parents need to follow these three rules:

- *Be consistent.* Parents need to be consistent in their expectations. If a behavior is off-limits, it must always be treated as off-limits. Otherwise, if a behavior is allowed one time and not another, a child becomes confused.
- *Keep both the child's and parents' welfare in mind.* What is needed for the child's safety? Will the limits help the child's personal growth? In addition, the needs of other family members should be considered.
- *Use positive reinforcement.* Taking this approach in discussing the child's behavior will reinforce and encourage behavior within the established limits. Positive reinforcement lets children know what behavior pleases their parents.

Establishing Routines

Learning to follow some regular routines is important for children. Routines give a feeling of security to a child's life. They help children know what to expect: after dinner every night, they are expected to brush their teeth, for instance.

Developing a routine that works takes time. Once the routine is established, it can save much time and conflict between parent and child.

Think About Your Reading

Think of an example in which one of your routines has helped you develop self-discipline.

Redirecting

Sometimes parents can guide a child away from an undesirable activity by substituting a more acceptable one. This method is called **redirecting** the child's behavior. Redirecting is accomplished by shifting the child's interest from something the parent does not want him or her to do to some other activity that is desired (**Figure 18.14**).

The key to redirecting is to replace the unacceptable activity with one that is acceptable and equally as interesting to the child. Redirecting is a good technique to use with toddlers, whose main desire is to explore. With children in this stage,

Copyright Goodheart-Willcox Co., Inc.

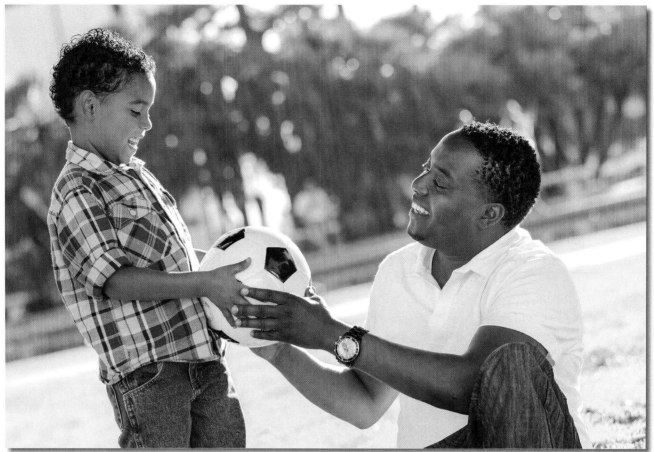

Andy Dean Photography/Shutterstock.com

Figure 18.14 Parents can sometimes guide behavior by redirecting the child's attention to a substitute toy or activity. *How could this method of guidance help older children develop thinking skills?*

a parent may physically move the child from an area that is unsafe to one that is safer. Parents can redirect older children by offering alternative activities. Reasoning and logic may be used to persuade children to follow their parents' advice.

Making Requests

One of the simplest ways a parent can guide a child's actions is through requests, expressing personal desires with I-statements. "Karin, I would like you to put your toys on the shelf," is one example. This kind of guidance gives the child a chance to please the parent by responding with the behavior. When she feels that she has pleased her parent, Karin's feelings of worth and importance increase.

Negative commands or you-statements tear down a child's self-esteem. "Don't leave your clothes on the floor!" is an example. Hearing

such commands continually will cause the child to have negative feelings of worth. Children are less likely to develop self-discipline if they do not believe they can carry out acceptable behavior.

Reinforcing

When a child performs a desired behavior, **reinforcement** can influence him or her to repeat it. For instance, when Karin picks up her clothes or cleans her room, her parents can praise her for doing a good job or give her some special privilege.

Reinforcing Desired Behavior

Reinforcement needs to occur right after the desired behavior is displayed. The child needs to remember that the good feelings that result from the response are linked to the particular behavior that prompted the response. Then the child will

want to repeat the desired behavior. The method a parent uses to reinforce behavior depends on the child's interests and level of development (**Figure 18.15**).

Reinforcing Negative Behavior

Sometimes parents may reinforce a child's negative behavior without realizing it. Think of some behaviors that a child may use to get his or her own way. For instance, Charlie has learned that if he keeps asking for what he wants in the grocery store, his mother will buy it. He has also learned that it only works to beg for one item; the second item will be a definite "no." Charlie's mother does not realize that she reinforces this behavior. Charlie, however, has learned that begging usually brings results.

One problem with reinforcement is that parents often let desirable behavior go unnoticed and only recognize undesirable actions. When siblings are playing together without conflict, a parent will probably not stop to praise them. If these siblings are pushing and tugging on the same toy, however, that attracts a parent's attention. This pattern of responding can have undesired consequences. If the child desires a parent's attention, he or she will show the negative behavior in order to receive that attention. In this way, ignoring desirable behavior and only correcting negative behavior actually results in more negative behavior.

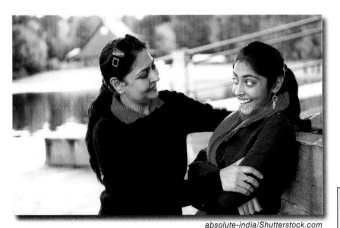
absolute-india/Shutterstock.com

Figure 18.15 Positive reinforcement results in both parent and child feeling good about a situation. *Why might parents fail to use positive reinforcement even though it could be very effective?*

Most children want their parents' attention but also want to please. The reinforcement that parents give can be a strong motivator. Parents need to watch their responses to be sure they reinforce desirable behavior only.

Think About Your Reading

Why do adults often fail to reinforce positive behavior?

Using Natural Consequences

Sometimes the natural consequences of an action are effective in helping a child control behavior. **Natural consequences** are the normal results of an action. For instance, suppose Jeremy is about to step on a balloon filled with air. Jeremy's father could pick him up and move him away from the balloon before he steps on it. Suppose, instead, he warns Jeremy that if he steps on the balloon, he will lose the balloon. He then lets Jeremy decide what to do. If Jeremy does indeed step on the balloon and bursts it, his father is letting him face the natural consequences of his actions.

For natural consequences to work, a direct relationship must exist between the child's choice of action and the result of that action. For instance, Abe spends all his money on a large box of popcorn at the movies. The natural consequence of this decision is feeling thirsty. Now Abe must wait until he is home to get a drink he wants.

Parents cannot rely on natural consequences in some situations because the consequences are dangerous to the child's health or welfare (**Figure 18.16**). Parents cannot let a child play in the street to learn that this behavior is harmful. They cannot let a child get burned to learn what hot means.

Think About Your Reading

Think of an example in which guidance with natural consequences is a good choice to develop a child's self-discipline.

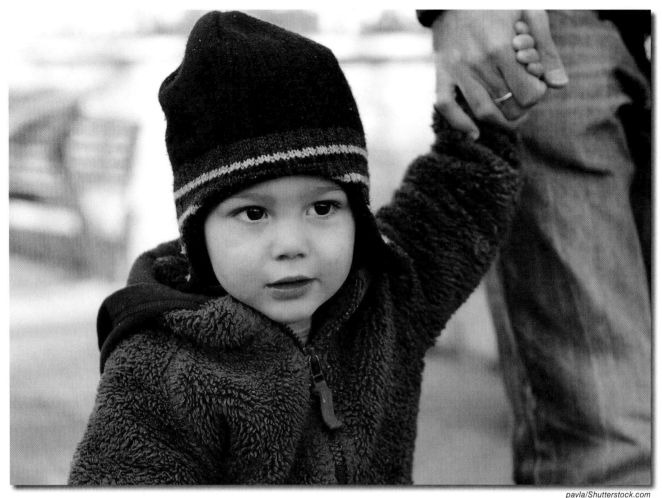

Figure 18.16 Natural consequences should not be used for guidance when the natural consequences are dangerous to a child's health or well-being.

Punishing

Punishment gives the child a reason to regret engaging in behavior he or she knew was wrong. For punishment to be effective, the child needs to be old enough to understand wrong behavior. For this reason, punishment is not appropriate for a very young child.

Parents should only use a punishment that *fits*, or directly links to, the wrong behavior. For example, parents might take a bike away for a period of time if a child repeatedly rides in the street instead of staying on the sidewalk. Some parents punish by giving a child a **time-out**, a period when he or she must be away from others to think quietly about the behavior. The time-out should take place in an area or room where the child has no toys or other distractions.

If some form of punishment is necessary, parents should discuss it with the child first. They need to make sure the child understands that the behavior was not acceptable. Parents also need to make clear *why* the behavior is unacceptable. As they talk about the behavior, they can help the child realize they love him or her but not the behavior.

Discussing behavior is difficult for parents if they are angry. The goal of punishment is not to give the parents a chance to vent their anger. Punishment dealt under these circumstances will likely tear down the child's self-esteem and may be abusive. Angry parents need to take time to calm down and control their emotions so they can address the child's behavior in a calm, firm, and loving manner. Calming down also helps ensure that the parent gives a punishment that is

proportionate to, or on the same level with, the behavior that earned it.

Think About Your Reading

What form of guidance do you think you would be most comfortable using with children?

Choosing a Guidance Method

When a child misbehaves, parents need to ask themselves two questions: Why did the child act this way? What can I do to help the child learn appropriate behavior? Identifying the problem can help parents choose an effective method of guidance (**Figure 18.17**).

Identify the problem first. Sometimes what appears to be undesirable behavior is really normal for the child's age. The child may just need to be redirected to play that is more acceptable. The child may be bored from not having enough to

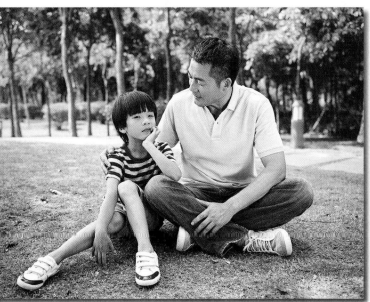

imtmphoto/Shutterstock.com

Figure 18.17 When children misbehave, they should be given a chance to explain their behavior. *How can parents use this discussion to help children develop self-discipline?*

do. At other times, there may be too much activity for the child to handle. In such cases, parents may need to change the child's environment.

Sometimes a child misbehaves to receive attention. If so, the child should be given love to fill that emotional need. Parents need to reassure a child that he or she will be loved even during periods of misbehavior.

If the problem resulted from a misunderstanding, the child may need some clear and simple instructions about what is acceptable. Sometimes the problem is a child wanting his or her own way. Then, parents need to ask if they are reinforcing the undesirable behavior by giving in.

Once the problem is identified, parents should then identify which guidance method will help the child learn self-discipline. Parents will most likely use all forms of guidance at some time during their parenting years. Limits, routines, positive models, and positive reinforcement help set guidelines for children's behavior. Sometimes children step outside those guidelines. Parents can guide them by redirecting them. At other times, natural consequences or punishments such as a time-out may be effective in helping children learn not to repeat a behavior.

Think About Your Reading

Why do you think parents often have a difficult time choosing an appropriate form of guidance?

Avoiding Accidents

Guidance skills can help parents teach children safe behaviors that can help them avoid common accidents. Accidents kill more young children than any one disease. Car accidents, fires and burns, and drowning are the three major causes of accidental death for children. Safety precautions for dealing with these and other dangers are described in the chart in **Figure 18.18**.

Child Safety Precautions	
Danger	**Safety Steps**
Car accidents	• Always buckle up for safety. • Use a restraint system that meets federal safety standards. • Use child safety seats and booster seats that are appropriate for the age and size of the child.
Fires and burns	• Place guards in front of fireplaces and open heaters and around registers and floor furnaces. • Keep hot liquids and foods out of children's reach. • Keep pot handles turned away from the edge of the stove or counter. • Avoid long tablecloths that a child could pull down to spill hot liquids. • Set hot water heater to no higher than 120°F (48.9°C). • Put covers on unused electrical outlets. • Keep matches out of child's reach. • Keep smoke and fire detectors working. • Keep fire extinguishers in the home.
Drowning	• Watch children when they are in or near water. • Never leave a baby or small child alone in a sink or tub. • Use life preservers at the beach, in or near a pool, or in a boat.
Falls	• Do not leave a baby unattended on a changing table, dresser, or bed. • Put safety gates at the tops and bottoms of stairs. • Remove ladders or objects that a young child may be tempted to climb.
Poisons	• Put poisonous substances such as the following out of a child's reach or in locked cabinets: cleaning agents (bleach, all-purpose cleaners, furniture polish, auto polish, or plant sprays); garage and garden products (antifreeze, fertilizers, gas, oil, paints, and pesticides); medicines, vitamins, and personal products (perfume, nail polish and remover, and lotions); and poisonous plants or plants with poisonous parts.
Large plastic bags	• Keep children away from large plastic bags. The child may suffocate if the child puts the bag over his or her face.
Unused freezers or refrigerators	• Fasten door when appliance is not in use so children cannot crawl in and shut the door.
Firearms	• Keep firearms and ammunition locked in separate places. Keep keys out of a child's reach.
Broken glass	• Pick up and dispose.
Tools	• Sharp or heavy tools should be put away where children will not play with them.

Figure 18.18 Children face safety risks every day. Many of these risks can be avoided with proper adult supervision. *How could guidance skills help parents promote safety in the environment?*

In addition to those precautions, these basic safety rules are important:

- Use proper car restraint systems. Toddler car seats and infant carriers are common child restraint systems.

- Never leave children alone. Young children should especially not be left alone near or in water, such as a full bathtub, or near a fire. Infants and toddlers should never be left alone on a surface above the floor unless there are raised sides that can prevent a fall.

- Never play roughly with infants, throw them in the air, or swing them upside down. These activities can cause brain damage.

- Learn first aid and emergency treatment. If an accidental injury does occur, a parent needs to be ready to respond.

Using Community Resources

Most communities offer support services to parents (**Figure 18.19**). Professionals are available to answer questions, teach new skills, or provide help. The services are provided by local support groups, the education system, and government agencies.

Support Groups

Some parents have special parenting situations. They may have a child who has a physical disability, who is gifted, or who has a certain illness. Their child may have a learning disorder and not be doing well in school. A child may have emotional problems because of a death or separation in the family. Parents handling these

---

Real-Life Scenario

Caring for Victor

Margarita and Ramon sat in the emergency room while the doctors quickly worked to pump Victor's stomach. Just a short time before, Victor, their three-year-old son, had swallowed a whole bottle of vitamin pills.

The hospital was a common sight to Victor and his parents. They had nearly lost him as a baby when he developed problems breathing. They could not forget the oxygen tent draped over his hospital crib. After that, they let him sleep in their bed so they could watch for any problems that might arise. That was two years ago, and he still insisted on sleeping in their bed—right between them.

Victor had become a handful. Margarita wondered if they had spoiled him while he was recovering from his illness. They felt sorry for him and usually let him do what he wanted. He cried when they laid him down for a nap, so they let him get back up and stay awake. Sometimes he would get so tired playing that he would fall asleep on the lawn or the floor.

Margarita had to watch Victor all the time. She could not trust him for a minute. When he began

climbing and walking, she never knew what he might do. He would tear the paper before they got a chance to read it. Once he crawled on top of the counter and emptied a jar of honey on the floor. He fell and, fortunately, only broke a leg.

Another time, he flushed a toy down the toilet and played in the water as it overflowed. She wondered if he would ever outgrow these pranks. Now she and Ramon had to deal with this crisis. How did Victor manage to eat the whole bottle of vitamins?

For Discussion

1. How could a child's serious illness cause parents to treat the child in a different or special way?
2. What techniques did Margarita and Ramon use to show their love for their child?
3. What techniques did they use to provide guidance?
4. Cite some specific examples of actions that Margarita and Ramon could take to help Victor learn self-discipline.

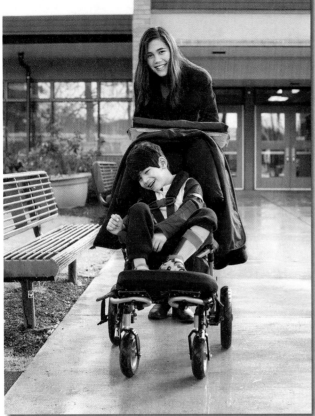

Jaren Jai Wicklund/Shutterstock.com

Figure 18.19 Community resources are available to assist parents in promoting their child's growth and development. *What community resources are available to all parents? What resources might be restricted to those with specific needs?*

situations often form support groups in which members help and encourage one another.

How can parents find a support group? The Internet or telephone directories are good sources. Parents can contact local social service organizations such as United Way to ask for names of suitable groups in the area. Religious institutions, social workers, welfare agencies, and medical or community health clinics can also provide this kind of information.

The Education System

Parents can contact the local school district for information and answers to many questions. The school district may offer special classes for parents as well as for children. Parents may also choose to get involved with school events or parent-teacher groups.

The education system is a vital resource for parents of children with special needs. When parents or teachers think that a child has special needs, the parent or teacher can ask to have the child tested. If a special need is identified, parents and school staff members work together to help the child.

Teachers, perhaps other professionals, and parents then work to design an **Individualized Education Plan (IEP)**. An IEP is a special plan for the particular child's education. Older children are sometimes involved in designing their own plans. The plan must be reviewed on a regular basis to see if the child is making progress or if changes should be made.

Education specialists use technologies to help students with special needs. These can be included in the IEP. For example, computers with programs that check for spelling and grammar can help students with disabilities that affect their writing skills. Auditory aids can be used for students with reading disabilities. Devices that enhance vision or hearing or address physical disabilities may be available to help a child with other kinds of needs.

Government Agencies

Sometimes parents have difficulty providing for the economic needs of their children. In these cases, they may be able to get some help from social service or welfare agencies. Some programs offer nutritious food, either free or at reduced costs. Some provide low-cost medical care for those who cannot afford a doctor's fee. Assistance with dental care and eye care is sometimes available.

Assess

LESSON 18.3

COMPREHENSION CHECK

1. Explain why guidance is an important skill for parents and others who relate to children.
2. List three principles that should apply to all guidance methods.
3. Name and briefly describe four methods of guidance.
4. When choosing a method of guidance for their child, what two questions should parents consider?
5. List three different community resources that could provide support services to parents.

CHAPTER 18 REVIEW AND ASSESSMENT

CHAPTER SUMMARY

Skills for relating to children can help parents and others who work with children provide an environment in which children can grow and develop to their potential. As parents provide care and guidance, they help their children mature physically, intellectually, socially, and emotionally. For children to develop to their full potential, they need to live in a nurturing environment that helps them feel secure and loved.

Children need a stimulating learning environment that provides them ample opportunity to play. A variety of play experiences and toys can stimulate development and learning. Play needs to be tailored to a child's stage of development. Toys and play activities should be chosen to ensure a child's safety.

Children need parental guidance so they can learn self-discipline. Parental guidance can also help them learn to be mature members in society. Parents can choose from among many different methods of guidance, and different approaches can be appropriate for different situations or children of different ages. Whatever method is used, it should always be communicated with love, uphold a child's self-esteem, and aim to develop the child's self-discipline. Parents who need support in their parenting role have access to many community resources, such as community support groups, local schools, and government agencies that offer services to parents and children.

VOCABULARY ACTIVITIES

1. Form into a pair with a partner. Write a list of all the terms that relate to guidance, with their definitions on a separate sheet of paper. Your partner will do the same with the terms related to play. Exchange papers and match the correct definitions to each term. Review the final answers to both lists and resolve any differences you and your partner have over the definitions.

Content Terms

associative play (18.2)
autonomy (18.2)
bonding (18.2)
cooperative play (18.2)
guidance (18.3)
Individualized Education Plan (IEP) (18.3)
infant (18.2)
mixed messages (18.1)

modeling (18.3)
natural consequences (18.3)
newborn (18.2)
nurturing environment (18.1)
nurturing relationship (18.1)
onlooker play (18.2)
parallel play (18.2)
preschooler (18.2)

redirecting (18.3)
reinforcement (18.3)
separation anxiety (18.2)

solitary play (18.2)
stranger anxiety (18.2)
time-out (18.3)
toddler (18.2)

2. Write a paragraph that uses each of the terms in relation to parenting.

Academic Terms

appropriate (18.2)
diminish (18.3)
input (18.2)

modify (18.1)
nurturing (18.1)
proportionate (18.3)

ASSESS

Your Knowledge

3. Name five types of play activities parents could provide for their child in order to stimulate growth and development.
4. Describe a different guidance strategy that parents could effectively use for a child from each age group—toddler, preschooler, elementary-age child, and teen—to help the child develop self-discipline.
5. List four community resources parents can use to find a local support group.

Your Understanding

6. Describe four actions a parent can take to help a child feel loved.
7. Choose two stages of development and explain how a parent can stimulate a child's development during each stage.
8. What should a parent consider when choosing a guidance method?

Your Skills

9. Use four different strategies together in a nurturing interaction between an adult and a child. Describe this interaction in detail.
10. Analyze the following play activities for their impact on the growth and development of a child between five and eight years of age: action figures, video games, and computer programs. Identify some guidelines for the activities' uses in a play environment.
11. Choose a selection of toys for a preschool child that are appropriate for stimulating development. Include a variety to promote growth in all areas.

CRITICAL THINKING

12. **Evaluate Assumptions.** Locate a toy catalog, either online or in print, and prepare a feature story for a newspaper in which you analyze popular toys

Copyright Goodheart-Willcox Co., Inc.

for preschool children. Identify qualities that make them popular. Then evaluate the toys, using toy-selection guidelines, characteristics of stimulating environments, and what children learn through play to make recommendations for parents to choose from among the toys. Cite evidence from the text or other resources to support your evaluation. *Choice*: Analyze electronic toys for this age group. *Choice*: Take the role of a television reporter, and deliver your report as an oral presentation. *Group option*: Work with a partner to evaluate toys for children of different ages.

13. **Predict Outcomes.** Research various technologies that are used for children's toys and entertainment. Choose five and evaluate the potential impact that each could have on a child's development, considering children at two different stages of development. Include the positive and negative effects that you predict the technology could have on a child. Cite evidence to support your predictions.

14. **Make Inferences.** Visit a child care center or nursery school. Observe and record examples of the following situations: using guidance techniques, using nurturing behavior, stimulating development, and following a routine. Describe your observations in a report and make a judgment as to whether you would recommend this child care center to a parent, explaining your reasoning for your recommendation. *Group option*: Work with a partner, compare observations, and collaborate on your report.

CORE SKILLS

15. **Writing.** Write a paper describing the methods of nurturing and guidance that you have experienced in your family. Summarize your paper by discussing which methods you feel were most effective in helping you learn self-discipline.

16. **Social Studies, Reading, Writing.** Write a paper addressing the impact of violence in U.S. society on the development of children. Include examples of ways that young children are exposed to violence on a daily basis, citing evidence from current newspaper articles. Describe how this exposure could impact a child's development. Make recommendations for ways parents can limit their children's exposure to violence. Cite references to support your analysis and recommendations.

17. **Writing.** Visit an elementary school classroom. Evaluate the classroom for its potential to provide a stimulating learning environment for children.

Support your evaluation, citing examples from the classroom and references from the text.

18. **Research, Writing.** Using the Internet, research and prepare a report on a community organization that offers educational or economic support to parents. Include a description of the following aspects: the type of support or resources provided, eligibility requirements, and application requirements. Identify the types of careers involved in providing these services.

19. **Research, Math.** Work in a team of four, with each person interviewing three adults about strategies they have found successful in helping children learn self-discipline. Combine your results in a spreadsheet, identifying the number of adults using each strategy. Convert the spreadsheet into a graph that shows how many adults use each strategy. Prepare a report for the class, summarizing your findings. *Group option*: Create a graph that includes all the statistics found by the entire class.

20. **Writing.** Create a chart outlining the steps a parent could use to reinforce desirable behavior for a preschooler and for a fourth-grade child. Include specific behaviors for each age (such as feeding the dog or picking up toys) that a parent might be trying to reinforce. With the chart, suggest a possible reward system to use. *Choice*: Use digital images to illustrate the chart.

CAREER READINESS

21. **Preparing a Day Care Schedule.** Take the role of the owner of a child care center that provides care for children three to five years of age. Prepare a schedule for a day's activities that gives the children a variety of play and other experiences. With each activity, write down any toys or materials that would be needed. Indicate how long each activity would last.

22. **Evaluating Personal Characteristics.** Observe child care workers at a child care center or a preschool teacher with a class of preschoolers. You should watch the professional for at least two hours and see him or her interact with several children in several different situations. Take notes on what you observe, thinking about the attitudes the worker shows toward the children and how he or she behaves, promotes age-appropriate play, guides behavior, handles problems, and provides nurturing care. Write a one-page paper in which you present your findings and assess whether you have the personal characteristics that would make you suitable for the career you observed.

THE AGING FAMILY

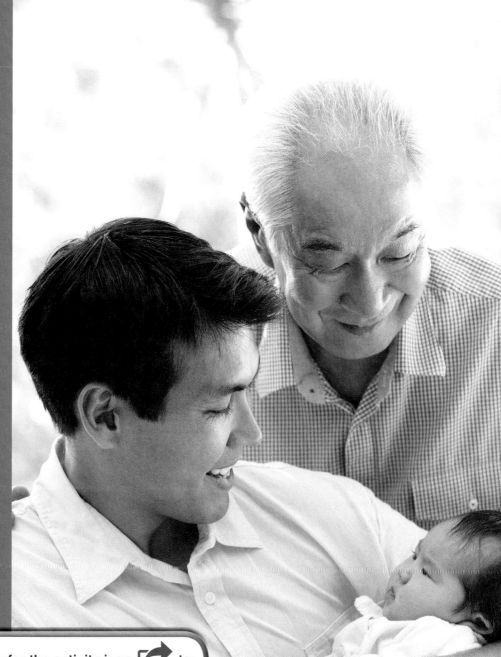

Reading Prep

Before reading the chapter, skim the headings and subheadings in each lesson. Write a sentence explaining what you think each section will be about. As you read, revise your sentences if necessary.

Key Questions

Questions to answer as you study this chapter:

- How can families adjust to the challenges of aging?
- How does grandparenting benefit all generations?
- How does understanding the grieving process help people accept a loss?

While studying this chapter, look for the activity icon   to:

- **build** vocabulary with e-flash cards, matching activities, and vocabulary games; and
- **assess** what you learn by completing the lesson comprehension checks online.

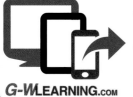

www.g-wlearning.com/humanservices/

Lesson 19.1 The Middle Years
Lesson 19.2 The Retirement Years
Lesson 19.3 The Elderly Years

AFTER STUDYING THIS CHAPTER, YOU WILL

KNOW:

- The effects of aging on the family system.
- The benefits of grandparents' participation in the family system.

UNDERSTAND:

- How families can adjust and balance the family system as adult members age.
- How technological advances impact the family in the later stages of the family life cycle.

BE ABLE TO DO:

- Formulate a plan for effectively managing resources in the later stages of the family life cycle.
- Locate federal and community resources to assist the elderly.

GETTING STARTED

Vi and Walter were both retired, yet they still led busy lives. Vi wanted to leave their home by 7:30 that morning because she had to give her granddaughter a ride to school. Then she had to be at the Bergstroms' home by 8:00 a.m. Martha Bergstrom, who was 84 years old, had fallen a few weeks earlier and broken her leg. Vi visited Martha three mornings a week to help her and her husband. She took Martha to the doctor for appointments, did some housework for Martha and her husband, or went shopping for them. On Tuesdays and Thursdays, Vi babysat two little girls. She enjoyed keeping busy and making a little money to cover her extra expenses.

Walter's first stop that day would be the church, where he mowed the lawn every week. After that, he planned to meet Rollie and Adolph for lunch at the senior center. There he would attend an afternoon meeting to help plan a group bus trip to the Ozarks. Walter was a member of the center's planning committee.

Aging does not mean that life becomes meaningless. Friends, family, and neighbors are all sources of meaningful relationships throughout a lifetime, and older adults can find many ways to remain active and involved in their families and communities.

Nevertheless, aging does bring about changes, and those changes affect the family system. The needs of individuals and couples change as people age. Resources change, often because of changes in technology. Strong, supportive relationships can help people adjust to these changes and make the aging years enjoyable and rewarding.

THE MIDDLE YEARS

Content Terms

Build Vocab

middlesence
midlife crisis

Academic Terms

intensify
rend

Objectives

After studying this lesson, you will be able to

- **describe** how middlescence affects the individual.
- **identify** changes in roles and responsibilities during the middle years.
- **predict** the possible impacts of changing technology on the middle-aged adult's career.
- **list** ways that grandparenting benefits different generations of a family.

Focus Your Reading

1. Develop a chart with three columns. Label column one *Changes That Take Place*. Label column two *How Changes Affect the Family System*. Label column three *Adjusting to the Changes*. As you read this lesson, fill in information under each column.
2. Compare middlescence with adolescence and list ways they are similar and different.

Between the ages of 35 and 40, most adults begin to see the first physical signs of aging. They may notice the appearance of a few wrinkles or gray hairs. Their reflexes may seem a little slower. Perhaps they cannot run quite as fast or as far as they did in the past. In a person's life span, these physical changes tend to mark the beginning of the middle-age years.

The middle-age years between 40 and 65 are sometimes called **middlescence**. This is because adults begin to ask many of the same questions they asked during adolescence, but from the perspective of looking back on life. They question who they have become, what they have accomplished in life, and what their purposes and goals for living are. "Who am I?" "What have I done so far in my life?" "Will I reach the goals I have set?" "Will I ever own my own business or travel around the world?" This questioning usually increases as the signs of aging become more evident (clearly seen).

For the middle-age adult, this period of questioning can be beneficial. It can encourage the adult to evaluate his or her progress in reaching life goals. This thinking can lead to revising goals, forming new goals, or reaffirming those goals and rededicating one's self to working toward them. It can also lead to planning and preparing for the retirement years. Questioning can encourage a couple to work together to strengthen their marital relationship as well. It can help them establish closer relationships with their children. Also, it can help them relate to their parents, who are already coping with the effects of aging.

The Effects of Change During Middlescence

Several changes take place in adults' lives during middlescence. Adults may experience multiple stages of the family life cycle during these years (**Figure 19.1**). Children of various ages may be at different stages of becoming independent. The adult's own parents, if alive, are aging and may be losing their independence. Working adults reach the peaks of their careers and look ahead to retirement. Each of these changes can trigger the questioning that takes place during middlescence.

Family Life Cycle Changes

Parents in their middle years may still have young children in the home, teenagers struggling with adolescence, or young adults anxious to launch out on their own. The challenges of fulfilling the multiple roles needed by these children in different stages add to the stress of the middle years. Parents may feel they have more questions than answers.

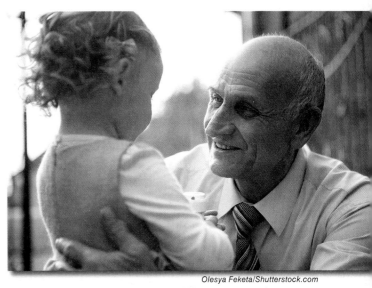

Olesya Feketa/Shutterstock.com

Figure 19.1 Adults in the middle years can have roles and responsibilities related to young children, teenagers, young adults, and elderly parents. *How could these multiple relationships impact the questioning that a middle-age adult might experience?*

Parents' roles and responsibilities during the later parenting stage focus on helping their children become independent, ready and able to launch their own lives. Making daily decisions to help children reach these goals can be challenging. How much supervision do children need? How much guidance is helpful, and how much might be seen as interference? How much financial support do children need? How does that support mesh with the middle-age parents' own goals? These questions may have different answers for each child, as each child is unique and has needs specific to her own abilities and goals. Finding answers that work for each child requires open, honest communication between parent and child and skills for solving problems jointly.

Parents want to be successful, and one of the measures that society uses to determine the success of parents is whether children are able to launch and live on their own. When children do not launch successfully, parents blame themselves, questioning what they should have done differently and what they should do now. Parents should keep in mind that their children are adults now and are responsible for their own lives (**Figure 19.2**).

Changes in the family life cycle remind the adult that time is passing. When the last child

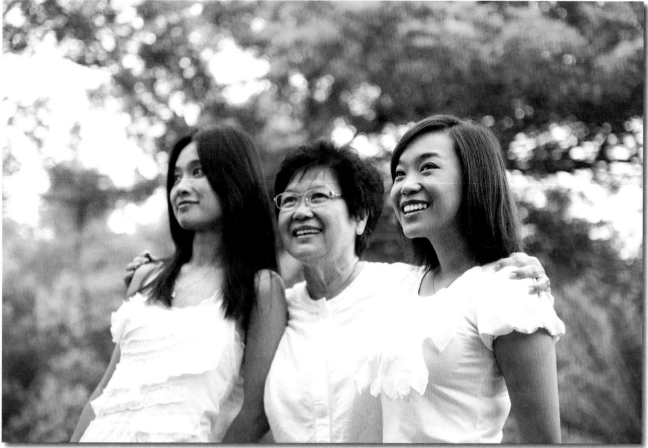
szefei/Shutterstock.com

Figure 19.2 Most adults in the middle-age years want their children to become independent. Middle-age parents, however, are not responsible for their adult children's decisions.

leaves home, parents enter the empty nest stage. This stage leads some middle-age adults to question the overall meaning of life, the time they have left, and what they want to do with the time that remains. The desire to have good relationships with their adult children and potential grandchildren can also bring more stress, depending on how successful parents and children were in communicating during the later parenthood stage.

The marriage of children brings more change to the middle-age adult, with the challenge of developing healthy relationships with sons- or daughters-in-law and their families. Building good relationships with in-laws requires all the relationship skills that are used to establish close friendships: being friendly, developing rapport, being willing to share one's self, building trust, and expressing empathy. In relationships with adult children, good listening skills are especially important, as older adults encourage and help younger adults think through and solve their own problems. The arrival of grandchildren brings new roles and potential responsibilities as well. Maintaining strong and healthy relationships can help the adult successfully make the transition through these many changes of middlescence.

Parental Relationship Roles

Middle-age adults also experience changes in their relationships with their own parents. The parent roles may even switch as the older adult loses some self-care abilities. The middle-age adult may then have to provide care and support for the aging parent. Doing so can demand a great deal of time and energy and cause deep emotional upheaval if the elderly parent is very ill or nearing death. This reminds the middle-age adult just how short life really is. The aging process cannot be avoided; it is inevitable. Reflecting on this fact

intensifies, or strengthens, the middle-age adult's questions about his or her own life.

Changes Affecting Careers and Finances

Changes in an adult's career may also influence questioning during middlescence. Some adults reach the peaks of their career achievement in middle age and are able to add to their savings for retirement. On the other hand, the middle-age adult may feel threatened by a younger employee climbing the career ladder. Self-esteem may drop if middle-age adults begin to see themselves as less capable professionally than others.

Changes in technology impact the workplace continually (**Figure 19.3**). Keeping up with these changes can be a challenge for middle-age adults. Yet it is essential that middle-age adults learn new skills and keep up-to-date with the technology that impacts their careers so they can maintain their positions. Losing a job at this age can be devastating to a family's finances, especially if the family is still supporting older children or helping young adults start out in their lives. It is often difficult for a person over 50 to find a new job that pays as well as the job that was lost. Such experiences can influence the adult to question his or her own self-worth.

Think About Your Reading
What resources increase for the family during middlescence? Which resources decrease?

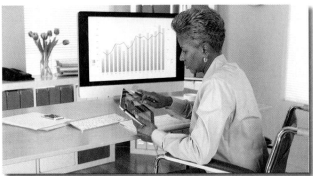
Rocketclips, Inc./Shutterstock.com

Figure 19.3 Technology changes can make an adult feel overwhelmed. *How could technology changes in the workplace affect an older worker's self-esteem?*

Midlife Crisis

Some adults have problems adjusting to the changes of the middle years and experience a midlife crisis. A **midlife crisis** is brought on by the stress from changes in the middle years of life. This stress is increased when the adult views youthfulness as more desirable than aging. To these adults, the signs of aging are proof that they are losing their youth. They may see themselves becoming less attractive or less capable and feel they have little worth.

During a midlife crisis, some middle-age adults try to regain their youthfulness. They may seek friends among youth, wear younger fashions, and listen to music that generally appeals to younger people. Some adults blame their loss of youthfulness on others. They may blame their family and desert them and the responsibilities that go with their middle-age roles. These actions *rend* (split) the family system apart. Some blame their job situation and change jobs or careers.

Most adults in middlescence are able to work through their questioning and avoid having a midlife crisis. Understanding from family members can help the adult cope with the stress and adjust to the changes of middle age. These adults can revise and set new goals. They may develop new interests and start a hobby they have always wanted to try. They may focus on areas of personal growth, learn a new skill, or take classes. They may set aside more time for important relationships. These experiences are enriching. They can help the adult rebuild feelings of esteem and enhance the years ahead.

Think About Your Reading
What could family members do to help a person experiencing a midlife crisis?

Grandparenting

When adults are in their middle years, their children will likely be having children. When they do, the adults take on the new role of *grandparents*.

For most families, this is an exciting transition filled with many joys.

Grandparent Roles

Most middle-age adults look forward to welcoming a new baby into the extended family. As grandparents, they may want to help the new parents with care expenses, such as clothing and furniture. They may help the new parents, who are adjusting to a new schedule during the baby's first weeks of life. Help with household chores, such as cooking, cleaning, and laundry, are often welcomed by the new parents. Most grandparents enjoy babysitting at this time so the new mother can get some extra rest. Even as children grow, grandparents can play important roles in their lives. In all of these roles, they provide benefits to their adult children and to their grandchildren (**Figure 19.4**).

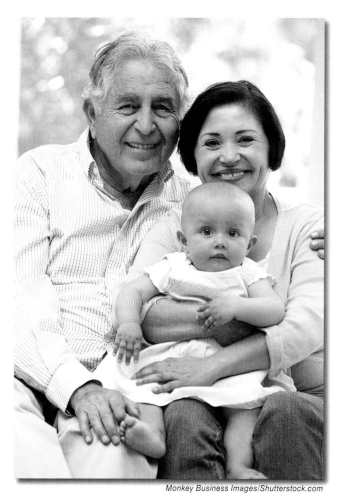

Monkey Business Images/Shutterstock.com

Figure 19.4 *In what ways can grandparents be an integral part of their grandchildren's lives?*

Provide Love and Acceptance

Grandparents can have a nurturing role. As they offer affection, they can help their grandchildren feel loved and wanted. Grandparents may attend special events, such as games, concerts, or plays, in which grandchildren take part. They may celebrate the grandchild's birthday with the family. Those who live far away can call or send letters, cards, or gifts to help make the grandchild feel important. Modern technology that allows video calls makes it easy for even distant grandparents to interact with their grandchildren more fully and observe how they have grown and changed. In all these ways, grandparents help build grandchildren's self-esteem and feelings of self-worth.

Give Focused Attention to Grandchildren

Grandparents who spend time with grandchildren can give them focused attention. They can center their attention on the grandchild, taking time to talk and listen. They may not have all the responsibilities that take most of the parents' time, especially if they are retired. Through such focused attention, grandparents build close bonds with their grandchildren. Many teens find it easier to talk to a grandparent about some topics. Close relationships benefit both grandparents and grandchildren.

Provide Child Care

Grandparents may also take part in the role of caring for grandchildren. They may provide child care while the parents work. At other times, they can give the grandchild's parents some time alone by offering to take care of the child so the parents can go out for an evening. These experiences benefit the parents and help the grandparents build relationships with their grandchildren.

Continue Family Traditions

Grandparents often play a role in keeping family traditions alive. They may take part in special celebrations on holidays or organize family reunions. Grandparents serve as a link to the family's past history, helping grandchildren feel a sense of belonging to the family.

Provide Some Financial Assistance

Sometimes grandparents help with the provider role as well. They may help purchase clothing and other gifts for their grandchildren. If they are financially secure, they may be able to help out with loans or finances for the children's education.

Benefits of Grandparenting

Grandparenting not only benefits the grandchildren and parents; it also benefits the older adult. It is a role most older adults enjoy.

Grandparenting relationships can be rewarding. They provide a source of love and affection for the aging adults, as well as for grandchildren (**Figure 19.5**). When grandparents become involved with their grandchildren's lives, they share many experiences together. Strong bonds can develop. In return, most young children will openly express their feelings of love, giving grandparents moments they treasure.

The role of grandparenting also provides the older adult an opportunity to feel needed and important. Helping with child care is a way in which older adults can give support to their own children. Their time and experience become valuable resources to their children.

Finally, grandparenting provides a feeling of satisfaction. Older adults feel satisfied in helping a grandchild learn and watching him or her grow. Contributing to the development of a new generation helps older adults feel their lives still have meaning.

LESSON 19.1

Assess

COMPREHENSION CHECK

1. Briefly describe what is meant by the term *middlescence*.
2. List four changes that take place in an adult's life during middlescence.
3. How could changes in technology impact the middle-age adult's career?
4. Identify five roles that grandparents fill in the family system.
5. List three benefits that the older adult can gain from grandparenting.

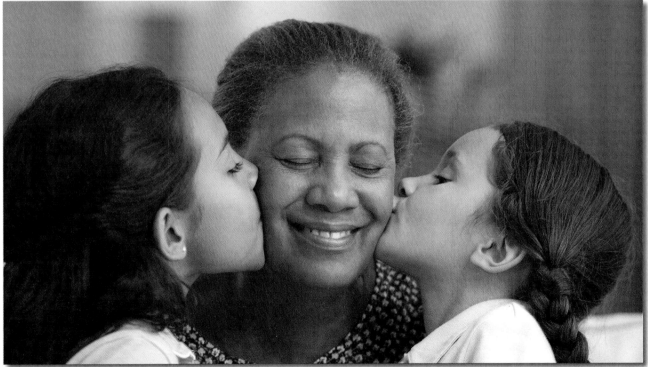

Figure 19.5 Grandchildren can be a source of love and affection for their grandparents. *For families who do not have grandparents nearby, where in a community could young families and older adults connect and build substitute grandparent relationships?*

LESSON 19.2

THE RETIREMENT YEARS

Content Terms Build Vocab

retirement

Social Security

Supplemental Security Income (SSI)

Medicare

pension

Academic Terms

file

eligible

Objectives

After studying this lesson, you will be able to

- **identify** the challenges of retirement.
- **formulate** a plan for addressing financial concerns of the retirement years.

Focus Your Reading

1. Continue the chart you started in Lesson 19.1, filling in the key information about the retirement years.
2. Interview a grandparent and ask questions about retirement income, Social Security, pensions, and Medicare. Summarize how each of these helps meet a retired person's needs.

When a family member retires, more changes occur. **Retirement** is the ending of paid employment. For most adults in U.S. society, retirement occurs around age 65. The trend to retire earlier has increased as companies replace those nearing retirement with younger workers. Some people retire later, depending on their health, job, and finances. Retirement affects people's lives in many different ways. It brings changes in daily schedules, social activities, and income (**Figure 19.6**). If older adults can adjust to these changes easily, retirement can be an enjoyable stage of their lives.

The Challenges of Retirement

"I can't wait to retire!" Many workers make this comment several times in life. When the reality of retirement draws near, however, and they think about the fundamental life changes they will experience, they may not feel the same way.

Changes in Work Roles

Many people are not ready to face retirement. They feel the loss of their job as a loss of part of their identity. For years, they may have found satisfaction in their work. They gained the respect

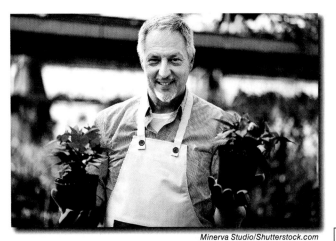
Minerva Studio/Shutterstock.com

Figure 19.6 People of retirement age look forward to having more control over how they spend their time. *Why do you think many older adults return to the world of work in some capacity?*

of others for their experience and expertise. When they retire, they may find themselves getting up in the morning with no place to go and no schedule to keep. They may feel worthless and suffer from a loss of self-esteem. Some miss the daily contact with other people they had when they were working.

All retirees do not feel this way, of course. Many find that the many roles they fill in the home can replace the activity and satisfaction they felt at work. Many retirees see retirement as a chance to spend more time on personal interests as well as on the role of grandparenting.

Adjusting to changes in work roles is easier if a retired person has other interests or hobbies to pursue. Some retirees develop a long-time hobby into a business. Others go to school to learn a new skill so they can pursue some new type of work. Others remain active by volunteering in community and religious organizations. These newfound interests can provide an older adult with great satisfaction. In some cases, these interests and activities may provide some income, as well as social contact with other people. Any of these activities helps people adjust to retirement.

Think About Your Reading

What are some hobbies that you will enjoy throughout your life?

Financial Changes

Adjusting to the loss of income is easier if people have planned ahead for their retirement years. Savings, investments, pension funds, and Social Security can all provide income during these years. When people have enough money to pay living expenses and pursue leisure activities, their retirement years are more enjoyable. The next section of this lesson discusses the financial aspects of retirement in more detail.

Think About Your Reading

At what age should a person start saving for retirement and invest in a pension plan?

Changes in Social Life

Keeping socially active and continuing relationships with others is important as people age (**Figure 19.7**). Relationships with children and

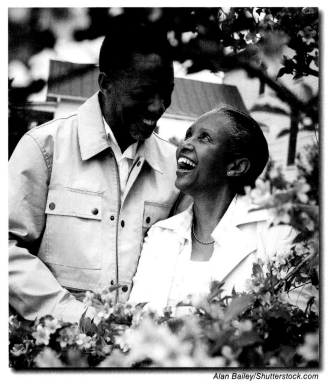
Alan Bailey/Shutterstock.com

Figure 19.7 Without the demands of work, a retired couple will have the time to renew the closeness in their relationship. *How would maintaining common interests over the years help make the retirement years more rewarding?*

grandchildren can provide closeness and bring much satisfaction. Relationships with other retirees can provide companionship. Involvement in organizations can help the retiree keep active in a community and develop friendships with people from many different age groups.

Activity in Retirement

The belief that older people are limited in what they can do stops many from exploring new interests and activities (**Figure 19.8**). New technologies can provide easy access to people and information so older adults can keep in touch with family, old friends, or new learning opportunities. Older adults may need to be encouraged to step out and try new things.

Diet and physical activity are important factors in staying active. Older adults need to continue eating a nutritious diet. Those who are physically active are more likely to stay healthy and retain ease of movement.

One factor other than poor health that might keep older adults from being active during retirement is attitude. Some retirees have a negative attitude. If they believe they are weak, have a poor memory, and cannot learn something new, they will likely act that way. Those who have a positive attitude about themselves, their abilities, and their worth can do almost anything they choose.

Think About Your Reading

What could you do to encourage a grandparent or other older adult to be active?

Planning for Financial Needs

A worker's paycheck stops at retirement, but living costs continue. Unfortunately, few adults actually save and invest enough money during their working years to prepare for retirement. As a result, their standard of living may change, perhaps dramatically, when they retire.

Wise money management, including savings and investments, is one key to having financial security in the later years (**Figure 19.9**). In addition, some financial assistance is available through federal and community programs. Learning about these programs before retirement can help older adults meet some of their financial needs.

Federal Programs

Social Security is a federal program that is run by the Social Security Administration and gives retired people and people with disabilities some income. Retired workers who paid Social Security taxes for a certain period are eligible for benefits, and these benefits are paid monthly. A

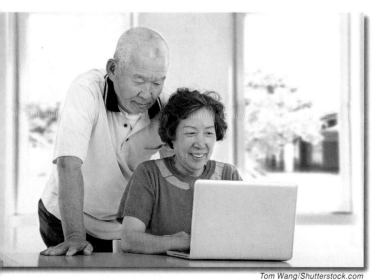

Tom Wang/Shutterstock.com

Figure 19.8 Continuing to learn new skills can help the elderly remain mentally alert. *How could technology be used to stimulate the older adult?*

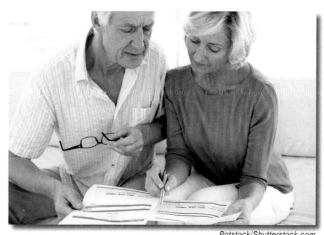

Potstock/Shutterstock.com

Figure 19.9 Financial planning can help couples have the money they need for activities during retirement. *When should a person begin financial planning for retirement?*

spouse, widow, or widower of an eligible worker can also receive Social Security benefits. Retired workers can *file*, or apply, for these benefits as early as age 62. The amount they receive each month, however, will be less than if they wait until full retirement age to begin collecting benefits.

People should apply for Social Security benefits about three months before they plan to retire. They can apply online at the Social Security website or can apply in person at a local Social Security office. Information regarding Social Security is also available at the Social Security website.

Supplemental Security Income (SSI) is another federal program administered through the Social Security Administration. Many people are not aware that this income source is available. The purpose of this program is to help people with low incomes who are 65 years of age or older, who are blind, or who have disabilities. SSI provides these people with extra income. It is not necessary to have worked and paid into Social Security to receive these funds, but people must meet an income test. To find out if they are *eligible*, or if they qualify, for benefits, people should contact their local Social Security office.

Medical expenses can take much of an older person's income and savings. Planning for health insurance can help with these expenses. Three months before they reach age 65, older persons receive information about **Medicare**. Medicare is a federal program that helps older people with health care expenses. Medicare includes coverage for inpatient care at a hospital as well as a portion of the expenses for doctor's visits and medications. Medicare does not cover all health care expenses, however, and those who receive it must have additional insurance.

Pensions and Retirement Accounts

Some retirees receive monthly pension checks from their former employers. **Pensions** are funds paid by employers to former employees who contributed to a special retirement fund while they were employed. Persons who do not have a company pension should build their own retirement account by saving and investing throughout their working years. The government offers income tax advantages to those who invest in retirement accounts to encourage workers to do so. The sooner individuals begin this kind of program, the better off they will be when they retire.

Community Programs

Through a local social service agency, older adults may also be able to receive help with some of their expenses. Aid such as food stamp programs or fuel assistance may be available if older adults qualify. Many public services, such as public transportation systems, help retirees by offering lower prices for their services (**Figure 19.10**). Retirees can also get discounts, or special prices, on meals in some restaurants; on tickets to events like movies or plays; and on admission to some special sites, such as museums.

LESSON 19.2
Assess

COMPREHENSION CHECK

1. Identify the changes retirement brings to a person's life.
2. Describe the benefits provided to a retired person by Social Security and Medicare.
3. List the strategies that could be included in a plan to meet financial needs after retirement.

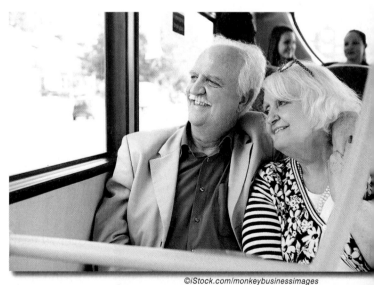
©iStock.com/monkeybusinessimages

Figure 19.10 Discounted public transportation aids elderly people's financial situations in some parts of the U.S.

LESSON 19.3

THE ELDERLY YEARS

Content Terms

Build Vocab

agency on aging
fraud
elder abuse
material abuse
durable power of attorney
adult day care
community-based day care
home health care
assisted living
hospice care

Academic Terms

detection
self-neglect

Objectives

After studying this lesson, you will be able to

- **determine** the challenges faced by the elderly.
- **predict** the impact of technological advances on the needs of the elderly.
- **locate** federal and community resources to assist the elderly.
- **explain** the concept of hospice.

Focus Your Reading

1. Summarize the changes of the elderly years, the effects on the family, and strategies the family can take to adjust to these changes.
2. Research one of the four sources of care (adult day, community-based, home health, and hospice) for elderly adults. Prepare a report with visuals to describe the care provided.

Just how long will each person live? No one knows that answer. If your past relatives lived long lives, your grandparents have a greater chance of living to an old age as well. Generally, each generation averages a slightly longer life span than the previous one (**Figure 19.11**). This means that you have a greater chance of facing the many challenges of old age.

Changes in Physical Health

Adults between the ages of 60 and 75 are healthier today than the same age group was in the past. The average life span of the population overall, including those with poor and good health, is over 79 years. Many outlive this estimate, even reaching 100 years.

As the result of aging, many physical changes take place during the elderly years. Increased illness, loss of strength, loss of vision and hearing, and loss of mental abilities are common. For most people, the physical changes linked to aging do not increase until after age 75.

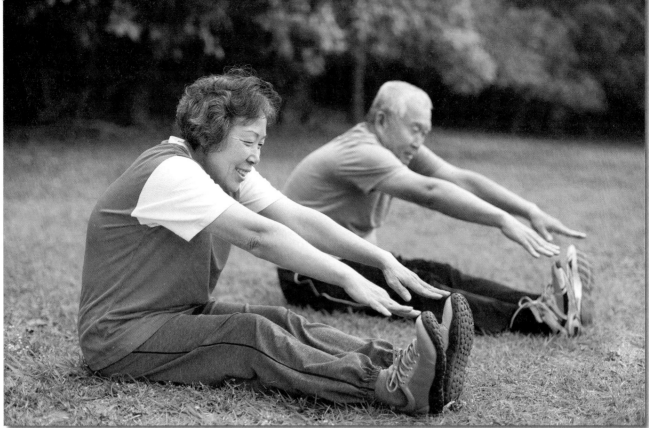

Figure 19.11 Due to medical advancements, people are living longer, healthier lives than ever before. *What other factors could be contributing to longer life spans?*

Think About Your Reading

What are some examples of increased needs in the family when grandparents lose their physical health?

Dealing with the Effects of Aging

What can older people do to counter the physical and mental decline caused by aging? Regular physical checkups can help detect some problems. With early *detection*, or identification, of health issues, health care professionals have a greater chance of curing some illnesses or at least treating them so that they do not worsen.

Eating a proper diet is important for the elderly. They need to eat nutritious meals with foods from all the food groups. Doing so provides proper nutrients so their bodies can continue the repairing and rebuilding processes.

Regular exercise is also important for staying healthy, but many elderly people avoid activity. Because of physical limitations, some may feel they cannot or should not exercise. Others, who live alone, may have no motivation to exercise. Lack of physical activity, however, speeds the aging process. Muscles and bones weaken quickly in the elderly if they are not used. Simply walking for a period of time a few days a week can help elderly people maintain health.

Plenty of rest can also help slow some of the effects of aging. A healthful lifestyle not only helps deter physical problems, but also enables many elderly people to stay mentally sharp and to keep active in society. Regular health care and a healthful lifestyle can help the elderly keep active and remain independent longer.

Using Technology to Assist with the Effects of Aging

Many elderly people use various technologies to assist with the effects of aging. Hearing and vision loss can often be managed with such solutions as hearing aids, telephone amplifiers, glasses, large-print books, and various surgical techniques (**Figure 19.12**). Technologies have been

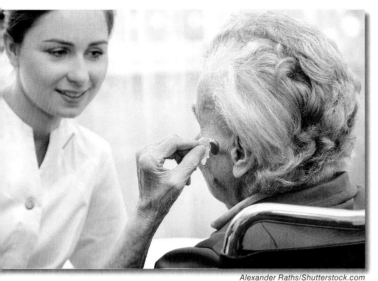

Alexander Raths/Shutterstock.com

Figure 19.12 Technologies such as hearing aids can help supplement the physical losses that come with aging.

developed to deal with various physical issues that limit mobility, too. Whether they are motorized wheelchairs, artificial limbs, or other devices, these technologies help individuals keep some measure of independence.

Other technologies are available to assist the elderly in their homes. Some are as simple as stools placed in the shower so that an older person can sit down while showering. Elderly people who have difficulty breathing may use machines that provide them with oxygen. Some elderly people have medical alert services, which allow them to contact a central office if they have a sudden injury, accident, or attack of an illness. These services enable many elderly people to live independently with the assurance that help is quickly reached if needed. It is likely that technological aids will continue to change and develop in the future to meet the needs of elderly people trying to live independently.

Medical technologies can help meet many of the physical health needs of the elderly and sustain life. The decision to use some of these technologies could result in ethical struggles for some family members. The desire to sustain life may be balanced with the quality of life expected after the medical technology is used. It is important for family members to talk about possible issues so they know the elderly person's desires and wishes for this stage of life.

Using Community Resources

Various **agencies on aging** bring many services to the elderly to help them handle the various issues of their daily lives. The agencies plan, fund, and coordinate senior citizen services. Some of these services include transportation, home-care workers, counseling, recreation, and information. The agencies also support community centers that provide activities and meals for the elderly. Elderly people can receive meals in community-center dining rooms and also in their own homes through the *Meals on Wheels* program. Information about these agencies can often be found online or in community telephone directories under the heading *senior citizens' services*.

Think About Your Reading

Why do you think more elderly people do not use community services such as Meals on Wheels?

Changes in Social Life

As physical health declines, so does the elderly person's social life. This is especially the case for elderly people whose spouses have died. Having children who are busy with work or live far away adds to the problem. Elderly people may not get out as often to visit friends and family. Those in poor health may be confined to their homes or bedridden, isolating them from much social contact.

Elderly family members still need the warmth and companionship of family relationships. Family visits and extra attention are important during these years. Parents and children can help elderly members by visiting regularly and helping with such tasks as running errands, doing housework, or providing transportation.

Most elderly people like to continue living in their own homes as long as possible (**Figure 19.13**). This keeps them in a familiar environment and near neighbors, friends, and family. Familiar surroundings and family support meet their needs for security.

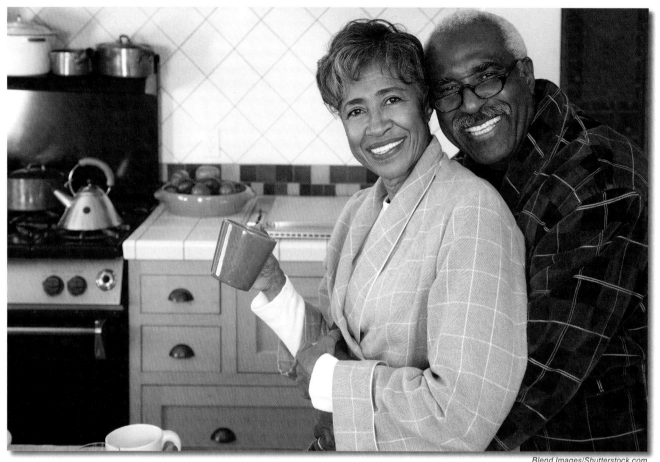
Blend Images/Shutterstock.com

Figure 19.13 Most elderly adults want to continue living independently in their own homes. *What are some technologies that could help families assist elderly people in reaching this goal?*

Think About Your Reading

What might family members need to do to help grandparents continue to live on their own?

Protecting the Rights of the Elderly

When the elderly feel lonely and isolated, they may open the doors of their home to anyone who knocks. They are so glad to have someone to talk to that they are prime targets for dishonest people looking to take advantage of them. Worried about their health or concerned about finances, many elderly people are curious about products and services that promise to improve their lives. For these reasons, elderly people are often the victims of **fraud**, the crime of using deceptive practices to cheat people out of their money. Even cautious people have been tricked by someone they thought they could trust.

Consumer Fraud

Door-to-door salespersons may exploit the elderly with promises of bargains, good deals, and cure-all remedies. The elderly may pay in advance for the promised goods, miracle drugs, repairs, or financial services. Finances are usually limited for the elderly. Salespersons who promise great money-saving bargains or money-making schemes often sound convincing. Using technology to commit theft or fraud can also be a hazard for the aging adult, who may be uncertain about how to navigate various computer applications, may click on fraudulent emails, and may find themselves a victim of computer hacking.

What can you do to help an elderly person avoid becoming a victim? Encourage the elderly

person to talk with a family member before making a commitment or signing a contract. Have a knowledgeable family member make sure the elderly person's computer virus-protection software is current. Educate older adults about the dangers of computer hackers and safety concerns when using the Internet. Also, identifying community experts that older adults can contact with questions about finances, health, and consumer services would help build the older adult's personal resources.

Cases of fraud or suspected fraud should be reported to the police. Often the elderly are embarrassed when they learn they have been victims of fraud. They do not want to appear foolish or incompetent. Fear of losing their independence keeps them quiet. Reporting the fraud, however, may protect others from being victimized.

Think About Your Reading

What are some ways you could help an older relative avoid consumer fraud?

Elder Abuse

Some people take advantage of the elderly who cannot see, hear, move well, or think clearly. Perhaps the elderly person is part of a family relationship that was not healthy in earlier years. Maybe the extra care he or she needs is more than the financial resources a family has available. Such situations increase the risk that elder abuse might take place. **Elder abuse** refers to intentionally or knowingly causing an elderly person to suffer physical harm or injury, unreasonable confinement, sexual abuse, or a lack of services or medical treatment needed to maintain health.

One form of elder abuse is material abuse. **Material abuse** means the misuse of an elderly person's property or financial resources. It may involve misusing the elderly person's money, taking valuables, or obtaining property. Material abuse also includes denying the elderly person's right to personal funds and interfering in financial decisions.

Elder abuse may also take the form of *neglect*, in which the elderly person's physical or mental health is in danger. It refers to cases in which the caregiver fails to provide adequate food, shelter, clothing, medical care, or dental care. Elderly persons living alone may cause *self-neglect* by taking actions that jeopardize their health.

Such offenses should be reported to a local agency on aging. The agency can also be contacted for free or low-cost legal service or other consumer problems.

Loss of Independence

As people age, they become more dependent on others. Many of those over 85 years old live in special care facilities that are equipped to handle the challenges of old age (**Figure 19.14**). For the safety and well-being of an elderly person, families must eventually make decisions about how to provide the best care.

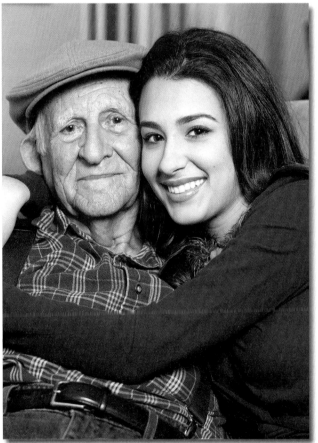

Fotoluminate LLC/Shutterstock.com

Figure 19.14 Close relationships with family members can be a protective factor for the elderly. *Why is this ongoing relationship important even when the elderly person is in a care facility?*

Elderly persons can help make these decisions by assigning a power of attorney for both medical and financial needs. A **durable power of attorney** is a legal document that allows a person to choose someone to act in his or her place in the event of becoming mentally incapable of handling his or her own affairs. By creating this document, the elderly person makes clear his or her wishes to this person to ensure that the person carries them out. Legal experts recommend that elderly people prepare two documents, one for financial decisions and one for medical decisions. Having these in place can help protect the desires, wishes, and finances of the elderly person in the later years. A lawyer can help an elderly person create these documents to include the desired instructions and have the correct language.

An Extended Family

Sometimes families choose to bring a grandparent into their own home. Doing so allows them to help on a daily basis with the physical, social, and financial issues that the elderly person faces. This can have a major effect on the family and should only be done after much thought and discussion. The elderly parent, other children, and all the family members should be included in the discussion.

Think About Your Reading

What are some factors that families should consider before moving an older relative into their home?

Community Resources for Providing Care

Many community programs are designed to give elderly people needed care and services while elderly people remain in their own homes and live as independently as possible. These programs can also help families that have taken an elderly relative into their homes to live with them. To locate a community-based service, you can visit the U.S. Department of Health and Human Services website or call your local agency on aging or

a social service agency. Three types of programs are commonly available:

- *Adult day care.* **Adult day care** is a program that provides care and companionship for elderly people who need help and supervision during the day. It may include transportation from elderly people's homes to centers that provide daytime group activities. These services are for elderly people who are impaired by physical or mental conditions. The centers provide activities, lunches, health screenings, and counseling.

- *Community-based day care.* **Community-based day care** is a program of activities for older people who are still somewhat independent. It may be sponsored by the local agency on aging and be run at a senior center. Social workers, nurses, and aides may be involved in providing a full program of activities.

- *Home health care.* **Home health care** is an arrangement in which nurses or aides go to the elderly person's home to provide assistance with health care (**Figure 19.15**). Services can involve helping the elderly take medicine, monitoring blood pressure, and changing dressings on a healing wound. Help with housekeeping chores, laundry, and personal needs is sometimes available through home-care services as well.

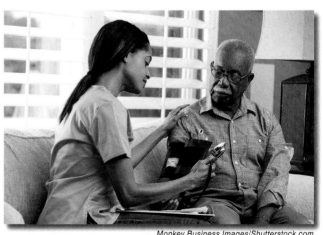
Monkey Business Images/Shutterstock.com

Figure 19.15 Home health care nurses or aides provide assistance to elderly adults in their homes. *What activities would you expect a home health care aide to carry out?*

Carmen's Grandparents

Carmen felt concerned as he left his grandparents' home Sunday afternoon. He knew that Grandpa's leg was really bothering him. Convincing his grandfather to go to the doctor had not been an easy task. Grandpa was afraid the doctor would put him in a hospital, and he was worried about leaving Grandma home alone. Who would take care of her? What if she forgot something important like turning off the oven?

Carmen's dad feared that the time had come when his parents no longer could live alone. How could the family handle this? Carmen's own home was already too small for his family of six. There just was no room for two more people. Also, who would care for Grandma and Grandpa during the day while everyone else was at work or school?

Carmen's dad thought about his brother in California. They had a large house, but that was thousands of miles away. His parents would be far from the friends and community they had known all their lives. He was sure that his parents did not have enough money to live in an assisted-living facility very long. What else could they do? Carmen's dad also thought about his plan to give Carmen some financial help as he started college next semester. He knew the family could not afford both assisted living for his parents and college for Carmen.

For Discussion

1. What factors did Carmen's dad consider as he thought about his parents' inability to take care of themselves?
2. What alternatives would there be in your community for a family in this situation?
3. How do you think each alternative might affect Carmen, his parents and siblings, and his grandparents? Consider both the positive and negative aspects of each alternative.
4. What alternative do you think would be best for this family? Explain your answer.

Sometimes the physical or mental effects of aging are so extensive that an elderly person requires constant care and attention. **Assisted living** can provide the around-the-clock care these people need. These elderly people live in special facilities, with nurses, doctors, dietary specialists, rehabilitation staff, and recreation workers providing the many services elderly people need around the clock. Every state requires assisted-living facilities to be licensed. Even so, the choice of assisted living should be researched and made with care.

Death and Dying

You may have already experienced the death of someone you love. Death can come suddenly and unexpectedly. On the other hand, death may be expected as a result of a long illness. When someone dies, the people affected by the loss must adjust. When someone becomes ill with an incurable condition, these adjustments may be spread over a longer period of time, prolonging the grieving process. Both the dying person and the loved ones must eventually accept the fact that the person's life will end.

Hospice

Hospice care is designed to help a dying person live the final days of life in comfort. It includes physical, emotional, and spiritual care that can help the person face death with dignity. Hospice programs also offer support to families as they face the death of a loved one. Sometimes hospice care is given to the elderly person in his or her home. In some situations, the person is so ill that he or she has to be moved to a hospice facility.

When a person feels that life has been full, death is easier to face. A hospice program helps a dying person focus on fulfilling experiences. These may be memories of special events or hobbies that can still be enjoyed in some way.

Hospice programs also focus on showing love and affection. Taking time to talk, listen, and touch the person can help meet social and emotional needs. Even simple physical contact, such as holding a hand, can give the person enormous

comfort. Hospice programs also provide comfort as professionals give pain medications when a dying person suffers extreme pain.

A doctor supervises the hospice care program. A team of nurses, volunteers, a home health aide, a social worker, and a spiritual leader may assist with care. The support and involvement of both the patient and the family are needed. The dying patient remains an important member of the family. Family members receive counseling to help them tend to the dying person's needs and accept the approaching death.

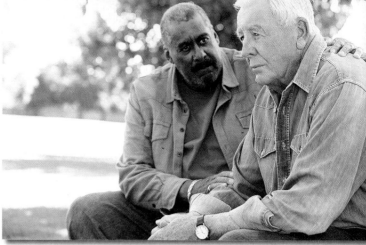
Monkey Business Images/Shutterstock.com

Figure 19.16 People experiencing the first stage of grief may have feelings of numbness or disbelief, even if the death was expected. *How could empathy and active listening skills help families work through these feelings of grief?*

Think About Your Reading

How are family members an important part of hospice care?

Coping with Death

When death occurs at a very old age or after a long illness, family members find it easier to accept. They can view the person's life as full and complete. Even then, they experience a grieving process.

The first stage of grieving brings feelings of emptiness and numbness even if death has been expected (**Figure 19.16**). Feelings of sorrow and loss may cause family members to weep without control for a long period of time after the loved one's death. Because this stage has such a numbing effect on family members, it is helpful if funeral and burial plans are arranged before the person dies.

In the weeks following the death of a loved one, family members pass through another stage. They may feel anxious, fearful, and abandoned by the loved one. They may feel angry that the loved one left them alone. Sometimes a grieving person wants to talk and share memories of the lost loved one. At other times, he or she wants to sit alone. Family members can help one another through this stage by listening and offering quiet support and understanding when someone needs to talk.

Brief periods of depression are normal after a loss. Talking with other people who have gone through similar experiences can help. Grief support groups may be located by contacting a local mental health agency or religious organization.

People who have mourned the loss of a loved one will gradually accept the loss and adjust to living without that person. They may continue to feel the loss and sadness sharply at certain times. Birthdays, anniversaries, holidays, or other events that were part of fond memories will bring back the pain of the loss.

Friends and family members are important to one another throughout the life cycle. In difficult times, they can provide support and encouragement. They can help one another focus on positive thoughts and memories. They can offer one another love and affection. They can help one another find satisfaction and fulfillment in living.

LESSON 19.3

Assess

COMPREHENSION CHECK

1. List four examples of physical and mental decline that can cause problems for the elderly, and identify technologies that could provide some help in meeting these needs.
2. Give three reasons why the elderly are susceptible to fraudulent sales practices.
3. Describe four community programs that provide care services to the elderly.
4. Describe two techniques used in hospice programs to help people cope with dying.
5. Identify the feelings that are common during the grieving process.

CHAPTER SUMMARY

Aging is inevitable; so are the effects that go with the aging process. In midlife, when these effects begin to appear, adults often find themselves questioning their achievements, purposes, and goals for living. Such evaluations can help adults set new goals for the years ahead.

The family continues to change as adults grow older. These changes, plus those at work, can increase the stress that middle-age adults feel. Sometimes these changes lead to a midlife crisis that is difficult to experience. Two major events may take place during this part of the life cycle: grandparenting and retirement. Many parents with married children become grandparents. At the same time, they may also provide care for aging parents who struggle with failing health and loss of independence. Grandparents can fill many roles that help their children and grandchildren. They benefit from these family relationships in several ways as well.

Retirement brings changes in practically every aspect of life. The extended family continues to be an important resource for adjusting to these changes in the life cycle. Close relationships with children and grandchildren can help adults adjust to the changes that go with aging and retirement. Close relationships in the family can also help members adjust to the grief and loss experienced over a death.

VOCABULARY ACTIVITIES

1. Divide the following terms with a partner. Each of you will write sentences that use your terms correctly, but leave a blank where each term goes. Exchange papers with your partner and fill in the correct term in each sentence.

Content Terms

adult day care (19.3)
agency on aging (19.3)
assisted living (19.3)
community-based day care (19.3)
durable power of attorney (19.3)
elder abuse (19.3)
fraud (19.3)
home health care (19.3)

hospice care (19.3)
material abuse (19.3)
Medicare (19.2)
middlesence (19.1)
midlife crisis (19.1)
pension (19.2)
retirement (19.2)
Social Security (19.2)
Supplemental Security Income (SSI) (19.2)

2. Work with a partner to write sentences that use each of the following terms correctly.

Academic Terms

detection (19.3)
eligible (19.2)
file (19.2)

intensify (19.1)
rend (19.1)
self-neglect (19.3)

ASSESS

Your Knowledge

3. How do the changes of middlescence affect the family system?

4. What are four benefits of having grandparents involved in the family system?

5. How is the family system affected by the changes of the elderly years?

Your Understanding

6. How can the family help members cope with the changes of middlescence and keep the family system balanced?

7. Give three examples of ways technology can be used to meet some of the needs of the aging adult.

8. Explain how the effect of technology on the elderly generation's health and finances can be managed by families.

Your Skills

9. Identify a plan a family could use to manage its resources to meet the various needs of the aging adult.

10. What resources would you use to help make sure an elderly grandparent gets nutritious meals? to help with health care costs?

CRITICAL THINKING

11. **Make Inferences.** Make a list of activities that you could do with a grandparent or another person of retirement age. For each activity, explain how it could provide mental, social, or physical stimulation for the older adult. Write a summarizing paragraph that explains how participating in these activities could help the aging adult avoid fraud. *Choice*: Explain how you or other teens could benefit from each activity. *Group option*: Form small groups and present your activities in a song, poem, rap, or visual presentation.

12. **Draw Conclusions**. Interview a grandparent or another older adult. Ask questions about how the person's family members help him or her (or could help him or her) with different aspects of aging. Summarize the responses and write a paragraph on how aging affects the family system. *Choice*: Present your information in a video or using presentation software.

13. **Make a Judgment**. Interview a middle-age person. Ask questions related to the person's goals for the next 20 years and retirement plans. Discuss the person's goals and plans in a written report. Judge whether you feel this person will be prepared for retirement. Identify any areas in which you think the person might struggle and explain why.

14. **Make Projections.** Write a paper describing your community 30 years from now, considering the future increases in the older population. Describe how this increase will impact the local economy, health care services, home-care services, housing needs, and the job market. *Group option*: Work in small groups, with each group member researching one of the topics. Present your information to the class.

CORE SKILLS

15. **Writing.** Visit a local assisted-living facility. Write a brief paper describing your visit. Include a description of the physical conditions of the residents, the activities available to them, and the care they received. Summarize your overall impression of life in an assisted-living facility.

16. **Social Studies, Writing.** Choose an older adult and carry out an activity with him or her. (You may choose an activity you listed in your response to question 11.) Summarize in a paragraph your thoughts and feelings about the experience. *Choice*: Share your reflection in a speech to the class.

17. **Research, Writing.** Contact a local agency on aging and identify services available in your community to help older adults. Develop a poster describing these services and give it to your local agency on aging for the public to see. *Choice*: Research online to identify the services that are available in your community.

18. **Writing, Publishing.** Interview a retired person in your community and ask questions about what he or she does to keep active. Find out what resources your community offers for retired people that this person takes advantage of. Summarize your interview in a written report. Evaluate the person's behavior and hobbies for effectiveness in keeping mentally and physically active. *Group option*: Work with a small group to tally all the resources identified in your community that might attract retired people. Prepare a handout summarizing these resources. *Choice*: Present your summary to your local chamber of commerce to post on their website.

19. **Research, Writing.** Identify a new technology that is designed to help older adults keep active or manage an issue of physical or mental health. Prepare a report that describes how this technology works and analyze the product for its potential to be effective. *Choice*: Obtain access to the technology and try it out with an older adult.

20. **Research, Writing.** Using the Internet, gather information on a hospice program. Prepare a report describing the services offered, their costs, and the qualifications of the people providing the services.

CAREER READINESS

21. **Calculating Retirement Payments for Various Careers.** Inquire at your local Social Security office for statistics on the average monthly payment for people retiring from various careers. Using a software program, prepare a chart with the statistics for the 10 careers that interest you most. *Choice*: In a written paragraph, evaluate what kind of lifestyle these monthly payments will support based on the cost of living in your community.

22. **Researching Careers in Elderly Services.** Using the Internet, research careers that will grow due to expanded services to the older population. Choose five different careers. For each, explain the nature of the work, potential employment sites, working conditions, average earnings, training and education needed, and the potential job outlook for your community. Present your information in a chart. *Group option*: Complete the activity as a group with each team member researching one service.

CONNECTING WITH CAREER CLUSTERS

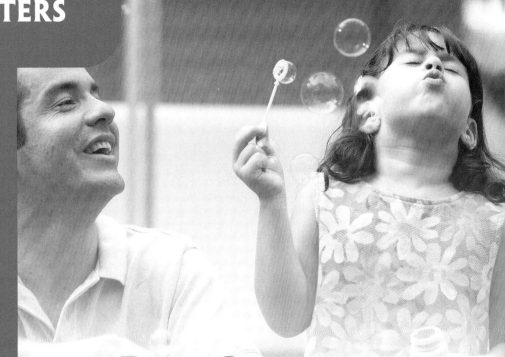

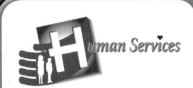

PATHWAYS

Early Childhood Development & Services

Counseling and Mental Health Services

Family and Community Services

Personal Care Services

Consumer Services

EARLY CHILDHOOD DEVELOPMENT & SERVICES

Professionals in early childhood development & services often work with children and their parents. One type of professional in early childhood development & services is the *child care provider*. Child care providers nurture children in small- or large-group settings. They provide custodial care (food, shelter, and a healthful and safe environment) and play an important role in a child's physical, emotional, intellectual, and social development. They help children develop their interests, independence, and self-esteem.

These professionals need to know the various stages of human development and methods for promoting growth through age-appropriate activities. Most children in child care are under six years of age, but ages range from infancy to the teenage years. Preschoolers generally spend full days in child care, while school-age children participate in before- and after-school programs.

Work hours are generally long and are usually set for the convenient drop-off and pickup times of working parents. The turnover rate for child care providers is high, as workers change jobs for better pay and work hours. With additional education and training, child care providers may become teacher assistants, teachers, or program directors—jobs with higher pay, better benefits, and shorter workdays.

Licensing requirements for child care providers vary by state. Most states require some formal training and work experience.

CAREER OUTLOOK

Child care providers must be interested in children; have immense energy; provide fair but firm treatment; communicate effectively with children, parents, and administrators; anticipate and prevent problems; and be patient and alert.

Employment for child care providers is expected to grow at an average rate. In 2014, the median annual earnings of child care providers were $19,730. Depending on the number of hours worked and the size and location of the facility, salaries range nationally from $16,600 to $30,100.

EXPLORE

Internet Research

Identify the website of a licensing agency in your area and review your state's procedures for making sure that caregivers meet those requirements. Identify the different options for providing licensed child care in your state. Research the training and education required for staff working in each different option, including the requirements for operating a licensed child care facility from your home. Then research and identify local community or technical colleges that provide the training and education needed to meet those state requirements. Also research the projected outlooks for child care jobs in your community and the potential wages that these jobs provide. Prepare a report describing your findings.

Job Shadowing

Spend one day in each licensed facility: a preschool and a child care center. Compare the facilities in a report, explaining their differences and giving specific examples. Include differences in staffing, licenses required by staff, hours of operation, programming, equipment, and costs of services. Identify when you would suggest either care setting for a working parent.

Community Service/Volunteer

Assist a local child care center after school for five different days and keep a journal describing the activities that take place. Inquire about preparing an activity in which you could take the lead, prepare the activity and all materials you will need, inform other staff about the activity and the role they will play in implementing the activity, and then carry out the activity with a group of children. Summarize your experience leading this group, describing how the activity promoted the growth and development of the participating children, how effective the activity was at reaching your goals, and how you could improve the activity.

Project

Organize a field trip for children in a child care program with the consent of the center's director. Plan transportation, food accommodations, and age-appropriate activities. Identify ways (intellectual, social, emotional, and physical) in which the field trip will stimulate the children. Take steps to obtain all required permission slips. Participate in the trip and write a summary, evaluating whether the planned activities met your learning objectives.

Interview

Interview working parents who use child care for preschoolers. Find out the extent of their child care needs, the ease with which they can obtain quality care, their concerns about available care and its costs, and what they expect from the care provider for their money. Summarize their responses in a report.

Part-Time Job

Start your own small business and offer babysitting services with an educational component. Prepare activities—physical, social, emotional, and intellectual—that match each child's level of development and promote growth. Develop lesson plans for these activities, including a description of how each activity will help a child grow and develop.

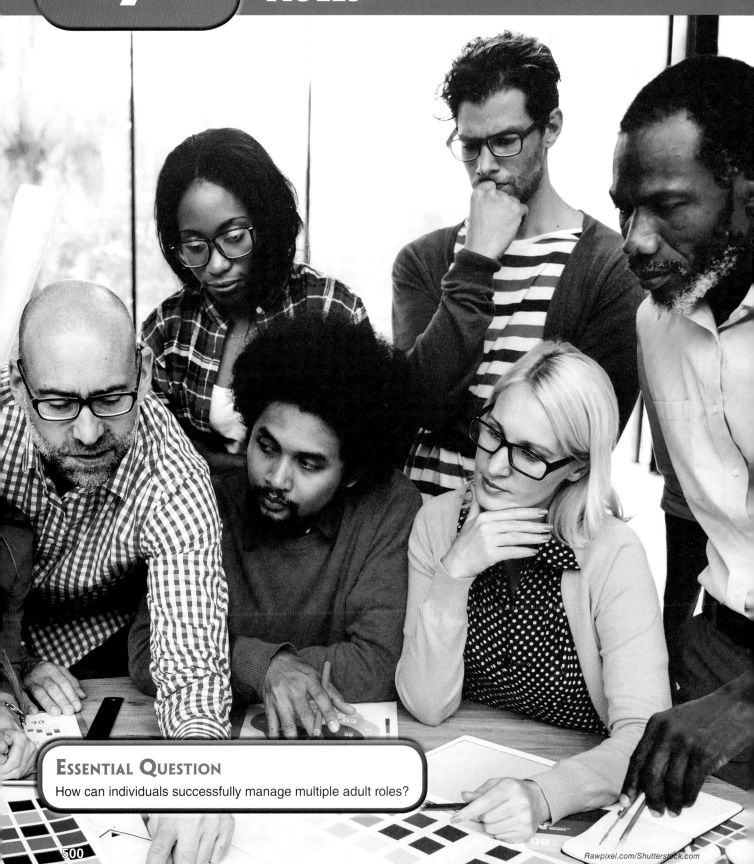

ESSENTIAL QUESTION

How can individuals successfully manage multiple adult roles?

CASE STUDY

How Do Families Manage Money?

Read the case study and discuss the questions that follow. After finishing the chapters in this unit, discuss the questions again and identify any answers you would change based on information you learned.

Not again, Echo thought. *How can there not be enough money to pay the rent* again? Val and Echo had both gone to college and found high-paying jobs. They were making a lot of money, but they also liked to spend money. They had moved to a high-rise apartment in Dubai and enjoyed the year-round water-skiing, night life, and amazing entertainment. They had purchased new furnishings for their apartment, a really nice BMW for Val, and a convertible for Echo—all on credit, of course. But with their salaries, it was easy to buy on credit. Echo wondered how they could possibly have maxed out their credit cards so they were left with nothing in the bank account to pay the rent. "We really need help," she said to Val. "We have to find a financial advisor to help us straighten out this mess."

Lorenzo counted out a week's salary and went to the bank to deposit some into his savings account and some into his other account, which he used for expenses. He was saving 25 percent of each paycheck so he would have enough for a down payment on a house in five years. That meant living in a small apartment for now, riding a bike to work when the weather cooperated, and taking the bus on rainy days. He used a credit card for all his expenses, but kept track of his account daily, checking it using his phone. He wanted to make sure he was not spending more on miscellaneous expenses than what he had budgeted. Every month he paid off the credit card in full when the bill came so he would not have to pay any finance charges. He and Abi were planning to marry within the year, and Abi was also putting money into savings for

furnishings for the house. They were fortunate her parents were paying for the wedding. That was a huge expense that would definitely have impacted their plan to purchase a home in the future.

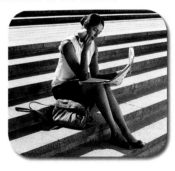

Eesha loved her new job at the University of Bangalore, where she and Rajah had studied agricultural sciences and technology. She enjoyed giving back to her community by applying new technologies to the needs of local farmers. Rajah supported her in her work, but now she was pregnant, and Rajah wanted Eesha to quit her job and stay home with the baby after it was born. She knew this would mean less income for their family and that she would likely not be able to return to her job. She wondered if her parents would be able to move in with them to watch the baby. Maybe Rajah would then agree that she could continue her work at the university. There certainly were not any other child care options near where they lived.

For Discussion

1. In what ways did day-to-day decisions impact each family's success in managing their adult roles?
2. Why are management skills critical to providing quality of life for all family members?

Volt Collection/Shutterstock.com

CHAPTER 20

SUCCEEDING IN THE CAREER WORLD

Reading Prep

Before reading the chapter, copy the headings down on a piece of paper in outline form. As you read, list the main ideas of each section under the appropriate heading.

Key Questions

Questions to answer as you study this chapter:

- What is required to carry out a career plan?
- What does it take to be successful in a job search?
- How can a career be managed to reach personal goals?

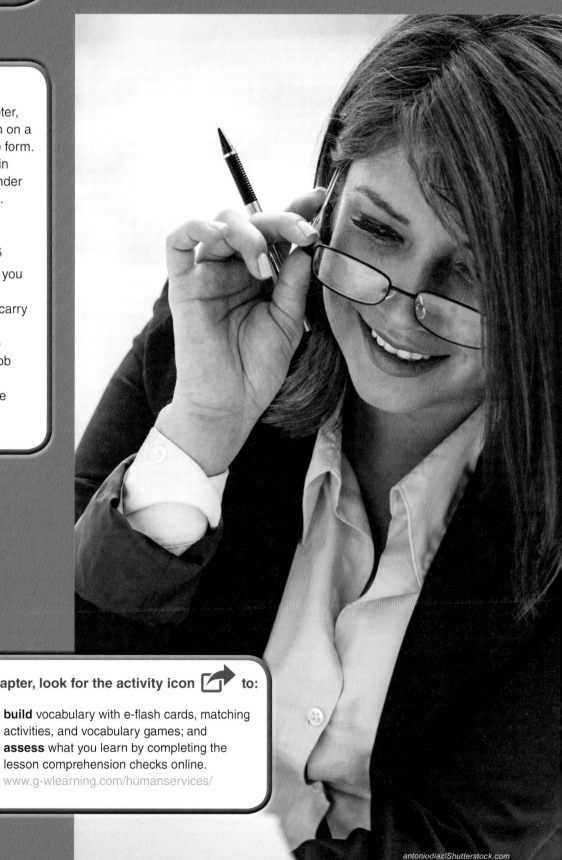

While studying this chapter, look for the activity icon ↗ to:

- **build** vocabulary with e-flash cards, matching activities, and vocabulary games; and
- **assess** what you learn by completing the lesson comprehension checks online.

www.g-wlearning.com/humanservices/

G-WLEARNING.com

502

antoniodiaz/Shutterstock.com

AFTER STUDYING THIS CHAPTER, YOU WILL

KNOW:

- Types of changes that could impact a career plan.
- Differences between various postsecondary educational options.
- Characteristics of successful workers.

UNDERSTAND:

- How personal skills and traits can impact job success.
- How to find and acquire a desired job.
- How to build work connections that will contribute to job success.

BE ABLE TO DO:

- Locate resources for funding an education.
- Prepare a résumé that reflects personal skills and accomplishments.
- Prepare a plan for managing a career.

GETTING STARTED

Joseph looked at his older brother. His brother was already 28 years old and was still living at home. He never seemed to have any money. He worked hard at his job, but still could not seem to make enough to find his own place.

"What happened?" Joseph asked his brother. "Why don't you have your own apartment?"

"I don't know," Joseph's brother replied. "Guess I'm just stupid."

Joseph knew that was not true. His brother was very gifted at fixing things. He fixed appliances in the house and kept the family car running. He was really good at working with his hands. He just could not seem to find a good-paying job.

"Why don't you go to school to become a mechanic?" Joseph asked his brother. "You could still work at nights and go to school in the daytime."

"It all takes money," his brother replied, "and I don't have any. And it just never has worked out. I'll make do."

Career success is more likely to happen with planning. Without planning, you probably will not reach your career goals. With planning and with carefully managing your time, you stand a good chance. In fact, the earlier you start with your career plan, the sooner in life you will reach career goals. But circumstances—yours and trends in society—change over time, so you also need to review and reexamine your career plan from time to time. A career plan can be started, changed, or adjusted at any time.

In this chapter, you will learn more about pursuing your career, carrying out your career plan, and finding success in the world of work. Even as you follow your career plan, you will make adjustments, set new goals, gain new experiences, and pursue more education if needed to meet your goals.

PURSUE YOUR CAREER CHOICE

Content Terms

Build Vocab

recruiter
technical college
remedial course
community college
open admissions
accredited
placement rate
grant
work-study program
scholarship

Academic Terms

trade union
subsidize

Objectives

After studying this lesson, you will be able to

- **identify** changes which could impact the success of a career plan.
- **recognize** the need for postsecondary education and training for many careers.
- **describe** options for meeting the educational requirements for your chosen career.
- **clarify** differences in admission to various education options.
- **identify** ways to fund a college education.

Focus Your Reading

1. List the various postsecondary educational options available to high school graduates. As you read, identify the benefits and the disadvantages of each option.
2. Choose five of the content terms and identify examples that depict the terms.

In Chapter 5, you learned about the importance of exploring careers, setting a career goal, and developing a career plan. Your career plan includes several *short-term goals* you have been working on through your years of high school. Succeeding in your high school courses is important, as these courses prepare you to succeed beyond high school, whatever direction you take.

Your career plan should also include a *long-term goal* for education or training required in your career. Working with your guidance counselor at school, you can evaluate your progress toward readiness for your postsecondary education or training options. Success in your high school courses is a requirement for entrance into most postsecondary institutions.

Reviewing Your Career Choice

While it is always important to keep your career goal in mind, you also need to review that goal from time to time. Your

thoughts, feelings, and desires related to a career can change over time. As you learn, grow, and gain experiences, your skills increase, you may develop new interests, and you may be exposed to career options you had not been aware of earlier in life. In addition, the world of work continues to change around you. New technologies create new careers or change the way work is done. Because of all these potential changes, it is helpful to review your career choice to be sure you are on a path that meets your goals and values (**Figure 20.1**). This review is part of keeping your career plan current and making sure it will help you reach your goals.

As you mature, it is helpful to review the characteristics of jobs in your career plan to see how they match the ways you have changed. For example, you may have developed leadership skills in a school club that you did not have when you made your career plan. If you have developed leadership skills, you may find yourself interested in a career that offers more leadership opportunities. In another example, as you have explored an initial career choice, you may have learned about related careers that offer more opportunities to use a particular strength you have developed, such as interpersonal skills. Making adjustments in your career plan could help you be more successful in reaching personal goals.

One question to consider is whether your career choice will help you live the lifestyle you desire. Changes in society can affect your plan. Has the future job outlook for your career choice changed? This will affect your ability to get a job in your field once you have finished your education and training. You can revisit the websites discussed in Chapter 5 to learn whether job-outlook projections have changed.

Another factor in the world of work that may affect your career goal is where potential

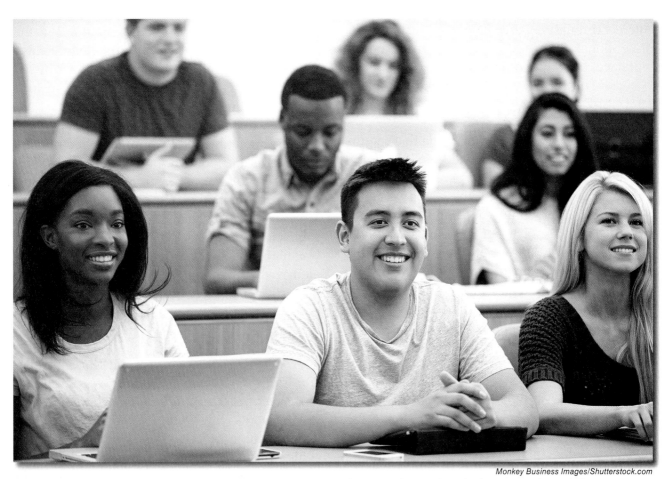

Figure 20.1 As young adults continue to learn and grow, they need to review their career plans. *What are some changes that could result in a needed adjustment to a career plan?*

jobs might be located. Has the market for workers in a particular career shifted to one region of the country? Would living in that region make it more likely for you to reach your goals? Workers should do this kind of analysis throughout their work lives. As you evaluate your career plan, you can review the statuses of potential employers to learn whether they expect to hire in the next five years. Reviewing your career goal is important as you make plans to take the next step in your career plan and obtain the needed training for that career.

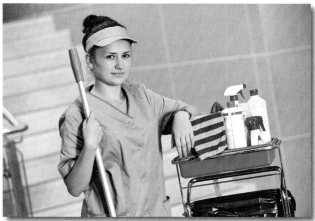

Figure 20.2 Some entry-level jobs are available that do not require any postsecondary education or training. *How could such jobs contribute to a career plan?*

Exploring Postsecondary Education and Training Options

What are the requirements for entering your chosen career? Is it a high school diploma, a certificate for a specific career program, a degree from a two- or four-year college, or completion of a master's or doctoral program? Can your career be entered through experience gained at the workplace alone? Each education or training option will have different requirements.

Immediate Employment

There are very few jobs available that require no training or education beyond high school. It is estimated that only about 10 percent of jobs fall into this category. Wages for these jobs are generally low, and opportunities for improved working hours, conditions, or benefits (such as paid holidays and sick days) are not likely (**Figure 20.2**). These jobs may offer little opportunity for promotions or raises in pay. Young adults should consider their career goals and desired lifestyles before choosing this option.

Military Training

Many young people choose to begin their training with service in the military. There are different branches in the military, and the requirements for entering these branches can vary. The military provides training and pay for the work that a person does while in the military. The armed forces also have multiple programs for helping service members receive a college education. Depending on the situation, military personnel can take advantage of these educational programs while in the military or after completing their service.

Of course, a career in the military requires the person enlisting to commit to remaining in the armed forces for a period of years. Recruits also have to undergo military training and have no say in where they are posted. Postings may include service in combat.

To learn about a military career, you can schedule an appointment with a military recruiter. A **recruiter** is a person who can explain about military careers, entrance requirements, training you can get through the military, requirements for active service, and benefits for those who have completed their service. Military recruiters often visit high schools to answer questions young people have about a military career. They also work in recruitment offices that people can visit.

Apprenticeships

For some trades, workers can learn the specific skills and knowledge they need through an *apprenticeship*. In this kind of program, a new worker works with an experienced worker, called a *master*, for a set period of time to develop the skills that are needed to perform tasks in the trade independently. In many cases, these starting workers also take classes through a technical

college or community college that specifically teaches skills related to the career. These classes may be offered in various schedules and formats to meet the needs of both the master worker and the apprentice.

School counselors can help you locate potential apprenticeships that are open in a career that interests you. Some might be sponsored by local *trade unions*, which are organizations that represent workers in a particular trade. Others might be promoted through a technical college.

Technical Colleges

A **technical college** is an educational institution that offers education and training in a career-focused program (**Figure 20.3**). All the courses students in one program take relate directly to the career they are pursuing and are designed to help them gain the skills and experience needed to succeed in that career. This approach can save time and money compared to other postsecondary options, as most programs in a technical college can be completed in less than two years.

Most technical colleges have specific entrance requirements, including courses that need to be completed in high school. Many also have entrance exams. Some offer remedial courses that students can take if they fail to meet the entrance requirements. **Remedial courses** are classes designed to help students gain basic knowledge and skills they lack so they can fully participate in a program of study. These courses cover basic communication, mathematics, or science concepts. Of course, these courses cost money, just like the job-preparation courses do. This means that needing to take them increases the cost of a student's postsecondary education.

Some technical colleges have aligned some of their programs with a four-year college, so that the two years completed at the technical college contribute toward the completion of a four-year degree. School guidance counselors can help you identify technical colleges that have programs in careers that interest you and can explain whether these colleges have such an arrangement with a four-year college.

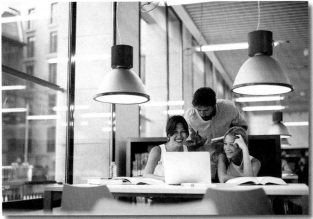

Figure 20.3 Taking courses at a technical college can help you gain specific skills. *What specific skills does your career require that could be gained at a technical college?*

GaudiLab/Shutterstock.com

> ## Think About Your Reading
> What career pathways do you think could be effectively connected through technical colleges and a four-year college?

Two-Year Community Colleges

A **community college** is a nonresidential college that offers courses leading to a certificate or a two-year associate's degree. Community colleges tend to cater to students who still live at home and commute to school or to part-time students who work while they attend college. Community colleges usually have **open admissions** policies, meaning anyone who has a high school diploma can be admitted as long as there is room available in the desired program. The cost of tuition at these schools is usually less than the tuition at a larger college or university.

The coursework offered at a community college usually is aligned with a four-year-degree program at a larger college or university (**Figure 20.4**). Thus, students can attend one of these schools, earn an associate's degree, and then use the course credits earned to help toward completing a four-year degree. This approach makes college more affordable by helping young adults save on the costs of living away from home and two years

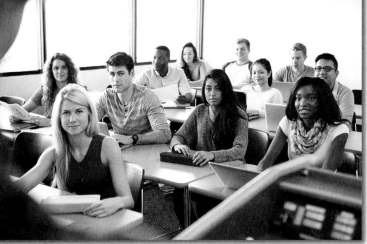

Monkey Business Images/Shutterstock.com

Figure 20.4 Most community colleges have curriculums aligned with larger four-year colleges or universities in order to facilitate ease of transferring credits from one institution to another. *What could be some benefits of starting your postsecondary education at a community college?*

of tuition. It is important, however, to check which courses will be accepted by the college or university you intend to transfer to. Not all courses are accepted for full credit.

A student who takes this approach must have a transcript sent from the community college to the four-year school. A *transcript*, as you learned in Chapter 5, is an official record of all the courses a student has taken at an institution and the grade received in each course. Some courses may apply to the desired program, and some may not.

Four-Year Colleges and Universities

Many careers require a degree from an accredited four-year college or university. If a college or university is **accredited**, this means that the college or university meets specific standards that have been set by an accreditation agency. Attending an accredited college ensures that the education received meets quality standards. It also provides access to federal and state funds, such as student aid, and makes it relatively easy to transfer credits to a different college if one wants to change institutions. When choosing a college, it is important to check its accreditation status. The Council for Higher Education Accreditation's website can help you find information related to accreditation.

In addition to being accredited, it is important that a college or university has a good placement

rate for students completing its programs. The **placement rate** is the percentage of graduates who find jobs in their field of study. If you spend the money to complete a degree, you want to be able to find a job that uses the skills and knowledge you have gained and paid for. The career services department at a college or university can provide information about the jobs their students have been able to obtain after leaving particular programs.

Most four-year colleges and universities have entrance requirements that include successfully completing specific coursework at the high school level. They also may require that applicants attain a minimum score on a nationally recognized exam, such as the ACT or SAT (**Figure 20.5**). Students can take these exams in their junior and senior years of high school. Entrance into many colleges and universities is competitive, meaning the qualifications of applicants are compared, and some are not accepted. Those with higher grades in high school, higher achievement scores on entrance exams, and greater participation in cocurricular activities usually have preference for admission. Some colleges and universities require that applicants also provide a written essay and letters of recommendation from teachers or other adults familiar with applicants' work and character. School counselors can explain about the various aspects of the application process.

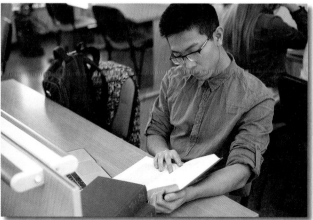

Dean Drobot/Shutterstock.com

Figure 20.5 Attaining a good score on the ACT or SAT is a good short-term goal. One way of achieving it is studying for the exams.

degree, it is important to choose an undergraduate program that is recognized and accepted by the graduate program. Also, you will have to work hard to excel in your undergraduate program, as acceptance into a graduate program is often competitive and very selective.

Master's and Doctoral Programs

Some careers require a master's or a doctoral degree. These advanced degrees are earned after completion of a bachelor's degree at a four-year college or university. If you are pursuing a long-term career goal that requires an advanced

Online Programs

Many colleges and universities offer online courses to help meet students' needs for flexibility in scheduling. Some offer a combination of in-class and online learning, and others offer complete online degree programs. If you are

Real-Life Scenario

Manny's Career

Manny smiled as he walked across the stage to accept his diploma. This was his third diploma—first high school, then college, and now his master's degree. He was already applying for jobs that required his new degree as a qualification. His new degree would mean a good salary increase. He was grateful he had reached this point in his career.

It had been a long road with many side trips. Manny started out in a private four-year college. He really had not been ready for school back then, he later realized. Still, his parents had said over and over again, "College is a must-do." So Manny had enrolled in college with his parents' encouragement and financial support. In the first semester, he managed to skate by, but he really did not take his classes seriously enough. He did not see any relevance to them. Second semester, he partied too much and flunked out. That had been a wake-up moment! His parents pulled the plug on funding for college and told him he needed to work until he was ready for the responsibility of school and knew what he wanted.

Manny's aunt worked at a high school and told him they had a need for a classroom aide for students in special education. She thought it might be a job he could enjoy while he figured out what he wanted to do. He applied, using his aunt as a reference. He got the job and found that he really liked working with kids. He found he could relate to these students, many of whom were smart but not motivated by school. He knew how they felt, and

he also knew the consequences of slacking off at school. Manny started working with the students on career planning and realized that was where he had missed the target. Manny decided he needed to get a career plan in place.

Manny enrolled in the community college and completed his associate's degree while he continued to work. Then he enrolled in a four-year college and completed his bachelor's degree in social work. He had returned to the same high school where he worked as an aide and was hired as a school social worker, working with students similar to those he had helped in his first job. After three years of social work, he had decided to move forward with a master's degree in mental health counseling. The knowledge and skills he had learned the last two years were very beneficial in his job at the school, but he was excited to knock on doors and see what opportunities were available with his new degree.

For Discussion

1. What could Manny have done in high school to help him find a career that interested him?
2. How did Manny's personal network help him find a job?
3. How did Manny's work experience help him develop his career?
4. How could a career plan in high school have saved Manny both time and money in developing his career?

considering online options, be sure to check the accreditation status of the program. It is important that your degree will be accepted by potential employers and by institutions that provide certifications or licenses. While online programs may be less expensive than a campus-based education, if the degree is earned from an institution that is not accredited, it may not do the graduate much good when looking for a job.

Pursuing Further Education and Training

Once you identify the type of program you need for the career you are interested in, you can use the decision-making steps to identify, research, and consider alternatives for getting that education or training. Many students take these specific steps in the process of choosing a postsecondary institution:

- *Narrow down your choices of schools.* Visit schools that interest you. Family members, friends, and guidance counselors all can help you in this decision-making process.

- *Apply to your top choice or choices.* Your school guidance counselor can help you access applications, answer questions, and make plans to meet deadlines. Applications often have to be submitted to the school a year or more in advance of the date you actually want to start attending the college.

- *Once accepted into a college, make plans to attend.* Visit the college and meet with a program advisor. Plan a program of study to follow in completing your degree requirements.

As you examine the different pathways for obtaining postsecondary education and training, you may make choices that combine several elements (**Figure 20.6**). The cost of tuition, the cost of living away versus at home, and the ease of coordinating education with an existing work schedule may all be factors in your decision for education and training.

For example, military personnel often take courses while they are still active in the military. As they transfer from one military base to another,

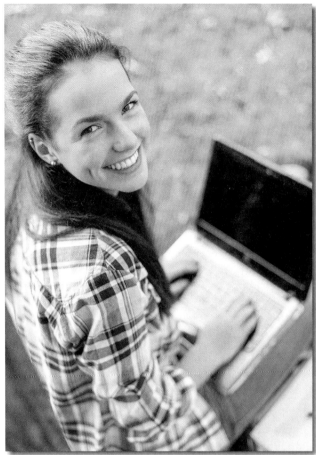

Figure 20.6 Online courses make it possible to pursue further education and training, especially when you need a flexible schedule. *What could be some benefits of taking online courses through the college where you intend to complete your degree?*

they may complete courses from several different colleges. Another student may take some courses at a community college, some online courses, and some courses at a technical college, and then transfer the credits to a larger college to finish a four-year degree. These students will need to have transcripts sent from each institution where they took courses.

When you develop your program of study as part of your career plan, it is helpful to examine the requirements for the degree program where you want to obtain your degree. Work with a program advisor at that college or university to learn what courses will be accepted. Identify whether the college has any agreements with community or technical colleges to accept certain courses for equal credit. This is vital in order to avoid taking courses that will not contribute to your career plan.

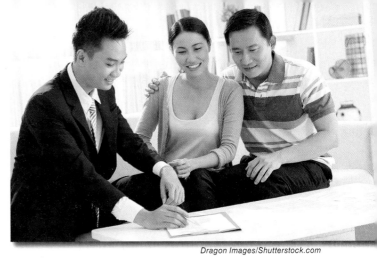

Dragon Images/Shutterstock.com

Figure 20.7 Early financial planning can help parents support their college-bound children.

Funding Your Education

Financing a postsecondary education is a major issue for many students. In fact, many students may feel the cost of tuition limits or controls where they can go to school and, thereby, controls the career choices they have.

Both federal and state governments recognize the huge benefit in obtaining postsecondary education to further a person's career choices. Even though they are highly *subsidized*, or supported financially, by government funding, state colleges are quite expensive, and many families find that tuition costs are beyond their family budgets. If you wish to attend a private college or university, the costs of tuition are likely to be even higher. Also, tuition is not the only cost to consider. Students who live on campus have to pay for room and board and transportation to and from the college. Even those who live at home and commute have to fund their transportation costs. In addition, all students have to buy books and pay other fees the institution might charge.

How can an average person fund his or her education? What are some of the resources available to help people pay for their education and reach their career goals? Most families use a combination of personal resources, federal and state resources, and possibly private or nonprofit resources to fund their education choice.

Savings and Earnings

Families can set aside money in an education fund for their children's or grandchildren's future use (**Figure 20.7**). This money is often not subject to income tax, giving this approach a clear financial advantage. Setting aside enough money each month to cover the projected cost of tuition is difficult for many families, however. The fact that tuition and other education costs rise over time compounds the problem.

Some families continue to provide assistance to students as they attend college, helping to pay for tuition, room and board, transportation, and other expenses incurred while living away from home. Sometimes this means adults work past retirement age in order to help children complete college and get established on their own. Other families are not able to provide such assistance.

Student Financial Aid

Students can obtain various kinds of financial aid provided by the federal government:

- *Grants.* **Grants** are forms of financial aid that do not have to be repaid. They are usually based on need, and students and their families must meet eligibility requirements to receive them.

- *Student loans.* Student loans are monies borrowed for college expenses that do need to be repaid, with interest.

- *Work-study programs.* **Work-study programs** are programs in which students work in a federally subsidized job at a college or university to earn money to help pay for school.

Students can only obtain this financial aid if they and their families complete an application called the *Free Application for Federal Student Aid* (*FAFSA*). This application can be found online at the U.S. Department of Education website. The application needs to be completed each year that a student wishes to be eligible for aid.

Even if you do not qualify for federal financial aid, you may qualify for financial aid through your state. Your school counselor can assist with applications for both federal and state financial aid.

Another source of financial aid could be the college or university you plan to attend. The school's financial-aid page on its website can help you learn what financial aid is available. Be sure to complete the school's applications and meet their deadlines (**Figure 20.8**).

Scholarships

Another source of funding for a postsecondary education could be scholarships. A **scholarship** is free money given to a worthy candidate to further his or her education. Like a grant, it does not have to be repaid. Many organizations offer scholarships or grants to help students pay for college.

The school or college where you plan to attend may have scholarships available for students in a particular field of study. Private or nonprofit organizations often offer scholarships. The requirements for different scholarships vary, but all require an application. Your school guidance counselor can be an excellent resource for helping you locate and apply for scholarships. Also, the U.S. Department of Labor sponsors a website, *CareerOneStop*, where people can also search for scholarships.

LESSON 20.1
Assess

COMPREHENSION CHECK

1. What changes could result in persons needing to adjust their career plan?
2. Explain why pursuing education and training past high school is important for most people.
3. List four different options for obtaining postsecondary education or training leading to a career.
4. What options might be available to a student who fails to get accepted into a four-year college of choice?
5. List three different ways a student could possibly fund his or her education.
6. Describe three different forms of financial aid subsidized by the federal government.

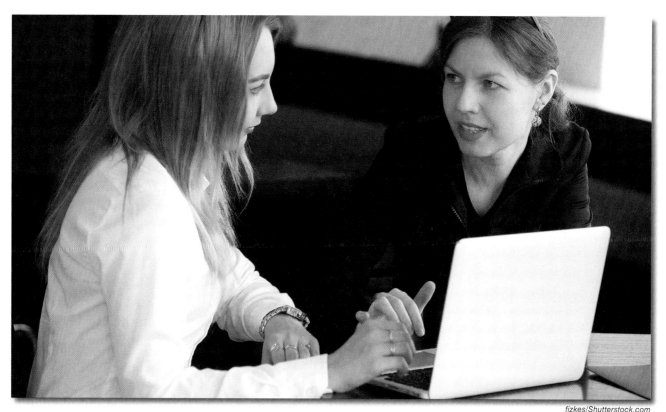

fizkes/Shutterstock.com

Figure 20.8 Financial aid to help fund college education can be obtained through several sources. *What is the benefit of seeking help from a school guidance counselor when searching for ways to fund your education?*

Objectives

After studying this lesson, you will be able to

- **identify** strategies for finding a job.
- **prepare** a résumé.
- **describe** how to prepare for an interview.
- **identify** keys to job success.
- **explain** the difference between business etiquette and business ethics.

Focus Your Reading

1. For each heading in this lesson, summarize the key points you could share with a friend who is trying to find a job or succeed at a new job.

2. Make a list of three people you could use as references. Include contact information for each person.

R ight now you spend little or no time in the workplace. During your adult life, however, most of your time will be spent in the workplace. Taking the time now to prepare for a satisfying career is important.

Searching for a Job

With the right preparation, you can find and secure the job that is best for you. The following steps will help you begin:

- ***Update your portfolio.*** As you learned in Chapter 5, a *portfolio* is a collection of materials that document achievements over time. Make sure your portfolio is current, with copies of diplomas, certificates, degrees, and other recent accomplishments. Add letters of reference or recommendations that support and promote you and your successes. If you can include examples of work that show particular job-related skills, that can also be helpful.

Content Terms

Build Vocab

networking
job fair
résumé
references
cover message
interview
business etiquette
business ethics
sexual harassment
equal opportunity

Academic Terms

screening
physical dexterity
confidentiality

- *Find out what jobs are available.* Check newspapers, online job listings, the career services department at your school or college, and employer and government websites. You can search for jobs by broad categories or specific job titles. For example, you could search under a broad category (for example, *human services*) or for a specific job (for example, *mental health counselor*). Using broad search words will show you more available jobs in the field. You may also be able to learn about openings by attending a **job fair**, an event where employers come together, often at a college or community center, to recruit potential employees for their organization or business (**Figure 20.9**).

- *Network with family, friends, and people in your career field.* **Networking** is talking to family members, friends, and other people you know about possible job openings. Social media websites can be an effective tool for networking. People in your network may hear about job openings or know someone who works for an organization that interests you. Membership in a professional organization can also provide networking opportunities.

- *Identify employers who offer the job you want.* You may locate this information

through a library, the Internet, or even the telephone directory.

- *Research the requirements needed for each position you consider.* The key requirements are usually listed in each job posting. If no openings are posted, try to identify organizations' needs through Internet or library research.

Think About Your Reading

What do you think would be the best source of information about job openings in which you might be interested?

Preparing Your Résumé

When you apply for a job, you will submit a résumé. A **résumé** is a summary of your skills, training, education, and past work experiences. A résumé allows an employer to quickly evaluate an applicant's qualifications (**Figure 20.10**). There are two types of résumés. A *chronological résumé* focuses on your employers and your work experiences listed in reverse chronological order. A *functional résumé* is most useful for those who have much experience and emphasizes your qualifications, skills, and achievements. In this lesson, we will discuss preparing a chronological résumé, as this will be the type of résumé you are most likely to create. Most chronological résumés include the following parts:

- *Personal information*—your name, address, telephone number, and e-mail address
- *Career objective*—a statement about the position you seek
- *Education*—the high school or postsecondary institution attended and the certificates or diplomas received or in progress
- *Work experience*—a job history, listing the years worked, the titles of your jobs, and the duties you performed in each position
- *Honors, awards, and achievements*—any honors you have won or distinctions you have been given, including any notable achievements

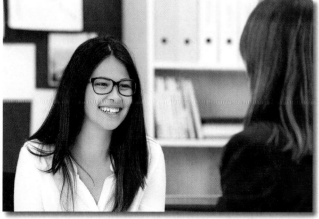

racorn/Shutterstock.com

Figure 20.9 Attending a job fair gives you an opportunity to meet potential employers face-to-face. *How could this be an advantage for both employer and employee?*

DENON P. CAPIKROLANKA
199 Eighth Avenue
Ellsworth, WI 54011
Cell: 715-123-4567
E-mail: dpcapikro@email.com

CAREER OBJECTIVE

Experienced and certified child care assistant seeking part-time employment in a licensed day care setting.

EXPERIENCE

Ellsworth School District   Ellsworth, WI
Student Aide, Prekindergarten Summer Program   June–August 20XX

- Prepared teaching materials for use with four-year-olds in kindergarten-readiness classes.
- Assisted teacher in kindergarten-readiness class.
- Worked with students who had special needs, reteaching concepts on a one-to-one basis.

Hillcrest Elementary School   Ellsworth, WI
Volunteer Teacher Assistant   January–May 20XX

- Assisted kindergarten teacher for one block per day.
- Helped prepare materials for instruction.
- Assisted kindergarten students with seatwork, reinforcing concepts.
- Taught remedial concepts to individual students in a one-to-one setting.

Bear Buddies Day Care   Hudson, WI
Child Care Assistant   September–December 20XX

- Completed practicum experience for the State of Wisconsin Child Care Teacher Assistant license.
- Prepared teaching materials and taught lessons to a group of 15 three- and four-year-olds.
- Participated in supervision of large-muscle activities.
- Participated in planning, preparing, and serving healthy, child-appropriate snacks.

EDUCATION

Ellsworth Senior High School

Ellsworth, WI, Junior, 20XX

- Child Care Teacher Assistant class—completed certificate May 20XX
- Ellsworth Honor Roll, 20XX

SPECIAL SKILLS

- Computer: Skilled with using iPad technology in early childhood instruction.
- Leadership: Served as president of FCCLA, 20XX, and as a member, 20XX–20XX.

Figure 20.10   All résumés follow a basic format to allow employers to quickly judge a job candidate's abilities. *How would your résumé be different after you completed your postsecondary education and training?*

- *Activities and memberships in professional associations*—the associations' or groups' names and your involvement, achievements, and leadership roles
- *Special skills and interests*—a list of your special skills and interests relating to the job you seek
- *References*—the phrase *References available upon request* can appear on your résumé to indicate that you have sought out references who can attest to your job skills. **References** are people who have direct knowledge of you and your past work. For references, you should choose at least three people who could give you a good recommendation. These people should not include relatives. Before you list people as references, be sure to ask their permission. You should be able to provide a list of references if asked by the employer.

Keep your résumé easy to review—use a bullet format, no full sentences, and clear bold headings. Many companies use applicant-tracking systems that perform *key word searches*. Typically, when an organization needs a new employee, it posts a job listing in various places. Résumés and applications are then searched for key words that were included in the job description. It is important to carefully select relevant words and education and work-history highlights when creating a résumé.

Some websites used in a job search ask you to post your résumé online. Remember that any information you put online has the potential of being accessed by anyone. *Never* put important personal information (such as your birth date, where you were born, or your Social Security number) on a website. Criminals can use this information to steal your identity. This type of information can be given to employers after you are hired.

Applying for a Job

When you find an interesting job, you will want to apply for it. Usually this requires writing a cover message and sending it with your résumé to the contact person listed in the job posting.

A **cover message** is a brief message that clearly states the position a job applicant seeks and highlights his or her relevant qualifications. The message should indicate how you learned about the position. The bulk of the message should state the most important reasons why you qualify for the job, focusing on the qualities, experiences, or skills that are most likely to attract the employer's interest. These skills should not be described in the same way the résumé describes them. A cover message should end with a request for an interview and should thank the employer for considering you for the position. Send your résumé with the message.

Application Forms

At some point before or during the interview, you will be asked to fill out an application form. Completing this form accurately is important. This form is a test itself. It represents you to the employer and demonstrates how well you follow directions.

When filling out the form, do not skip any questions. If a question does not relate to you, write "does not apply." Be sure to answer all other questions accurately.

You may be asked for specific names, dates, and addresses—details beyond the facts on your résumé. Create a list of facts about your education, work experience, and outside activities. This list is often called a *personal fact sheet*. Keep this fact sheet with you and refer to it when extra details are needed, such as when filling out an application. By keeping this list handy, you will be able to answer any question that arises.

> **Think About Your Reading**
> What might an employer think if you do not bring what is needed to accurately complete an application form?

Employer Screening

Employers use several strategies to identify the best candidates for job openings (**Figure 20.11**). First, they review all résumés to see which applicants have the knowledge and personal skills

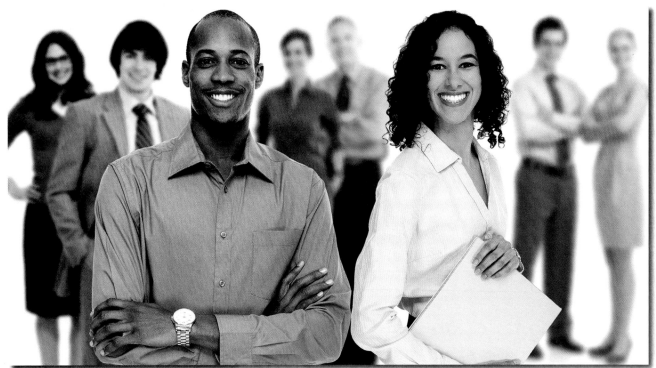

Figure 20.11 Employers use multiple strategies to identify whom they should hire for open positions in their business or company. *How could you build positive networks that could potentially help you get a job?*

needed for the job. Then they may take further steps to narrow down their list of potential hires. If you pass all these *screening*, or initial evaluation, procedures and emerge in the top group, an employer will contact you for an interview.

Preemployment Tests

Sometimes employers give *preemployment tests* before making a hiring decision. Employers use these assessments to try and identify matches between applicants and a job's requirements. Some preemployment tests assess skill levels and measure some basic skills, such as math, reading, or dexterity. *Physical dexterity* refers to how quickly you can work with your hands and fingers. These tests are usually designed to measure your abilities to use skills that are specific to the job you are seeking.

Some preemployment tests are *psychological tests* and measure interests, personal traits (for example, honesty and loyalty), and personality patterns. These tests can help the employer learn more about you and judge how well you might get along with others on the job. They also can help identify whether you are ready for a particular job.

In many cases, these tests have neither right nor wrong answers, but there are answers that could make you appear to be a strong candidate, and there may be answers that would raise concerns for the employer. When you take a preemployment test, try to answer questions in a positive, truthful manner, using responses that emphasize your strengths and positive character traits.

Social Media Search

Some employers find information about job applicants by accessing social media websites and evaluating applicants' digital footprints. Items the individual posts can provide examples of the way he or she communicates, solves problems, or makes decisions. Items posted by friends give employers a view of the types of people the applicant associates with. One danger of this use for social media is that an applicant may be given no opportunity to explain away something negative. Some pictures may not present an applicant in the best light. If a person is applying for a job that involves working with young children or young adults, for example, the employer may

view online material as a critical factor in his or her fit for the job.

The fact that employers use social media in these ways emphasizes the importance of being careful what messages and pictures you post online. Chapter 7 includes suggestions on how to manage your digital footprint.

Think About Your Reading

In what ways could you use social media to advance career opportunities? In what ways could some social media websites hurt your career opportunities?

Interviewing for a Job

An **interview** gives the employer an opportunity to talk with job applicants. Before an interview, do some research about the position you are seeking (**Figure 20.12**). Be able to explain why you want to work for that particular organization. Be prepared to tell the interviewer what you will be able to do to help that employer reach its goals. If you know what skills and qualities the employer wants, think about your strengths in these areas. You should also prepare some questions about the job or organization that show genuine interest.

Your appearance at the interview can make a difference in whether you get the job. Cleanliness, neatness, and appropriate apparel are important in any interview. As a rule, observe what the employees of an organization wear to work and dress slightly better for your interview.

It can help if you practice interviewing ahead of time. This will help you feel more relaxed and able to answer questions with confidence. Have a friend or family member ask you some common interview questions as you prepare for your interview. Whomever you ask to help you should be someone who has been through the experience of

Interview Tips
Prepare for the interview.
• Learn all you can about the employer.
• Prepare some questions to ask about the job.
• Bring a folder with materials needed for the interview (pen, résumé, list of references, personal fact sheet to fill out application form, and a notepad with your list of questions).
• Prepare to answer questions the interviewer might ask, such as these: *Can you start by telling me about yourself? Why do you want this job? What are your strengths and weaknesses? Are you willing to work evenings and weekends? What are your future plans?*
• Practice your answers to the above questions before the interview.
Make a positive impression.
• Wear neat, clean clothes that help you look your best.
• Comb and neatly style your hair.
• Shave or trim a beard.
• Wear makeup sparingly.
• Be sure hands and fingernails are clean.
• Brush your teeth and be sure your breath is fresh.
Be on time for the interview.
• Know the exact time and place of the interview.
• Allow extra travel time to arrive a few minutes early.

Figure 20.12 Being prepared, well groomed, and on time will help you interview successfully. *How could preparing for an interview help calm your feelings of nervousness?*

having a job interview so they know what kinds of questions interviewers ask.

When you arrive for the interview, introduce yourself and thank the interviewer for his or her time. Be sure to indicate your pleasure and enthusiasm for the opportunity. Offer a strong first impression by making direct eye contact and offering a firm handshake (**Figure 20.13**). Let the interviewer lead the interview as you discuss yourself, your education, and your skills. When given the opportunity, ask the questions you prepared before the interview. Asking these questions communicates interest and shows the interviewer you have done your research. If prompted, you may also present your portfolio during an interview. At the interview, be ready to provide a list of references, either to the interviewer or on an application form. List your references, including their names, titles, office addresses, phone numbers, and e-mail addresses. Be sure to ask permission to list a person as a reference.

Send a short *thank-you message* to the interviewer immediately after the interview. Express appreciation for the interviewer's time and thank him or her for considering you. Such a note shows that you know how to treat people with kindness and respect. It may be the final step that gets you the job.

Employment decisions can take a long time. Some companies notify all applicants after making an employment decision, but some do not. If you have not heard anything a week or two after the interview, it is appropriate to send an e-mail to follow up and inquire about an update on the position.

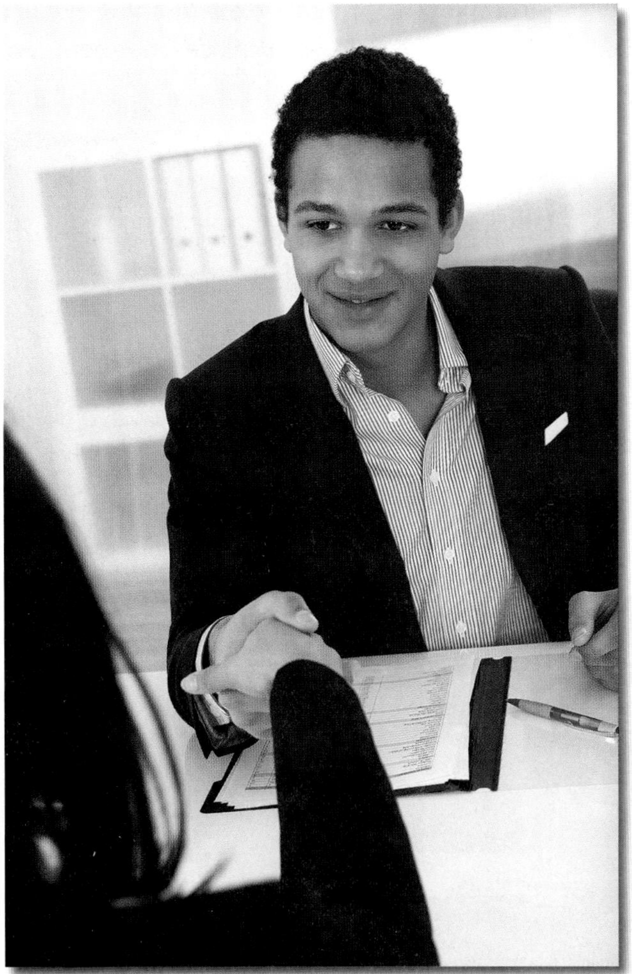

Andrey_Popov/Shutterstock.com

Figure 20.13 The interview is your chance to offer a strong, professional first impression. *What body language could help you give a good first impression?*

Think About Your Reading

What information would you like to know about an organization before working there?

Succeeding on the Job

Most people want to meet their employers' expectations and succeed in their work. Learning all the responsibilities of a new job takes time, so do not be too critical of yourself if it takes several weeks to adjust to a new job. The key is to stick to it and work hard at learning your duties.

One factor in career success is learning and following the *code of conduct* that your employer expects on the job. You can learn this code of conduct by reading the employer's employee manual, reading other internal communications, and observing the behaviors of respected coworkers. Knowing this code of conduct can help you follow the rules and carry out the responsibilities of your job, as well as understand what practices are expected of employees at your place of work. Common practices included in an organization's code of conduct include regular attendance, productive work habits, professional behavior, business etiquette, and business ethics.

Regular Attendance

Being to work on time each day shows your employer that you are dependable (**Figure 20.14**). You can be counted on to carry out the responsibilities of your job. Good attendance from employees is critical for an employer to meet an organization's goals. Employers will instruct new employees on their policies for calling in to work if they must be absent. Taking care of your health and well-being can help you meet the responsibility of being at work on a regular basis.

Productive Work Habits

Doing good-quality work will help you feel good about your work as well as impress your employer. You will build a reputation of having a strong work ethic. A strong work ethic includes habits such as using your time well and making sure that the quality of your work meets your employer's expectations. One characteristic that employers like very much in workers is initiative to ask for more work when workers complete an assigned task.

Professionalism

Job success requires that workers show *professionalism*, the behaviors that are suitable for the workplace. Good workers act like professionals in their fields, utilizing knowledge and skills specific to their fields. This includes performing responsibilities competently, following directions, and working cooperatively with supervisors and coworkers. It also includes dealing professionally with customers or clients.

Business Etiquette

All employees are expected to show proper manners on the job. Workplace manners are

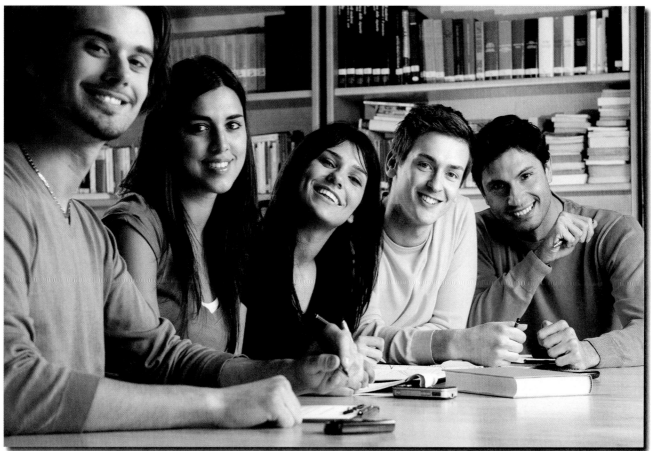

Rido/Shutterstock.com

Figure 20.14 Several skills essential to job success can be practiced in the school setting. *What are some classroom requirements that could relate to expected conduct on a job?*

called **business etiquette**. They include showing respect, being polite, and taking time to listen and communicate clearly. Using business etiquette will help you make positive impressions and should help you be successful. Showing up at meetings on time and listening without interrupting are ways of showing respect. Being polite makes a difference in the way others see you.

One aspect of business etiquette that you will probably use often is introducing people to others properly. In introductions, always name the person to whom you show the most respect first. It may be the company president, a well-respected customer, your supervisor, or an older coworker compared to a younger one. For example, you would say, "Mr. Carmichael, I would like to introduce to you my friend, Melissa Bach. She is a reporter with our daily newspaper. Melissa, this is Mr. Carmichael, the owner of our company." By making proper introductions, you show your ability to treat people respectfully.

Business Ethics

Good character traits are highly valued by employers. When these traits influence business activities, an organization and its employees are said to have high standards of **business ethics**. Honesty and integrity are apparent when you do what you say you will. Your teammates and supervisor know that you stand by your word. You do not lie to customers, clients, or coworkers (**Figure 20.15**). You do not steal property such as office supplies. You do not steal time from the organization by leaving early, taking extra-long breaks, or making personal phone calls while at work.

Employee conduct that reflects high moral principles is important to employers. Employers expect employees to treat everyone in the workplace with respect. They especially ask all employees to avoid behavior that may be viewed as **sexual harassment**. This is unwelcome or unwanted advances, requests for favors, or other verbal or physical conduct of a sexual nature. All forms of sexual harassment are illegal and should be reported to the proper authority within the organization, such as the human resources manager. The employee handbook given to new

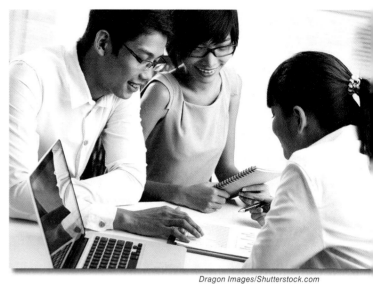
Dragon Images/Shutterstock.com

Figure 20.15 Good business ethics foster positive relationships between employees.

employees usually lists the proper procedures for reporting sexual harassment. It also summarizes an organization's rules and policies.

Fairness and a sense of justice are important in job decisions that impact others. Employees have a better attitude toward work if they feel they are treated fairly. This is the basis of equal opportunity, which is required by law. **Equal opportunity** forbids employers to discriminate against workers based on race, color, sex, national origin, age, religion, or disability. Opportunities in the workplace should be open to all qualified individuals. Salaries should be equal for those who have similar qualifications and perform similar jobs. Organizations that focus on workers' abilities report greater loyalty and productivity from their employees.

Confidentiality

Information gained at work needs to be kept confidential. *Confidentiality* means limiting the knowledge and use of information to those who are authorized to have it. In a work setting, the only people who should know about projects you are working on are those authorized to do so.

Many jobs today deal with confidential information about clients or customers as well as about employers. It is important that the organization you work for has a system in place to protect that

information, and that you follow the procedures to do so. Talking about confidential information to a family member could result in you losing your job. Thus, many conversations about what you do at work need to be general, without details. Family members need to be supportive in helping maintain that confidentiality.

> ## Think About Your Reading
> How can you demonstrate high standards of business ethics in your chosen career?

Performance Ratings

Feelings of job success will be influenced by the performance ratings you receive from your supervisor. Most employees are evaluated formally, in writing, once or twice a year. They are rated on how well they do their job and work cooperatively with others (**Figure 20.16**). Many employers use a rating scale of *excellent, good, fair,* or *poor* for each area. Some include more descriptive evaluations. Usually, a worker's supervisor does his or her evaluation.

Besides doing your job well, your conduct on the job is important, too. Being dependable, loyal, getting along with coworkers and supervisors, and following company rules all merit a high rating.

Hard work on the job pays off. It will help you succeed at your job, feel positively about your work, and obtain good recommendations from your supervisor and coworkers. It will also help you move up in your career as you successfully gain skills and experience in applying those skills. You will be prepared for the next step on your career ladder.

Sometimes a performance rating may not be as high as you desire. It is important to ask a supervisor to explain areas in which improvement is needed. There may be specific skills you need to improve, certain knowledge you need to do the job better, personal traits that you need

Keys to Job Success

- Be dependable; avoid unnecessary lateness or absenteeism.
- Follow directions.
- Do not let personal life interfere with working hours.
- Perform your responsibilities competently.
- Be open to learning from criticism.
- Be cooperative with supervisors and coworkers.
- Be courteous; show concern for others.
- Keep a neat, clean appearance.
- Look for opportunities to advance in your career.

Figure 20.16 Positive personal traits can be your key to job success. *How could personal maturity help you develop these traits and succeed on the job?*

to develop, or attitudes you need to change. It is important that you work to maintain a positive attitude at these times. The steps for building a positive attitude, discussed in Chapter 3, may help you become confident that you can set goals and take steps to address these areas needing improvement. A positive attitude can help you keep a positive self-concept and believe in yourself and in your abilities to learn, grow, and meet your goals to carry out a job well.

LESSON 20.2

Assess

COMPREHENSION CHECK

1. List three places to search for a job.
2. Identify the parts of a chronological résumé.
3. Briefly explain what to write in a cover message.
4. Describe how to prepare for an interview.
5. List four behaviors that will help you succeed on the job.
6. What is the difference between business etiquette and business ethics?

MANAGE YOUR CAREER

Objectives

After studying this lesson, you will be able to

- **identify** relationships that could help a person succeed on a chosen career path.
- **explain** how job changes can contribute to progress up a career ladder.
- **describe** steps for terminating a position with an employer.
- **identify** skills needed to be an entrepreneur in a chosen field.

Focus Your Reading

1. For each heading in this section, identify persons who could help you manage your own career.
2. For each method of building connections, identify persons who have filled that capacity in your life to date.

Content Terms

coach
mentor
role model
promotion

Academic Terms

mentee
lateral

Times of performance ratings are good opportunities for self-evaluation. In addition to learning how your supervisor views your progress on the job, you can ask yourself some questions related to your own career plans: How am I doing at this job? Do I find it satisfying? Are there opportunities for me to grow and better myself? Throughout your career, it is a good idea to review your progress to make sure you are reaching your career goals. These periods of evaluation can also be times of preparing to move up the career ladder.

Building Connections

Developing relationships with people who can help you succeed in your career can be an important piece of moving up a career ladder. These are relationships that help you connect, gain support, develop personally, and excel in your career. *Coaches*, *mentors*, *role models*, and *feedback providers* are common terms that people may use to describe someone serving in this type of relationship.

Coaches

Coaches are people who help you learn specific skills. A coach is likely the person who will train you in a new position, teaching you the skills needed for a job and supervising you while you are learning to master the skills (**Figure 20.17**). Good communication with a coach is important and should involve effective speaking and listening skills to make sure shared communication takes place. I-statements can help you clarify what you understand and areas where you need further information. By using active listening skills, you can make sure that you decoded your coach's messages accurately. Being a good listener and a quick learner, as well as doing high-quality work, can help you gain a good recommendation from a coach.

Mentors

Mentors are people who serve as advisors to you with the goal of helping you be successful. Working with a mentor is a way of learning from experiences that you do not yet have and thereby gaining insight that can help you make better work-related decisions. A mentor is someone you can go to for advice, to seek insight into a situation, or to identify approaches that others have used successfully when faced with a particular situation or issue. In careers where your job is to help people grow or change in some capacity (for example, a teacher or counselor), having a mentor is very helpful as you learn to identify and apply solutions to many varied situations. The relationship between the mentor and *mentee* (the person being mentored) can also be helpful to the mentor, as a new worker in the field often brings new ideas and new approaches to the workplace.

Role Models

As you look around you at others in your career area, who serves as an example of what you would like to do? A **role model** is a person who carries out his or her roles and responsibilities in a way that you would like to imitate. A person who serves as a role model might be someone farther up the career ladder, a person in a position of leadership, or a person who inspires you and others to be the best you can be. A person can serve as a role model for you even though you may not know him or her personally. You may simply observe the person in action at work, noting the way he or she makes decisions, leads a group, or carries out work responsibilities (**Figure 20.18**). You may be able to learn about that person's career path and the steps he or she took to reach the current position. If you get an opportunity to talk with this person about that career path, you will probably find him or her willing to share. He or she may also be willing to give you advice on how to follow a similar path.

> ## Think About Your Reading
> Who has served as a role model in your life to date? Where would you locate a potential role model for your career?

Feedback Providers

As your position and work responsibilities change, you may benefit from having people who provide feedback for you. These may be individuals or a small group of people who are willing to give you feedback on how you are doing. You

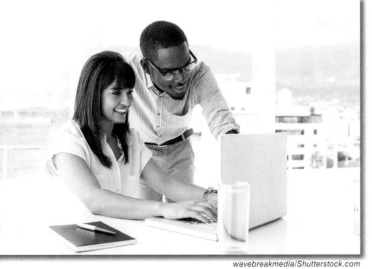

wavebreakmedia/Shutterstock.com

Figure 20.17 A coach is a person who helps train you in a new position. *What leadership qualities would you expect in a person who is a good coach?*

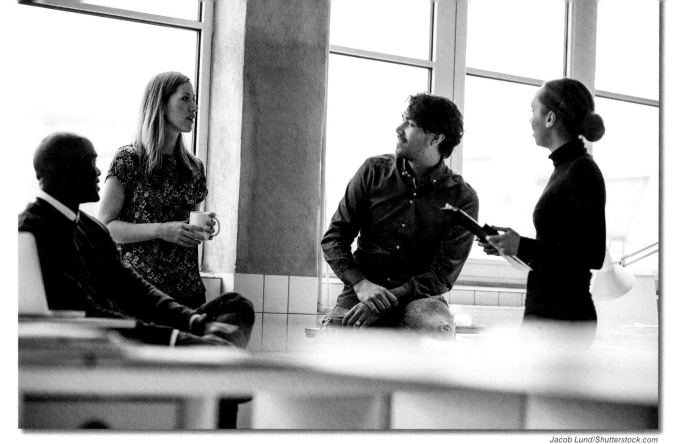

Figure 20.18 Because role models are exemplary in their work, you can learn from them by observing them in action.

can ask questions such as: How did my presentation go? Was there something I could have done to improve my performance? Seeking input from other professionals whom you respect can help you be better at your job and increase your success at work.

Working Up Your Career Ladder

Most people experience several different jobs over their working years. Each position you have throughout your work life can add to your skills, knowledge, and life experiences. New positions may bring you increased pay, better working conditions, more leadership opportunities, or other qualities you desire in your job. You can easily see how these contribute to your career ladder, as the characteristics of each new position build on ones from the previous position.

Sometimes, new positions may not bring any of these desired traits. The job you get may be the only one you can find or the only one open for a person with your skills or in your current location. Keeping a positive attitude through these events is important. No matter what the job, there are skills that can be learned and improved; there are experiences to be gained. There are positive references and recommendations to be earned. Look for ways to use these skills and experiences to build on each other and become part of a step upward on your career ladder.

Changing Jobs

A change in your work position at the same employer may occur in several ways. You may be assigned to another position in a different department or group but at the same pay level. This is called a *lateral*, or sideways, move and often is used when an organization wants workers to understand different aspects of its work. Such a move can make you a more valuable employee, with more insight and understanding of the organization's goals. In the long run, it can give you more experience to contribute to decision making and problem solving (**Figure 20.19**).

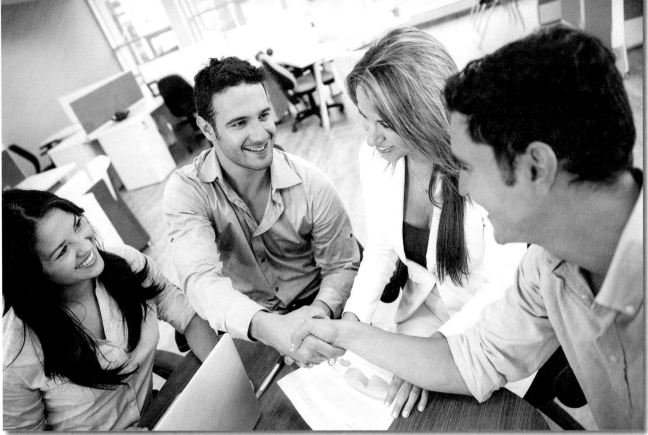

Figure 20.19 Experience gained in employment can increase your success on the job. *How could positive evaluations as an employee help you work up your career ladder?*

Another kind of job change is a **promotion**, in which you are assigned to a different position in the same organization that has more responsibility and increased pay. Both lateral moves and promotions can help you move up your career ladder, gaining skills and experiences which can be valuable in your next step.

Moving to a New Employer

In some situations, you may find yourself having to seek a new position with a different organization in order to progress up your career ladder. This will require following the steps of applying for, interviewing for, and getting hired in a new position. It will also require taking appropriate steps to end your employment with your current employer in a professional manner. Part of handling this in a professional manner is continuing to do quality work during the job search. You should also keep your job search confidential until it reaches a final outcome and avoid making negative statements about your employer or supervisor.

If you have been hired by a new employer, it is typical to give the current employer a two-week notice of termination of employment. Some jobs require more than that. For instance, a teacher is required to sign a contract or a letter of intent to return several months before the new school year. In most cases, employers like to have enough time to fill a position with a replacement by the time a worker leaves.

The letter giving notice should indicate your desired last day of work and express gratitude for the opportunities to learn and grow that you have had with the employer. Being courteous in this way helps maintain good relationships with your former employer, supervisor, and coworkers. Those positive relationships may prove useful to you in the future.

Asking for a Recommendation

Once you have given written notice of your intention to leave your job, continue working throughout that remaining period. It may be tempting to come in late or skip work when you know the end is near, but your reputation as a dependable worker is at stake. Keep a positive attitude and continue to put forth full effort at your job. Your employer will appreciate it, and your recommendation will show it.

Be sure to ask for a written recommendation before you leave so you can add it to your work file. Your immediate supervisor is the most common person to provide a letter of recommendation, although letters from coworkers, a team leader, or the human resources department all could be potential sources.

Exploring Entrepreneurship

Starting a new business has many risks and responsibilities as well as potential rewards. Establishing a new business is referred to as *entrepreneurship*. You may consider entrepreneurship as part of your career ladder (**Figure 20.20**).

After working in a field and increasing your skills and knowledge, you may think about going to work for yourself. You may desire to be your own boss, make your own decisions, and be more in charge of your daily schedule. You may have ideas about how to improve a process, create something new, or increase your income by owning your own business rather than working for someone else.

Launching a new business, no matter how small, requires the investment of at least some money. A business owner needs to pay rent on a place to conduct the business and the furnishings and equipment needed. When the business starts, the owner needs to buy supplies and perhaps materials. He or she may need to pay licensing fees or spend money on advertising. It can take some time before these expenses begin to generate any profits. Anyone starting a new business needs to have some money saved to survive the difficult times at startup.

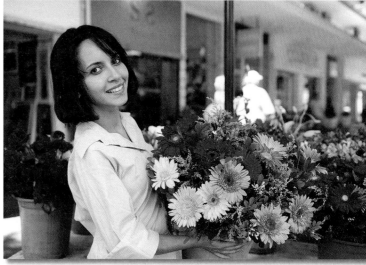

mangostock/Shutterstock.com

Figure 20.20 Owning your own business may be a career goal that you have. *What skills would you need to successfully run a business in your career area?*

Operating a business is a lot of work and requires many different skills, not only those related to the type of work the business does, but also those related to the operation of the business. To keep costs down, a new entrepreneur may need to carry out all aspects of the business, including the production or service tasks, bookkeeping, sales, and management tasks. It may take some time before the business can support hiring workers to assist with these various jobs.

Owning one's own business can be satisfying, but it is a lot of work. A successful entrepreneur needs many different skills as well as the determination to work hard and make the business succeed.

LESSON 20.3

Assess

COMPREHENSION CHECK

1. List four types of relationships that could help you succeed on the job.
2. Explain how a lateral move in a company could benefit a career.
3. Explain how a promotion can contribute to progress on a career ladder.
4. List two steps a person should take to show professionalism when leaving a job.
5. Describe how entrepreneurship could fit into a career ladder.

CHAPTER SUMMARY

A career plan needs to be frequently reviewed as personal interests and goals change, the outlooks for jobs change, and personal needs and desires change. There are various postsecondary options that individuals can access to help them gain the education and training needed to pursue their career goals. Choosing options that build on each other can help individuals create a pathway that meets their needs and resources. There are several sources for funding postsecondary options of choice.

Being successful in the workplace requires knowing how to find and apply for a job and successfully interview for it. Once on the job, doing the best work possible as a professional in your field will help you keep it and advance in your career.

Relationships with coaches, mentors, role models, and feedback providers can help people experience success as they climb their career ladder. Reaching career goals often requires changes in jobs, either inside a company, moving to a different company, or starting your own business as an entrepreneur.

VOCABULARY ACTIVITIES

1. Divide the terms into those related to education and training, those related to finding a job, and those related to succeeding at work. Partner with two other students. Each of you should take one set of terms and quiz each other until you all thoroughly understand each term.

Content Terms

accredited (20.1)	open admissions (20.1)
business ethics (20.2)	placement rate (20.1)
business etiquette (20.2)	promotion (20.3)
coach (20.3)	recruiter (20.1)
community college (20.1)	references (20.2)
	remedial course (20.1)
cover message (20.2)	résumé (20.2)
equal opportunity (20.2)	role model (20.3)
grant (20.1)	scholarship (20.1)
interview (20.2)	sexual harassment (20.2)
job fair (20.2)	technical college (20.1)
mentor (20.3)	work-study program (20.1)
networking (20.2)	

2. Write a paragraph or two that correctly uses each of these terms.

Academic Terms

confidentiality (20.2)	lateral (20.3)
mentee (20.3)	screening (20.2)
physical dexterity (20.2)	subsidize (20.1)
	trade union (20.1)

ASSESS

Your Knowledge

3. What changes could result in a revised career plan?
4. What are four potential sources for funding a postsecondary education?
5. Describe the characteristics of a successful worker.

Your Understanding

6. Describe steps a person could take to find and acquire a desirable job.
7. Explain how a person's job performance could impact his or her success in moving up a career ladder.
8. List four different types of work relationships and explain how each could help a person succeed with a career plan.

Your Skills

9. Analyze your needs for postsecondary education and training and identify two possible sources for that education.
10. Develop a plan for climbing a career ladder to a high-salary end job in your chosen career. Include possible sources of needed education and jobs along the pathway that could provide the knowledge and skills needed to reach the top-level job.
11. Complete a personal fact sheet and develop a résumé that can be added to your portfolio.

CRITICAL THINKING

12. **Make Judgments.** Create a rating scale from 1 to 10 to evaluate available jobs in a career of your choice. Identify 10 factors that you would like your job to have. Include specifics related to hours of work, working conditions, salary range, location, benefits, and vacations. Then research three available openings for new hires in your chosen career, reviewing the job descriptions and other details. Rate each job. Write a summary describing how well each of these three positions would fulfill your career goals. *Choice:* Post your rating scale and your summary for one of the jobs on your school guidance department's website.

13. **Make Predictions.** Write a paper identifying how your preferences for work hours and working conditions could change over your life span. Include factors that are important to you now,

factors that you think will be important when you graduate from college, and factors that could make a difference if you marry and have a family. Then analyze your career choice and evaluate whether it has the potential to meet your needs and preferences for the future. Cite evidence from the text and other resources to support your analysis. *Choice*: Create a digital presentation that describes how your chosen career can meet various demands over a person's life span.

14. **Make Generalizations**. Identify five different jobs in a career pathway of your choice. Research the educational requirements for each job and identify a salary range for each of these jobs. Look for any correlations between salary ranges and the amount of education needed for the job. Write a paragraph generalizing about your findings. *Choice*: Put your information in a spreadsheet with generalizations stated below.

CORE SKILLS

15. **Reading, Writing.** Interview a business owner or a manager about what makes a successful employee. Ask specifically about how an employee applies interpersonal communication skills, time management, ethics, and professionalism. Compare your findings with the information in the text and at least one other resource. Write a paper describing a successful employee, citing evidence from your sources. *Group option*: Working with a small group, combine information from several interviews and resources. Role-play the qualities of a successful employee.

16. **Research, Writing.** Research the requirements for admission into three different postsecondary options that interest you. Analyze your own high school program of study and evaluate your readiness for meeting the requirements for each postsecondary option based on your successfully completing that program. Write a paragraph explaining your evaluation. *Choice*: Meet with your guidance counselor and discuss your readiness.

17. **Research, Writing.** Research the skills and knowledge needed for a person to be an entrepreneur in a career field that interests you. How does professionalism apply in this job setting? Summarize your findings in a paper, citing your sources.

18. **Reading, Writing.** Identify a newspaper or magazine article that deals with a possible violation of business ethics. Read the article and write a

paragraph describing the ethical principles that were potentially violated. Summarize by describing what ethical actions the workers could have taken in the same situation. *Choice*: Share your article with the class, describe the ethics violation, and summarize actions that would have been ethical.

19. **Writing.** Interview one or more persons who recently got hired in a new job. Ask questions about how they located their job, what information they put in their résumé, what education and experience they had for their job, and how they prepared for an interview. Summarize your findings in a paper. *Group option*: Work in a group with each person interviewing one recent new hire. Combine your findings and write a group paper summarizing successful strategies for getting a new job.

20. **Writing.** Interview a successful employee or business owner who is at the peak of his or her career. Ask questions about the steps in that individual's career ladder that helped him or her reach the current position. Ask if he or she had persons who served as a coach, mentor, or role model. Write a paper summarizing your interviewee's advice about working up a career ladder.

CAREER READINESS

21. **Practicing Interviewing.** Work with a partner. You will work together to research two careers, one in which you are interested and one that interests your partner. Learn about an initial job on the pathway of each career and an organization that employs workers in that job. You will take the role of a manager working for that organization who is preparing to interview your partner for the job in his or her career pathway. Your partner will prepare for that interview as a job applicant. Conduct the interview. Then reverse the roles and conduct a second interview with your partner as the manager and you as the interviewee. Write a brief report analyzing what you learned from the experience.

22. **Writing an Employee Manual.** Assume you are the owner of a small retail store that sells cell phones and other electronic equipment and has 10 employees who work different shifts so that the store has workers every day of the week from 10:00 a.m. until 9:00 p.m. You have an assistant manager. Write a brief manual for your employees that explains what kind of behavior you expect from them.

BALANCING FAMILY, CAREER, AND COMMUNITY ROLES

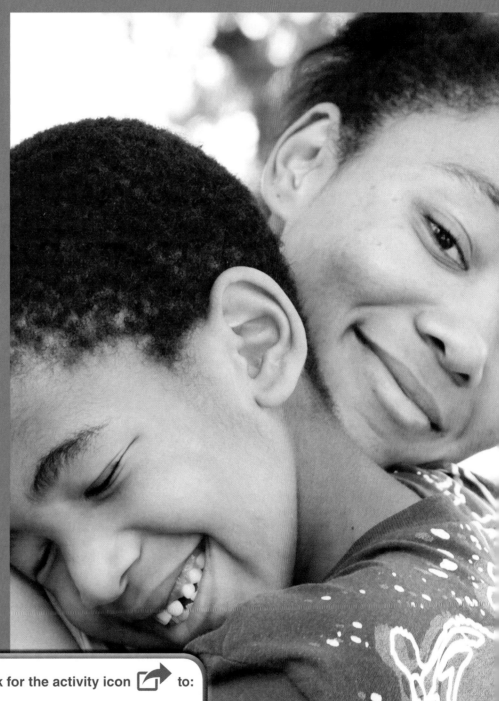

Reading Prep

Before reading the chapter, skim the headings, subheadings, and charts in each lesson. On a sheet of paper, write down three things you want to learn or skills you want to gain from reading each lesson. After you read each lesson, note what you learned under each statement.

Key Questions

Questions to answer as you study this chapter:

- How can a person balance family and career goals?
- How can a person find quality child care?
- How does being a responsible citizen benefit families?

While studying this chapter, look for the activity icon ⬆ **to:**

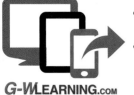

- **build** vocabulary with e-flash cards, matching activities, and vocabulary games; and
- **assess** what you learn by completing the lesson comprehension checks online.

www.g-wlearning.com/humanservices/

G-WLEARNING.com

AFTER STUDYING THIS CHAPTER, YOU WILL

KNOW:

- Factors that can affect a person's work patterns.
- The characteristics of quality child care for each age group.
- The rights and responsibilities of citizenship.

UNDERSTAND:

- How personal goals and values affect a family's work patterns.
- How employer policies can help families balance family and career goals.
- How laws protect the rights of families.

BE ABLE TO DO:

- Evaluate a source of child care for its potential for meeting the needs of a child.
- Develop a plan for managing household tasks.
- Analyze contract language for legal obligations.

GETTING STARTED

When her mother graduated from college, Rita was very proud. The whole family attended the graduation ceremony. Rita's mother looked so happy as she marched down the aisle in her cap and gown! The job she got as a result of her degree meant more money for the family to spend. They were able to take a family vacation. Now, with their mother working, Rita and her brother Jon both had extra chores to do to help the family. Each night they traded meal, cleanup, and laundry tasks. Rita didn't mind because the benefits of her mother's job made up for any extra work.

Lollie lived next door. She did not feel so positive about her mother's job. In fact, she resented it. She hated to come home after school to an empty house. She was alone until her dad arrived at 6:00 every evening. She was supposed to do homework and housework until then, but she felt too lonely to do anything. Instead, she sat and watched television to make the time pass quickly. Lollie felt like her parents were always working. She wished her parents could spend more time with her.

Decisions about balancing family and career have different effects on children, as well as on adults. In Rita's family, both parents working outside the home had a positive effect on the whole family. In Lollie's case, the same circumstances had a negative impact.

Why was there a difference? Every child is unique and may respond differently to the same situation. Also, parents are unique. They have their own personalities, so their responses to the pressures of work and family can differ. In addition, families have different resources and skills for managing those resources. Communities also have different resources available. All these factors need to be considered when families make decisions about balancing career and family roles.

CHOOSING A WORK PATTERN

Objectives

After studying this lesson, you will be able to

- **describe** various work patterns.
- **identify** factors that may affect a family's choice of work patterns.
- **explain** how employer policies can impact families.

Focus Your Reading

1. As you read this lesson, identify an example of someone you know who fits each work pattern. After reading, share your examples with a partner.
2. Contact the human resources department of a company and interview a worker there about family-friendly options for employees. Ask questions using the content terms in this lesson.

Families have many factors to consider when choosing a **work pattern**, or a system in which a person balances the activities of work life and home life over the course of adulthood. These factors include families' goals and values and their expectations for work and for parenting roles. The birth of children, employer policies that benefit the work of the family, the roles that family members take, and the earning potential of each family member also affect choices related to work patterns.

Types of Work Patterns

There are many different types of work patterns that adults can choose. Some of these patterns include career to retirement, career to family-focused, and interrupted work patterns. All of these work patterns have advantages and disadvantages.

Career to Retirement

Many adults follow a work pattern in which they start working full time after completing their education, build their career,

and then work until retirement age or longer. This pattern is *conventional*, or common to many people, and is followed by both men and women, single and married. A person's work history may be broken by periods of unemployment, changes in jobs, or various types of leave, but most people following this work pattern expect to return to the job market as soon as possible.

Throughout history, men have been expected to be wage earners so long as they are productive and healthy, and most men do choose the career-to-retirement work pattern. When women first started working outside the home, few of them chose to do so permanently. Today, however, increasing numbers of women are choosing to work from the time they finish their education until retirement.

Career to Family-Focused

Some adults follow a career-to-family-focused work pattern, in which they start work when they leave school and work until they marry or have children. This work pattern is more common with women than with men, although some men do stay home and carry out the work of the family as their main job (**Figure 21.1**). Adults who choose this work pattern tend to be very involved in raising children. They are often involved in their children's education, and some may do volunteer work in the community.

Although being a full-time *homemaker* is work, a homemaker is not classified in government statistics as a working person. The reason is that this work does not earn an income. This does not mean a homemaker's work has no value. Instead, the opposite is true. Work within and for the family includes different important tasks, including housekeeping, laundering clothing, food preparation, child care, and preschool teaching. These and other homemaker tasks command a wage when the work is done in the workplace for others.

Interrupted Work Pattern

In an **interrupted work pattern**, adults devote full-time attention to their careers after leaving school, then quit work for a period of time to carry

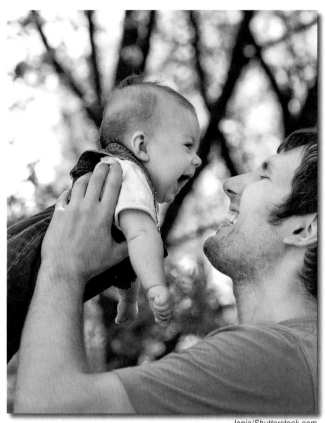

Figure 21.1 When husbands choose the career-to-family-focused work pattern, they are the primary caregivers for the family. *Why might this work pattern be less common than other options?*

out the work of the family (**Figure 21.2**). Then, at a later time, they resume their careers. Reasons vary why one spouse or the other chooses to quit work, but childrearing is the most common reason. Caring for a sick or aging parent is another common reason. In this type of situation, the person who earns the higher income may continue to work so that the other spouse does not have to. Other adults make this choice based on their values, personal desires, and role expectations. This work pattern is quite common for women and less common for men.

The length of time adults stay out of the workforce varies. Many female workers following the career-to-retirement work pattern take a maternity leave when they have a baby and then return to work. The length of a maternity leave may vary from at least 6 weeks to 12 weeks or even longer, depending on the employer. In an interrupted work pattern, parents may take time off to raise their children, waiting until they are older before

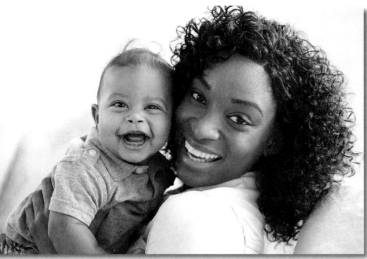

Monkey Business Images/Shutterstock.com

Figure 21.2 An interrupted work pattern is more common for women than for men.

they resume their careers. Even within that group, there are variations. Some parents go back to work when the youngest child goes to school because the children are no longer at home all day long. Others wait until the youngest child is in college.

When people following this pattern decide to return to the workforce, many find that their career plans must change. Depending on how many years they spend at home with children or sick and aging parents, they may no longer have the skills that were needed in their old jobs. Even if that is not the case, many find that they are no longer on the same career track in terms of opportunities for advancement as before. Couples considering having one parent stay at home to care for children need to examine these options before making a decision.

> ## Think About Your Reading
> What impact would it have on society if work within and for the family earned wages?

When both spouses pursue careers, this is called a **dual-career family**. Both work outside the home to earn income. Their jobs place demands on their time, energy, skills, and other resources. In addition, they are responsible for the work of the family. When dual-career families include

children, parents must make child care arrangements for the time they are at work. The home still needs to be managed, and household tasks must be done. For these families, balancing family needs and work demands can be challenging.

Factors in Choosing a Work Pattern

One work pattern may interest you more than another. One may match your expectations for the roles you will take in the future. Once you marry, however, choices about work patterns become influenced by your partner's desires as well. Couples need to share their thoughts and feelings about work patterns before they consider marriage. During the engagement period, a couple should discuss their values, goals, and views about work and child care issues, as well as their expectations for work.

When children are older, they should also be included in work-pattern decisions since they are affected by the choices made. Children may be required to do extra household chores or care for siblings if both parents work. Positive attitudes are fostered when children are involved in collaborative decision making. It helps when each person can see how the decision will benefit the whole family.

> ## Think About Your Reading
> What would the benefit be to your family if you were included in a discussion about who should fulfill which work patterns?

Values and Goals

Choices about family work patterns are influenced by what family members value and what goals they want to achieve. Most families want to meet their basic needs for food, clothing, shelter, health care, and transportation. Just meeting basic needs often requires both parents to earn incomes. Single-parent families often have incomes too low to support their families.

Balancing Family and Work

Linda and Abby sat at the table, talking with their younger sister, Wendy. They were all excited that the due date for Wendy's baby was near. "What have you decided to do about work?" asked Linda.

Before Wendy answered, Abby chimed in, "It's a hard decision to make. You can be sure of that. I really liked my job at the airport, and we needed the income, too. That's why I transferred to the night shift, so Ed and I could take turns caring for the baby. That way we were both able to keep our jobs."

Linda smiled. "That's a hard schedule to keep. I don't think I could do it. I really enjoyed staying home with Kim the first three months. Then Scott took a three-month leave from his job. After that, our childrearing leave was all used up. We were lucky to get Grace as a babysitter. She comes to our home to take care of Kim. That works great since we both are gone quite a bit. I have tried to cut down on the time that I have to travel, though. I don't like to be away from the baby so much. I wish Scott could cut back on his schedule, too."

Wendy thought about what her sisters were saying. They were raising their families differently from the way the three of them had been raised.

Wendy looked forward to staying home and being a full-time mother. Her job at the store would not allow her enough time at home to raise a family, so she decided to quit. Her husband, Bill, supported her decision and felt they could manage without her income. They wanted at least one of them to be home with the children. Bill's job was also very demanding, and he would not have much time to help her with the housework. It was a tough decision, but she was sure they had made the right one for them.

For Discussion

1. Identify the work patterns of the three sisters: Linda, Abby, and Wendy. What are their husbands' work patterns?
2. In each situation, what factors influenced the sisters' choices of work pattern?
3. For each situation, how was the choice of child care arrangements related to the child's needs? How likely is it that the child's needs were met?
4. How was each choice about child care affected by the demands of the parents' work?
5. How did work patterns affect the roles taken by the spouses?

Some people value work highly and regard it as an important part of their lives and identities. They like the opportunities for growth, creativity, or self-expression their work provides. They appreciate the social stimulation or the mental challenges they receive at work (**Figure 21.3**). They enjoy opportunities to benefit others through their work. Others place a very high value on being a full-time parent, and they make work choices that help them focus on that role.

The Arrival of Children

The arrival of children significantly affects a family's work patterns. The responsibility of caring for children puts demands on parents that must be met in some way. Some families choose to have one parent consistently care for the young children. Other families adjust their work schedules so parents can take turns being home with the children. Many families access child care in or outside the home to balance the demands of both work and family.

The availability of good child care alternatives may affect a couple's choice of work patterns. If a family cannot find satisfactory child care during the hours it is needed, the demands of family and work are difficult to balance. Sometimes a parent will choose to provide child care for his or her own children as well as for others. In this way, families care for their children while earning extra income.

The arrival of children can impact a parent who continues working outside the home as well. Caring for children when they are sick, taking them to appointments, or attending special events at school all take time away from work. This can impact an employee's productivity and affect the workplace.

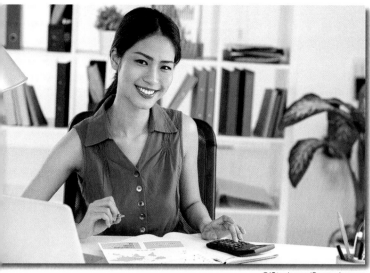

Figure 21.3 Work can be a fulfilling and stimulating experience for some people. *What do you think determines whether work is stimulating for a person?*

©iStock.com/DragonImages

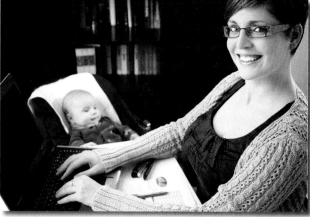

c12/Shutterstock.com

Figure 21.4 Company policies which allow some flexible scheduling can benefit families trying to balance career and family roles. *Are there some careers more suited to flexible scheduling than others?*

On the other hand, when the needs of the family are met, employees will find it easier to focus on their jobs. Thus, both employers and families benefit when workplace policies support families.

Employer Policies and Trends

Employer policies and trends have a direct effect on a family's options for balancing career and family. Most workplaces have fairly rigid schedules—generally eight-hour workdays, five days a week. When schedules are rigid, workers must work at the time and place specified by the employer. With such schedules, a worker may need to request special leave to take care of some family responsibilities, such as doctor's or dentist's appointments. Company policies that allow personal leave without *penalizing* (inflicting disadvantage on) the employee's work record are helpful to the family. Some employers have other policies that support employee efforts to care for their families, which help workers meet both family and work demands.

Some companies offer **flexible scheduling**, which allows workers to choose the hours they work, within reason (**Figure 21.4**). For example, some employers require employees to be at their worksites during core periods, such as 10:00 a.m. to 12:00 p.m., Monday through Thursday. Then

employees do the rest of their work at whatever hours suit them. Technology has affected career options available to family members. For some jobs, employees are allowed to work from home part of the time, using a digital device and the Internet to complete work and to connect with coworkers. Such flexibility can help families adjust their schedules so one parent is available to care for children and meet various needs that arise, or take time to attend special school events.

Job sharing is another alternative to a rigid 40-hour workweek. With this work arrangement, two people split a full-time job. This arrangement makes more part-time work available to those who want it. Job sharing offers a parent the income benefits of working while allowing more time for parenting and household tasks. Of course, each worker earns less income than he or she would from a full-time job.

Some employers even make child care services available to employees with **employer-sponsored child care**. They may also have special arrangements when children of employees are ill. These services are extremely helpful because many child care centers do not allow sick children to attend.

Parental leave is an employee benefit that permits parents to be away from work while involved in full-time parenting for a specified period. Parental leaves may be paid or unpaid, depending on the employer's policies. *Maternity leave* is when a mother is away from her job to give birth

and recover. *Paternity leave* is the period when a father is away from his job immediately following the birth of his child. *Adoption leave* refers to time allowed away from a job when parents adopt a child. A **childrearing leave** is a longer period of time that a parent may be absent from work to provide full-time care for a young child.

Think About Your Reading

Which family-friendly work policies do you think are most essential for an employer to have?

The Family and Medical Leave Act

Government policies, such as the Family and Medical Leave Act, sometimes influence employer policies. The *Family and Medical Leave Act* helps parents balance work and family responsibilities. Its mandates apply to employers with 50 or more workers, so not all employees are covered. This law allows workers to take up to 12 weeks of unpaid leave in any 12-month period without the leave impacting their employment status or group health insurance coverage. Leave can be taken for any of the following reasons:

- having and caring for a baby
- adopting a child or adding a foster child to the family
- caring for a sick child, spouse, or parent
- being unable to work because of serious illness

Roles of Family Members

The roles that spouses take can affect their choices about work patterns. One spouse may be the main wage earner; the other may work part time and carry most of the roles that go with the work of the family—cleaning, making meals, shopping, and doing laundry.

Some families expect the husband and wife to have equal roles as wage earners. Their incomes are considered to be equally important to the family. In these couples, other roles of homemaking and providing child care are also shared equally (**Figure 21.5**).

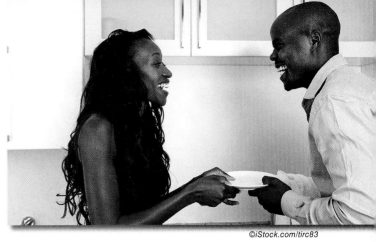
©iStock.com/tirc83

Figure 21.5 When both spouses fulfill roles as wage earners, they typically share homemaking and child care responsibilities.

Earning Potential

In many families, the potential income of each spouse is a major factor in choices about work. For instance, dual-income families have a higher amount of taxable income than they would if only one spouse worked. Therefore, they are taxed at a higher rate. Paying more income tax reduces some of the benefit gained from having a second income. The cost of child care also reduces the amount of money a second worker actually adds to the family income. Sometimes families decide that the amount of money left over after taxes and extra expenses is not enough to merit having both spouses work. The family may not benefit from trying to balance the extra demands on time and energy when both spouses work. For other families, the extra income is needed for family expenses, even if the addition is small.

LESSON 21.1

Assess

COMPREHENSION CHECK

1. Describe how family life impacts workplace productivity.
2. Explain the term *dual-career family*.
3. List five factors that may affect a family's choice of work patterns.
4. Identify employment practices and trends that support families.
5. For what four reasons may a person take a work leave under the Family and Medical Leave Act?
6. Explain how technology could impact a person's choice of work patterns.

Content Terms

Build Vocab

nanny
family child care
group child care
cooperative child care
latchkey children

Academic Terms

regulation
foremost

Objectives

After studying this lesson, you will be able to

- **explain** how families can manage multiple roles.
- **describe** various substitute child care arrangements.
- **evaluate** child care services for age-appropriate child care.

Focus Your Reading

1. Use a graphic organizer to identify key points and supporting ideas that would help a person identify quality child care for the family.
2. Interview a child care provider who fits one of the categories that is a content term. Write a summary of the characteristics of the care offered in that setting and share it with a partner or the whole class.

Healthy families are made of members who show love, affection, and appreciation for each other. They spend time together as companions. They are committed to each other, offering support and encouragement. They use good communication skills to express thoughts, share feelings, listen, and solve problems. They work together to build strong family relationships. The goal of healthy family living requires each family member to use many personal resources in meeting these needs.

Work also places a demand on these resources, however. Work requires time and effort and draws on physical, mental, social, and emotional resources. These resources are limited. Family members must find a way to balance this combination of demands on their resources.

Identifying Resources

Managing multiple roles requires planning. People need to plan the use of their resources to carry out the responsibilities of these various roles. First, family members need to identify all

the resources they have to help them meet their needs. That includes resources inside the family, such as the time, energy, and skills of each member. It may include resources outside the family as well. Substitute child care, housekeeping services, or laundry services may be necessary to handle the jobs that family members cannot do. Second, families must manage their resources to meet the needs of all family members. This management task requires flexibility in roles, sensitivity to each other, and cooperation (**Figure 21.6**).

Outside resources and management skills become very important for a single parent trying to balance family and work. Good child care at a low cost is a necessity, but it is not always available. Assistance from family and friends can help the single parent manage the home. Within single-parent families, older children often carry a major part of the responsibility for housekeeping tasks and child care.

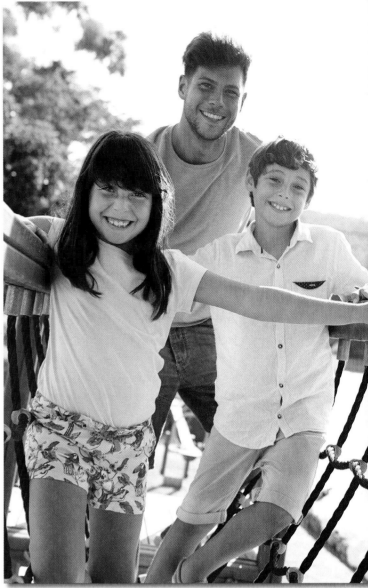

©iStock.com/monkeybusinessimages

Figure 21.6 Family success in managing multiple roles requires family members to be flexible and sensitive to each other. *What are some signs that family members are succeeding at managing their roles? What are some signs that they are not succeeding?*

Think About Your Reading

What could families do if they always found themselves lacking resources needed to meet all the needs of the family?

Exploring Substitute Child Care Options

The decision to go to work when children are young is often a difficult choice for parents. They recognize the importance of a main caregiver in the young child's life and want to fulfill this role. Sometimes one parent will choose to postpone his or her career plans until the child is older. Some adjust their schedules so that one parent provides care while the other is working. Some are even able to take the child to work with them. For many families, though, such options will not work. Instead, they must rely on resources outside the immediate family to meet child care needs.

Finding a quality caregiver who is able to stimulate a child's growth and development and provide a nurturing environment is important to parents. Even when parents do find such a

caregiver, parents also need to give the child love, affection, and guidance when they are with him or her. They need to take time to talk with their child, do activities together, and be a role model. When parents and caregivers work together to provide the best care possible, a child's growth and development usually benefit.

A variety of child care arrangements are available in each community. These might include care in the child's home or in the home of a caregiver.

Child care can also be provided in group settings, such as child care centers. Whatever arrangements are considered, the family must carefully decide what is best for their child.

Child Care in the Child's Home

Sometimes child care is provided in the child's own home, often by a grandparent or other relative (**Figure 21.7**). One benefit of this arrangement is that relatives usually have a personal interest in, love for, and attachment to the child. Their previous contact with the child can reduce feelings of insecurity that the child, especially an infant or toddler, might feel in being cared for by someone other than the parent. Also, relatives often have childrearing viewpoints similar to those of the parents. For these reasons, relatives or close friends are often relied upon to provide child care for infants and toddlers. For older children, parents may consider group care. Another benefit of a relative providing child care is that relatives usually do so for free.

Sometimes families obtain the service of a **nanny**. A nanny is a person who comes into the child's home to provide child care as a paying job. A live-in nanny actually stays at the child's home. This child care service has many benefits for

parents who work long hours, travel away from home, or work irregular schedules. The nanny can provide consistent care and often becomes attached to the whole family. The cost of hiring a nanny, however, is often too high for most families.

Think About Your Reading

What could be the advantages and the disadvantages of having child care in the child's home?

Family Child Care

Sometimes child care is offered in a caregiver's home. This is called **family child care**. Children have the benefit of a homelike setting. In addition, if the person is providing care to more than one child, children have opportunities to play with other children. The group of children should be small, especially if the children are younger. Another benefit of this arrangement is that children from the same family can be together, even though they are different ages. Family child care may also offer flexible hours, which is an advantage to parents who work irregular hours.

Most states have regulations for family child care. Licensing agencies check that a caregiver is following the rules about the number of children permitted and meets standards regarding safety, nutrition, and activities. Parents should question whether a family child care program is registered or licensed. They should also inquire about the nutritional program, scheduled activities, and liability insurance in case of an accident. Before enrolling a child, they should also ask for references from other parents who use or have used the service and talk to some of those parents about their evaluation of the caregiver.

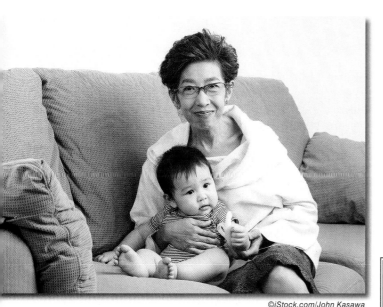

©iStock.com/John Kasawa

Figure 21.7 Leaving a child with a close family member can help reduce everyone's anxiety over the separation. *What strategies can parents use to help a young child adjust to a new environment?*

Think About Your Reading

What could parents do to learn about the quality of care in a family child care program if they are new to the community?

Copyright Goodheart-Willcox Co., Inc.

Child Care Centers

Care for a fairly large number of children is provided in **group child care** centers. Children in these settings have the benefit of interacting with others the same age. In addition, child care centers usually offer educational programs with activities for children in each age group (**Figure 21.8**). Another advantage is that these centers have facilities and equipment that are varied and appropriate for children of all ages. Such centers are usually open during daytime hours.

Child care centers are licensed by state agencies. They must meet minimum standards for space, nutrition programs, activity programs, group size, and staff. Special facilities must be available for infant and toddler programs. Certain *regulations*, or rules, apply to public programs funded by government agencies as well as to private programs.

Cooperative child care centers are organized, managed, and funded by the parents who use the center. Usually the center has a board of parents who handle administrative tasks. Teachers and caregivers are hired to work at the center. Sometimes parents donate services to keep the costs down. Profits from the service are channeled back into the center.

As discussed in Lesson 21.1, some employers provide child care for their employees. Often the child care facility is in or near the worksite, so workers can spend breaks and lunch hours with their children (**Figure 21.9**). These employer-sponsored centers are more likely to have care hours that match the various work hours of employees. Also, this child care alternative is usually lower in

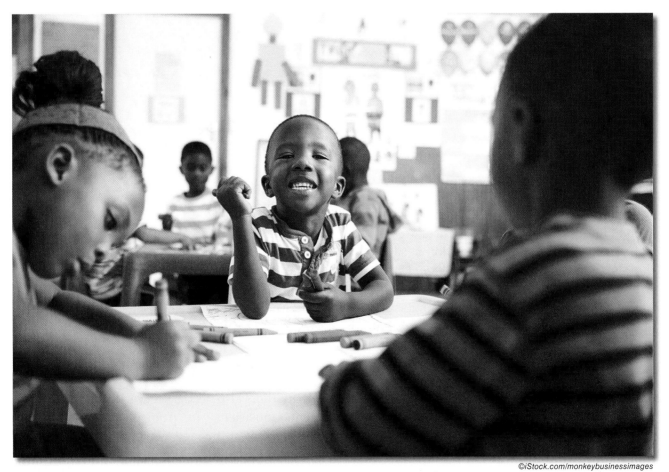

©iStock.com/monkeybusinessimages

Figure 21.8 In a child care center, children benefit from interacting with other children and participating in educational activities.

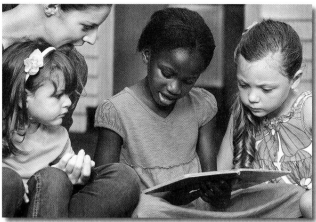
Robert Kneschke/Shutterstock.com

Figure 21.9 Parents can easily pick up and drop off their children if an employer-sponsored child care facility is located in the worksite. *How do before- and after-school programs meet similar needs?*

cost to the family since the employer sponsors the program as an employee benefit.

Think About Your Reading

Why might involvement in a cooperative child care center be difficult for most working parents?

Choosing a Child Care Program

All children need consistent and loving care, both at home and away from home. Parents need to help children make the transition between the two as smoothly as possible. The goal for families and caregivers is to help the child continue to grow and develop in both environments. Choices about child care need to be based on the following:

- needs of the child
- services available
- parents' work schedules
- family budget

The best way to evaluate a child care program is to visit the home or center. Observe the staff and the children and evaluate the space and the equipment. Ask for a description of the program and the types of activities offered. The center should provide a warm, nurturing, child-centered environment.

Specific needs for child care will depend on a child's age and developmental stage. Young infants, toddlers, preschool children, and elementary-age children need child care with unique qualities. The needs of the young infant and toddler are the most difficult to meet in child care arrangements.

Child Care for Infants

Infants need to develop feelings of trust and security in their environment away from home. Adjustment to a caregiver could first be made in the infant's home with a parent present. If that is not possible, the parent should spend time with the infant in the new environment. New sights, sounds, and smells should be added slowly to the infant's environment, preferably with the parent present to make it easier for the infant to adjust.

With infants, caregivers must enjoy holding, cuddling, and talking to the child while they provide care. They need to be relaxed and able to spend time nurturing as well as caring for the infant's physical needs. Consistency in the infant's caregiver is important. Parents often choose an extended family member, neighbor, friend, or nanny to care for infants, but if these are not options, consistency in the person providing the care is important in a group setting.

Think About Your Reading

What actions can parents take to help infants develop a strong attachment for their caregivers?

Child Care for Toddlers

Toddlers also need a secure, intimate environment. Consistent care from one main caregiver is important at this age as well. Parents can help their toddler adjust to a new caregiver by spending time with the child in the care setting. Leaving a small personal item that belongs to the parent at the child care setting can also increase the

toddler's feelings of security. The item becomes a visual reminder that the parents will return.

In addition to needs for security, a toddler needs to explore the environment and move about. The needs of toddlers can make child care challenging. Caregivers must understand the toddler's need for nurturing one minute and exploring the next. This takes both patience and flexibility on the part of the caregiver.

Child Care for Preschoolers

Preschoolers—children between three and five years of age—need a greater variety of experiences with both people and objects. They need more opportunities to explore their environment. They need larger spaces to exercise their large muscles. Opportunities to play with other children are important for children in this age group.

They enjoy play companions and develop close friendships at this age (**Figure 21.10**). They are able to feel more secure away from their parents. This opens up more opportunities for child care arrangements.

Child Care in the Elementary Years

Once children start school, parents are responsible for fewer hours of the children's days. They still are responsible, however, for how the children spend their time after school.

Sometimes children participate in school-sponsored activities directly after the school day. If not, they need someone to whom they are accountable after school. Some families arrange for their child to go to the home of a neighbor, grandparent, or family friend. Others make arrangements for a neighbor or grandparent to

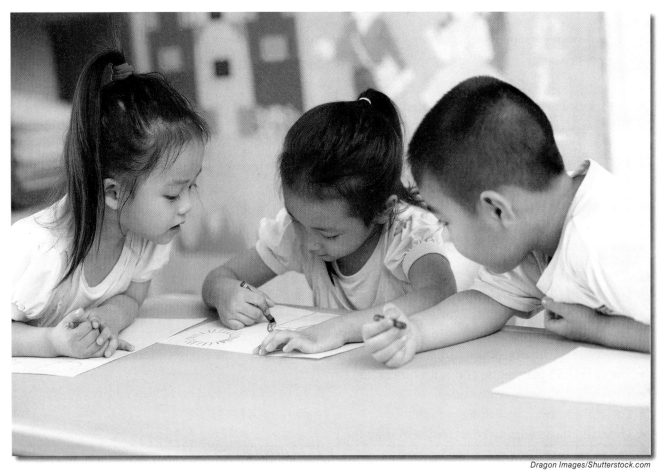

Dragon Images/Shutterstock.com

Figure 21.10 Preschool children enjoy opportunities to play with their peers in a child care setting. *How can this setting help prepare children for the school years?*

check on the child shortly after the child gets home. This may be done with a telephone call or visit. Some have their children go to after-school care programs, which may be run in the school itself or in a separate location.

Latchkey children are children who regularly go home after school to empty homes without adult supervision. They are often alone until a parent returns from work. Loneliness and boredom are common problems for the child who is home alone. Worry and fear that the parents will not come home on time is another. The way the child spends this time of day should be planned. Parents and the child can discuss activities that are appropriate for the child to engage in and how much time is suitable for each one. Whatever the activities planned—homework, special hobbies, or household tasks—a method of checking the child's progress should be developed. This helps the child to be accountable for time and it helps parents set guidelines for the child's activities.

If children go to a child care center or family child care after school, parents should inquire about the activities offered. Elementary-age children need activities appropriate for their age. Some public schools are addressing the problem of latchkey children by offering supervised activities in a relaxed atmosphere in an after-school program.

Think About Your Reading

What could be the advantages and disadvantages of having before- and after-school care provided by your school?

Meeting the Needs of Parents

Finding substitute child care that meets both the child's and parents' needs can be a challenge (**Figure 21.11**). Several factors, such as cost,

Child Care Services
Parents' Needs
• The service is available when needed.
• The service is easy to reach from home or work.
• The service is within the parents' budget.
• The caregiver has a childrearing philosophy similar to the parents'.
• The caregiver is competent.
• The caregiver is willing to talk about the child's progress regularly.
• The caregiver shows love and affection for the child.
• The caregiver appears relaxed and free of anxiety.
Children's Needs
• The child is happy and comfortable with the caregiver.
• The child feels loved by the caregiver.
• The child is developing self-care skills.
• The child is learning about himself or herself, other people, and the environment.
• The child can play alone and with others, too.
• The child has positive attitudes.
• The child knows the limits for behavior.
• The child has a variety of activities to keep busy.

Figure 21.11 Child care services should meet both parents' and children's needs. *Why is it often difficult to find desirable child care services?*

available hours, location, and the quality of the caregivers, must be considered. Finding a caregiver who provides quality care at a cost the parents can afford is probably the *foremost* (greatest) need that working parents face.

Managing Household Tasks

An organized home does not happen automatically. Achieving that goal requires everyone working to the degree that each is capable. The keys to managing household roles are flexibility and cooperation. Family members need to be flexible, because needs and resources change, sometimes daily. They also need to cooperate and work together to determine what tasks to address and how to accomplish them.

Problems develop when one person tries to handle too many tasks. Then, all tasks probably do not get done, and the person becomes exhausted trying. This often is the dilemma faced by the heads of single-parent families who do not have other adults with whom to share work and family demands. Task overload can be avoided by developing a family schedule, prioritizing tasks, and following a home-management plan.

Develop a Family Schedule

Families can work collaboratively to meet their needs by developing a family schedule. It can help to hold weekly family meetings to create this schedule. Each person in the family can put on the calendar all the extra activities that he or she plans. Then the family can review the calendar to see if any one person's plans are taking too many resources. If the demand is too great, family members must make choices. Sometimes, activities will need to be limited to those most preferred or necessary. Looking at the calendar together will also reveal if two or more events conflict and give the family a chance to see how to resolve the situation.

Think About Your Reading
How do families get into the position of having too many activities to attend?

Prioritize Tasks

Another home-management technique is to separate the important tasks that must be done from those less important. The important daily tasks, such as preparing meals, doing dishes, or picking children up from school, can be written on a primary list. Then family members can divide these tasks according to their schedules (**Figure 21.12**). Following such a plan helps make sure that necessary work gets done.

In this system, the family prepares a second list for less important tasks. These are tasks that need to be done, but may be less urgent. For instance, doing laundry and vacuuming are often tasks that can be rescheduled for another day.

Make and Follow a Plan

After tasks are listed, the family should establish a plan for completing them. Each family member may be assigned certain tasks. Another approach is to set a certain time aside, such as between 9:00 and 11:00 on Saturday mornings, for everyone to work together until all tasks are completed. Another approach is to set up a 10-minute

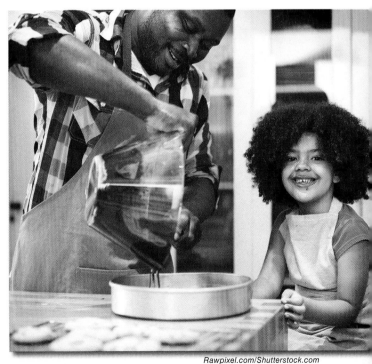

Rawpixel.com/Shutterstock.com

Figure 21.12 Work responsibilities for the family should be shared by all capable members. *What tasks of caring for the family are shared most often?*

period each evening to pick up personal items before going to bed. Such techniques help to put a plan into practice and keep the responsibilities for housework shared among all family members.

Think About Your Reading

What plan does your family have to make sure the work of the family is distributed evenly to all family members?

Use Technology to Manage the Home

Families can take advantage of many electronic devices, appliances, and gadgets to make fulfilling family roles easier. Technology, such as cell phones, has improved families' abilities to communicate, no matter what the family's schedule is or where members are. Technology will continue to change. Some new products will help families reach their goals. Some will add challenges for families to manage (**Figure 21.13**). All new products come with a price. Family meetings can provide a good time for members to weigh the costs and the benefits of new products to ensure balance between the family's needs and resources.

Think About Your Reading

What new technologies make the work of the family easier? Which ones add responsibilities for the family to manage?

LESSON 21.2

Assess

COMPREHENSION CHECK

1. Explain why family and work roles need to be managed.
2. List the types of substitute child care available and describe the characteristics of each.
3. List the characteristics of preschoolers that make finding substitute child care easier at this age.
4. Name three resources that working parents may use to care for elementary-age children after school.
5. List three common responses of latchkey children who are home alone after school.
6. What are two keys to managing household tasks successfully in a changing family?
7. What are three activities that families can use to help manage household tasks?

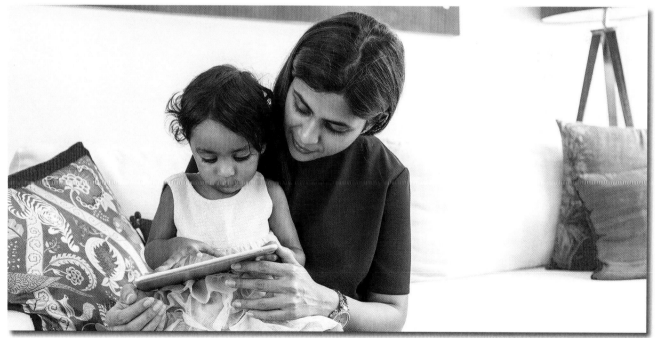

leungchopan/Shutterstock.com

Figure 21.13 Technology, such as electronic games and programs for children, can both benefit families and cause challenges. *What benefits and challenges are associated with technologies for children?*

Objectives

After studying this lesson, you will be able to

- **identify** the roles and responsibilities of citizens in a community.
- **describe** the functions of law within a society.
- **explain** the need for taxes at various levels of government.
- **relate** environmentally safe practices and volunteering to citizenship.

Focus Your Reading

1. Create two columns with the headings *Citizen Rights* and *Citizen Responsibilities*. As you read the lesson, summarize key ideas under the appropriate heading.
2. Identify where you would vote in your community and find out what you would need to do to register to vote.

Content Terms

Build Vocab

citizen
register
legislature
ordinance
felony
misdemeanor
violation
contract
tort
volunteer

Academic Terms

elect
federal

The community you live in can help you manage multiple roles in your career and family. Your community offers resources to help families reach their goals. These resources are paid for through various forms of taxation and monitored through laws and court systems. Decisions about how communities use resources are made by persons who are *elected* (chosen for office) by citizens in the communities where they live. A **citizen** is a person who formally owes allegiance to a government. By connecting with others in your community and participating as a citizen, you can make a difference in the way your community and the larger society functions.

Your Role as a Citizen

Citizens have both rights and responsibilities. The laws of the government protect your rights. You also have the responsibility to obey these laws. Citizens have the right to be informed about laws that are being considered. They have the right to provide input

into decisions made by local, state, and federal governments. This input is usually demonstrated through voting, when citizens indicate whom they want to hold a government office. Writing letters to officials in charge can be another effective way to influence government decisions.

Citizens also have the responsibility to pay taxes. Taxes are used by the local, state, and federal governments to provide a variety of public services. Some examples include fire and police protection, education, and highway construction and maintenance. As a citizen, you also have the responsibility to stay involved in your community and help improve your community by volunteering and caring for the environment.

Your Voting Rights

The right to vote is one of the most basic and important rights of a U.S. citizen. Voting allows you to express your opinions on public issues. Often this is done by voting for a person who has views similar to yours. When you vote for someone, you are saying, "I choose this person to represent me in government."

Voting enables you to elect leaders at all three levels of government—local, state, and federal. The power of your vote makes it important to be informed about candidates running for any government office. Compare their views with your own and then make an informed decision about whom you want to represent you (**Figure 21.14**).

Registering to Vote

At age 18, you are eligible to vote, but in order to vote, you must register. When you **register**, you are placing your name on the list of citizens who can vote in elections. To register, you must be a citizen of the United States. You must also meet a residency requirement. This means you must have lived for at least 30 days in the state and county where you register.

Just before a major election, registration booths are often set up in high-traffic areas to encourage citizens to register and to speed the process. At other times, you can register to vote at the government office of the county commissioner, municipal clerk, or election supervisor.

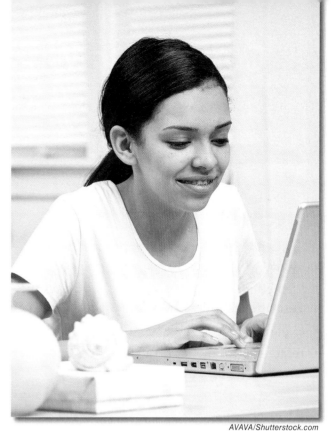
AVAVA/Shutterstock.com
Figure 21.14 Researching candidates is an important step in making an informed voting decision. *What resources are available to help you learn about various candidates' positions during an election?*

Some states also register voters at driver's license facilities. Voter registration forms are available on most state websites.

On election day, you go to the local site chosen for voting. Election officials at the site will check if you have registered. If your name is on the list of registered voters, you will be allowed to vote.

Think About Your Reading
Why is it important to become involved in voting?

Levels of Government and Their Laws

Laws are written and enforced so that people in the country can live in harmony. Laws are designed to protect the rights and safety of individuals as well as to benefit society as a whole. The government bodies that make laws are called **legislatures** at the federal and state levels. You can

contribute your input into these laws through voting in state and national elections, and through communicating with your representatives in the government. Laws are carried out and enforced by the *executive branch* of government. A city's mayor, a state's governor, and the nation's president are all officials of the executive branch.

Federal Laws

The U.S. Congress is the legislature that makes federal laws. *Federal* laws apply to an entire nation—in this case, the United States. For instance, there are federal laws against spying, airplane hijacking, mail fraud, and other crimes affecting more than one state. Other federal laws apply to military service, to protecting the civil rights of U.S. citizens, and to the collection and use of federal tax money.

State Laws

Each state's legislature makes laws that apply to that state and its residents. Some examples include laws against robbery, drunken driving, murder, and shoplifting. Other areas of state law include laws about the use of state funds, state highways, motor vehicle registration, and traffic (**Figure 21.15**). Laws relating to family life, such as marriage and divorce laws, are also made at the state level.

Local Laws

Local laws are usually called *regulations* or **ordinances**. These are made by local legislatures such as city, town, or county councils or boards. Zoning regulations, building codes, and curfews for minors are a few examples of local laws.

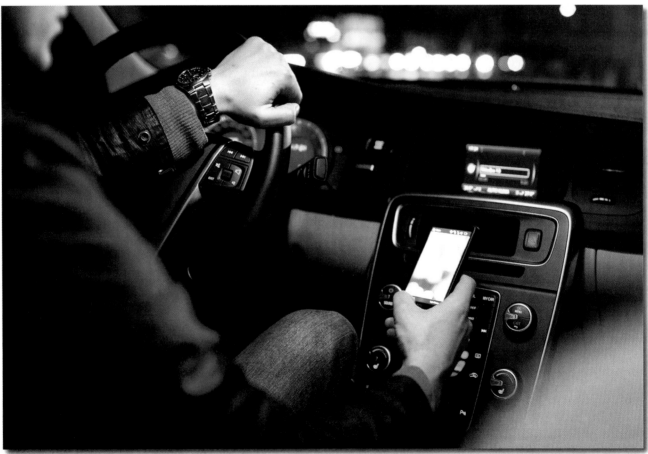

lightpoet/Shutterstock.com

Figure 21.15 Laws against texting and driving at the same time are an example of state laws. *Why is it important that people obey local, state, and federal laws?*

Constitutional Laws

Constitutional laws refer to the basic laws of a nation. In the United States, constitutional laws are based on the U.S. Constitution and the constitutions of the states. *Constitutions,* as they are written by the government, are documents that set out the basic rights all citizens possess and the structure and powers of government. Laws passed by a legislature cannot go against the principles set out in constitutions. If individuals think a law does violate a constitution, they can challenge that law in court. Judges hear arguments on both sides and issue a decision. If the judges agree with the claim, they declare the law *unconstitutional*, which means the law cannot be enforced.

Think About Your Reading
How does having constitutional law benefit individuals at the local level?

Public Laws

Federal and state legislatures make two types of laws: public laws and civil laws. The laws that govern a person's rights relative to the government are called *public laws.* These laws affect society as a whole, whether the entire community, state, or nation. Some public laws identify actions that are crimes. These criminal laws also set the punishment society gives to those who break the law. Crimes are classified into three types based on their seriousness:

- *Felonies.* A **felony** crime is considered most serious and can result in a sentence of more than a year in prison or even death. Some examples of felonies include murder, rape, kidnapping, armed robbery, arson, and sale of illegal drugs.

- *Misdemeanors.* A **misdemeanor** is a less serious crime, such as speeding or disorderly conduct. Such crimes may be punished by a fine or a short prison term of less than a year.

- *Violations.* A **violation** (sometimes called a *petty offense*) is an act that violates or breaks a local ordinance. For instance, failing to clear the snow off the sidewalk or littering may be violations in some towns. Punishments for violations are not severe. Examples are a fine or a short jail term.

Think About Your Reading
In what ways do public laws benefit citizens?

Civil Laws

Civil laws govern your rights in relation to other people. Issues such as divorce, child custody, inheritances, and personal injury are all covered by civil law. Most civil laws fall into two groups: contract laws and torts. Contract laws cover agreements that people make with each other. Torts refer to wrongdoings against another person.

Contract Laws

A **contract** is a mutual agreement between two consenting people. You may think of contracts as something that only big businesses are involved in, but there are many situations in life where you will have to sign a contract. For instance, you usually have to sign a service contract when you purchase cellular phone service. A bank requires you to sign a contract to take out a loan to buy a car or a house. Understanding your rights and responsibilities according to the terms of a contract is important.

A contract must meet several conditions for it to be legal and binding:

- *Both parties must sign the contract agreement willingly.* That is, one party cannot force the other party to sign it.

- *Both parties must be competent.* This means both parties must be able to understand the terms of the contract and the consequences of accepting those terms (**Figure 21.16**). State laws define who is considered legally competent. In most states, you must be at least 18 years old to be legally bound by a written contract. To make a contract involving a minor (a person under age 18) valid, a parent

Cellular Service Agreement

Customer Information

Name   Reginald Hall

Address   456 Chayes Court, Unit 210

City, State, Zip   Chicago, IL 60645

Service Information

Mobile #   (321) 456-7891

Plan   Individual Nationwide   Minutes Included   600

Term   24 months

Monthly Fee $59.99

Customer Acceptance

By signing this service agreement, I acknowledge and agree that:

- I am of legal age (at least 18 years old).
- I have read and understand the terms and conditions.
- I give permission to obtain information about my credit history.

Signature   *Reginald Hall*   Date   04/05/20XX

Terms and Conditions

1. Your service begins when you accept by signing this agreement. There is a $40 activation fee for each mobile phone.
2. If you terminate your service before the end of your term, you will be charged an early termination fee of $150.
3. If you cancel your service within 10 days of signing a service agreement, you will not be charged an early termination fee. You will be responsible for paying for all charges, fees, and taxes incurred through the date of cancellation.
4. We can change the terms of this agreement at any time. If we make any changes, we will provide you with 30 days' notice. You may terminate service without paying an early termination fee, provided you notify us within 30 days of receiving the notice. By failing to terminate within 30 days, you accept the changes.
5. You will receive a bill summarizing your charges each month. If we do not receive payment in full by the due date, you will be charged a late fee of $6 a month. If we need to use a collection agency to collect payment, you agree to pay any collection agency fees incurred.

Figure 21.16   Be sure you understand all of the terms and conditions before signing a contract. *What contracts have you or your parents signed in the past?*

or another adult must cosign it. Then the adult would be held responsible for the terms of the contract. Minors who lie about their ages and sign a contract are legally bound to the contract.

- **Both parties must give consideration.** *Consideration* means giving up something to obtain something else. For instance, a renter

gives money in the form of monthly rent to obtain a place to live, which is what the landlord gives.

- **A valid contract must relate to a legal activity.** For instance, a contract between two parties asking one party to commit a theft or a murder is not valid or legally binding.

Once you sign a contract, you are legally responsible to abide by it, even if you did not read it or understand it (**Figure 21.17**). Before you sign your name, carefully read all parts of the contract. Be sure you understand all the terms. Ask for explanations of anything that seems unclear. Keep a copy of the signed contract for your own records.

Think About Your Reading

What are some common contracts that you may sign in your lifetime?

Torts

A wrongful act committed against another person is called a **tort**. Some examples include injuries to another person's body, emotional well-being, reputation, property, or business. Another wrongdoing that is considered a tort is fraud. *Fraud* is intentional trickery, lies, or misrepresentation to make a person give up a right or something of value.

Taxes

Citizens enjoy many services paid for, in part, by local, state, or federal government funds. The money to pay for them is obtained through the taxes that these governments collect. U.S. government funds are used to help pay for the following programs and services:

- public schools, community colleges, state universities, and other educational programs
- social services and welfare programs
- public health care facilities and services
- police and fire protection and emergency services
- unemployment and job services

Government funds provide many other types of programs and services as well. Four different types of taxes help the U.S. government raise funds. These are income-based, employer-paid, sales, and property taxes.

Income-based taxes are withheld from, or taken out of, your paycheck. The federal government collects a personal income tax from wage earners. Many, though not all, states and some cities have income taxes as well. Income taxes are used to pay for many state and federal programs and services. The funds are also used for Social Security and Medicare, which provide income and medical benefits to older retired citizens. Early in the year, wage earners must file a tax form, state their income, and calculate the total tax they should have paid. If more than that amount was withheld from their pay during the year, they get a refund. If less than the amount owed was withheld, they have to pay the difference.

Employer-paid taxes are paid by employers on the employees' behalf. Employer-paid taxes are used for unemployment benefits. Also, employers pay taxes that go into Social Security and Medicare funds, just as workers do.

Contract Tips

Before you sign a contract:

- Be sure you understand all the terms of the contract. If you need help, ask for a copy of the contract and take it to a lawyer or consumer-help agency. Have them explain the terms of the contract in language you understand.
- Never sign a contract that has blank spaces in it. Either have the blanks filled in or cross them out.
- Be sure all verbal promises are included in writing on the contract.
- If any changes are made to the written contract, make sure that both you and the other person write your initials next to the change.
- Be sure the total amount of money you have to pay and the amount of monthly payments are clearly stated.

After you sign a contract:

- Always get a copy of the contract after it is signed by both parties. Keep it with your other important records.

Figure 21.17 A contract is a legally binding document. *How could following these tips protect an individual?*

Sales taxes are added to the value of purchases that consumers make. They are used by state and local governments to raise money to pay for the services they provide. The rate of sales tax will vary from one state to another. The rate may also vary within a state, as some counties and cities add their own sales taxes (**Figure 21.18**). What items are taxable may also vary from state to state. For instance, some states do not tax necessities like food, clothing, and medicines.

Property taxes are usually collected by local governments and provide funds for education and other services. The amount of property tax a property owner must pay is determined by two factors: the taxation rate in the area and the assessed value of the property. Government officials estimate the value of property.

Paying taxes is one way to be a responsible citizen. It enables you to support programs that benefit you, others in the community, and the country as a whole.

Think About Your Reading

What items are taxed a sales tax in your county?

Citizen Involvement

Voting and paying taxes are not the only ways that citizens get involved in government. You can take a number of steps to be an involved citizen:

- *Check in your local newspaper or online to see when local government meetings are scheduled.* These may be school board, county board, or city council meetings. These meetings usually have periods of time open to public comment when citizens can speak out on issues the government body is discussing or those that citizens want them to discuss.

- *Attend area meetings held by state representatives.* Members of the state

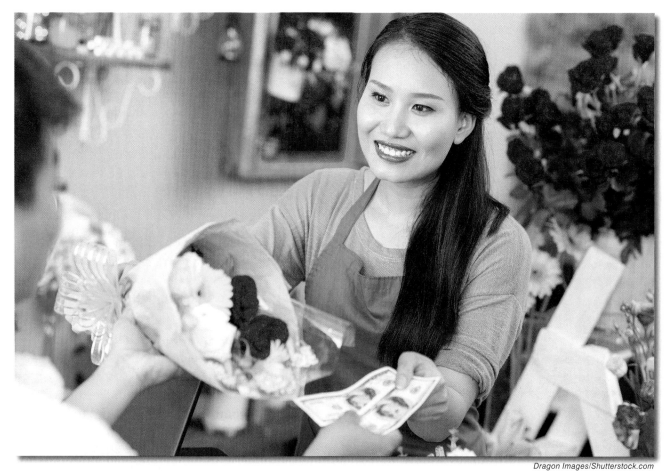

Dragon Images/Shutterstock.com

Figure 21.18 Sales taxes are typically added to your total in store when you purchase goods or services.

legislature often come back to their districts to meet with the people they represent. These meetings are often advertised online, in mail flyers, or through the local newspaper. By attending these meetings, you can become informed about issues being considered at the state level.

- *Write letters stating your opinions.* You can write letters to the editor of the local newspaper. Contact members of your local government on local issues. Let school board members know your views on school issues, for instance. Send letters or e-mails to your representative in the state legislature or in the U.S. Congress (**Figure 21.19**). Use social media to share your point of view. You may be only one voice, but as one with many others, you can have a powerful impact.

- *Practice critical thinking.* Analyzing your own thinking, as well as the ideas of others, can help you identify false assumptions in various points of view. Critical thinking requires listening to others' perspectives in order to identify what assumptions a person may have that are not accurate. People have different life experiences and have seen different outcomes from various decisions.

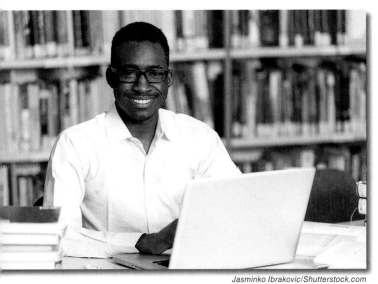

Jasminko Ibrakovic/Shutterstock.com

Figure 21.19 You can let those in government positions know your opinion by writing letters or e-mails. *What tone do you think you should take when writing a message to a government official?*

Sharing your experience and your analysis can help others in leadership make better decisions.

- *Run for a leadership position in your community.* At times, you may identify skills and knowledge you possess that you believe could benefit your community. You may have a desire to participate in leadership decisions. In some settings, that means running for an elected office and sharing your viewpoints with others who could vote you into office. In other situations, it may be a job for which you apply and are hired to carry out some aspects of the government's activities.

Think About Your Reading

What issues in your community are important to you? How could you let others know how you feel about these issues?

Volunteering in Your Community

Volunteers are people who donate their time, talents, and energy to serve others. By volunteering, you can improve your community while making new friends and developing new skills. Choosing a volunteer opportunity that matches your interests is a good way to decide where to devote your efforts. The following examples are just a few ways that you could give back to your community:

- Participate in an outdoor cleanup event at a park or forest preserve (**Figure 21.20**).

- Distribute food at a food pantry or serve a meal at a soup kitchen.

- Organize a blanket or clothing drive for a shelter.

- Be a mentor for a younger person through programs such as Big Brothers Big Sisters and the Boys & Girls Club.

You can find out about volunteer opportunities in your community by searching the Internet for local branches of national charities. Joining a service-oriented club at your school is another way to give back to your community. In addition,

the community section of your local newspaper may have listings of volunteer opportunities.

Protecting the Environment

Another way to improve your community is to take action to protect the environment. Protecting the environment can mean keeping water and air clean and preserving a healthy food supply, to name just a few ways. Taking these steps is important for everyone's health and well-being—now and in the future. As an individual citizen, your actions have a worldwide impact on the environment, not just a local one. Through personal support, wise purchasing decisions, and recycling, everyone can make a difference. Some ways of protecting the environment include those that follow:

- Contact your representatives in all levels of government and let them know that you support the need to protect the environment.
- Contact companies who may have an impact on your local environment to see what they are doing to control pollution.
- Make wise purchasing decisions. Choose items that have recyclable packaging such as glass, paper, aluminum, and cardboard. Check plastic containers for the recycling symbol. Plastics with a recycling classification of 1 or 2 are easiest to recycle.
- Choose reusable items rather than disposable products.
- Buy only what you will use, especially for items such as cleaning agents, solvents, and paints.

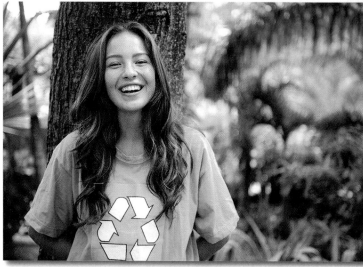
mangostock/Shutterstock.com

Figure 21.20   Volunteering for a cleanup event at a local park is one way to stay involved in your community. *How could connections made as a volunteer have an impact on your success in a job?*

- Sort recyclable items. Having items clean and ready for recycling can assist a community recycling program.
- Follow local regulations for disposing of items that cannot be recycled. This is especially important for hazardous substances such as motor oil and house paint.

LESSON 21.3
Assess

COMPREHENSION CHECK

1. Name three requirements that citizens must meet to vote.
2. What does a citizen accomplish by voting?
3. Describe the difference between a felony and a misdemeanor.
4. List four conditions of a legal contract.
5. List four types of taxes that are collected by local, state, or federal governments. Then give an example of services that are provided through each tax.
6. Describe three steps a person can take to protect the environment.

Chapter Summary

Work patterns for both men and women have more variations today than in past generations. Families weigh several factors as they make choices about work patterns. Managing multiple roles becomes a greater challenge when both parents hold jobs. Resources such as time and energy become limited, and outside resources such as substitute child care may be required. Families need to consider the needs of each child, the services available, their costs, and the parents' schedules when choosing substitute child care.

In the home, family members must be flexible. They need to share roles and work together to carry out household tasks. Community resources also can help families balance career and family roles and meet goals. Through your role as a citizen, you can impact decisions made at local, state, and federal levels of government. Citizens have a responsibility to obey the laws of the land and pay taxes. It is important that individuals be involved in their communities by connecting with their local representatives in government, volunteering, and caring for the environment. The input of one person, multiplied by many, can have a far-reaching and powerful impact.

Vocabulary Activities

1. Create a crossword puzzle that defines all the terms correctly. Exchange puzzles with a partner and solve the one your partner created. Resolve any disagreements you and your partner have over the meanings of any of the terms.

Content Terms

childrearing leave (21.1)
citizen (21.3)
contract (21.3)
cooperative child care (21.2)
dual-career family (21.1)
employer-sponsored child care (21.1)
family child care (21.2)
felony (21.3)
flexible scheduling (21.1)
group child care (21.2)

interrupted work pattern (21.1)
job sharing (21.1)
latchkey children (21.2)
legislature (21.3)
misdemeanor (21.3)
nanny (21.2)
ordinance (21.3)
parental leave (21.1)
register (21.3)
tort (21.3)
violation (21.3)
volunteer (21.3)
work pattern (21.1)

2. Create flash cards and review the meanings of these terms with a partner.

Academic Terms

conventional (21.1)
elect (21.3)
federal (21.3)
foremost (21.2)

homemaker (21.1)
penalize (21.1)
regulation (21.2)

Assess

Your Knowledge

3. What factors could affect spouses' work patterns when they are expecting their first child?

4. What should a parent look for when searching for quality child care for the following children: an infant, a toddler, a preschooler, and an elementary-age child?

5. What are the rights and responsibilities of citizenship?

Your Understanding

6. How do personal values and goals affect work patterns when a couple has small children?

7. How can employer policies and trends support families? How has technology affected family career options and roles in the home?

8. Give an example of how a civil law could protect a citizen's rights.

Your Skills

9. Imagine that you have visited a group child care facility for children of all ages. The space for infants is separated from the other children. When children are able to walk, they are moved to a toddler area. There is a crib for each infant, and the ratio of child care providers to infants is one to four. The sleep and play areas are in adjoining rooms, with a glass window between them. The center appears clean, and the staff is friendly. Evaluate the child care program described. Write a brief paper explaining why this program would or would not meet the needs of both an infant and a toddler, and identify any additional questions you would want to have answered to make a judgment.

10. Develop a family schedule for one week for the following family: Both parents work 8 hours a day and commute 30 minutes to and from work. The children are ages 4, 7, and 12. The youngest child goes to a group child care center. The older children take the bus to school and go to an after-school program. Include the following items in the schedule: shop for groceries,

prepare meals, keep up with household chores, drop off and pick up children, help children with homework, do family leisure activities.

11. Write a legal contract between you and a friend in which you agree to lend him $50.00 and he agrees to pay you back in one month. If you are under 18, identify what additional steps you would need to take to make this legal.

CRITICAL THINKING

12. **Make Judgments.** Prepare a list of questions for a panel of working mothers and fathers about how they balance family needs and work demands. Summarize their responses in a paper and make a judgment about whether some strategies for balancing career and family worked more effectively than others. Cite evidence to support your judgment.

13. **Analyze Projections.** Imagine your future career and identify your desired work pattern. Explain why you would choose this work pattern. Identify the particular challenges that this work pattern presents to families and explain how you plan to meet those challenges. Cite evidence from the text to support your analysis.

14. **Make Inferences.** Create a list of indoor and outdoor household tasks. Identify who is likely to carry out each task in a dual-career family with children. Then evaluate your list. Would all members in that family experience a balance between family and work demands? Write a paragraph describing the division of work in the family and suggest ways to create a better balance between family and work demands.

CORE SKILLS

15. **Social Studies, Writing**. Survey three families about their work patterns. Ask about their reasons for choosing their specific work patterns. Include a question addressing each of the five factors affecting work patterns. Write a report that states the questions you asked relating to each factor, the results of your survey recorded in a table, and a summarizing paragraph explaining your results. *Group option*: Work in small groups and combine your individual survey results. Evaluate your data to see if families with the same work patterns have similar reasons for their choices.

16. **Research, Writing**. Research three different child care services in your community. Describe the important characteristics of each, including the

caregivers and the environment. Identify the ages of children served, the programs offered, food service provided, and the type of license held.

17. **Writing.** Interview a locally elected official, asking him or her to discuss the following topics: the procedure for registering to vote, the local government's structure and operating procedure, and how to become actively involved in local government. Summarize the results of the interview in writing. Discuss why you think more people do not become actively involved in local government.

18. **Research, Writing**. Identify an issue in your community related to protecting the environment. Research various opinions on the issue and the reasons given. Then write a letter to the editor of your local newspaper expressing your position. Be sure to present information to support your position.

19. **Research, Writing**. Using the Internet, obtain a copy of the regulations for child care services in your state for the following: family child care services, group child care centers, cooperative child care centers, and other types of licensed child care. Prepare a brief written report.

20. **Writing.** Prepare a flyer to advertise a new child care service, either real or imaginary. Highlight the special features of the service and the ages of the children served. Add pictures and graphics to your flyer.

21. **Writing.** Choose one of the following stages of child development: infant, toddler, preschooler, or elementary years. Create a digital checklist to use when evaluating a child care service for your chosen age group. Then visit a center and evaluate it using your checklist.

CAREER READINESS

22. **Evaluating the Availability of Child Care.** Contact social services in your community to learn about the need for child care services. Then prepare a report on the availability of licensed child care in your community, average wages earned as a child care provider, and ease of becoming a licensed child care provider. Identify what community resources are available for training persons to become licensed child care providers.

23. **Researching Family Policies.** Choose a company in your community and research its policies related to families (such as sick leave, maternity or paternity leave, childrearing leave, or employer-sponsored child care). Prepare a one-page report describing these policies. *Choice*: Present your information in an electronic presentation.

CHAPTER 22

MANAGING AND PROTECTING YOUR RESOURCES

Reading Prep

Arrange a study session to read the chapter aloud with a classmate. At the end of each lesson, discuss any words you do not know. Take notes of words you would like to discuss in class.

Key Questions

Questions to answer as you study this chapter:

- How can a person balance income and expenses?
- How can a budget help individuals and families meet the responsibilities of living as independent adults?
- What services can help individuals and families protect their resources?

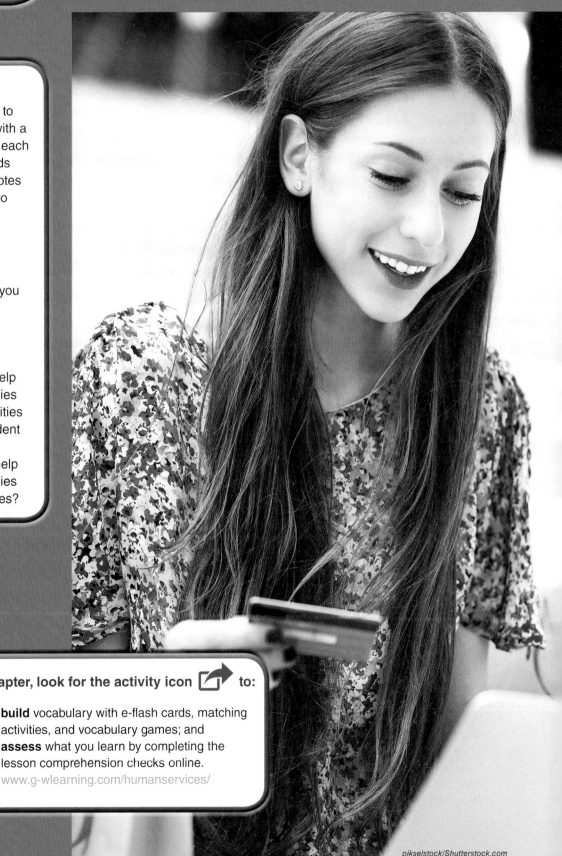

 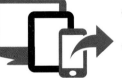
pikselstock/Shutterstock.com

AFTER STUDYING THIS CHAPTER, YOU WILL

KNOW:

- The main sources of income.
- The factors to consider when choosing a savings account.
- The components of a budget.
- The types of insurance individuals and families need.

UNDERSTAND:

- How interest rates affect earnings and the cost of credit.
- How a budget can help persons manage spending.
- How current credit choices can impact financial goals.
- How types of risk affect a person's need for different types of insurance.

BE ABLE TO DO:

- Calculate net income.
- Create a budget and use it to make appropriate spending decisions.
- Calculate the cost of credit.
- Analyze an insurance plan for the protection it provides.

GETTING STARTED

Sharise and Milo planned to go shopping after work, and their list of needs was long. They had recently rented a larger apartment and needed new furniture. Both had good jobs, so the move to the larger apartment seemed like a good idea. It was farther to work for both of them. Since driving each other to work was out of the way and public transportation was not available to them, they also felt they needed another car.

During her lunch hour, Sharise bought two lamps on sale and looked at a couch and two chairs. Sharise liked the furniture, but she wanted Milo to see the furniture before she used their credit card to make such a costly purchase.

Sharise wondered how much they would need for a down payment on a car. The dealer said they could buy a new car and finance it through the manufacturer. She knew they would save considerable time if they had their own cars.

Sharise and Milo's needs are common to many young adults. These needs often come all at once—when people first live on their own, are newly married, or start a new job. Meeting all these needs at once may seem important, but spending without a plan can result in financial disaster.

Learning to manage your money will enable you to live within your means and reach your goals. Managing money involves creating a budget, planning how to use your income, and controlling your spending. In addition, using credit wisely can help you reach your financial goals.

Identifying personal risks and the cost of protecting your resources is also part of budgeting and managing your money. Insurance can protect individuals and families from the financial impact of major losses.

LESSON 22.1

USING A BUDGET

Content Terms

Build Vocab

budget
gross income
net income
interest
compounding
liquidity
disability insurance
fixed expense
variable expense

Academic Terms

constant
utility

Objectives

After studying this lesson, you will be able to
- **explain** the benefits of using a budget.
- **describe** sources of income.
- **identify** the different parts of a budget.
- **explain** the function of savings in a budget.

Focus Your Reading

1. As you read, create a list of the different pieces of information you would need to develop an individual or family budget.
2. Interview a parent and ask which items in the family budget are fixed expenses and which items are variable expenses.

A **budget** is a plan for the use of income. Whether your income is small or large, a budget is a tool that can help you do the following:
- Control spending so you live within your income.
- Guide decision making about purchases.
- Set aside money for special purchases, future plans, and emergencies.
- Reach financial goals.

When planning a budget, you need information related to your income, potential expenses, individual or family needs, and specific short-term and long-term goals (**Figure 22.1**). The more accurate your information, the more useful your budget will be in helping you make good financial decisions.

Estimating Your Income

You need income to be independent and to purchase the goods and services needed to live on your own (**Figure 22.2**). Income can come from several sources. You can work for an employer and earn a *wage*. You can work for yourself in your own business and

Planning a Budget	
Income	
Gross monthly income from paychecks	$3,200.00
Deductions	
Federal tax	316.20
State tax	175.00
Social Security and Medicare	244.80
Net income	$2,464.00
Expenses	
Expense	**Amount**
Housing	
Rent (includes water)	$700.00/mo
Rental insurance	$23.00/mo
	($276 a year, paid annually)
Utilities	
Gas*	$45.00/mo
Electric*	$67.00/mo
Cable	$40.00/mo
Internet access	$25.00/mo
Cellular phone	$65.00/mo
Food*	$333.00/mo
Personal	
Health insurance	$135.00/mo
Other medical expenses*	$25.00/mo
Clothing*	$58.00/mo
Recreation and entertainment*	$125.00/mo
Miscellaneous*	$70.00/mo
Transportation	
Car payment	$226.00/mo
Car insurance	$102.00/mo
	($1,224 a year, paid quarterly)
Gas, oil, tolls*	$146.00/mo
Other	
Debt payment on student loan	$150.00/mo
Savings	$100.00/mo
Total monthly expenses	$2,435.00
Balance (income minus expenses)	$29.00

* Flexible expenses

Figure 22.1 This budget might be typical for a young person beginning a career. *How could experience with budgeting be helpful to a young person transitioning to independence?*

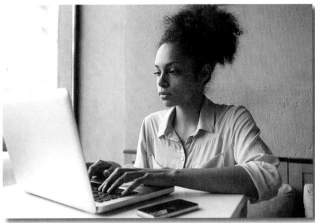

Figure 22.2 Succeeding at work will help you earn income to support your desired lifestyle. *What are some factors that could impact how much income you will earn?*

mimagephotography/Shutterstock.com

earn a *profit*. Income can also come from savings and investments.

Think About Your Reading

What would be the benefits of having income from more than one source?

Income from Work

Most people earn income by working and are paid wages. *Wages* include money payments—in the form of an hourly wage, a salary, a commission, or a profit—and any benefits an employer provides. Vacation pay, bonuses, and tips are also considered part of a person's wages. Some types of wages include the following:

- *Hourly wage.* Some workers are paid by the hour. Many beginning workers are paid hourly, and many of them receive a minimum wage. The *minimum wage*, which is set by governments, is the lowest amount per hour that an employer must pay. You can learn what the federal minimum wage is by contacting a Job Service office or the U.S. Department of Labor. Your state or city may also have a minimum-wage law. Employers must meet any legal requirements for their location. Workers paid an hourly wage are

paid the same rate for every hour they work unless they are paid extra for overtime hours.

- *Salary.* A *salary* is a set amount of money that is paid for all the work an employee does. It is usually stated as an annual or weekly amount, whereas wages are stated in terms of hourly rates. Most people who earn a salary are not paid extra if they work more than an employer's official number of work hours in a week.

- *Commission.* Many workers in sales jobs are paid a *commission*, which is often stated as a certain percentage of each sale made by the worker. The amount of income they earn, then, depends on how much they sell. In some sales jobs, the worker receives a base salary that is guaranteed and then a commission in addition to that.

- *Profit.* Some people are self-employed and earn an income through their own businesses. As entrepreneurs, they sell goods or services for money. *Profit* is the amount of money earned from sales minus all business expenses.

Think About Your Reading

What is the annual starting income for a person employed in a job that is connected with your chosen career plan? Divide this starting income by 12 to identify the income you might have to develop a monthly budget.

The wage or salary you make is called your **gross income**. The amount of money you actually receive, however, is less than that amount (**Figure 22.3**). From your gross income, your employer will take off certain payroll deductions. Some of these deductions are required by law, such as federal and state income taxes and Social Security tax. The Social Security tax is mandated under *FICA*, which stands for the *Federal Insurance Contributions Act*. All workers have these deductions. Some workers have additional deductions, such as contributions to employer-provided health insurance. Your take-home pay is your net

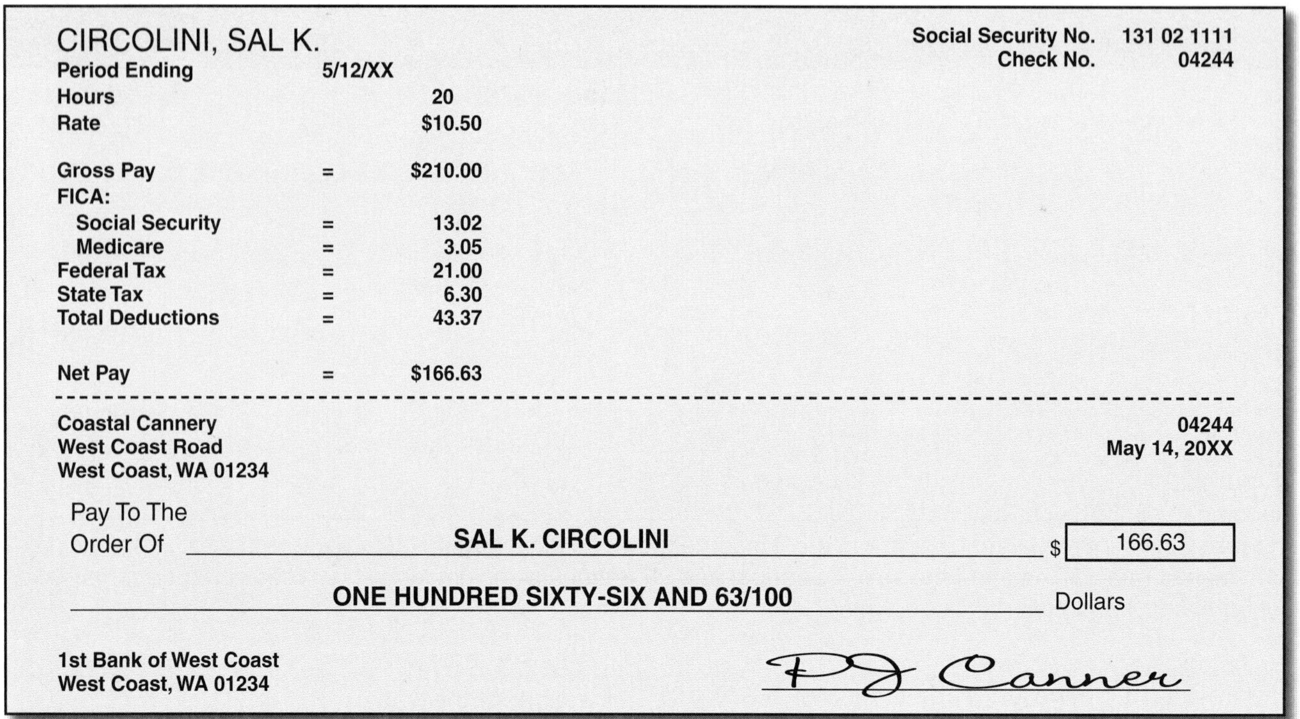

CIRCOLINI, SAL K.

Period Ending	5/12/XX	
Hours		20
Rate		$10.50
Gross Pay	=	$210.00
FICA:		
Social Security	=	13.02
Medicare	=	3.05
Federal Tax	=	21.00
State Tax	=	6.30
Total Deductions	=	43.37
Net Pay	=	$166.63

Social Security No. 131 02 1111
Check No. 04244

Coastal Cannery
West Coast Road
West Coast, WA 01234

04244
May 14, 20XX

Pay To The
Order Of _____ **SAL K. CIRCOLINI** _____ $ 166.63

ONE HUNDRED SIXTY-SIX AND 63/100 _____ Dollars

1st Bank of West Coast
West Coast, WA 01234

PJ Canner

Figure 22.3 Your paycheck, like Sal's, should reflect deductions for income taxes. *What is the benefit of having money withheld from paychecks on a regular basis?*

income. **Net income** is the amount of money left in a paycheck after subtracting the deductions from your gross income.

To begin planning a budget, you must first estimate your monthly net income. How much money did you take home last month? That total should be a guide as to how much you will make this month if you expect to do the same amount of work and have the same deductions. Also include all other sources of income. These might include bonuses, tips, allowances, gifts, or interest earnings.

Income from Savings and Investments

Income can also be earned by placing money in various savings and investment plans. The money earned from these savings may be subject to income taxes.

Savings Income

Money placed in a savings account earns interest. **Interest** is a charge for the use of money, usually expressed as a percentage. Income earned on a savings account is called *interest income*. For instance, if you had $10,000 in a savings account

with an annual interest rate of 4 percent, you would earn $400 in interest in one year. How much interest income a savings account earns is based on four factors:

- the amount saved
- the length of time the savings are in the account
- the interest rate
- the type of compounding used

Compounding is when the interest previously earned is added to the total before new interest earnings are calculated (**Figure 22.4**). Therefore, interest is paid on your original deposit plus the amount of interest previously earned. Interest may be compounded annually (once a year), semi-annually (twice a year), quarterly (four times a year), or monthly. The more often interest is compounded, the more interest income the savings account earns.

The primary benefit of a savings account is that you earn interest on your money as you save toward your goals. The savings accounts offered by each financial institution may vary, but you can shop around to find the one that best fits your needs. You may even use different accounts

How Interest Income Grows

	Principal		Interest Rate		Time		Interest Earned
	100.00 ↓	X	2½%	X	6 months	=	$1.25
1. Increase in principal	200.00	X	2½% ↓	X	6 months	=	$2.50
2. Rate increase	200.00	X	3%	X	6 months ↓	=	$3.00
3. Time increase	200.00	X	3%	X	1 year	=	$6.00 ↓
4. Compounded quarterly	200.00	X	3%	X	1 year	=	$6.07

Figure 22.4   This chart shows how interest income grows as the following factors are increased: (1) principal, (2) interest rate, (3) length of the savings period, and (4) frequency of compounding. *What would be a benefit of starting a savings plan at a young age?*

for different purposes. Your choice of a savings account can depend on the following factors:

- *Interest rate and type of compounding.* The higher the interest rate, the more interest income you will earn. The more often interest is compounded, the more you will earn.

- *Liquidity.* The ability to take out your money on short notice is **liquidity**. Some savings accounts allow you to withdraw money whenever you want and even write checks on the account. These accounts have high liquidity. They usually pay the lowest rate of interest, however. Other savings plans require that you leave your money in the account for a period of time, but usually pay a higher interest. If you need to take out your money before the time is up, you have to pay a penalty (**Figure 22.5**).

- *Convenience.* Some savings accounts provide additional benefits. They may allow you to transfer money from your savings account to your checking account, for instance. Such convenience may influence you to open a savings account at the same place you have a checking account.

Think About Your Reading

What is the benefit of having your money earn interest over a long period of time?

Investment Income

Investments include stocks, bonds, mutual funds, retirement accounts, and real estate. Money put into these investments is usually kept there for several years, sometimes until retirement age.

Investments differ from savings in terms of both safety and potential reward. Savings placed in a bank are very safe because they are guaranteed by the government. That means that if the bank should go out of business, you do not lose your savings. The government insurance fund will send you the amount you had saved. Most investments are not protected in this way. In fact, money that has been invested can be lost if the investment does not perform well. On the other hand, investments have the advantage of being able to grow much larger over time, even though this growth is not guaranteed. Investments tend to have less liquidity than savings, too.

Another way to make money with investments is through buying and selling them, which is called *trading*, rather than holding them for a long period of time. The key to successful trading is buying an investment at a low price and selling it at a higher price. Successful trading requires a great deal of knowledge and experience, however. While the financial rewards can be high, so are the risks. Consequently, trading is recommended only for experts.

Comparing Savings Plans		
Types	Liquidity	Interest
Regular account	Can withdraw on notice.	Pays lowest interest rates.
Club account	Can withdraw on club due date.	Interest rates fairly low.
Certificate of deposit (CD)	Withdrawal depends on terms of CD.	Higher rates for longer terms.
Money market account	Is less liquid; requires minimum balance.	Rates vary with market rates.

Figure 22.5 Savings plans vary in liquidity and rate of interest. *What type of savings account would be suitable for your emergency fund?*

Income During Emergencies

Sometimes people lose their sources of income. They may lose their jobs or become ill or injured. Families in these situations may be able to get help from local social service or human service agencies. Social Security insurance provides some income for workers who have disabilities, as well as for their spouses and children. Some families purchase their own insurance to provide income during emergencies, such as short-term or long-term **disability insurance**. With this kind of insurance, for a fee, the insurance company pays a weekly or monthly amount to an individual who cannot work.

Financial experts recommend having enough savings set aside to cover living expenses for three to six months in the event of an emergency. Establishing such an account and contributing to it regularly can help you avoid financial problems.

Think About Your Reading

What sources of income would be available to you in an emergency?

Establishing Goals for Your Income

The expense side of a budget includes all the goods and services you buy with your income. Deciding what you need is the first step in planning a budget. Identifying goods and services you want is the next step. Your needs and wants will determine your short- and long-term financial goals.

Most people expect their income to provide for their needs. They need to have food, shelter, and clothing—goals that must be taken care of immediately (**Figure 22.6**). Most people do not have enough money for everything they need and want at once. Putting money into a savings account can help you build up a fund for these purposes:

- meeting short-term goals, such as buying a car or taking a vacation
- meeting long-term goals, such as a college education, buying a house, or retirement
- preparing for an emergency

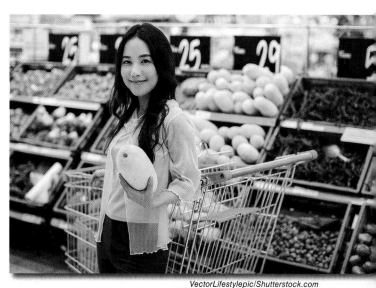

VectorLifestylepic/Shutterstock.com

Figure 22.6 Basic life necessities, such as food, are a need. *How can you distinguish between needs and wants?*

Planning and controlling the use of your income by following a budget can help you meet your needs, as well as short- and long-term financial goals.

Think About Your Reading

What are some of your goals that are needs?
What are some of your goals that are wants?

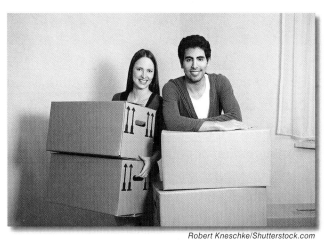

Robert Kneschke/Shutterstock.com

Figure 22.7 Your choice of housing will depend on what is available for a price you can afford. *How could a budget help you identify suitable housing?*

Planning Expenses

In addition to your income, your budget should include the categories in which you spend money. Keep a record of your expenditures for a few weeks if you are not sure how you spend it. Then use that history to identify your spending patterns.

Most people have both fixed and variable expenses. **Fixed expenses** are expenses that are *constant*, or unchanging, each month. Fixed expenses could include rent, a car payment, and insurance payments. A weekly lunch ticket or bus ticket is also a fixed expense.

Variable expenses are expenses that change from month to month. Clothing costs, food, and other expenses may depend on personal needs and desires. Estimate your variable expenses as accurately as you can. Ask other family members or friends what they budget for various expenses such as phone service, food, or personal items. Compare charges for services from different providers such as telephone, cable, or Internet companies. The closer you can project the cost of these items, the more useful your budget will be.

Housing Costs

To live independently, you will need your own housing. Many different types of housing are available, but the type you choose will depend on what is available in your price range that best meets your needs.

You need to know what type of housing you can afford before you start looking (**Figure 22.7**).

Should you rent or buy a home? Your decision will be affected by the following factors:

- family members' annual income
- family size
- family members' ages
- lifestyle
- housing availability in the area
- housing preferences
- job mobility (how often you change jobs)

The cost of housing includes many expenses. First, there is the cost of monthly payments for rent or to repay money borrowed to buy a house. The cost of utilities, taxes, insurance, furnishings, and repairs must also be considered. *Utility* charges include electricity, natural gas, water, sewer, telephone, and garbage-disposal services. These costs vary depending on how much you use the services, but need to be included in your budget.

Sometimes people cannot afford the type of housing they really want. They may find that rents in the neighborhood where they want to live are too high, for instance. In this situation, they may need to compromise and choose an alternative, such as a different neighborhood or a smaller housing unit. Cost is often the biggest factor in determining which housing choices a family can consider. Therefore, obtaining affordable housing that meets a family's needs and expectations requires careful thought and planning.

Think About Your Reading

Which of the housing costs discussed would be fixed expenses? Which would be variable expenses?

Food Costs

Food costs take a significant portion of the family income—as much as 25 percent. Spending less on food, then, can help you reach other goals.

Having an eating plan can help you control food costs. Such a plan includes planning what you eat, making informed purchases, and knowing how to prepare healthful foods. Eating out at restaurants is generally more expensive than preparing your own meals at home.

It is important to ensure good nutrition while controlling food costs. Planning meals can help you make sure that what you do eat is healthful and meets your nutritional needs. *MyPlate*, a food guidance system run by the U.S. Department of Agriculture, can help you identify a food plan that is nutritious.

All food expenses should be in your food budget, including both the costs of buying food and of dining out. As you track the amount of money you spend on food, you will become more accurate at estimating how much money to set aside in your food budget (**Figure 22.8**).

Transportation Costs

Getting back and forth to school, work, home, shopping, and other activities is a routine part of life. The costs of this travel can vary, depending on both your needs and your wants. You may have different options for getting around, such as taking a bus, driving a car, or walking. Each option comes with its particular cost. Even walking,

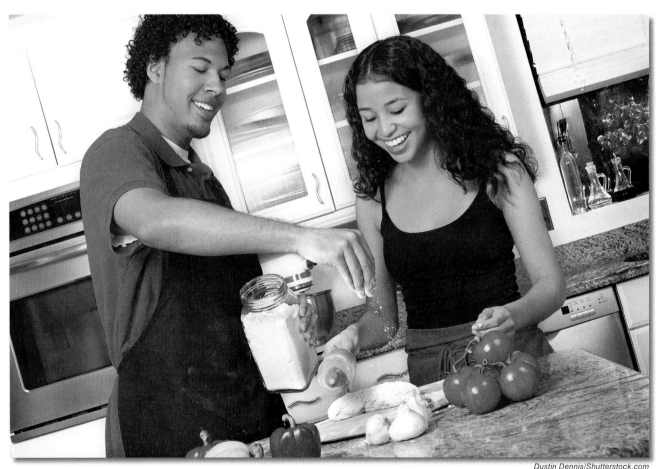

Dustin Dennis/Shutterstock.com

Figure 22.8 A family's food budget depends on personal preferences, the cost of groceries, and how often the family eats at restaurants. *How could cooking skills help a family reduce their food costs?*

which is free, carries the cost of time. Once you have identified what method of transportation you need and want to use, you can calculate your transportation expenses.

Transportation expenses can be both fixed and variable. For example, if you take out a loan for a car, your payment will be a fixed expense in your budget. The cost of gas each month will be a variable expense, depending on how much you use and the price of gas. Insurance for your car would be another fixed expense. Lesson 22.3 has detailed information on buying car insurance.

REAL-LIFE SCENARIO

Hans and Britta's Budget

Hans and Britta both work and attend college classes part time. They have tried to keep their spending as low as possible in order to finish school. After graduation, they look forward to finding better-paying jobs and higher incomes.

Hans and Britta have a joint gross income of $2,550 per month. Their monthly paycheck deductions equal $222 for Social Security and Medicare taxes, $160 for state income taxes, and $244 for federal income taxes. They also have taken out $5,000 in student loans to help with tuition and living expenses.

Housing in a college town is not cheap, but they found a small apartment for $690 per month, including heat and water. Their electricity and telephone bills average about $150 per month. Their food bill is about $400 per month. They pay $110 per month for student health insurance. They drive a used car that took about $340 worth of repairs last year. They try to put aside money each month in an emergency fund to cover such expenses. They hope the car will keep going until they graduate. Gas costs about $135 each month. Their car insurance is $900 annually. Britta pays $90 a month to use the local bus system to get to her job.

They spend about $50 each month for entertainment and as little as possible on clothing or extra household items. To pay for tuition, they must set aside $400 each month. They also need to save $125 a month to cover the cost of textbooks they need at the beginning of each semester. They hope they can save this money during their last semester to pay for new clothes for job hunting and moving expenses.

Hans and Britta's budget is somewhat different from that of their friends, who also have an income of about $30,000 per year. A financial advisor suggested their friends should plan an average budget, based on the following figures:

Expenses as Percent of Net Income	
Rent	28%
Utilities	9%
Food	15%
Transportation and car insurance	15%
Health care	8%
Entertainment/recreation	5%
Clothing	4%
Gifts	3%
Miscellaneous personal	2%
Debt payments	5%
Savings	6%

For Discussion

1. How much net income do Hans and Britta have?
2. How much should they put in savings each month to cover car repairs if those expenses will be the same as last year?
3. Prepare a budget for Hans and Britta using the amounts they have set aside for fixed and variable expenses and savings.
4. Compare Hans and Britta's budget to the average budget the advisor prepared for their friends. In which areas do Hans and Britta spend more than average? In which areas do they spend less than average?
5. Do you think Hans and Britta could continue with their budget long-term? In which areas are expenses likely to increase over a period of time?
6. If they continue to take out the same amount in student loans for three more years, how much will they be in debt when they finish school?
7. How will their student loans affect their financial planning for future goals?

Other Expenses

Individuals and families will have other expenses unique to their own situations. Some may have school-loan payments; some may have higher medical expenses or different needs for such items as clothing or uniforms for work. Whether these additional costs are fixed or variable expenses, they all need to be identified and included in your budget.

Planning for Savings

Financial experts recommend treating savings as a fixed expense. When you get your paycheck, put a certain amount into savings immediately. This helps you control spending, save for future goals, and develop a habit of saving.

The amount you save depends on your goals. You may need to save enough money for a down payment on a car, a security deposit on a rental unit, or a down payment on a home. You may put money in savings for a special purchase you want to make. It is also important to have money in an emergency savings account, so you have some resources to live on in an emergency. The more money you are able to save each month, the faster you will be able to reach your short-term and long-term financial goals.

Finalizing the Budget

Gathering accurate information about income and expenses is essential to making a budget work for you. After you total both, you need to compare the two. In a well-planned budget, the amounts reserved for spending and saving should equal income. They should never surpass your income.

If your expenses are higher than your income, you need to do some adjusting, either by finding a way to increase the income or by cutting variable expenses. If the income is higher than the expenses, you can set aside more for savings and perhaps add a little to the variable expenses, too.

After preparing your budget, use it for a trial period. Keep track of your income and expenses and compare them with your budget's estimates. If necessary, revise your budget to keep your spending and income in line. If you spend more than you make, some decisions will be needed. How can you cut your spending? Can you increase your income?

Your budget will be different from another person's plan for spending. That is because a budget is based on each individual's income, expenses, and savings plans. Your income may be identical to another person's, but your expenses will differ because of your needs, values, and goals. These factors will also influence how much you save and how you use your savings.

A family budget will likely include more expenses than an individual budget. Usually, the expenses of all family members must be met with one or two incomes. Involving the whole family in the planning process can lead to greater success in developing a budget.

Assess

LESSON 22.1

COMPREHENSION CHECK

1. List four benefits of planning a budget.
2. Name and describe four ways to earn income from work.
3. Explain the difference between gross and net income.
4. Explain why savings needs to be a part of a budget.
5. List three factors to consider when choosing a savings account.
6. Explain the difference between fixed and variable expenses in a budget. Give two examples of each.

MAKING A BUDGET WORK FOR YOU

Content Terms

Build Vocab

credit
credit limit
revolving credit
installment credit
collateral
annual percentage rate (APR)
credit rating

Academic Terms

thorough
repossess
security

Objectives

After studying this lesson, you will be able to

- **explain** how a budget is used to make good buying decisions.
- **describe** two advantages and two disadvantages of using credit.
- **explain** the difference between installment and revolving credit.
- **identify** the costs of using credit.
- **explain** how to build and maintain a good credit rating.

Focus Your Reading

1. Create a graphic organizer by writing the word *Credit* in the center of a blank sheet of paper. Draw branches coming out from the center and write a main heading on each branch. As you read the lesson, write key ideas about credit under the appropriate branch.

2. Create a chart with three columns. Write the content terms in the first column and the corresponding text definitions in the second column. In the third column, write how each term relates to using credit wisely.

The first key to budgeting is to be *thorough* (careful and complete) and thoughtful in constructing the plan. The second key is to follow the plan. It is not enough to make a budget; you have to use it. Following your budget means making sure that your budget is realistic and that it changes as your circumstances change. By following the budget that you carefully thought out, you ensure that you make wise buying decisions and control your spending. You can use some technology to help you manage your money. You also can use credit as part of your financial plans—but to take advantage of the benefits of credit, you have to use credit wisely.

Keeping Your Budget Realistic and Flexible

To be useful, a budget must be realistic. You need to use figures that truly reflect your income, spending needs, and ability to save. You need to include all spending categories that are important to you. A budget is not much help if it looks great on paper, but does not really match your situation.

Be flexible in your planning. When expenses or income change, you need to adjust your budget to reflect those changes. If income goes up, you will be able to increase your savings, your spending, or both. If income goes down, you need to adjust expenses and savings to reflect that change. As your financial picture changes, so should your budget.

Using Technology for Money Management

Some people prefer to use technology to track spending habits, carry out banking, pay bills, or manage savings and investments (**Figure 22.9**). Many banking institutions have software connected to their accounts that can help people with accounts track their spending. Most banks also offer online bill paying, which makes it easy to make regular payments. Some offer notifications when monthly bills are due so consumers can be sure to pay their bills on time.

Some people purchase personal finance software to build a budget and track spending. These programs can be linked to a bank account to automatically download and categorize expenses. Various online sites offer free budgeting tools. Electronic budgeting tools make it easy to view reports of spending and track progress toward savings goals.

Making Buying Decisions

A well-planned budget can help you make wise buying decisions. For instance, suppose a pair of sneakers that you want is on sale. Take a look at your variable expenses. Have you budgeted

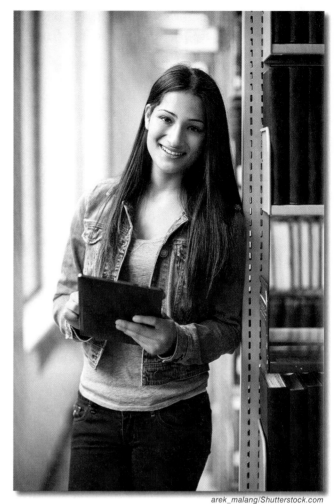

arek_malang/Shutterstock.com

Figure 22.9 Technology can help you organize financial data and quickly calculate expenses.

any amount for this type of expense? Have you set aside enough money in savings for this purchase? If your budget cannot handle the expense, do not make the purchase. Instead, consider setting aside a small amount of money each month until you have enough to purchase the shoes. Saving to make a purchase is the least costly way of meeting a goal.

Choosing to Use Credit

Credit is a financial agreement that allows consumers to borrow money or make a purchase and pay for it in the future. Whenever you use credit to purchase an item, you need to have room in your budget to make the monthly payment. Before using credit, you need to weigh its advantages and disadvantages. By doing so, you may

find it advantageous for some situations, but not for others. These are the main benefits of using credit:

- **You can make large purchases.** For instance, most people would not be able to purchase a home or even a car if they had to pay the full amount.

- **You can use goods and services while you pay for them.** With credit, you can have the use of a computer or a smartphone before you have finished making all the payments.

- **In emergencies, credit lets people purchase needed goods or services.** You may have an emergency car repair, for example, but not have enough money saved to pay it. Credit can make it possible to get the repair done.

- **Credit is convenient.** Credit cards allow you to charge the purchase of many different goods and services (**Figure 22.10**).

- **Credit cards can be safer than carrying large amounts of cash.** For instance, a family may use a credit card on a vacation rather than carry cash. Using credit in this way will also give the family a record of how much was spent, where, and when.

Using credit has disadvantages as well. Wise consumers consider these drawbacks before deciding to use credit. If credit is taken for granted or used unwisely, it can lead to financial problems. The disadvantages of using credit include the following:

- **Using credit can encourage overspending.** Credit is sometimes too convenient. Unplanned spending can easily occur if a person buys on impulse, which can lead to a high burden of debt.

- **Using credit costs money.** Credit is not free. Lenders charge people for the privilege of buying now and paying later. Also, the longer

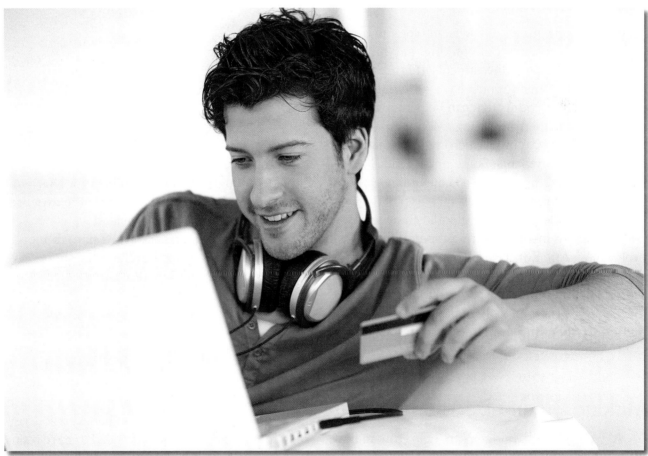

Goodluz/Shutterstock.com

Figure 22.10 Credit cards offer the convenience of being able to purchase goods and services from the comfort of your own home. *How could the ease of using credit result in financial problems?*

borrowers take to repay credit, the higher the cost of using it.

- *Credit reduces future income.* Buying on credit is a promise to pay in the future. People sometimes become unemployed or face emergency expenses. When that happens, their financial commitments may well exceed what they are able to pay back.

- *Misusing credit can cause serious financial problems.* Sometimes when payments are missed, the lender may *repossess*, or take back, the good that was purchased. You would then lose the money you had already paid for it. Bankruptcy and a bad credit rating are other financial risks.

Think About Your Reading

How many of these issues do you think people consider before using credit?

Credit Cards

Credit cards are one of the most common ways that people use credit. Many financial institutions, companies, and stores offer credit cards.

Using credit cards wisely can help you avoid financial problems (**Figure 22.11**).

A credit card has a **credit limit**, or a maximum amount of money that you can borrow. The credit limit is based on the individual's income and credit record. A minimum payment is due each month (usually 2 to 4 percent of the balance). If the balance is not paid off in full, interest is added to the amount owed. This interest adds to the cost of whatever you purchased with your credit card. Credit cards are a kind of **revolving credit**, which means you can continuously borrow and repay money, as long as you stay under the credit limit.

When you have a credit card, you receive a monthly billing statement. It shows any purchases made in the previous month and states how much has been borrowed and how much of the credit limit remains. The statement also states the minimum payment and the payment due date. The payment must be received by the company issuing the card by that date at the latest to count as being on time. If payment is not made on time, the card issuer may add a late fee.

If you find an error in your bill, notify the creditor in writing within 60 days of the billing date. Be sure to write to the correct address for billing inquiries. Include your name, account number,

---

Tips for Using Credit Cards Wisely

- Shop around for a low annual percentage rate and low or no user fees. Fees for credit card services vary from one institution to another and may be more than the rewards that are offered for using the card.
- Look for an institution that does not charge interest from the time of purchase to the first billing.
- Pay your bill in full each month and avoid interest charges.
- Be aware of institutions that do not charge a yearly user fee, but instead charge each time the card is used.
- Budget your credit spending carefully.
- Pay your bills on time to build your credit rating.
- Keep your receipts and compare them with your monthly statement.
- Notify the institution in writing if any incorrect charges are on your statement.
- Keep a list of your credit card numbers and the issuers' phone numbers in your file, where you can find them easily.
- Report loss or theft of a credit card at once. Call by telephone; then follow up with a message.

Figure 22.11 Following these tips can make credit cards work for you. *Which tip do you think consumers fail to follow most often?*

---

and a complete and clear explanation of the error in the correspondence. If you take these steps, you do not need to pay the amount in question until the matter is settled. You are still responsible for paying the rest of your bill on time.

If your credit card is stolen or lost, report it immediately to the business that issued the card. In such cases, federal law usually limits your responsibility for purchases made without your permission to $50. Once you have notified the creditor of the loss, you cannot be held responsible for any charges thereafter.

Loans

Loans are a type of credit often used to finance cars, homes, education, or a new business. When you take out a loan, you borrow a set amount of money and agree to pay it back over time, plus interest. Loans are **installment credit**, which means the loan is paid back in equal installments, usually as monthly payments. Knowing the exact terms of the loan before signing any credit agreement is important.

Loans often require collateral. **Collateral** is a form of *security*, or financial protection, on a loan. When a consumer takes out a car loan, the car serves as collateral. If the borrower stops making loan payments, the lender can repossess the collateral and take ownership of the car.

Think About Your Reading

Why would a lender want to have collateral on a large loan like a car loan?

The Cost of Credit

When you take out a loan or use a credit card, it usually costs more than if you had paid cash for the purchase (**Figure 22.12**). That is because lenders charge interest on the amount you owe. The cost of using credit can vary from one lender to another. The Truth in Lending Act requires lenders to disclose the exact cost of using credit, including interest and other charges, such as annual fees. Also, lenders are required to disclose

The Cost of Credit		
Item Purchased	Time to Pay Off	Real Cost of Item (Approximate)
$100.00 boots	11 months	$107.00
$300.00 game system	38 months (about 3 years)	$371.00
$1,500.00 computer system	124 months (about 10 years)	$2,334.00
$3,000.00 vacation	162 months (13½ years)	$4,788.00

Figure 22.12 This chart shows the cost of purchasing items using a credit card with an APR of 14 percent and making the minimum payment every month (3 percent of the balance). *How could credit card debt impact your financial goals?*

the **annual percentage rate (APR)**, which is the annual cost of credit.

Some experts recommend keeping credit expenses under 20 percent of net income; most recommend holding it in the 10 to 15 percent range. This includes all debt payments other than expenses for buying a home (which is under *housing* in the budget) or a car (under *transportation* in the budget). A lower amount is certainly safer. To figure how much credit you can afford, you need to look at your budget. Buying on credit adds another fixed expense. If you do not have enough money to cover a credit payment and other expenses, you cannot afford to buy on credit.

Think About Your Reading

How do credit card companies fulfill the Truth in Lending Act through billing statements?

Applying for Credit

Credit is offered to people who have a good record of paying their bills on time. They have

a regular income and are able to show that this income will likely continue in the future. When you apply for credit, the lender will ask for information about your job, length of employment, and your income. The lender will also check your credit rating.

Your **credit rating** is a record of how well you paid your bills in the past. To establish a credit rating, you need to apply for credit and use it wisely. If you are considered a good credit risk, many retail stores will issue a first credit card quite easily. You can begin using this credit wisely to build a good credit rating. Experts recommend beginning by using credit to make a small purchase that you could buy with cash. Then repay it as soon as the bill comes in. Doing this a few times to make small purchases for which you have the money will help you build your credit rating.

A person's credit rating can change over time. To *keep* a good credit rating, you need to pay bills on time (**Figure 22.13**). If you make late payments, fail to pay, or have items repossessed, you will have a poor credit score, which results in a poor credit rating. Negative information about your credit history cannot be erased from your file. A poor credit rating can result in being turned down for any type of credit. A poor credit rating can also lead lenders to charge higher interest rates than they would to someone with a better credit score.

The Fair Credit Reporting Act gives you the right to receive one free credit report each year to verify the information in your report. That report comes from one of several *credit bureaus*, which are companies that maintain credit records on individuals. You have the right to ask the credit bureau to investigate any information that is not correct or complete. The bureau must then correct its records if there are errors. If you apply for credit and are turned down, you have the right to know the specific reasons why.

The Equal Credit Opportunity Act states that certain factors cannot be used against you in determining whether you are granted credit. These include race, color, sex, age, and marital status. To gain credit, you must be old enough (age 18 or 21) to sign a binding contract in your state.

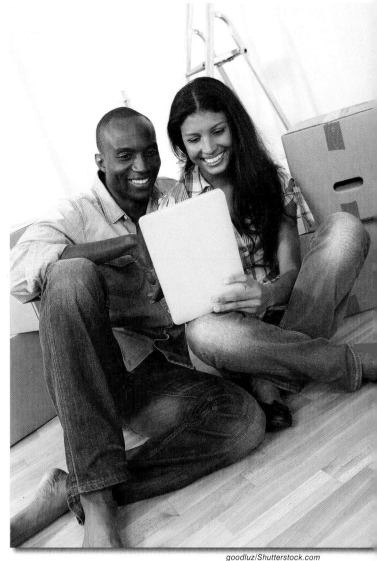
goodluz/Shutterstock.com

Figure 22.13   No matter how you use credit, you should pay your bills on time to maintain a good credit rating.

LESSON 22.2
Assess

COMPREHENSION CHECK

1. Describe two advantages and two disadvantages of using credit.
2. Explain the difference between installment and revolving credit.
3. Explain how the Truth in Lending Act helps the consumer.
4. Explain how a person can build and keep a good credit rating.

PROTECTING RESOURCES THROUGH INSURANCE

Content Terms

Build Vocab

insurance
premium
policy
liability
financial responsibility law
medical payments coverage
bodily injury liability
uninsured motorists protection
no-fault insurance
property damage liability
collision insurance
comprehensive physical damage
deductible
face value
guaranteed replacement value
coinsurance
co-pay
group health insurance
term insurance
beneficiary
whole life insurance
universal life insurance

Academic Terms

insured
maximum
adequate

Objectives

After studying this lesson, you will be able to

- **explain** how types of risk affect a person's need for different types of insurance.
- **describe** various types of insurance individuals and families may need.
- **explain** how personal factors impact the need for and cost of insurance.

Focus Your Reading

1. As you read, develop a checklist for each type of insurance. Include key points you should know or questions you should ask before agreeing to buy that type of insurance coverage.

2. Create a chart with three columns. Put each content term in the first column. In the second column, write the text definition for each term. In the third column, give an example of that term.

When Lola came home from school Thursday afternoon, she had no idea how her life was about to change. Her dad had been in a car accident on the way home from work. He was pronounced dead on arrival at the hospital. Suddenly, their family had become a single-parent family. Their lives were torn by the tragic event.

Such events do happen. They may be due to dangers such as an accident, storm, violence, or illness. There is always a chance that such an event could affect you or your family, resulting in a loss.

Buying Insurance

Insurance is a form of protection against financial loss. This protection is purchased from an insurance company, or insurer. The individual who purchases that protection is called the *insured*.

The main types of insurance for consumers are for cars, the home and property, health care, disability, and life.

How Insurance Works

When selling insurance, an insurance company charges a fee called a **premium** to assume a financial loss that is described in the policy. The **policy** is a contract between the insurance company and you as a policyholder.

A basic policy will describe the exact risks against which you are being insured and the dollar amount of your protection. If you want more coverage for other risks or perils, you may be able to add extra insurance. This extra protection is added to the policy as a *policy rider*. Knowing what coverage a basic policy provides and the risks included by any riders is important (**Figure 22.14**).

In an insurance company, all the people who buy the same kind of insurance from the same company are putting their money together into a pool. When one policyholder gets sick or has an accident, money is taken from that pool to cover that person's expenses or loss. The insurance company's goal is to have enough money in the pool to cover the needs of the members. If many people have high expenses at the same time, the pool runs dry. When this happens, insurance rates increase.

When purchasing insurance, it is important to identify your risks of loss, which risks you could cover through savings, and which risks are large enough that you would need additional funds to help manage the effects of the loss and avoid a crisis. The costs of insurance premiums need to be included in your budget as a fixed expense.

Risks Leading to Financial Loss

Risk of financial loss comes from several sources. There is the risk of damage to personal property, such as a car or home. Protection against such losses can be purchased with car and home insurance. There is the risk that you may lose your health, your income, or your life. Protections against the financial burdens that result from such losses are purchased through health, disability, and life insurance.

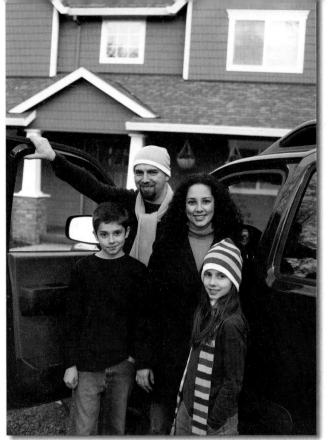
Hurst Photo/Shutterstock.com

Figure 22.14 Most families purchase several types of insurance to protect them against the risk of losing their costly purchases, such as a home or vehicle.

Think About Your Reading
How much money would your family need to live for one month without any income? What resources do they have that would provide this money?

You may also have the risk of liability. **Liability** is the legal responsibility for another person's financial costs due to a loss or injury for which you are responsible. You can become legally responsible if the loss or injury results from your actions or neglect. For instance, if the work you do for a business could result in a loss to someone, you would need to carry liability insurance. This coverage would protect you against the liability risk. You have liability for losses caused by your property, such as your car or even your pet dog. A loss caused by a person for whom you are responsible, such as your child, is also your responsibility. Protection against these liability risks is typically purchased with property insurance.

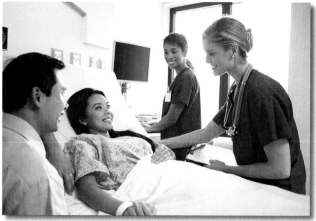

Insuring Your Car

All states have a **financial responsibility law**. These laws require drivers to prove that they are able to pay for the cost of any damages or injuries that might be caused in a car accident. Most people buy car insurance to meet the financial responsibility law. Car insurance provides protection against the risks of bodily injury to the driver and others and of property damage to your own or others' property.

Bodily Injury Risks

Your risks for bodily injury can be protected under three different sections in your car insurance policy. These three sections include medical payments coverage, bodily injury liability, and uninsured motorists protection.

Medical payments coverage pays for the medical expenses resulting from injuries to you and others in your car in a car accident. It also covers you if you are injured as a passenger in or as a pedestrian by someone else's car. This coverage pays these costs no matter who is at fault for the accident.

Bodily injury liability protects against major financial losses resulting from an accident for which you are responsible (**Figure 22.15**). The insurance pays medical costs, legal expenses, lost wages, or compensation for suffering. Since these losses can total hundreds of thousands of dollars, this protection is very important. Bodily injury liability coverage is usually stated on a policy as part of three numbers, such as *50/100/25* or *100/300/100*. The first two numbers of the liability coverage are for bodily injury liability. The third number is for property damage liability. The first number is the *maximum*, or highest, amount (in thousands of dollars), that the insurance company

Monkey Business Images/Shutterstock.com

Figure 22.15 The person at fault in an accident is responsible for the costs of injuries to others. *Why is it important that motorists be insured for these costs?*

will pay for one person in an accident. The second number is the maximum amount that will be paid for all people injured in a single accident.

Uninsured motorists protection covers bodily injuries to you and your family caused by someone else driving without car insurance. This insurance also protects you if that driver does not have enough insurance to cover the cost of your injuries.

Some states have **no-fault insurance** plans, offering personal injury protection (PIP) instead of, or in addition to, medical payments coverage. PIP plans may also pay for funeral expenses, loss of income, and other expenses related to injury or death from a car accident.

Property Damage Risks

Your car and the items in it are at risk for property damage. The same is true for any items your car may hit, such as someone else's car or property. Your car may also be damaged by hail, wind, a storm, a falling tree, or other perils. These risks are covered by *property damage insurance*, which has three parts.

Property damage liability is protection to cover losses to someone else's property caused by you and your vehicle. The amount of your coverage is the third number of the liability limits. For example, the policy of *50/100/25* covers damage to someone else's property for $25,000.

Collision insurance covers the cost of damage to your car when it is involved in an accident (**Figure 22.16**). The amount of coverage depends on the vehicle and its worth. The most you can collect is the retail value of your car at the time of the accident. If someone else is at fault for the accident, your insurance company will try to collect the repair costs from that person's insurance company.

Comprehensive physical damage covers the risk of damage to your car by perils other than a collision. For instance, the damage caused by a fallen tree is covered under comprehensive damage. This protection covers loss or damage from perils such as fire, theft, glass breakage, falling objects, vandalism, wind, hail, or animals.

Controlling Car Insurance Costs

The cost of your car insurance will depend on several factors. The amount of liability coverage you carry is a major factor. The more protection you buy, the higher the premium; the lower the coverage, the lower the premium. The insurance company is charging you for the amount of risk they are taking. The legal limits for liability vary from state to state, but they are generally lower than what experts say is *adequate*, or enough. Legal advisors recommend *100/300* for bodily injury liability and $50,000 or $100,000 for property damage liability.

> ## Think About Your Reading
> What would happen if you did not carry enough liability insurance to cover the cost of an accident? Who would be responsible to pay the uncovered expenses?

The type of car you own and its value affect the amount of risk the insurance company covers.

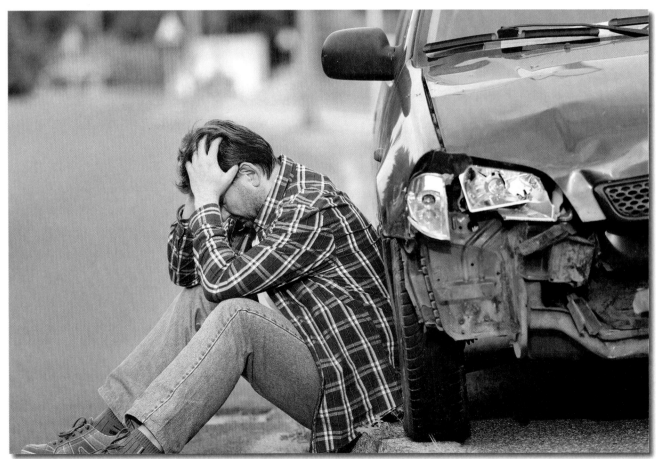

wideonet/Shutterstock.com

Figure 22.16 Collision insurance covers damage to the insured's vehicle.

The more expensive the car, the higher the premium for collision or comprehensive coverage. You can reduce the cost of your premium by having a larger deductible. In insurance policies, a **deductible** is an amount that the insured has to pay before the insurance company pays any money. For instance, suppose an accident resulted in $1,500 in damages to your car. If you had a $250 deductible, you would be responsible for the first $250. The insurance company would pay the remaining expense of $1,250. If you carry a high deductible, it will lower the cost of your collision and comprehensive insurance.

Insurance companies will compare you with other drivers to determine how risky it will be to insure you. The classification you are given will depend on your age, sex, marital status, driving record, and driving habits. Young unmarried males tend to have more accidents (**Figure 22.17**). As a result, if you are a young, unmarried male, you will be classified in a group that pays higher premiums. A driver who has had a number of accidents or received tickets for traffic violations in the past three years will have a poor driving record. That driving record would put him or her in a classification with those who pay higher premiums.

Your risk of having an accident increases the more often you drive. That risk is reflected in your insurance premium as well. For instance, if you drive to work or school every day, your premium will be higher than if you just drive your car for pleasure.

Insuring Your Home

To protect against financial loss due to damage to a home and its contents, families purchase *homeowner's insurance*. Two basic types of coverage are provided: property protection and liability protection.

Basic *property protection coverage* insures you against the damage or loss of your home and your personal property (such as home furnishings and clothing) caused by certain dangers. These include fire or lightning, windstorms or hail, explosions, riots, aircrafts, vehicles, smoke, vandalism, and theft. The policy may include loss-of-use protection. This coverage pays for the family's living expenses while the home is being repaired or rebuilt.

Most policies also include *liability protection* in case someone is hurt on or by your property. If you or your property accidentally causes damage to someone else's property, it provides this coverage as well.

Value of Loss

Knowing exactly what your insurance company will pay in case of a loss is important. Some policies provide *replacement cost*. This means they will pay enough to replace what was damaged up to the face value of the policy. The **face value** of your policy is the largest amount the company will pay for a loss. Other policies insure for the actual cash value of the property at the time of the loss.

Suppose you carry insurance on your entertainment system for a loss due to theft or fire for up to $600. Nine months later, that entertainment system is stolen. The present cash value of your entertainment system may be $500 because of nine months of use, even though a new one costs $600. The insurance company will pay only $500 (present cash value) unless your policy states that replacement value is covered. Then it will pay the $600. If replacement cost is now $700, the company

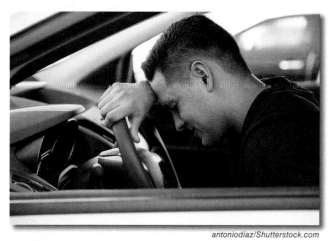

antoniodiaz/Shutterstock.com

Figure 22.17 A young unmarried male is a high insurance risk and will pay higher premiums for car insurance.

will only pay $600 because that is the face value of your policy.

Some policies offer **guaranteed replacement value**. In this case, the company replaces the item even if the cost of the new item is higher than the face value of the policy. With guaranteed replacement value, the insurance company would pay the $700 for your entertainment system if that is the cost of a new one.

Think About Your Reading

Do you think the coverage provided by a policy with guaranteed replacement value would be worth the additional cost in insurance?

Renter's Insurance

Even if you do not own a home, you still face the risk of property loss and of liability. Renters should carry insurance to cover loss of personal belongings and property that they have inside the home. Liability protection should also be considered since there is a risk that guests may be harmed by your property. Such a policy would protect you if someone slipped in your shower or was bitten by your dog, for example.

Insuring Your Health

Without good health, working at a job, caring for a family, or even caring for yourself is difficult. Making daily living choices that contribute to good health is the best method of protecting your health. At some time in your life, however, you likely will need health care, which can be very costly (**Figure 22.18**). For this reason, you need to be covered by some form of health plan. Since 2014, individuals have been required by law to have health insurance, though the law has been challenged and may be changed.

How Health Insurance Works

When looking for a health insurance plan, it is important to know how various plans function so you can identify the best plan for your situation.

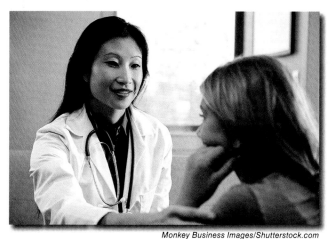

Monkey Business Images/Shutterstock.com

Figure 22.18 Health care can be very costly, exceeding many people's budgets. *What are the risks of not having health insurance?*

Most health insurance plans cover a portion of medical expenses. The amount the company pays and the specific services covered differ by plan. All plans will have a *premium*, the fixed amount you pay monthly for coverage.

A basic level of benefits is usually covered by all health plans. These essential health benefits include services such as hospitalization; pregnancy, maternity, and newborn care; mental health and substance abuse services; laboratory services; children's services; rehabilitation services; prescription drugs; and preventive and wellness services. Coverage for other types of health care, such as vision and dental services, must be purchased in addition to these basic benefits.

If a plan has a deductible, you have to pay for services until that deductible is met. For example, an insured person with a policy that has a $500 deductible may have to pay for doctor's visits, drugs, or laboratory visits until the total payments made reach the $500. Some services, such as preventive care, may be exempt from the deductible. Plans that cover families offer both an individual deductible and a deductible for the whole family.

Some plans have **coinsurance**, which means the insured person pays a percentage of each bill. For example, if your coinsurance rate is 20 percent, and the bill for an office visit is $150, you pay $30. Some plans have **co-pays**, which are flat fees for some services, such as office visits. Many drug plans have co-pays, often with different fees for different classifications of drugs.

Group Health Insurance

Group health insurance policies are available through employers, unions, and professional associations. These group policies provide more coverage at a lower cost than individual policies. Employers may pay all or part of the insurance costs. Although groups can provide health insurance for members in different ways, many choose health maintenance organizations (HMOs), preferred provider organizations (PPOs), or high-deductible health plans (HDHPs) with health savings accounts.

- *Health maintenance organizations (HMOs).* HMOs provide all health services through a network of medical personnel and facilities. With an HMO, you choose a primary doctor to oversee your care. Most HMOs require you to get a referral to see a specialist. Depending on your plan, there may be deductibles and co-pays for care.

- *Preferred provider organizations (PPOs).* PPOs offer another option for health care. A PPO is a group of doctors and hospitals that contract with the insurance company or employer to provide health care services to group members for certain fees. All the physicians and hospitals that sign such a contract with an insurer are in that insurer's network; those who are not signed up are out of the network. With a PPO, the insurer pays a higher share of the cost when you receive care from a doctor or hospital in the network than if you receive care out of the network (**Figure 22.19**).

- *High-deductible health plans (HDHPs).* HDHPs provide services just as HMOs or PPOs do, but offer a lower premium in return for a high deductible. These deductibles range from amounts of $1,300 to $6,400 for an insured person. These are high deductibles and need to be included in your budget. If you choose an HDHP for health insurance, there will be a cap on the amount you have to pay out of pocket (with your own money). Once that cap is met, the plan pays 100 percent of medical expenses. HDHP plans are sometimes available with a *health savings account (HSA).* An HSA can be used to set aside money to pay your deductible. The money you put into a

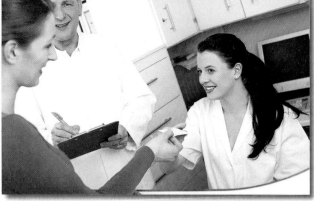

Kzenon/Shutterstock.com

Figure 22.19 If you are insured by a PPO, you should verify a provider is in your network before going to that provider. Providers can also check this information.

health savings account is not taxed, which can lower the amount of income tax you owe.

In all states, *Medicaid* provides free or low-cost health care for some individuals and families with low incomes. Coverage and costs may vary from state to state. The *Children's Health Insurance Program (CHIP)* also provides low-cost health coverage for children in some low-income families.

Think About Your Reading

In what ways do you think HMO and PPO programs benefit a medical organization?

Controlling Health Insurance Costs

Health insurance has become a large expense for individuals and families, as well as for employers. You can take several steps to control your health care costs.

Most importantly, take steps to keep healthy. Health insurance costs increase the more people use health care. Preventive care can help you avoid many major health problems.

Second, shop around. Before choosing a health insurance plan, be sure you understand what services are provided, where they are offered, and how the plan covers the cost of services. What provisions are made for emergency health care if you are not able to reach your preferred provider or assigned doctor? Compare the costs and services with other health care providers and insurance companies. Then choose the plan that works best for you.

Third, choose a higher deductible, a higher rate of coinsurance, or higher co-pays. In these

cases, it is important to set aside money in your budget to cover the portion of each bill you might have to pay as well as the premium.

Disability Insurance

Disability insurance protects against loss of income if a person gains a disability (**Figure 22.20**). The premium cost depends on the individual's income. Some policies cover disability due to accident; some include disability due to illness. The amount of benefit the policy pays will vary, with some paying 70 to 90 percent of a person's regular income. The waiting period before benefits begin also varies. Check the details of a disability policy to know what protection you have.

Insuring Your Life

Life insurance protects against the loss of income due to death. Its main purpose is to provide income for family members (spouse, children, elderly parents) who depend on a wage earner's income.

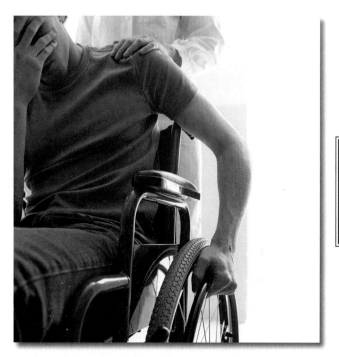

Stokkete/Shutterstock.com

Figure 22.20 Loss of income due to an accident or illness can mean financial disaster if a wage earner has no disability insurance.

There are two main types of life insurance: term and cash value. Policies may have many different names, but they all represent variations or combinations of these two.

Term Insurance

A **term insurance** policy insures your life for a set number of years. The term may be 1, 5, 10, or more years; then it expires. Term insurance gives you the most protection for the least amount of money. Premiums are lower for those who are younger and higher for those who are older.

A term policy is taken out for a certain face amount indicating the amount of insurance purchased. At death, the policy pays a death benefit to a **beneficiary**, who is the person named in the policy to receive the money. In a term policy, the death benefit is equal to the face amount of the policy. For instance, if you buy a $100,000 term insurance policy at age 25, the death benefit to your beneficiary is $100,000 if you should die.

Usually, a term policy can be renewed after it expires, although the premium may go up since the insured person is older. Some employers that provide life insurance may require that employees have a physical before renewing the policy. If the employee's health is poor, the company may not renew the policy. Some policies are guaranteed renewable term policies. With these policies, the employee would not have to meet the company's medical standards after each term.

Think About Your Reading

Why might term insurance be a good choice of family protection for a young couple with preschool children?

Cash Value Insurance

Cash value insurance provides coverage for a death benefit just as term insurance does. It differs in acting as a type of savings plan and having a cash value. The cash value of the policy is the amount you would receive if you should drop or surrender the policy. In the early years, that

cash value grows slowly. The longer you hold the policy, the more the cash value increases. Even if the cash value increases, however, the death benefit remains the same.

The cash value gives the insured person some flexibility because it can be used in several ways:

- You can take out a loan from the insurance company based on the cash value.
- You can turn in (surrender) your policy, and the company would pay you the cash value.
- If you wanted to stop paying premiums, you could use the cash value to buy a certain amount of protection for a certain number of years.
- You could put the cash value into an *annuity*, which provides you a guaranteed income for life.

Whole life insurance is the best known form of cash value insurance. In a straight whole life policy, the premium stays the same as long as you carry the policy. The cost of the protection is spread evenly over the years of the policy. This occurs even though the risk of death is lower during the younger years.

Universal life insurance is a combination term and cash value policy which offers more flexibility than a straight whole life policy. If you bought a universal life policy, you would pay a set premium each month. Part of the premium goes toward the death benefit protection (the term part of insurance). Most of the remaining amount earns a variable rate of interest and forms the cash value part of the policy. The company also deducts part of the premium for administrative costs.

When you are young, the actual charge for the death benefit is lower, and the policy earns more interest. As you age, the charge for the death benefit increases, and the amount earning interest decreases. Policyholders can sometimes change either their death benefits or their premiums, depending on how much cash value the policy has accumulated.

When considering a universal life policy, be sure to ask what rate is charged for the death benefit. A regular term policy usually offers the same amount of protection for a lower premium. Also ask what the administrative costs are. Most companies charge a one-time fee for setting up the policy. They may charge a percentage of all premium payments to pay for company expenses. Also, they may charge a fee for withdrawing funds from your cash value. All these costs reduce the amount that actually earns interest.

Understanding the difference between cash value insurance and term insurance will help you choose the plan that is best for you (**Figure 22.21**).

Comparing Term and Cash Value Insurance		
	Term Insurance	**Cash Value Insurance**
Advantages	• Has lower premiums in the early years. • Provides more coverage with fewer dollars. • Can be flexible by being converted to cash value insurance.	• Has constant premiums over the years. • Cannot be canceled because of age. • Builds a cash value. • Has increases in value that are tax free. • Is a type of forced savings.
Disadvantages	• After a certain age, policy cannot be renewed. • Premiums increase when a person reaches an older age bracket. • Has no buildup of cash value.	• Early premiums are higher even though risk of death is low. • A person may not carry enough protection because costs are higher. • Higher interest rates may be available in other investments. • Comparing rates of return is difficult because of administrative costs.

Figure 22.21 Comparing life insurance can help you determine which policy best suits your needs.

Cash value insurance is a type of forced savings plan, but the interest rate paid is usually quite low. The difference in premium costs between term and cash value insurance could produce a higher return in a savings or investment plan. To get the most protection for the money, consider term insurance.

How Much Life Insurance Is Needed?

When considering how much life insurance to purchase, the key question is what the extent of the family's financial loss would be with the death of a wage earner. The death benefit can provide funds for funeral and burial expenses. It can provide funds for family living expenses during the years that children are growing up. Such funds can also provide income for the surviving parent after the children are grown. The size of the death benefit should relate to the policyholder's responsibilities in these areas. In a family with children at home, higher amounts of life insurance are needed for each wage earner than is the case for a family with few or no dependents.

If a family has a good savings and investment plan, it probably needs less return from life insurance. That is because these funds can be used to provide income for the family.

Filing an Insurance Claim

The types of insurance discussed in this lesson can protect people from various types of losses. When you do experience a loss, you need to file a claim to access the money guaranteed by insurance. This step starts the process of being compensated for your loss. Filing an insurance claim requires some prior record keeping on your part. With the proper papers in hand, file an insurance claim by following the appropriate steps. See **Figure 22.22**.

Lesson 22.3
Assess

Comprehension Check

1. Identify three different types of potential risks that could result in financial losses and give an example of each.
2. Explain how car insurance and homeowner's insurance can protect individuals and families.
3. Identify five factors that impact the cost of car insurance.
4. List three ways individuals and families can reduce health insurance costs.
5. Explain why term insurance is the best buy for a young family with a limited income.
6. Describe why a person might choose a cash value life insurance policy.

Filing an Insurance Claim

- Keep an up-to-date file of your insurance policies. Be sure family members know where the files are.
- For property loss, keep receipts from purchases to prove the value of your property. Also keep an inventory of all personal property. For health care costs, keep records of your appointments and receipts for any *out-of-pocket expenses* (expenses that you have paid) that might be reimbursed by insurance. These receipts may also be needed for filing income taxes.
- For property loss, contact the police as soon as possible. Be sure to obtain a copy of the written police report describing your loss. In a car accident, write down the names, addresses, and telephone numbers of the people involved. Include witnesses as well. Get the license plate number(s) from the other car(s) and get the driver's license number(s).
- Contact your appropriate insurance agent as soon as possible.
- In the event of property loss or damage, locate original receipts to determine original costs. Obtain estimates to repair the property or get estimates of the value of the property. Share your information with your agent at the insurance company.

Figure 22.22   To file an insurance claim, follow these steps.

CHAPTER SUMMARY

Using a budget can help individuals and families plan and control spending, make buying decisions, and save money. A well-planned budget can work for you if you follow it. You also need to evaluate it often to make sure it is working. Being realistic and flexible in your planning will enable you to reach your financial goals.

Credit allows you to buy now and pay later. Before using any type of credit, you need to consider the pros and cons of credit. Always know the total cost of using credit and the amount of credit you can afford. Paying bills on time helps you establish credit and keep a good credit rating.

Families can protect themselves from the risk of financial loss by purchasing various types of insurance. Insurance may be purchased to protect against loss due to some property risks, personal risks, or liability risks. A family's need for such protection will depend on what risks they can afford to absorb and various factors that affect the cost of insurance.

VOCABULARY ACTIVITIES

1. Categorize the terms into those related to insurance and those related to other financial issues.

Content Terms

annual percentage rate (APR) (22.2)
beneficiary (22.3)
bodily injury liability (22.3)
budget (22.1)
coinsurance (22.3)
collateral (22.2)
collision insurance (22.3)
compounding (22.1)
comprehensive physical damage (22.3)
co-pay (22.3)
credit (22.2)
credit limit (22.2)
credit rating (22.2)
deductible (22.3)
disability insurance (22.1)
face value (22.3)
financial responsibility law (22.3)
fixed expense (22.1)

guaranteed replacement value (22.3)
gross income (22.1)
group health insurance (22.3)
installment credit (22.2)
insurance (22.3)
interest (22.1)
liability (22.3)
liquidity (22.1)
medical payments coverage (22.3)
net income (22.1)
no-fault insurance (22.3)
policy (22.3)
premium (22.3)
property damage liability (22.3)
revolving credit (22.2)
term insurance (22.3)
uninsured motorists protection (22.3)

universal life insurance (22.3)
variable expense (22.1)
whole life insurance (22.3)

2. Write two sentences for each term, one that uses the term in relation to one of the topics in this chapter, and one that correctly uses the term in another context.

Academic Terms

adequate (22.3)
constant (22.1)
insured (22.3)
maximum (22.3)
repossess (22.2)
security (22.2)
thorough (22.2)
utility (22.1)

ASSESS

Your Knowledge

3. What are the main sources of income?
4. What information is needed to create a budget?
5. What four factors impact how much money you would earn in a savings account?
6. What are the types of insurance that most families need?

Your Understanding

7. How could a budget help a person make buying decisions?
8. Explain why a high interest rate is a benefit when saving money, but hurts financially when borrowing money.
9. How can credit decisions affect your financial future?
10. Why does a person need to carry insurance even if he or she does not own very much property?

Your Skills

11. If a person earns $10 per hour and works 40 hours a week, what is the gross monthly income? If FICA deductions are 7.65 percent of gross income and tax deductions are 15 percent of gross income, what would the person's monthly net income be?
12. Create a budget to meet your individual needs if you earned $290 net income every two weeks at a part-time job. Include your current expenses and assume you don't pay for housing because you live with your family. Determine if you could afford to buy a car with a monthly loan payment of $185.
13. Calculate the amount due on a credit card with a $557 balance and a minimum payment requirement of 3 percent. If the minimum amount was paid this month, and the card charges a monthly interest rate of 1.5 percent, what would the balance be next month? How much interest was charged?

14. Assume your renter's policy has a face value of $50,000, a deductible of $500, and a premium of $125 per year. How much would the insurance policy pay out if lightning struck the apartment and destroyed your $1,000 laptop computer?

CRITICAL THINKING

15. **Compare Findings.** Interview a financial advisor about recommended amounts to budget for various living expenses in your community. Compare the advice with the example in your textbook. For additional information, research recommended amounts for budgeting on the Internet. In a report, identify similarities and differences between recommendations. Explain how unique characteristics of your community could contribute to the differences. Make generalizations for recommended budgeting categories and percentages in your community.

16. **Gather and Analyze Data.** Record all your purchases for a month. Group them into categories and identify how much you spend a month in each category. Write a report summarizing your data and your analysis, including a total of the amount you spent in a month and a total annual income you would need to cover your current expenses. Prepare an individual budget based on this information.

17. **Create an Eating Plan and a Food Budget.** Using the Internet to find guidelines for a healthful diet, create an eating plan for one week. Include specific foods you would eat throughout the day. Create a shopping list for the food in your eating plan and calculate the cost of your eating plan by visiting a grocery store and pricing each item on your list. Multiply the cost of your weekly eating plan by four to calculate a monthly cost of grocery bills. Add in the cost of any meals you would eat at a restaurant to create a monthly food budget.

18. **Make Judgments.** Acquire information on whole life and term life insurance policies for a 25-year-old male or female from two different insurance companies. Make a chart comparing the features of both companies' policies. Summarize their similarities and differences in a written report and make a recommendation for the policy you would choose as a young adult.

CORE SKILLS

19. **Research, Math.** Research the various costs of housing-related expenses, such as the monthly or annual costs of rent, heating and cooling, electricity, cable service, telephone service, garbage pickup, and insurance. Add these payments and identify how much monthly take-home income you would need if your housing and utility costs equaled 37 percent of your income.

20. **Math, Financial Literacy.** Locate a website related to financing a used car. Enter the cost of a car and print out various payment plans based on four-year and five-year loans. Compare the total cost of purchase at various interest rates, including a low-interest rate loan from the manufacturer and a loan from your local bank. Write a paragraph in which you identify your findings and explain what you feel would be the best choice. Identify the monthly payment needed in a budget in order to purchase this vehicle.

21. **Speaking, Listening.** Prepare questions to ask an insurance representative regarding needs for families at different stages. Ask about housing, car, health, and life insurance. Write a summary of the representative's recommendations.

22. **Financial Literacy, Math.** Plan a family budget using recommended percentages for your area (based on your findings in question 15). Identify an income figure close to the amount you expect to make at the beginning of your working career. Identify gross pay, subtract deductions, and identify net income to use in your budget. Then identify realistic figures for the cost of food and housing in your area (see questions 17 and 19). Identify the monthly cost of a choice of transportation and of both health and life insurance (see questions 20 and 21). Budget for the following: emergency expenses, one short-term goal, and the long-term goal of buying a home. Figure what percent of your income you planned for each budget expense.

CAREER READINESS

23. **Evaluating Health Insurance.** Find out what kind of health insurance plans are offered by three local employers. Learn what coverages they offer; what the individual and family deductibles are for those insured; what the coinsurance and co-pay rates are; and how much, if any, employees have to contribute to the premiums. Compare the three plans. Which one is a better benefit for employees?

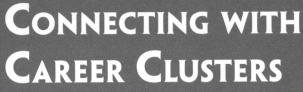

CONNECTING WITH CAREER CLUSTERS

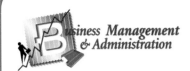

PATHWAYS

General Management

Business Information Management

Human Resources Management

Operations Management

Administrative Support

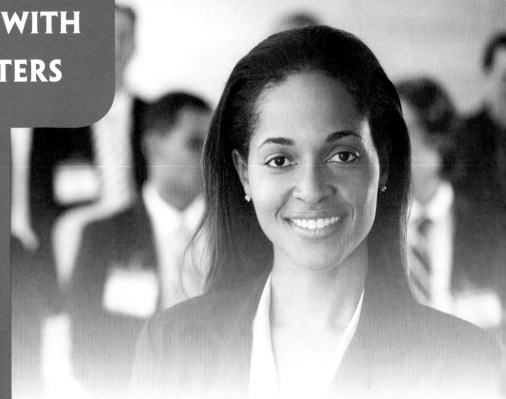

HUMAN RESOURCES MANAGEMENT

Human resources managers and *human resources specialists* handle the routine tasks of interviewing, hiring, and explaining company benefits and policies to employees. These specialists also provide training opportunities to personnel and help firms make the best of their employees' skills. Many also write employee newsletters and develop programs to boost employee morale.

A big part of this career is staying informed of laws and guidelines pertaining to equal employment, affirmative action, health insurance, pension planning, and other workplace programs. Human resources managers also negotiate labor issues between workers and managers and resolve employee conflicts.

People in this career work normal office hours, except when labor contracts are being prepared. Most work in an office setting, but may travel extensively to discuss labor contracts or recruit new employees. Human resources positions are found in every industry, with about 13 percent of workers in state, federal, and local governments.

A bachelor's degree is needed for entry-level jobs, but specialized and top positions require an advanced degree. Courses in business, psychology, management, labor law, and employee training and development are important.

CAREER OUTLOOK

A career in human resources requires good communication, persuasion, presentation, and technology skills; a talent for functioning well under pressure, coping with opposing viewpoints, and resolving conflict; an ability to work with people from various backgrounds; and integrity and fair-mindedness.

The overall growth of new jobs through 2022 is expected to be average. Salaries for human resources managers ranged from $60,400 to $183,600 in 2014, with a median salary of $102,780. Salaries vary according to the type of employer, level of experience, and area of specialty.

EXPLORE

Internet Research

Find a company that interests you and search online for information about working in its human resources department. What career information can you find? What positions does the department utilize? Research the postsecondary education needed for at least one of these positions. Then identify a college that offers this program and review the list of courses that such a program includes. Finally, write a letter (as though you were applying for a job) indicating how you, as a potential human resources specialist, could benefit the business.

Job Shadowing

Spend some time with an employee who handles human resources tasks for a local business, organization, or school. Ask questions about what he or she likes about the job, the challenges that go with the job, and what specific skills he or she feels are especially valuable in carrying out the job. Also, gather information about the types of employee benefits that the company provides and what family-friendly policies the company has (for example, flexible hours, job sharing, employer-sponsored child care, or parenting leaves). Summarize your impressions of the job in a one-page paper. Report the person's title and identify 10 qualities the person possesses.

Community Service/Volunteer

Volunteer to referee children's games for a summer camp, youth-group outing, or recreation department program. Afterward, report the type of training you received before starting the assignment and the lessons you learned from the experience. Summarize your report with a description of how the programs in which you participated benefit various members in your community.

Project

Identify a problem in your school involving two or more people that needs to be resolved. Then, take on the role of a human resources manager and determine the steps to take to solve the problem. Write a report describing what you would do in each step and how much time the project would take.

Interview

Ask a human resources manager for a 15-minute telephone interview about his or her job. Find out the main responsibilities of the job and the skills required to accomplish them. Also, learn what the job requires in terms of education, training, and experience, including ongoing training to keep current in the field. Prepare a report summarizing your information.

Part-Time Job

Prepare a training manual that could be used to train a person who does your job. Include techniques that would help the new worker become efficient and productive. Identify training workshops held in the area that could be beneficial to you and similar jobholders.

GLOSSARY

A

abilities: Skills that a person learns and develops as a result of training and practice.

absorb: To take in.

abstinence: Not having sexual relations.

abstract thinking: A type of thinking related to something you cannot see, touch, taste, smell, or hear.

abuse: Behavior used in a relationship to exert power and control over another person; endangers the safety of the person being abused.

accommodation: A pattern of adjustment in which a spouse agrees to accept and live with his or her partner's differences.

accountability: Being responsible to another for action that is taken.

accredited: A status in which the college or university meets specific standards that have been set by an accreditation agency.

acquaintance: A person whom you know, but who is not a close friend.

acquired immunodeficiency syndrome (AIDS): A disease caused by HIV, which attacks the cells that normally help the body fight off infection and other diseases.

acting out: Using extreme behavior to express oneself rather than expressing feelings and thoughts in words.

active interaction: An interaction in which two people have physical and verbal exchanges during an activity.

active listening: Listening that involves giving the message sender some type of feedback, including such techniques as clarifying, paraphrasing, and reflecting.

activities preference inventory: A test designed to help people learn whether their interests are centered on people, ideas, or objects.

addiction: Physical dependence of the body on a drug.

adequate: Having enough to meet one's needs.

adolescence: The teen years.

adolescent growth spurt: A period of sudden growth marking the beginning of several physical changes and puberty in early adolescence.

adoptive family: A family structure that consists of one or more parents and an adopted child or children.

adult day care: A program that provides care and companionship for elderly people who need help and supervision during the day.

advanced placement course: A high school course that, if completed, allows students to skip entry-level college courses based on completion with a specific level of success.

agency adoption: An adoption that is handled through a public or private adoption agency.

agency on aging: An organization that brings many services to the elderly to help them handle the various issues of their daily lives.

agenda: A list prepared by a group leader that outlines what the group will be doing and discussing at the meeting.

aggressive: The quality of expressing thoughts, needs, and wants in a way that hurts others.

alcoholic: A person who is addicted to alcohol and cannot control its use.

alienated: Feeling alone, without hope, or cut off from others who care.

alimony: A financial settlement paid to a spouse.

alternative: A possible choice to consider when making a decision.

anemia: A condition of weakness and fatigue, often caused by an iron-deficient diet.

annual percentage rate (APR): The yearly cost of using credit.

anonymous: The state of being unknown or unidentified.

anxiety: The uneasy feeling people experience when they believe something terrible will happen.

appreciation: Showing approval with positive feedback.

apprenticeship: A position in which the worker learns skills and gains experience while under the supervision of an experienced worker.

appropriate: Being suitable for a specific situation.

aptitudes: A person's natural talents.

artifact: An item that represents achievements over time.

assault: A threat to cause physical harm to a person.

assertive: The quality of clearly expressing thoughts, needs, and wants in a way that is considerate of others; involves using I-statements, direct eye contact, and genuine expressions and gestures.

assessment: An evaluation of a situation.

assisted living: Around-the-clock care for elderly people in which people live in special facilities and receive support with daily living tasks.

assistive technology: A device that assists a person who has a disability with hearing, vision, or mobility tasks.

associative play: Stage of play in which two or more children play at one activity that is not organized.

assumption: An idea you take for granted, without thinking about it.

attitude: A pattern of thinking, feeling, and responding that develops as a person interacts with his or her environment.

author: One who creates and sends a written message.

authoritarian: An approach to leadership in which the leader dictates how the group operates.

autism spectrum disorder: A developmental disorder that results in children having difficulty with social interactions.

automatic: A behavior that occurs without thought or conscious intention.

autonomy: The child's realization that he or she has control over his or her own body and is a separate person.

available: Able to be used.

axon: A long fiber in a neuron that carries information away from the cell body to the dendrites of other nerve cells or to other cells in the body.

B

balance: A state in which there is an even distribution of weight or power.

barrier to divorce: Any factor that keeps a couple from moving ahead with a divorce.

battery: The use of force resulting in physical contact with a person that the individual did not permit.

beneficiary: A person who benefits from a situation; the person who receives money from an insurance policy in the event of the death of the policyholder.

blaming: A pattern of communication in which people accuse others for everything that goes wrong as a way of preserving their own self-esteem.

blind spot: An area of awareness in which your knowledge or understanding is limited.

bodily injury liability: Type of insurance that protects against major financial losses resulting from an accident for which the policyholder was responsible.

body language: The expression of thoughts, feelings, and emotions through body movements and position.

bonding: The development of strong feelings of attachment between the parent and the newborn.

brain plasticity: The ability of the brain to respond to changes.

brainstem: Part of the brain that controls life functions such as the beating of the heart and breathing.

budget: A plan for the use of income.

bullying: Using aggressive behavior to intentionally harm or intimidate another person.

business ethics: A guiding set of good character traits that influence high standards in business activities.

business etiquette: Workplace manners, including showing respect for others, being polite, and taking time to listen and communicate clearly.

bylaws: Additional guidelines for group activities that state when meetings are held, how often, when elections are held, what procedures are used, and any other information related to the group's organization.

C

career: The work done over several years while a person holds different jobs within a particular career field or area.

career clusters: Sixteen broad groupings of occupational and career specialties.

career fair: An event in which employers or professional organizations provide career-related information to attendees.

career ladder: A series of jobs in which each job builds on the experiences of the previous job.

career pathway: A series of education, training, and services that advance, over time, to successively higher levels of education and employment in a given career area.

career plan: A list of steps to take to reach a career goal.

carrier: A person who has a recessive gene for a certain disease and can pass the disease on to his or her children, but who does not have the disease.

cerebellum: Part of the brain that controls automatic movements and some complex thinking processes.

ceremonial wedding: A marriage ceremony in which friends and family witness the couple's vows being taken before a religious official.

certificate of completion: A statement that verifies you have mastered a set of specific skills.

certification: A confirmation of completion of a formal course of study or success in showing that a specific set of knowledge and skills has been mastered.

chairperson: A group leader; also called a *president.*

channel: The means by which a message is conveyed to a receiver; either the air if it is spoken, or through technology or print if the message is written.

character: The set of principles and beliefs that shape one's conduct; developed as part of the socialization process.

child abuse: Any physical or mental threat or injury to a child under the age of 18.

childrearing leave: A period of time that a parent may be absent from work to provide full-time care for a young child; typically refers to a longer period of leave than parental leave.

child sexual abuse: Any sexual contact or interaction between an adult and a child or teenager.

child support: Payments that a noncustodial parent is legally required to pay toward the expense of raising children under age 18.

chlamydia: A sexually transmitted infection that can damage a woman's reproductive organs; one of the most common bacterial STIs in the United States.

chromosomes: Rod-shaped structures that carry hereditary information from each biological parent to the child.

chronic illness: A medical problem that cannot be cured.

chronic stress: Ongoing stress that continues over time.

circumstance: A condition of living.

citizen: A person who formally owes allegiance to a government. In return, he or she gains rights and responsibilities that are protected by the laws of the government.

civil ceremony: A marriage ceremony in which family members and a few friends witness a couple's wedding vows being taken before a judicial or public official.

clarifying: An active listening strategy in which you use questions to make sure you understand a message communicated by a sender.

closed adoption: Type of adoption in which the child does not know the identity of the birthparents and an adoption agency makes the decisions.

coach: A person who helps you learn a specific skill.

cocurricular: Learning opportunities outside of the classroom.

code of conduct: An expected pattern of behaving and acting.

codependent: A relationship in which one person tries to rescue and enable others to continue with problematic behaviors instead of letting them take responsibility for their own choices.

cohesive: The quality of sticking together because group members feel they belong to the group.

coinsurance: An arrangement in which the insured person pays a percentage of each health care bill.

collaborate: To work together to perform a task or reach a goal.

collateral: A form of security on a loan in which the lender can repossess goods if a person fails to make payments.

collision insurance: Insurance that covers the cost of damage to the policyholder's car if it is involved in an accident.

commitment: A decision to dedicate yourself to someone or something.

communication: An exchange of information among two or more people; involves the sending and receiving of messages through spoken or written words, facial expressions, or gestures.

communication style: A pattern of speaking and listening in which a person feels comfortable; often affected by temperament, traits, and personality.

community-based day care: A program of activities for older people who are still somewhat independent.

community college: A nonresidential college that offers courses leading to a certificate or a two-year associate's degree.

compensation: A technique in which a person focuses on a strength to make up for a weakness in another area.

complementary quality: A difference between people that attracts one person to another and benefits the relationship.

complementary role: A role in a marriage that harmonizes with or supports the roles the other person takes.

complication: An increased concern, problem, or difficulty resulting from and affecting a woman's pregnancy.

compounding: The accumulation of interest in which interest previously earned is added to the total before new interest earnings are figured.

comprehensive physical damage: A type of insurance that covers the risk of damage to the policyholder's car by perils other than collision.

compromise: A give-and-take method of resolving differences that allows all people involved to express themselves and reach a solution that is satisfactory to all.

compulsory: Required by law.

conceited: Thinking one is better than others.

concession: A pattern of adjustment in which one spouse gives in to the other, rather than working to reach a joint agreement.

concrete thinking: A type of thinking that is related to specific objects that can be seen or touched.

conditional: Dependent upon behavior or another factor.

confidentiality: Limiting the knowledge and use of information to those who are authorized to have it.

conflict: When two people disagree on an issue.

conflict resolution: A communication skill that encourages a better understanding of the other person's point of view, helping to resolve conflicts in a positive way.

conform: To adapt to certain standards of appearance, dress, and behavior.

consensus building: A process in which a group works together to find a solution that is acceptable to all involved.

consequence: The end result of a choice.

consider: To think about or view in a certain way.

consistent: Regular, ongoing, and reliable.

constant: Unchanging.

constitution: A formal written statement that explains a group's purpose and goals and governs its functions.

constructive: Having a positive impact.

constructive feedback: Responses that provide information that would help improve a situation.

contention: Disagreement.

context: The situation in which an action is taking place.

continuum: A range in which qualities exist all of the time at one end of the range, and never exist at the other end of the range, with many variations in between.

contract: A mutual agreement between two consenting people.

conventional: Common to many people.

conversion: Transferring an emotion into a physical symptom.

cooperative child care: Child care centers that are organized, managed, and funded by the parents who use them to care for their children.

cooperative play: Stage of play in which children work together to reach common goals.

coordinate: To organize different pieces of a task.

co-pay: A flat fee for some health care services, such as office visits.

coping behavior: Planned behavior that helps persons adjust as quickly as possible to changes that have taken place.

corpus callosum: The cable of neurons that connects the two halves of the brain; changes and grows during the teen years.

cortex: Part of the brain that controls thinking, decision making, and judgment; also called the *cerebrum*.

courteous: The quality of being polite.

cover message: A message sent with a résumé to clearly state the position a job applicant seeks and highlight his or her relevant qualifications.

credit: A financial agreement that allows consumers to borrow money or make a purchase and pay for it in the future.

credit limit: The maximum amount of money a person can borrow on a credit card.

credit rating: A record of how well a person has paid his or her bills in the past.

crisis: An experience or event affecting an individual, family, community, or society that could lead to an unstable or dangerous situation; causes a person to make major changes in his or her life.

crisis-care center: A safe, short-term shelter for abused children.

critical thinking: The active process of improving your own thinking by analyzing your thoughts, assessing your logic, judging your assumptions, and restructuring your own thoughts based on your reasoning and reflection.

cultural heritage: Learned behavior that is passed from generation to generation.

cultural identity: The way a person sees himself or herself as a member of a specific cultural group.

custom: An accepted way of acting.

customer relations: All the interactions that take place when you are providing services to the people who are your employer's customers.

customer service: Meeting customers' needs in an efficient, effective, and courteous manner.

cyber-acquaintance: A person you talk to whom you have met online.

cyberbullying: Using technology, such as the Internet or mobile devices, to send hurtful or threatening messages to another person.

D

date rape: Sexual intercourse with a dating partner against one person's will.

deadline: The date at which a task must be completed.

decision-making process: A step-by-step method to guide thinking when a planned decision is needed.

decoding: The process of receiving a message and interpreting its meaning; a step in the communication process.

deductible: An amount that the insured has to pay before the insurance company pays any money.

defense mechanisms: Methods people unconsciously use to deal with life situations; may hide or balance people's feelings and actions.

democratic: A style of leadership in which group members are involved in making decisions.

democratic decision making: Process in which group members take part in the selection of one choice and help carry out the plan of action.

demographic: A characteristic of a population.

dendrite: The fingerlike extension of a neuron through which information is sent to the nerve cells.

denial: The refusal to accept the reality of something that has happened.

depressant: A substance that slows the activity of the brain by knocking out control centers.

depression: An overwhelming attitude of sadness, discouragement, and hopelessness that can cause difficulty in making decisions and in trying to lead a normal life.

designated: Assigned or appointed to a particular position.

detached: Distant.

detection: Identification of a symptom.

developmental task: A skill that society expects of individuals at various stages of life.

digital footprint: A collection of information about a person and the various websites that he or she has visited over time.

diminish: To make smaller or less important.

direct attack: A method used to face a problem, recognize it, and try to solve it.

direct eye contact: Looking directly at a person when you are speaking or listening.

disability: A condition that interferes with certain intellectual or physical abilities.

disability insurance: A type of insurance in which, for a fee, the insurance company pays a weekly or monthly amount to an individual who cannot work.

disbanded: Having been broken up.

displacement: Taking out feelings on someone or something else rather than facing the real problem.

distracting: A pattern of communication in which people ignore unpleasant situations and put them aside as not really being important.

diversity: The unique qualities of people from different backgrounds.

divorce: The ending of a marriage.

DNA: The unique pattern of genes in all of your cells; made up of approximately three billion base pairs of genetic material.

dominant gene: A gene that determines how a certain trait is expressed in a person.

double date: A date in which two couples attend a planned event together.

drug: Any substance that chemically changes structures or functions in living organisms.

drug abuse: Using drugs in ways for which they were not intended.

dual-career family: Type of family in which both husband and wife pursue careers outside the home while maintaining their family roles.

durable power of attorney: A legal document that allows a person to choose someone to act in his or her place in the event of becoming mentally incapable of handling his or her own affairs.

dwell: To focus your attention on an issue.

E

early parenthood stage: The second stage of the family life cycle that begins with the birth of the first child and continues through the toddler, preschool, and elementary years of the youngest child in the family.

elder abuse: Intentionally or knowingly causing an elder person to suffer physical harm or injury, unreasonable confinement, sexual abuse, or a lack of services or medical treatment to maintain health.

elect: To choose for office.

eligible: Able to be considered; meeting the qualifications.

emotional abuse: Any behavior that tears at a person's core being or sense of self and destroys self-esteem.

emotional development: A developmental process that refers to the ability to experience, express, and control emotions.

emotional divorce: The first stage of marriage breakdown in which one or both spouses withdraw from the relationship and fulfill emotional needs outside the marriage.

emotional stability: The ability to withstand common minor stressors in life without becoming upset, angry, nervous, or anxious, as well as the ability to control behaviors and return to an even emotional state in a short period of time after a major stress event.

empathy: An emotion in which you feel what another person is feeling.

employer-sponsored child care: Care offered for children of employees that is funded by the employer.

empty nest stage: The fourth stage of the family life cycle in which the last child becomes independent and begins living on his or her own.

encoding: The process of thinking about what you want to say and how to say it and then transmitting or sending the message; a step in the communication process.

endometriosis: A disease in which uterine tissue grows outside the uterus, often resulting in pain and infertility.

endorsement: A statement or symbol indicating mastery or completion of a specific program.

engagement: The final stage in the dating process leading to marriage.

enthused: Excited.

entrepreneur: A person who is self-employed and earns income through his or her own business.

environment: A person's surroundings and everything in them, including human and nonhuman factors.

equal opportunity: A requirement in the workplace to treat all people fairly regardless of race, color, sex, national origin, age, religion, or disability.

escalate: To increase rapidly, becoming more intense or serious.

estimate: To guess based on past experiences and outside input.

ethical decision making: Making personal decisions that are guided by ethical standards which help to develop communities and a society where mutual respect, honesty, caring, justice, and fairness benefit all.

ethics: Moral principles or standards a person uses to judge what is right or wrong.

etiquette: Appropriate behaviors that will help a person succeed in a group.

evidence: Information or facts to support a thought, point of view, or conclusion.

exclusive dating: Dating in which a person commits to date only one person.

expertise: An area in which a person has specialized knowledge.

extended family: (1) Relatives beyond the immediate family; grandparents, aunts, uncles, cousins, and other relatives. (2) A family structure in which several generations of one family live together, sharing the home and family activities.

extent: The amount to which a quality exists.

external stress: Stress caused by factors outside the family.

extrovert: A person who is very outgoing and enjoys being with people.

F

face-to-face interaction: Communication in which you read another person's nonverbal signs.

face value: The largest amount an insurance company will pay for a loss, as determined by the type of policy purchased.

factor: A quality or feature that needs to be considered for its potential impact.

family: Two or more people living in the same household who are related by blood, marriage, or adoption.

family child care: Child care that is provided in a caregiver's home.

family life cycle: Five stages in the life of a family that include common events and adjustments that families go through over time.

family routines: Small events or activities that are repeated on a regular basis in the family.

family structure: The form that the family takes in terms of the makeup of parents, children, and other family members.

family system: The interactions of all family members with one another and the effects of these interactions.

family traditions: Established patterns of behavior or customs handed down through generations.

family tree: A list of several generations of blood relatives; often used to trace hereditary factors and traits from one generation to another.

fantasy: Defense mechanism in which people use their imaginary thoughts as an escape to fill their personal needs.

federal: The level of government at the national level; applying to an entire nation.

feedback: A signal the receiver gives back to the sender to indicate how the message communicated was understood.

felony: A serious crime that can result in a sentence of more than a year in prison or even death.

fight-or-flight response: The body's natural response to stress in which it reacts to a perceived danger by sending out stress hormones to give the body increased strength and speed.

file: To apply for benefits by completing an application.

financial responsibility law: Law that requires drivers to prove their ability to pay for the cost of any damages or injuries that might be caused in an auto accident.

fixed expense: An expense that is constant each month.

flexibility: The willingness to change and negotiate differences with another person.

flexible scheduling: An employee benefit that allows workers the ability to choose their work hours, within reason.

foremost: Greatest.

formal date: A date in which two people attend a planned event together.

foster care: Temporary care for children under 18 years of age.

founding family: The newly formed family at the beginning of the family life cycle.

fraud: The crime of using deceptive practices to cheat people out of their money.

free society: A community where policies and actions are promoted to bring about better living conditions for all people.

function: A purpose.

G

gene: The basic unit of heredity that determines human characteristics or traits.

genetics: The scientific study of heredity.

genital herpes: An incurable and widespread sexually transmitted infection caused by a virus that produces painful sores or blisters.

genital warts: Small bumps or clusters of bumps in the genital area caused by a virus.

genotype: The genetic makeup of an individual or group.

goal: Something a person wants to do, have, or achieve at a certain point.

gonorrhea: A sexually transmitted infection caused by bacteria that can produce damage to the male and female organs and result in sterility.

grant: A form of financial aid that does not have to be repaid.

grief: A process in which a person identifies and accepts a loss; consists of emotional stages.

gross income: A person's total wage or salary before any deductions are made.

ground: A legally acceptable reason.

group: Two or more people interacting in ways that affect each other.

group child care: Care provided for a number of children, usually of the same age, in a child care center.

group dating: Dating in which a group of people spend time together, developing friendships with others in the group.

group health insurance: A health insurance policy available through an employer, union, or professional association; provides more medical coverage at a lower cost than individual policies.

group home: A place available for children or teens who live in abusive families. Counselors provide care and counseling to cope with problems stemming from abuse.

group values: The ideals and beliefs that are important to a specific group of people within a culture.

guaranteed replacement value: The assurance that an insurance company will replace an item even if the cost of the new item is higher than the face value of the policy.

guidance: All that parents do and say as they influence their children's behavior in a positive way and lead them into maturity.

H

harmonize: To go well with or support.

helpless: Needing care and provision from others to grow toward maturity.

hepatitis B: A sexually transmitted infection caused by a virus that attacks the liver; can also be transmitted by exposure to infected blood.

hectic: Busy or chaotic.

heredity: The sum of the qualities that are passed to a person from his or her ancestors.

high-growth industry: A career area that is expected to provide many new job openings in the future.

home health care: An arrangement in which nurses or aides go to the elderly person's home to provide assistance with health care.

homemaker: A person who conducts work in the home. Although a homemaker is not classified as a working person, homemaking involves important tasks, such as housekeeping, laundering clothing, food preparation, child care, and preschool teaching.

home study: Process in which an agency or a social worker conducts an evaluation of a couple's home to determine its suitability for a child.

homogamy: A principle that people who have similarities in certain areas, or much in common, are more likely to have a satisfying marriage.

hospice care: Physical, emotional, and spiritual care designed to help a dying person live the final days of life in comfort.

hostility: A pattern of adjustment in which a couple continually argues or quarrels without settling conflicts or agreeing on solutions.

household: All the persons occupying a living unit.

human immunodeficiency virus (HIV): The AIDS-causing virus, which attacks cells that normally help a person fight off infection and disease.

human papillomavirus (HPV): A sexually transmitted infection that infects the skin and mucous membranes and can cause genital warts or cancer.

human resource: A personal quality and characteristic that comes from within a person; also a person who provides support in some way.

I

icebreaker: A short interaction that helps you connect with another person.

idealization: Valuing someone or something far more than its true worth.

immunizations: Injections or drops given to a person to prevent a specific disease.

impending: Upcoming.

implement: To carry out or put into practice.

inconvenient: Coming at a bad time.

independence: The chance to live alone as one wishes.

independent adoption: An adoption that is arranged privately, usually though a doctor or lawyer.

independent living: Living on one's own and being responsible to care for oneself. An option for abused teens whose parents agree to give up legal control; only for mature, emotionally stable teens who can provide for themselves financially.

Individualized Education Plan (IEP): A plan set up by parents and school staff members for the education of a child with special needs.

inevitable: Certain to occur or happen.

infant: A child from three months to one year old.

infatuation: A strong feeling of attraction that tends to be self-centered or one-sided.

infertility: A couple's inability to conceive a child after trying for a year or more, or a woman's inability to carry a child to full term.

input: Information coming in.

installment credit: A type of credit in which money is paid back in equal installments, usually as monthly payments.

institution: A structure that is part of society.

insurance: A form of protection against financial loss.

insured: An individual who purchases insurance protection.

integrity: The quality of being completely honest and doing the right thing in a reliable way.

intellectual development: A developmental process that refers to the growth of the brain and the use of mental skills.

intelligence: A person's capacity for mental activity.

intensify: To increase or make stronger.

intentional: Acting with purpose or intent to make something happen.

interdependent: Being interconnected with, depending on, and being affected by and able to affect others.

interest: A charge for the use of money, usually expressed as a percentage.

interests: The subjects, activities, or events that a person enjoys.

internal stress: Stress that comes from inside the family.

international adoption: Type of adoption in which a family adopts a child from another country and culture.

internship: On-the-job training where a student learns to put to practice the skills and knowledge gained in an educational program.

interpersonal adjustment: A change that a couple makes as they learn to adjust to each other's differences.

interpret: To construct a personal understanding of.

interrelated: A quality in which two objects, concepts, or people cannot exist without the other.

interrupted work pattern: A pattern of work in which adults devote full-time attention to their careers after leaving school, quit work for a period of time to carry out the work of the family, and then resume their careers.

interview: A meeting in which an employer talks with a job applicant.

intimate: Close and honest.

intrauterine insemination (IUI): A procedure in which a doctor uses a syringe to deposit sperm directly into the uterus.

introvert: A person who is shy, withdrawn, or anxious about meeting new people.

inventory: A list of items or activities.

in vitro fertilization (IVF): An assisted reproductive technology in which multiple eggs are stimulated to mature and then fertilized in a laboratory before being placed directly into the uterus.

I-statement: A statement that directly expresses your thoughts, feelings, and ideas from a personal point of view.

J

job: A position in which a person works to earn a living.

job fair: An event where employers come together, often at a college or community center, to recruit potential employees for their organization or business.

job outlook: The potential for finding a job in an area and in the future.

job shadow: An opportunity to follow a person in a particular career for a day, listening in and observing what he or she does in the course of the job.

job sharing: A full-time job split between two people.

joint custody: An arrangement in which both parents in a divorce share the rights and responsibilities of legal custody of their children.

L

latchkey children: Children who regularly go home after school to an empty home without adult supervision.

lateral: Sideways.

launching stage: The third stage of the family life cycle in which parents help young adults complete their education, become financially independent, and move out on their own; also known as the *later parenthood stage*.

leader: A person who is placed in charge or takes charge of a group and is responsible for helping the group succeed.

learning disorder: A disability in which a child has difficulty learning to carry out certain skills, even though his or her intelligence is average.

lease: A legal contract between the renter and the landlord that states the terms and conditions of the agreement.

legal custody: Having the legal rights and responsibilities of providing for each child's care until he or she reaches age 18.

legal divorce: The ending of a marriage through the legal process.

legal separation: A legal agreement for a couple to live apart, divide their property, and provide for their children but remain legally married.

legislature: A law-making governmental body at the federal or state level.

leisure: Activities done for enjoyment and relaxation.

letter of recommendation: A letter addressed to a potential future employer that explains the skills and behaviors that a person showed on a job or in a class.

liability: The legal responsibility for another person's financial costs due to a loss or injury for which you are responsible.

license: The right to work in a particular profession; is gained after a person follows the process laid out by the state government.

lifelong learning: Education and training throughout one's work life.

life span: The time between a person's birth and death.

lifestyle: The way a person chooses to live.

limbic system: Four main structures in the brain that control emotions and hormone production; eating, drinking, and sleeping; and long-term memory storage.

liquidity: The ability to withdraw money from an account on short notice.

logic: Connecting several abstract ideas to support a decision or build a viewpoint.

long-term goal: Something a person wants to do, have, or achieve in the distant future.

M

marital adjustment: The process couples use to modify their relationship as needed throughout their married life.

marital role: A responsibility that a person may be expected to fulfill after marriage, such as spouse, friend, wage earner, cook, caregiver, or housekeeper.

marriage counseling: Meeting with a professional to try to improve a couple's relationship.

marriage enrichment program: A program sponsored by community service agencies or religious or educational groups to help couples strengthen their marriages.

material abuse: The misuse of an elderly person's property or financial resources.

mature love: A long-lasting, caring, and giving type of love.

maximum: The highest amount.

media: Sources of information and entertainment, such as television, radio, movies, videos, newspapers, magazines, and the Internet.

mediator: A third party who works with others to help them negotiate and reach a solution that all can accept.

medical payments coverage: A type of insurance that pays the medical expenses resulting from injuries to you and others in your car in a car accident.

Medicare: A federal program that helps older people with health care expenses.

mental disorder: A type of disability that affects social or emotional functioning; examples include anxiety disorders and phobias, bipolar disorder, depression, mood disorders, and personality disorders; also called a *mental illness*.

mental health: The overall condition of your social and emotional well-being; is impacted by how well you deal with feelings about yourself, others, and the world around you.

mentee: Someone who is being mentored.

mentor: Someone who serves as advisor to you with the goal of helping you be successful.

method: A way of doing something.

middlescence: The years between the ages of 40 and 65.

midlife crisis: An event caused by trouble adjusting to the changes that occur during the middle years of life.

minutes: A written description of what took place at a meeting.

miscarriage: Loss of a fetus during the first twenty weeks of development.

misdemeanor: A less serious crime that may be punished by a fine or a short prison term of less than a year.

mixed messages: Words and actions that do not match each other.

model: An example from which others can learn.

modeling: Acting in a way that sets a good example for children to follow.

modify: To change in some way.

monitor: To observe what is happening.

moral development: A person's development of the ability to distinguish between good and bad, or acceptable and unacceptable, behaviors.

motivation: A reason for taking action.

multiculturalism: A society with people of different cultural backgrounds.

N

nanny: A person who comes into the child's home to provide care as a paying job.

natural consequences: The normal results of an action.

neglect: Failure to give a child proper shelter, clothing, food, medical care, supervision, love, or affection.

negotiation: A communication process in which people alternate between sending and receiving messages for the purpose of reaching a mutually agreeable solution.

net income: The amount of money left after subtracting deductions from gross income.

networking: Talking to family members, friends, or acquaintances about possible job openings.

neuron: A nerve cell in the brain.

neurotransmitter: A chemical in the nerve synapse that allows messages to be carried from one neuron to another.

newborn: A child between birth and three months.

newly married stage: The first stage of the family life cycle in which two people marry; also called the *beginning stage*.

no-fault divorce: A legal term for a divorce in which neither spouse is blamed for the divorce.

no-fault insurance: Insurance that eliminates the legal process of proving who was at fault in a car accident. No-fault insurance offers personal injury protection instead of medical payments coverage. The actual costs of medical expenses, lost wages, and related expenses are covered by each person's own insurance.

nonfamily household: A type of single living that encompasses a one-person household, a person living alone, and a household in which unrelated people share the home.

nonhuman resource: An item available to help a person reach a goal, such as money, a car, tools, time, or information.

nonverbal communication: A way of sending a receiving messages without using words, such as through body motions, facial expressions, and eye contact.

nuclear family: A family structure that includes a married couple and their biological children.

nurture: To care for.

nurturing: Caring and attentive.

nurturing environment: An environment in which children feel secure, protected, and loved.

nurturing relationship: A relationship in which children's needs for feeling secure, protected, and loved are met.

O

obstacle: Something that stands in the way of achieving a goal.

onlooker play: Stage of play in which young toddlers watch other children play but will not join in.

open admissions: A policy that anyone who has a high school diploma can be admitted to a college as long as there is room available in the desired program.

open adoption: Type of adoption in which birthparents may select and meet the adoptive parents and in which the adopted child will have information about his or her birthparents.

optimistic: Looking at events and life experiences positively.

ordinance: A local law or regulation.

organization: The process of arranging things in a systematic way so you can deal with them efficiently.

ovulation: The process in which the ovaries release a mature egg.

P

pair adjustment: A change that a couple makes to adjust their individual lifestyles to have a satisfying life together.

pair dating: Dating in which two people spend time as a couple building their friendship.

parallel play: Stage of play in which older toddlers play side by side without interacting with each other.

paraphrasing: Repeating in your own words what you think another person has said.

parental leave: An employee benefit that permits parents to be away from work while involved in full-time parenting for a specified period.

parenting: Using skills to care for and raise a child to adulthood.

parliamentary procedure: An orderly way of conducting a meeting and discussing business.

participate: To take part in.

passive interaction: An interaction in which a person is involved only as an observer or listener.

passive listening: Listening that involves hearing words without listening for meanings.

peer: A person in your age group.

penalize: To inflict disadvantage on.

pension: A fund paid by an employer to a former employee who contributed to a special retirement fund while he or she was employed.

personal boundaries: Limits for behavior that a person will accept in a relationship.

personal identity: A sense of your individuality and personality.

personality: The sum of all personal and behavioral traits that combine to make a person unique.

personal space: The amount of space that you need between yourself and another person for both of you to feel comfortable.

perspective: A point of view.

petitioner: The person who files for divorce.

phenomenon: A notable occurrence.

phobia: An intense fear.

physical abuse: The intentional harm or threat of harm to a person's body.

physical custody: A legal term for where children live and which parent in a divorce provides the routine daily care and control of the children.

physical development: A developmental process that refers to the body's physical growth, which affects height, weight, and internal body systems.

physical dexterity: The skill of working quickly with one's hands or fingers.

pileup effect: Stress that builds up and produces a crisis.

placating: A pattern of communication in which people say or do things just to please others or keep them from getting upset.

placement rate: The percentage of graduates who find jobs in their field of study.

planned decision: A decision that requires more time and energy to make the best choice.

point of view: The personal way a person sees things; involves the person's position of knowledge, experiences, background, and culture.

policy: A contract between the insurance company and the policyholder.

portfolio: A collection of materials that document achievements over time.

postsecondary: Relating to after high school.

potential: The maximum development that can take place.

praise: To express appreciation for.

preeclampsia: A condition during pregnancy characterized by swelling and high blood pressure; also called *toxemia* or *pregnancy-induced hypertension (PIH)*.

prejudice: The formation of an opinion about another person or group of people without complete knowledge or facts.

premature baby: A baby born before the 37th week of pregnancy.

premium: A fee charged by an insurance company to assume a financial loss that is described in the policy.

prenatal: Referring to the months before birth.

preschooler: A child between three and five years of age.

prestige: Feelings of importance or high status.

principle: An accepted idea that can be applied to a situation.

prioritize: To list in order of importance.

problem ownership: Identifying the person who is most bothered and affected by a problem.

procedure: A set step in a process.

procrastinate: To put off doing a project until the last minute.

professional relationships: Relationships which are maintained at a professional level and usually focus on specific tasks or types of work.

profile: A report with specific details.

program of study: The sequence of courses you take in high school aligned with the courses you will take at a postsecondary institution.

project: To plan or think about ideas for the future.

projection: Placing the blame for failures on others.

promotion: A job change in which a person is assigned to a different position in the same organization that has more responsibility and increased pay.

property damage liability: Protection to cover losses to someone else's property caused by the policyholder and his or her vehicle.

proportionate: On the same level; a proper relationship between two things.

prospective: Likely to happen or be.

puberty: A process through which reproductive organs mature during adolescence. Sexual maturity takes place when certain hormones are released in the body.

public policy: A government action meant to achieve certain goals.

Punnett square: A graph used to determine what possible gene pairs may result from combining two genes.

Q

qualified: Trained and experienced to meet a certain standard.

quarrel: To argue.

R

rape: Forced sexual intercourse.

rapport: A balanced, harmonious atmosphere between two people.

rate of development: The pace at which a person proceeds through the stages of the growth sequence.

rationalization: Explaining weaknesses or failures by giving socially acceptable excuses.

reap: To gain.

receiver: The person in the communication process who hears and interprets the message.

recessive gene: A gene that determines the nature of a trait only when two recessive genes are present.

recruiter: A person who can explain about military careers, entrance requirements, training you can get through the military, requirements for active service, and benefits for those who have completed their service.

redirecting: Focusing a child's interest away from one activity to a more acceptable one.

references: People who have direct knowledge of a person and his or her past work.

reflecting: Mirroring and restating the sender's feelings as well as thoughts, using words.

register: To place your name on the list of citizens who can vote in elections.

regress: To go backward in development.

regression: Returning to childish or immature behavior when difficulties or frustrations occur.

regulation: A rule that governs various activities of a program.

reinforcement: Praising a child who does well in order to encourage continued behavior.

relationship-oriented leadership: A style of leadership that places emphasis on the feelings, thoughts, and needs of each group member.

reliable: Consistently accurate.

remedial course: A class designed to help students gain basic knowledge and skills they lack so they can fully participate in a program of study.

rend. To split.

repossess: To take back.

reputation: The beliefs or opinions that others have of you.

resent: To be angry about.

reserve: An amount set aside for emergency expenses.

resilience: The quality of being able to adjust to setbacks and make changes to survive and reach maximum growth and development.

resource: Anything available to help carry out decisions and reach goals.

respondent: The spouse against whom a divorce is filed.

responsible parenting: Making choices that will help a child develop fully in all areas of life.

résumé: A summary of a person's skills, training, education, and past work experiences.

rigid: Inflexible.

retirement: The ending of paid employment.

retirement stage: The last stage of the family life cycle in which one or both spouses retire from their careers.

revolving credit: A type of credit in which you can continuously borrow and repay money, as long as you stay under the credit limit.

Robert's Rules of Order: A book that details the process of parliamentary procedure.

role: A way of acting to fulfill certain responsibilities in life; most often taught by the family.

role model: A person who carries out his or her roles and responsibilities in a way that you would like to imitate.

role overload: Having too many roles and responsibilities to carry them all out well.

role sharing: A way of handling responsibilities by partners working together to carry out a task.

romantic love: The exhilarating feeling that can spark a relationship to then grow into mature love.

routine decision: A decision made every day without much thought.

routine stress: Stress that comes from everyday events.

S

sandwich approach: A communication method in which a criticism is expressed between two positive statements.

sandwich generation: A generation of people who are between and often supporting their older parents and their own children; also called the *middle generation*.

scapegoating: Blaming someone else for a problem instead of taking ownership.

scholarship: Free money given to a worthy candidate to further his or her education.

scope: The overall extent of a subject.

screening: Initial evaluation to narrow down the list of potential applicants for a job.

secretary: A person who records the minutes of each group meeting.

security: Something that is used for financial protection on a loan; also called *collateral*.

self-actualization: The experience of reaching your potential and feeling fulfilled.

self-concept: The mental picture people have of themselves; their opinions about or views of themselves.

self-discipline: The ability to control your behavior, words, or actions in a responsible way; also called *self-control*.

self-esteem: Your feelings of value and importance.

self-neglect: The failure of a person to provide his or her own adequate food, shelter, clothing, medical care, or dental care.

self-perpetuating cycle: The process of attitudes producing actions that may cause those same attitudes to increase.

self-pity: Feeling sorry for yourself.

self-sufficient: Able to meet one's own needs.

self-talk: Brief comments a person makes to himself or herself in his or her mind that can be either negative or positive.

sender: The person in the communication process who transmits or sends the message.

sensitive: The quality of being personal or delicate.

sensitivity: Being aware of how another person thinks and feels and taking those thoughts and feelings into consideration when responding with words or actions.

separation anxiety: An infant's fear of being any distance from parents, or the fear that parents who leave will not return.

sequence: The specific order in which steps occur.

service activity: An activity that someone does to help or benefit others.

sex roles: A culture's definition of how males and females should behave.

sex stereotypes: Oversimplified opinions or beliefs about the characteristics shared by all members of one sex.

sexual abuse: Forcing another person to be sexually involved in any way.

sexual harassment: Any unwelcome or unwanted advances, requests for favors, or other verbal or physical conduct of a sexual nature.

sexually transmitted infections (STIs): Infections that are passed from one person to another through sexual contact.

Shaken Baby Syndrome: A form of physical abuse in which brain damage is caused by a fast and forceful shaking of an infant, blows to the head, or dropping or throwing a child.

shelter: A short-term place of safety that provides an escape from a family crisis.

short-term goal: Something a person wants to do, have, or achieve in a relatively short amount of time, such as a day or week.

sibling: A brother or sister.

significant adults: Nonparental adults who play some important part in a person's life.

single living: A lifestyle in which a person lives alone.

single-parent family: Family structure that includes one parent and one or more children.

social abuse: Any behavior that destroys the ability of a person to develop healthy relationships with others.

social development: A developmental process that refers to the way people relate to others around them.

socialization: The process through which people learn behavior that is acceptable in their society, including the beliefs and standards of that society.

social media: Media and technology used for interacting with many people at once.

Social Security: A federal program run by the Social Security Administration that is designed to give retired people or people with disabilities some source of income.

sole custody: An arrangement in which one parent is assigned the legal and physical custody of children.

solitary play: Stage of play in which infants tend to play alone and ignore other children playing nearby.

spatial: Space-related.

split custody: An arrangement in which children are divided between the divorced parents.

stage: A period of time or a step in a process.

standards: Levels of quality that are used to measure progress toward meeting goals or determine whether a goal has been reached.

state: A condition in which something exists.

stepfamily: A family structure that includes two spouses, one or both of whom have been married before and have children from one or more previous marriages.

stepparent: The new spouse of a parent with children from a previous marriage.

stereotype: An oversimplified opinion or prejudiced attitude.

sterility: The inability to have a child.

stillbirth: The death of the fetus after 20 weeks of development.

stranger anxiety: An infant's reaction of crying in fear when an unfamiliar person is near.

stress: The body's response to the events of a person's life that cause physical, mental, and emotional tensions.

stress hormones: Body chemicals that cause the heart to beat harder and faster, open wide the airways to the lungs, increase metabolism, increase the flow of blood to large muscles, and suppress the immune system.

stressor: A life event that causes stress and may lead to a crisis.

student and professional organizations: Organizations, either for students or for professionals, that offer the opportunity to develop skills while learning about future careers.

subgoal: A step that brings a person closer to achieving a long-term goal.

subsidize: To support financially, often by government funding.

substance abuse: Drug or alcohol abuse.

substantial: Significant.

substitute family: Nonrelatives who encourage or help a person in a way that family members would if they were present.

suicide: Taking one's own life.

supervisor: The person who serves as a leader for a permanent work team; someone to whom you are responsible for the work you complete.

Supplemental Security Income (SSI): A federal program that provides extra income for people who are 65 years of age or older, who are blind, or who have disabilities.

support network: A group of people who help one another with child care, parenting, and daily problems.

surrogate mother: A woman hired by a couple to carry the couple's child to birth.

synapse: The space between the axon of a sending neuron and the dendrite of a receiving neuron.

syphilis: A sexually transmitted infection caused by bacteria that produces a sore called a *chancre*; if left untreated, can damage body organs and lead to death.

T

task-oriented leadership: A style of leadership that focuses on specific tasks needing to be done.

teamwork: Work done by several members doing their parts to help a group accomplish its goals.

technical college: An educational institution that offers education and training in a career-focused program.

technology: The practical application of knowledge; the process of using knowledge to solve problems.

temperament: Consistent, predictable behavior based on inborn patterns of response.

temporary: Short-term; not permanent.

term insurance: A policy that insures a policyholder's life for a set number of years.

texting: The practice of sending and receiving short messages through mobile phones; also called *text messaging*.

thorough: Careful and complete.

time management: Controlling the way time is used.

time-out: A form of guidance in which a child spends time alone to think quietly about his or her wrong behavior.

toddler: A child between one and three years of age.

tort: A wrongful act committed against another person.

trade union: An organization that represents workers in a particular trade.

traits: Inherited characteristics.

transcript: An official record of all the courses a student has taken at an institution and the grade received in each course.

transferable skills: Basic job skills that can be applied to various work situations.

transition: A process of moving between two stages.

transitional stress: Stress that results from the normal process of growing and developing.

traumatic: Causing emotional stress and intense emotional upset.

trivial: Minor or less important.

U

unconditional love: The ability to love another under any circumstance, such as the love of a parent for a child.

uninsured motorists protection: Insurance that covers bodily injuries to the policyholder and family members if an accident is caused by someone who has no insurance.

unique: Unlike that of any other person.

universal life insurance: A policy that combines both term and cash value life insurance.

utility: A charge for services that concern a house; includes electricity, natural gas, water, sewer, telephone, and garbage-disposal services.

V

validated: The feeling that your input has been considered to be just as important as another person's.

values: All the ideals and beliefs that a person considers important and that influence his or her decisions and actions.

variable expense: An expense that changes or varies from month to month.

verbal communication: The use of words to send and receive messages.

victimhood: Living as a victim, a person who has been wronged, harmed, or hurt by others.

violation: An act that violates or breaks a local ordinance and can result in a fine or a short jail term; sometimes called a *petty offense*.

visitation rights: Arrangements for the noncustodial parent in a divorce settlement to visit the children.

visualizing: The process of picturing something in your mind.

vital: Very important.

volunteer: A person who donates time, talents, and energy to serve others.

vow: A statement that specifically expresses a couple's commitment to each other.

W

whole life insurance: A form of cash value insurance in which the premium stays the same during the life of the policy.

window of opportunity: The most efficient time for learning to take place.

withdrawal: Discomfort, nausea, pain, and convulsions that occur when a person stops using an addictive drug.

work: Any mental or physical activity that produces or accomplishes something.

work pattern: A system in which a person balances the activities of work life and home life over the course of adulthood.

workplace: A large group in which all the employees are members of the group.

work-study program: A program in which students work in a federally subsidized job at a college or university to earn money to help pay for school.

work team: A group that is brought together to complete a task as a result of the jobs that members do.

Y

you-statement: A statement that tries to dictate another person's thoughts, feelings, or intentions; usually commands, judges, or blames another person and tears down the listener's self-esteem.

INDEX

A

abandonment, 441
abilities, 115
abstinence, 252–254
abstract thinking, 37
abuse
    accepting problem
        ownership, 266
    assault, 359
    battery, 359
    breaking the cycle of abuse,
        362–363
    bullying, 193
    child abuse, 359–362
    confronting abuse in a
        relationship, 265–266
    definition, 263
    elder abuse, 492
    emotional abuse, 263–264,
        360
    material abuse, 492
    overcoming victimhood, 363
    physical abuse, 264, 360
    recognizing abuse, 262–266
    setting personal boundaries,
        265
    sexual abuse, 264–265, 360
    Shaken Baby Syndrome, 360,
        455
    social abuse, 264
abuse, substance. *See* substance
    abuse
accommodation, 297–298
accountability, in marriage, 307
accreditation, 508
acquaintance, 185
acquired immunodeficiency
    syndrome (AIDS), 256
acting out, 61
active interaction, 303
active listening, 161–162, 167,
    170–171, 357
activities preference inventory,
    115
addiction, 101. *See also* substance
    abuse

adolescence, developmental
    tasks of, 7–8
adolescent growth spurt, 34
adoption, 441–445, 537
    adoption leave, 537
    adoptive families, 336–337
    agency adoption, 442
    costs of, 444
    independent adoption, 442
    international adoption, 445
    rights of birthparents, 441–
        442
    single-parent adoption,
        444–445
    steps in adoption, 443–444
    types of, 442–443
adult day care, 493
advanced placement courses, 126
age at marriage, 277–278
agency adoption, 442
agency on aging, 490
agenda, meeting, 225
aggressive communication, 161
aging process, 478–495. *See also*
    elderly years
alcohol abuse. *See* substance
    abuse
alimony, 403
alternatives, decision making,
    95–97
American Academy of Pediatrics
    (AAP), 462
anemia, 431–432
anger, 71–72
    problems caused by, 72
    steps for handling, 72
annual percentage rate (APR),
    574
annuity, 584
anxiety, 72–74
    causes of, 73
    definition, 72–73
    handling, 73–74
    mild and major anxiety, 73
apprenticeships, 120–121, 127,
    506–507
aptitudes, 115

artifacts in a portfolio, 129
assault, 359. *See also* abuse
assertive communication, 159
assisted living, 494
assisted reproductive technology
    (ART), 440–441
assistive technology, 383–384, 473
associative play, 461
attitudes
    definition, 58
    developing attitudes that
        lead to mental health,
        58–65
    how attitudes develop, 60
    influence on behavior, 59–60,
        377
    in marriage, 306
    positive and negative
        attitudes, 58–60
authoritarian leadership, 216
authority figures, relationships
    with, 232–233
autism spectrum disorder, 383
automobile insurance. *See* car
    insurance
autonomy, toddlerhood, 457
axon, 14

B

background. *See* cultural
    background
barrier to divorce, 394
battery, 359. *See also* abuse
beneficiary, 583
blaming, 62, 164, 359
blended family. *See* stepfamily
blind spot, 190
bodily injury liability, 578
body language, 156–157. *See also*
    nonverbal communication
    skills
    body movements and
        position, 157
    definition, 156
    facial expressions, 156
    gestures, 156

bonding, 455
brain
    development, 14, 27, 36–37
    emotional responses, 39
    structures of, 13–14, 35–36
brain plasticity, 27
brainstem, 35
budget, 560–575. *See also* finances
    definition, 560
    establishing goals for income,
        565–566
    estimating income, 560–565
    finalizing, 569
    making a budget work for
        you, 570–575
    planning expenses, 566–569
    planning for savings, 569
    using credit, 571–575
    using technology, 145, 571
bullying, 173, 193. *See also* abuse
business ethics, 521–522
business etiquette, 521
business management &
        administration careers, 588
buying decisions. *See* budget;
        finances
bylaws, 225

C

career clusters, 117
career fair, 118
CareerOneStop, 119, 512
career plan, 125–129, 504–506
career roles, managing. *See*
        multiple roles
careers
    applying for a job, 516–518
    building a portfolio, 129
    changing jobs, 525–527
    connecting within, 228–233,
        523–525
    definition, 109
    developing a career plan,
        125–129, 504–506
    education and training for,
        120–121, 506–510
    entrepreneurship, 121–122,
        527
    factors affecting job outlook,
        120
    funding education, 511–512

    in business management &
        administration, 588
    in education and training,
        236
    in human services, 78, 148,
        314, 416, 498
    interviewing, 518–519
    making a career choice,
        123–129
    personal factors affecting,
        102, 112–115, 287–288
    preparing a résumé, 514–516
    researching, 117–120
    searching for a job, 513–514
    student and professional
        organizations, 122
    succeeding in, 135–137,
        519–522
career skills
    attendance, 520
    being part of a work team,
        230–233
    building connections, 523–525
    communication skills, 154–179
    conflict resolution, 174–179
    customer relations, 233
    decision-making skills,
        84–103
    ethical conduct, 521–522
    etiquette, 520–521
    group interaction skills,
        212–233
    professionalism, 520
    relating to fellow employees,
        229–230
    time management, 135–137
    work habits, 520
career-to-family-focused work
        pattern, 533
career-to-retirement work
        pattern, 532–533
car insurance, 578–580
    bodily injury risks, 578
    controlling costs, 579–580
    property damage risks,
        578–579
carrier, 15
cash value insurance, 583–585
cerebellum, 35
cerebrum. *See* cortex
ceremonial wedding, 291
certificate of completion, 125

certification, 121. *See also*
        education
chairperson, 225
changes. *See also* crises
    in the family life cycle,
        422–428, 436, 478–495
    marital adjustments, 296–311
    preparing for and managing,
        8–10
channel, 154
character development, 41–45
child abuse
    definition, 359
    reporting child abuse, 361
    signs of, 360–361
    sources of help, 361–362
    types of, 360
child care
    child care centers, 541–542
    child care in child's home,
        540
    choosing a child care
        program, 542–545
    employer-sponsored child
        care, 536, 541–542
    family child care, 540
    needs of elementary-age
        children, 543–544
    needs of infants, 542
    needs of parents, 544–545
    needs of preschoolers, 543
    needs of toddlers, 542–543
    planning for, 438
childless family, 335–336
childrearing leave, 537
children
    community resources for
        nurturing, 472–473
    developing a nurturing
        relationship with,
        450–453
    importance of play, 459–462
    providing guidance, 464–470
    safety, 461–462, 470–472
    selecting toys, 461–462
    socialization of, 326–327
    stimulating development
        of elementary-age
        children, 459
    stimulating development of
        infants, 455–456

role of technology, 462–463
toddlers, 456–457, 542–543
digital footprint, 172–173
direct attack of an issue, 64
disabilities, 382–384
assistive technology, 383–384
autism spectrum disorder, 383
coping with, 383–384
education for children with disabilities, 473
hereditary health conditions, 15–16
influence on personal identity, 26–27
learning disorders, 383
mental disorders, 74, 382–383
disability insurance, 565, 583
discipline. *See* guidance
displacement, 63
distracting, 164
diversity, 41, 206–207. *See also* cultural backgrounds
divorce
adjusting to, 405–410
barriers to, 393–394
custody settlements, 402–403
definition, 392
divorce counseling, 401
effects of, 392–393
factors contributing to, 394–396
financial settlements in, 403–404
remarriage and the stepfamily, 411–413
single-parent families, 410–411
stages of a marriage breakdown, 399–402
strengthening the family after divorce, 405–413
DNA, 6
domestic adoption, 441–445
dominant gene, 12–13
double date, 246
Down syndrome, 15–16
drug abuse. *See* substance abuse
drugs, 100–102, 265, 384. *See also* substance abuse
dual-career family, 534
durable power of attorney, 493

E

early parenthood stage, 424–425
education
certification, 121
education and training for careers, 120–121, 510
education and training options, 127, 506–510
apprenticeships, 120–121, 127, 506–507
four-year colleges and universities, 127, 508
master's and doctoral programs, 509
military training, 127, 506
online programs, 509–510
technical colleges, 127, 507
two-year community colleges, 127, 507–508
education for children with special needs, 473
funding education, 511–512
licenses, 121
education and training careers, 236
elder abuse, 492
elderly years, 488–495
changes in physical health, 488–490
changes in social life, 490
community resources, 490, 493–494
consumer fraud, 491
dealing with effects of aging, 489
death and dying, 494–495
impact of technology, 489–490
protecting rights of elderly, 491–493
elections. *See* voting
elementary-age children, 459, 543–544
emergency plan, 382
emotional abuse, 263–264, 360
emotional development, 38–41
emotional divorce, 399
emotional stability, 275
emotions

controlling emotional responses, 39
emotional adjustments during divorce, 406–408
emotional needs, 52, 304, 325, 451–453
emotional responses and the brain, 39
handling anger, 71–72
handling anxiety, 72–74
handling depression, 74–75
identifying emotions, 39
impact on communication, 165
impact on decision making, 85
reaching emotional maturity, 40–41, 85, 434
empathy, 186
employees, relating to, 228–233, 519–525
employer-paid taxes, 552
employer policies and trends, 536–537
employer-sponsored child care, 536, 541–542
employment. *See* careers
employment outlook, 117, 120
empty nest stage, 426–427
encoding, 154
endometriosis, 439
endorsement, 125–126
engagement, 285–290
entrepreneurship, 121–122, 527
environment
brain plasticity, 27
impact on communication, 165–166
influence on personal identity, 17–27
influence during the adult years, 26
influence of community, 24
influence of cultural heritage and society, 21
influence of family environment, 17–21
influence of media, 25
influence of peers, 23

influence of religious beliefs, 24
influence of school environment, 21–22
influence of stress, violence, and the global environment, 25–26
influence of technology, 24–25
providing a stimulating environment for children, 454–463
responding with resilience, 26–27
environment, protecting the, 555
Equal Credit Opportunity Act, 575
equal opportunity, 521, 575
ethics
    character and ethics, 42
    definition, 42
    ethical communication, 179, 191, 205
    ethical decision making, 103
    ethical questions about reproductive technology, 441
    ethics in the workplace, 521–522
etiquette, 223, 520–521
exclusive dating, 245
executive branch, 549
expenses, 566–569. *See* budget; finances
extended family, 200–201, 334–335
external stress, 375
extrovert, 49
eye contact, 157, 452–453

F

face-to-face interaction, 171
face value, insurance, 580
FAFSA, 511
Fair Credit Reporting Act, 575
family
    benefits of family living, 324–325
    crises in the family, 368–387, 392–413

dealing with problems in the family, 355–363
definition, 320
family as a system, 346–349
family life cycle, 422–428, 478–495
family structures, 330–337
functions of, 326–329
history of, 320–324
impact on society and community, 328–329, 349
influence on personal identity, 17–21
public policies and laws supporting families, 337, 537
relating to and guiding children, 450–473
strengthening positive patterns of interaction in families, 350–354
    family decision making, 352–353
    maintaining family communication, 350–351
    maintaining trust, 351–352
    setting time to talk, 351
    sharing, 353–354
trends affecting the family, 320–325
violence and abuse, 359–363. *See also* abuse
Family and Medical Leave Act, 537
family child care, 540
family court, 401
family life cycle, 422–428, 478–495
    definition, 422
    early parenthood stage, 424–425
    empty nest stage, 426–427
    impact of technology, 428
    later parenthood stage, 425–426, 478–483
    newly married stage, 423–424
    retirement stage, 427–428, 484–495
family roles, managing. *See* multiple roles
family routines, 354
family structures, 330–337

adoptive family, 336–337
childless family, 335–336
definition, 19, 330
extended family, 334–335
influence on personal identity, 19
nuclear family, 330–331
single-parent family, 331–332, 410–411
stepfamily, 333, 411–413
family traditions, 328–329, 354
family tree, 16
family trends, 320–325
fantasy, 63
Federal Insurance Contributions Act (FICA), 562
feedback, 154
felony, 550
FICA, 562
fight-or-flight response, 26, 67
finances
    financial crises, 386–387
    financial settlements in divorce, 403–404
    funding education, 511–512
    in marriage, 286–287, 307–308, 396
    in the family, 377, 438, 481, 485–487
    making a budget work, 570–575
    protecting resources through insurance, 576–585
    using a budget, 560–569
    using technology to manage, 145, 571
financial responsibility law, 578
fixed expense, 566
flexibility, 275–276, 377, 435
flexible scheduling, 536
food costs, 567
formal date, 246
foster care, 362, 442
founding family, 423
fraud, 491–492, 552
Free Application for Federal Student Aid (FAFSA), 511
free society, 346
friendships
    as a resource, 379, 411
    benefits of, 185–187

developing friendships
with communication
technology, 191
healthy versus unhealthy
friendships, 194
in romantic relationships,
260, 310
in the community, 202–203
peer relationships, 191–193
quality of a friend, 185, 187
skills for developing
friendships, 187–191
types of, 184–185
with people of other cultures,
206–207

G

genes, 6, 12–13, 15–16
genetic counseling, 16
genetic disorders. *See* hereditary
health conditions
genetics, 12
genital herpes, 256
genital warts, 256
genotype, 12
goals, 87–88, 113–114, 132–149
definition, 87
developing a plan to reach a
goal, 88
establishing goals for income,
565–566
group goals, 221
handling obstacles to goals,
88
identifying goals, 139–140
influence on decision
making, 87–88
in romantic relationships, 278
types of, 87, 139–140
gonorrhea, 256
government
agencies, 473
laws, 547–552
levels of, 548–549
policies, 337, 537
taxes, 552–553
voting, 548
grandparenting, 481–483
grandparents, relationships with,
200–201
grant, 511

grieving process, 371–372, 494–495
gross income, 562
group child care, 541
group dating, 245–246
group health insurance, 582
group home, 362
group interaction skills, 210–237
being part of a work team,
230–233
evaluating a group, 226–227
leading a group, 212–219
organizing a group, 224–227
planning a group, 224
qualities of successful
groups, 221–223
roles and responsibilities
of group members,
222–223
solving problems as a group,
178, 231–232
group values, 85–86
growth and development. *See*
development
guaranteed replacement value,
581
guidance
avoiding accidents, 470–472
choosing a method, 470
community resources, 472–473
definition, 464
methods for guiding
children, 465–470
need for guidance, 464–465
reinforcement, 467–468

H

health and well-being
decisions about alcohol, 100
decisions about sexual
activity, 252–257
decisions about tobacco, 100
decisions about using drugs,
100–102
effects of decisions on, 99–102
mental health, 60–61, 71–75
stress management, 69–70,
373–379
health insurance, 581–583
health maintenance
organizations (HMOs), 582

health savings account (HSA),
582
healthy relationships. *See*
relationships
hepatitis B, 256
hereditary health conditions,
15–16, 382–384
heredity, 6, 11
definition, 11
dominant and recessive
genes, 12–13
hereditary health conditions,
15–16
heritage, 26
high-deductible health plans
(HDHP), 582
high-growth industry, 120
HMO, 582
home health care, 493
homemaking. *See* household
tasks
homeowner's insurance, 580–581
home study, 444
homogamy, 278–281
honeymoon, 291
hospice care, 494–495
hostility, 297
hourly wage, 562
household, definition, 320
household tasks
developing a family
schedule, 545–546
making and following a plan,
545–546
managing family resources,
347
prioritizing tasks, 545
using technology, 546
human immunodeficiency virus
(HIV), 256
human intelligences, 37–38
human needs, influence of, 52,
304. *See also* needs
human papillomavirus (HPV),
256
human resources, 90
human resources management,
588
human services careers, 78, 148,
314, 416, 498

I

icebreaker, 188
idealization, 63
identity. *See* personal identity
immaturity, marital breakdown, 395
income
    establishing goals for, 565–566
    estimating amount of, 560–566
    sources of, 109
income-based taxes, 552
independence
    definition, 339
    loss of, 492–493
    preparing for, 8
independent adoption, 442
independent living, 362
Individualized Education Plan (IEP), 473
Industrial Revolution, 322–323
infants
    child care for, 542
    definition, 455
    stimulating development of, 455–456
infatuation, 250
infertility, 439–441
    causes of, 439–440
    definition, 439
    emotional effects of, 440
    technology and treatments for, 440–441
installment credit, 574
insurance, 576–585
    buying insurance, 576–577
    car insurance, 578–580
    definition, 576
    disability insurance, 583
    filing a claim, 585
    health insurance, 581–583
    homeowner's insurance, 580–581
    life insurance, 583–585
    renter's insurance, 581
integrity, 42
intellectual development, 34–38
intellectual maturity, 37–38, 85
intelligence, 13, 37–38
interest, monetary, 563–564, 573–574
interests, 114–115

internal stress, 374–375
international adoption, 445
Internet. *See also* technology
    developing friendships, 191
    online educational programs, 509–510
    researching careers, 119
    social media, 171–173, 247–248
internship, 129
interpersonal adjustments in marriage, 296–306
interpersonal communication skills. *See* communication skills
interpersonal skills. *See* communication skills; decision making; relationship skills
interrupted work pattern, 533–534
interviewing, 518–519
intrauterine insemination (IUI), 440
introvert, 49–50
inventory of time use, 138–139
investments, 564–565
in vitro fertilization (IVF), 441
I-statements, 159–160, 357

J

job fair, 514
job outlook, 120
jobs
    applying for a job, 516–518
    building a portfolio, 129
    changing jobs, 525–527
    connecting within, 228–233, 523–525
    definition, 109
    developing a career plan, 125–129, 504–506
    education and training for, 120–121, 506–510
    entrepreneurship, 121–122, 527
    factors affecting job outlook, 120
    funding education, 511–512
    in business management & administration, 588
    in education and training, 236

    in human services, 78, 148, 314, 416, 498
    interviewing, 518–519
    making a career choice, 123–129
    personal factors affecting, 102, 112–115, 287–288
    preparing a résumé, 514–516
    researching, 117–120
    searching for a job, 513–514
    student and professional organizations, 122
    succeeding in, 135–137, 519–522
job shadow, 119
job sharing, 536
job skills
    attendance, 520
    being part of a work team, 230–233
    building connections, 523–525
    customer relations, 233
    ethical conduct, 521–522
    etiquette, 520–521
    professionalism, 520
    relating to fellow employees, 229–230
    time management, 135–137
    work habits, 520
joint custody, 403

L

laparoscopy, 440
latchkey children, 544
later parenthood stage, 425–426
launching stage, 426
laws
    civil laws, 550–552
    constitutional laws, 550
    contract laws, 550–552
    divorce laws, 401–402
    federal laws, 549
    local laws, 549
    marriage laws, 290
    public laws, 550
    public policies and laws supporting families, 337, 537
    state laws, 549
leadership

midlife crisis, 481
military training, 127, 506
minimum wage, 562
minutes, meeting, 225
miscarriage, 431
misdemeanor, 550
mixed messages, 166, 451
modeling, 331, 465
money management. *See* budget; finances
moral development, 41
motivation, 52, 214–215
multiculturalism, 206–207. *See also* cultural backgrounds; diversity
multiple roles
    child care options, 539–545
    employer policies benefiting families, 536–537
    factors in choosing a work pattern, 534–537
    managing households tasks, 545–546
    role overload, 410
    types of work patterns, 532–534
MyPlate, 567

N

nanny, 540
natural consequences, 468
needs
    emotional needs, 52, 304, 325, 328, 451–453
    financial needs. *See* finances
    human needs, basic, 52, 304
    managing resources to meet. *See* resources
    meeting needs in marriage, 304
    meeting needs in the family, 327–328, 544–545
    meeting needs of children, 450–473, 542–544
    need for friendship, 185–187
    of the stepfamily, 412–413
    physical needs, 52, 325, 327, 347, 435
    social needs, 328
    special needs, 15–16, 26–27, 74, 382–384, 473

negative attitude, 58–59
negative communication patterns, 164–165
neglect, 360, 492. *See also* abuse
negotiation, 178, 199–200, 244. *See also* conflict resolution; problem solving
net income, 563
networking, 514, 523–525
neural connections, 14
neuron, 13
neurotransmitter, 14
newborns, stimulating development of, 455
newly married stage, 423–424
no-fault divorce, 401
no-fault insurance, 578
nonfamily household, 338
nonhuman resource, 90–91. *See also* management
nonverbal communication skills, 155–158
    body language, 156–157
    eye contact, 157–158
    tone, 158
nuclear family, 330–331
nurturing environment, 450–463
nurturing relationship, developing, 450–453

O

obstacles to goals, handling, 88
occupational and career specialties. *See* career clusters
Occupational Information Network, 119
Occupational Outlook Handbook, 119
O*NET, 119
onlooker play, 461
open admissions, 507
open adoption, 442
ordinances, 549
organization, 143, 145
organizing a group, 223–227
over-the-counter drugs. *See* drugs
ovulation, 440

P

pair adjustments, 299–306
pair dating, 245
parallel play, 461
paraphrasing, 162
parental leave, 536
parental relationship roles, 480–481
parenthood. *See* parenting
parenthood stage, 424–426
parenting
    adoption, 441–445
    community resources for, 472–473
    considering child care, 438, 539–545
    decisions about whether to parent, 430–431
    definition, 429
    developing nurturing relationships with children, 450–453
    infertility, 439–441
    parenting in the teen years, 432–433
    preparing for children, 437–439
    providing a stimulating environment, 454–463
    providing guidance, 464–473
    qualities needed by parents, 434–436
    reasons for not parenting, 431–433
    reasons for parenting, 433–434
    roles of parents, 429–430
parents and guardians, relationships with, 197–199, 425–426
parliamentary procedure, 225
passive interaction, 304
passive listening, 162
paternity leave, 537
patterns of adjustment to conflict, 296–298
    accommodation, 297–298
    compromise, 298
    concession, 297
    hostility, 297
peer pressure, 191–193

peer relationships, 191–193. *See also* friendships
    handling bullying, 193
    influence on personal identity, 23
    peer pressure, 191–193
    resisting negative peer pressure, 192–193
pension, 487
performance ratings, 522
personal boundaries, 252, 257, 265, 358–359, 398–399
personal identity, 7
    influence of community, 24
    influence of cultural heritage and society, 21
    influence of family environment, 17–21
    influence of global environment, 24–25
    influence of heredity, 11–16
    influence of media, 25
    influence of peers, 23
    influence of personality, 46–53
    influence of religious beliefs, 24
    influence of school environment, 21–22
    influence of stress, 25–26
    influence of technology, 24–25
    influence of violence, 24–25
personality, 46–53, 113. *See also* personal identity
    definition, 46
    healthy personality, 52–53
    impact on career choice, 113
    impact on leadership style, 217
    influence of human needs, 52
    influence of self-concept, 46–51
personal priorities, 113
personal space, 157
personal values, 113. *See also* values
petitioner, 401
phobia, 383
physical abuse, 264, 360
physical custody, 403
physical development, 34

physical dexterity, 517
physical intimacy, 304–305
physical maturity, 34
pileup effect, 369–370
placating, 164
placement rate, 508
placenta abruptio, 432
planned decision, 84
play
    guidelines for toy selection, 461–462
    importance of, 459–462
    stages of play, 461
point of view, 159
policies
    civil laws, 550–552
    constitutional laws, 550
    contract laws, 550–552
    divorce laws, 401–402
    employer policies, 536–537
    federal laws, 549
    local laws, 549
    marriage laws, 290
    public laws, 550
    public policies and laws supporting families, 337, 537
    state laws, 549
policy, insurance, 577
policy rider, 577
portfolio, 129
positive attitude, 64–65
    compensating, 64
    directly attacking an issue, 64
    interpreting information, 65
    selecting friends, 65
    setting reasonable expectations, 64
    using positive self-talk, 64–65
positive communication pattern, 163–164
postsecondary education and training options, 127, 506–510
    apprenticeships, 120–121, 127, 506–507
    four-year colleges and universities, 127, 508
    master's and doctoral programs, 509
    military training, 127, 506
    online programs, 509–510

    technical colleges, 127, 507
    two-year community colleges, 127, 507–508
PPO, 582
preeclampsia, 432
preemployment tests, 517
preferred provider organizations (PPOs), 582
pregnancy
    complications of, 255, 431–432
    during the early parenthood stage, 424–425
    infertility, 439–441
    teen pregnancy, 254–255, 432–433
pregnancy-induced hypertension (PIH), 432
prejudice, 166
premarital counseling, 289–290
premature baby, 432
premium, insurance, 577, 581
prenatal care, 255
prenatal environment, 18
preschoolers
    child care for, 543
    definition, 457
    stimulating development of, 457–459
prescription drugs. *See* drugs
primary and secondary sex characteristics, 34
problem ownership, 176
problems. *See also* crises; stress
    chronic illness and disabilities, 382–384
    definition, 368
    difficult events and emotions, 71–75
    divorce, 405–406
    drug and alcohol abuse, 384–386
    effects on individuals and families, 370–371
    grieving process, 371–372
    individual and family resources, 377–379
    managing, 373–387
    problems caused by anger, 72
    responding to, 380–382
    types of, 368–369
    unemployment and financial crises, 386–387

unhealthy adjustment
    patterns, 372
problem solving. *See also* conflict
    resolution; decision
    making
  conflict resolution, 174–179
  group problem solving, 178,
    231
  handling difficult events and
    emotions, 71–75
  in romantic relationships,
    282, 296–298, 302–303
  in the family, 199, 355–359
  in the workplace, 231–232
  managing problems and
    crises, 373–387
  negotiating a solution, 178–179
  responding to problems,
    380–382
procrastination, 142
professionalism, 520
professional relationships, 205
profit, 562
program of study, 125–127. *See
    also* education
projection, 62
promotion, 526
property damage liability, 578
property protection coverage, 580
property taxes, 553
puberty, 34
public policies. *See* policies,
    public
Punnet square, 13

Q

quality time, 453
quarrel, 297. *See also* conflict
    resolution

R

rape, 264–265
rapport, 187–189, 251
rate of development, 33. *See also*
    development
rationalization, 63
receiver, 154
recessive gene, 12
recruiter, 506
redirecting, 466

references, 516
reflecting, 162
regression, 63, 360
regulations. *See* laws; ordinances
reinforcement, 467–468
relationship-oriented leadership,
    216
relationships
  dating relationships, 249–269
  developing, 8
  friendships, 184–194, 202–203
  in group settings, 220–227
  in the community, 202–207
  in the family, 195–201, 350–363
  in the workplace, 228–233,
    519–525
  marriage, 272–311
  professional relationships,
    205
  with grandparents, 200–201
  with parents and guardians,
    197–200
  with peers, 191–193
  with people of other cultures,
    206–207
  with siblings, 200
  with significant adults,
    204–205
relationship skills, 182–209
  communication skills, 154–179
  conflict resolution, 174–179
  dating relationships, 249–269
  decision-making skills,
    84–103
  developing friendships,
    184–194
  group interaction skills,
    212–233
  marriage, 272–311
  relationships in the
    community, 202–207
  relationships in the family,
    195–201
  relationships in the
    workplace, 228–233,
    519–525
religious beliefs, 24, 280
remarriage and the stepfamily.
    See stepfamily
remedial course, 507
replacement cost, 580
repossess, 573

residential care. *See* group home
resilience, 26–27
resources, 90–92
  community resources, 379,
    472–473
  definition, 90
  education system, 473
  family support, 379
  financial resources, 91–92,
    377, 558–589
  for coping with financial
    crises, 386–387
  for coping with substance
    abuse, 385–386
  friendships, 379
  government agencies, 473,
    486–487
  human resources, 90
  information, 91
  interpersonal skills, 378–379
  nonhuman resources, 90–91
  optimistic viewpoint, 377
  personal characteristics,
    377–378
  support groups, 379, 472–473,
    487, 490, 493–494
  time management, 134–145
respondent, 401
responsibilities
  in dating, 245–246
  in parenting, 435–436
  of family members, 347,
    422–428
  of group leaders, 212–213
  of group members, 222–223
résumé, 514–515
retirement stage, 427–428
retirement years, 427–428, 484–487
  activity in retirement, 486
  challenges of, 484–486
  changes in social life, 485–486
  changes in work roles, 484–485
  community programs, 487
  federal programs, 486–487
  financial changes, 485
  pensions and retirement
    accounts, 487
  planning for financial needs,
    486–487
revolving credit, 573
rights and responsibilities, family
    systems, 347

Robert's Rules of Order, 225
role model, 523–524
role overload, 410
roles, 41, 286
    adjusting to marital roles, 306
    of family members, 347–348,
        422–428, 537
    of group members, 222–223
    of leaders, 214–216
    role expectations, 286
role sharing, 286
romantic love, 249–250
romantic relationships. *See* dating
    relationships; marriage
routine decision, 84
routine stress, 66

S

safety
    abuse. *See* abuse
    child safety, 461–462, 470–472
    emergency plan, 382
    influence on personal
        identity, 52
    Internet safety, 172–173
    workplace safety, 519
salary, 562. *See also* income
sales taxes, 553
sandwich approach, 301
sandwich generation, 426
savings, 563–565, 569
scapegoating, 359
scholarship, 512
school environment, influence on
    personal identity, 21–22.
    See also peer relationships
screening, 517
secretary, 225
security on loans, 574
self-actualization, 304
self-awareness circle, 160
self-concept. *See also* personal
    identity
    definition, 46
    four areas of temperament,
        48–50
    influence on personality,
        46–51
    understanding response
        patterns, 50–51

your temperament's
    influence, 48
self-control. *See* self-discipline
self-discipline, 42, 266, 465
self-esteem
    definition, 7
    impact on communication
        patterns, 163–164
    influence of other people, 46,
        186
    influence of physical traits, 47
    influence of skills and talents,
        47–48
    influence of special needs, 27
    influence of the family
        environment, 17–21
    influence of work, 111
self-neglect, 492
self-perpetuating cycle, 60
self-pity, 74
self-talk, 64–65
sender, 154
sensitivity, 165, 274
separation, 400–401
separation anxiety, 456
service activity, 139. *See also*
    volunteering
sex roles and stereotypes, 75
sex stereotype, 75
sexual abuse, 264–265, 360
sexual decisions
    abstinence, 252
    psychological consequences
        of, 253–254
    responding to pressures,
        257–258
    sexually transmitted
        infections, 255–257
    unwanted pregnancy, 254–255
sexual harassment, 521
sexually transmitted diseases
    (STDs), 255–257
sexually transmitted infections
    (STIs), 255–257
Shaken Baby Syndrome, 360, 455
shelters, 362
short-term goal, 87, 504
siblings
    definition, 19
    influence on personal
        identity, 19–21

learning to compromise with,
    358
only child, 20
relationships with, 200
rivals for parent attention, 20
sibling position, 20
twins and other multiple
    siblings, 21
significant adults, relationships
    with, 204–205
single living, 338–341
    advantages of, 340
    changes leading to, 340
    concerns of single people,
        340–341
    definition, 338
    reasons for choosing, 339–340
    social relationships, 340–341
    stereotyped images, 341
single-parent families, 331–332,
    410–411
    coping with loneliness,
        410–411
    definition, 331
    role overload from added
        responsibilities, 410
    supportive friendships, 411
social abuse, 264
social adjustments in marriage,
    308–310
    adjusting to new community,
        310
    adjusting friendships, 310
    keeping family counsel in
        perspective, 309–310
    relating to family, 309
    supporting parents in
        adjustment, 310
social development, 41–45
socialization, 41, 326–327
social maturity, 45, 85
social media, 171, 247–248,
    517–518
Social Security, 486, 552
Social Security tax, 562
sole custody, 403
solitary play, 461
special needs
    assistive technology, 383–384
    autism spectrum disorder,
        383
    coping with, 383–384

education for children with
disabilities, 473
hereditary health conditions,
15–16
influence on personal
identity, 26–27
learning disorders, 383
mental disorders, 74, 382–383
spousal support agreements. *See*
alimony
standards, 88–89
stepfamily, 333, 411–413
stepparenting, 411
stereotypes, 75, 341
sterility, 256
stillbirth, 432
stranger anxiety, 456
stress, 66–70
definition, 66
effects of, 67–69
identifying sources of stress,
374–375
influence on personal
identity, 25–26
reducing amounts of stress,
375–376
reducing effects of stress, 70,
376
responding with resilience,
26–27
sources of, 67
stress management, 69–70,
373–387
types of, 66–67, 374–375
stress hormones, 67
stressor, 368
student and professional
organizations, 122
subgoal, 88
substance abuse, 100–102, 384–386
alcohol, 100
community resources for
coping with, 385–386
definition, 384
drugs, 100–102
effects on family, 384–385
tobacco, 100
substitute family, 310
suicide, 74–75
supervisors, relationships with,
232–233

Supplemental Security Income
(SSI), 487
support groups, 379, 472–473
support network, 198
surrogate mother, 441
synapse, 14
syphilis, 256

T

task-oriented leadership, 216
taxes, 548, 552–553
teamwork, 221. *See* group
interaction skills
technical college, 127, 507
technology
communication technology,
24–25, 170–173, 191,
199, 247–248
cyberbullying, 173
definition, 24
digital footprint, 172–173
impact on children's
development, 462–463
impact on family functions,
327–329
impact on family
relationships, 199
impact on the family life
cycle, 428
influence on personal
identity, 24–25
in the history of the family,
323–324
medical technologies, 440–441,
490
social media, 171, 247–248,
517–518
use for time management,
144–145
use to manage home, 546
using for money
management, 571
using to assist with effects of
aging, 489–490
using to research careers, 119
teen marriages, 396
temperament
areas of, 48–50
definition, 48
influence of, 48
term insurance, 583

texting, 171. *See also*
communication
technology
time management, 134–135
avoiding time wasters,
142–144
benefits of, 134–136
definition, 134
making a time management
plan, 138–142
using time management
tools, 144–145
workplace time management
skills, 137
time-out, 469
toddlers
child care for, 542–543
definition, 456
stimulating development of,
456–457
tort, 552
toxemia, 432
trade union, 507
trading, investments, 564
traditions, 328–329, 354
traits, 12–13. *See also* heredity
transcript, 126, 508
transferable skills, 115. *See also*
career skills
transitional stress, 67
transportation costs, 567–568
traumatic events, 67. *See also*
stress
trends affecting the family, 320–325

U

U.S. Bureau of Labor Statistics,
119
U.S. Congress, 549
U.S. Constitution, 550
U.S. Department of Agriculture,
567
U.S. Department of Education
website, 511
U.S. Department of Labor, 119,
562
U.S. workforce. *See* career
clusters
unconditional love, 434–435
unemployment, 386–387. *See also*
finances

uninsured motorists protection,
578
universal life insurance, 584
utility, 566

V

values, 85–87, 113
    definition, 85
    how values develop, 85–86
    identifying values, 86–87
    influence on career choice,
        113
    influence on decisions, 87
    influence on work patterns,
        534–535
    in romantic relationships,
        278–279
variable expense, 566
verbal communication skills, 155,
    158–161. *See also* written
    communication skills
    communication style, 159
    I-statements, 159–160, 357
    word choice, 159
    you-statements, 161
victim. *See* victimhood
victimhood, 363
violation, 550
violence, influence on personal
    identity, 25–26
violence in relationships. *See*
    abuse
visitation rights, 403
volunteering
    in the community, 128,
        554–555
    opportunities, 79, 149, 237,
        315, 417, 499, 589
voting, 548
vow, 291

W

wages, 562
wedding ceremony, 290–291
whole life insurance, 584
window of opportunity, 14
withdrawal, 101
work, 513–522
    applying for, 516–518
    building a portfolio, 129
    changing jobs, 525–527
    connecting within, 228–233,
        523–525
    definition, 108
    developing a career plan,
        125–129, 504–506
    education and training for,
        120–121, 506–510
    entrepreneurship, 121–122,
        527
    factors affecting job outlook,
        120
    funding education, 511–512
    in business management &
        administration, 588
    in education and training,
        236
    in human services, 78, 148,
        314, 416, 498
    interviewing, 518–519
    making a career choice,
        123–129
    personal factors affecting,
        102, 112–115, 287–288
    preparing a résumé, 514–516
    researching, 117–120
    searching for a job, 513–514
    student and professional
        organizations, 122
    succeeding in, 135–137,
        519–522
    why people work, 109–111

work ethics, 521–522
work experience, 128–129
work pattern
    definition, 532
    factors in choosing, 534–537
    types of, 532–534
workplace skills
    attendance, 520
    being part of a work team,
        230–233
    building connections, 523–525
    communication skills, 154–179
    conflict resolution, 174–179
    customer relations, 233
    decision-making skills, 84–103
    ethical conduct, 521–522
    etiquette, 520–521
    group interaction skills,
        212–233
    professionalism, 520
    relating to fellow employees,
        229–230
    time management, 135–137
    work habits, 520
work-study program, 511
work team, 230–233
work values. *See* values
written communication
    skills, 168–173. *See*
    also communication
    technology; verbal
    communication skills
    communication technology
        and social media,
        170–173
    reading and comprehension
        skills, 170

Y

you-statements, 161